T0291561

Behavioral Economics

Arthur O'Sullivan

OXFORD
UNIVERSITY PRESS

OXFORD
UNIVERSITY PRESS

Oxford University Press is a department of the University of Oxford.
It furthers the University's objective of excellence in research, scholarship,
and education by publishing worldwide. Oxford is a registered trade mark
of Oxford University Press in the UK and in certain other countries.

Published in the United States of America by Oxford University Press
198 Madison Avenue, New York, NY 10016, United States of America.

For titles covered by Section 112 of the US Higher Education Opportunity Act,
please visit www.oup.com/us/he for the latest information about
pricing and alternate formats.

Library of Congress Cataloging-in-Publication Data
Names: O'Sullivan, Arthur, author.
Title: Behavioral economics / Arthur O'Sullivan.
Description: New York, NY : Oxford University Press, [2023] | Includes
    bibliographical references and index.
Identifiers: LCCN 2022006935 | ISBN 9780197515921 (paperback) | ISBN
    9780197515938 (epub) | ISBN 9780197515976 (pdf)
Subjects: LCSH: Economics—Psychological aspects.
Classification: LCC HB74.P8 O88 2023 | DDC 330.01/9—dc23/eng/20220214
LC record available at https://lccn.loc.gov/2022006935

Printing number: 9 8 7 6 5 4 3 2 1
Printed by Sheridan Books, Inc., United States of America

To Conor and Maura

CONTENTS

Preface   xx

Acknowledgements   xxi

PART 1   INTRODUCTION

1   Introduction and Key Concepts of Microeconomics   1

1.1	What Is Behavioral Economics?	2
	Review the Concepts 1.1	3
1.2	Key Concepts: Marginal Reasoning	4
	Opportunity Cost	4
	The Marginal Principle	4
	The Equimarginal Principle	6
	Review the Concepts 1.2	8
1.3	Key Concepts: Equilibrium and Efficiency	8
	Nash Equilibrium	8
	Comparative Statics	10
	Pareto Efficiency	11
	Review the Concepts 1.3	12

Key Terms 12 · Takeaways 13 · Discuss the Concepts 13 · Apply the Concepts 15

2   Insights from Behavioral Science   16

2.1	Social Preferences and Social Norms	17
	Adam Smith on Social Norms and the Impartial Spectator	18
	Rule-Following Task: Avatar Pedestrian	19

Sharing the Rewards of Collaboration   20

Incurring a Cost to Enforce a Social Norm   22

Review the Concepts 2.1   25

2.2   Mental Shortcuts   26

Mental Accounting   26

Default Options   27

Review the Concepts 2.2   27

2.3   Cognitive Bias   28

The Decoy Effect   28

Present Bias   30

Review the Concepts 2.3   31

2.4   Problems with Probabilities   32

Rare Events   32

The Gambler's Fallacy   32

Review the Concepts 2.4   34

2.5   Instinctive Urges and Thoughtful Deliberation   34

Apple versus Cupcake   34

Hunting Practices of the Ju/'hoansi   35

Why Do We Do That?   35

Review the Concepts 2.5   36

Key Terms 36 · Takeaways 36 · Discuss the Concepts 37 · Apply the
Concepts 38

Appendix to Chapter 2: More Insights from Behavioral Science   40

1   Anchors   40

2   Confirmation Bias   40

3   Overconfidence Effect   41

4   Availability Heuristic   41

Review the Concepts 2A   42

Key Terms 43

PART 2   SOCIAL PREFERENCES AND PRO-SOCIAL BEHAVIOR

3   Social Norms: Sharing and Enforcement   44

3.1	Utility Maximization with a Social Norm	45
	Trade-Off Between Material Benefit and Norm-Violation Cost	46
	Utility Maximization	47
	Review the Concepts 3.1	49
3.2	Sharing Behavior: The Dictator Game	49
	Game Structure and Results	49
	Variation in Sharing Behavior	50
	Review the Concepts 3.2	52
3.3	Costly Norm Enforcement	52
	Third-Party Punishment of Norm Violators	53
	Structure of the Ultimatum Game	54
	A Norm-Sensitive Responder	55
	Equilibrium Responder Share	56
	A Norm-Sensitive Proposer	58
	Review the Concepts 3.3	59
3.4	Results from Ultimatum-Game Experiments	59
	Meta-Analysis of Ultimatum Experiments	59
	Crosswalk Rules and the Ultimatum Game	60
	Review the Concepts 3.4	60
3.5	Market Engagement and Social Norms	61
	Review the Concepts 3.5	63

Key Terms 63 · Takeaways 63 · Discuss the Concepts 64 · Apply the Concepts 65 · Math Solutions 66

Appendix to Chapter 3: Fehr-Schmidt Inequity Cost	68

Key Terms 70

4   Trust   72

4.1	The Trust Game: Investment and Production	73
	Game Structure	74
	Outcome in the Absence of a Sharing Norm	75
	Review the Concepts 4.1	75

4.2   A Sharing Norm for the Producer   76

The Producer's Trade-Off: Material Benefit versus Norm-Violation Cost 76

Varying Norm Sensitivity and Return Fractions   79

The Investor Decision   79

Review the Concepts 4.2   80

4.3   A Sharing Norm for the Investor   81

The Investor's Trade-Off: Material Benefit versus Norm-Violation Cost   81

Relative Norm Sensitivity and Equilibrium   82

Social Norms, Efficiency, and Social Capital   83

Review the Concepts 4.3   84

4.4   Experiments and Implications   84

Experimental Results   85

The Trust Game and Social Capital   87

The Trust Game and Oxytocin   88

Review the Concepts 4.4   89

Key Terms 89 · Takeaways 89 · Discuss the Concepts 90 · Apply the
Concepts 90 · Math Solutions 92

5 Public Goods and Voluntary Contributions   94

5.1   Free Riding and Economic Experiments   96

The Free-Rider Problem   96

Results from Voluntary-Contribution Experiments   98

Review the Concepts 5.1   99

5.2   Social Norms and Voluntary Contributions   99

Norm: Efficient Contribution   100

Norm: Equal Contribution   103

Explaining a Path of Decreasing Contributions   104

Review the Concepts 5.2   105

5.3   Punish Free Riders?   106

Punishing Norm Violators   106

Summary of Experimental Results   107

Review the Concepts 5.3   107

Key Terms 108 · Takeaways 108 · Discuss the Concepts 108 · Apply the
Concepts 109 · Math Solutions 110

6   Identity, Norms, and Reciprocity in the Workplace   112

6.1   Worker Reciprocity and Social Capital   114

Perfect or Imperfect Information in the Workplace?   114

Social Norms and Pareto Improvements   115

Review the Concepts 6.1   115

6.2   Worker Identity and Effort   115

Utility Maximizing Effort   116

Insiders versus Outsiders   119

Producer Investment in Identity Management   121

Review the Concepts 6.2   121

6.3   Response to a Higher Wage   122

Wages and a Sharing Norm   122

Wages and the Work-Effort Norm   123

Review the Concepts 6.3   125

6.4   Evidence of Worker Reciprocity   125

Field Experiments   125

A Gift-Exchange Experiment   126

Review the Concepts 6.4   127

Takeaways 128 · Discuss the Concepts 128 · Apply the Concepts 129 ·
Math Solutions 129

7   Voluntary Prices   131

7.1   Voluntary Prices: Pay What You Want   132

The Equal-Sharing Price and Norm-Violation Cost   132

Sustainability of PWW Systems   136

Economic Experiment: Pay What You Want versus Pay It Forward   137

Review the Concepts 7.1   137

7.2   Public Broadcasting: Free Riders and Guilt-Tripping Pledge Drives   138

Payoffs to Members and Free Riders   138

Choosing the Length of a Pledge Drive   141

Review the Concepts 7.2   143

Key Terms 143 · Takeaways 143 · Discuss the Concepts 143 · Apply the
Concepts 144 · Math Solutions 145

8 Imitation and Cultural Learning   146

8.1   Imitation and Conformity   147
      Over-Imitation by Humans   147
      Over-Imitation: Humans versus Chimpanzees   148
      Conformity and Matching Pennies   149
      Review the Concepts 8.1   151
8.2   Faithful Imitation and Cultural Learning   151
      Manioc and Obscure Production Processes   151
      Social Learning: Humans versus Chimpanzees   153
      Review the Concepts 8.2   154
      Key Terms 155 · Takeaways 155 · Discuss the Concepts 155 · Apply the
      Concepts 156

PART 3   TIME PREFERENCES AND INTERTEMPORAL CHOICE

9 Discounting and Present Bias   157

9.1   Conventional Discounting and Present Bias   158
      The Quasi-Hyperbolic Discount Function   158
      Present Bias and Doubling Your Apples   160
      Time Inconsistency   161
      Time Inconsistency and the Relative Values of Bundles   162
      Present Bias and Regret   163
      Review the Concepts 9.1   164
9.2   Estimates of Discounting Parameters   164
      Estimates of Conventional Discounting and Present Bias   164
      Economic Experiment: Patience among Mothers and Children   165
      Review the Concepts 9.2   166
9.3   Illustrations: Cupcake, Weed, Bucket List   167
      Cupcake versus Apple   167
      Homeowner versus Weed   168
      The Bucket List   170
      Review the Concepts 9.3   172
      Key Terms 173 · Takeaways 173 · Discuss the Concepts 173 · Apply the
      Concepts 174 · Math Solutions 175

10   Time Preferences and Saving   177

10.1 Discounting and Intertemporal Choice	178
Saving and the Equimarginal Principle	178
Present Bias and Regret	180
Review the Concepts 10.1	181
10.2 Saving Mandates and Nudges	182
Response to Mandate: Active Saver	182
Response to Mandate: Non-Saver	183
Nudges: Defaults, Save More Tomorrow, and Saving Lotteries	184
Review the Concepts 10.2	185
10.3 Clueless versus Savvy Consumers	186
Three-Period Model of Intertemporal Choice	186
Consumption Path of the Clueless	187
Regret of the Clueless	189
Consumption Path of a Savvy Consumer	190
Commitment Devices and Saving	191
Review the Concepts 10.3	191
10.4 Impulse Control by Pigeons	192
Review the Concepts 10.4	193

Takeaways   193 · Discuss the Concepts   194 · Apply the Concepts   194 ·
Math Solutions   197

11   When to Act   200

11.1 Procrastination: Waiting Too Long	201
Present Bias and a Clueless Decision-Maker	202
Conditions for Procrastination	204
Review the Concepts 11.1	204
11.2 Self-Awareness and Procrastination	205
Backward Induction	205
Evidence of Present Bias and Self-Awareness	206
Clueless versus Self-Aware: How to Tell the Difference	207
Review the Concepts 11.2	208
11.3 Preproperation: Acting Too Soon	209
Present Bias and a Clueless Decision-Maker	209

Conditions for Preproperation   211

Review the Concepts 11.3   212

11.4 Self-Awareness and Preproperation   212

Backward Induction   212

Is Being Clueless Better?   215

Review the Concepts 11.4   215

Key Terms 215 · Takeaways 216 · Discuss the Concepts 216 · Apply the Concepts 217

12   Application of Present Bias—Sin Taxes and Fertilizer   219

12.1 Personally Harmful Products and Sin Taxes   220

A Model of a Personally Harmful Good   220

Present Bias and a Personally Harmful Good   221

Savvy Consumers and Hobbling   223

Support for Sin Taxes   223

Review the Concepts 12.1   225

12.2 Present Bias and Fertilizer Investment   226

Review of Intertemporal Choice Model   226

Present Bias and the Fertilizer Investment   227

Policy Options: Subsidy versus Nudge   230

Review the Concepts 12.2   231

Takeaways 231 · Discuss the Concepts 232 · Apply the Concepts 232 · Math Solutions 233

PART 4   MENTAL ACCOUNTING AND THE POWER OF LOSS

13   Mental Accounting for Consumers   236

13.1 Mental Accounting and Fungibility   237

Consumer Budgets and Fungibility   237

Mental Accounting and Coupons   239

Review the Concepts 13.1   242

13.2 Other Implications of Consumer Mental Accounting   242

Mental Accounting and Sunk Cost   242

Decoupling Cost and Benefit: Credit Cards and Ride-Hailing Services 243

Regular versus Premium Gasoline   244

Review the Concepts 13.2   245

Key Term 245 · Takeaways 245 · Discuss the Concepts 246 · Apply the
Concepts 247

14 Loss versus Gain   249

14.1 Asymmetric Influences of Loss and Gain   250

The Greater Weight of Loss   250

Measuring the Greater Weight of Loss   251

Reappraisal and the Weight of Loss   252

Review the Concepts 14.1   252

14.2 The Endowment Effect   253

Willingness to Pay versus Willingness to Accept   253

Classic Endowment Experiment   254

Evidence for the Endowment Effect   254

Endowment Effect for Chimpanzees and Capuchin Monkeys   255

The Endowment Effect and Exchange   256

Greater Weight of Loss and Loss Aversion   257

Review the Concepts 14.2   258

Key Terms 258 · Takeaways 258 · Discuss the Concepts 259 · Apply the
Concepts 259

PART 5   RISK PREFERENCES AND DECISIONS IN UNCERTAIN ENVIRONMENTS

15 Risk Preferences and Prospect Theory   261

15.1 Features of Prospect Theory   262

Utility Function for Prospect Theory   263

Utility Value and Certainty Equivalent   264

Review the Concepts 15.1   266

15.2 Risk Aversion and Risk Neutrality   266

   Risk Aversion and the Risk Premium   267

   Risk Neutrality: Linear Utility and Equal Weight of Loss and Gain   268

   Sources of Risk Aversion   269

   Review the Concepts 15.2   270

15.3 The Values of Key Parameters   270

   Relative Weight of Loss   271

   Decreasing Sensitivity to Gain and Loss   271

   Measuring Sensitivity to Stimulus   273

   Economic Experiment: Risk Preferences and Cognitive Ability   274

   Review the Concepts 15.3   275

15.4 Risk Preferences for Rats   275

   Review the Concepts 15.4   277

Key Terms 277 · Takeaways 278 · Discuss the Concepts 278 · Apply the
Concepts 279 · Math Solution 281

16   Problems with Probability   282

16.1 Probability in Prospect Theory   283

   Prelec Probability Weighting   283

   Psychological Foundations   284

   A Closer Look at Rare Events   285

   Review the Concepts 16.1   286

16.2 Learning by Description versus Learning by Experience   287

   Review the Concepts 16.2   289

16.3 Solving Puzzles with Probability Weighting   289

   The Numbers-Game Puzzle   289

   Solving the Numbers-Game Puzzle   290

   The Longshot Puzzle   292

   Review the Concepts 16.3   294

Key Terms 295 · Takeaways 295 · Discuss the Concepts 296 · Apply the
Concepts 296

17   Prospect Theory and Asset Markets   298

17.1 Decreasing Sensitivity and Attitudes toward Risk   299

Decreasing Sensitivity to Gain and Risk Aversion   299

Decreasing Sensitivity to Loss and Risk Seeking   300

Constant Sensitivity and Risk Neutrality   302

Review the Concepts 17.1   304

17.2 The Disposition Puzzle   305

Reservation Price in a Winner Market   306

Reservation Price in a Loser Market   306

Reservation Prices and Time on the Market   307

Evidence for the Disposition Puzzle   308

Review the Concepts 17.2   308

17.3 Disposition Puzzle Disappears?   309

Let Bygones Be Bygones   309

Constant Sensitivity to Gain and Loss   310

Review the Concepts 17.3   311

17.4 The Equity Premium Puzzle   311

Greater Weight of Loss and Loss Aversion   311

Loss Aversion Solves the Equity Premium Puzzle   312

Professional Traders: Too Much Information?   314

Review the Concepts 17.4   314

Key Terms 315 · Takeaways 315 · Discuss the Concepts 315 · Apply the Concepts 316

18   Prospect Theory and Insurance   319

18.1 Decreasing Sensitivity and the Willingness to Pay for Insurance   320

Decreasing Marginal Disutility of Loss   320

Certainty Equivalent and Willingness to Pay for Insurance   322

Willingness to Pay for Insurance versus Break-Even Price   322

Economic Experiment: Willingness to Pay for Insurance   323

Review the Concepts 18.1   323

18.2 Probability Weighting and Insurance Puzzles   324

Decreasing Sensitivity and Probability Weighting   324

Conflicting Forces: Decreasing Sensitivity and Probability Weighting   326

The Hazard-Insurance Puzzle   328

The Insurance-Deductible Puzzle   328

Review the Concepts 18.2   330

Key Terms 331 · Takeaways 331 · Discuss the Concepts 332 · Apply the Concepts 332 · Math Solution 333

19   Reference Points and Goals   335

19.1 Goals and the Marginal Principle   336

Goal-Related Marginal Benefit   337

Full Marginal Benefit and Choice   338

Goals on the Golf Course   340

Review the Concepts 19.1   341

19.2 Applications: Rainy-Day Taxis and Abstinence   341

Rainy-Day Taxis   342

Inefficiency and a Pareto Improvement   343

Abstinence   344

Review the Concepts 19.2   346

Takeaways 347 · Discuss the Concepts 347 · Apply the Concepts 348 · Math Solution 349

PART 6   NATURAL SELECTION AND CULTURE

20   Natural Selection and Co-Evolution of Genes and Culture   351

20.1 Background Concepts from Evolutionary Biology   352

DNA, Genetic Mutations, and Natural Selection   353

Illustration: A Fire-Building Manual   354

Review the Concepts 20.1   355

20.2 A Closer Look at Fitness and Evolution   355

Fitness, Natural Selection, and Evolution   356

Fitness Contests and Geometric Mean Fitness   357

Economics versus Biology: Spider Somersaults   360

Review the Concepts 20.2   361

20.3 Genes, Environment, Norms, Culture, and Cognition   361

Genes and the Environment   361

Genes and Culture   362

Genes and Social Norms   363

Instinctive Urges versus Thoughtful Deliberation   364

Review the Concepts 20.3   364

Key Terms 365 · Takeaways 365 · Discuss the Concepts 365 · Apply the Concepts 366 · Math Solution 366

21 Cooperation   367

21.1 Humans versus Chimpanzees   368

Cooperation: Skills and Motivation   368

Sharing   369

Bearing a Cost to Enforce Norms   370

Review the Concepts 21.1   372

21.2 Consumption and Production Benefits of Cooperation   372

Benefits from Consumption Smoothing   373

Benefits from Economies of Scale   374

Review the Concepts 21.2   375

21.3 Co-Evolution of Genes and Culture   375

Genes and Culture   375

Cultural Learning   376

Review the Concepts 21.3   378

Key Term 378 · Takeaways 378 · Discuss the Concepts 379 · Apply the Concepts 379

22 Loss Aversion and Time Preferences   380

22.1 Natural Selection and Loss Aversion   381

Steady versus Fluctuating Reproduction   382

Gain Equals the Loss   382

Gain Exceeds the Loss   384

Fitness Equivalence   386

Environmental Conditions and Genetic Mixes   388

Review the Concepts 22.1   389

22.2 Natural Selection, Culture, and Time Preferences   390

Trade-Offs from Investment   390

Low Investment Productivity   391

High Investment Productivity   392

Lessons from Historical Data   393

Review the Concepts 22.2   395

Key Terms 396 · Takeaways 396 · Discuss the Concepts 396 · Apply the
Concepts 397 · Math Solution 398

23   Natural Selection and Risk Preferences   400

23.1 Small Reward and Risk Aversion   401

Geometric Mean Fitness   402

Natural Selection and Risk Aversion   403

Review the Concepts 23.1   404

23.2 Large Reward and Risk Neutrality   404

Greater Fitness for Risk Takers   405

Natural Selection Favors Risk Taking   405

Fitness Equivalence   407

Risk Aversion in Bonobos, Shrews, and Other Creatures   408

Review the Concepts 23.2   408

23.3 Subsistence and Risk Seeking   409

Subsistence and Risk Preferences   409

The Flexible Risk Preferences of Juncos   410

Review the Concepts 23.3   411

Takeaways 411 · Discuss the Concepts 412 · Apply the Concepts 412 ·
Math Solution 414

24   Bargaining and the Endowment Effect   415

24.1 A Hunter-Gatherer Exchange Economy   416

Hunter-Gatherer Fitness   416

Edgeworth Box and Gains from Exchange   416

Bargaining and Equilibrium   418

Review the Concepts 24.1   420

24.2 Natural Selection: Bargaining Outcomes   420

Endowment Effect and Nash Equilibrium   420

Disagreement Value and the Nash Bargaining Solution   422

The Endowment Effect and Group Fitness   423

Egalitarian Economy and the Endowment Effect   424

Review the Concepts 24.2   424

Key Terms   424 · Takeaways   425 · Discuss the Concepts   425 · Apply the
Concepts   426 · Math Solutions   427

Glossary   429

References   432

Index   439

PREFACE

This book is designed for a course in behavioral economics, the discipline that incorporates insights of behavioral science—from psychology, anthropology, biology, and neuroscience—into models of economic choice. Over the last few decades, behavioral scientists and economists have noticed patterns of behavior that appear to be inconsistent with traditional models of economic choice. Behavioral economics identifies these patterns of behavior and extends models of economic choice to explain them. Behavioral economics is not a catalog of quirky behavior, but instead a systematic inquiry into the causes and consequences of observed behavior that does not fit neatly into a traditional model of economic choice.

The book is organized into six parts. Part 1 reviews some key concepts of microeconomics and some key observations from behavioral scientists. Part 2 explores the role of social norms in behavior such as cooperation, trust, reciprocity, voluntary contributions to public goods, and voluntary prices. Part 3 explores inter-temporal choice, focusing on the role of present bias in behavior such as meager saving, procrastination, smoking, and under-investment in fertilizer. Part 4 discusses mental shortcuts that simplify the decision-making process and explores the notion that losses loom larger than gains. Part 5 introduces prospect theory—a framework for decision-making in an environment of uncertain benefits and costs—and applies the theory to decisions about investment, asset prices, insurance, gambling, and behavioral goals. Part 6 explores the roles of natural selection and culture in shaping human behavior, with the co-evolution of genes and culture as a recurring theme.

The text is accompanied by 24 interactive widgets that promote understanding through active learning. There are three types of widgets:

- *Roll Your Own Graph.* Drag a slider to change the value of a key parameter, and the widget shows the implications for a familiar graph.
- *Calculator.* Drag a slider to change the value of a key parameter, and the widget computes the values of relevant economic variables.
- *Find an Equilibrium.* Drag a slider to search for an equilibrium outcome.

 You can access the widgets at www.oup.com/us/osullivan1e. Some of the widgets are referenced in the book, while others are not. Here is a list of chapters that have supporting widgets on the website: 3, 5, 7, 9, 10, 11, 12, 15, 16, 17, 18, 19, 22, 23, and 24.

ACKNOWLEDGEMENTS

I am indebted to many people who reviewed the first and second drafts of the manuscript that became this book. Their insightful comments and suggestions improved the coverage and exposition, and I deeply appreciate their efforts. The appearance of their names does not necessarily constitute their endorsement of the text or its methodology.

Sean Crockett, Baruch College, City University of New York
Benjamin Ho, Vassar College
Matthew Kovach, Virginia Tech
Jim Leitzel, University of Chicago
Jeffrey Naecker, Wesleyan University
Joe Price, Brigham Young University
Steven M. Sheffrin, Tulane University
Katie Sobota, Bowling Green State University
Julide Yazar, Ohio Wesleyan University

Introduction and Key Concepts of Microeconomics

This first chapter introduces behavioral economics as a field in economics and provides an overview of the book. In addition, the chapter reviews six key concepts of microeconomics that are deployed in behavioral economics. As we'll see throughout the book, the starting point for a model in behavioral economics is a conventional model of microeconomics that can be extended to account for behavioral considerations. The following six key concepts are typically covered in a course in intermediate microeconomics.

1. Opportunity cost

2. Marginal principle

3. Equimarginal principle

4. Nash equilibrium

5. Comparative statics

6. Pareto efficiency

Learning Objectives: The Explainer

After mastering this chapter, you will be able to explain each of the following statements.

1. Economic choice is based on thinking at the margin.

2. We have reached an equilibrium when no single individual has an incentive to change his or her choice.

3. A change in the value of a parameter changes an economic outcome.

4. An outcome is inefficient if we could make at least one person better off without harming anyone.

1.1 What Is Behavioral Economics?

Over the last few decades, behavioral scientists (economists, psychologists, anthropologists, neuroscientists, and biologists) have noticed patterns of behavior that appear to be inconsistent with traditional models of economic choice. There are five assumptions that people sometimes violate.

1. People are selfish, and ignore the consequences of their actions on others.
2. People evaluate future benefits and costs in a logically consistent way, and never regret past actions.
3. People perform thorough benefit–cost analysis of alternative actions, and don't take shortcuts.
4. Calculations of benefits and costs are correct, and are not subject to systematic bias.
5. People base choices on total wealth, not on gains and losses per se.

Behavioral economics provides evidence that people violate these assumptions, and develops models of choice that are more consistent with observed behavior.

Behavioral economics uses the standard toolbox of neoclassical economics, including models of constrained optimization. The workhorse model of behavioral economics is the model of individual utility maximization, in which an individual chooses the best feasible allocation of a resource, such as time or money. In many cases, a behavioral model simply extends a standard neoclassical model to incorporate assumptions that are consistent with observations of human behavior. In other words, behavioral economics is an extension of microeconomic analysis.

The book is organized into six parts. After two introductory chapters, the next four parts use models of constrained optimization to explore four topical areas of behavioral economics. In the last part, we use concepts from natural selection to gain some insights into human behavior.

Part 1: Introduction. Chapter 1 reviews six key concepts of microeconomics that are used throughout the book. Chapter 2 introduces key observations from behavioral scientists that provide the foundation for behavioral economics.

Part 2: Social Preferences and Pro-Social Behavior. Behavioral economics relaxes the assumption of strictly selfish behavior and explores pro-social behavior such as cooperation, trust, reciprocity, and voluntary contributions to public goods.

Part 3: Time Preferences and Intertemporal Choice. Behavioral economics explores decisions about how to allocate resources across time, including (i) how much to save for retirement, (ii) whether to consume unhealthy products such as cigarettes, (iii) when to perform a costly task, and (iv) when to collect a benefit. A common thread running through these choices is present bias, the tendency of a decision-maker to over-weight present benefits and costs and under-weight future benefits and costs.

Part 4: Mental Accounting and the Power of Loss. People use mental short-cuts (also known as heuristics) to simplify and shorten the decision-making process. Mental accounting organizes economic life into separate categories, with mental accounts that must be periodically balanced. In making decisions, the disutility of loss exceeds the utility of gain: losses loom larger than gains.

Part 5: Risk Preferences and Decisions in Uncertain Environments. Prospect theory is based on the observations that (i) many decisions are based on the possible gains and losses, (ii) individuals experience decreasing sensitivity to gains and losses, (iii) the disutility of loss exceeds the utility of gain, and (iv) humans are biased in their estimation and application of probabilities in making decisions. Prospect theory provides insights into investment choice, asset pricing, gambling, insurance, and goal setting.

Part 6: Natural *Selection and Culture.* Evolution during the roughly 2.4 million years of the hunter-gatherer era shaped human genomes and culture. The legacy of evolution during the hunter-gatherer era influences modern human behavior, including loss aversion, time preferences, and risk preferences.

Behavioral economics is a new and rapidly changing field in economics. The ongoing efforts of behavioral economists to develop and test theories of behavior are reported in articles in academic journals and summarized in books. The book by Dhami (2016) provides a rigorous and comprehensive summary of the field, and other books provide less technical discusions of the field and related ideas.

Dhami, Sanjit. *Foundations of Behavioral Economics*. Oxford University Press, 2016.

Henrich, Joseph. *The Secret of Our Success*. Princeton University Press, 2016.

Kahneman, Daniel. *Thinking Fast and Slow*. Farrar, Straus, and Girox, 2011.

Lewis, Michael. *The Undoing Project*. W.W. Norton & Company, 2015.

Sapolsky, Robert M. *Behave: The Biology of Humans at Our Best and Worst*. Penguin, 2018.

Thaler, Richard and Cass Sunstein. *Nudge: Improving Decisions About Health, Welfare and Happiness*. Penguin, 2009.

Thaler, Richard. *Misbehaving*. W.W. Norton & Company, 2015.

Review the Concepts 1.1

1. Conventional economic analysis is based on the assumption that decision-makers are [___]. (selfish, generous, irrational, logically consistent).

2. Conventional economic analysis is based on the assumption that an individual's benefit–cost analysis is [___]. (thorough, incomplete, biased, unbiased).

3. Behavioral economics [___] standard models of economics. (abandons, narrows, adopts, extends)

4. The workhorse model of behavioral economics is a model of [___]. (social welfare maximization, individual utility maximization, cost minimization, profit maximization)

1.2   Key Concepts: Marginal Reasoning

In this part of the chapter, we review three of the key concepts of microeconomics, listed below, that are used extensively in the book. The foundation of economic choice is marginal reasoning—thinking in terms of **marginal benefit** and **marginal cost**. As we'll see throughout the book, we can use marginal reasoning to get insights into decision-making and behavior.

1. Opportunity cost
2. Marginal principle
3. Equimarginal principle

Opportunity Cost

Economic cost is **opportunity cost**, and the opportunity cost of something is what you sacrifice to get it. We can state this more precisely.

> *The opportunity cost of using a resource is the value of that resource in its next-best use.*

Here are some upcoming examples of opportunity cost in behavioral economics.

- The opportunity cost of a contribution to support a public good is the utility value of private goods that could have been purchased instead.
- The opportunity cost of product purchased this year is the utility value of products that could be purchased next year instead.
- For a farmer, the opportunity cost of money spent on fertilizer is the utility value of the consumer goods that could be purchased instead.
- The opportunity cost of time spent performing a task such as pulling a weed is the value of time in its next-best use, such as leisure or earning income.
- For a worker, the opportunity cost of joining a risky start-up firm is the forgone certain salary in an established firm.

The Marginal Principle

Economic reasoning often focuses on marginal or incremental change. The marginal benefit of an activity is the additional benefit resulting from a one-unit increase in the activity. The marginal cost of an activity is the additional cost resulting from a one-unit increase in the activity. The **marginal principle** allows a decision-maker to fine-tune a decision by making small changes that improve the outcome.

The marginal principle provides a simple decision-making rule for choosing the appropriate level of an activity.

> *Marginal principle: Choose the level of an activity at which the marginal benefit equals the marginal cost.*

Suppose you start from a relatively low level of some activity. The marginal principle says that if the marginal benefit of the activity exceeds the marginal cost (if the additional benefit exceeds the additional cost), you should do more. And you should continue to increase the level of the activity until the marginal benefit equals the marginal cost. If at some point the marginal benefit is less than the marginal cost, you've gone too far, and the rational response is to do less.

To illustrate the marginal principle, consider a housing firm that will build a residential tower and rent the dwellings to households. The firm could use the marginal principle to determine how tall a structure to build. Figure 1.1 shows how to use the marginal principle to determine the profit-maximizing building height.

- *Marginal benefit.* The benefit of the building is the revenue generated by renting space to tenants, and the marginal benefit of height equals the rent collected on the additional (marginal) floor. As building height increases, the amount of space devoted to vertical transportation increases (more elevator shafts and wider staircases), so the rentable space per floor decreases. Each additional floor adds less to rental revenue than the previous floor, so marginal revenue decreases as building height increases. In Figure 1.1, the marginal-benefit curve is negatively sloped.
- *Marginal cost.* The marginal cost of building height equals the additional construction cost from building one more floor. A taller building requires more reinforcement to support its more concentrated weight, so each additional floor adds more to the construction cost than the previous floor. In other words, the marginal cost increases as building height increases. In Figure 1.1, the marginal-cost curve is positively sloped.

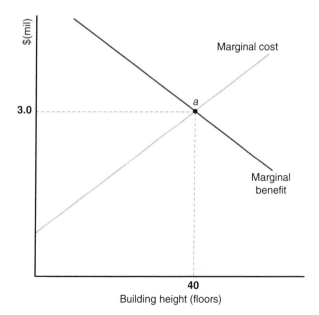

FIGURE 1.1: The Marginal Principle

The firm maximizes profit at point *a*, with 40 floors at a marginal cost of $3 million. The firm stops at 40 floors because the cost of adding the 41st floor (greater than $3 million) exceeds the rental revenue from the additional floor (less than $3 million).

Behavioral economics applies the marginal principle in all sorts of decision-making environments. Here are some upcoming applications of the marginal principle.

- A worker chooses the level of effort at which the marginal benefit equals the marginal cost. In behavioral economics, the calculation incorporates the benefit of adhering to a social norm of equal sharing of the gains from exchange. As a result, a worker may respond to an increase in the wage by working harder, even if the employer does not observe the increase in effort.
- A consumer of a product subject to voluntary pricing (pay what you want) chooses the price at which the marginal benefit equals the consumer's marginal cost. In behavioral economics, the calculation incorporates the benefit of adhering to a social norm of equal sharing of the gains from exchange. As a result, a consumer may pay a positive price, even though paying nothing is an option.
- A consumer with a goal of abstaining from a harmful product abstains as long as the marginal benefit exceeds the marginal cost. In behavioral economics, the marginal benefit may increase as the consumer gets closer to the abstinence goal. As a result, the consumer is more likely to reach the goal.

The Equimarginal Principle

The **equimarginal principle** is a variation on the marginal principle, and is a useful tool for the task of allocating a fixed quantity of a resource to two or more activities.

> *Equimarginal principle: To allocate a fixed amount of a resource to competing uses, choose the feasible bundle (adding-up constraint) that equates the marginal benefit across the competing uses (**equimarginal rule**).*

The equimarginal principle is versatile and can be used to allocate all sorts of resources, including time, physical resources, and financial resources.

To illustrate the equimarginal principle, consider a student who allocates a fixed number of hours to study for exams in anthropology (A) and biology (B). The student's objective is to maximize the sum of the two exam grades. The marginal benefit of study time is the increase in the exam score resulting from one additional hour of study. To maximize the sum of the exam scores, the student chooses the bundle of hours in anthropology and biology that satisfies two conditions.

- *Equimarginal rule.* The marginal benefit of an hour in anthropology equals the marginal benefit of an hour in biology.
- *Adding up.* The hours allocated to the two courses add up to the fixed number of study hours.

To summarize, the student chooses a feasible mix of study hours that makes the marginal benefit in one course equal to the marginal benefit in the other course.

Figure 1.2 applies the equimarginal principle to the allocation of 24 hours to the two exams. The right panel shows the marginal benefit per hour on biology (B), with the number of hours increasing as we move from left to right. The negative slope reflects the assumption of diminishing marginal returns to study: the first hour of study increases the exam score by more than the second hour, and the second hour increases the exam score by more than the third hour, and so on. The left panel shows the marginal benefit per hour on anthropology (A), with the number of hours increasing as we move from right to left. The positive slope reflects the assumption of diminishing marginal returns to study time. The equimarginal principle is satisfied at points *a* and *b*, with 8 hours for anthropology and 16 hours for biology.

- *Equimarginal rule.* For each course, the marginal benefit per hour is 3 points.
- *Adding up.* The student allocates 8 hours to anthropology and 16 hours to biology, for a total of 24 hours.

The allocation of study hours (8, 16) satisfies both conditions, so it is the best feasible allocation.

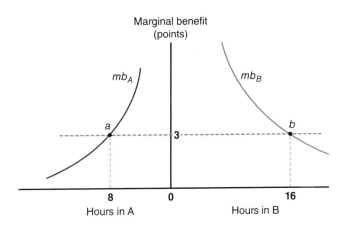

FIGURE 1.2: Equimarginal Principle

Behavioral economics applies the equimarginal principle to all sorts of decisions. Here are some upcoming applications of the equimarginal principle.

- A person chooses the level of retirement saving at which the marginal benefit of consuming now equals the marginal benefit of consuming later. In behavioral economics, present bias causes people to under-weight the benefits of future consumption. As a result, some people don't save much for retirement, and later regret their meager saving.
- A consumer chooses the mix of healthy and unhealthy products (sugary drinks, cigarettes) at which the marginal benefit per dollar spent on a healthy product equals the marginal benefit per dollar spent on an

unhealthy product. In behavioral economics, present bias causes people to under-weight the future health costs of smoking and other unhealthy products. As a result, some people later regret their unhealthy consumer choices.

Review the Concepts 1.2

1. Economic cost is [___]. (average cost, accounting cost, opportunity cost, fixed cost)

2. In economic analysis, an optimizing decision-maker chooses the level of an activity at which [___]. (total benefit = total cost, average benefit = average cost, marginal benefit = marginal cost, total benefit is maximized, total cost is minimized)

3. A decision-maker has a fixed number of hours to allocate to two activities J and K. The equimarginal rule is [___] benefit of J = [___] of K. (average, average; marginal, average; marginal, marginal; total, total)

4. A decision-maker has 24 hours to allocate to two activities J and K. The adding-up constraint is [___]. ($J = K = 12$, $J = K/2$, $24 = J + K$, $K = J/2$)

1.3 Key Concepts: Equilibrium and Efficiency

In this part of the chapter, we review three more key concepts of microeconomics. Individual choices occur in environments where many decision-makers interact to allocate scarce resources among competing users. These interactions result in an equilibrium outcome—a situation in which no single individual has an incentive to change his or her behavior. Once we reach an equilibrium outcome, two questions arise.

1. *Comparative statics.* How would a change in the decision-making environment affect the equilibrium outcome?
2. *Pareto efficiency.* Is the equilibrium efficient?

Nash Equilibrium

In microeconomics, an equilibrium is defined as an outcome such that there is no incentive for any single individual to change his or her behavior.

> *Nash equilibrium: An allocation such that there is no incentive for unilateral deviation.*

We have reached a **Nash equilibrium** if no single participant has an incentive to change his or her behavior, given the choices made by other participants. The word "unilateral" captures two features: (i) there is no incentive for a single participant to deviate, and (ii) the choices of other participants are assumed to be given. In more casual terms, we have a Nash equilibrium if there are no regrets: no single participant wishes that he or she had made a different choice, given the choices made by other participants.

As an illustration of Nash equilibrium, suppose two vendors sell ice cream along a beach that is 11 blocks long. Consumers are uniformly distributed along the beach, with two customers in each block. Each consumer patronizes the closest ice-cream vendor, and the firm's profit per customer is $1. Figure 1.3 shows an initial location pattern and the transition to the Nash equilibrium.

- *Panel 1: Initial location pattern.* Vendors Lefty and Righty divide the beach into two equal market areas, and each locates at the center of its market. Lefty is closer to consumers in blocks 1 through 5 (a total of 10 customers), while Righty is closer to customers in blocks 7 through 11 (a total of 10 customers). The vendors are equally distant from the two consumers in block 6, and each firm gets one indifferent consumer. Each vendor has 11 customers, so the profit per firm is $11.
- *Panel 2: Unilateral deviation increases Lefty's profit.* Suppose Lefty moves to block 6. This is the median location, defined as the location that splits consumers into two equal groups: 5 consumers are to the left and 5 customers are to the right. Lefty is now closer to all consumers in block 1 through block 7, meaning that the unilateral deviation increases Lefty's number of customers to 14 and increases profit to $14. In contrast, Righty now has only 8 consumers and an $8 profit.
- *Panel 3: Unilateral deviation increases Righty's profit.* If Righty moves to the median location (block 6), the two firms again split the market equally, so Righty's profit increases from $8 to $11, and Lefty's decreases to $11.

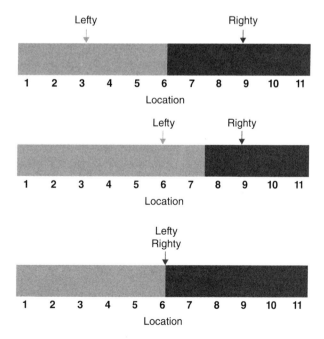

FIGURE 1.3: Nash Equilibrium on the Beach

When both vendors reach the median location, there is no incentive for unilateral deviation. Suppose a vendor moved away from the median location. The vendor would move away from a majority of consumers and toward a minority of consumers, so the number of customers would decrease. In the Nash equilibrium, both vendors are located at the median location, and each gets half the market.

As we'll see in later chapters, the introduction of behavioral concerns can change a Nash equilibrium. To illustrate, we will start by deriving a Nash equilibrium in a particular economic environment under the conventional assumptions of selfish and fully rational choice. Then we introduce pro-social behavior or other departures from the conventional assumptions, and show how the Nash equilibrium changes. For example, under the conventional assumptions, the Nash equilibrium price for a product sold under voluntary pricing (pay what you want) is zero: if you're selfish, why pay anything when you can get it for free? But if buyers are sensitive to a social norm of sharing the gains from exchange, the Nash equilibrium price will be positive. As we'll see, the introduction of behavioral concerns affects the Nash equilibrium in all sorts of economic environments.

Comparative Statics

Economists use **comparative statics** to explore the effects of a change in the value of one economic variable on the value of another variable. In the economic analysis of rational choice by individuals, firms, and other decision-makers, we can distinguish between two types of variables.

- *Choice variable.* The value is chosen by the decision-maker. For example, a consumer chooses how much coffee to drink.
- *Parameter.* The value is beyond the control of the decision-maker. For example, a consumer takes as given the prices of coffee, milk, tea, and other goods.

We can use comparative statics to explore the effect of a change in the value of a single **parameter** (choice environment) on the value of a **choice variable**. For example, we can explore the effect of an increase in the price of coffee (a parameter) on the utility-maximizing quantity of coffee (a choice variable).

Economics also explores the economic forces that generate a market equilibrium. In the economic analysis of market equilibrium, we can distinguish between two types of variables.

- *Equilibrium variable.* The value is determined within the market under consideration, for example, the equilibrium price of coffee.
- *Parameter.* The value is determined beyond the market under consideration. For the coffee market, the parameters include the amount of rainfall, the price of fertilizer, and the wage of farm workers. The values of these variables are determined outside the coffee market, and are taken as given in determining the equilibrium price and quantity of coffee.

We can use comparative statics to predict the effect of a change in the value of a single **parameter** (equilibrium environment) on the value of an **equilibrium variable**.

For example, we could predict the effect of an increase in the wage of farm workers (a parameter for the coffee market) on the equilibrium price of coffee (an equilibrium variable).

The label "comparative statics" is revealing. The word "static" is a synonym for "equilibrium," and comparative statics compares two equilibria. The equilibria differ because they are generated by different sets of parameter values. Specifically, we change the value of a single parameter while holding the values of the other parameters fixed, and compare the two outcomes.

Here are some upcoming applications of comparative statics in behavioral economics. In each case, we underline the parameter and italicize the equilibrium or choice variable.

- An increase in the sensitivity to violating a social norm of sharing increases the *price paid by a consumer* who can choose any price, including zero.
- An increase in the strength of present bias decreases *saving*, increases *smoking*, and increases *procrastination*.
- An increase in the pain of loss relative to the pleasure of gain decreases *investment in risky assets such as stocks and start-ups*.

Pareto Efficiency

The notion of economic efficiency is embodied in the concept of **Pareto efficiency**, named after Italian economist Vilfredo Pareto. The concept of Pareto efficiency is based on a simple thought experiment. Starting from some initial allocation of resources, could we do better? We could do better if there is a **Pareto improvement**.

> *Pareto improvement: a reallocation of resources that makes at least one person better off without making anyone worse off.*

To determine whether an allocation is Pareto efficient, we check for Pareto improvements.

- An allocation is **Pareto inefficient** if there is a Pareto improvement.
- An allocation is **Pareto efficient** if there are no Pareto improvements.

We can illustrate the notion of Pareto efficiency with an example from a workplace. Consider a producer with 100 workers, each of whom chooses his or her worker effort. The total quantity produced is determined by the collective efforts of the workers. Consider the implications of a one-unit increase in effort by each worker.

- The marginal cost of effort is $3: the disutility of the additional effort is equivalent to a $3 loss of wealth.
- The increase in worker effort increases the quantity produced, increasing total revenue by $7 per worker.

There is an opportunity for a Pareto improvement: a one-unit increase in effort has a cost of $300 to workers ($3 ×100 workers) and a benefit of $700 to the producer ($7 ×100 workers). So workers and the producer have an opportunity to share a $400 gain.

In a world of perfect information in the workplace, the Pareto improvement is likely. Suppose the producer and the workers agree to share the $400 gain equally. The wage increases by $5, and each worker increases effort by one unit, at a cost to the worker of $3. As a result, the gain per worker is $2 = $5 – $3. The producer monitors each worker (at zero cost) to verify that each worker increases his or her effort. The producer gets $700 in additional revenue at a cost of $500, generating a gain of $200 = $700 – $500.

As we'll see later in the book, there is a problem with this potential Pareto improvement, and there is also a possible solution. The problem is that it may be costly or impractical to monitor the efforts of individual workers. As a result, individual workers may fail to increase their effort levels in response to the higher wage. The possible solution is that workers may observe a social norm of sharing the benefits of exchange. If so, workers may increase their effort levels in response to the higher wage, even if they are not being monitored.

Review the Concepts 1.3

1. In a Nash equilibrium, there is no incentive for [___] (unilateral, bilateral, multilateral, devious) deviation.

2. Economists use comparative statics to predict the effect of a change in the value of a(n) [___] on the value of a(n) [___] variable. (parameter, equilibrium; choice, parameter; parameter, choice; equilibrium, parameter)

3. A Pareto improvement makes [___] better off. (at least two individuals, a majority of individuals, at least one individual)

4. A Pareto improvement makes [___] worse off. (no one, only one individual, at least one individual, a minority of individuals, at least one individual)

5. A Pareto improvement [___]. (makes at least one individual better off, makes a majority of individuals better off, harms only one individual, harms no one, harms a minority of individuals)

Key Terms

choice variable, p. 10
comparative statics, p. 10
equilibrium variable, p. 10
equimarginal principle, p. 6
equimarginal rule, p. 6
marginal benefit, p. 4
marginal cost, p. 4

marginal principle, p. 4
Nash equilibrium, p. 8
opportunity cost (economic cost),
   p. 4
opportunity cost, p. 4
parameter (choice environment),
   p. 10

parameter (equilibrium
   environment), p. 10
Pareto efficient allocation, p. 11
Pareto improvement, p. 11
Pareto inefficient allocation, p. 11

Takeaways

1. Behavioral scientists have noticed patterns of behavior that appear to be inconsistent with traditional models of economic choice based on the assumptions of (i) selfish behavior, (ii) logically consistent evaluation of future benefits and costs, (iii) thorough benefit–cost analysis, (iv) unbiased calculations of benefits and costs, and (v) using total wealth as a basis for decisions.

2. In many cases, a model in behavioral economics simply extends a standard neoclassical model to incorporate assumptions that are consistent with observations of human behavior.

3. Economic cost is opportunity cost, and the opportunity cost of something is what you sacrifice to get it.

4. A decision-maker who applies the marginal principle chooses the level of an activity at which the marginal benefit equals the marginal cost.

5. A decision-maker who applies the equimarginal principle allocates resources to two activities to ensure that the marginal benefit in one activity equals the marginal benefit in the other activity.

6. In a Nash equilibrium, there is no incentive for unilateral deviation: no single participant has an incentive to change his or her behavior, given the behavior of other participants.

7. We can use comparative statics to explore the effect of a change in the value of a single parameter on the value of a choice variable or the value of an equilibrium variable.

8. An allocation is Pareto efficient if there are no Pareto improvements, where a Pareto improvement is a reallocation of resources that makes at least one person better off without making anyone worse off.

Discuss the Concepts

1. *Expedition Cost.* The five members of the BukoUlo tribe differ in their productivity in harvesting coconuts: one coconut harvested per day for worker 1, two coconuts per day for worker 2, and so on up to five coconuts per day for worker 5. The tribe will choose two people to serve as scouts in a one-day expedition to explore the island.

    a. If the tribe randomly picks two members to serve as scouts, the economic cost of an expedition could be as low as [___] or as high as [___] coconuts.

    b. Suppose the tribe will use a market system to choose scouts. The market-clearing wage is [___] and the cost of the expedition is [___] coconuts.

    c. An increase in the scout wage [___] (↑, ↓, does not change) the economic cost.

2. *Driving Speed.* For Khrash, the marginal benefit of driving speed is mb(s) = $3. As speed increases, the expected cost associated with an accident increases at an increasing rate: the marginal cost of speed is mc(s) = (s/10). The utility-maximizing speed is $s^* =$ [___]. Illustrate.

3. *Equimarginal Principle in the Factory.* A firm has 60 workers to allocate to the production of two products, small solar panels and large solar panels. The marginal benefit from workers producing small panels is mb(S) = 600/S, where S is the number of workers producing small panels. The marginal benefit from workers producing large panels is mb(L) = 300/L, where L is the number of workers producing large panels. The profit-maximizing mix is S^* = [___] and L^* = $[___]. The common marginal benefit is $[___]. Illustrate.

4. *Median Voter.* Consider a school-board election in which each citizen votes for the candidate whose proposed school budget is closest to the citizen's preferred budget. The distribution of voter preferences is uniform, with 10 voters in each $1 interval from $1 through $7. There are two candidates, Left and Right.

   a. The Nash equilibrium is a proposed budget of $[___] for Left and $[___] for Right. The outcome of the election is [___] votes for Left and [___] votes for Right.

   b. Starting from the Nash equilibrium, suppose Right increased his or her proposed budget by $1. The new election outcome is [___] votes for Left and [___] votes for Right. Illustrate.

5. *Airbags and Speed.* Khrash just replaced the old car with a new car that has mandated safety equipment such as air bags.

   a. The new mandate for air bags [___] (↑, ↓, does not change) the marginal cost of speed, from mc(s) = s/10 to mc(s) = [___] (s/10, s/20, s/5).

   b. The mandate for airbags [___] (↑, ↓, does not change) the driving speed from [___] mph to [___] mph. Illustrate.

   c. For bicyclists and pedestrians, a mandate to install airbags brings [___] (good, bad) news because [___].

6. *Twins Outrun a Bear?* Dash and Slog are identical twins, so they have the same shoe size. On a camping trip, the twins awake in their tent to the sound of a rustling, pawing bear. Slog calmly puts on his running shoes and starts stretching.

   Dash: What are you doing? You can't outrun a hungry bear.
   Slog: I don't have to outrun the bear. I just have to outrun you.

   Dash is a faster runner if either (i) both twins wear shoes, or (ii) neither twin wears shoes. A person wearing shoes outruns a person without shoes. The bear will eat one person and his or her shoes.

   a. In the Nash equilibrium, [___] campers wear shoes.

   b. In the Pareto-efficient outcome, [___] campers wear shoes.

   c. The efficiency gain from switching from the Nash equilibrium to the Pareto-efficient outcome is [___].

Apply the Concepts

1. *Barbershop Hours.* Suppose the marginal cost of operating your barber-shop (for wages, electricity, heating/cooling) is constant at $20 per hour. The marginal benefit of operating the barbershop is mb(h) = 240/h, where h is the number of hours. The profit-maximizing number of hours is $h^* =$ [___]. Illustrate.

2. *Equimarginal Principle on the Farm.* A farmer has 100 hours to allocate to two crops, alfalfa (A) and barley (B). The marginal benefit of time spent on alfalfa is mb(A) = 600/A, where A is the hours on alfalfa. The marginal benefit of time spent on barley is mb(B) = 200/B, where B is the hours on barley.

   a. The profit-maximizing mix is $A^* =$ [___] and $B^* =$ [___]. Illustrate.

   b. The common marginal benefit is $[___]. Illustrate.

3. *Comparative Statics and Barbershop Hours.* Suppose the marginal cost of operating your barbershop (for wages, electricity, heating/cooling) is constant. The marginal benefit of operating the barbershop is mb(h) = 240/h, where h is the number of hours. If the marginal cost increases from $20 to $30, the profit-maximizing number of hours [___] (↑, ↓, does not change) from [___] to [___]. Illustrate.

4. A proposed neighborhood park would generate a benefit of $6 for each of 100 households. The cost of the proposed park ($300) is to be covered by voluntary contributions. If the contribution campaign fails to raise $300, the park will not be built, and all contributions will be returned. Any excess contributions will be returned to contributors in a proportionate fashion.

   a. Suppose each household contributes $4. This [___] (is, is not) a Nash equilibrium because [___].

   b. Suppose each household contributes $3. This [___] (is, is not) a Nash equilibrium because [___].

   c. Suppose 75 households contribute, and the contribution per household is $4. This [___] (is, is not) a Nash equilibrium because [___].

5. *Nash, Pareto, and a Land Auction.* A hectare of land will be auctioned by its owner to the highest bidder among 90 farmers. Farmers vary in their value for the land: the value ranges from $v =$ $10 to $v =$ $100, with one farmer for each integer value.

   a. The Nash equilibrium price is $p^* =$ $[___].

   b. The Pareto-efficient price is [___]. Hint: the absence of "=" is deliberate.

2 Insights from Behavioral Science

The Ju/'hoansi are mobile hunter-gatherers in the Kalahari Desert in southern Africa. Members of a tribe engage in group hunting, and the harvested meat is shared in accordance with social norms. The owner of the arrowhead that takes down an animal takes ownership of the harvest, and is responsible for distributing the meat to members of the tribe. Hunters often use an arrowhead owned by someone else, and thus avoid the politically sensitive task of dividing the harvest. In many cases, elderly men and women loan their arrowheads to hunters, so non-hunting elders divide the harvest among members of the tribe (Henrich 2016).

Behavioral economics is distinguished from traditional economics in a number of respects. Over the last few decades, behavioral scientists (economists, psychologists, anthropologists, neuroscientists, and biologists) have noticed patterns of behavior that seem inconsistent with traditional models of economic choice. Behavioral economists have responded by developing decision-making models that are more compatible with observed human behavior. In this chapter, we introduce some of these observed patterns of behavior and set the stage for the rest of the book.

The traditional model of economic choice deploys a number of assumptions about human behavior. These assumptions are useful abstractions from reality and provide many important insights into decision-making.

1. *Perfectly selfish motives.* An individual maximizes personal utility, and ignores any consequences of his or her actions on other individuals. In the language of behavioral economics, an individual has **self-regarding preferences**.

2. *Comprehensive benefit–cost analysis.* A decision-maker considers many alternative actions, and computes the benefit and cost of each possible action. The individual chooses the action that generates the largest gap between benefit and cost.

3. *Correct benefit–cost analysis.* An decision-maker correctly computes the benefit and cost of each possible action. There are no systematic errors in computing benefits and costs.

These assumptions are widely used in economics, but are not universal. Some economists have developed models that explore the choices of individuals who are not perfectly selfish. Other models consider the choices of individuals whose benefit–cost analysis is imperfect. But in many cases, these assumptions provide the starting point for models of economic choice.

This chapter is organized around alternatives to these traditional assumptions. Part 1 introduces the notion of social preferences as embodied in social norms, providing an alternative to the assumption of selfish behavior. Part 2 introduces the idea of mental shortcuts, which simplify the decision-making process and provide an alternative to comprehensive benefit–cost analysis. Parts 3 and 4 discuss some systematic errors in the decision-making process that can lead to faulty benefit–cost analysis and misguided decisions. In Part 5, we discuss the notion that decisions do not emerge from cool-headed rational thinking, but instead emerge from a complex mix of instinctive urges and thoughtful deliberation.

Learning Objectives: The Explainer

After mastering this chapter, you will be able to explain each of the following statements.

1. Decision-makers in behavioral economics differ from decision-makers in traditional economics in three respects.

2. Adam Smith used the impartial spectator to represent the effects of social norms on individual behavior.

3. Youngsters (two- to three-year-olds) are inclined to share some types of rewards but not others.

4. Decision-makers sometimes use mental shortcuts rather than comprehensive benefit–cost analysis.

5. Decision-making is affected by a number of cognitive biases, including the decoy effect and present bias.

6. Humans have trouble in applying probabilities in making decisions: rare events are particularly troublesome, and the gambler's fallacy distorts decisions.

2.1   Social Preferences and Social Norms

A key innovation of behavioral economics is to introduce **other-regarding preferences** as an alternative to purely selfish motives. A person with other-regarding preferences considers the consequences of his or her actions on other individuals, and a synonym is "social preferences." As we'll see in Part 2 of this book, the introduction of social preferences allows us to explore pro-social behavior such as cooperation, trust, and reciprocity.

We use the notion of a **social norm** to incorporate other-regarding preferences into the decision-making process of an individual. A social norm is a context-specific rule for the behavior of members of a social group. Individuals in a group are expected to (i) conform to group norms and (ii) enforce conformity on other members of the group (Tomasello 2019). Social norms are collective expectations for individual behavior, and are taken as given by a member of the group. In this part of the chapter, we tap the wisdom of Adam Smith, who wrote in 1759 about the role of social preferences in a market economy. In addition, we present the results of modern experiments that demonstrate the power of social norms to influence decisions.

Adam Smith on Social Norms and the Impartial Spectator

The writings of Adam Smith provide insights into the role of social preferences in decision-making. In *The Theory of Moral Sentiments*, Smith focuses on individual decision-making in a social context. In the first sentence of the book, Smith notes that our sentiments include both self-interest and interests in the welfare of others (Smith 1982, 9).

> How selfish soever a man may be supposed, there are evidently some principles in his nature, which interest him in the fortune of others, and render their happiness necessary to him, though he derives nothing from it, except the pleasure of seeing it.

Later in the book, Smith identifies the human virtues associated with concerns for self and concern for others. (Smith 1982, 262).

> Concern for our own happiness recommends to us the virtue of prudence; concern for that of other people, the virtues of justice and beneficence . . .

In Smith's framework of socially aware decision-making, individual choice incorporates the judgement of what he calls an impartial spectator (Smith 1982, 113).

> When I endeavor to examine my own conduct, . . . to approve or condemn it, . . . I divide myself . . . into two persons . . . the judge, and the person whose conduct is . . . judged. . . . The first is the spectator, whose sentiments with regard to my own conduct I endeavor to enter into, by placing myself in his situation . . .

Smith notes the trade-off between self interest and the actions favored by the impartial spectator (Smith 1982, 82).

> Every man is . . . by nature, first and principally recommended to his own care . . . If he would act so . . . that the impartial spectator may [approve] his conduct . . . he must . . . humble the arrogance of his self-love, and bring it down to something which other men can go along with.

The sentiments of the impartial spectator reflect social norms, many of which require an individual to suppress selfish behavior (humble the arrogance of self-love) and act in the social interest (something that others can go along with).

Rule-Following Task: Avatar Pedestrian

The power of a norm is demonstrated by an experiment performed by Kimbrough and Vostroknutov (2016). Each subject in the experiment controls an avatar on a computer screen that must cross five crosswalks, each with a red/green (wait/walk) light. The subject hits the START button, and the avatar proceeds to the first crosswalk, where the red light is illuminated for five seconds, followed by a green light. The subjects are told, "The rule is to wait at each stop light until it turns green." The subject can press the WALK button any time to get the avatar to cross the crosswalk. A subject who crosses during a red light violates the rule, while a subject who waits five seconds for the green light obeys the rule. The process is repeated for the second through the fifth crosswalks: each subject has five opportunities to obey or violate the rule.

Figure 2.1 illustrates the crosswalk experiment. The rectangles show the lights, with the upper circle showing a "wait" light and the lower circle showing a "walk" light. The dots show walking time, with one dot per second. There are five dots for crossing each of the five crosswalks. The diamonds show waiting time, with one second per diamond. A faithful rule follower waits five seconds at each light (five diamonds shown below the red light), and then takes five seconds to cross each crosswalk (five dots from the green light to the next red light). As a result, the total time spent to complete the course is 50 seconds: 25 waiting diamonds + 25 walking dots. A rule breaker avoids the waiting diamonds. In the extreme case of never following the rule, an individual takes only 25 seconds to cross all five crosswalks. For an individual who follows the rule at four of five lights, the total crossing time is 45 seconds: 20 waiting diamonds + 25 walking dots.

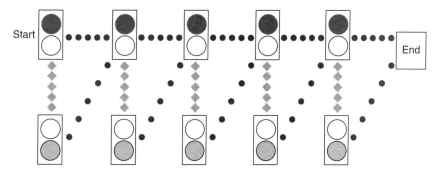

FIGURE 2.1: Crosswalk Experiment

The subjects in the experiment face a trade-off between following the rule and a material benefit. Each subject starts with 8 euros, and each second spent walking or waiting on the crossing task reduces the payoff by 0.08 euro. Over the course of the five crosswalks, walking time reduces the payoff by 2 euros (equal to 25 times 0.08). Therefore, a person who violates the rule for all five crosswalks (crosses while the light is red) gets a payoff of 6 euros. For a subject who always obeys the rule, the total waiting cost is 2 euros, so the payoff is only 4 euros.

The waiting cost of 0.08 euro per second incorporates the notion that observing a social norm can be costly.

The results of the experiment revealed the power of a rule to affect behavior. The average waiting time was 22.5 seconds (22.5 orange waiting diamonds), compared to a maximum waiting time of 25 seconds (25 orange waiting diamonds).

1. *Strict rule followers.* Five-eighths of the subjects (62.5 percent) waited the full 25 seconds, and thus bore a waiting cost of 2 euros that could have been avoided by violating the rule.
2. *Rule breakers.* Three-eighths of the subjects (37.5 percent) violated the rule at least once.
3. *Frequent rule followers.* Many of the rule-breakers followed the rule for several of the five crosswalks. On average, the waiting time for a member of a rule-breaking group was 19 seconds.

The experiment illustrates the inclination of people to adhere to a rule, even when it means sacrificing material gains. As we'll see later in the book, this inclination plays an important role in pro-social behavior supported by a sensitivity to social norms.

Sharing the Rewards of Collaboration

As documented by behavioral scientists, a key manifestation of other-regarding preferences is sharing. Experiments with youngsters (two- to three-year-old humans) provide insights into sharing in an environment of collaboration. Evidence for sharing comes from the rope-pulling experiment (Hamann et al. 2011).

- If two youngsters pull the two ends of a rope simultaneously, the collaborative effort delivers a total of four toys (marbles) to the youngsters.
- If only one youngster pulls the rope, the rope runs through the mechanism without delivering any toys.

Youngsters quickly figure out how to collaborate to get the rewards. When the reward comes in a single bundle, youngsters usually share the reward equally.

What happens when by chance one youngster gets more marbles than the other? For example, suppose the lucky youngster gets three marbles, compared to only one for an unlucky youngster. In roughly three-fourths of trials in the rope-pulling experiment, the lucky youngster transfers a marble to the unlucky youngster to equalize the rewards. The frequency of the equal-sharing outcome is roughly the same (75 percent) for both repeated games and one-shot games. In other words, even when youngsters realize that there is no future collaboration—and thus no motivation for strategic sharing—they equalize rewards at the same rate. A similar experiment (Warneken et al. 2011) explored responses to greedy behavior. When a lucky youngster is greedy (tries to keep more than half the reward), the unlucky youngster typically protests the unequal allocation, and the greedy youngster typically relents and equalizes the reward.

The key to the equal-sharing outcome is collaboration. Figure 2.2 shows the results of the experiment for two cases: collaboration (pull together on a common board to get toys) and parallel (pull separately on individual boards to get toys). As we've seen, the collaborative case generates equal sharing in 75 percent of trials. In contrast, when the youngsters work in parallel, a lucky youngster equalizes the reward in only 25 percent of trials. The authors note, "Taken together, these studies show that collaborative work encourages equal sharing in children much more than does working in parallel or acquiring resources in a windfall" (Hamann et al. 2011, 328).

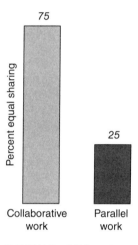

FIGURE 2.2: Collaboration and Sharing

The results from the rope-pulling experiment for youngsters suggest that instincts play a role in a social norm of sharing the fruits of a collaborative activity. Equal sharing occurs frequently, despite the fact that youngsters don't have the cognitive ability or lengthy experience to learn a sharing norm from adults or other children. When the sharing norm is violated, most shortchanged youngsters protest, and most greedy youngsters relent and divide the reward equally. Experiments in a wide variety of cultural environments generate the same results, suggesting that the equal sharing of a reward generated by collaboration is a human universal, at least for three-year-olds (Tomasello 2019). Later in life, older children develop sharing norms that vary from one culture to another, and differences in behavior emerge.

How do the results of the rope-pulling experiment fit into Adam Smith's framework of social norms? In the case of collaboration, the high frequency of equal sharing is consistent with an impartial spectator who expects equal sharing in a collaborative environment. When people work together to get a reward, the social norm is equal sharing. In the case of parallel work, the lower frequency of equal sharing is consistent with an impartial spectator who expects less sharing of the rewards of independent effort.

The 50–50 Norm

Andreoni and Bernheim (2009) document the widespread use of the equal-sharing norm (also known as the 50–50 norm) in dividing resources. Equal sharing is common in joint business ventures, tenancy in agriculture, and restaurant tabs. These are all cases of collaboration in the pursuit of a reward, and a high frequency of equal sharing is consistent with frequent sharing among collaborating youngsters in the rope-pulling experiment.

The Andreoni-Bernheim theory of the 50–50 norm is based on the notion that people like to be perceived as fair, that an individual's social image matters. Their experimental results suggest that the likelihood of equal sharing increases as the observability of sharing increases. In the experiment, an adult (the donor) receives $20 to keep or share with an adult recipient. The observers to the sharing outcome are the participants (donor and recipient) and individuals working in the lab. In other words, there are actual impartial spectators observing the donor's sharing behavior. In the baseline case, all the observers know for certain that the donor makes the sharing decision. In this case of full observability, 57 percent of donors followed the 50–50 norm, and only 30 percent gave nothing to the recipient.

To test the role of observability, the experimenters developed a randomized process to make it unclear whether the sharing decision was made by the donor or a computer. Specifically, the probability that a decision was made by the donor was 0.25: only one of four decisions was made by the donor, and the other three were made by a computer. All the observers (participants and lab workers) observed the actual sharing outcome, but didn't know whether the decision was made by the donor or the computer. The observers did know that the likelihood of a donor decision was only 25 percent. In this randomized case with incomplete observability, only 34 percent of donors followed the 50–50 norm, while 48 percent gave nothing.

These experimental results are consistent with a social norm of sharing. The experiments with youngsters suggest that a social norm of sharing is at least partly instinctive. Between childhood and adulthood, social norms are shaped by education and social interactions. Recall that Adam Smith's impartial spectator is an internal judge that promotes pro-social behavior. The Andreoni and Bernheim results suggest that actual spectators matter too: they promote pro-social behavior because an individual may be sensitive to the judgement of others.

Incurring a Cost to Enforce a Social Norm

As we've seen, a member of a social group is expected to (i) conform to group norms and (ii) enforce conformity on other members of the group. Recall part of an earlier quote from Adam Smith:

> Every man . . . must . . . humble the arrogance of his self-love, and bring it down to something which other men can go along with.

When a person fails to bring down selfish behavior to a level that other people "can go along with," he or she violates a social norm and may be punished.

Punishment is costly for a punisher, who incurs an opportunity cost for the resources (including time) allocated to punishing a norm violator. Boyd, Bowles, and Gintis (2010) explore the role of punishment in promoting cooperation.

Experiments with young children show that five-year-olds are willing to bear a cost to punish a violator of social norms. In one experiment with middle-income American children, a youngster was joined by two puppets in a three-way sharing game (Robbins and Rochat 2011). The players shared poker chips, which the youngster used to purchase toys at the end of the experiment. In each round, each player received nine chips to keep or share with the two other players. The puppets differed in their sharing behavior.

- *Stingy.* One puppet regularly kept seven chips and gave one to the other puppet and one to the youngster.
- *Generous.* One puppet regularly kept one chip and gave four to the other puppet and four to the youngster.

After several rounds of sharing, the experimenter reported the total number of chips for each player. The youngster then had an opportunity to direct the experimenter to take some chips away from the puppets and remove them from the experiment. Punishment was costly to the youngster: for each set of five chips taken from the puppets, the youngster paid one chip to the experimenter.

The key question is whether youngsters are willing to bear a cost to punish a puppet that violated a social norm of sharing. Costly punishment by the youngsters was frequent and selective: youngsters punished stingy puppets more frequently. In other words, the five-year-olds in the experiment incurred costs to punish norm violators. In contrast, three-year-olds did not discriminate between stingy and generous puppets. There was similar non-discriminatory punishment in a parallel experiment with five-year-olds from rural Samoa. The lack of discriminatory punishment by three-year-old Americans and five-year-old Samoans suggests that learning and culture play important roles in the punishment of norm violators.

Salali, Juda, and Henrich (2015) explore the role of cultural learning in the costly punishment of norm violators. The participants (youngsters aged 3 to 8 years) observed an interaction in which one individual (the donor) either (i) shared four stickers equally with another individual (the recipient) or (ii) kept three of the four stickers and gave only one to the recipient. A participant was given six stickers to start, and then had the opportunity to incur a cost (lose one sticker) to punish the donor (decrease the donor's stickers by two). Children of all ages punished both types of donors—those who shared equally, and those who were greedy (kept three of four stickers). Younger children (age 3 to 5) punished both types of donors at roughly the same frequency, while older children punished the greedy donors more frequently. In other words, the selective punishment of unequal outcomes begins to emerge at age 5 years.

To explore the role of cultural learning, the experimenters allowed some participants to observe another child making a punishment decision. Before making their own decisions, participants in the treatment group observed another child deciding whether to punish a donor or not. The question is whether a participant would be influenced by the decision of another child. For both equal-sharing donors and greedy donors, the participants imitated other children.

1. *Equal sharing.* Seeing another child punish an equal-sharing donor increased the frequency of punishment, while seeing another child not punish an equal-sharing donor decreased the frequency of punishment.
2. *Greedy.* Seeing another child punish a greedy donor increased the frequency of punishment, while seeing another child not punish the greedy donor decreased the frequency of punishment.

Salali, Juda, and Henrich (2015) summarize their results as follows.

> Our findings support the view that cultural learning builds on existing aspects of an evolved social psychology, as children can readily acquire social norms (for or against) punishing either equal or unequal distributions via cultural transmission.

In other words, a norm of punishing norm violators can be acquired by observing the actions of others.

Self-Domestication

Henrich (2016) uses the notion of self-domestication to explain the role of social norms in human behavior.

> Over our evolutionary history, the sanctions for norm violations and the rewards for norm compliance have driven a process of self-domestication that has endowed our species with a *norm psychology* that has several components. (Henrich 2016,189)

A key component of norm psychology is that humans learn social norms by observing others. At an early age, humans develop the cognitive abilities and motivations to (i) learn the local rules for social interaction, (ii) identify norm violations, and (iii) monitor our reputations in terms of adhering to social norms. A second component is that a learned norm is at least partly internalized.

> This internalization helps us navigate the social world more effectively and avoid temptations to break the rules to obtain immediate benefits. . . . This means that our automatic and unreflective responses come to match the normatively required ones. Other times, internalized preferences may merely provide an additional motivation that goes into our calculations. (Henrich 2016, 189)

To illustrate the automatic or reflexive nature of norm adherence, consider a simple experiment (Rand, Greene, and Mowak 2012). Each subject in the experiment is given some money, and then chooses either a selfish action (keep the money) or a pro-social action (contribute to support a public good whose benefits are shared equally by the four members of the group). The subjects are randomly assigned into three treatments in terms of decision times: (i) forced to decide within 10 seconds, (ii) no constraint on decision time, and (iii) forced to delay the decision for 10 seconds and encouraged to think about the options. The fraction of the money contributed to the public good was highest for subjects who were forced to choose quickly (roughly 67 percent) and was lowest for subjects who were forced to delay and reflect (roughly 53 percent). The experiment suggests that in a small-group setting, automatic responses tend toward prosocial behavior, and thoughtful responses tend toward selfish behavior.

Harmful Social Norms

With a bit of knowledge of history, it's obvious that a social norm can be harmful to a society. Human history has many examples of social norms that persisted over long periods, despite substantial harm to societies that observed and enforced the norm. One challenge in dealing with a harmful social norm is that even if everyone would be better off if the norm were abandoned, any single individual who violates the norm may be punished. In other words, a harmful social norm may be a Nash equilibrium: No individual has an incentive for unilateral deviation. As we know from microeconomics, many Nash equilibria are inefficient.

The persistence of some harmful social norms has led to research into possible solutions. As noted by Mackie and Lejeune (2009), experiences in China and Africa suggest a strategy for the abandonment of a harmful social norm.

> An initial core group, called the critical mass, recruits others through organized diffusion, until a large enough proportion of the community, referred to as the tipping point, is ready to abandon. A moment or process of public commitment is essential to ensure a stable abandonment.

The key observation is that to eliminate a social norm that promotes collective action, a collective effort is required.

Review the Concepts 2.1

1. In Adam Smith's *Theory of Moral Sentiments*, an individual decision-maker considers [___]. (self interest, consequences for others, viewpoint of the impartial spectator, justice)

2. The crosswalk experiment reveals [___]. (independent decision-making, the power of a rule to affect behavior, the trade-off between material benefit and following a rule, infrequent rule-following)

3. The rope-pulling experiment shows that youngsters [___] the rewards of [___]. (don't share, independent effort; don't share, collaboration; give away, collaboration; share equally, collaboration)

4. In the puppet-punishing experiment [___]-year-olds were willing to bear a cost to enforce social norms. (3, 5, 20, 50)

5. In the four-person public good experiment, a subject who was forced to to decide within 10 seconds contributed [___] than a participant who was forced to delay the decision by 10 seconds. (more, less, the same)

2.2   Mental Shortcuts

The second key assumption of traditional microeconomics models is that decisions are based on thorough benefit–cost analysis. A decision-maker carefully considers all the alternative courses of action, generating a comprehensive evaluation of benefits and costs. Behavioral scientists have documented all sorts of decisions that are based on mental shortcuts or "heuristics." Mental shortcuts allow an individual to make quick decisions without precise calculations of all the benefits and costs. The brain has many tasks to perform, and a mental shortcut can be advantageous because it allows the brain to quickly return to other tasks.

Mental Accounting

Mental accounting is the practice of organizing economic life by setting up separate mental accounts for different activities. As in a real bank account, there are deposits and withdrawals, and a key feature is that eventually each mental account must be balanced at a zero value. This form of compartmentalization simplifies the decision-making process because an individual can deal with one thing at a time. The trade-off is that simplicity can also bring inflexibility. In this chapter we introduce the notion of mental accounting, setting the stage for more detailed analysis later in the book.

Mental accounting starts when an individual places some quantity of resources such as money in a named account. For example, when a worker gets a paycheck, he or she could place $60 in a "coffee" account, and place the rest in an account for everything else (food, housing, fuel, and so on). The mental accountant then debits the coffee account $2 for each cup of coffee, and by the end of the accounting period, the balance falls to zero to balance the account. The consumer's decision is simple: buy coffee until the account balance reaches zero. If the price of coffee doubles, a strict mental accountant will buy half as much coffee. In other words, the consumer observes the rules of accounting rather than the logic of constrained utility maximization.

Sometimes mental accounting goes in the other direction. A person incurs a cost, and then starts a mental account with a negative balance that must be eventually raised to zero. Consider two consumers who have tickets for a basketball game. Pedro paid $100 for his ticket, while Freida got her ticket for free. The two consumers have similar preferences, and the tickets are for similar seats. Suppose a blizzard on game night makes travel to the game equally hazardous and costly for both people. Frieda stays home because the hazardous weather makes the cost of attending the game greater than the benefit. In contrast, Pedro decides to brave the weather and attend the game. He explains his choice by saying, "I paid $100 for the ticket, so of course I'll go."

In conventional economic analysis, Pedro's decision is irrational. The $100 paid for the ticket is a sunk cost, defined a cost that was incurred in the past and cannot be recovered. A decision-maker can't do anything about costs incurred in the past, so a fully rational person ignores sunk costs. In popular language, a rational decision-maker "lets bygones be bygones." But in fact, people regularly incorporate sunk costs in their decision-making.

Mental accounting could explain Pedro's seemingly irrational choice (Thaler 1999). When a person purchases a $100 ticket, he or she opens a mental account labeled "basketball game" and starts with a negative balance of –$100, reflecting the cost of the ticket. Attending the game allows a mental accountant to add a $100 benefit to the account, which balances the account and allows it to be closed and forgotten. In contrast, if Pedro does not attend the game, the account remains open with a negative balance, a bothersome outcome for a mental accountant. Pedro braves the bad weather to attend the game because that's better than living forever with a nagging negative balance in his basketball-game account.

Default Options

Another mental shortcut is to defer to others in decision-making, allowing someone else to decide what an individual will do. For some decisions, there is a **default option**, defined as what happens if an individual does not take any action. For example, a new student could be automatically enrolled in a specific meal plan, one of several options. Or a new employee could automatically be enrolled in a specific health-insurance plan, one of several available plans. The employee can opt out of the default health-insurance plan, but opting out requires taking an action—choosing a different plan. If the individual does nothing, the default option takes effect.

In traditional economic analysis, a default option is irrelevant. We assume that a rational person precisely computes all the relevant benefits and costs of alternative actions, and chooses the action with the largest gap between the benefit and the cost. If a rational person determines that the default option is the best option, no action is taken. But if a thorough benefit–cost analysis reveals a better option, the individual will reject the default option in favor of the better option.

Behavioral economics suggests that the conventional analysis of default options is faulty. A key empirical result is that default options are "sticky" in the sense that a relatively large number of decision-makers simply accept default options. This suggests that many people don't carefully consider alternatives, but instead passively accept the choices of others. As a result, there is much more at stake with the choice of default options, as a relatively small number of people "opt out" of the default option in favor of other options. In contrast, an option with an opt-in is likely to attract fewer participants because it requires a careful evaluation of alternatives, and then action.

Review the Concepts 2.2

1. A mental accountant with a monthly coffee account periodically [___] the account. (balances, ignores, inverts, replenishes)

2. Mental accounting sometimes runs afoul of [___]. (headaches, floating cost, flying cost, sunk cost)

3. Suppose a treasure hunter pays a fee to search for sunken treasure. For a fully rational hunter, an increase in the fee [___] treasure-hunting time. (increases, decreases, does not change)

4. Suppose a treasure hunter pays a fee to search for sunken treasure. For a mental accountant, an increase in the fee [___] treasure-hunting time. (increases, does not change, decreases)

5. In traditional economic analysis, the designation of a default option [___]. (is decisive, identifies the best choice, is irrelevant)

6. The power of a default option illustrates that many people [___]. (passively accept the choices of others, perform rigorous cost-benefit analysis, don't carefully evaluate options, don't trust experts)

2.3   Cognitive Bias

The third key assumption of traditional microeconomics models is that decisions are based on correct calculations of benefits and costs. In evaluating alternative courses of action, we assume that a decision-maker doesn't make any systematic errors. Behavioral scientists have documented all sorts of cognitive biases that generate misguided choices. A **cognitive bias** is a systematic pattern of faulty thinking that tilts an individual's decision-making in a predictable direction. In this chapter we consider two of the most prominent cognitive biases. The appendix to the chapter introduces four cognitive biases that are part of the broad field of behavioral economics, but are not covered in the rest of this book.

The Decoy Effect

Another puzzle of decision-making is known as the **decoy effect**. In the classic experiment, one set of subjects is shown images of two models, A and B, and each subject is asked to choose which is more attractive. The subjects are equally split, with half preferring A and half preferring B. A second set of subjects is shown images of three models, including A and B (the same images as seen by the first set of subjects), and a third model who is identical to B except for a small but obvious defect such as a slightly altered nose. Let's label the third model B–, indicating slight inferiority to model B. A large majority of the second set of subjects choose B as the most attractive model. In other words, adding an inferior alternative to one of the options (B–) tipped preferences in favor of the option that obviously dominates the decoy. Adding a decoy changes preferences.

Figure 2.3 illustrates the decoy effect for a consumer good. Suppose two car models (A and B) differ in two features: interior space (on the vertical axis) and fuel economy (on the horizontal axis). Given the trade-offs—A has less fuel economy but more space—neither car is a dominant choice. Suppose consumers are equally split between the two models, with half preferring A and half preferring B. Alternatively, consumers could be indifferent between the two models. When we introduce B− to the choice set, the decoy effect means that more consumers will choose B instead of A, as B is clearly superior to the decoy B−. Although no one will choose B−, its presence affects preferences, with a tilt toward model B.

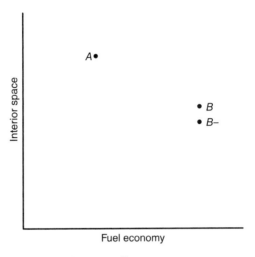

FIGURE 2.3: The Decoy Effect

A compelling explanation for the decoy effect has proven elusive. One contender is called "decision justification," the notion that a decision-maker expects to explain and justify a decision to a casual observer. It's easy to justify B, because it's obviously superior to B−: "I chose B because it has the same fuel economy as B−, but more interior space." In contrast, it may be difficult to justify A, as the explanation requires a discussion of trade-offs: "Compared to B, A has lower fuel economy but more space, and my marginal rate of substitution between the two features . . ."

Connolly, Reb, and Kausel (2013) test the decoy effect in an experiment in which participants choose one of three hypothetical jobs. Jobs A and B are designed to make them equally appealing in terms of the nature of the work (how "interesting" the work is) and the prospects for promotion. In the absence of a decoy, roughly half the participants choose A, and half choose B. The decoy (B−) was slightly inferior to job B in terms of the nature of the work: job B− was a bit less interesting, but had the same prospects for promotion. The introduction of the decoy tipped the balance in job choice: 87 percent of the participants chose B, and only 13 percent chose A.

The authors used a second experiment to explore the reasons for the decoy effect. The experimenters told the participants in advance that they might choose the wrong job, and regret it: "You could find yourself in a job you don't like, regretting the decision you made and wishing you had picked one of the other jobs." This warning reduced the decoy effect: only 62 percent of the participants chose job B, and 38 percent chose job A. The authors suggest that the thought of regret shifts a participant's focus from what other people might think to what is best for the participant. Perhaps the participants shifted from thinking about how to easily justify their choices to others, to thinking about how to justify their choice to themselves. This change in perspective could weaken the decoy effect.

Based on crafty experiments, biologists have discovered the decoy effect in other forms of life—including birds, bees, and slime mould. To test the decoy effect for gray jays, Shafir, Waite, and Smith (2002) started with two options—a large reward (two raisins) at a long distance (0.56 meters) within a tube, and a small reward (one raisin) at a short distance (0.28 meters). A bird faces a trade-off: getting the large reward requires more time and effort. The options were designed to generate a roughly 50–50 split between the two options. Then the experimenters added a decoy—a third option with the large reward (two raisins) and an extra-long distance (0.84 meters). The introduction of the decoy tilted preferences in favor of large-long option (two raisins at 0.56 meters). In other words, gray jays experience the decoy effect: their choices are influenced by the presence of inferior options. The discovery of the decoy effect in birds, bees, and slime mould suggest that it "may be an intrinsic feature of biological decision-making" (Latty and Beekman 2011, 312).

What are the implications of the decoy effect for marketing products to consumers? A seller can manipulate prices to tilt a consumer toward a particular product. A used-car seller who wants to sell car B today can price a virtually identical car at a slightly higher price. The higher-priced decoy (B–) could tilt a buyer's preferences in favor of car B. The decoy effect can also be deployed through product design. A seller of mobile phones can market two models (B and B–) with roughly the same price, but with a bit less performance or storage capacity in the B– model. The decoy tilts preferences in favor of model B. One advantage of this approach is that a single B– phone can be used repeatedly to help sell B phones.

Present Bias

Another cognitive bias occurs in intertemporal choice—the *when* of decision-making. For example, an individual could decide in the present how much to save now for retirement. An individual who exhibits present bias overplays the present benefit of consumption now and underplays the future benefit of consumption in retirement. As a result, the individual doesn't sacrifice much now to save for the future. And when the future becomes the present, an individual regrets earlier choices that led to meager savings in a retirement account.

We can illustrate present bias with a simple example developed by Richard Thaler. Suppose we offer a person some choices of apples delivered at different times.

- *One apple today versus two apples tomorrow.* The typical person would prefer one apple today to two apples tomorrow. In the present, the typical person is not willing to wait one day to get an extra apple.

- *One apple in 50 days versus two apples in 51 days.* The typical person would prefer two apples in 51 days to one apple in 50 days. In the future, the typical person is willing to wait an additional day to get an additional apple.

The typical person is impatient in the present, indicating the power of instant gratification. In contrast, the typical person is patient when looking to the future because instant gratification is not possible. When gratification is delayed, a bit more delay is not very costly. If a one-day delay doubles the apple payoff, it's worth waiting.

What happens when day 50 arrives, and the choice is between one apple today and two apples tomorrow? For the typical person, the power of instant gratification will cause a change in plans: grab the single apple today rather than wait for two apples tomorrow. The plan changes because when day 50 switches from the future to the present, instant gratification becomes an option. A person affected by present bias up-plays the newly present benefit, and chooses instant rather than delayed gratification.

As we'll see in Part 3 of this book, present bias affects all sorts of behavior. Present bias leads to meager retirement accounts, as individuals up-play the benefits of present consumption and downplay the benefits of future consumption. Present bias also causes procrastination (bear a cost later) and preproperation (collect a benefit sooner). Present bias also increases the consumption of products that generate relatively large costs in the future. In general, present bias triggers instant gratification when delayed gratification would ultimately be more gratifying.

Review the Concepts 2.3

1. For the decoy effect, the introduction of option 3, which is clearly inferior to option 2, tilts preferences toward option [___]. (1, 2, 3)

2. Experiments with birds, bees, and slime mould suggest that the decoy effect may be [___]. (confined to humans, confined to primates, an intrinsic feature of biological decision-making, a hoax)

3. *True or false.* An individual who experiences present bias will choose one apple on day one instead of two apples on day two, and plan on choosing two apples on day 51 rather than one apple on day 50. (true, false)

4. On day 50, an individual who experiences present bias is likely to [___] a plan to choose two apples on day 51 rather than one apple on day 50. (execute, abandon)

5. A person who experiences present bias [___] a present benefit and [___] a future benefit. (overplays, underplays; underplays, overplays)

Problems with Probabilities

Another set of cognitive biases occurs when a decision requires an individual to assess the likelihood of some future event. Humans are terrible at (i) estimating the probabilities of alternative outcomes and (ii) applying probabilities in making decisions. For example, many humans have trouble acting on information about the likelihood of a major flood. Similarly, many humans have trouble calculating the numbers associated with playing a lottery. We devote several chapters of the book to decision-making when benefits and costs are uncertain. In those chapters, we explain a number of ways that humans struggle to accurately estimate and correctly apply probabilities. In this chapter, we highlight two key cognitive biases related to probability.

Rare Events

Humans have trouble in thinking about low probabilities. Suppose that all homeowners in a coastal area know that in any given year, the probability of a major flood is 0.01. In any given year, the probability of a major flood is low but positive. Some homeowners (type Z for zero) will act as if the probability is zero, and decide not to purchase inexpensive flood insurance. Other homeowners (type E for excessive) will act as if the probability is much higher (say 0.03 or 0.04), and will spend an excessive amount on flood insurance. In the words of Kahneman and Tversky (1979), "Because people are limited in their ability to comprehend and evaluate extreme probabilities, highly unlikely events are either ignored or overweighted . . ." In our example, Z homeowners ignore the possibility of a flood, and type E homeowners over-weight the probability of a flood.

The Gambler's Fallacy

The **gambler's fallacy** is that the probability of a future outcome is determined by the past frequency of the outcome. In other words, history affects probability. The label comes from the idea that a gambler who has lost several consecutive times is "due" for a win. To illustrate, the probability of "heads" on the flip of an unbiased coin is one-half. A person who suffers from the gambler's fallacy believes that after five consecutive "tails," the probability of "heads" on the next flip is greater than one-half. This fallacy is based on the assumptions that (i) the coin has a memory, and (ii) the coin has a preference for balanced outcomes. A coin doesn't have neurons for memories or preferences, so its flipping history doesn't affect the probability of future outcomes.

The gambler's fallacy is sometimes known as the erroneous "law of small numbers" (Tversky and Kahneman 1971). Recall the law of large numbers: if we flip an unbiased coin a large number of times, we expect the fraction of heads will be close to one-half. The erroneous law of small numbers suggests that the roughly 50–50 frequency will occur even for a small number of coin flips. To ensure a roughly 50–50 frequency in the small-number case, a coin must make mid-air corrections to keep the frequency of heads close to one-half. A coin does not have wings to alter its flight path, so there is no reason to expect a roughly 50–50 frequency for a small number of coin flips.

Figure 2.4 illustrates the gambler's fallacy (Rabin and Vayanos 2010). Each bar represents the assessment of a typical individual of the probability that a coin toss will generate heads (H) for a particular sequence of earlier tosses. For example, in the case of three previous heads (HHH), the typical person believes that the probability of a heads on the fourth toss is only 0.30. At the other extreme, the assessed probability of heads after three tails is 0.70. For an unbaised coin, the actual probability is 0.50. In the middle, the assessed probability is less than 0.50 when two of the three previous tosses were heads, and greater than 0.50 when only one of the three previous tosses was heads. These numbers are consistent with the stylized fact the typical person believes that the probability of "tails" after "heads" is roughly 0.60 (Rabin and Vayanos 2010).

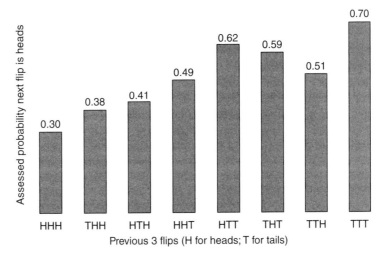

FIGURE 2.4: The Gambler's Fallacy

There is evidence that the gambler's fallacy affects both personal and professional judgment. Before choosing a lotto number, many players check the winning numbers from the previous week, and are less likely to bet on last week's winners. (Suetens, Galbo-Jorgensen, and Tyran 2016). A recent study (Chen, Moskowitz, and Shue 2016) shows the cognitive bias among judges and baseball umpires. For example, an asylum judge is 3.3 percentage points more likely to reject a current case if he or she approved the previous case. In calling balls and strikes, a baseball umpire is less likely to call a pitch a strike if the previous pitch was a strike (controlling of course for the location of the pitch). For pitches close to the edge of the strike zone, the decrease in the probability of a strike is over 0.03.

Review the Concepts 2.4

1. For many people, highly unlikely events are [___]. (ignored, over-weighted)

2. The gambler's fallacy is based on the assumption(s) that a flipped coin has neurons for [___]. (memories, hearing, olfactory events, preferences)

3. The gambler's fallacy is also known as the erroneous law of [___] numbers. (large, prime, zoroastrian, small)

4. Evidence for the gambler's fallacy comes from baseball umpires, who are less likely to call a strike if the previous pitch was called a [___]. (ball, wilding, strike, blooper)

2.5 Instinctive Urges and Thoughtful Deliberation

In traditional economics, we assume that economic choice is rational in the sense that decisions are based on calm and careful benefit–cost analysis. We assume that decisions are not affected by emotions or instincts, but instead emerge from an emotion-free cognitive processing of the trade-offs associated with alternative actions. As shown by behavioral scientists, things are not so simple. Many decisions result from a complex mix of emotions, instincts, and thoughtful deliberation.

Apple versus Cupcake

We can illustrate the complexities of the decision-making process with a simple example. Imagine that you are hungry and will choose either an apple or a large cupcake. For the typical person, the choice triggers a complex mix of instinctive urges and thoughtful deliberation.

- *Instincts.* An instinctive urge to grab the cupcake is the result of millions of years of natural selection when food resources were scarce. For our hunter-gatherer ancestors, grabbing a big packet of sugar and fat would improve the prospects for survival and reproduction, so instinctive grabbing of enticing food is natural.
- *Thinking.* The thoughtful deliberation incorporates the long-term health consequences of the two foods. You might recall your recent dietary choices and wonder whether a recently consumed chunk of broccoli would offset the ill effects of the cupcake. Or you might picture your older self struggling to fit into your current clothing.

Your choice—apple or cupcake—depends on the relative strengths of instincts and thoughtful deliberation. In some cases, thoughtful deliberation overpowers the instinctive urge, and you choose the apple. But sometimes those instinctive urges dominate, and you choose the cupcake. As we'll see in later chapters, this conflict between instinctive urges and thoughtful deliberation plays out in all sorts of decisions, including how much to save, when to take an action, whom to trust, whether to contribute to public radio, and how to do your part (or not) in combating climate change.

Hunting Practices of the Ju/'hoansi

The hunting practices of the Ju/'hoansi illustrate the role of thoughtful deliberation in enforcing social norms. To support the social norm of sharing harvested meat, the Ju/'hoansi implement a rule that the owner of the decisive arrowhead divides the harvest among members of the tribe. A hunter who decides to use an arrowhead owned by someone else engages in thoughtful deliberation before the hunt. The hunter anticipates the possibility of selfish behavior (grab a large share of the harvest), and takes steps to avoid violating the social norm of sharing. Thinking ahead, a hunter uses an arrowhead owned by someone else to avoid the temptation. In the Adam Smith framework of social preferences, the arrowhead owner is like the impartial spectator who promotes adherence to social norms.

Why Do We Do That?

In the first five parts of this book, we encounter all sorts of curious and puzzling human behavior. Some patterns of behavior seem short-sighted, illogical, and misguided. A recurring question is "why do we do that?"

1. Why do humans—even three-year-olds—voluntarily share the rewards of joint efforts?
2. Why do humans voluntarily contribute to public goods such as disaster relief and public radio?
3. Why do some humans have a short-term orientation, leading to smoking and meager saving?
4. Why is the pain of loss greater than the pleasure of gain?
5. Why are some humans oddly possessive of their assets?
6. Why are many humans risk averse, preferring $30 for sure to a 50 percent chance of getting $70?

Recent work by economists, biologists, anthropologists, and neuroscientists provides some insights into these questions. As we'll see in Part 6 of this book, many of the insights arise from considering the role of natural selection and cultural evolution. The genetic makeup of modern humans reflects natural selection over the roughly 2.4 million years of the hunter-gatherer era, when small nomadic bands foraged for edible plants and meat. Only 12,000 years have passed since the end of the hunter-gatherer era, so the genetic differences between modern humans and our hunter-gatherer ancestors are relatively small. To get insights into modern behavior, we can look back to our hunter-gatherer ancestors. In addition, the co-evolution of genes and culture has been happening for many generations, and our current behavior reflects the legacy of this lengthy co-evolution.

Review the Concepts 2.5

1. Traditional economic analysis is based on the assumption that decisions emerge from [___] cognitive processing of trade-offs. (emotional, irrational, emotion-free)

2. As shown by behavioral scientists, many decisions result from a complex mix of [___]. (emotions, instincts, thoughtful deliberation)

3. The hunting practices of the Ju/'hoansi illustrate the role of [___] in enforcing [___]. (penalties, formal laws; thoughtful deliberation, social norms; respect for elders, generosity)

Key Terms

cognitive bias, p. 28
decoy effect, p. 28
default option, p. 27

gambler's fallacy, p. 32
mental accounting, p. 26
other-regarding preferences, p. 17

self-regarding preferences, p. 16
social norm, p. 18

Takeaways

1. In the Adam-Smith framework of other-regarding behavior, (i) individuals consider both self-interest and consequences for others, (ii) decisions are guided by social norms, and (iii) there may be a trade-off between self-interest and the interests of others.

2. The crosswalk experiment demonstrates the power of rules and social norms.

3. The rope-pulling experiment shows that youngsters share the rewards of collaboration.

4. The puppet-punishing experiment shows that youngsters are willing to bear a cost to enforce social norms.

5. Experiments with adults suggest that a social norm of 50–50 sharing is motivated in part by social image.

6. Mental accounting is a system of organizing economic life by setting up mental accounts and periodically balancing the accounts.

7. Mental accounting can make sunk costs relevant to decision-making.

8. A key empirical result in behavioral economics is that default options are sticky in the sense that many decision-makers simply accept default options.

9. Sellers can use the decoy effect to influence consumer behavior by the strategic placement of inferior products.

10. An individual who exhibits present bias overplays present benefits and costs, and underplays future benefits and costs.

11. In a world of uncertain benefits and costs, humans have trouble in (i) estimating probabilities and (ii) applying probabilities to decision-making.

12. The gambler's fallacy (sometimes known as "the law of small numbers") is that the probability of a random event is determined by the past frequency of the event.

13. The gambler's fallacy has been observed in behavior of lottery players, judges, and baseball umpires.

14. Many decisions result from a complex mix of emotions, instincts, and thoughtful deliberation.

Discuss the Concepts

1. *Speed Spectator.* Smithian Insurance Company allows its customers to enroll in a safe-driver program that (i) offers a safe-driver discount of 15 percent and (ii) installs an internet-connected speed monitor on the car. In the language of Adam Smith, a driver has an incentive to humble the arrogance of [____] down to something that [____].

2. *Enforcing a Social Norm.* Two youngsters are in a rope-pulling exercise with three trials, with 6 gummie bears per trial. If one youngster does not collaborate (pull to get the reward), no gummies are retrived. A youngster will not collaborate on a particular trial if he or she received fewer than three gummies (half the total) in the previous trial. On each trial where both youngsters cooperate, Lucky gets five gummies, and can either keep the larger share (K) or equalize rewards (E) by giving two gummies to Unlucky.

   a. Under a social norm of equal sharing, the total reward over the three trials is $R^{Norm} = $ [____].

   b. Suppose in trial one, Lucky doesn't share, but instead keeps five gummies. The total reward over the three trials is $R^{Greed} = $ [____]. Unlucky's cost of enforcing a norm of equal sharing is $c = $ [____].

3. *Climate Change and Quick Thinking.* An experimenter gives each subject $10, and then allows the subject to (i) keep the $10 or (ii) donate some or all the money to a project that is combating climate change by planting trees. Some subjects are forced to decide within 10 seconds, and others are forced to delay the decision for 10 seconds. We would expect the fraction of the money contributed to the public good to be higher for subjects who were forced to [____]. (decide quickly, delay the decision)

4. *Hike Accounting.* Twink and Tohs are mental accountants with watches that record distances hiked. Suppose the price of a hiking permit for a national forest is $9. At this price, Twink and Tohs hike three miles on their weekly

hike. If the price of a permit increases to $25, we expect the length of the weekly hike to [____]. (increase, decrease, not change)

5. *Bicycle versus Unicycle.* Predict the results of a survey of cycling skills. The typical person believes that his or her:

   - bicycle skills are better than the bicycle skills of [____] (30%, 50%, 70%) other people.

   - unicycle skills are better than the unicycle skills of [____] (30%, 50%, 70%) other people.

   - quad-cycle skills are better than the quad-cycle skills of [____] (30%, 50%, 70%) other people.

6. *Completing an Unpleasant Task.* It's Tuesday, and Dleigh must complete an unpleasant task today (Tuesday), Wednesday, or Thursday. The time required to complete the task is 10 minutes today, compared to 13 minutes on Wednesday and 16 minutes on Thursday. Suppose on Tuesday Dleigh makes a plan to complete the task on Wednesday. If Dleigh experiences present bias, we'd expect him or her to complete the task on [____] and regret the loss of [____].

7. *Vaccination Law.* Consider a group of 1000 people whose limited fractional skills cause them to round small numbers to the nearest hundredth. Suppose the probability that an unvaccinated individual experiences a severe case of COVID-19 is 0.003, compared to 0.0001 for a vaccinated individual. The personal cost of a severe COVID-19 case is $60,000. At the personal level, the perceived benefit of vaccination = [____] .

Apply the Concepts

1. *Mental Accounting and Treasure Hunting.* Each year, a group of treasure hunters purchases a license to search for sunken treasure off a tropical island. Last year, the price of the permit was $1000, and they searched for 30 days. If the price of the permit doubles this year, we expect the group to spend [____] (more, less, the same) time in the search for sunken treasure.

2. *Mental Accounting and Law of Demand.* Consider a consumer with mental account for coffee, with a fixed budget $b = \$60$.

   a. Draw the individual demand curve, including points for prices $2, $4, $5, and $6.

   b. The individual demand curve [____] (is, is not) consistent with the "law of demand."

3. *The Marginal Rate of Substitution (MRS) for Apples Today and Tomorrow.* Consider the apple thought experiment. An individual prefers one apple today

to two apples tomorrow, and is indifferent between one apple today and three apples tomorrow. The individual prefers two apples in 51 days to one apple in 50 days, and is indifferent between 1.40 apples in 51 days and one apple in 50 days. When day 50 arrives, the individual's marginal rate of substitution (MRS) between apples today and tomorrow [____] (↑,↓↑, does not change) from [____] to [____].

4. *Seat-Belt Mandate.* Consider a group of 1000 people whose limited fractional skills cause them to round small numbers to the nearest hundredth. Suppose over a one-year period, the probability that a person experiences an automobile collision is 0.003. The injury cost per collision is zero if the driver is wearing a seat belt, and $12,000 otherwise. A seat-belt law that generates full compliance decreases the cost of collision injuries by $[____].

5. *Name That Sequence.* An instructor gives seven students a fair coin and asks each student to flip the coin 20 times and record the sequence of outcomes—the sequence of "heads" and "tails." The instructor asks seven other students to each fabricate a plausible sequence of 20 coin tosses, a list of "heads" and "tails." The instructor leaves the room while the students generate their sequences. The instructor returns and correctly identifies the real sequences and the fabricated sequences. How does the instructor do that?

6. *Shuffling Tunes.* Consider a person with 100 tunes on a phone. The person chooses "Shuffle," anticipating a random sequence of tunes. When a tune A plays twice in a set of 30 tunes, the person contacts you (the customer-service representative of phone maker) to complain that the shuffling algorithm is defective.

   a. What's your response?

   b. Suppose the phone maker receives similar complaints from thousands of customers. How would you expect the CEO of the phone maker to respond?

Appendix to Chapter 2: More Insights from Behavioral Science

This appendix to Chapter 2 covers a few cognitive biases that are relevant to the broad field of behavioral economics but not discussed elsewhere in this book.

1 Anchors

A consumer will purchase a good if the willingness to pay exceeds the price of the good. One puzzling result from behavioral economics is that a consumer's willingness to pay for a product can be manipulated by irrelevant information. In the classic experiment, each subject writes down the last two digits of his or her social security number, and then expresses a willingness to pay for a common product such as a coffee mug. The puzzling result is that there is a positive correlation between the two-digit number and the bid on the product: people with relatively large two-digit numbers bid more, on average, than those with low numbers. In the language of behavioral economics, the last two digits of the social security number provides an anchor for the bid on the product. The **anchoring effect** is that a person's valuation of an object is positively correlated with recently generated—and irrelevant—numbers.

2 Confirmation Bias

A person subject to **confirmation bias** is selective in acquiring information, focusing on information that confirms prior beliefs. Such a person (i) searches for information that confirms prior beliefs and (ii) downplays any information that contradicts prior beliefs. Confirmation bias sometimes involves selective memory: facts that confirm prior beliefs are recalled more readily than facts that contradict prior beliefs.

To illustrate, consider the issue of policy responses to climate change. Consider two regular citizens who are not fully informed on environmental issues, but hold prior beliefs on a carbon tax: Nona believes the tax is unwise, while Yaya believes that the tax is wise. Suppose both citizens watch an informative video on the trade-offs associated with using a carbon tax to address the problem of climate change. A citizen subject to confirmation bias will focus on facts that confirms his or her prior belief. Nona will commit to memory any facts that suggest the carbon tax is a bad idea, while ignoring facts that suggest the tax is a good idea. Similarly, Yaya will be selective in incorporating facts, embracing facts that support her position and ignoring facts that don't. As a result, the informative video will not change beliefs. In fact, the video may strengthen the opposing beliefs, despite the fact that both people are exposed to the same information.

3 Overconfidence Effect

Another troubling cognitive bias is that people are generally overconfident in their productivity in everyday tasks and in cognitive processing. In the classic study of the **overconfidence effect**, scientists administered spelling examinations and asked the participants about their confidence in their spelling (Adams and Adams 1960). In the typical case, a person who expressed 100 percent confidence in the spelling of a word spelled the word incorrectly 20 percent of the time. Another manifestation of overconfidence is that people generally believe that they perform better than the average person. For example, in a survey of young adults, 93 percent of the participants believed that they were above-average drivers (Svenson 1981).

More recent research challenges the conclusion that people are comically over-confident (Greenberg and Stephens-Davidowitz 2019). Although people are generally over-confident in performing familiar tasks, they are under-confident in performing unfamiliar tasks. For example, on average, people believe that they can outperform 75 percent of others in using a computer, compared to only 37 percent in knitting a sweater. Similarly, people are over-confident in driving a car, but under-confident in riding a unicycle. Another result is that confidence decreases as the difficulty of the task increases. For example, on average, people believe that they can out-perform 66 percent of others for regular driving, compared to 52 percent for driving on ice, and 42 percent for driving a racing car.

4 Availability Heuristic

The **availability heuristic** is a mental shortcut that relies on easily recalled memories to estimate probabilities. Strong memories are easily recalled, and have a relatively large effect on the estimated probability of an event. A memory can be strong because (i) it is recent, or (ii) it is associated with strong emotions.

1. *Recent memories.* Memories fade over time, so recent memories have a relatively large effect on probability assessments. For example, suppose that over the last several years, a worker has been late on one of 100 days, suggesting that the probability of being late on any day is 0.01. If the worker was late yesterday, the boss might believe that the probability of being late tomorrow is greater than 0.01. Over time, the memory of the late event fades, and the employer is likely to revise the probability of being late, downward toward 0.01.

2. *Emotional memories.* An event that triggers strong emotions is relatively prominent in a person's memory and thus receives a relatively large weight in estimating probabilities. If a worker arrives late dressed as a gorilla, the boss is likely to over-estimate the probability the worker will be late in the future, and the over-estimate is likely to persist.

Tversky and Kahneman (1974) developed the notion of the availability heuristic by asking lab subjects various questions. The classic question is about the words with the letter K.

> If a random word is taken from an English text, is it more likely that the word starts with a K, or that K is the third letter?

The typical person estimated that a randomly chosen word was twice as likely to begin with K than it was to have K as the third letter. In fact, the reverse is true: the probability that a word has K as the third letter is three times times the probability that the word begins with K. This systematic error is explained by the availability heuristic: for the typical person, it is easier to recall words starting with K (king, kangaroo, kick) than it is to recall words with K as the third letter (inkling, likelihood, lake). The availability of K-beginning words biases the person's assessment of the probabilities.

The availability heuristic affects probability assessments and decisions in many economic environments.

1. A person may overestimate the probability of being attacked by a shark or being struck by lightning because shark attacks and lightning strikes are sensational.
2. A driver may respond to witnessing a traffic accident by driving more slowly for some time, and then gradually restore his or her regular speed.
3. A report of a heinous crime by a recent immigrant may cause a citizen to believe, incorrectly, that the crime rate among recent immigrants exceeds the crime rate of citizens.

Review the Concepts 2A

1. The [___] effect is that a person's valuation of an object is positively correlated with recently generated—and irrelevant—numbers. (sailing, drifting, propeller, anchoring)

2. A person subject to [___] bias is selective in acquiring information, focusing on information that confirms prior beliefs. (baptism, communion, extreme unction, confirmation)

3. The typical person is [___]-confident in driving a car and [___]-confident in riding a unicycle. (under, over; over, over; over, under; under, under)

4. The availability heuristic explains why people generally over-estimate the probability of [___]. (being struck by lightning, crime by recent immigrants, global warming after a cold winter)

Key Terms

anchoring effect, p. 40

availability heuristic, p. 41

confirmation bias, p. 40

overconfidence effect, p. 41

3 Social Norms: Sharing and Enforcement

> The Golden Rule: Do to others what you would have them do to you.
>
> The Golden Rule is illustrated by the allegory of the long spoons. There is a huge pile of delicious and nutritious food at the center of a large round table. The hungry people seated around the table have very long spoons: the spoons are long enough to reach the food, but too long to deliver food to a person's mouth. It is impossible to feed yourself with a spoon that is longer than your arm.
>
> - *Selfish preferences.* In a society with self-regarding preferences, each person scoops food onto a long spoon, but is unable to eat because the spoon is too long. As a result, everyone in the selfish society perishes.
>
> - *Social norms.* In a society with social norms that promote sharing and cooperation, each person scoops food onto a long spoon and then feeds another person. As a result, everyone in the cooperative society thrives.

As we saw in the previous chapter, social norms promote pro-social behavior such as sharing and cooperation. In this chapter, we show how to incorporate social norms into models of economic choice. We present a utility function that captures the trade-off between personal material benefits and adhering to social norms. We use the utility function to explain behavior related to social norms of (i) sharing the rewards of collaboration and (ii) punishing norm violators.

It is important to note that the social-norm approach is just one of several ways to incorporate pro-social behavior into economic analysis. A prominent alternative uses the notion of "other-regarding preferences" as a counterpoint to self-regarding preferences. A person with other-regarding preferences acts in a pro-social fashion because the individual's utility function includes the material payoff to other individuals in society. This approach leads to a framework known as "inequity aversion," which distinguishes between advantaged inequity (you have more wealth than another person) and disadvantaged inequity (you have less wealth than another person). We present this approach (Fehr-Schmidt inequity cost) in the appendix to this chapter.

Learning Objectives: The Explainer

After mastering this chapter, you will be able to explain each of the following statements.

1. A utility function incorporates the trade-off between material benefits and acting on a social norm.

2. We can use the marginal principle to show the utility-maximizing choice for an individual who is sensitive to a social norm.

3. The dictator game provides evidence of a social norm of sharing.

4. The ultimatum game provides evidence of a social norm of punishing norm violators.

5. The outcome of the ultimatum game is determined by the relative norm sensitivity of the proposer and the responder.

6. There is substantial variation in pro-social behavior across individuals.

7. A study of societies around the globe suggests a correlation between market engagement and sensitivity to the social norms of sharing and of punishing norm violators.

3.1 Utility Maximization with a Social Norm

As Adam Smith (1982) noted, there is often a trade-off between an individual's material benefits and adhering to social norms. In his words, "Every man . . . must humble the arrogance of his self-love, and bring it down to something which other men can go along with." In other words, an individual must sacrifice personal material benefits to satisfy social norms. Akerlof and Kranton (2008) incorporate a social norm into an individual utility function, and thus represent a trade-off between personal material benefits and responding to a social norm. More recently, Kimbrough and Vostroknutov (2016) develop a utility function that captures the trade-off. In this part of the chapter, we describe a utility function that incorporates the trade-off between material benefits and acting on a social norm.

We can illustrate the frameworks developed by Akerlof and Kranton (2008) and Kimbrough and Vostroknutov (2016) with a highly simplified version of their models. Suppose a fixed gain X = 1 unit of resources is to be divided between two individuals, 1 and 2. The word "gain" is used deliberately, as we will focus on norms for sharing a change in wealth rather than norms for sharing wealth *per se*. The budget constraint for distributing the gain is

$$1 = x_1 + x_2$$

Suppose that individual 1 starts with the full gain, and then decides how much to transfer to individual 2, who simply accepts whatever individual 1 transfers. Suppose the social norm is that the gain is to be shared equally: to strictly adhere to the social norm, $x_1 = x_2 = 1/2$.

Trade-Off Between Material Benefit and Norm-Violation Cost

The utility function for individual 1 includes the material benefit and a cost associated with violating the social norm. The material benefit is simply the quantity x_1. The cost of violating the norm is

$$norm-violation\ cost = \psi \cdot \left(x_1 - \frac{1}{2}\right)^2$$

The expression in the brackets is the gap between the amount kept by individual 1 and the equal-sharing quantity. Because the gap is raised to a power greater than one, the cost of violating the norm increases at an increasing rate. The parameter ψ measures an individual's sensitivity to norm violations: $\psi = 0$ for a perfectly selfish person (self-regarding preferences); the parameter is positive for a person who is influenced by social norms. Utility equals material consumption (x_1) minus the moral cost incurred by violating the social norm of equal sharing:

$$u(x_1) = x_1 - \psi \cdot \left(x_1 - \frac{1}{2}\right)^2$$

Figure 3.1 shows the two components of utility for individual 1. The horizontal axis measures the amount kept by individual 1. The curve with slope equal to one is the material benefit: as x_1 increases, the material benefit of individual 1 increases linearly. The U-shaped curve shows the cost of violating the norm. At point a, the individual adheres to the social norm by keeping half the gain ($x_1 = 1/2$), so the norm-violation cost is zero. As the gap between x_1 and $1/2$ increases, the norm-violation cost increases at an increasing rate.

Figure 3.1 also shows the individual's utility curve. Recall that utility equals the material benefit minus the cost of violating the norm.

1. *Keep less than half: $x_1 < 1/2$.* Suppose we start with $x_1 = 0$, meaning that individual 1 transfers the entire gain to individual 2. Starting from $x_1 = 0$, an increase in the amount kept by individual 1 has two effects: (i) the material benefit increases, and (ii) the norm-violation cost decreases. This double dividend from increasing x_1 means that the utility curve is positively sloped as long as individual 1 keeps less than half the gain.
2. *Keep half: $x_1 = 1/2$.* The utility curve meets the material-benefit curve at $x_1 = 1/2$: under equal sharing, the norm-violation cost is zero, so utility equals the material benefit.
3. *Keep more than half: $x_1 > 1/2$.* When person 1 keeps more than half the gain, the norm-violation cost makes utility less than the material benefit. As x_1 increases beyond $1/2$, norm-violation cost increases at an increasing

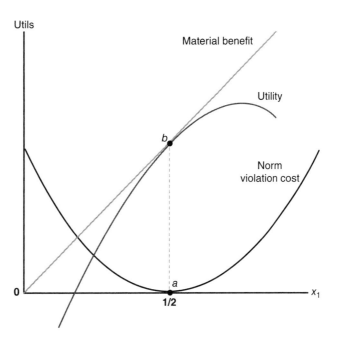

FIGURE 3.1: Material Benefit, Norm-Violation Cost, and Utility

rate, so the gap between the material benefit and utility increases. Eventually, the rapidly increasing norm-violation cost more than offsets the increasing material benefit, so the utility curve is negatively sloped.

Utility Maximization

Figure 3.2 shows utility maximization for individual 1, given the trade-off between material benefit and norm-violation cost. In the upper panel, the utility curve reaches its maximum at point c, with individual 1 keeping x_1^* of the gain. The lower panel applies the marginal principle. The marginal-benefit curve is horizontal, reflecting the linear material-benefit curve. The marginal-cost curve is positively sloped, reflecting the assumption that as the gap between x_1 and the social norm $x_1 = 1/2$ increases, the norm-violation cost increases at an increasing rate. Applying the marginal principle, the marginal benefit equals the marginal cost at point d, so the rational individual 1 keeps x_1^* of the gain.

The utility function generates a straightforward expression for the marginal cost of x_1 associated with violating a sharing norm. As shown in Math 3.1, the marginal cost is

$$mc = \psi \cdot (2 \cdot x_1 - 1)$$

For the equal-sharing outcome ($x_1 = 1/2$), marginal cost is zero, and as the share kept by individual 1 increases (as x_1 increases), the marginal cost increases. For an individual who keeps it all ($x_1 = 1$), marginal cost $= \psi$.

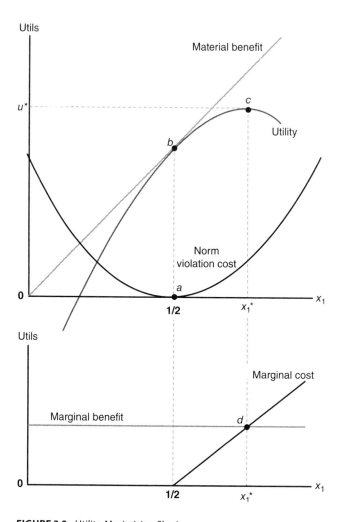

FIGURE 3.2: Utility-Maximizing Sharing

Why does the marginal-cost curve in Figure 3.2 start at 1/2, the equal-sharing outcome? We can ignore any choices below 1/2 because choosing any $x_1 < 1/2$ would be irrational. Starting from the equal-sharing outcome, a $1 decrease in x_1 decreases the material benefit and increases the norm-violation cost, so utility will decrease. The equal-sharing outcome is clearly superior to any $x_1 < 1/2$, so we can ignore the inferior outcomes.

We can relate the logic of Figure 3.2 to the moral-sentiments framework of Adam Smith. A perfectly selfish individual would not consult the impartial spectator for a social-norm assessment, and would instead be driven by full-fledged self-love to choose $x_1 = 1$. At the other extreme, an individual who strictly adheres to a social norm of equal sharing would keep only half the gain: $x_1 = 1/2$. In Figure 3.2, the individual chooses an intermediate value, keeping roughly two-thirds of the gain. The individual experiences some disapproval by the impartial spectator, but the benefit of stopping short of equal sharing (a larger material benefit) exceeds the cost (a disapproving look and perhaps a few mutters from the impartial spectator).

Review the Concepts 3.1

1. For a utility function that incorporates social norms, utility equals [_____] minus [_____]. (material benefit, material cost; material benefit, norm-violation cost; social benefit, social cost)

2. In Figure 3.1, in the case of equal sharing, [_____] = [_____]. (utility, material benefit; norm-violation cost, zero; utility, zero; material benefit, norm-violation cost)

3. For utility maximization under a social norm of equal sharing, the [_____] associated with material consumption equals the [_____] associated with violating the social norm. (average, average; total, total; marginal, average; marginal, marginal)

4. In Figure 3.2, a perfectly selfish individual would choose $x_1 = $ [_____], while an individual who strictly observes the social norm would choose $x_1 = $ [_____]. ($x/2$, x; x, 0; $x/2$, $x/4$; x, $x/2$)

5. In Figure 3.2, the utility-maximizing individual chooses roughly [_____] of the gain x. [1/3, 1/2, 2/3, 7/8]

3.2 Sharing Behavior: The Dictator Game

As we've seen, we can incorporate social norms into a person's decision about how to share a gain with another person. In this part of the chapter, we discuss economic experiments in which one individual has an opportunity to share a gain with a second individual. The experiments provide evidence that in some circumstances, sharing is a social norm.

Game Structure and Results

The **dictator game** has a long history in behavioral economics, starting with the first experiment by Kahneman, Knetsch, and Thaler (1990). In the dictator game, one player receives additional resources (a gain) and decides how much of the gain to transfer to a second player. The second player is passive, and simply accepts the transfer from the dictator. If the dictator has self-regarding preferences, the rational choice is to keep the entire gain and not transfer anything to the second player. Alternatively, if the dictator is influenced by a social norm of sharing, a positive transfer is likely.

Engel (2011) uses a meta-analysis to summarize the results of hundreds of dictator experiments. The overall average transfer is 28 percent of the gain. As shown in Figure 3.3, there is substantial variation in the individual transfers. Over one-third of participants (36 percent) gave nothing, while roughly one-sixth (17 percent) chose equal sharing. Roughly one in 20 participants (5 percent) transferred the entire gain. Roughly 47 percent of participants transferred at least 30 percent, and roughly 39 percent of participants transferred at least 40 percent.

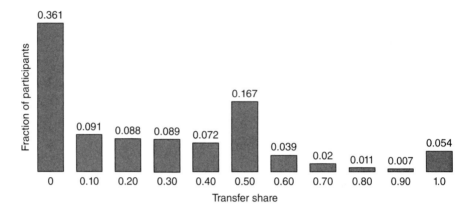

FIGURE 3.3: Distribution of Transfers in the Dictator Game

One advantage of the Kimbrough-Vostroknutov framework is that it allows variation across individuals in the sensitivity to social norms. Given a common social norm, the parameter ψ measures an individual's sensitivity to violating the norm. The curves in Figure 3.2 are based on norm sensitivity measured by $\psi = 3$.

$$u(x_1) = x_1 - 3 \cdot \left(x_1 - \frac{1}{2}\right)^2$$

As shown in Math 3.2, the dictator's utility-maximizing transfer increases as the value of the norm-sensitivity parameter increases. The fraction of the gain transferred is

$$t^* = \frac{\psi - 1}{2 \cdot \psi}$$

In this case, a utility-maximizing dictator transfers one-third of the gain and keeps two-thirds:

$$t^* = \frac{3-1}{3 \cdot 2} = \frac{1}{3}$$

Variation in Sharing Behavior

Figure 3.4 shows two other cases. An individual with a high sensitivity to social norms has a relatively large value of ψ. As a result, the marginal-cost curve is relatively steep and the utility-maximizing x_1 is closer to the equal-sharing norm (point s and x_1^{**}). In contrast, an individual with a low sensitivity to social norms has a relatively flat marginal-cost curve, so utility is maximized with a relatively large value of x_1 (point i and x_1^{***}). In other words, an insensitive individual deviates from the social norm of equal sharing by a relatively large amount.

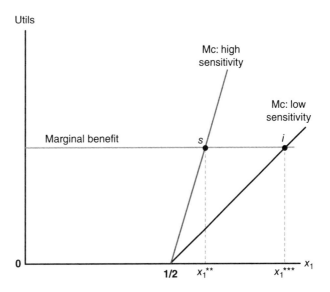

FIGURE 3.4: Variation in Utility-Maximizing Sharing

Recall the Andreoni and Bernheim (2009) results from Chapter 2. In a dictator game with full observability, 57 percent of dictators shared half the endowment. As the observability of the sharing outcome decreased, so did the fraction of the dictators who shared half the endowment. In the case of a one-in-four chance that the observed sharing outcome was chosen by the dictator (a three-in-four chance it was chosen by a computer), only 34 percent of dictators shared half the endowment. In Figure 3.4, the steeper marginal-cost curve (high sensitivity) could represent the case of full observability, and the flatter marginal-cost curve (low sensitivity) could represent the case of low observability.

Engel (2011) explores variation in sharing behavior related to participant characteristics. In most dictator experiments, the participants are college students, but some experiments use non-students. On average, students transfer less: the average transfer from a student dictator is 25 percent, compared to 40 percent for non-students. In addition, students are more likely to keep all the gain: roughly 40 percent of students transfer nothing, compared to roughly 10 percent of non-students. In terms of gender effects, women transfer more as dictators and receive more as recipients. The age of the dictator has a significant effect on transfers.

1. The average transfer increases with age. Although transfers by children are roughly equal to the transfers of college students, transfers increase rapidly with age beyond college age.

2. The frequency of transferring zero is highest for college students, followed by children, middle-aged adults, and the elderly.
3. For middle-aged dictators, the mode (highest frequency) is equal sharing.
4. For elderly dictators, the mode is full transfer (giving it all).

Recall from Chapter 2 the rule-following experiment with stoplights and crosswalks. Kimbrough and Vostroknutov (2016) ran the dictator game with subjects who vary in their adherence to the rule of waiting for a green light before crossing the crosswalk. For the strongest rule followers (the top 10 percent of crosswalk waiters), the average transfer by a dictator was roughly 34 percent of the gain. For the weakest rule followers (the bottom 10 percent of crosswalk waiters), the average transfer by a dictator was roughly 18 percent of the gain. In other words, there is a positive correlation between following the crosswalking rule and conforming to a social norm of sharing a gain.

Review the Concepts 3.2

1. A meta-analysis of the dictator game revealed an overall average transfer of roughly [___] percent. (10, 28, 50, 75)

2. A meta-analysis of the dictator game revealed [___] variation in transfers across individual participants. (zero, small, substantial)

3. Using the results shown in Figure 3.2 as a starting point, an increase in norm sensitivity from $\psi = 3$ to $\psi = 5$ changes the dictator's utility-maximizing transfer share from 1/3 to [___]. (4,10, 1/2, 9/20, 6/10)

4. In the dictator game, the transfer share generally [___] with the dictator's age. (increases, decreases, does not change).

5. Suppose you are about to play a dictator game as a recipient and can choose your dictator. Your best choice is [___]. (a college student, a middle-aged adult, a teenage student)

3.3 Costly Norm Enforcement

We turn next to interactions that allow the punishment of individuals who violate social norms. Recall that a member of a social group is expected to (i) conform to group norms and (ii) enforce conformity on other members of the group. Recall part of an earlier quote from Adam Smith (1982):

> Every man . . . must . . . humble the arrogance of his self-love, and bring it down to something which other men can go along with.

When a person fails to bring down selfish behavior to a level that other people "can go along with," he or she violates a social norm and may be punished. Punishment is costly for a punisher, who incurs an opportunity cost for the resources (including time) allocated to punishing a norm violator.

Third-Party Punishment of Norm Violators

Consider first the case of punishment by a member of society who does not have a direct stake in an interaction that triggers a norm violation. Suppose individual 1 violates a social norm in interacting with individual 2. For example, in the dictator game, individual 1 could transfer a relatively small amount—or nothing—to individual 2. Under **third-party punishment**, individual 3, an individual without any financial stake in the dictator game, punishes individual 1 for his or her violation of a social norm of sharing. The punishment is costly to the third party.

Evidence for third-party punishment comes from experiments with children and adults. Based on dozens of experiments, the consensus is that third-party punishment happens in a wide variety of environments. It is clear that individuals are willing to bear a cost to punish others who violate a social norm, even if the punisher has no material stake in the violation. In other words, some individuals who are not victims of a particular norm violation punish the norm violator anyway, even when punishment is costly to the punisher.

A recent study performs a number of experiments to test for third-party punishment (Jordan, McAuliffe, and Rand 2016). The participants were recruited through the online labor market Amazon Mechanical Turk (MTurk), which allows individuals to earn small payments for completing brief tasks. In a dictator game, participants were randomly assigned to be either dictator, recipient, or third party. Each dictator received 50 cents and made a binary decision to give either 0 or 25 cents to the recipient. Each third party received an endowment of at least 25 cents, After observing a dictator's allocation decision, the third party had the opportunity to spend up to 10 cents to punish the dictator. For each cent spent by the third party on punishment, the dictator lost 3 cents.

As expected, third parties punished selfish dictators more frequently. As shown in Figure 3.5, third parties spent an average of 2.08 cents to punish selfish dictators, compared to 0.21 cents to punish dictators who shared equally. The difference is statistically significant. In a follow-up experiment, the authors explored dictators' expectations about the likelihood of third-party punishment. Most

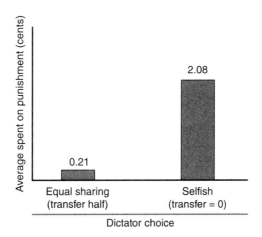

FIGURE 3.5: Third-Party Punishment in a Dictator Game

dictators anticipated punishment for selfish behavior, and dictators who anticipated more severe punishment were more likely to share the endowment equally.

Structure of the Ultimatum Game

Consider next the case of punishment by an individual who has a stake in the interaction that triggers a norm violation. The **ultimatum game** is a widely used experiment that provides evidence that people are willing to bear a cost to punish norm violators. In the ultimatum game, two people interact to share an endowment (X): one person (the proposer) proposes a division of X, and a second person (the responder) either accepts the offer or rejects it. Rejection means that each person gets nothing. If the proposer is greedy and proposes to keep a relatively large share of X, the responder can punish the proposer by rejecting the offer, ensuring that the greedy proposer gets nothing. Punishment is costly, as a responder who rejects an offer doesn't get anything either.

Figure 3.6 illustrates the mechanics of the ultimatum game. Two people interact to divide a fixed amount X. The proposer (1) offers a share of X to the responder (R). The proposed transfer to the responder is

$$x_R = s \cdot X$$

where $0 \le s \le 1$ is the share of the gain offered, and x_R is the responder's material payoff. If the responder accepts the offer, the material payoff to the proposer is what remains after the transfer:

$$x_1 = (1 - s) \cdot X$$

In the second stage of the game, the responder either accepts or rejects the offer. Rejection means that each person gets a zero material payoff: $x_1 = x_R = 0$. To simplify the numerical example, we assume that X = 1. In the right panel of Figure 3.6, the acceptance of an offer with $s = 1/10$ generates a material payoff of 0.90 for the proposer and 0.10 for the responder.

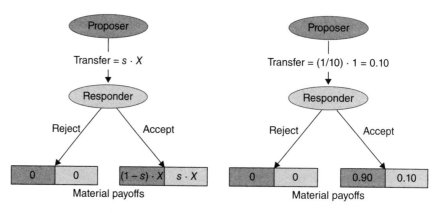

FIGURE 3.6: Game Tree for the Ultimatum Game

A Norm-Sensitive Responder

Suppose for the moment that the proposer is perfectly selfish, and observes no social norms regarding sharing the gain. As a result, the proposer acts in a strictly strategic fashion, acting to maximize his or her material payoff. In this case, the proposer will keep at least half the gain, so $x_R < 1/2$. In contrast, assume that in this environment, the responder observes a social norm of equal sharing. The utility of the responder equals his or her material benefit minus the cost associated with participating in a transaction that violates the social norm. We can use the Kimbrough-Vostroknutov utility function, with the sensitivity to the sharing norm measured by $\psi = 3$. In this case, the utility of the responder is computed as the material payoff minus the norm-violation cost:

$$u\left(x_R\right) = x_R - 3 \cdot \left(\frac{1}{2} - x_R\right)^2$$

Note that the responder incurs a cost by participating in a transaction in which the proposer violates the norm of equal sharing.

Figure 3.7 incorporates norm-violation cost into the ultimatum game. For the perfectly selfish proposer, utility doesn't change. For the responder, the norm-violation cost is 0.48 and utility is negative, at −0.38:

$$u\left(x_R\right) = 0.10 - 3 \cdot \left(0.50 - 0.10\right)^2 = 0.10 - 0.48 = -0.38$$

The responder's utility from the proposed transaction is negative because the norm-violation cost (0.48) exceeds the material gain (0.10). As a result, the responder rejects the offer: zero is better than −0.38.

Figure 3.7 illustrates a fundamental idea in behavioral economics. A person may forgo a material payoff in the interest of promoting a social norm of

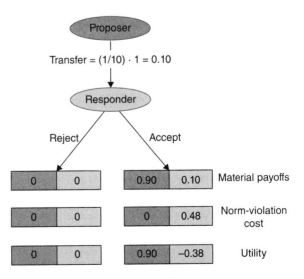

FIGURE 3.7: Rejecting a Proposed Allocation

sharing. In our example, the responder incurs a cost of 0.10 (the forgone material benefit) to impose a punishment of 0.90 on the proposer, whose offer is far from the equal-sharing offer of 0.50. Because the utility function features a trade-off between material benefit and norm-violation cost, the responder would actually accept an offer less than 0.50. In other words, equal sharing is not required. But a share of 0.10 is too far from equal sharing for the responder to accept. The proposer's large deviation from the social norm triggers punishment, which is costly for both the punisher (responder) and the punished (proposer).

Equilibrium Responder Share

In this bilateral environment where the responder has veto power over a transaction, a selfish proposer will act strategically. In choosing its offer to the responder, the proposer's objective is to maximize his or her utility, subject to the constraint that the responder accepts the offer. In other words, a selfish proposer's target offer will be just high enough to get the responder to accept the offer.

Figure 3.8 shows the relevant curves for the responder. The horizontal axis measures the transfer to the responder, from zero to the equal-sharing outcome 1/2.

- *Material benefit.* The material benefit equals the transfer $x_R = s$.
- *Norm-violation cost.* The norm-violation cost is zero when the responder receives half the endowment ($x_R = 1/2$). Therefore, the negatively sloped curve showing the norm-violation cost is anchored at zero at point a, where the equal-sharing norm is satisfied. Starting from $x_R = 1/2$, as the transfer

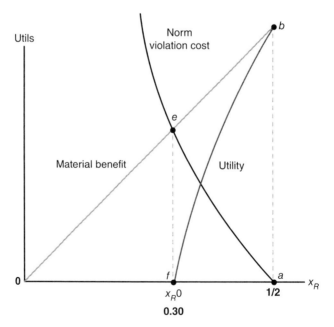

FIGURE 3.8: Responder Utility in the Ultimatum Game

decreases and the gap between x_R and 1/2 increases, the norm-violation cost increases at an increasing rate.

- *Utility curve.* The responder's utility equals the material benefit minus the norm-violation cost. The positively sloped curve showing the responder's utility is anchored at point *b*, where equal sharing eliminates norm-violation cost and makes the responder's utility equal to the material benefit. Starting from equal sharing, a decrease in x_R decreases utility for two reasons: the material benefit decreases, and norm-violation cost increases.

As frequently happens in economics, intersection points are important. At point *e*, the curve showing the cost of norm violation intersects the curve showing the material benefit, indicating that at the transfer x_R^0, norm violation cost equals the material benefit. As shown by point *f*, that means that the responder's utility is zero, as the norm-violation cost exactly offsets the material benefit of the transfer. The responder's utility is positive for a larger transfer and negative for a smaller transfer.

Recall that the responder can either accept or reject the proposer's proposed transfer. How large a transfer is required for the responder to "go along with" the proposed transfer? The responder will accept an offer if the utility from the transaction is greater than or equal to zero, after accounting for both the material benefit and any norm-violation cost. The minimum acceptable transfer x_R^0 is the transfer that generates zero utility for the responder, meaning that the responder is indifferent about the transaction. In Figure 3.8, this happens at point *f*, where the utility curve crosses the horizontal axis.

Let's switch to the proposer's perspective. Imagine that the proposer is savvy and knowledgeable. The proposer is savvy in the sense that he or she knows that the responder is sensitive to a social norm of equal sharing, but is willing to accept a transfer that falls short of equal sharing. The proposer is knowledgeable in the sense that he or she can compute the responder's minimum acceptable transfer x_R^0. In this case, the proposer's rational (utility-maximizing) response is to offer a transfer of x_R^0. The responder is indifferent about the transaction, and we assume that he or she will accept the offer. When the proposer is savvy and knowledgeable, the equilibrium transfer is the responder's minimum acceptable transfer:

$$s^* = x_R^0$$

We can use some simple algebra to derive an expression for the equilibrium transfer fraction as a function of the responder's norm-violation parameter ψ. As shown in Math 3.3, the equilibrium transfer fraction is

$$s^* = \frac{1 + \psi - \left(1 + 2 \cdot \psi\right)^{1/2}}{2 \cdot \psi}$$

In Figure 3.8, $\psi = 15/2$, so the equilibrium transfer is 0.30.

$$s^* = \frac{1 + \left(15/2\right) - \left(1 + 15\right)^{1/2}}{15} = \frac{9}{30} = 0.30$$

The equilibrium transfer increases with the value of ψ, the norm-violation parameter. Consider our ongoing numerical example.

1. *Weaker norm sensitivity:* $\psi = 3/2$. The equilibrium transfer is $s^* = 1/6$, meaning that the responder will accept any offer that provides at least one-sixth of the gain.
2. *Stronger norm sensitivity:* $\psi = 12$. The equilibrium transfer is $s^* = 1/3$, meaning that the responder will accept any offer that provides at least one-third of the gain.

The equilibrium transfer satisfies the conditions for a Nash equilibrium. In other words, neither party has an incentive for unilateral deviation.

1. *Responder.* A unilateral deviation by the responder means that the responder rejects the offer. In this case, the responder gets nothing, so the responder is not better off.
2. *Proposer.* There are two possible unilateral deviations. An increase in the transfer to an amount greater than x_R^0 would decrease the proposer's material payoff without affecting the outcome. In the other direction, a decrease in the transfer would cause the responder to reject the offer, so the proposer would get nothing.

In the Nash equilibrium, the proposer offers a transfer that is just large enough to get the responder to accept the offer.

A Norm-Sensitive Proposer

So far we have assumed that the proposer is purely selfish, and acts strategically to maximize his or her material benefit. Suppose instead that the proposer is sensitive to violations of an equal-sharing norm. As we saw earlier for the dictator game, when the dictator is highly sensitive to the sharing norm, the utility-maximizing transfer is relatively large. When the proposer in an ultimatum game is sensitive to a sharing norm, there are two possibilities.

1. *Strong sensitivity.* In the case of a strongly sensitive proposer, the proposer will favor a transfer that exceeds the responder's minimum acceptable transfer (x_R^0).
2. *Weak sensitivity.* In the case of a weakly sensitive proposer, the proposer will favor a transfer that is less than the responder's minimum acceptable transfer (x_R^0), and the outcome of the ultimatum game is x_R^0. In this case, a savvy proposer will act strategically, and choose the responder's minimum transfer x_R^0 rather than a smaller transfer that would be rejected by the responder. Something is better than nothing.

Review the Concepts 3.3

1. In a test for third-party punishment, a third party must [___] (receive a reward for, incur a cost for, be unaffected by) punishing a dictator.

2. Using Figure 3.7 as a starting point, suppose the transfer increases to 0.20. The utility of the recipient equals [___]. (−0.10, −0.07, 0, 0.20)

3. In the ultimatum game, the equilibrium transfer makes the responder's utility equal to [___]. (the proposer's utility, half the endowment, one-third the endowment, 0)

4. Using Figure 3.8 as a starting point, suppose norm sensitivity decreases, making $\psi = 4$. The equilibrium transfer in the ultimatum changes to $s^* =$ [___]. (1/6, 1/5, 1/4, 3/8)

5. Suppose that both players in the ultimatum game are sensitive to a social norm of equal sharing. The proposer's norm sensitivity will affect the outcome of the game if the proposer is [___] (more, less, equally) sensitive than the responder.

3.4 Results from Ultimatum-Game Experiments

We turn next to the results from economic experiments with the ultimatum game. Dozens of experiments have been performed around the world in different cultural and economic environments. Most of the experiments have been bilateral, with one proposer and one responder, but there have been some studies with competing responders.

Meta-Analysis of Ultimatum Experiments

Oosterbeek, Sloof, and van de Kuilen (2004) performed a meta-analysis of dozens of studies of the ultimatum game. The mean (average) transfer share is roughly 0.40, and roughly two-thirds of the transfer shares are between 0.30 and 0.50. The mean (average) rejection rate by responders is roughly 0.16. For the United States, the authors compare the results from eastern states to western states. Although the mean transfer shares are similar (0.405 for the east and 0.426 for the west), the average rejection rate is lower in the west (0.094 in the west versus 0.171 in the east).

Oosterbeek, Sloof, and van de Kuilen (2004) conclude that responders are responsive to changes in the relative payoff from the ultimatum game. A decrease in either X (the size of the endowment) or x_R/X (the share of the endowment transferred to the responder) increases the rejection rate. But a decrease in the transfer share has a stronger effect on the rejection rate. In other words, responders are willing to bear a cost to penalize proposers whose offers involve relatively large deviations from equal sharing.

Crosswalk Rules and the Ultimatum Game

Recall the rule-following experiment with stoplights and crosswalks. Kimbrough and Vostroknutov (2016) ran the ultimatum game with subjects who vary in their conformity to the rule of waiting for a green light. For proposers, the transfer share did not vary significantly with the subject's conformity to the waiting rule. In contrast, for responders there was a high correlation between rule conformity and the minimum acceptable transfer.

- *Strong rule following.* For the top 10 percent of crosswalk waiters, the minimum share was roughly 32 percent. These subjects rejected offers less than 32 percent of the gain: they were willing to bear a relatively large cost to punish norm violators. Individuals who strongly conform to norms are willing to bear a large cost to enforce conformity on others.
- *Weak rule following.* For the bottom 10 percent of crosswalk waiters, the minimum transfer share was roughly 13 percent of the gain. People who are lackadaisical in conforming to norms aren't willing to pay much to enforce conformity on others.

In other words, conforming to norms and enforcing conformity on others go together.

The results of Kimbrough and Vostroknutov (2016) illustrate the difference between the dictator game and the ultimatum game. The dictator game provides evidence of a sharing norm, as the dictator transfers resources to a passive recipient. On average, the transfer in the dictator game is roughly 25 percent of the gain. In contrast, the proposer in an ultimatum game faces an active responder, who can reject an offer that he or she considers inequitable. On average, the transfer in the ultimatum game is roughly 40 percent of the gain. This suggests that strategic behavior plays an important role in the ultimatum game: the typical proposer boosts the transfer to avoid rejection by a responder who is willing to incur a cost to promote a social norm of sharing.

Review the Concepts 3.4

1. In a meta-analysis of the ultimatum game, the average transfer share is roughly [___]. (0.10, 0.20, 0.40, 0.50)

2. The crosswalk-ultimatum game results show that [___] and [___] go together. (conforming to norms, enforcing conformity; violating norms, enforcing conformity; conforming to norms, ignoring norm violations)

 3. Consider Widget 3.1 (available at www.oup.com/us/osullivan1e). For the starting point, the potential responder utility is [___] and the proposer utility is [___]. (zero, negative; positive, zero; negative, zero; negative, positive)

 4. Consider Widget 3.1 (available at www.oup.com/us/osullivan1e). For the equilibrium transfer share, responder utility is [___] and proposer utility is [___]. (positive, zero; zero, positive; zero, negative; negative, positive)

3.5 Market Engagement and Social Norms

A recent research program explores the connection between participation in markets and pro-social behavior (Ensminger and Henrich 2014). A collaboration among roughly two dozen anthropologists and economists performed behavioral experiments on 15 societies around the globe, including hunter-gatherers (from Tanzania, Indonesia, and Paraguay), herders (from Mongolia, Siberia, and Kenya), subsistence farmers (from South America and Africa), wage laborers (from Ghana and Missouri in the U.S.), and slash/burn horticulturists (from New Guinea, Oceania, and Amazonia). The question is, "How does participation in markets affect behavior in the dictator, third-party punishment, and ultimatum games?"

Consider first the correlation between market participation and behavior in the dictator game. In Figure 3.9, the horizontal axis measures market integration, computed as the percent of household food (in calories) purchased in markets, as opposed to produced by the household itself (grown, hunted, gathered, fished). The vertical axis measures the dictator's transfer share. In general, there is a positive correlation between market involvement and the transfer share: the greater the market engagement, the larger the dictator's transfer to the recipient.

- At the lower end, the Hazda people in Tanzania have a market-integration value of zero (no food purchased in markets) and the average transfer share is roughly 0.26.
- At the upper end, in a small rural community in Missouri (in the U.S.), households are fully engaged in the market, and the average transfer share is roughly 0.47.

The authors estimate that on average, a six percentage point increase in market integration increases the transfer share by 0.01.

Why does greater participation in markets increase the dictator's transfer? An individual who participates in a market engages in exchange with people outside his or her family and kin group. As noted by Henrich (2020), market-based norms (rules for behavior in markets) cause individuals to broaden their pro-social behavior to include interactions with people outside the family and kin group.

> Market norms establish the standards for judging oneself and others in impersonal transactions and lead to the internalization of motivations for trust, fairness, and cooperation with strangers and anonymous others. (Henrich 2020, 293)

To succeed in market exchange—as buyer and seller—an individual must observe market norms.

> . . . individuals succeed in part by cultivating a reputation for impartial fairness, honesty, and cooperation with acquaintances, strangers, and anonymous others because it's these qualities that will help them attract

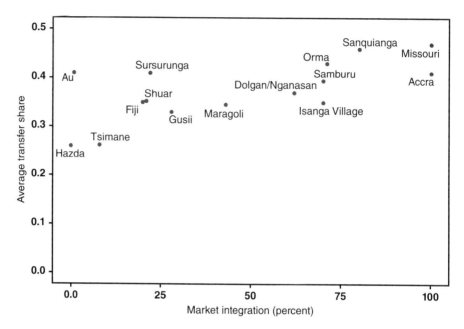

FIGURE 3.9: Market Integration and the Dictator Transfer

the most customers as well as the best business partners, employees, students, and clients. (Henrich 2020, 294)

The formula for success in market exchange includes impartial fairness and cooperation with anonymous others, which translates into greater sharing with an anonymous partner in the dictator game.

Recall from an earlier chapter the results of the rope-pulling experiment. Two youngsters (three-year-olds) can earn a reward, but only if they collaborate by pulling the rope together. The youngsters usually share the rewards of collaboration equally, but rarely share rewards generated individually. This identifies a possible factor in the positive relationship between market engagement and sharing in the dictator game: a person who regularly engages in mutually beneficial exchange in markets may acquire a relatively broad notion of collaboration that includes strangers and anonymous others. A broad notion of collaboration could promote sharing and fairness in a variety of environments, including the artificial environment of the dictator game.

Experiments with other economic games generate similar correlations between market integration and pro-social behavior. Experiments with third-party punishment show that greater market engagement is associated with stronger punishment of norm violators. Figure 3.10 shows the results of experiments with the ultimatum game. The horizontal axis measures market integration (percent of food purchased in markets), and the vertical axis measures the average proposed transfer from the proposer. The positive correlation between market engagement and the average transfer share reflects two pro-social norms: sharing and costly punishment of norm violators.

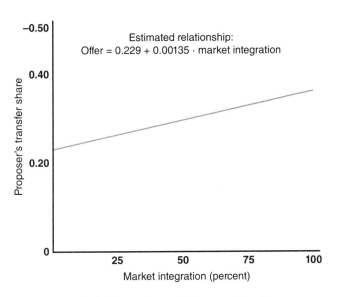

FIGURE 3.10: Market Integration and the Proposer Transfer

Review the Concepts 3.5

1. The results of behavioral experiments around the globe suggest a [____] correlation between participation in markets and the transfer share in the dictator game. (positive, negative, zero)

2. The results of behavioral experiments around the globe suggest a [____] correlation between participation in markets and the transfer share in the ultimatum game. (positive, negative, zero)

3. One explanation for the correlation between market engagement and pro-social behavior is that market participants internalize market norms of [____] with strangers and anonymous others. (trust, fairness, cooperation)

4. The correlation between market engagement and pro-social behavior is [____] with the key result from the rope-pulling experiment with youngsters: equal sharing is triggered by [____]. (consistent, independent work; inconsistent, independent work; consistent, collaboration)

Key Terms

dictator game, p. 49   third-party punishment, p. 53   ultimatum game, p. 54

Takeaways

1. A simplified version of the Kimbrough-Vostroknutov utility function incorporates the trade-off between material benefits and the cost of violating a social norm.

2. For the utility-maximizing amount of a gain kept, the marginal benefit from material benefits equals the marginal cost of violating a social norm of sharing.

3. The dictator game demonstrates the power of a social norm of sharing rewards.

4. In the dictator game, the observed transfer increases with the age of the dictator and the observability of the sharing outcome.

5. The third-party-punishment game demonstrates the social norm of enforcing norm conformity.

6. The ultimatum game demonstrates the social norms of sharing and enforcing norm conformity.

7. When the proposer in an ultimatum game is relatively insensitive to a social norm of sharing, the equilibrium transfer generates zero utility for a norm-sensitive responder.

8. Compared to the dictator game, the ultimatum game has greater transfers: the threat of rejection by a norm-sensitive responder increases the transfer.

9. Experiments with the dictator game and ultimatum game show a positive correlation between participation in markets and pro-social behavior.

Discuss the Concepts

1. *Dictator in Jerseyville.* Everyone in Jerseyville wears a jersey displaying his or her allegiance to a sports team. Consider an individual who plays the dictator in the dictator game twice, each time with a stranger. Recipient M's jersey matches the jersey of the dictator. Recipient D's jersey comes from a different team. The dictator is likely to keep a larger fraction (a larger x_1^*) in the dictator game with recipient [___] because we expect ψ_M [___] ψ_D. Illustrate with the marginal principle.

2. *Choose Your Dictator.* You have agreed to participate in a dictator game as a recipient. A dictator has $24 to share with a recipient. When you enter the experiment room, you see dictators at tables around the room. You can choose your dictator: either a 20-year-old college student or a 40-year old college graduate. Your best choice is [___] because [___]. Use the marginal principle to illustrate your choice.

3. *Game the Ultimatum Game.* Tomorrow you will play an ultimatum game as a responder. The proposer doesn't know your true ψ value. When you discover that the proposer is eavesdropping on your conversation with a friend, you have an incentive to disclose a fake ψ value that is [___] (greater than, less than, equal to) your true value. Use a graph like Figure 3.8 to show the effects of your deception. Draw your true utility curve and your fake utility curve. Label your true minimum transfer x_R^0 and your fake minimum transfer x_R^{fake}. Label your utility with a successful fake as u^{**}.

4. *Choose Your Game.* You have an opportunity to participate in one of two economic experiments. You can be a recipient in a dictator game or a responder in an ultimatum game. The dictator has $40 to share. The proposer in the ultimatum game has $30 to share. The best choice is [___] because [___] > [___].

Apply the Concepts

1. *Dictator and Language.* Consider an individual who plays the dictator in the dictator game twice, each time with a stranger. Recipient S speaks the same language as the dictator, while recipient D speaks a different language.

   a. Predict the outcomes of the dictator game with the two recipients in terms of the fraction transferred to the recipient: t_S [___] t_D.

   b. In terms of norm sensitivity, ψ_S [___] ψ_D.

   c. Use the marginal principle to illustrate.

2. *Marginal Principle.* In an economic experiment, a dictator has X = 1 to share. Consider a dictator whose sensitivity to a norm of equal sharing is measured by $\psi = 1/3$. For a utility-maximizing dictator, $x_1^* = $ [___] and $t^* = $ [___]. Illustrate with the marginal-benefit and marginal-cost curves.

3. *Decibels and Dictator.* A dictator has received $120 to share with a recipient. The impartial spectator is the town crier, who observes the transfer of the dictator to the recipient, and sounds off with volume $v = 0.02 \cdot (x_1 - 60)^2$. The dictator's utility equals material utility x_1 minus the noise cost ($\psi \cdot v$), where ψ is a measure of the dictator's hearing acuity.

   a. Suppose $\psi = 1$. Draw the curves for material benefit, norm-violation cost, and utility. In this case, $x_1^* = $ [___].

   b. Suppose $\psi = 2$. Draw the curves for material benefit, norm-violation cost, and utility. In this case, $x_1^{**} = $ [___].

4. *Decrease in Responder Sensitivity.* Using Figure 3.8 as a starting point, suppose the value of the responder's norm-sensitivity parameter decreases from $\psi = 15/2$ to $\psi = 4$. The equilibrium transfer [___] ($\uparrow$, $\downarrow$, does not change) to $s^{**} = $ [___]. Illustrate.

5. *Game the Ultimatum Game.* You are about to play the ultimatum game (X = 1), and your role is responder. Your value for norm-sensitivity parameter is $\psi = 4$. The proposer in the game doesn't know your ψ value.

   a. You will reject any offer that is [___].

   b. The proposer is snooping around, trying to determine your ψ value. When you realize that the proposer is eavesdropping on your conversation with a friend, you have an opportunity to deceive the proposer by stating either your true value ($\psi = 4$) or a fake value ($\psi = 12$). The benefit of successful deception is [___]. Illustrate.

6. *Ultimatum Game with Sensitive Proposer.* Consider an ultimatum game ($X = 1$) with a proposer and a responder who differ in their sensitivity to the social norm of equal sharing. For the proposer, $\psi_P = 10$. For the responder, $\psi_R = 6$. The equilibrium transfer fraction is $s^* = $ [___], so the responder gets $x_R = $ [___] and the proposer gets $x_1 = $ [___].

7. *A Second Responder.* Consider an ultimatum game with responders who vary in their sensitivity to a social norm of equal sharing: Melo has weak sensitivity, Avar has average sensitivity, and Salut has strong sensitivity. In Round 1, there is a game between the proposer and Avar. In Round 2, we add a second responder, generating a game between the proposer and two responders. Assume that the proposer is insensitive to a social norm of sharing.

   a. If the second responder is Melo, the move from round 1 to round 2 [___] (↑, ↓, does not change) the equilibrium transfer because [___].

   b. If the second responder is Salut, the move from round 1 to round 2 [___] (↑, ↓, does not change) the equilibrium transfer because [___].

   c. Consider the following values of the norm-sensitivity parameter: $\psi = (3/2, 4, 12)$. Match each value to the appropriate responder. The equilibrium transfer for the single-responder game with Avar is $s^* = $ [___]. The equilibrium transfer for a two-responder game with Avar and Melo is $s^{**} = $ [___]. The equilibrium transfer for a two-responder game with Avar and Salut is $s^{***} = $ [___].

Math Solutions

Math 3.1: Marginal Cost of Violating an Equal-Sharing Norm

The norm-violation cost is

$$c = \psi \cdot \left(x_1 - \frac{1}{2}\right)^2$$

Marginal cost is the change in norm-violation cost per unit change in x_1. Differentiate the expression for norm-violation cost with respect to x_1 to get an expression for marginal cost:

$$\frac{dc}{dx_1} = \psi \cdot (2 \cdot x_1 - 1)$$

$$mc = \psi \cdot (2 \cdot x_1 - 1)$$

For equal sharing ($x_1 = 1/2$), marginal cost is zero:

$$mc = \psi \cdot (1-1) = 0$$

For no sharing ($x_1 = 1$), marginal cost is ψ:

$$mc = \psi \cdot (2-1) = \psi$$

Math 3.2: Amount Kept and Transferred by a Utility-Maximizing Dictator

Differentiate the dictator's utility function with respect to the choice variable x_1:

$$\frac{du}{dx_1} = 1 - 2 \cdot \psi \cdot \left(x_1 - \frac{1}{2} \right)$$

Set the derivative equal to zero to solve for the utility-maximizing value of x_1:

$$x_1^* = \frac{1+\psi}{2 \cdot \psi}$$

The transfer fraction is $t = 1 - x_1^*$:

$$t^* = \frac{\psi - 1}{2 \cdot \psi}$$

Math 3.3: Equilibrium Transfer Fraction for the Ultimatum Game

Expand the responder's utility function to identify the components of the expression relevant to the quadratic formula $y = a \cdot x^2 + b \cdot x + c$:

$$u(x_R) = -\psi \cdot x_R^2 + (1+\psi) \cdot x_R - \frac{\psi}{4}$$

Set utility equal to zero and use the quadratic formula to generate the roots of the quadratic function (where utility = 0). The relevant root (for zero utility) is

$$x_R^0 = \frac{1 + \psi - (1 + 2 \cdot \psi)^{1/2}}{2 \cdot \psi}$$

A savvy and knowledgeable proposer will offer the minimum acceptable offer (responder utility = 0). The equilibrium transfer fraction equals the minimum acceptable transfer:

$$s^* = x_R^0 = \frac{1 + \psi - (1 + 2 \cdot \psi)^{1/2}}{2 \cdot \psi}$$

Appendix to Chapter 3: Fehr-Schmidt Inequity Cost

As explained in Chapter 3, a convenient way to incorporate pro-social behavior is to refine traditional benefit–cost analysis to include a cost associated with violating a social norm in a utility function. In this appendix to the chapter, we introduce a second framework to represent the trade-off between material benefits and the psychological cost associated with inequality in economic outcomes. This second framework is based on the notion of other-regarding preferences—the notion that an individual has preferences concerning the economic welfare of another person (Fehr and Schmidt 1999; Fehr and Schmidt 2004). An individual's decisions are based on both self-regarding and other-regarding preferences.

The Fehr-Schmidt inequity function measures two sorts of costs from an unequal distribution of wealth. Consider an economy with two people, person 1 and person 2, and define x_i as the wealth of person i. If person 2 has lower wealth $(x_1 > x_2)$, he or she experiences **disadvantaged inequity** cost equal to

$$disadvantaged\ inequity = \epsilon \cdot (x_1 - x_2)$$

For example, if $x_1 = 50$, $x_2 = 10$, and $\varepsilon = 8/10$, the inequity cost experienced by person 2 is $32:

$$disadvantaged\ inequity = 8/10 \cdot 40 = 32$$

If instead person 2 has higher wealth $(x_2 > x_1)$, he or she experiences **advantaged inequity** cost equal to

$$advantaged\ inequity = \gamma \cdot (x_2 - x_1)$$

For example, if $x_1 = 15$, $x_2 = 45$, and $\gamma = 1/3$, the inequity cost experienced by person 2 is $10:

$$advantaged\ inequity = 1/3 \cdot 30 = 10$$

We can use a general expression to include both possibilities—disadvantaged and advantaged inequity cost. The inequity cost experienced by person 2 is computed as

$$z_2(x_1, x_2) = \epsilon \cdot Max[0, x_1 - x_2] + \gamma \cdot Max[0, x_2 - x_1]$$

Only one part of the right-hand side will be relevant. The first part incorporates disadvantaged inequity $(x_1 > x_2)$, and will be in play only when person 2 has lower wealth. If instead person 2 has higher wealth, $x_1 - x_2 < 0$, and ε will be multiplied by zero. We use the Greek letter ε for disadvantaged inequity as a reminder that ε could represent (i) the second person's envy of the higher wealth of the other person, or (ii) the second person's sense of being exploited by the other person. The second part incorporates advantaged inequity $(x_2 > x_1)$, and will be in play only when person 2 has higher wealth. We use the Greek letter γ for disadvantaged inequity as a reminder that γ could represent the second person's guilt generated by his or her greater wealth.

Figure 3A.1 illustrates inequity cost from the perspective of person 2, assuming the wealth of person 1 is $x_1 = 30$. The values of the parameters are $\varepsilon = 2/3$ for disadvantaged inequity (envy/exploitation) and $\gamma = 1/3$ for advantaged inequity (guilt). As shown by point b, when $x_2 = x_1$, inequity cost is zero. For $x_2 < x_1$, person 2 experiences disadvantaged inequity, as shown by the negatively sloped portion of the inequity-cost curve. For the extreme case $x_2 = 0$, inequity cost is $z_2 = 20 = 2/3 \cdot 30$ (shown by point a). For $x_2 > x_1$, person 2 experiences advantaged inequity, as shown by the positively sloped portion of the inequity-cost curve. For the extreme case $x_2 = 60$, inequity cost is $z_2 = 10 = 1/3 \cdot (60 - 30)$ (shown by point f).

Figure 3A.1 also shows how to incorporate inequity cost into the calculation of utility of person 2. The positively sloped curve that includes the origin, point c, and point d shows the material payoff of person 2, which is simply the person's wealth x_2. The kinked curve with a vertical intercept -20 that includes points c

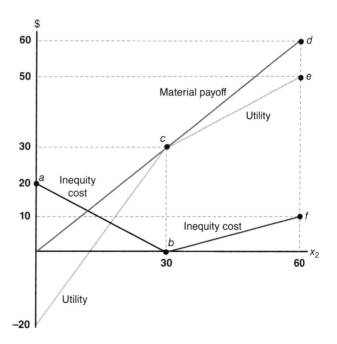

FIGURE 3A.1: Inequity Cost, Material Payoffs, and Utility

and e shows the person's utility, equal to the material payoff minus inequity cost. As shown by point c, when $x_2 = x_1$, inequity cost is zero, so utility equals the material payoff. For $x_2 < x_1$, person 2 experiences disadvantaged inequity, so utility is less than the material payoff: the utility curve is below the material-payoff curve. For $x_2 > x_1$, person 2 experiences advantaged inequity, and utility is again less than the material payoff: the utility curve is below the material-payoff curve. For the extreme case $x_2 = 60$, the utility is $10 less than the material payoff (shown by point e).

The notion of inequity in the Fehr-Schmidt framework is narrow and self-centered. It is narrow in the sense that a person compares his or her wealth to the wealth of one other person. In other words, inequity is defined in a bilateral fashion. This notion of equity is self-centered in the sense that each person uses his or her own wealth as the reference point in computing differences in wealth and the resulting inequity. Each person ignores any wealth inequalities beyond the simple bilateral comparison.

Key Terms

advantaged inequity, p. 68   disdvantaged inequity, p. 68

Apply the Concepts

1. *Compute Envy Cost.* According to Tupac, "I am indifferent between the bundles {0,0} and {70,30}, where the first element in each bundle is Wanda's wealth (x_1) and the second element in each bundle is Tupac's wealth (x_2).

    a. Tupac's value of the exploitation parameter is $\varepsilon =$ [____].

    b. Suppose Wanda's value for the exploitation parameter is 2/3 the value of Tupac's. Wanda will be indifferent between {0,0} and $\{x_1, x_2\}$, where $100 = x_1 + x_2$. The values for Wanda indifference are $x_1 =$ [____] and $x_2 =$ [____].

2. *Decrease in Inequity Cost.* Using Figure 3A.1 as a starting point, suppose the value of the inequity parameter decreases from $\varepsilon = 3/4$ to $\varepsilon = 1/4$. The equilibrium share [____] (↑, ↓, does not change) to $s^{**} =$ [____]. Illustrate. Use Widget 3.2 (available at www.oup.com/us/osullivan1e) to verify your calculations.

3. Gaming the Ultimatum Game. You are about to play the ultimatum game with an endowment of $1000, and your role is responder. Your value for the envy/exploitation parameter is $\varepsilon = 0.45$. The proposer in the game doesn't know your ε value.

    a. You will reject any offer that is [____].

    b. The proposer is snooping around, trying to determine your ε value. When you realize that the proposer is eavesdropping on your conversation with a friend, you have an opportunity to deceive the proposer by stating either your true value ($\varepsilon = 0.45$) or a fake value ($\varepsilon = 0.90$). The benefit of deception is roughly $[____].

4. *Sharing a Lottery Prize.* You just won a lottery prize of $800 and will share it with a friend. Ignoring any guilt cost, your utility function is $u(x_1, x_2) = a \cdot \log[x_1] + b \cdot \log[x_2]$, where x_1 is the lottery money you keep for yourself, x_2 is the lottery money you give to your friend, and log[ ] is the natural logarithm.

   a. For $a = 6$, $b = 2$, the utility-maximizing allocation is $x_1 =$[____] and $x_2 =$ [_____].

   b. Suppose you experience linear Fehr-Schmidt inequity in the form of guilt for $x_1 > x_2$. If $\gamma = 0.10$, your guilt cost for the allocation in (a) = [____]. For a $1 transfer to your friend, the marginal benefit is [_____], and the marginal cost is [_____].

   c. The rational response to your guilt is to give $[_____] of the lottery prize to your friend.

4 Trust

Imagine that you are in your favorite coffee shop, and a behavioral economist invites you to play a little game. The economist will give you $10. You can keep the money or give any amount to a randomly selected customer in the coffee shop (your game partner, a person you will never meet again). For each dollar you give your partner, the behavioral economist will add two dollars: each dollar from you becomes three dollars to your partner. Your partner then decides how much to return to you. In other words, every $1 you invest becomes $3 that your partner divides between the two of you. For example, if your partner returns half, you get $1.50 back on every dollar invested. Or if the partner returns 10 percent, you get back $0.30 for every dollar invested.

1. How much of the $10 would you give your game partner?

2. How much would you expect to get back?

3. How would your answers vary, depending on whether your partner is a 20-year-old college student or a 40-year-old college graduate whose work involves transactions that require mutual trust?

Write your numbers in a secure location. Later in the chapter you can compare your choice and expectation to the experiences of other people who participated in the Trust Game.

This is the second of several chapters that explore the effects of social norms on economic behavior. In this chapter, we explore the role of social norms in interactions that require trust and trustworthiness. Trust is a component of **social capital**, defined as features of social organization that improve cooperation and promote efficiency. In the absence of trust between two parties involved in exchange, a transaction may require detailed contracts and costly monitoring to ensure compliance with the terms of trade. Trust reduces transaction cost because it reduces the need for costly contracts and monitoring. Lower transaction cost translates into larger gains from trade and thus more trade. An increase in trade increases aggregate wealth as an economy more fully exploits economies of scale and comparative advantage.

Learning Objectives: The Explainer

After mastering this chapter, you will be able to explain each of the following statements.

1. **In an environment of perfectly selfish individuals, investments that require trust are unlikely.**

2. **An investor prefers a collaborator (a producer) who has a relatively strong sensitivity to a norm of sharing the rewards of collaboration.**

3. **When an investor is less sensitive to a sharing norm than his or her collaborator (a producer), investment is more likely.**

4. **When an investor is more sensitive to a sharing norm than his or her collaborator (a producer), investment is less likely.**

5. **In trust-game experiments, there is substantial variation across participants in investment fractions and return fractions.**

6. **In trust-game experiments, the investment fraction is relatively large when an investor is paired with a producer with a past history of trust or trustworthiness.**

4.1 The Trust Game: Investment and Production

As we saw in the previous chapter, the ultimatum game and the dictator game are zero-sum games about how to divide a fixed amount of resources—how to slice a pie. In contrast, the **trust game** illustrates the role of pro-social behavior in deciding how much of a resource to invest in a production process that increases the total value of the economy. Two agents engage in transfers to and fro. Agent 1 is a resource owner who starts the game by transferring resources to agent 2. Agent 2 is a producer who transforms the invested resources into output, and then returns a fraction of the output back to agent 1.

1. Agent 1: Investor. The traditional tag for agent 1 is "trustor." We will instead use the tag "investor" as a reminder that agent 1 invests resources in anticipation of a return on the investment.
2. Agent 2: Producer. The traditional tag for agent 2 is "trustee." We will instead use the tag "producer" because the agent's role is to transform resources into output.

Because the trust game includes production, it is a positive-sum game that illustrates the implications of pro-social behavior for both efficiency (the size of the pie) and equity (the slicing of the pie).

It will be useful to introduce some terms. We can distinguish between trust and trustworthiness. In the trust game, an investor displays *trust* by investing resources without a guarantee of getting anything back. A producer who returns a fraction of output to the investor displays *trustworthiness*.

Game Structure

Consider a two-agent economy with a resource endowment X and two roles, investor (#1) and producer (#2). The economy's resource endowment is held by the investor, and the production process is controlled by the producer. In the first stage of the game, the investor transfers a fraction of the resource endowment to the producer as an investment:

$$invest = i \cdot X$$

where $0 \le i \le 1$ is the investment fraction. Agent 2 is a producer, and the production process increases the value of the invested resources:

$$output = i \cdot X \cdot \theta$$

where the productivity parameter is $\theta > 1$. In the second stage of the game, the producer returns a fraction of the output to the investor:

$$returned\ to\ investor = i \cdot X \cdot \theta \cdot r$$

where the return fraction is $0 \le r \le 1$.

Consider the perspective of the investor. To simplify the calculations, we'll assume that the endowment is $X = 1$. What is the minimum acceptable return for the investor? The investor will simply hold on to the endowment if the payoff from investment (the amount returned to the investor) is less than 1. The investor will be indifferent about investing if the payoff is 1. This happens when

$$\theta \cdot r = 1$$

The production process increases the one unit invested to $\theta > 1$ and the producer returns a fraction $r < 1$ to the investor. For the investor, the minimum acceptable return fraction is

$$r^0 = \frac{1}{\theta}$$

For example, for $\theta = 3$, the return is positive for a return fraction of at least 1/3. In the absence of norm concerns, an investor will be willing to invest with a producer whose return fraction is at least $1/\theta$.

Figure 4.1 shows a simplified version of the trust game, with limited choices for each actor. The endowment is one unit of the resource. The investor chooses either $i = 0$ or $i = 1$, choosing between investing nothing or investing all the resources. If the investor chooses $i = 0$, the game is over and the payoffs shown by rectangle A are 1 for the investor (keep the resources) and zero for the producer. Alternatively, if the investor invests, the producer triples the value of the resources ($\theta = 3$). The producer has four options: with r equal to {0, 0.10, 0.40, 0.50}, generating four additional payoff rectangles.

1. B: $r = 0$. The producer keeps all 3 units of output.
2. C: $r = 0.10$. The producer returns 0.30 units and keeps 2.70 units.
3. D: $r = 0.40$. The producer returns 1.20 units and keeps 1.80 units.
4. E: $r = 0.50$. The producer returns half and keeps half.

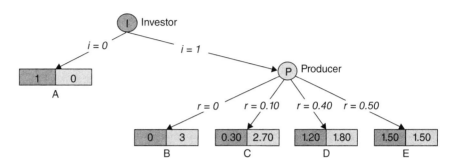

FIGURE 4.1: A Simplified Trust Game

Outcome in the Absence of a Sharing Norm

Consider the outcome of the trust game in an economy with self-regarding preferences. The objective of a selfish person is to maximize his or her material benefit. The investor (resource owner) is the first mover, and naturally anticipates the choice of the producer. A selfish producer will keep all the output rather than sharing it with the investor. In Figure 4.1, if the investor transfers resources to the producer, the producer will triple the value and take it all: $r = 0$, leading to payoff rectangle B, with zero for the investor and 3 for the producer. Thinking ahead, the investor anticipates that a selfish producer will not share, so a similarly selfish investor will choose $i = 0$. As a result, the outcome of the game is payoff rectangle A: the investor payoff is 1 rather than zero in rectangle B.

What would happen if the producer promised in advance to return half the output ($r = 0.50$) to the investor? If the investor believes the promise, he or she would anticipate a payoff from investment of 1.50 (rectangle E). The problem with this scenario is that the producer's promise to return some output to the investor is not a credible promise. In the absence of a binding contract, a producer's rational response to any investment is to keep all the output. In other words, a positive return fraction is not a Nash equilibrium. A selfish producer has an incentive to unilaterally deviate from $r = 0.50$ and choose $r = 0$ instead.

Review the Concepts 4.1

1. In the trust game, trust is measured by the [____] fraction and trustworthiness is measured by the [____] fraction. (investment, return; return, investment)

2. Consider an investor in the trust game. If $\theta = 4$, the minimum acceptable return fraction is $r_0 = $ [____]. (1/4, 1/3, 1/2, 3/4)

3. In a trust game, $i = 0.60$, $\theta = 3$, and $r = 0.10$. The amount returned to the investor is [____].
(0, 0.10, 0.18, 1.80)

4. In Figure 4.1, investment makes the investor better off if the producer chooses a return fraction
$r = $ [____]. (0, 0.10, 0.40, 0.50)

5. In an economy with self-regarding preferences, the Nash equilibrium investment fraction in a
trust game is [____]. (0, 0.10, 0.50, 1)

4.2   A Sharing Norm for the Producer

We turn next to the role of social preferences in the trust game. As in the ultimatum game, the social norms observed by the second mover in the game (the producer) play a key role in the outcome of the game. The decision of the first mover (the investor) is based on his or her expectations about how much the producer will return to the investor. As we'll see, a social norm of sharing the rewards of collaboration affects the return fraction of the producer.

The Producer's Trade-Off: Material Benefit versus Norm-Violation Cost

Let's assume that the producer has internalized a social norm of equal sharing of the output generated by an investment. This assumption is in the spirit of the rope-pulling experiment with youngsters described in an earlier chapter. Like the youngsters, the investor and producers are collaborating to get a reward, and each person is required for success. The investor provides resources, and the producer provides the technology and human capital to transform the resources into output. So a norm of equal sharing is a reasonable starting point.

To avoid double negatives and other awkward language, we introduce the hold fraction h as the choice variable of the producer. The hold fraction is defined as the fraction of the investment retained by the producer rather than returned to the investor. Naturally, the hold fraction and the return fraction add to 1:

$$h + r = 1$$

When a producer chooses the utility-maximizing hold fraction h^*, he or she simultaneously chooses the utility-maximizing return fraction r^*:

$$r^* = 1 - h^*$$

As we saw in an earlier chapter, we can use a utility function to incorporate social norms into a decision-making process. The utility function captures the trade-off between material benefits and the cost of violating a social norm. In the trust game, equal sharing by the producer generates a hold fraction $h = 1/2$. We can represent the cost of violating the equal-sharing norm as

$$norm\ violation\ cost = \theta \cdot \psi_2 \cdot \left(h - \frac{1}{2}\right)^2$$

where ψ_2 measures the producer's sensitivity to the equal-sharing norm. The norm-violation cost is zero for $h = 1/2$. As the hold fraction h rises above $1/2$ and the producer keeps more than half, the norm-violation cost increases at an increasing rate. The productivity parameter θ scales up the norm-violation cost for comparison to the material benefit. For material benefits, one unit of resources invested grows to θ units, so the producer's material benefit is $\theta \cdot h$. The producer's utility equals the material benefit minus the norm-violation cost:

$$producer\ utility = \theta \cdot h - \theta \cdot \psi_2 \cdot \left(h - \frac{1}{2}\right)^2$$

Figure 4.2 illustrates the choice of a utility-maximizing hold fraction. The horizontal axis measures the hold fraction (increasing from left to right) and the return fraction (decreasing from left to right). We can ignore hold fractions less than half because $h = 1/2$ satisfies the equal-sharing norm, and the producer has no incentive to retain less than half. The numbers in the figure are based on productivity measured by $\theta = 3$ and norm sensitivity measured by $\psi_2 = 5$.

- *Material benefit.* As the hold fraction increases, the material benefit of the producer increases, as shown by the linear material-benefit curve. As shown by the vertical intercept of the material-benefit curve, when the producer keeps half ($h = 1/2$), the material benefit is $\theta/2 = 1.50$. As shown by point g, when the producer keeps it all ($h = 1$), the material benefit is $\theta = 3$.
- *Norm-violation cost.* The norm-violation cost is zero when the producer strictly adheres to the social norm of equal sharing ($h = r = 1/2$), and increases as an increasing rate as the hold fraction increases. At point i, the norm-violation cost is 0.15.
- *Utility.* The producer's utility equals the material benefit minus norm-violation cost.

Given the interplay of material benefit and norm-violation cost, the utility curve reaches its peak at $h^* = 0.60$, shown by point j. In this case of relatively strong sensitivity to the norm of equal sharing, the producer maximizes utility with a hold fraction not far from half ($h^* = 0.60$) and a return fraction close to half ($r^* = 0.40$).

The lower panel of Figure 4.2 applies the marginal principle to the producer's choice of a hold fraction. Suppose we start at $h = 1/2$, and consider the effects of increasing the hold fraction. The marginal-benefit curve incorporates the producer's gain of material benefits: an increase in h increases the material benefit at a constant rate, so the marginal-benefit curve is horizontal. The positively sloped marginal-cost curve incorporates norm-violation cost: an increase in the hold fraction increases inequality (the gap between the hold fraction and $1/2$), and

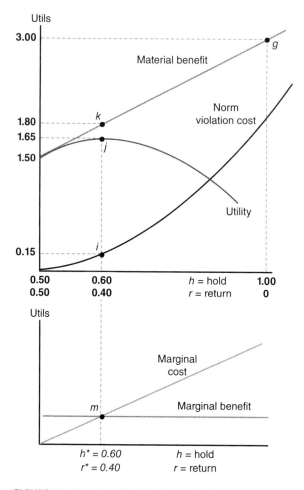

FIGURE 4.2: Norm-Sensitive Producer in the Trust Game

increases norm-violation cost. Because the norm-violation cost increases at an increasing rate, the marginal-cost curve is positively sloped. The marginal principle is satisfied at point m, with the utility-maximizing hold fraction $h^* = 0.60$ and return fraction $r^* = 0.40$.

The utility-maximizing hold fraction is determined the norm-sensitivity parameter ψ_2. As shown in Math 4.1, we can use the marginal principle to derive an expression for h^*:

$$h^* = \frac{\psi_2 + 1}{2 \cdot \psi_2}$$

As shown in Figure 4.2, for $\psi_2 = 5$, the utility-maximizing hold fraction is $h^* = 0.60$:

$$h^* = \frac{5+1}{2 \cdot 5} = \frac{6}{10}$$

The utility-maximizing return fraction is

$$r^* = 1 - h^* = 1 - \frac{6}{10} = \frac{4}{10}$$

Using the producer's utility function, this modest deviation from the norm of equal sharing generates a utility level of 1.65:

$$producer \; utility = 3 \cdot 0.60 - 3 \cdot 5 \cdot (0.60 - 0.50)^2 = 1.65$$

This is shown by point j in Figure 4.2: utility is 1.65, compared to a material benefit of 1.80 (point k).

Varying Norm Sensitivity and Return Fractions

If producers vary in their norm sensitivity, they will maximize utility with different hold fractions. The variation across producers is reflected in different values of the norm-sensitivity parameter ψ_2. Figure 4.3 shows the utility-maximizing hold fractions and return fractions for three producers. One citizen has strong norm sensitivity, generating a large ψ_2 and a hold fraction h_S close to half, and a return fraction close to half. At the other extreme, another citizen has weak sensitivity to the equal-sharing norm, so the marginal-cost curve is everywhere below the marginal-benefit curve. As a result, the utility-maximizing hold fraction is h* = 1 and the return fraction is r* = 0. A third citizen has middling sensitivity to the equal-sharing norm, generating a medium hold fraction h_M and medium return fraction.

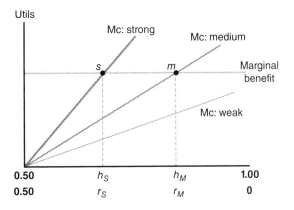

FIGURE 4.3: Varying Norm Sensitivity and Return Fractions

The Investor Decision

The investor's decision about whether to invest is based on the anticipated return fraction chosen by the producer. The investor will invest if the producer's utility-maximizing return fraction r* = 1 − h* exceeds the investor's minimum return fraction r^0. In our example, this condition is satisfied, as the norm-sensitive producer chooses a return rate $r^* = 0.40$, which exceeds the investor's minimum return rate $r^0 = 0.33$.

Figure 4.4 shows the game tree for the case when the producer is sensitive to an equal-sharing social norm, but the investor is not. The producer chooses either $r = 0$ or $r = 0.40$. As we've seen, the producer's payoff for $r^* = 0.40$ is 1.65 (rectangle D). In contrast, full deviation from equal sharing ($r = 0$) generates a negative payoff (-0.75 in rectangle B) because the cost of violating the norm overwhelms the material benefit:

$$producer\ utility = 3 - 3 \cdot 5 \cdot (0.50)^2 = -0.75$$

For the investor, choosing $i = 1$ generates a payoff of 1.20:

$$investor\ utility = \theta \cdot r = 3 \cdot 0.40 = 1.20$$

The utility from investment (shown in rectangle D) exceeds the utility of not investing (rectangle A), so the rational choice is to invest. The lesson is that the introduction of a sharing norm for the producer can cause the investor to invest.

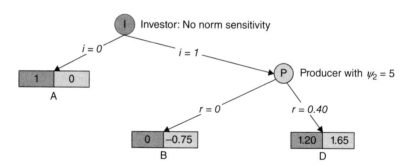

FIGURE 4.4: Investment Happens with a Norm-Sensitive Producer

Review the Concepts 4.2

1. In Figure 4.2, the slope of the material-benefit curve = [____]. (0.50, 1, 1.50, 3)

2. Start from the equal-sharing outcome shown in Figure 4.2. For a marginal increase in the hold fraction, the increase in [____] is greater than the increase in [____]. (norm-violation cost, material benefit; utility, material benefit; material benefit, norm-violation cost)

3. Suppose $\psi_2 = 4$. The utility-maximizing hold fraction is $h^* = $ [____]. (1/4, 3/8, 1/2, 5/8)

4. In Figure 4.3, the marginal-cost curve represents the change in [____] from an increase in the hold fraction. (material benefit, norm-violation cost)

5. In Figure 4.3, the marginal-benefit curve represent the change in [____] from an increase in the hold fraction. (material benefit, norm-violation cost)

6. *Comparative statics.* The relationship between the norm-violation parameter ψ_2 and the utility-maximizing hold fraction h^* is [____]. (positive, negative, zero)

7. *Comparative statics.* The relationship between the norm-violation parameter ψ_2 and the utility-maximizing return fraction r^* is [____]. (positive, negative, zero)

8. Consider Figure 4.4. The producer chooses a positive return fraction because [____]. The investor invests because [____]. (1.65 > –0.75, 1.20 > 0; 1.65 –0.75, 1.20 > 1; 1.65 > 0, 1.20 > 1)

4.3 A Sharing Norm for the Investor

So far we have assumed that the investor is insensitive to social norms of sharing. We turn next to a case where both producer and investor are sensitive to an equal-sharing norm. The investor anticipates that the producer will return less than half of the output, so the investor expects to experience a norm-violation cost. Will the investor still invest, despite the norm violation? In the framework of Adam Smith, will an investor go along when a producer chooses r* = 0.40? In this case, the producer has humbled the arrogance of his or her self-love by moving from $r = 0$ to $r = 0.40$. Is that enough humbling to get the investor to collaborate?

The Investor's Trade-Off: Material Benefit versus Norm-Violation Cost

We can use a utility function to incorporate the cost of norm violations into the investor's decision. The investor's material benefit from investment is $r \cdot \theta$. For the investor, the norm-violation cost is

$$norm-violation\ cost\ for\ investor = \theta \cdot \psi_1 \cdot \left(h - \frac{1}{2}\right)^2$$

where ψ_1 measures the investor's sensitivity to the equal-sharing norm. The norm-violation cost is positive if the producer holds on to more than half (returns less than half). The investor's utility function is

$$investor\ utility = \theta \cdot r - \theta \cdot \psi_1 \cdot \left(h - \frac{1}{2}\right)^2$$

For $h = 0.60$, $r = 0.40$, and $\theta = 3$, the investor's utility is the material benefit $(1.20 = 0.40 \cdot 3)$ minus the norm-violation cost:

$$investor\ utility = 1.20 - 3 \cdot \psi_1 \cdot \left(0.60 - 0.50\right)^2 = 1.20 - \psi_1 \cdot 0.03$$

The investor will invest if the utility from investment exceeds the utility level of one util from not investing. In our example, investment is sensible if

$$1.20 - \psi_1 \cdot 0.03 > 1$$

This happens if the investor's sensitivity to the equal-sharing norm is relatively weak (small value for ψ_1):

$$\psi_1 < \frac{20}{3}$$

In this numerical example, the investor will collaborate (invest) if ψ_1 is less than 20/3, roughly 6.67.

Relative Norm Sensitivity and Equilibrium

Suppose the investor and producer are equally sensitive to a social norm of equal sharing. Figure 4.5 shows the game tree associated with a common sensitivity to a equal-sharing norm, with $\psi_1 = \psi_2 = 5$. As we saw earlier, the utility-maximizing return fraction is $r^* = 0.40$ and the producer's utility after accounting for the cost of violating the norm is 1.65 (shown in the right-side part of rectangle D):

$$producer\ utility = 3 \cdot 0.60 - 3 \cdot 5 \cdot (0.60 - 0.50)^2 = 1.65$$

For the investor with $\psi_1 = 5$, utility after accounting for the cost of the norm violation is 1.05 (shown in the left-side part of rectangle D):

$$investor\ utility = 1.20 - 3 \cdot 5 \cdot (0.60 - 0.50)^2 = 1.05$$

In other words, each player experiences a norm-violation cost of 0.15: the producer incurs a cost from taking more than half, and the investor incurs a cost from getting less than half. The investor's payoff from investing exceeds the payoff from not investing (1.05 > 1.00), so investment happens.

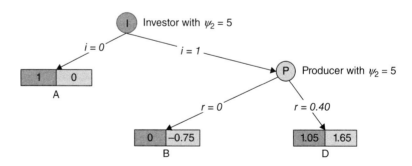

FIGURE 4.5: Investment Happens with Common Norm Sensitivity

What happens when the investor has relatively strong norm sensitivity? Such an investor will have a relatively low tolerance for inequality, and will require a relatively high return rate. To illustrate, suppose the investor's norm-sensitivity is measured as $\psi_1 = 7$. Given the strong norm sensitivity, the utility generated by a return rate of $r = 0.40$ is less than the utility of not investing (1):

$$investor\ utility = 1.20 - 3 \cdot 7 \cdot (0.60 - 0.50)^2 = 0.99$$

This is shown in payoff rectangle D in Figure 4.6: a return rate of 0.40 generates a payoff less than the no-investment payoff of 1 (rectangle A). In this case, the equilibrium investment fraction is zero, just as in the case of a perfectly selfish producer. Investment doesn't happen when the investor's norm sensitivity is strong relative to the producer's norm sensitivity.

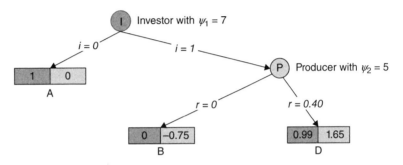

FIGURE 4.6: Investment Doesn't Happen with a Highly Sensitive Investor

The general lesson is that what matters for investment is the norm sensitivity of the producer relative to the norm sensitivity of the investor. For investment to happen, the producer sensitivity must be strong enough to offset any norm sensitivity of the investor. When the investor is insensitive, it doesn't take much producer sensitivity to generate a high enough return fraction to make investment worthwhile. But when the investor is strongly sensitive and has a relatively low tolerance for inequality, the producer must be strongly sensitive too, resulting in a return return fraction that is high enough to make investment worthwhile for a sensitive investor.

Social Norms, Efficiency, and Social Capital

We can measure the efficiency gain from the social norm of sharing. The introduction of the common social norm and a common sensitivity to violating the norm moves the economy from the no-investment outcome in rectangle A to the investment outcome in rectangle D. The total utility in the economy increases from 1 = 1 + 0 to 2.70 = 1.05 + 1.65. As another measure of the effect of the social norm, the total output of the economy increases from 1 (no investment) to 3 (investment and productivity measured by $\theta = 3$).

This scenario illustrates the role of social norms in promoting social capital. Social capital is defined as features of social organization that promote cooperation and efficiency. In the trust game, the feature of social organization is a norm of sharing, which promotes cooperation (the investor and producer collaborate to increase the value of the economy) and efficiency (each individual gets a higher payoff). The general lesson is that pro-social behavior triggered by social norms can improve the efficiency of an economy.

It is important to note that cooperation happens even though the producer does not strictly adhere to the social norm of equal sharing. The producer falls short of equal sharing: $r = 0.40$ rather than $r = 0.50$. But the return fraction is positive and is high enough to induce investment by the norm-sensitive investor. Adam Smith's impartial spectator may gaze disapprovingly at a producer who doesn't share equally, but the spectator's reaction is mild relative to the freak-out that would be triggered by greater selfishness (for example, $r = 0.10$). For the producer, the disapproving gaze may be bothersome, but the norm-violation cost is less than the additional material benefit.

Review the Concepts 4.3

1. In Figure 4.5, the norm-violation cost for the producer is [___] and the norm-violation cost for the investor is [___] (0.10, 0.10; 0.15, 0.15; 0.01, 0.01; 0.15, 0.10)

2. Consider the move from Figure 4.4 to Figure 4.5. When we add norm-violation cost for [___], his or her utility [___]. (producer, decreases; investor, increases; producer, increases; investor, decreases)

3. As shown by Figure 4.5, a common social norm of equal sharing increases total output by [___] and increases total utility by [___]. (1, 0.70; 2, 1.70; 3, 1.70)

4. Using Figure 4.6 as a starting point, suppose the value of the investor's norm-violation parameter increases from $\psi_1 = 7$ to $\psi_1 = 10$. The investor's norm-violation cost changes to [___] and the investor's utility changes to [___]. (0.30, 0.90; 0.30, 0.70; 0.20, 1.0)

5. *True or false.* For a social norm to promote efficiency, strict adherence to the social norm is required. [___] (true, false)

4.4 Experiments and Implications

We turn next to the results of economic experiments of the trust game. As we'll see, the results are inconsistent with a model of perfectly selfish behavior. Although some producers are selfish, many producers return a positive faction of output to investors. In other words, some producers are trustworthy. And although some investors fail to entrust their resources to producers, many investors trust producers to provide positive returns on their investments. In other words, the results are consistent with pro-social behavior and a social norm of sharing the rewards of collaboration.

Experimental Results

Figure 4.7 shows the mechanics of the full trust game. In contrast with the simplified version we've discussed, so far, the players are flexible: the investor chooses an investment fraction i, and producers choose a return fraction r. The investment $i \cdot X$ grows to $i \cdot X \cdot \theta$, and the producer returns a fraction r of the output to the investor while keeping a fraction $(1 - r)$. For the investor, the final wealth equals the endowment, minus the amount invested, plus the the amount returned:

$$investor\ wealth = X - i \cdot X + i \cdot X \cdot \theta \cdot r$$

The final wealth of the producer equals the quantity of output kept:

$$producer\ wealth = i \cdot X \cdot \theta \cdot (1 - r)$$

The lower panel of Figure 4.7 provides a numerical example of the trust game based on the results of experiments. The endowment is $X = 200$, and the investment fraction is $i = 1/2$, and the producer triples the 100 investment to 300 ($\theta = 3$). The producer returns 37 percent of the output, generating final wealth of 211 for the investor and 189 for the producer.

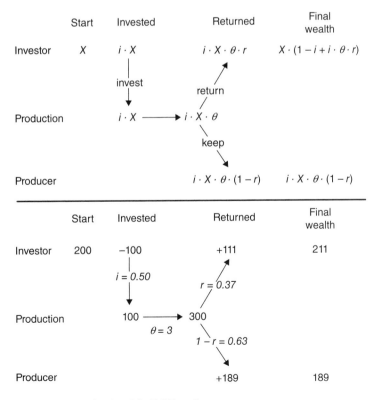

FIGURE 4.7: Mechanics of the Full Trust Game

Economists and anthropologists have run many experiments with the trust game. Johnson and Mislin (2011) performed meta-analysis on dozens of replications of the original trust experiment. The average investment fraction was $i = 0.502$, and roughly 68 percent of investors transferred between 38 percent and 62 percent of the endowment. The average return fraction was $r = 0.372$, and roughly 68 percent of producers returned between 26 percent and 48 percent of the investment. This average outcome is shown in Figure 4.7.

Johnson and Mislin (2011) explored the influence of various factors on trustworthiness, as measured by the return fraction. Several patterns emerge from the studies.

1. College students have lower return fractions, with an average return fraction of roughly 28 percent.
2. A decrease in the productivity of investment (θ) decreases the return fraction.
3. Participants in Sub-Saharan Africa than have lower return fractions than participants in North America.

Participants in Sub-Saharan Africa also have lower investment fractions, consistent with the lower return fractions.

Figure 4.8 shows the results from the original study of the trust game (Berg, Dickhaut, and McCabe 1995). There were 32 pairs of participants (investor and producer), and each investor received an endowment of $10. The value of the productivity parameter is $\theta = 3$, so each dollar invested grew to $3 in the hands of a producer. For each pair, the first bar shows the amount invested by the investor, and the second bar shows the amount returned by the producer. The pairs are arranged in declining order of the amount invested. For example, the first four investors fully invested ($10). Moving from left to right, investment decreases, and reaches zero for investors 31 and 32. The average investment fraction is 0.52.

Consider the investor perspective. The payoff from investing is positive if the amount returned exceeds the amount invested. In Figure 4.8, the investor's payoff is positive when the investment bar is shorter than the return bar. The payoff was positive for roughly one-third of investors (11/32), negative for roughly half the investors (16/32), and zero for the remaining 5 investors. On average, the investor payoff is negative, at –$0.50 per investor. On average, producers returned 28 percent of the output to investors, a fraction that is not high enough to generate a positive payoff from investment. Given the productivity of investment in the experiment ($\theta =3$), a positive payoff from investment requires that the return fraction exceeds 1/3.

Figure 4.8 reveals substantial variation in trustworthiness across participants in the original trust experiment. One explanation for the differences is that participants vary in their sensitivity to social norms of sharing the rewards of collaboration. The return fraction will be relatively high for producers who have internalized a social norm of equal sharing, and are sensitive to violations of the norm. In contrast, the return fraction will be relatively low for producers who

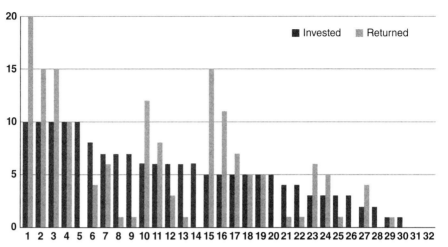

FIGURE 4.8: Results of the Original Trust Experiment

are relatively insensitive to a sharing norm or have internalized a norm of low sharing.

A recent study explores the role of reputation in promoting trust (Charness, Du, and Yang 2011). An investor had the opportunity to get information about the past behavior of his or her partner producer. If the producer had a history of being trustworthy (relatively high return fractions), the investor acted with more trust (relatively high investment fraction). For a partner producer who had a history as an investor, the current investor could get that history too. If the partner producer had a history of relatively high trust, the current investor acted with more trust. In other words, when an investor is partnered with a producer with a past history of either high trustworthiness or high trust, the response is to invest more.

The Trust Game and Social Capital

Why study the trust game? People regularly play trust games when they engage in transactions that are not covered by contracts or other legal obligations. In the consumer world, a restaurant provides a meal in anticipation of being paid a specified price, plus a tip chosen by the consumer. In a conventional model of economics, everyone has self-regarding preferences, and the utility-maximizing tip for a restaurant a person will never patronize again is zero. The fact that people regularly leave tips at restaurants they patronize once suggests that the assumption of self-regarding preferences is problematic.

We also play trust games at work. An employer pays a worker in anticipation of work effort that generates revenue for the employer. Suppose an employer cannot detect a low work effort (shirking) by a worker. In this work environment, a perfectly selfish worker would shirk rather than work. The fact that some workers work when they could shirk questions the validity of the assumption of perfectly selfish behavior. In a later chapter, we will explore pro-social behavior in the workplace. As we'll see, some workers respond to an increase in the wage by working harder, even if the employer cannot detect their additional effort.

As noted earlier in the chapter, a system of trust is a key component of social capital. The two features of a trust system—trust and trustworthiness— promote efficiency because in an economy where investors trust and producers are trustworthy, fewer resources are used on contracts, lawsuits, monitoring, and other costly actions to ensure that the terms of exchange are met. In a trusting economy, lower transaction costs facilitate exchange and increase the gains from trade.

The Trust Game and Oxytocin

You may have heard about oxytocin, a molecule produced in mammal brains that acts as both a neurotransmitter in the brain and a hormone in other parts of the body. Over the last few decades, scientists have discovered that oxytocin plays several roles in the physiology and social behavior of mammals. In reproduction, oxytocin promotes partuition (giving birth) and lactation. In the realm of mammal social behavior, animal studies have shown that oxytocin promotes maternal behavior in rats and pair bonding in voles; it also promotes social recognition. In other words, oxytocin promotes pro-social behavior—trust and cooperation—in non-human mammals.

What about humans? In response to the results from numerous animal studies, scientists decided to look for a connection between oxytocin and human social behavior. Many of the human projects focused on trust and used the familiar trust game to explore the effects of oxytocin on trust and trustworthiness. For example, consider a subject who receives a dose of oxytocin in a nasal spray before playing the trust game. Some studies suggested that the spritzed subject will be more trusting as an investor (making a relatively large investment) or more trustworthy as a producer (returning a relatively large share to the investor). The results of these studies have been widely cited as providing evidence that oxytocin promotes pro-social behavior in humans, including trust and cooperation.

Not so fast! In a review of the oxytocin-trust literature, Nave, Camerer, and McCullough (2015) explain that matters are more complex. The human studies have generated conflicting evidence about the connection between oxytocin and trust. Many of the studies deploy unreliable research methods, and few of the results have been replicated. Conlisk (2011) identifies some methodological issues with the most prominent work on oxytocin and human trust. Nave, Camerer, and McCullough (2015) conclude that ". . . the cumulative evidence does not provide robust convergent evidence that human trust is reliably associated with oxytocin (or caused by it)." Nonetheless, the reviewers note that given the results from the animal studies, it seems likely that oxytocin plays a role in some human social behaviors. The reviewers provide several recommendations on how to develop rigorous studies of the role of oxytocin in regulating human behavior.

Review the Concepts 4.4

1. In trust-game experiments, a plausible number for the investment fraction is i = [____]. (0, 0.20, 0.50, 0.70)

2. In trust-game experiments, a plausible number for the return fraction is r = [____]. (0, 0.17, 0.37, 0.73).

3. In the original study of the trust game, there was [____] variation across participants in trustworthiness. (zero, trivial, substantial)

4. *True or false*. There is compelling evidence that a nasal spray of oxytocin promotes trust and cooperation in humans [____]. (true, false)

Key Terms

social capital, p. 72   trust game, p. 73

Takeaways

1. An investor displays trust by investing resources without a guarantee of getting anything in return.

2. A producer displays trustworthiness by returning a fraction of the output produced by an investment.

3. When players in a trust game are perfectly selfish, the utility-maximizing return fraction is zero, and the equilibrium investment is zero.

4. When the producer in a trust game is sensitive to a norm of equal sharing of the rewards from collaboration, the utility-maximizing return fraction may be positive, and the equilibrium investment may be positive.

5. When both players in the trust game are sensitive to the social norm of sharing the rewards of collaboration, investment happens when the norm sensitivity of the producer is strong relative to the norm sensitivity of the investor.

6. In experiments of the trust game, the average investment fraction is i = 0.50 and the average return fraction is r = 0.37.

7. A key component of social capital is the combination of trust and trustworthiness.

Discuss the Concepts

1. *Credible Promise?* Use Figure 4.1. Suppose the producer promises $r = 0.25$ on any investment. As a result, the investor forms a belief (a conjecture) that the producer will return 25 percent: $r_? = 1/4$.

   a. If the investor acts on the conjecture, he or she will invest [____]. (0, 1)

   b. The promise is [____]. (credible, not credible)

2. *Norm Sensitivity and Return Fraction.* Suppose the range of values of the norm-sensitivity parameter is $1/20 \leq \psi_2 \leq 10$.

   a. Draw a curve showing the utility-maximizing hold fraction as a function of ψ_2. For $\psi_2 = 1$, $h^* = $ [____]; for $\psi_2 = 10$, $h^* = $ [____].

   b. Draw a curve showing the utility-maximizing return fraction as a function of ψ_2. For $\psi_2 = 1$, $r^* = $ [____]; for $\psi_2 = 10$, $r^* = $ [____].

3. *Matching Investors and Producers.* Consider a trust experiment with productivity measured as $\theta = 3$. Each of the participants has already participated in the crosswalk-waiting experiment discussed in an earlier chapter. Investor I25 waited the full 25 seconds, while investor I15 waited 15 seconds, and investor I0 didn't ever wait. Producer P25 waited the full 25 seconds, while producer P15 waited 15 seconds, and producer P0 didn't ever wait. These crosswalk performances are common knowledge to all participants in the trust game.

   a. When I0 is paired with P0, investment is [____] (likely, unlikely) because [____].

   b. When I15 is paired with P25, investment is [____] (likely, unlikely) because [____].

   c. When I25 is paired with P15, investment is [____] (likely, unlikely) because [____].

4. *Choose Your Producer.* Consider the chapter opener about the trust experiment. Suppose you have the opportunity to play the game with one of three producers: a 20-year old college student, a 40-year old college graduate, or a 40-year old college graduate whose work requires frequent exercises in mutual trust. The best choice is [____] because [____].

Apply the Concepts

1. *Marginal Principle.* In a trust experiment, an investor has an endowment $X = 1$ and $\theta = 3$. Consult Math 4.2 for expressions for the marginal benefit and the marginal cost of the hold fraction.

a. Suppose as in the text, the producer's $\psi_2 = 5$. Draw the marginal-benefit and marginal-cost curves for h from 1/2 to 1, and show the utility-maximizing hold fraction.

b. Suppose the producer's $\psi_2 = 1$. Draw the marginal-benefit and marginal-cost curves for h from 1/2 to 1, and show the utility-maximizing hold fraction.

c. Suppose the producer's $\psi_2 = 1/2$. Draw the marginal-benefit and marginal-cost curves for h from 1/2 to 1, and show the utility-maximizing hold fraction.

2. *Rank Producers and Investors.* Consider a trust experiment with productivity measured as $\theta = 3$. Each of the participants has already participated in the crosswalk-waiting experiment discussed in an earlier chapter. Investor I25 waited the full 25 seconds, while investor I15 waited 15 seconds, and investor I0 didn't ever wait. Producer P25 waited the full 25 seconds, while producer P15 waited 15 seconds, and producer P0 didn't ever wait.

a. Suppose the crosswalk performances of producers are common knowledge. For investors, the ranking of the producers, in declining order of attraction, is [____].

b. Suppose the crosswalk performances of investors are common knowledge. For producers, the ranking of the investors, in declining order of attraction, is [____].

3. *Mismatched Investor and Producer?* Suppose productivity in a trust game is measured as $\theta = 3$. The investor's endowment is 1. The investor is relatively sensitive to a sharing norm, with $\psi_1 = 6$. The producer is relatively insensitive to a sharing norm, with $\psi_2 = 4$.

a. For the producer, the utility-maximizing hold fraction is $h^* = $ [____] and the utility-maximizing return fraction is $r^* = $ [____].

b. The investor [____] (will, will not) invest because the payoff from investment is [____] = [____] material benefit − [____] norm-violation cost.

4. *Consensus Values.* An investor has up to $100 to invest in a start-up business with a productivity value $\theta = 3$. Suppose the values of choice variables in the trust game are $(i, r) = (0.50, 0.40)$. Illustrate with a graph like Figure 4.7

a. The investor's final wealth is $[____], compared to $[____] for the producer.

b. The rate of return on investment is [_____] percent.

5. *Start-up Business.* You have one unit of resources to invest in a startup business with a productivity value $\theta = 5/2$. The common value for norm sensitivity is $\psi_1 = \psi_2 = 8$. You either invest it all or not invest ($i = 1$ or $i = 0$).

a. The minimum return fraction is $r^0 = $ [____].

b. The producer's utility-maximizing hold fraction is $h^* = [\_\_]$ and the utility-maximizing return fraction is $r^* = [\_\_]$.

c. Investment $[\_\_]$ ($\uparrow$, $\downarrow$, does not change) your material benefit from 1 to $[\_\_]$.

d. Investment $[\_\_]$ (($\uparrow$, $\downarrow$, does not change) your utility from 1 to $[\_\_]$.

6. *Minimum Return Fraction for Investor.* Your task is derive an expression for an investor's minimum return fraction r_{MIN} as a function of the parameters θ and ψ_1. Note that r_{MIN} makes the investor indifferent between keeping the endowment (1 unit of resources) and investing.

a. The expression is $r_{MIN} = [\_\_]$

b. To illustrate, for $(\theta, \psi_1) = (3, 7)$, $r_{MIN} = [\_\_]$.

Math Solutions

Math 4.1: Utility-Maximizing Return Fraction for Norm-Sensitive Producer

The producer's utility function is

$$\text{producer utility} = \theta \cdot h - \theta \cdot \psi_2 \cdot \left(h - \frac{1}{2} \right)^2$$

Differentiate the utility function with respect to the choice variable h:

$$\frac{du}{dh} = \theta - 2 \cdot \theta \cdot \psi_2 \cdot \left(h - \frac{1}{2} \right)$$

Set the derivative equal to zero to solve for the utility-maximizing h:

$$h^* = \frac{\psi_2 + 1}{2 \cdot \psi_2}$$

Since the return fraction is $1 - h$, the utility-maximizing return fraction is

$$r^* = \frac{\psi_2 - 1}{2 \cdot \psi_2}$$

Math 4.2: Marginal Benefit and Marginal Cost for Norm-Sensitive Producer

The producer's utility function is

$$\text{producer utility} = \theta \cdot h - \theta \cdot \psi_2 \cdot \left(h - \frac{1}{2} \right)^2$$

Differentiate the utility function with respect to the choice variable h:

$$\frac{du}{dh} = \theta - 2 \cdot \theta \cdot \psi_2 \cdot \left(h - \frac{1}{2} \right)$$

The marginal benefit of h is the constant θ:

$$mb(h) = \theta$$

The marginal cost of h is the change in norm-violation cost per unit change in h:

$$mc(h) = 2 \cdot \theta \cdot \psi_2 \cdot \left(h - \frac{1}{2} \right)$$

Suppose $\theta = 3$. The expression for marginal cost simplifies to

$$mc(h) = 6 \cdot \psi_2 \cdot h - 3 \cdot \psi_2$$

5 Public Goods and Voluntary Contributions

A recent economic experiment in Ethiopia (Rustagi, Engel, and Kosfeld 2010) explored the motives for voluntary contributions to support public goods. The experimenters gave each participant 6 birr bills (the local currency), an amount equal to the local daily wage. Each participant was assigned an anonymous partner and given the opportunity to contribute between 0 and 6 birr to a public-good project with a benefit-cost ratio of 1.50. The efficient action is for each partner to fully contribute and get 9 birr back. The selfish action is to be a free rider—contribute nothing, hang on to your 6 birr, and hope the other individual contributes something. If both partners think this way, neither contributes anything, and they both miss an opportunity to get 9 birr instead of 6.

Each participant was given the opportunity to engage in **conditional cooperation** by linking his or her contribution to a partner's contribution. One possibility is to match the partner's contribution, birr for birr. In contrast, a free rider would contribute zero, regardless of the partner's contribution. At the other extreme, an altruist would contribute up to 6 birr, regardless of the partner's contribution. Across a population of 679 participants:

1. Roughly half engaged in conditional cooperation.

2. Only 2 percent acted altruistically.

3. Roughly 12 percent were free riders.

4. The remaining participants adopted other contribution strategies.

This chapter explores pro-social behavior in the form of voluntary contributions to support public goods. We define a **public good**, broadly, to include any good that is available for more than one person to consume, regardless of who pays and who doesn't. More precisely, a public good has two features.

1. *Non-rival.* One person's benefit from a public good does not reduce another person's benefit from the good. For example, your listening to a radio program doesn't reduce the listening benefits of other people. Similarly, if an environmental organization reduces air pollution, everyone benefits from cleaner air.

2. *Non-excludable.* It is impractical to exclude people who don't pay for the good. You can listen to public radio even if you don't join as a paying member. You benefit from clean air even if you don't contribute to the environmental organization responsible for reduced air pollution.

The analysis in this chapter is relevant to public goods supported by voluntary contributions rather than taxes or other payment systems. Many organizations that provide public goods solicit contributions from people who benefit from the public goods. The list of public goods supported by voluntary contributions includes public broadcasting, environmental protection, disaster relief, income support for the poor, and economic-development programs in less developed countries. In each case, one person's benefit from the public good doesn't reduce the benefit for another person (non-rivalry), and a person can benefit from the public good even if he or she does not provide financial support to the organization that provides the public good (non-excludability).

In conventional models of economic choice, we assume that decision-makers have self-regarding (selfish) preferences. In other words, each person's utility depends solely on his or her material payoff. One implication of self-regarding preferences is the free-rider problem. In a purely selfish world, everyone would exploit the non-excludable feature of a public good and try to get the benefit of a public good without paying. People would listen to public radio and use Wikipedia without becoming paying members. When a natural disaster strikes, people would ignore requests for donations of goods and money. Charitable organizations and environmental organizations would fail to raise money to support their missions. In general, the assumption of self-regarding preferences is at variance with the reality of billions of dollars contributed to support all sorts of public goods.

This chapter uses models of social norms to explain voluntary contributions to public goods. The norms include concerns for efficiency and fairness, and the punishment of norm violators plays a key role in solving the free-rider problem. As we've seen in earlier chapters, individuals vary in their adherence to social norms, which makes matters complex and interesting.

Learning Objectives: The Explainer

After mastering this chapter, you will be able to explain each of the following statements.

1. In a world of perfectly selfish citizens, the utility-maximizing contribution to a public good is zero.

2. A social norm of efficient contributions for a public good increases the utility-maximizing contribution.

3. A social norm of equality in contributions for a public good tends to decrease the utility-maximizing contribution.

4. Individuals vary in their utility-maximizing contributions to a public good.

5. Over the course of a public-good experiment, the average contribution typically decreases from one round to the next, and eventually approaches zero.

6. Conditional cooperation increases contributions in public-good experiments and promotes efficient management of forest resources in Ethiopia.

5.1   Free Riding and Economic Experiments

A **free rider** is a person who gets a benefit from a public good but does not pay for it. To illustrate, consider a two-citizen community with a public good that is supported by voluntary contributions. Each dollar contributed to the public good increases the per-capita benefit of the public good by g:

$$1/2 < g < 1$$

For example, if $g = 0.60$, an additional dollar increases the per-capita benefit by $0.60. The marginal private benefit of a dollar contributed ($g = 0.60$) is less than the $1 marginal cost, so a selfish citizen will not provide the public good. The marginal social benefit of a dollar contributed ($2 \cdot g = 1.20$) exceeds the $1 marginal cost, so the provision of the public good is efficient.

The Free-Rider Problem

Figure 5.1 uses a game tree to illustrate a two-person contribution game. The productivity of the public good is represented by $g = 0.60$, and each citizen contributes either $1 or zero. Citizen 1 chooses first, followed by citizen 2.

- *Payoff rectangle A*. Citizen 1 contributes ($c_1 = 1$), and so does citizen 2. Each citizen has a payoff of $0.20 = 1.20 - 1.00$, computed as the 1.20 per-capita benefit of the public good ($2 \cdot g$) minus the $1 contribution.
- *Payoff rectangle B*. Citizen 1 contributes, but citizen 2 does not. The payoff for the contributor (citizen 1) is -0.40, computed as the 0.60 benefit g minus the $1 contribution. The payoff for the free rider (citizen 2) is 0.60: the free rider gets the benefit of citizen 1's contribution ($g = 0.60$) without paying.
- *Payoff rectangle C*. Citizen 1 does not contribute, but citizen 2 does. Roles are reversed relative to rectangle B: citizen 1 gets a free ride on citizen 2's contribution.
- *Payoff rectangle D*. Neither citizen contributes, so the payoff for each citizen is zero.

To find the Nash equilibrium in the contribution game, we check each payoff rectangle to see if either citizen has an incentive for unilateral deviation. For payoff rectangles A, B, and C, at least one citizen has an incentive to change.

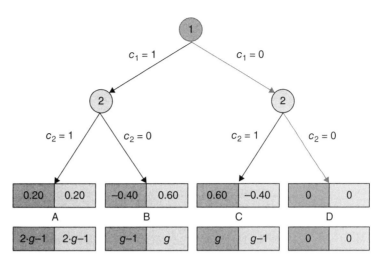

FIGURE 5.1: The Free-Rider Problem

- *Payoff rectangle A.* A unilateral deviation by citizen 2 (switch to not contributing) increases the payoff from 0.20 in rectangle A to 0.60 in rectangle B. In other words, citizen 2 has an incentive to get a free ride on citizen 1's contribution.
- *Payoff rectangle B.* A unilateral deviation by citizen 1 (switch to not contributing) replaces a negative payoff (−0.40) in rectangle B with a zero payoff in rectangle D. In other words, citizen 1 has an incentive to switch to avoid giving a free ride to citizen 2.
- *Payoff rectangle C.* A unilateral deviation by citizen 2 (switch to not contributing) replaces a negative payoff in rectangle C (−0.40) with a zero payoff in rectangle D. In other words, citizen 2 has an incentive to switch to avoid giving a free ride to citizen 1.

The Nash equilibrium in the contribution game is shown by payoff rectangle D, with neither citizen contributing. Starting from rectangle D, a unilateral deviation would decrease the deviator's payoff by replacing a zero payoff in rectangle D with a negative payoff. For example, citizen 1 would switch to rectangle B, and get a payoff = −0.40. Similarly, citizen 2 would switch to rectangle C, and get a payoff = −0.40. In the Nash equilibrium, each citizen tries to get a free ride on the other citizen's contribution. Of course, neither citizen actually gets a free ride because the other citizen has a similar incentive to seek a free ride.

The Nash equilibrium is inefficient because both citizens would be better off if each citizen contributed to the public good. If each citizen contributed $1 and they reached rectangle A, each citizen would be better off by 0.20. The contributors' dilemma (the analog of the prisoners' dilemma) is that both citizens would be better off if each contributed, but neither citizen has an incentive to contribute. The contributors' dilemma is a consequence of self-regarding preferences.

Results from Voluntary-Contribution Experiments

Behavioral economists use lab experiments to explore the free-rider problem and how it can be overcome. Here is an example of a simple classroom experiment.

1. The instructor selects 10 students and gives each student 10 dimes.
2. Each student can contribute money to support a public good by dropping up to three dimes into a public-good pot. The contributions are anonymous and strictly voluntary.
3. For each dime in the public-good pot, the instructor adds two dimes. For example, if the students contribute a total of 20 dimes, the instructor adds 40 dimes, for a total of 60 dimes in the pot. The two-for-one match represents the idea that the benefit of a public good exceed its cost. In this case, the benefit/cost ratio is three to one.
4. The instructor divides the money in the public-good pot equally among the 10 students. For example, if there are 60 dimes in the pot, each student receives 6 dimes.

Steps 2 through 4 can be repeated several times.

Consider the contribution strategy for a person with self-regarding preferences. For each dime contributed, the public-good pot grows by $0.30, so the payout to each of the 10 students increases by $0.03. The $0.03 benefit is less than the $0.10 cost, so a selfish person will not contribute. If other students contribute, a free rider would benefit from the other contributions. For example, suppose that 2 of 10 students each contributes $0.30. The total contribution is $0.60 and after the instructor adds $1.20, there is $1.80 in the pot. A free rider will gain $0.18 (one tenth of $1.80), while a contributor will lose $0.12 = $0.30 − $0.18. For a purely selfish person, the best strategy is not to contribute anything.

Economists have done variations on this experiment in a wide variety of settings. The general conclusion is that some participants contribute money to the public good, contrary to the prediction of free riding from purely selfish individuals. In the first round of the typical experiment, the contribution level is roughly half the efficient level: on average, participants contribute half the maximum. Naturally, some participants contribute more than half, while others contribute less, and some participants contribute nothing. In the second round, the average contribution decreases, and so does the number of contributors. As the game proceeds from one round to the next, the decreases in contributions continue in a downward spiral of free riding. After roughly 10 rounds, the average contribution is close to zero, the purely selfish outcome.

The conclusion from the contribution experiment is that many people are willing to contribute to promote the social interest, but no one wants to be exploited. Here is a plausible interpretation of the pattern of decreasing contributions. Many participants in public-good experiments start under the assumption that most other people will contribute, and many but not all participants actually contribute. But once a contributor realizes that he or she is being exploited by free riders, the response is to contribute less. Over the course of the game, the recognition of exploitation spreads to more and more contributors, and the average contribution decreases to an amount close to zero.

Review the Concepts 5.1

1. In the public-good experiment involving birr, the most frequent action was [___]. (altruism, conditional cooperation, free riding)

2. A public good is [___]. (non-rival, rival, non-excludable, excludable)

3. In a two-person community, the productivity of a public good is $g = 0.70$. The marginal social benefit of a dollar contributed is [___]. (0, 0.70, 1.35, 1.40, 1.70)

4. In a two-person community, the productivity of a public good is $g = 0.70$. If citizen 1 contributes \$1 and citizen 2 does not contribute, the payoff for citizen 1 is [___] and the payoff for citizen 2 is [___]. (−0.30, 0.70; 0.70, −0.30; 0.30, 1.40; 0.30, 0.70)

5. In a two-citizen environment, the contributor dilemma is that [___] would be better off if [___] contributed, but [___] has an incentive to contribute. (neither, both, each; both, each, neither; both, neither, each)

6. In a classroom contribution public-good experiment, the average contribution typically [___] from one round to the next, and eventually gets close to [___]. (increases, the maximum; decreases, zero; doesn't change, half the maximum; decreases, one-fourth the maximum)

5.2   Social Norms and Voluntary Contributions

In this part of the chapter we develop a model of contributions to public good that is consistent with the stylized facts of public-good experiments. We represent conditional cooperation with two social norms.

1. *Efficient contribution.* Suppose that for the efficient level of a public good, there is some per-citizen contribution required to support the efficient level. A citizen who strictly adheres to the efficiency norm simply contributes the efficient amount.
2. *Equal contributions.* A citizen who strictly adheres to the equal-contribution norm matches the average contribution of other citizens.

As in our earlier discussions of social norms, an individual faces a trade-off between material benefits and observing a norm, and uses the marginal principle to choose the utility-maximizing deviation from the norm. People vary in their sensitivity to violating social norms, so they vary in their contributions to support public goods.

Norm: Efficient Contribution

Consider an economy with many citizens and a public good. To simplify matters, we assume that the number of citizens is large enough that an individual citizen ignores the effect of his or her contribution on the level of the public good. For example, in an economy with 10,000 citizens, suppose the per-capita benefit of a $1 contribution is $0.0002. The marginal social benefit of a $1 contribution is $2, but the benefit for the individual contributor is tiny—small enough to be ignored in our discussion. We assume that the maximum contribution to support the public good is one unit of resources (money, time, other resources). We start our discussion with a model that incorporates the first norm (efficient contribution) and incorporate the second norm (equal contributions) later in the chapter. In other words, we assume for now that a citizen is not concerned about the contributions of other citizens.

Suppose that the efficient contribution is $1. A citizen must decide whether to strictly adhere to the social norm or to keep part of the potential public-good dollar to purchase private goods. In other words, the citizen divides one dollar between private consumption (h) and a contribution to the public good (c):

$$h + c = 1$$

When a citizen chooses the utility-maximizing private consumption h^*, he or she simultaneously chooses the utility-maximizing contribution c^*:

$$c^* = 1 - h^*$$

As we've seen in earlier chapters, we can use a utility function to incorporate social norms into a decision-making process. The utility function captures the trade-off between material benefits and the cost of violating a social norm. In the public-good game, strict adherence to the efficiency norm generates a contribution $c = 1$ and $h = 0$: the entire dollar is spent on the public good. We can represent the cost of violating the efficiency norm as

$$norm - violation\ cost = \psi \cdot (1 - c)^2$$

In our simple framework, $h = 1 - c$, so we can state this as

$$norm - violation\ cost = \psi \cdot h^2$$

where as usual ψ measures the sensitivity to the efficiency norm. The norm-violation cost is zero for $c = 1$ and $h = 0$. As private consumption increases and the contribution to the public good decreases, the norm-violation cost increases at an increasing rate. The citizen's material benefit equals the amount spent on the private good, and utility equals the material benefit minus the norm-violation cost:

$$\text{utility} = h - \psi \cdot h^2$$

Figure 5.2 illustrates a citizen's choice of the utility-maximizing private consumption. The horizontal axis measures private consumption (increasing from left to right) and the contribution (decreasing from left to right). The numbers in the figure are based on norm sensitivity measured by $\psi = 5/8$. The upper panel shows the trade-off between material benefits and norm-violation cost.

- *Material benefit.* As private consumption increases, the material benefit increases, as shown by the linear material-benefit curve.
- *Norm-violation cost.* The norm-violation cost is zero when the citizen strictly adheres to the social norm of $h = 0$ and $c = 1$, and increases at an increasing rate as private consumption increases at the expense of the contribution to the public good.

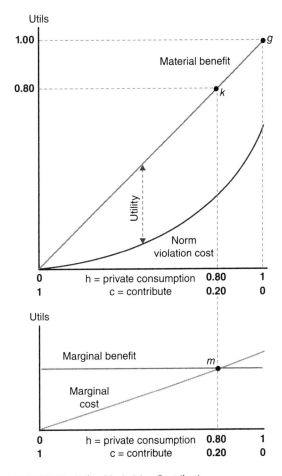

FIGURE 5.2: Utility-Maximizing Contribution

The citizen's utility is shown by the gap between the material-benefit curve and the norm-violation cost.

The lower panel of Figure 5.2 applies the marginal principle to the citizen's choice. Suppose we start at $h = 0$ and $c = 1$, and consider the effects of increasing private consumption at the expense of the contribution. The marginal-benefit curve incorporates the citizen's gain of material benefits: an increase in h increases the material benefit at a constant rate, so the marginal-benefit curve is horizontal. The marginal-cost curve incorporates the cost of violating the social norm, and is positively sloped because the norm-violation cost increases at an increasing rate. The marginal principle is satisfied at point m, with private consumption $h^* = 0.80$ and contribution $c^* = 0.20$. In this case of relatively weak sensitivity to the efficiency norm, the citizen maximizes utility with a relatively small contribution.

If citizens vary in their norm sensitivity, they will maximize utility with different contributions to the public good. Figure 5.3 shows the utility-maximizing contributions for three citizens with varying norm sensitivities. As shown by point s, a citizen with strong norm sensitivity chooses a large contribution c_S. For a citizen with weak sensitivity to the norm, the marginal-cost curve is everywhere below the marginal-benefit curve, so the utility-maximizing contribution is zero. A citizen with middling sensitivity chooses a medium contribution c_M.

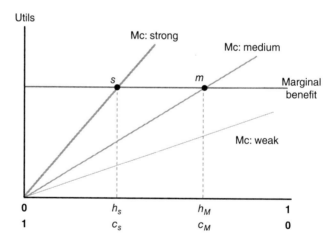

FIGURE 5.3: Varying Norm Sensitivity and Contributions

We can use a bit of calculus to derive an expression for the utility-maximizing contribution. Math 5.1 shows how to derive expressions for the utility-maximizing private consumption and the utility-maximizing contribution. The expressions show the connection between norm sensitivity and contribution choices.

$$h^* = \frac{1}{2 \cdot \psi}$$

$$c^* = 1 - \frac{1}{2 \cdot \psi}$$

A citizen with sufficiently weak norm sensitivity contributes nothing to the public good. For $\psi \leq 1/2$, the utility-maximizing contribution is zero.

Norm: Equal Contribution

We turn next to the second social norm--equal contributions across citizens. To incorporate the equal-contribution norm into the individual's utility function, we add a cost associated with contributing more or less than the average:

$$utility = h - \psi \cdot h^2 - \phi \cdot \left(c - \bar{c}\right)^2$$

where $\bar{c}$ is the average contribution, and the parameter ϕ represents a citizen's sensitivity to the equal-contribution norm. The cost of violating the equal-contribution norm is positive for anyone who doesn't contribute the average.

1. *More than average.* A citizen who contributes more than $\bar{c}$ feels exploited by citizens who contribute less.
2. *Less than average.* A citizen who contributes less than $\bar{c}$ feels guilty about exploiting citizens who contribute more.

Naturally, citizens vary in their sensitivity to the equal-contribution norm, with a higher value of ϕ indicating greater sensitivity and a higher norm-violation cost.

The equal-contribution norm makes the calculation of a citizen's utility-maximizing contribution a bit tricky. Before choosing a contribution, a citizen must form a belief—a conjecture—about the average contribution $c_?$, where the question mark reminds us that the conjecture may turn out to be correct or incorrect. The utility-maximizing contribution reflects the trade-offs between (i) the material benefits of private consumption, (ii) the cost of violating the efficiency norm, and (iii) the cost of violating the equal-contribution norm. As shown in Math 5.2, the utility-maximizing is determined by the two parameters representing norm sensitivity (ψ and ϕ) and the conjectured average contribution $c_?$.

$$c^{**} = \frac{c_? \cdot \phi + \psi - 1/2}{\phi + \psi}$$

The key insight is that there is a positive relationship between the conjectured average contribution and a citizen's utility-maximizing contribution.

- An increase in the average contribution increases an individual's contribution as (i) below-average contributors contribute more to reduce their guilt and (ii) above-average contributors contribute more because they feel less exploited.

- A decrease in the average contribution decreases an individual's contribution as (i) below-average contributors contribute less because they feel less guilty and (ii) above-average contributors contribute less because they feel more exploited.

The strength of the relationship between the average contribution and the individual contribution increases with the sensitivity to the equal-contribution norm, as reflected in the parameter ϕ.

Explaining a Path of Decreasing Contributions

Recall the path of decreasing contributions over the course of public-goods experiments. We can use our model of dual social norms to explain why contributions decrease from one round to the next. To illustrate, we develop a numerical example with three assumptions.

1. Half the participants are relatively insensitive to social norms, so they contribute zero. For these habitual free riders, $\psi \leq 1/2$ (low sensitivity to the efficiency norm) and $\phi = 0$ (insensitivity to the equal-contribution norm).
2. Half the participants have intermediate values for the norm parameters, with $\psi = 0.60$ and $\phi = 0.80$.
3. In the first round, the common conjecture is that the average contribution is $c_? = 0.75$ (three-fourths of the efficient contribution).

Consider the actual contributions in round 1 and round 2. Using the equation for c^{**}, the typical contributing citizen (with intermediate values of the norm parameters) contributes 0.50:

$$c^{**} = \frac{c_? \cdot \phi + \psi - 1/2}{\phi + \psi} = \frac{0.75 \cdot 0.80 + 0.60 - 0.50}{0.80 + 0.60} = 0.50$$

The relatively insensitive citizens contribute zero, so the actual contribution is 0.25, or only one-third the conjectured contribution (0.75). Citizens were overly optimistic about contributions, and they revise their conjectures for round 2. Suppose that for round 2, the conjectured average contribution equals the actual contribution in round 1: in round 2, $c_? = 0.25$. The decrease in the conjectured contribution decreases the utility-maximizing contribution to 0.214:

$$c^{**} = \frac{0.25 \cdot 0.80 + 0.60 - 0.50}{0.80 + 0.60} = 0.214$$

The relatively insensitive citizens continue to contribute zero, so the actual contribution in round 2 is 0.107, or less than half the conjectured contribution (0.25).

Figure 5.4 shows how this process plays out over ten periods. The calculations are based on the assumption that the conjectured quantity in each period equals the actual contribution from the previous period. By period 10, the contribution of a norm-sensitive citizen has dropped to 0.10 and the average contribution is only 0.05.

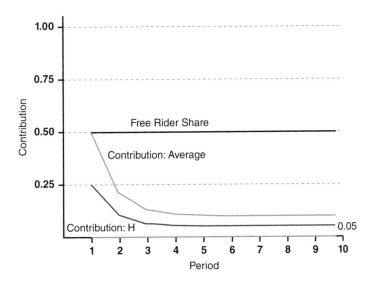

FIGURE 5.4: Decreasing Contributions

The decreases in the average contribution happens as contributors adjust their contributions downward to avoid contributing too much more than the average citizen. The contribution is positive rather than zero because (i) some citizens contribute in response to the efficiency norm and (ii) the difference between the typical contribution and the average contribution (half the typical contribution) is relatively small.

Review the Concepts 5.2

1. In Figure 5.2, starting from full contribution ($h = 0$; $c = 1$), a small increase in the private consumption [____] utility because the change in [____] exceeds the change in [____]. (increases, norm-violation cost, material benefit; increases, material benefit, norm-violation cost; increases, utility, material benefit; decreases, norm-violation cost, utility)

2. For a citizen with sensitivity to the efficiency norm measured as $\psi = 3$, the utility-maximizing contribution is $c^* = $ [____]. (0, 1/6, 1/2, 2/3, 5/6)

3. *Comparative statics.* The relationship between ψ (sensitivity to the efficiency norm) and c^* (the utility-maximizing contribution) is [____]. (positive, negative, zero, ambiguous)

4. The utility-maximizing contribution to a public good will be zero if the marginal [____] is always less than the marginal [____] (cost of norm violation, benefit of private consumption; benefit of private consumption, cost of norm violation, cost of private consumption, benefit of norm violation)

5. To act on a norm of equal contributions, a citizen must form conjectures or beliefs about [___]. (the number of free riders, the maximum contribution of other citizens, the average contribution of other citizens)

6. In Figure 5.4, the average contribution [___] from one period to the next because norm-sensitive citizens [___] the value of the conjectured average contribution. (decrease, increase; decrease, decrease; increase, decrease; increase, increase)

7. Use Widget 5.1 (available at www.oup.com/us/osullivan1e). An increase in the sensitivity of type H to the equality norm [___] the average contribution in period 10. (increases, decreases, does not change)

8. Use Widget 5.1 (available at www.oup.com/us/osullivan1e). An increase in the initial conjectured average contribution c_2 [___] the average contribution in period 1 and [___] the average contribution in period 10. (increases, increases; increases, decreases; does not change, increases; increases, does not change)

5.3 Punish Free Riders?

We've seen that over the course of a voluntary-contribution game, contributions decrease from one round to the next. In economic experiments, the average contribution approaches zero. In the model of dual social norms, utility-maximizing contributions decrease over time as contributors respond to free riding. So far, our citizens have been passive in acting on the second norm: they respond to free riding by reducing their own contributions. In this part of the chapter we explore a more activist approach: What happens if the victims of free riding punish free riders?

Punishing Norm Violators

As we saw in the chapter that introduced social norms, a key component of a system of social norms is a norm to punish norm violators. A violation of a social norm may trigger punishment by a victim of a norm violation, as well as punishment by third parties. Recall a quote from Adam Smith (1982):

> Every man … must … humble the arrogance of his self-love, and bring it
> down to something which other men can go along with.

Free riding is an example of unbridled self love. For a fellow citizen who is not willing to "go along with" unbridled self love, one possible response is to punish the norm violator. As we've seen in earlier chapters, economic experiments provide evidence that some individuals who are harmed by norm violations incur costs to punish norm violators, and so do third parties.

Recall the experiment described in the chapter opener (Rustagi, Engel, and Kosfeld 2010). Roughly half the participants in the public-good experiment engaged in conditional cooperation by linking their contributions to partners' contributions. The experiment was conducted in a forest area with 49 separate groups that tapped forest resources. There was substantial variation across user groups in the extent of conditional cooperation. For roughly one-fifth of the groups, at least 60 percent of participants were conditional cooperators. As we'd expect, user groups with relatively large shares of conditional cooperators manage the forest resources more efficiently: a one percent increase in the share of conditional cooperators increased the number of trees by 0.27 percent.

The forest experiment also shows the connection between cooperation and norm enforcement. Naturally, each user group has some free riders, and groups with relatively large shares of conditional cooperators invested more resources in forest patrols to monitor behavior and punish free riders. A one percent increase in the share of conditional cooperators increases the time spent monitoring by 0.28 percent. The authors note that

> In sum, better forest management outcomes are not only a result of conditional cooperators being more likely to abide by the local rules of the group but also being more willing to enforce these rules at a personal cost. (Rustagi, Engel, and Kosfeld 2010, 964)

This illustrates the notion that a member of a social group is expected to (i) conform to group norms and (ii) enforce conformity on other members of the group.

Summary of Experimental Results

Behavioral economists have run experiments to test the effects of punishing free riders. The punishment of a participant who contributes zero or a relatively small amount typically involves a monetary penalty. In the classic work on the subject, Fehr and Gatcher (2000) report the distribution of contributions in the final round of a voluntary-contribution experiment.

- When there is no punishment for free riding, 53 percent of participants contribute zero, and an additional 16 percent contribute no more than 15 percent of the efficient contribution.
- When there is punishment for free riding, 83 percent of participants contribute the maximum amount to support the public good.

The lesson from the experiments is that a punishment for free riders promotes efficiency by reducing the free-rider problem.

Review the Concepts 5.3

1. In the language of Adam Smith, free riding is an example of unbridled [___]. (generosity, cycling, horse racing, self-love)

2. The public-good experiment with forest groups in Ethiopia illustrates the role of [___] to solve the free-rider problem. (conditional cooperation, norm enforcement, public-service announcements, pledge drives)

3. Consider the experiments with monetary penalties for free riders. In the final round, roughly [____] percent of players contributed the maximum amount. (3, 23, 53, 83)

Key Terms

conditional cooperation, p. 94   free rider, p. 96   public good, p. 94

Takeaways

1. The free-rider problem is that although a contribution to a public good is efficient, the selfish response is not to contribute.

2. In experiments with the voluntary contribution game, the average contribution starts at roughly half the efficient level and then decreases in successive rounds, reaching close to zero after roughly 10 rounds.

3. Under an efficiency norm, an individual faces a trade-off between material benefits and the cost of violating the norm.

4. Under an equal-contribution norm, an individual incurs a norm-violation cost when (i) contributing more than the average (a sense of being exploited) or (ii) contributing less than the average (a sense of exploiting others).

5. Free riding happens when some citizens are relatively insensitive to a efficiency norm.

6. The insensitivity of some citizens to an efficiency norm decreases the average contribution and thus decreases the contributions of citizens sensitive to an equal-contribution norm.

7. In an experiment with forest users, conditional cooperation increased productivity, in part by increasing the enforcement of a social norm of cooperation.

8. In experiments with the voluntary contribution game, the punishment of free riding increases the average contribution by a relatively large amount.

Discuss the Concepts

1. *Payoffs with More Citizens.* In the example presented in Figure 5.1, suppose there are three citizens (A, B, C) rather than two. Consider the payoffs of citizen A.

   a. Suppose B and C contribute. A's payoff from contributing is [____], compared to [____] for not contributing.

    b. Suppose B contributes, but C does not contribute. A's payoff from contributing is [___], compared to [___] for not contributing.

    c. Suppose no one else contributes. A's payoff from contributing is [___], compared to [___] for not contributing.

2. *Floods versus Asteroids.* Suppose the marginal-cost curves in Figure 5.3 are for a single individual and three different public goods:

- F: Local flood protection (building levees to protect a neighborhood)

- D: System of national defense against foreign invaders

- A: System to divert asteroids from collisions with the earth

Match the curves and utility-matching contributions to the public goods.

3. *Compete to Cooperate?* Consider two low-elevation neighborhoods that stage campaigns for voluntary contributions to build flood-control levees. For every $1000 raised, the height of the levee increases by one centimeter. Each neighborhood covers 25 blocks and has 250 households.

- Neighborhood T has a traditional campaign, with weekly updates on total neighborhood contributions.

- In neighborhood B, the weekly updates on total contributions are disaggregated by individual block.

The levee is likely to be taller in neighborhood [___] because [___].

Apply the Concepts

1. *Free-Rider Problem.* Consider a two-citizen economy with contributions to support a public good. The productivity of the public good is measured by $g = 0.80$.

    a. Suppose both citizens are perfectly selfish. Draw a game tree like the one shown in Figure 5.1 and predict the outcome of the contribution game. The total payoff is [___].

    b. Starting from the Nash equilibrium in (a), a unilateral deviation by a citizen changes the citizen's payoff by [___].

2. *Marginal Principle.* Use the results from Math 5.1. Consider a trio of citizens that vary in their sensitivity to violating the efficiency norm (W for weak, M for medium, S for strong). The values of the norm-sensitivity parameter are $\psi_W = 1/3$ for W, $\psi_M = 5/8$ for M, and $\psi_S = 3$ for S. Consider the utility-maximizing private consumption and contribution to the public good.

    a. Draw the marginal-benefit curve and a trio of marginal-cost curves.

b. The utility-maximizing contributions are $c^*_W = [\_\_\_]$, $c^*_M = [\_\_\_]$, $c^*_S = [\_\_\_]$.

3. *Downward Spiral.* Consider the text example of the utility-maximizing contribution for an individual who is sensitive to both norms (efficiency and equal sharing). In round 1, a conjecture $c_? = 0.75$ generates $c^{**} = 0.50$. In round 2, a conjecture $c_? = 0.25$ generates $c^{**} = 0.214$. Using the same logic for round 3, the conjecture is $c_? = [\_\_\_]$ and the utility-maximizing contribution is $c^{**} = [\_\_\_]$.

4. *One Rotten Apple (or Free Rider).* Consider a 10-person community that each month collects voluntary contributions for a public good. For each citizen, the sensitivity to the efficiency norm is measured as $\psi = 2$, and the sensitivity to the equal-contribution norm is measured as $\phi = 3$. Suppose $c_? = 0.75$.

   a. Based on $c_?$, the utility-maximizing contribution for month 1 is $c^{**}_1 = [\_\_\_]$. Draw the time path of average contributions for 3 months.

   b. Suppose that just before the contributions are collected for month 4, a single citizen loses all sensitivity to social norms, so $\psi = \phi = 0$. The average contribution for month 4 is [___]. The average contribution in month 10 is [___].

   c. A single free rider (10 percent of the population) decreases the average contribution by [___] (more than, less than, exactly) ten percent because [___].

5. *Free-Rider Solution.* Consider a two-citizen economy where the productivity of the public good is measured by $g = 0.80$. Each citizen either contributes $1 or zero. Both citizens are perfectly selfish. To ensure the efficient outcome, the minimum penalty for a free rider is [___]. Illustrate with a game tree.

Math Solutions

Math 5.1: Utility-Maximizing Contribution for Efficiency Norm

Differentiate the utility function

$$\frac{du}{dh} = 1 - 2 \cdot \psi \cdot h$$

Set the derivative equal to zero and solve for the utility-maximizing private consumption:

$$h^* = \frac{1}{2 \cdot \psi}$$

Because $c = 1 - h$, the utility-maximizing contribution is

$$c^* = 1 - \frac{1}{2 \cdot \psi}$$

For the marginal principle, the marginal benefit is derivative of the material-benefit with respect to h, which is constant at 1.

$$mb(h) = 1$$

The marginal cost is the derivative of the norm-violation cost with respect to h:

$$mc(h) = 2 \cdot \psi \cdot h$$

Math 5.2: Utility-Maximizing Contribution for Efficiency and Equality Norms

Differentiate the utility function with respect to private consumption h with $h_?$ representing the conjectured average private consumption:

$$\frac{du}{dh} = 1 - 2 \cdot \psi \cdot h - 2 \cdot \phi \cdot (h - h_?)$$

Set the derivative equal to zero and solve for the utility-maximizing private consumption:

$$h^* = \frac{1/2 + \phi \cdot h_?}{\psi + \phi}$$

Because $c = 1 - h$, the utility-maximizing contribution is

$$c^{**} = \frac{c_? \cdot \phi + \psi - 1/2}{\phi + \psi}$$

6 Identity, Norms, and Reciprocity in the Workplace

Imagine that you are participating in an experiment with anonymous employers and workers. Your task as a worker is to solve mazes on a computer. Each maze requires roughly 1.5 minutes to solve, and for each maze you solve, your anonymous employer gets $1. Before you get to work on the mazes, you receive a payment of $5 from your employer. If you like, you can simply take the $5 and walk away without solving any puzzles. Or you can solve puzzles and make money for your employer. This experiment generates three questions.

1. Will you take the money and walk away, or will you solve some puzzles?

2. How many puzzles will you solve?

3. If the payment from your employer doubles to $10, will you solve more puzzles?

This chapter explores the role of norms in the work environment. We focus on norms concerning work effort, which may be important in environments where it is costly or impractical for an organization to monitor its workers and measure individual contributions to the organization's output. In production environments where teamwork is important, it may be impossible to figure out how much each worker contributed to the team output. In environments of costly or impractical monitoring, workers have some flexibility in choosing how hard they work. As explained by Akerlof and Kranton (2000, 2008), an individual worker's choice of an effort level may be influenced by norms forged in the workplace.

The consideration of workplace norms raises questions about labor–management practices. The most obvious labor–management tool is the wage. An organization can use a relatively high wage to attract new workers and retain existing workers. In this case, an organization taps material incentives to develop a workforce. This chapter explores two other labor–management practices.

1. *Higher wage for increased effort.* An organization may increase its wage to get its workers to work harder. In the case of relatively strong group norms, an individual may work harder at a higher wage, even if effort is not monitored.

2. *Identity management.* An organization may invest resources to get a worker to include the organization as part of the worker's self-image or identity. The potential payoff is that the worker will embrace an organizational norm of high work effort. A norm-sensitive individual will work harder, even if effort is not monitored.

When a worker responds to a higher wage by increasing effort, that's an example of workplace reciprocity. We can relate workplace reciprocity to a social norm of sharing the fruits of collaboration. As we saw earlier in the book, youngsters in the rope-pulling experiment share equally the rewards of collaboration. In a workplace, the employer and workers collaborate to produce a product, so workers may act on a social norm of sharing the benefit of a higher wage by working harder. As we've seen in earlier chapters, individuals vary in their adherence to social norms, and we can expect workers to vary in their responsiveness to an increases in the wage.

Another possible source of workplace reciprocity is a social norm of gift exchange. In some social groups, a gift from A to B obligates B to give a gift to A. The recipient of a gift is indebted to the donor, and can clear the debt by giving back. Studies by anthropologists show the power of a gift-exchange norm (Mauss [1924]; Gouldner [1960]; Wiessner [2002]). In societies that rely heavily on gifts rather than formal economic exchange, responders in the ultimatum game reject offers of 50 percent or more because the acceptance of an unsolicited gift puts the recipient in debt to the donor (Henrich et al. 2014). In the economics literature, Malmendier and Schmidt (2017) invoke a social norm of gift exchange in a model of commercial gifts. In this chapter, when a worker receives the gift of a higher wage, he or she may feel obligated to give the gift of higher productivity to the employer.

Learning Objectives: The Explainer

After mastering this chapter, you will be able to explain each of the following statements.

1. A worker whose self-image (identity) is strongly tied to a work group will internalize workplace norms.

2. A worker's utility-maximizing effort increases with the share of the worker's self-image (identity) tied to the work group: an insider works harder than an outsider.

3. An organization may have an incentive to invest resources to boost its share of a worker's self-image (identity).

4. For a worker who acts on a norm of sharing the rewards of collaboration, an increase in the wage will increase work effort.

5. For an organization whose workers respond to a higher wage by working harder, an increase in the wage may increase or decrease profit.

6. Experiments in labs and in the field provide evidence of worker reciprocity: an increase in the wage or other compensation sometimes increases work effort.

6.1 Worker Reciprocity and Social Capital

Reciprocity is a component of social capital, defined as features of social organization that facilitate cooperation and improve efficiency. We can illustrate the social-capital feature of workplace reciprocity with a simple example. Suppose a producer has 100 workers, each of whom chooses his or her worker effort. The total quantity produced is determined by the collective efforts of the workers. Consider the implications of a one-unit increase in effort by each worker.

1. The marginal cost of effort is $3: the disutility of an increase in effort is equivalent to a $3 loss of wealth.
2. The increase in worker effort increases the quantity produced, increasing total revenue by $7 per worker.

There is an opportunity for a Pareto improvement: a one-unit increase in effort has a cost of $300 to workers ($3 times 100 workers) and a benefit of $700 to the producer ($7 times 100 workers). So workers and the producer have an opportunity to share a $400 gain.

Perfect or Imperfect Information in the Workplace?

In a world of perfect information in the workplace, the Pareto improvement will happen. Suppose the producer and the workers agree to share the $400 gain equally. The wage increases by $5, and each worker increases effort by one unit, at a cost of $3. As a result, the gain per worker is $2 = $5 − $3. The producer monitors each worker (at zero cost) to verify the anticipated increases in effort. The producer gets $700 in additional revenue at a cost of $500, generating a gain of $200 = $700 −$500.

There is one problem with this scenario. The producer may be unable to monitor the effort and productivity of each worker. In a team of 100 workers, measuring the individual contributions to production and total revenue may be impractical. Suppose the increase in the wage does not increase total revenue by $700, meaning that at least one worker has not increased work effort by one unit. In a world of imperfect monitoring, it will be impossible for the producer to identify which workers did not boost their work efforts. Suppose workers have self-regarding preferences. For a selfish worker, the rational response to the increase in the wage in an unmonitored workplace is to collect the higher wage and not change the effort level: after all, $5 is better than $2. Knowing this, the producer will not pay the higher wage, and the Pareto improvement will not happen.

Social Norms and Pareto Improvements

A social norm that triggers reciprocity can make the Pareto improvement happen. Suppose that in the collaborative work environment, workers observe an equal-sharing norm. In our example, a $5 increase in the wage will cause each worker to increase effort by one unit ($3), which leaves the worker with a $2 gain. The producer gets a benefit of $700 and pays $500 in higher wages, leaving a $200 gain, or $2 per worker. Knowing that each worker will increase effort by one unit, the rational response by a profit-maximizing producer is to increase the wage. As a result, the economy realizes the Pareto improvement: after accounting for the extra effort, each worker gains $2; after accounting for the higher wage, the producer gains $200.

This example illustrates the connection between social norms and social capital. A social norm of sharing the rewards of collaboration triggers reciprocity that addresses the problem of imperfect information in worker effort and productivity. In contrast, the monitoring response to imperfect information in the workplace—developing a system of monitoring workers to measure individual productivity—is likely to be costly and may be impractical. The alternative to monitoring workers is to tap worker reciprocity in response to a higher wage. Social capital in the form of worker reciprocity increases the efficiency of the economy because it makes Pareto improvements possible.

Review the Concepts 6.1

1. Workplace reciprocity is consistent with experimental evidence showing that youngsters who [___] to earn a reward [___]. (act independently, don't share; collaborate, share equally; compete, share equally)

2. When it is costly to monitor the effort of individual workers, worker reciprocity can promote [___]. (efficiency, Pareto improvements, social capital)

3. In a workplace where workers respond to an increase in the wage by increasing work effort, an increase in the wage [___]. (will increase profit, will decrease profit, may increase profit)

6.2 Worker Identity and Effort

Akerlof and Kranton (2008) developed a model of work effort that incorporates a sense of identity and group norms. The term "identity" is used to describe a person's self-image. If you consider yourself a member of a work group, the group is part of your self-image, part of your identity. As a member of the group, you internalize the group's norms of workplace conduct. If the group norm is to arrive for work five minutes early, that will be your target arrival time. If the group norm is to be fully focused on work tasks for seven-eighths of the workday, that determines your target effort level. If you identify with a group, violating a group norm is costly because it erodes your self-image.

As we've seen in earlier chapters, there is typically a trade-off associated with following any group norm. The trade-off for work effort is subtle. Consider a worker who has the following constraint:

$$T = e + d$$

where e is work effort and d incorporates the opportunity cost of effort. To increase e, a worker with a fixed T must decrease d. In this simple case, there is a one-for-one trade-off between work effort and d. The variable d could take many forms.

- For a manual laborer, d could be energy reserved for leisure activity. Working at a slower pace reserves energy for after-work softball or dancing. Alternatively, working at a high energy level for an entire workday may leave little energy for evening activities.
- For an off-hours environmental monitor (sometimes known as a night watchman), d could be dozing time—time spent sleeping on the job rather than monitoring the environment for suspicious activity.
- For a professional, d could be time spent on leisure or social activities rather than thinking about work issues. A medical worker who on a bus ride home reads a novel rather than the latest edition of a medical journal chooses d over e.
- For an office worker, d could be daydreaming time—time spent thinking about non-work phenomena rather than focusing on work tasks.

In our discussion, we will use the office-worker example: the worker has a fixed amount of time to allocate to work-related thinking (e) and daydreaming (d). Naturally, the analysis is applicable to other trade-offs between work effort and other aspects of life.

Utility Maximizing Effort

We can use the framework of Akerlof and Kranton (2008) to develop a utility function that incorporates the trade-offs associated with a group norm. Consider a worker whose utility increases as the wage (w) increases. An increase in work effort (e) decreases utility, while an increase in daydreaming (d) increases utility. In Figure 6.1, the horizontal axis measures daydreaming and effort: d increases from left to right, and e increases from right to left. In this example, $T = 1$, so effort and daydreaming add up to 1. The linear curve shows the benefits from the wage and daydreaming, which of course increase with d. The vertical intercept is w: for a job without daydreams, the only benefit is the wage.

In the spirit of Akerlof and Kranton (2008), the worker identifies with a work group and is sensitive to the group's norm for work effort. The work-effort norm is $\hat{e}$.

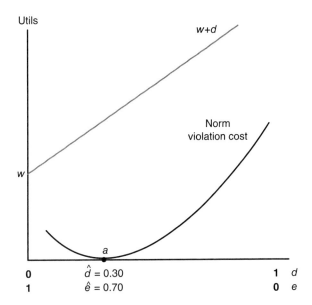

FIGURE 6.1: Components of Worker Utility

Given the one-for-one trade-off between e and d, the group norm can be expressed as a daydreaming norm:

$$\hat{d} = T - \hat{e}$$

The cost of violating the norm is

$$norm-violation\ cost = \psi \cdot (d - \hat{d})^2$$

where ψ is a norm-violation parameter that varies across workers. For a worker who strictly adheres to the norm, $d = \hat{d}$, and the norm-violation cost is zero. In Figure 6.1, the norm is $\hat{d} = 0.30$, and point a shows the case of strict adherence to the norm. As the gap between actual daydreaming and the daydreaming norm increases, norm-violation cost increases at an increasing rate.

The worker's objective is to maximize utility. The utility function incorporates the trade-off between material benefit and the cost of violating the norm:

$$utility = w + d - \psi \cdot (d - \hat{d})^2$$

The worker's choice variable is d. Given the one-for-one trade-off between daydreaming and effort, the choice of the utility-maximizing d^* is also a choice of the utility-maximizing e^*:

$$e^* = T - d^*$$

In the upper panel of Figure 6.2, the utility curve shows the gap between the benefit curve and the norm-violation cost curve. At point a, the norm-violation cost curve is zero, so at point b, utility equals the benefit $w + d$. As d increases, the benefit increases at a constant rate, while the cost increases at an increasing rate. As d increases, utility increases as long as the increase in benefit exceeds the increase in cost. The utility curve reaches its peak at point c, with $d^* = 0.55$ and $e^* = 0.45$. Beyond point c, the increase in norm-violation cost exceeds the increase in benefit, so utility decreases.

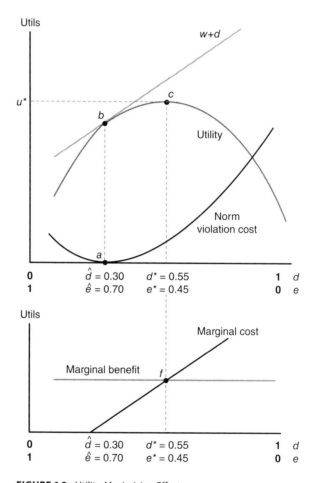

FIGURE 6.2: Utility-Maximizing Effort

The lower panel of Figure 6.2 deploys the marginal principle. The marginal-benefit curve is horizontal because the benefit $w + d$ increases at a constant rate as d increase. The marginal-cost curve is positively sloped because as d increases (and e decreases), norm-violation cost increases at an increasing rate. The marginal principle is satisfied at point f, where the marginal benefit equals the marginal cost.

Insiders versus Outsiders

Akerlof and Kranton (2008) distinguish between insiders and outsiders. An insider is a worker who identifies with a work group and shares the group norm with respect to effort. In the context of our model, an insider has a relatively large value for the norm-violation parameter ψ. The worker strongly identifies with the group, so violating the group norm by choosing an effort level that falls short of the norm $\hat{e}$ is costly. In other words, the norm-violation cost curve is relatively steep. In the left-side panel of Figure 6.3, an insider's sensitivity to the group norm is so strong that utility is maximized with an effort level close to the norm: at point s, $d*$ is close to $\hat{d}$, and $e*$ is close to $\hat{e}$.

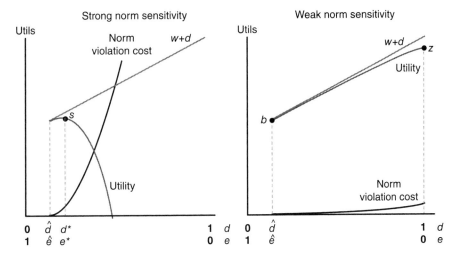

FIGURE 6.3: Insider versus Outsider

An outsider is defined as a worker who does not identify with a work group. Therefore, and outsider is relatively insensitive to violating a group norm about work effort. The right-side panel of Figure 6.3 shows a case of relatively weak norm sensitivity. The norm-violation cost curve is positively sloped but relatively flat, so an increase in d increases the benefit $w + d$ by more than it increases the norm-violation cost. As a result, utility is maximized at point z: the utility-maximizing effort level is zero. A worker with relatively weak norm sensitivity will exert the minimum effort required.

Norm Sensitivity and Effort

Figure 6.4 uses the marginal principle to summarize the connection between norm sensitivity and work effort. For a given group norm $(\hat{d}, \hat{e})$, the utility-maximizing effort is determined by a worker's sensitivity to the norm.

- *Strong sensitivity.* The marginal-cost curve is relatively steep, generating a relatively small gap between the utility-maximizing effort (e^*) and the norm.
- *Moderate sensitivity.* The marginal-cost curve has a moderate slope, generating a moderate gap between the utility-maximizing effort (e^{**}) and the norm.
- *Weak sensitivity.* The marginal-cost curve is relatively flat and never rises above the marginal-benefit curve. The utility-maximizing effort is zero.

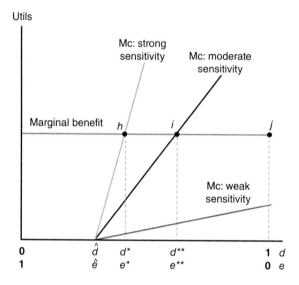

FIGURE 6.4: Variation in Norm Sensitivity

We can use some simple math to show the relationship between norm sensitivity and the utility-maximizing work effort. As shown in Math 6.1, the utility-maximizing daydreaming is

$$d^* = \hat{d} + \frac{1}{2 \cdot \psi}$$

Daydreaming exceeds the norm $\hat{d}$ by an amount that depends on norm sensitivity. As ψ increases, the gap decreases, and the utility-maximizing daydreaming moves closer to the norm.

Looking back to Figure 6.2, the numbers are based on parameter values $\psi = 2$ and $\hat{d} = 0.30$:

$$d^* = 0.30 + \frac{1}{2 \cdot 2} = 0.55$$

A switch to stronger norm sensitivity (with $\psi = 5$) decreases daydreaming to 0.40:

$$d^* = 0.30 + \frac{1}{2 \cdot 5} = 0.40$$

Recall that daydreaming comes at the expense of focused effort. As shown in Math 6.1, the utility-maximizing effort level is

$$e^* = \hat{e} - \frac{1}{2 \cdot \psi}$$

The utility-maximizing effort (focused time) exceeds the norm by an amount that depends on norm sensitivity. As ψ increases, the gap decreases and the utility-maximizing effort moves closer to the norm. In Figure 6.2, $e^* = 0.45$:

$$e^* = 0.70 - \frac{1}{2 \cdot 2} = 0.45$$

A switch to stronger norm sensitivity (with $\psi = 5$) increases effort to 0.60:

$$e^* = 0.70 - \frac{1}{2 \cdot 5} = 0.60$$

Producer Investment in Identity Management

An organization may have an incentive to invest resources to get workers to more tightly identify with the organization. To do so, an organization could persuade an individual that a larger share of the worker's identity is tied to the organization. In our simple model, a boost in the organization's contribution to an individual's self-image increases the worker's sensitivity to violating the group norm for work effort. As we've seen, an increase in norm sensitivity (an increase in ψ) increases the utility-maximizing work effort.

Akerlof and Kranton (2005) describe a number of ways that organizations use resources to link their workers' self-image to the organization. If an identity-management program increases work effort and increases total output of the organization, the next question is whether the increase in output is large enough to offset the resource costs of the identity-management program.

Review the Concepts 6.2

1. The opportunity cost of work effort is incorporated into the work-effort model with [___]. (norm-violation cost, $T = d + e$, the wage)

2. For the utility-maximizing work effort, [___]. (norm-violation cost is minimized, utility equals the norm-violation cost, marginal benefit of d equals the marginal cost of d)

3. An insider has relatively [___] norm sensitivity, reflected in a relatively [___] value for ψ. (weak, small; strong, small; weak, large; strong, large)

4. The utility-maximizing effort level will be zero if the marginal-cost curve [___] (is relatively flat, lies below the marginal-benefit curve, is relatively steep, has a moderate slope)

5. An increase in the sensitivity to a work-effort norm [___] ψ and [___] the utility-maximizing work effort. (increases, decreases; increases, increases; decreases, increases; decreases, decreases)

6. An organization uses an identity-management program to [___]. (issue ID cards, encourage workers to think independently, get workers to more tightly identify with the organization)

6.3   Response to a Higher Wage

We can extend our model of workplace norms to explore the effects of an increase in the wage on worker effort. There are many possible reasons for a producer to increase its wage. The organization may use a higher wage to (i) retain workers who have received better offers at other organizations or (ii) recruit new workers. As we'll see in this part of the chapter, a producer may increase the wage to increase the work effort of an existing workforce. In other words, a producer may use the wage as motivational tool.

Wages and a Sharing Norm

Consider an organization with a stable workforce, with no concerns about retention or recruitment of additional workers. Suppose each worker incorporates the organization as part of his or her identity. Each worker collaborates with other members of the organization in the pursuit of common goals such as profit, citizen satisfaction with public goods, or a sustainable environment. As we saw in the rope-pulling experiment, working together promotes sharing the rewards of collaboration.

Figure 6.5 shows indifference curves for the wage and d, the variable that incorporates the opportunity cost of work effort. In our example, d is daydreaming, but it could represent other activities that are reduced by work effort. For example, an evening of softball or dancing may be feasible for a worker who eases back on work effort during the day. In contrast, the evening activities may be impossible for a worker who goes full-tilt all day long. Each curve shows the (*wage*, d) combinations that generate a fixed level of utility. The negative slope shows the trade-off between the *wage* and d. If the wage increases, the worker will achieve the same utility level if daydreaming decreases (work effort increases).

Consider the effects of an increase in the wage. Suppose a worker starts at point a, with a wage w', daydreaming d_H, and utility u_1. If the wage increases to w'', the worker has three options for daydreaming.

- *Point* b. No change in daydreaming, and a large increase in utility. The worker moves to a higher indifference curve, indicating greater utility. The

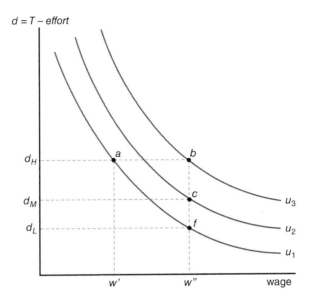

FIGURE 6.5: Tradeoff between Wage and Daydreaming

worker's effort doesn't change, so the worker gets the full benefit of the wage increase.

- *Point* f. Large decrease in daydreaming, and no change in utility. The worker remains on the same indifference curve, indicating constant utility. The worker responds to the higher wages by working harder, with less day-dreaming and more time focused on work tasks. In other words, the higher wage is fully offset by less daydreaming and greater effort. In this case, the worker shifts the full benefit of the higher wage to the organization.
- *Point* c: Moderate decrease in daydreaming and a moderate increase in utility. The worker shifts to a higher indifference curve (increase in utility) and moves downward along the new curve (less daydreaming and more effort). By increasing effort, the worker shares the benefit of the higher wage with the organization.

In a work environment where workers' identities include the organization, it is possible that workers will share the benefit of a higher wage by working harder.

Wages and the Work-Effort Norm

We can incorporate workers' responses to a higher wage into our norm-based utility function. Suppose the organization's norm for effort is determined by the wage: the higher the wage, the greater the effort required to satisfy a work-effort norm. In other words, an increase in the wage increases $\hat{e}$ and decreases $\hat{d}$. When an organization increases wages, the consensus among the workers is that every-one should work harder.

Figure 6.6 shows the implications of a higher wage for the utility-maximizing effort. At the low wage, the norm is $\hat{d} = 0.50$ and $\hat{e} = 0.50$ (shown by point *a*). Norm sensitivity is measured by $\psi = 2$. The marginal principle is satisfied at point *h*, so the utility-maximizing effort is $e^* = 0.25$. At the higher wage, the norm is $\hat{d} = 0.10$ and $\hat{e} = 0.90$ (shown by point *b*). The marginal principle is satisfied at point *i*, so the utility-maximizing effort is $e^* = 0.65$. In other words, an increase in the wage increases the work-effort norm, and the utility-maximizing effort increases from 0.25 to 0.65.

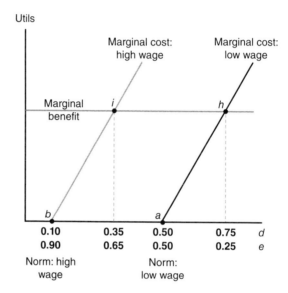

FIGURE 6.6: Wages and Work Effort

Wages and Profit

Figure 6.6 shows that an increase in the wage is at least partly offset by an increase in worker effort. An increase in worker effort presumably increases the quantity produced by an organization, increasing the organization rewards such as profit, citizen satisfaction, public health, and environmental quality. This is applicable for a producer with a workforce that internalizes (i) a group norm for work effort and (ii) a norm of sharing the gains from collaboration. An increase in the wage will increase a producer's profit if

- The increase in effort is large relative to the increase in the wage. This requires strong sensitivity to the norms of work effort and sharing.
- The increase in productivity from the increase in effort is relatively large.
- The increase in revenue from an increase in the quantity produce is relatively large. This requires a relatively high output price.

Review the Concepts 6.3

1. To share a higher wage with an employer, a worker [____]. (moves to a higher indifference curve, decreases daydreaming, increases work effort, stays on the same indifference curve, does not change work effort)

2. If workers are sensitive to a social norm of sharing the rewards of collaboration, an increase in the wage increases [____]. (the daydream norm $\hat{d}$, the utility-maximizing daydreaming, the effort norm $\hat{e}$)

3. In Figure 6.6, suppose that starting from the low wage, an increase in the wage increases the work-effort norm to $\hat{e} = 0.60$. The utility-maximizing effort is $e^* = $ [____]. (0.35, 0.60, 0.65, 0.90, 1)

6.4   Evidence of Worker Reciprocity

Behavioral economists have used lab and field experiments to explore the relationship between wages and work effort. The experiments provide robust evidence of a positive relationship between effort and wages. There is evidence that the effect of a decrease in the wage is stronger than the effect of an increase in the wage. Kube, Marechal, and Puppe (2006) estimate the elasticities of effort with respect to changes in wages. The estimated elasticity is 0.30 for a wage increase, compared to 0.80 for a wage decrease.

Field Experiments

Field experiments provide empirical support for a positive relationship between wages and work effort. Gneezy and List (2006) explore the effects of an unexpected increase in the hourly wage for a library data-entry task. An increase in the wage from $12 to $20 boosted effort by roughly 25 percent for the first 90 minutes of work. The effort boost diminished over time, and dissipated after roughly 270 minutes. This is consistent with reference dependence: under a reference wage of $12, an increase to $20 triggers reciprocity in the form of higher effort. But over time, the reference wage presumably drifts upward, and once the reference wage reaches $20, the effort has drifted back to the original level.

A second set of field experiments by Kube, Marechal, and Puppe (2013) provides insights into why many firms are reluctant to cut wages, even when the demand for labor is weak. In the experiment, workers were hired with the understanding that the hourly wage for a data-entry task was to be 15 euros. The control group was paid the 15-euro reference wage, but some workers were instead paid 20 euros, and others were paid only 10 euros. The wage hike (from 15 to 20 euros) did not significantly increase work effort. In contrast, the wage cut (from 15 to 10 euros) decreased work effort by an average of 21 percent.

A third field experiment illustrates the notion of gift exchange when workers are paid piece rates rather than hourly wages (Bellemare and Shearer 2009). A tree-planting firm that paid its workers a piece rate of $0.20 per tree gave each worker a surprise gift of $80. Workers responded to the one-time gift by planting more trees: on average, a worker planted an additional 132 trees per day, which translates into an 11 percent increase in effort. In other words, workers reciprocated the employer gift by increasing productivity, resulting in a gift to the employer in the form of increased revenue. The increase in revenue was not large enough to offset the $80 gift, so the firm's profit decreased.

The tree-planting experiment illustrates the role of worker tenure in the responsiveness of worker effort to changes in compensation. A key insight is that worker reciprocity is stronger for workers in long-term labor relationships. In the experiment, an increase in worker tenure (a longer time working for the firm) was associated with larger increase in effort in response to the $80 gift. For example, the average productivity boost was roughly 90 trees for workers with a tenure of one year, compared to roughly 284 trees for workers with a tenure of 14 years.

A Gift-Exchange Experiment

The chapter opener introduced a gift-exchange experiment that gives a "worker" the opportunity to perform a task that generates revenue for the "employer." The key question is whether an increase in the payment from the employer to the worker increases worker effort. Gneezy (2002) ran the experiment by pairing MBA students (employers) with undergraduates (workers). Each employer received $10 at the start of the experiment and then chose one of three payments (0, $5, or $10) to an anonymous worker. Each worker was informed of the payment from his or her anonymous employer and then decided how much time to spend solving mazes on a computer. For each maze solved, the employer earned $1.

Figure 6.7 shows the average number of mazes solved for the three payments. As shown by the positively sloped curve, doubling the payment from $5 to $10 more than doubled the average number of mazes solved, from 4.80 to 11.95. Productivity increased because the average time spent on the maze-solving task more than doubled. The results of the study provide evidence for a positive relationship between wages and work effort. In the experiment, employers had no control over their workers' efforts, and yet an increase in the payment increased work effort.

How did an increase in the payment to workers affect employer profit? As shown in the V-shaped profit curve in Figure 6.7, the average profit from a zero payment was $12.30, compared to $9.80 for the $5 payment and $11.95 for the $10 payment. In other words, profit was highest for employers who paid nothing to their workers. The average quantity of unpaid workers was 2.3 mazes, so a non-paying employer kept the $10 endowment and added $2.30 from mazes solved by

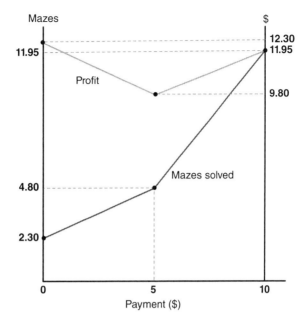

FIGURE 6.7: Results of Maze Experiment

unpaid workers. Although an increase in the payment to $5 increased output, the additional revenue to the firm was less $5, so profit decreased. Moving to the $10 payment, the increase in revenue exceeded $5, so profit increased.

There are two lessons from this experiment. First, an increase in the wage can increase worker effort and productivity. Second, an increase in effort is necessary but not sufficient for higher wages to translate into higher profit. The increase in worker productivity must be large enough that the increase in revenue exceeds the increase in labor cost.

Review the Concepts 6.4

1. Field experiments on worker reciprocity suggest that a decrease in the wage has a [___] effect on worker effort compared to an increase in the wage. (weaker, roughly equal, stronger)

2. In the tree-planting experiment, worker reciprocity is stronger for workers in [___] labor relationships. (short-term, involuntary, contentious, long-term)

3. Experiments on worker reciprocity illustrate that an increase in wages can increase [___] and decrease [___]. (worker effort, producer profit; worker productivity, producer profit; producer profit, worker effort)

Takeaways

1. Worker reciprocity is a component of social capital in the sense that reciprocity promotes cooperation and efficiency.

2. A worker whose identity is tied to an organization may be sensitive to a group norm concerning work effort.

3. The utility-maximizing work effort increases with the worker's sensitivity to the workplace effort norm.

4. For a worker who is sensitive to a norm of sharing the rewards of collaboration, an increase in the wage increases work effort.

5. Empirical studies of worker reciprocity suggest asymmetry in worker reciprocity: the decrease in effort from a wage reduction is large relative to the increase in effort from a wage increase.

Discuss the Concepts

1. *Contractor Janitors?* An organization can either hire its own janitorial staff or pay a contractor to provide janitorial services. The hourly wage of a hired janitor is $w_I = 20$ while the hourly cost of a contract janitor is $w_O = 12$. The contractor [___] (is, is not) the obvious choice because [___].

2. Suppose a group of 50 workers has proposed a company softball team to compete in a city softball league, and has requested $5000 in financial support from the company. The company does not advertise because it sells its products overseas. The company agrees to provide the support with one condition: the company logo must be prominent on the team's uniforms.

   a. The funding of the softball team will increase the company's profit if [___].

   b. The logo requirement is sensible because [___].

3. *Worker Reciprocity.* Consider a worker whose indifference curve for effort and wages is $d(w) = 240/w$ and $2 = d + e$. Suppose the wage increases from 240 to 300.

   a. To keep worker utility constant, worker effort [___] (↑, ↓, does not change) from [___] to [___].

   b. In terms of work effort, the worker's willingness to pay for the wage increase is $\Delta e = $ [___].

   c. For a worker who shares half the willingness to pay with the employer, worker effort [___] (↑, ↓, does not change) from [___] to [___].

Apply the Concepts

1. *Insider Janitors?* An organization can either hire its own janitorial staff or pay a contractor to provide janitorial services. The daily cost of a hired janitor is $w_I = 200$ and the daily cost of a contract janitor is $w_O = 120$. The output of a janitor is $q = \theta \cdot (1 + e)$, where e is the effort level. The norm sensitivity of an insider is $\psi = 10$, and the norm sensitivity of an outsider is $\psi = 0.50$. The effort norm is $\hat{e} = 0.70$.

    a. The [___] (hired, contract) janitor is a better choice because [___].

    b. Suppose $\theta = 100$. The benefit-cost ratio of a hired janitor is [___], compared to [___] for a contract janitor.

2. *Swag and Effort.* Consider an organization that can invest S in logo swag (ball caps, sweatshirts, mugs with the organization logo) to increase its share of the identities of its workers. The identity boost increases the value of the common norm-sensitivity parameter from $\psi = 1$ to $\psi = 5$. The organization's profit from a worker equals $\theta \cdot e$, where e is the worker's utility-maximizing effort. Suppose $\theta = 50$ and the organization has 100 workers. The investment in identity will be profitable if the cost of the logo swag program is $S < $ [___].

3. *Wage, Effort, and Organizational Reward.* Consider an organization whose workers include the organization as part of their identities. The common value of the norm-sensitivity parameter is $\psi = 4$. The initial work-effort norm is $(\hat{d}, \hat{e}) = (0.30, 0.70)$. The firm is considering an increase in the wage from $w_L = 20$ to $w_H = 36$. Assume that the increase in the wage changes the work-effort norm to $(\hat{d}, \hat{e}) = (0.15, 0.85)$. The organization's benefit per worker (profit, output, or other reward) is $q = \theta \cdot e$, where e is the worker's effort level and θ is a productivity parameter. Suppose $\theta = 100$.

    a. The increase in the wage [___] ($\uparrow$, $\downarrow$, does not change) the effort per worker per worker from [___] to [___].

    b. On a per-worker basis, the benefit of the wage increase is $B = $ [___], compared to a cost $C = $ [___].

Math Solutions

Math 6.1: Utility-Maximizing Effort

The utility function is

$$utility = w + d - \psi \cdot (d - \hat{d})^2$$

Differentiate the utility function with respect to the choice variable d:

$$\frac{du}{dd} = 1 - 2 \cdot \psi \cdot (d - \hat{d})$$

Set the derivative equal to zero and solve for the utility-maximizing d:

$$d^* = \frac{1 + 2 \cdot \psi \cdot \hat{d}}{2 \cdot \psi}$$

This can be rewritten as

$$d^* = \hat{d} + \frac{1}{2 \cdot \psi}$$

Effort (e) and daydreaming (d) add up to the time constraint T, so the utility-maximizing effort level is

$$e^* = \hat{e} - \frac{1}{2 \cdot \psi}$$

For the marginal principle, the marginal benefit of d is constant at 1.

$$mb(d) = 1$$

The marginal cost is the derivative of the norm-violation cost with respect to d:

$$mc(d) = 2 \cdot \psi \cdot (d - \hat{d})$$

Voluntary Prices

It's the first Tuesday of the month, and people who visit the Cartoon Art Museum in San Francisco get to choose how much to pay for admission. Each visitor is randomly selected into one of two types, **pay what you want (PWW)** and **pay it forward (PIF)**. A museum employee gives each visitor in the PWW group a card that describes a pay-what-you-want program.

> Today is a Pay-What-You-Wish Day, so all visitors will be admitted regardless of how much they pay. Today, all visitors, including you, can pay any price they want for their own admission. How much do you want to pay?

Similarly, a museum employee gives each customer in the PIF group a card that describes a pay-it-forward program.

> Today is a Pay-What-You-Wish Day. A visitor who came earlier paid for your admission. Since you are paid for, you now have a chance to pay forward the admission for another person who will come later today. How much would you like to pay forward for another persons's admission?

Imagine that you visit the museum on a first Tuesday, and get a PWW card. How much would you voluntarily pay for yourself? If you instead get a PIF card, how much would you voluntarily pay for someone else?

This chapter explores the role of social norms in the realm of voluntary prices. Under a pay-what-you-want pricing system, consumers decide for themselves how much to pay for a product. Some providers of public goods solicit voluntary contributions to help support the public good. For example, public-radio stations encourage listeners to pay an annual membership fee, and use pledge drives to increase membership. The chapter addresses several questions about voluntary pricing.

1. If a consumer is sensitive to a social norm of sharing the benefit of exchange, what are the implications for the utility-maximizing voluntary price?

2. Under what circumstances will pay-what-you-want pricing be profitable?

3. How do public-radio pledge drives tap into a social norm of contributing to support a public good?

Learning Objectives: The Explainer

After mastering this chapter, you will be able to explain each of the following statements.

1. When consumers choose their own prices for a product, the price will be positive for consumers who are relatively sensitive to a norm of sharing the gains from exchange.

2. A system of voluntary pricing will be profitable if a relatively large number of buyers are relatively sensitive to a norm of sharing the gain from exchange.

3. A public-radio pledge drive imposes costs on members and free riders.

4. A public-radio pledge drive can convert free riders into paying members.

7.1   Voluntary Prices: Pay What You Want

Some producers allow each consumer to choose how much to pay for a product. Under a pure PWW (pay-what-you-want) system, there is no lower limit on the transaction price. In a traditional economic model with purely selfish agents (self-regarding preferences), "pay what you want" translates into "pay nothing." In the case of a purely selfish consumer, consumer surplus is maximized with a voluntary price equal to zero. In this case, a producer experiences a loss equal to the marginal cost of production.

As a variation on pure PWW, some sellers set a minimum price to ensure that they recover at least part of their production costs. In another variation, the producer lists several price options, with information about the consequences of paying different prices. For example, a seller could say that (i) the low price allows the producer to cover its marginal cost, (ii) the medium price allows the producer to pay its workers higher wages, and (iii) the high price allows the producer to invest in capital to expand its operation.

For a producer considering a PWW system, the key question is, "How low will the voluntary price go?" The producer will earn a profit when the voluntary price exceeds the marginal cost, but will lose money when the voluntary price is less than marginal cost. In this part of the chapter, we consider a social norm under which buyers and sellers share equally the gains from exchange. As we'll see, sensitivity to this social norm causes consumers to voluntarily choose positive prices.

The Equal-Sharing Price and Norm-Violation Cost

Consider a transaction between a consumer and a producer. The consumer's value of the product (the willingness to pay or marginal benefit) is v, and the producer's marginal cost of production is c. The social gain from exchange equals the difference between the consumer value and marginal cost:

$$gain\ from\ exchange = v - c$$

For equal sharing of the gains from exchange, the voluntary price paid by the consumer equals the consumer value minus half the social gain:

$$p_0 = v - \frac{v-c}{2}$$

We can use simple algebra to generate an expression for the **equal-sharing price**. We can rewrite the expression for p_0 as

$$p_0 = \frac{2 \cdot v - v + c}{2}$$

Simplify the numerator to generate the equal-sharing price:

$$p_0 = \frac{v+c}{2}$$

For example, if $v = 1$ and $c = 1/5$, the equal-sharing price is $p_0 = 3/5$.

A consumer who chooses a voluntary price faces a trade-off between material benefits and the cost of violating a social norm of equal sharing. The consumer starts by computing the equal-sharing price (p_0). Then the consumer decides how much to pay for the PWW product (p_V) and how much to spend on other products (h):

$$p_0 = p_V + h$$

For strict adherence to the equal-sharing norm, $p_V = p_0$, so other consumption is $h = 0$. A consumer who pays less than the equal-sharing price has more money to spend on the other product.

As we've seen in earlier chapters, we can use a utility function to capture the trade-off between material benefits and the cost of violating a social norm. We can represent the cost of violating the equal-sharing norm as

$$norm - violation \; cost = \psi \cdot \left(p_0 - p_V \right)^2$$

The expression in parentheses is the gap between the equal-sharing price and the voluntary price. As usual, ψ measures the consumer's sensitivity to the norm. Consumer utility equals the material benefit from consuming the other product minus the norm-violation cost:

$$utility = h - \psi \cdot \left(p_0 - p_V \right)^2$$

Figure 7.1 illustrates a consumer's choice of the utility-maximizing voluntary price. The horizontal axis measures consumption of the other good (increasing from left to right) and the voluntary price (decreasing from left to right). Note that at the origin, the voluntary price is the equal-sharing price (3/5 in our example) and other consumption is zero. At the other extreme, when the voluntary price is zero, other consumption is the equal-sharing price (3/5).

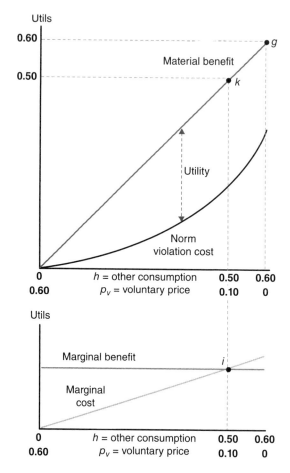

FIGURE 7.1: Utility-Maximizing Voluntary Price

The upper panel of Figure 7.1 shows the consumer's trade-off between material benefit and norm-violation cost.

- *Material benefit.* As the consumption of the other product increases, the consumer's material benefit increases, as shown by the linear curve.
- *Norm-violation cost.* The norm-violation cost is zero when the consumer strictly adheres to the equal-sharing norm ($p_v = p_0$) and increases at an increasing rate as the consumption of the other product increases at the expense of the voluntary price.

Consumer utility equals the material benefit minus norm-violation cost. This is shown by the vertical gap between the material-benefit curve and the norm-violation cost curve.

The lower panel of Figure 7.1 applies the marginal principle to the consumer's choice. The marginal-benefit curve is horizontal because an increase in other consumption increases the material benefit at a constant rate. The marginal-cost curve is positively sloped because as the voluntary price decreases, the norm-violation cost increases at an increasing rate. The marginal principle is satisfied at point *i*, with other consumption $h* = 0.50$ and a voluntary price $p_V^* = 0.10$. In this case, the consumer maximizes utility with a positive but relatively low voluntary price.

Why does a norm-sensitive consumer pay less than the equal-sharing price? Suppose we start with strict adherence to the norm of equal sharing ($h = 0$ and $p_V = p_0$). As other consumption increases and the voluntary price decreases, the norm-violation cost increases slowly at first, meaning that the marginal cost is relatively low. Starting from the equal-sharing price, the marginal cost of paying less (getting more other consumption) is less than the marginal benefit, so the consumer will pay less than the equal-sharing price. As shown by point i, utility maximization happens when the consumer pays 0.50 less than the equal-sharing price.

If consumers vary in their norm sensitivity, they will maximize utility with different voluntary prices. Figure 7.2 shows the utility-maximizing voluntary prices for three consumers. A consumer with strong norm sensitivity chooses point s, with a high voluntary price p_{VS}. For a consumer with weak norm sensitivity, the marginal-cost curve is everywhere below the marginal-benefit curve, so the consumer chooses a voluntary price of zero. A consumer with middling norm sensitivity chooses point m, with a medium voluntary price p_{VM}.

We can relate the logic of Figure 7.2 to the moral-sentiments framework of Adam Smith. A perfectly selfish individual will ignore the impartial spectator, and will instead be driven by full-fledged self-love to choose a voluntary price of

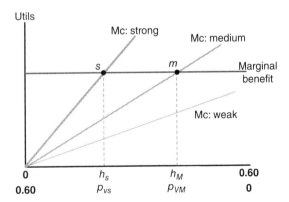

FIGURE 7.2: Varying Norm Sensitivity and Voluntary Prices

zero. At the other extreme, an individual who strictly adheres to the social norm of equal sharing will voluntarily pay the equal-sharing price p_0. In Figure 7.2, two consumers choose a positive voluntary price that falls short of the equal-sharing price. These consumers experiences some disapproval by the impartial spectator, but the benefit of stopping short of the equal-sharing price (more consumption of the other product) exceeds the cost (the disapproval of the impartial spectator).

We can use a bit of calculus and algebra to derive an expression of the utility-maximizing voluntary price. As shown in Math 7.1, the utility maximizing price is determined by the equal-sharing price p_0 and the consumer's sensitivity to the equal-sharing norm:

$$p_V^* = p_0 - \frac{1}{2 \cdot \psi}$$

Continuing our numerical example, suppose $v = 1$ and $c = 1/5$, so $p_0 = 3/5$. If $\psi = 1$, the voluntary price is 1/10:

$$p_V^* = \frac{3}{5} - \frac{1}{2} = \frac{1}{10}$$

As norm sensitivity and ψ increases, the utility-maximizing voluntary price gets closer to the equal-sharing price. For $\psi = 5$, the voluntary price is 1/2:

$$p_V^* = \frac{3}{5} - \frac{1}{10} = \frac{1}{2}$$

The utility-maximizing voluntary price also depends on production cost. Using the expression for the equal-sharing price p_0, an alternative expression for the voluntary price is

$$p_V^* = \frac{v + c}{2} - \frac{1}{2 \cdot \psi}$$

An increase in the marginal cost of production increases the equal-sharing price, increasing the voluntary price. For example, if marginal cost increases from 1/5 to 3/5, the equal-sharing price increases to $p_0 = 4/5$ (up from 3/5).

$$p_0 = \frac{v + c}{2} = \frac{1 + 3/5}{2} = \frac{4}{5}$$

For $\psi = 1$, the utility-maximizing voluntary price increase to 3/10 (up from 1/10):

$$p_V^* = \frac{1 + 3/5}{2} - \frac{1}{2 \cdot 1} = \frac{4}{5} - \frac{1}{2} = \frac{3}{10}$$

Sustainability of PWW Systems

Under what circumstances will a PWW pricing system be profitable? For profitability, the mix of customers must include some people who pay at least the marginal cost of production, and the number of profitable customers must be large enough to offset the losses associated with customers who pay less than marginal cost. One response to the problem of underpaying customers is to set a minimum price equal to marginal cost. Another approach is to track customers' voluntary prices, and give favorable treatment to profitable consumers to encourage them to buy more.

Economic Experiment: Pay What You Want versus Pay It Forward

The chapter opener introduced two programs of voluntary pricing: pay what you want (PWW) and pay it forward (PIF). The key question is which pricing program generates higher voluntary prices. The field experiments of Jung et al. (2014) show that prices are higher when people pay for others. Figure 7.3 shows some key results. For the Cartoon Art Museum in San Francisco, the average price was $2.17 for paying what you want, compared to $3.07 for paying it forward. For a coffee vendor at a farmer's market in Oakland, the average price was $1.93 for paying what you want, compared to $2.33 for paying it forward. In general, prices were significantly higher under the pay-it-forward program.

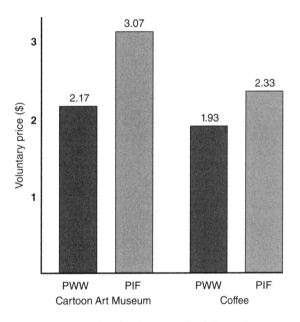

FIGURE 7.3: Pay What You Want versus Pay It Forward

Review the Concepts 7.1

1. The equal-sharing fair price makes [___] = [___]. (profit, zero; consumer surplus, profit; consumer surplus, profit/2; profit, consumer surplus/2 profit)

2. Consider a product with marginal cost = 1/12 and consumer value = 9/12. The equal-sharing price is $[___]. (1/12, 3/12, 5/12, 8/12)

3. Consider a product with marginal cost = 1/12 and consumer value = 9/12. For a consumer with norm sensitivity measured as $\psi = 3$, the equilibrium voluntary price is [___]. (0, 1/12, 3/12, 5/12)

4. Consider a product with marginal cost = 1/12 and consumer value = 9/12. For a consumer with norm sensitivity measured as $\psi = 1$, the equilibrium voluntary price is [___]. (0, 1/12, 3/12, 5/12)

5. *Comparative statics.* The relationship between the marginal cost of production and the equilibrium voluntary price is [___]. (positive, negative, zero)

6. *Comparative statics.* The relationship between the consumer value of a product and the equilibrium voluntary price is [___]. (positive, negative, zero)

7. Use Widget 7.1 (available at www.oup.com/us/osullivan1e). Suppose marginal cost is $c = 0.20$. The equilibrium voluntary price is zero for ψ less than or equal to [___]. (0.80, 1.5, 2, 3)

7.2 Public Broadcasting: Free Riders and Guilt-Tripping Pledge Drives

As another example of a good subject to voluntary pricing, consider public broadcasting, which includes public radio and public television. Many public-radio stations use on-air pledge drives to encourage listeners to become paying members. A pledge drive comes at the expense of programming, so it impose a cost on all listeners—paying members and free riders. In this part of the chapter, we explore the link between a social norm and a pledge drive.

In our simple model, a radio station uses a pledge drive to make free riders feel guilty about violating a social norm of contributing to support a public good. A study by Levati (2006) explores guilt as a motivation to contribute to support public goods. A survey of public-radio contributors by Asturias (2006) suggests that guilt plays an important role in supporting public radio. Among the reasons for contributing were (i) because I want to do my share, (ii) because I feel obligated to contribute, (iii) because it is the right thing to do, and (iv) so I do not feel guilty when I listen.

Payoffs to Members and Free Riders

Consider the payoff to a person who becomes a member of a public radio station by paying a membership fee. The payoff to a member is

$$\pi_M = v \cdot m - p$$

where v is the listening value per minute of programming, m is the minutes of programming over some time period (a year), and p is the membership price. The station has a fixed number of minutes to allocate to programming and pledge drives, and the time constraint is

$$M = m + d$$

where M is the fixed on-air time in minutes and d is the minutes allocated to pledge drives. An increase in the length of the pledge drive (an increase in d) decreases the member payoff because pledge time comes at the expense of programming. We can rewrite the member payoff function as

$$\pi_M = v \cdot (M - d) - p$$

In other words, using a pledge drive to reduce free riding is costly to all listeners, including people who pay the member price.

Figure 7.4 shows the negative relationship between the length of the pledge drive and the member payoff. As shown by the vertical intercept of the upper curve, in the absence of a pledge drive and a membership fee, the payoff is $150. A membership price of $40 means the payoff curve is $40 below the listening-benefit curve. As the length of the pledge drive increases, both the listening benefit and the payoff decrease in a linear fashion.

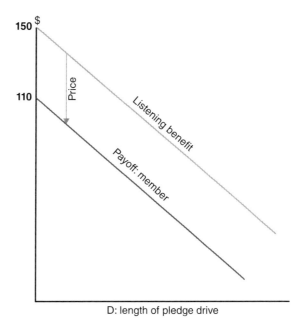

FIGURE 7.4: Payoff for Paying Member

Consider next the payoff to a free rider, someone who listens to public radio without paying the membership price. The benefit of free riding equals the listener value ($v \cdot m$) minus the member price (p) that a free rider avoids paying:

$$free - riding \ benefit = v \cdot m - p$$

For every minute of pledge time, the free rider experiences a norm-violation cost:

$$norm - violation\ cost\ per\ minute\ of\ pledge\ time = \psi \cdot (v \cdot m - p)$$

where $\psi \geq 1$ is the norm-violation parameter. The total cost of violating the social norm equals the norm-violation cost per minute multiplied by the length of the pledge drive (d).

$$norm - violation\ cost = \psi \cdot (v \cdot m - p) \cdot d$$

The purpose of an on-air pledge drive is to boost membership by making free riders feel guilty about violating the social norm. Figure 7.5 shows norm-violation cost as a function of the length of the pledge drive. As d increases, the norm-violation cost is affected by two factors.

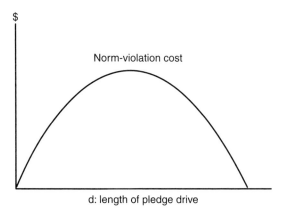

FIGURE 7.5: Norm-Violation Cost for a Free Rider

- *More reminders.* Over the course of a longer pledge drive, a free rider experiences more reminders of his or her free riding. For a given free-rider benefit ($v \cdot m - p$), norm-violation cost increases.
- *Shrinking free-rider benefit.* As programming time decreases (as pledge time increases), a free rider gets a smaller listener benefit and thus a smaller free-rider benefit. As a result, the norm-violation cost from free riding decreases.

The net effect of these two factors is the hill-shaped cost curve. For small values of d, the first effect (more reminders) dominates, and norm-violation cost increases as d increases. For large values of d, the second effect (the shrinking free-rider benefit) dominates, and norm-violation cost decreases as d increases.

Figure 7.6 shows the payoff for a free rider. The payoff equals the listening benefit minus the norm-violation cost:

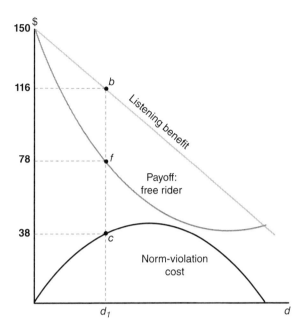

FIGURE 7.6: Payoff for Free Rider

$$\pi_F = v \cdot (M - d) - \psi \cdot (v \cdot (M - d) - p) \cdot d$$

For a pledge drive of length d_1, the listening benefit is $116 (point b) and the norm-violation cost is $38 (point c), so the payoff is $78 (point f). As the length of the pledge drive increases, the payoff curve is initially negatively sloped, and eventually is positively sloped. The shape of the payoff curve reflects the effects of an increase in the length of the pledge drive on the listening benefit and norm-violation cost.

1. Over most of the negatively sloped portion, decreasing listening benefits are reinforced by increasing norm-violation cost, so the payoff decreases.
2. Over the positively sloped portion, decreasing listening benefits are more than offset by decreasing norm-violation cost, so the payoff increases. When norm-violation cost is zero, the payoff equals the listening benefit.
3. In the intermediate range, decreasing listening benefits are partly offset by decreasing norm-violation cost, so the payoff decreases by a modest amount.

Choosing the Length of a Pledge Drive

Figure 7.7 shows the payoff curves for a listener and a free rider. In the absence of a pledge drive ($d = 0$) there is no norm-violation cost from free riding, so the payoff from free riding ($150) exceeds the payoff from membership ($110 after paying the $40 membership price). Our simple model predicts that if the radio station does not have an on-air pledge drive, the lack of guilt-tripping of free riders means that no one would pay the membership fee. In other words, no guilt tripping means free riding without any norm-violation cost.

A pledge drive that makes free riders feel guilty can make the payoff for a free rider less than the payoff for a member. In Figure 7.7, this happens for values of d from d^* to d^{**}. For values less than d^*, the relatively short pledge drive provides few guilt reminders for free riders, so the norm-violation cost is relatively low and free riding is the rational choice. For values of d greater than d^{**}, the free-rider benefit ($v \cdot m - p$) is relatively low, so norm-violation cost is relatively low and free riding is rational. For intermediate pledge drives (between d^* and d^{**}), the member payoff exceeds the free-rider payoff, so it is rational to become a member. The task for a radio station is to stage a pledge drive that is longer than d^* but shorter than d^{**}.

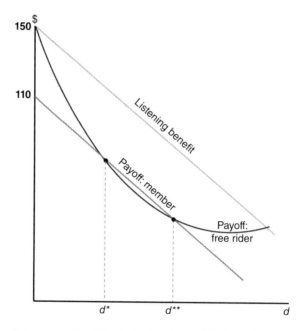

FIGURE 7.7: Payoffs for Paying Member and for Free Rider

Our discussion of pledge drives for public broadcasting illustrates a subtle cost of free riding and other norm violations. Any action taken to enforce a social norm is costly because it uses resources that could be used in other activities. So even if a policy eliminates free riding, the presence of potential norm violators still imposes cost on a society. On the flip side, when the adherence to a social norm is relatively high, the cost of enforcing the norm will be relatively low. In the case of public radio, a successful pledge drive mitigates the free-rider problem, but imposes costs on paying members as they are deprived of programming and forced to listen to repeated guilt-tripping pitches to free riders.

Review the Concepts 7.2

1. A pledge drive for public radio [___] listener benefits and [___] norm-violation costs for free riders. (does not affect, increases; decreases, increases; decreases, does not affect)

2. A public-radio station has an incentive to choose the length of a pledge drive to make [___]. (benefit of listening = zero, cost of free riding = membership fee, payoff from membership > payoff from free riding)

3. For a pledge drive that makes the payoff from membership greater than the payoff from free riding, [___] bear a cost because of the threat of free riding. (members, free riders)

4. For a free rider of public radio, the guilt-cost curve is shaped like a [___] because of the conflicting effects of more reminders of free riding and [___]. (hill, increasing listener benefits; hockey stick, decreasing listener benefits; ramp, decreasing listener benefits; hill, decreasing listener benefits)

Key Terms

equal-sharing price, p. 133   pay it forward (PIF), p. 131   pay what you want (PWW), p. 131

Takeaways

1. A consumer will pay a positive voluntary price if his or her sensitivity to a norm of sharing the gain from exchange is sufficiently strong.

2. A system of pay-what-you-want pricing will be profitable if a relatively large number of consumers are relatively sensitive to a norm of sharing the gain from exchange.

3. A pledge drive by a public-radio station (i) decreases the member payoff because it decreases program time and (ii) decreases the free-rider payoff because it decreases program time and increases the cost of violating a social norm of paying for a public good.

4. The purpose of a public-radio pledge drive is to reduce the number of free riders by making the payoff from being a paying member greater than the payoff of free riding.

Discuss the Concepts

1. *PWW and County Accents.* A candlemaker uses a PWW (pay-what-you-want) pricing system to sell hand-crafted candles from a booth at music fairs in two counties in Ireland—Kerry and Derry. Each county has a distinct accent

for the Irish language. The candlemaker is fluent in the Derry accent, and can enroll in a course to learn the Kerry accent. The cost of the course is 33 euros.

a. The benefit of learning the Kerry accent is [____].

b. Under what circumstances will learning the Kerry accent increase the candlemaker's profit?

2. *Guilt-Tripping Podcast Curves.* You produce a podcast that is available in two versions. The free version comes with frequent reminders to listeners that (i) producing a podcast is costly and (ii) responsible people pay for services they enjoy. The reminders reduce programming time by g minutes per month. The paid version costs $6 per month and is free of guilt-tripping reminders. For each listener, the value of the podcast is $20 per month.

a. Draw the payoff curves for the two types of listeners, with g on the horizontal axis and the dollar payoff on the vertical axis.

b. The intersection of the payoff curves shows [____].

Apply the Concepts

1. *PWW and Profit.* You are providing a product on a PWW platform. Your marginal cost is $c = \$0.40$ and the common material value for consumers is $v = \$1$. The social norm is equal sharing of the gain from exchange. You have two types of customers. Type S has strong sensitivity to the social norm, with $\psi = 5$. Type W has weak sensitivity to the social norm, with $\psi = 2$. You have six customers of each type. Your profit on type S customers = $[____]. Your profit on type W customers = $[____].

2. *Norms versus Marginal-Cost Pricing.* Consider two producers of a product. Firm M sets its price at its marginal cost of production. Firm N has customers that are sensitive to a social norm of sharing, with $\psi = 5$. The initial marginal cost is $c = 0.40$.

a. The price for producer M is $p_M = [____]$ and the price for producer N is $p_N = [____]$.

b. Suppose the marginal cost of production increases to $c = 0.50$. The price for producer M changes by [____]. The price for producer N changes by [____].

c. The change in the price of the product with norm-sensitive consumers changes by a [____] (larger, smaller, the same) amount because [____].

3. *Public Radio Station and Free Riders.* Consider the model of free riding for public broadcasting. Suppose the parameter values of the model are $(v, p, \psi, M) = (25, 60, 0.25, 10)$. The station's choice variable is d, the minutes devoted to a pledge drive.

a. Draw the payoff curves for a member for d in the range $(0, 8)$.

b. Draw the payoff curves for a free rider for d in the range $(0, 8)$.

c. The payoff of a contributor exceeds the payoff of a non-contributor for values of d from [___] to [___].

4. *Guilt-Tripping Podcast Numbers.* You produce a podcast that is available in two versions. The free version comes with frequent reminders to listeners that (i) producing a podcast is costly and (ii) responsible people pay for services they enjoy. The reminders reduce programming time by g minutes per month. The paid version costs $6 per month and is free of guilt-tripping reminders. Based on data from other podcasts, the listener payoff for $g = 0$ is $20, and the payoff for free riders is

$$\pi_R = 20 - \frac{d^{1/2}}{2}$$

Your task is to choose the number of guilt-tripping minutes at which the payoff to a free rider equals the payoff to a listener who pays $6 for the guilt-free paid version. The threshold value is [___]. Illustrate.

Math Solutions

Math 7.1: Utility-Maximizing Voluntary Price

In our simple framework, $h = p_0 - p_V$, so utility is

$$utility = h - \psi \cdot h^2$$

Differentiate the utility function with respect to the choice variable h:

$$\frac{du}{dh} = 1 - 2 \cdot \psi \cdot h$$

Set the derivative equal to zero and solve for the utility-maximizing other consumption:

$$h^* = \frac{1}{2 \cdot \psi}$$

Recall that $h = p_0 - p_V$, so

$$p_0 - p_V = \frac{1}{2 \cdot \psi}$$

Solve for the utility-maximizing voluntary price:

$$p_V^* = p_0 - \frac{1}{2 \cdot \psi}$$

8 Imitation and Cultural Learning

In the game of **matching pennies**, one individual plays the role of the matcher and receives a reward if the choices match (heads-heads or tails-tails). The second individual plays the role of the mismatcher and receives a reward if the choices are different (heads-tails or tails-heads). According to the rules of the game, the players reveal their choices simultaneously. But sometimes one individual accidentally reveals a choice early, so the second player gets a sneak preview of the first player's choice. Suppose you are about to play a matching-pennies game as the mismatcher. When someone offers you a blindfold to use while you play, will you use it?

In this chapter we explore the connection between imitation and **cultural learning**. As we'll see, humans are unusual among primates in our inclination to imitate the behavior of others, even when imitation is counter-productive to the task at hand. We will explore the role of **over-imitation** in cultural learning across generations. **Faithful imitation** facilitates the transmission of complex processes from one generation to the next, so the second generation can implement an inherited process without fully understanding the underlying causal relationships. One generation builds on the accomplishments of earlier generations, resulting in technological progress. To best understand cultural learning triggered by imitation, it is useful to contrast humans with chimpanzees, our closest genetic relatives. As we'll see, faithful imitation helps explain why humans are so successful in transmitting knowledge and culture across generations.

Learning Objectives: The Explainer

After mastering this chapter, you will be able to explain each of the following statements.

1. Humans tend to over-imitate: we sometimes imitate when it is counter-productive for the task at hand.

2. In a game of matching pennies, a mismatcher may do better by wearing a blindfold.

3. When the causality in a production process is obscure, faithful imitation may be best formula for success.

4. The three-stage puzzle experiment illustrates the advantages of imitation and sharing the rewards from collaboration.

Imitation and Conformity

We start our discussion of cultural learning by summarizing the results of experiments that show humans are skillful imitators, and so are chimpanzees. The difference is that humans tend to over-imitate: we tend to imitate even when imitation does not promote success in completing a task. In other words, humans sometimes imitate when it is counter-productive. In contrast, chimpanzees are more selective in their imitation and less inclined to over-imitate. As we'll see, over-imitation can promote social learning.

Over-Imitation by Humans

Scientists use simple experiments to show that young humans over-imitate adults (Lyons, Young, and Keil 2007). In a classic experiment, an adult shows a youngster (three to five years old) how to extract a toy turtle from a transparent box. The turtle is in the lower compartment of the box, and the upper compartment is empty. The adult takes four steps to remove the turtle. The first two steps are irrelevant—they are unnecessary to remove the turtle.

1. Use a wand to remove a red bolt that plays no role in opening the box.
2. Tap the wand on the floor of the empty upper compartment.
3. Pull out a round plug in the door to create an opening into the lower compartment.
4. Use the wand to remove the turtle.

After demonstrating the four steps, the experimenter puts the turtle back into the box. The experimenter then leaves the room after telling the child, "If you want to, you can get the turtle while I'm gone. You can get it out however you want." Left on their own to extract the turtle, 93 percent of children executed all four steps, including the two irrelevant steps. This over-imitation occurred despite the fact that the children received training beforehand on relevant and irrelevant steps. For example, in an illustration with a toy dinosaur in a jar, the experimenter tapped the side of the jar with a feather and then unscrewed the lid to remove the dinosaur. The experimenter discussed the "silly" feather tapping, helping the child distinguish between relevant and irrelevant steps.

What happens if the experimenter alerts the child about possible irrelevant steps? In a second experiment, the experimenter warns the child, "I want to you watch really carefully, because when I open this box, I might do something that's silly and extra, just like the feather." As shown in Figure 8.1, over-imitation decreased by a modest amount (from 93 percent to 80 percent) but roughly four-fifths of youngsters continued to execute all four steps, including the two

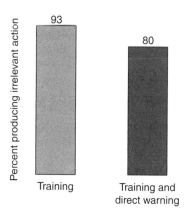

FIGURE 8.1: Over-Imitation by Young Humans

irrelevant steps. The authors note, "Children are largely unable to circumvent over-imitation, even when explicitly instructed to do so, because the adults' irrelevant actions have already been absorbed into their representation of the puzzle object's causal structure." (Lyons, Young, and Keil 2007, 19755).

Wait a minute! Youngsters over-imitate, but surely everyone outgrows over-imitation. In a series of experiments by Nicola McGuigan, Janet Makinson, and Andrew Whiten (2011), over-imitation actually increases with age. The experimenters used a transparent box with a reward in a lower compartment and an empty upper compartment. A demonstrator showed how to retrieve the reward and included irrelevant steps involving the empty top compartment. The fraction of subjects who executed irrelevant steps was 15 percent for three-year-olds, 32 percent for five-year-olds, and 56 percent for adults. In the case of the punishment of norm violators, we saw in an earlier chapter that imitation increases with age (Salali, Juda, and Henrich 2015).

Over-Imitation: Humans versus Chimpanzees

What about chimpanzees? In a similar puzzle-box experiment, experimenters showed chimpanzees how to extract a reward from a box and included irrelevant actions (Horner and Whiten 2005). In the first stage, the experimenters used an opaque box, so the chimpanzees could not see that the reward was in the lower compartment. When the demonstrator took the irrelevant step of probing the upper compartment, the chimpanzees had no reason to suspect that this step was irrelevant. When the chimpanzees got their turn to get the reward, they repeated all the steps, including the irrelevant steps involving the upper compartment.

The test for over-imitation came in stage two, when the experimenters replaced the opaque box with a clear box. In this case, the chimpanzees could clearly see that the actions with the upper compartment were irrelevant. Given another chance to get the rewards, most of the chimpanzees skipped the irrelevant steps. In short, most chimpanzees did not over-imitate, but instead executed

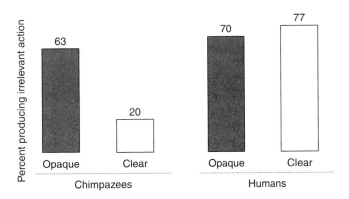

FIGURE 8.2: Over-Imitation in Chimpanzees and Humans

only the steps required to retrieve the reward. As shown in Figure 8.2, the frequency of executing irrelevant steps decreased from roughly 63 percent with the opaque box to 20 percent with the clear box.

How did young humans do with the opaque-clear box experiment? As in other experiments, the youngsters over-imitated. Their strategies to retrieve the reward didn't change much when the opaque box was replaced by the clear box. In contrast with the chimpanzees, the youngsters executed steps that were clearly irrelevant. As shown in Figure 8.2, the median frequency of executing the irrelevant steps was roughly 70 percent with the opaque box compared to roughly 77 percent with the clear box. The difference was not statistically significant.

Conformity and Matching Pennies

Over-imitation is an example of the human tendency to conform to choices of others in a group. Conformity in humans starts at an early age. In one experiment (Haun, Rekers, and Tomasello 2014), an apparatus has three boxes (yellow, red, blue), with a hole on the top of each box. For one of the three boxes, dropping a ball through the hole generates a reward (chocolate for children; peanuts for chimpanzees). A subject learns from experience which of the boxes generate the reward, for example the blue box. Then the subject observes three demonstrators (other children or other chimpanzees) place their balls in a different box (the yellow box) and get a reward. What happens on the next turn?

1. *Human children.* On next turns, roughly two-thirds of children switched to the yellow box. Most children switched from the box that always worked for them (blue box) to a box chosen by someone else (yellow box). The number of switchers was greater when the other children (yellow-box children) were watching.
2. *Chimpanzees.* On next turns, only 1 in 12 chimpanzees switched to the yellow box. Most chimpanzees continued the action that worked for them, rather than switching to an action chosen by others.

These experiments suggest strong conformity among children and little conformity among chimpanzees.

As another example of conformity, consider the game of matching pennies. One player is the *matcher* and receives a reward if the choices match (heads-heads or tails-tails). The other player is a *mismatcher* and receives a reward if the choices are different (heads-tails or tails-heads). The rules of the game specify that the choices of the two players are to be revealed simultaneously. But sometimes one player accidentally reveals a choice early, so the second player gets a sneak preview of the first player's choice. What happens next?

Experiments with matching pennies show that some sneak previews trigger conformity by the second player (Belot, Crawford, and Heyes 2013). A player who gets a sneak preview of the other player's choice is more likely to make the same choice, so the frequency of heads-heads and tails-tails increases. This is good news for the matcher, but bad news for the mismatcher.

1. *Matcher: Good news.* When a matcher sees the other person's choice, the matcher wins either by making the perfectly rational choice (match to win) or by acting instinctively (match to conform).
2. *Mismatcher: Perhaps bad news.* When a mismatcher sees the other person's choice, the perfectly rational choice is to make the opposite choice and thus mismatch for a win. But if a mismatcher acts on instinctive conformity, the mismatcher will match the other player's choice and lose.

In other words, a sneak preview is beneficial for a player who acts rationally but harmful for a mismatcher whose instinctive conformity is strong enough to overcome rational choice.

Suppose you are ready to play matching pennies as a mismatcher. If someone hands you a blindfold, will you use it while you play the game? Under the assumption that people are perfectly rational, more information is clearly better. So under the assumption of perfect rationality, blinding yourself to some information would be irrational. But suppose you experience instinctive conformity: if you see a heads you tend to match by choosing heads. If the tendency is strong enough to offset your rational choices (see a heads and mismatch by choosing tails), you'll be better off with the blindfold. If you can't avoid conforming, it's best to strap on the blindfold and take your chances with less information.

A recent study of the rock-paper-scissors game demonstrate the power of imitation (Cook et al. 2012). In each round of the game, each player chooses one of the three options. In the absence of imitation, we'd expect that close to one-third of the plays will generate a draw (a match: rock-rock or paper-paper or scissors-scissors). That's what happens when both players are blindfolded. But when only one player is blindfolded, the frequency of draws increases to roughly 36.4 percent, suggesting that the sighted player sometimes instinctively matches the blindfolded player's choice. In the experiment, blindfolded players won 32.4 percent of the plays, while a sighted player won only 31.3 percent of the plays. Players with less information won more money.

Review the Concepts 8.1

1. Compared to chimpanzees, young humans over-imitate [___]. (less frequently, with roughly the same frequency, more frequently)

2. Compared to chimpanzees, young humans conform [___]. (less frequently, with about the same frequency, more frequently)

3. Two individuals are ready to play a game of matching pennies. A blindfold might be beneficial for [___]. (the matcher, the mismatcher, neither player)

4. In the game rock-paper-scissors, the frequencies of ties is [___] the number that would occur by chance. (greater than, less than, roughly equal to)

8.2   Faithful Imitation and Cultural Learning

We've seen that humans over-imitate the actions of others and have a strong inclination to conform to others' behavior. Over-imitation can be problematic because there is an opportunity cost of time spent executing irrelevant steps in a completing a particular task. Conformity can be problematic because being guided by others' choices may lead to misguided choices. In this part of the chapter, we explore some positive aspects of imitation. As we'll see, what appears to be misguided behavior can promote cultural learning across generations.

It will be useful to introduce a bit of new language concerning imitation. As we've seen, over-imitation is defined as the execution of clearly irrelevant steps in a production process. As a slight variation, let's define faithful imitation as imitating a trusted authority in executing all the steps in a production process. A faithful imitator has faith in a trusted authority who demonstrates the steps, and the imitator executes each step without questioning its relevance. This may be a sensible approach for a production process where the causal relationships between actions and consequences are obscure. When it's impossible for an individual to distinguish between relevant and irrelevant steps, the best strategy may be to imitate an individual with a record of success.

Manioc and Obscure Production Processes

To illustrate the benefits of faithful imitation, consider the case of manioc (also known as casava) (Henrich 2016). Manioc thrives in drought-prone tropical environments and can support high population densities. Some bitter varieties of manioc are rich in cyanide chemicals that provide protection against insects and other pests. From the perspective of a manioc plant, humans are on the list of "other pests." So, unfortunately for humans, eating raw manioc causes acute and chronic cyanide poisoning, with symptoms such as neurological problems, paralysis, and immune suppression. For many generations, Indigenous groups in South America have used a multi-step, multi-day process to reduce the cyanide content of manioc, resulting in nutritious edibles. The tuber is scraped, then grated, and then washed to separate the fiber, starch, and liquid. Then the liquid is boiled while the fiber and starch are set aside for two days. After two days, the solids are baked and then eaten.

This multi-step detoxification process developed over many generations without any assistance from biochemists. The development of the process resulted from many trials and errors, and it is unlikely that any of the people who developed the process understood the chemistry behind the many steps. What mattered is that the process worked: people who ate the processed manioc did not suffer from cyanide poisoning. Once the successful process was in place, it was sensible for youngsters to faithfully imitate the experienced processors by strictly following all the steps. The process was faithfully imitated in one generation after another, even though no one understood the chemistry. Although a shortcut might be tempting ("Do we really have to wait two days?"), it could also be deadly.

The benefit of faithful imitation is illustrated by what happened when the cultivation of manioc was extended from South America to Africa. In South America, many generations of Indigenous people faithfully executed the many complex steps required for detoxification, so cyanide poisoning was rare. When the Portuguese transported manioc to Africa in the early 1600s, they did not transplant the intricate detoxification methods. Although the manioc growers in Africa may have received a set of instructions, they did not have the opportunity to observe the Indigenous people of South America as they performed the complex process of transforming toxic tubers into healthy edibles. In other words, the African farmers did not have an opportunity for faithful imitation, so they did not follow all the intricate steps required to produce healthy food. Manioc thrived in the hospitable tropical environment in Africa and so did cyanide poisoning.

The general lesson is that when the causality in a production process is obscure, faithful imitation may be the best formula for success. In casual terms, "If it isn't broken, don't try to fix it." Over time, a production process can be refined as the benefits of trial and error accumulate. Along the way, increasing complexity in the production cost is likely to make the connection between cause and effect more obscure. A faithful imitator taps into the knowledge accumulated over many generation of experimenters who used trial and error to develop complex processes. Faithful imitation means that a producer doesn't need to know how a complex production process works, but just needs to know that it works. Henrich (2016, 112) summarizes the notion of social learning.

> . . . as a cultural species, we have an instinct to faithfully copy complex procedures, practices, beliefs, and motivation, including steps that may appear causally irrelevant, because cultural evolution has proved itself capable of constructing intricate and subtle cultural packages that are far better than we could individually construct in a lifetime. Often people don't even know what their practices are doing, or that they are doing anything.

Naturally, it is sometimes useful to deviate from faithful imitation to try alternative processes. An innovation that improves a production process can result in a different set of steps for faithful imitation. The faithful imitators can benefit from the contribution of innovators without understanding how a particular innovation works, and each faithful imitator "pays it forward" by passing on the accumulated knowledge to the next generation. Social learning results from faithful imitation blended with occasional innovation.

Social Learning: Humans versus Chimpanzees

An elegant experiment illustrates social learning in humans and contrasts humans and chimpanzees in terms of imitation and learning (Dean et al. 2012). In the experiment, youngsters (age three to four years) and chimpanzees had the opportunity to earn rewards by solving a three-stage puzzle. The three stages are (i) slide a door, (ii) push a button, and (iii) rotate a dial. At each stage, an actor (chimpanzee or youngster) who took the correct action received a reward: a chimpanzee got food and a youngster got a sticker. The reward increased from one stage to the next, so each actor had an incentive to fully solve the puzzle by completing all three stages. Experimenters formed groups of five subjects, and members of a group could work together to solve the puzzle.

How would an independent decision-maker fare in solving the three-stage puzzle? Suppose that for each stage of the puzzle, an individual's probability of success is one-third. For example, there is a one in three chance that an individual will figure out how to slide the door to succeed in stage one. For an individual to fully solve the puzzle (succeed in all three stages), the probability of success is $1/27 = (1/3)^3$. An individual who works independently has a relatively low probability of success.

In the experiment, only 1 of 33 chimpanzees fully solved the puzzle. As expected, chimpanzees worked independently for the most part, and didn't do much imitation. Although many chimpanzees observed other chimpanzees succeed on the first stage, the typical chimpanzee did not imitate successful chimpanzees. As a result, the chimpanzees were unable to build on the success of others and the independent approach generated a relatively low success rate. To further test for imitation, the experimenter showed the chimpanzees the correct sequence of actions to solve the puzzle. The demonstration did not affect the performance of the chimpanzees. In general, the lack of imitation by the chimpanzee means that success was a matter of luck, and only 1 chimpanzee in 33 got lucky.

Consider the implications of faithful imitation for solving the three-stage puzzle. To illustrate, consider a group of five youngsters (A, B, C, D, E), and imagine that the probability that an individual solves a stage of the puzzle is 1/3. Suppose A, B, and C try to solve stage one and A succeeds. Then B, C, and D imitate A for stage one and try to solve stage two. If B succeeds on stage two, that allows imitation of B by C, D, and E for stages one and two, allowing them to try to solve stage three. If C succeeds on stage three, the group now has an algorithm for fully solving the puzzle: imitate A for stage one, B for stage two, and C for stage three. With perfect imitation, everyone in the group can fully solve the puzzle and get all the rewards.

In the experiment, young humans were more successful than the chimpanzees. The youngsters imitated others who solved the early stages of the puzzle, so they built on each others' success. Compared to the chimpanzees, youngsters imitated each other three times as frequently. The overall success rate for youngsters (solving all three stages) was 15/36, compared to only 1/33 for the chimpanzees. For five of the eight groups, at least two of five youngsters fully solved the puzzle. This greater success occurred despite the fact that youngsters worked on the puzzle for only 2.5 hours, compared to 30 hours for the chimpanzees.

The experiment also highlights the role of social norms in promoting cooperative success. Youngsters shared the rewards of collaboration. The late-stage puzzle solvers received larger rewards, and some youngsters used voluntary transfers to early-stage solvers to compensate them for paving the way to the large rewards. In our example, youngster C fully solved the puzzle after imitating youngster A for stage one and youngster B for stage two. Based on the results of the experiment, we would predict youngster C to voluntarily transfer some of his or her larger reward to A and B. The results of the experiment indicated this sort of redistribution of rewards.

1. Roughly 47 percent of youngsters voluntarily transferred retrieved rewards to others, with a total of 215 voluntary transfers.
2. The frequency of transfers was higher among youngsters who reached later stages of the puzzle.
3. For chimpanzees, there were no voluntary transfers.

The multi-stage puzzle experiment reveals two fundamental differences between humans and chimpanzees, our closest genetic relative. Humans are more inclined to imitate others and more inclined to share the rewards of collaboration. This combination of traits promotes cultural learning and facilitates the development of progressively more complex—and obscure—production techniques across generations.

Review the Concepts 8.2

1. Faithful imitation promotes cultural learning when a production process involves [___]. (complexity, simplicity, obscure causality)

2. The problem with manioc as a source of nutrition is that the plant's defense against insects also works against [___]. (unsuspecting humans, humans who take processing shortcuts, humans who faithfully imitate ancestral processing practices)

3. The multi-stage puzzle experiment shows that compared to chimpanzees, humans are [___] inclined to imitate others and [___] inclined to share the rewards of collaboration. (less, more; more, less; less, less; more, more)

Key Terms

cultural learning, p. 146

faithful imitation, p. 146

matching pennies, p. 146

over-imitation, p. 146

Takeaways

1. Humans engage in over-imitation, imitating irrelevant steps in a task.

2. Chimpanzees are less inclined than humans to over-imitate.

3. Evidence for human over-imitation comes from the games of matching pennies and rock-paper-scissors.

4. Over-imitation promotes cultural learning, defined as the transmission of knowledge from one generation to the next.

5. When the causality in a production process is obscure, faithful imitation may promote success.

6. Young humans solve multi-stage puzzles by (i) imitating success of others and (ii) rewarding those who contribute to cumulative learning.

Discuss the Concepts

1. *WTP for Blindfold.* You are about to play 200 rounds of rock-paper-scissors, and will gain $30 for each win. There is a single blindfold available, and will go to the highest bidder. You are willing to pay up to $[___] for the blindfold.

2. *Chimp versus Young Human.* In a puzzle-box experiment, the reward for a young human is a gummie bear and the reward for a chimpanzee is a grape. Suppose experimenters have several puzzle boxes, each with a different set of steps for retrieving the reward. The boxes are clear, and as the experimenters demonstrate the retrieval steps, they include a few irrelevant steps. Once a subject retrieves a reward on a particular puzzle, the experimenter moves on to the next puzzle. Each subject is given three minutes to retrieve rewards for the sequence of puzzles.

   a. On average, we expect the number of gummie bears retrieved to be [___] (>, <, =) the number of grapes retrieved.

   b. To reverse the outcome of the experiment, we would change the experiment by [___].

Apply the Concepts

1. *WTP for Blindfold.* You are about to play 100 rounds of the matching-pennies game as a mismatcher against a matcher who prematurely reveals his or her choice on 24 percent of rounds. In each round, the winner gets a prize of $1 from a third party.

   a. Suppose your instinctive conformity is $c = 2/3$. In other words, your instincts to conform overcome your rational thought on two of three premature reveals. You are willing to pay $[___] for a blindfold to use while playing.

   b. To be indifferent about wearing a blindfold (WTP = 0), the frequency of instinctive conformity is $c^* = [___]$.

2. *Imitation in Rock-Paper-Scissors.* Suppose you are observing a series of 150 rock-paper-scissors contests between two individuals. For every draw (rock-rock, paper-paper, scissors-scissors), you will gain $2, and for each mixed outcome, you will lose $1. You have two blindfolds, and you can use one or both of them on the players.

   a. If both players use blindfolds, your expected payoff from the 120 contests is [___].

   b. If only one player uses a blindfold, your expected payoff from the 120 contests is [___].

3. *Rock-Paper-Scissors for Millions.* In 2005, a game of rock-paper-scissors between two auction houses (Christie's and Sotheby's) determined which house had the rights to auction an art collection worth roughly $20 million. At stake was roughly $2 million in auction fees for the winner. Rather than the conventional hand signals, the contestants wrote their plays on paper. This approach reduced the probability of [___]. Christie's winning play was based on the advice of 11-year-old twins: [___] (rock, paper, scissors) defeated [___].

4. *Five-Stage Puzzle.* Consider a five-stage puzzle in which the probability that any individual (human or chimpanzee) will solve a stage is one in five. The active group (working on the task) is five individuals, and once an individual solves a stage of the puzzle, he or she no longer participates in the task. (The individual is busy eating a reward.)

   a. Consider a team of human youngsters. To ensure that a single individual will fully solve the puzzle (all five stages), the minimum team size is $s = [___]$ youngsters.

   b. The probability that a chimpanzee fully solves the puzzle is $p = [___]$.

Discounting and Present Bias 9

Consider an economic experiment designed to determine the degree of patience of mothers and their young children. The researcher asked the mothers, "Would you prefer $100 now, or $101 in one year?" If the answer was $100 now, the researcher increased the proposed later payment, dollar by dollar (to $102, $103, $104, and so on), until the mother switched to preferring the larger later payment (LL) to the smaller sooner payment (SS). The most patient mothers switched early and accepted a relatively small LL, for example $110. The least patient mothers held out longer and required a relatively large LL, for example $200. For the kids, the researcher gave each child one pack of gummy bears, and promised two packs if the child waited roughly 50 minutes before eating any gummy bears. This experiment generates three questions.

1. If you were asked the SS-LL question, at what point would you switch? At what later payment would you be indifferent between $100 now and the later payment?
2. What's your guess about the fraction of children who waited the 50 minutes to double the gummy-bear reward?
3. Would you expect a correlation—positive or negative—between the patience of mothers and their children?

Later in the chapter, you can determine whether you are more or less patient than the average mother in the experiment. And you can check your answers to the gummy-bear questions.

This is the first of four chapters on intertemporal choice, defined as decisions about how to allocate resources across time. In this chapter we introduce a framework for intertemporal choice that will be useful as we explore three sorts of intertemporal choices.

1. *Product choice*. A person can consume a product now, and incur the cost later. Our discussion highlights regrets associated with instant gratification.
2. *When to incur a cost*. A person can bear a cost now, or wait to incur it later. Our discussion highlights regrets associated with procrastination.

3. *When to spend wealth.* A person decides how much to spend now, and how much to save for later. Our discussion highlights regrets associated with meager savings.

For each of these choices, a person must compare a future value (benefit or cost) to a current value. This comparison requires a system to translate a future value into an equivalent current value. This chapter is about discounting, defined as the translation of a future value into a current value.

Learning Objectives: The Explainer

After mastering this chapter, you will be able to explain each of the following statements.

1. Present bias causes plan switching: an individual's plan changes when the future becomes the present.

2. Present bias causes regret.

3. Present bias favors products with relatively high future cost.

4. Present bias causes procrastination for tasks with rising costs.

5. Present bias increases present consumption at the expense of future consumption.

9.1 Conventional Discounting and Present Bias

Behavioral economics uses utility functions to translate future outcomes into current values. The key feature of the most commonly used utility function is **present bias**—a bias in favor of present consequences and thus a bias against future consequences. In making intertemporal choices, a person subject to present bias underplays future benefits or costs. The underplaying of future consequences causes choices that a person is likely to regret.

The Quasi-Hyperbolic Discount Function

A discount function translates a future payment or consumption bundle into its current value. Consider a product that is to be consumed t years later. For example $c_2 =$ 100 apples means that a consumer will consume 100 apples in 2 years. The current value of future consumption depends on how far into the future the consumption is to occur. The quasi-hyperbolic utility function was developed by Phelps and Pollak (1968) and later revived and applied by Laibson (1998). The current value of a consumption amount c_i depends on the time of consumption in years (t).

$$U(c_i) = u(c_i) \quad for \quad t = 0$$

$$U(c_i) = \beta \cdot \delta^t \cdot u(c_i) \quad for \quad t \geq 1$$

In this utility function, $u(c_i)$ is the utility experienced during the actual consumption of the product at time t, $\delta \leq 1$ is the **conventional discounting** factor, and $\beta \leq 1$ distinguishes between now ($t = 0$) and the future ($t \geq 1$). Naturally, for product consumed now ($t = 0$), the current utility is simply the utility of consuming the product. For a product consumed later ($t \geq 1$), the current value is discounted to translate a future benefit into an equivalent current benefit.

Consider δ, the conventional discounting parameter. Another label for conventional discounting is "exponential discounting." If $\delta = 0.90$, then one apple to be received one period later (period $t + 1$) generates the same utility as 0.90 apples in period t. More distant consumption is discounted more heavily: one apple consumed two years later is equivalent to $0.81 = 0.90 \cdot 0.90$ apples today. The same discount factor δ applies to any two successive time periods. Table 9.1 shows an example of discounting with the simplest utility function, $u(c) = c$: one apple generates one util of utility. In the δ discounting row, the table shows the current value of 100 apples received at various times: now ($t = 0$), in one year ($t = 1$), in two years ($t = 2$), and in three years ($t = 3$). The current value of the future amount decreases from 100, to 90 for $t = 1$, to 81 for $t = 2$, and to 72.90 for $t = 3$.

TABLE 9.1   **Discounting and Present Bias**

	Current value of 100 apples received at ...			
	t = 0	t = 1	t = 2	t = 3
δ discounting alone ($\delta = 0.90$)	100	90	81	72.90
β discounting alone ($\beta = 1/2$)	100	50	50	50
δ and β discounting	100	45	40.50	36.45

Consider next the role of the present-bias parameter β, which distinguishes between now ($t = 0$) and later ($t \geq 1$). The discounting represented by β applies equally to all future time periods: an apple received in one year is treated the same as an apple in 2 years, 10 years, or even 100 years. In the β discounting row in Table 9.1 , the value of the present-bias parameter is $\beta=1/2$. The current value of 100 apples received now is 100, and the current value of 100 apples received in one year is 50. As t increases beyond $t = 1$, the current value doesn't change from 50 because present bias doesn't distinguish between different versions of "later." Present bias with $\beta =1/2$ means that the current value of 100 apples received in the future is 50 apples, regardless how far in the future the apples will be received. As we'll see in this and later chapters, present bias helps solve many puzzles in human behavior.

The last row in Table 9.1 combines conventional discounting ($\delta < 1$) and present bias ($\beta < 1$). For each time period t, we multiply the number for conventional discounting (100, 90, 81, 72.90) by $\beta < 1$. In our example, $\beta = 1/2$, so each number in the last row (for $t \geq 1$) is half the number in the first row. In other words, β applies equally to all future periods, but does not apply to the present. The tag "present bias" is apt because β discounting separates time into just two periods—now and later—and everything that happens later is discounted (downplayed) by a factor β < 1.

The sliders control the value of the conventional discount parameter δ and the value of the present-bias parameter β. Dragging the sliders illustrates 3 lessons.

1. A decrease in δ means that future bundles are more heavily discounted, so the current value of a future bundle decreases and both curves shift downward. For example, if δ decreases to 0.84 and β = 1/2, the current value for a bundle received in five years is $42 under conventional discounting (down from 59), and $21 when we incorporate present bias (down from $29.50).
2. For δ = 1, there is no conventional discounting, so the current value of a bundle does not decrease as the bundle becomes more distant. Both curves are horizontal, and the present-bias curve is horizontal at β · 100.
3. A decrease in β strengthens present bias, so the current value of any future bundle decreases. As a result, the gap between the two curves widens. For example, if β decreases to 0.40 (and δ = 0.90), the current value of a bundle received in five years is $23.6 (down from $29.5).

Present Bias and Doubling Your Apples

Nobel Laureate Richard Thaler provides a compelling example of time preferences that are consistent with β < 1. The results of behavioral experiments suggest that the typical person would prefer one apple today to two apples tomorrow, but would prefer two apples in 51 days to one apple in 50 days. In other words, the typical person is not patient enough to wait until tomorrow (one additional day) to get an extra apple. But looking to the future (50 days from now), the typical person says that he or she will be patient enough to wait an additional day to get an extra apple.

We can illustrate this classic example with some numbers. Suppose the utility of an apple when it is consumed is 1 util. Present bias is represented by β = 2/5. Over a one-day interval, conventional discounting is represented by δ = 0.99, meaning that delaying the consumption of an apple by one day decreases its value by one percent. The first scenario is one apple today or two apples tomorrow. Naturally, the value of one apple today is one apple:

$$Apple\ today : utility = 1\,util$$

The current value of two apples received tomorrow is lower, at 0.792 util:

$$2\,apples\ tomorrow : utility = 2 \cdot \beta \cdot \delta = 2 \cdot \frac{2}{5} \cdot 0.99 = 0.792\,util$$

The value of two apples tomorrow is less than the value of one apple today, so the person is not willing to wait a day to double the apples. Because of present bias (β = 2/5) and a bit of conventional discounting (δ = 0.99), the value of each apple tomorrow is less than 40 percent of an apple today, and the number of apples only doubles.

Things are different for the second scenario—one apple on day 50 or two apples on day 51. The difference is that both day 50 and day 51 are in the future, so present bias applies to both days. Today (day 1), the current value of one apple to be received in 50 days is 0.242 util:

$$apple\ in\ 50\ days : utility = \beta \cdot \delta^{50} = \frac{2}{5} \cdot 0.99^{50} = 0.242\ util$$

Today (day 1), the current value of two apples to be received on day 51 is almost twice as large, at 0.479 util:

$$2\ apples\ in\ 51\ days : utility = 2 \cdot \beta \cdot \delta^{51} = 2 \cdot \frac{2}{5} \cdot 0.99^{51} = 0.479\ util$$

Looking ahead 50 days, a person believes that he or she will be willing to wait a day to double the apples. In general, when considering two future successive time periods (day 50 and day 51), a person is likely to believe that he or she will be willing to wait a day to double the payment.

So what happens when day 50 arrives and is now the present? Will the person grab one apple on day 50, or wait to get two apples on day 51? Present bias no longer applies to the single apple on day 50, but present bias continues for the pair of apples on day 51. The value of the single apple today (on the now-present day 50) is one util, compared to a current value of 0.792 util for two apples tomorrow (the still-future day 51). Therefore, the person will act on day 50 just as he or she acted on day 1: grab a single apple on day 50 rather than waiting one day to double the apples.

The apple example illustrates **time inconsistency**, a key implication of present bias. A person who experiences time inconsistency makes an intertemporal plan, and then later changes the plan. In the apple example, the person makes a plan on day 1 to get two apples on day 51 rather than grabbing a single apple on day 50. But when day 50 arrives and loses its present-bias feature, the person changes the plan and grabs the single apple rather than waiting a day to double the apples.

Time Inconsistency

We can use a simple example to illustrate the time inconsistency generated by present bias. Consider a person who must decides when to acquire a basket of apples, when the number of apples in the basket increases over time. The number apples increases from four in January, to six in February, to 10 in March. To simplify matters, suppose there is no conventional discounting ($\delta = 0$), but present bias represented by $\beta = 1/2$. Table 9.2 shows the decision-making process, with three vantage points.

- *January vantage point.* Wait until March. The utility of 10 apples in March is 5 utils (10/2), which exceeds the utility of the four apples in January (4 utils) and the utility of six apples in February (3 utils = 6/2). The highest utility is achieved by waiting until March.

TABLE 9.2 Present Bias and Time Inconsistency

Vantage point	January benefit	February benefit	March benefit
January	4	$3 = 6 \cdot (1/2)$	$5 = 10 \cdot (1/2)$
February	—	6	$5 = 10 \cdot (1/2)$
March	—	—	10

- *February vantage point.* Immediate gratification. The utility of the 10 apples in March is still 5 utils, but the six apples in February apples are now in the present, so the utility is 6 utils (up from 3 utils). Viewed in the present, the six-apple bundle looks like the best choice. So instead of waiting for 10 apples in March, the present-biased person chooses immediate gratification in February, resulting in six apples.
- *March vantage point.* Get 10 apples. If the person had adopted the original plan to wait until March, the benefit would have been 10 apples.

In this example, time inconsistency involves a change in the consumption plan. In January, the utility-maximizing plan is for 10 apples in March. But one month later, the person changes the plan in favor of instant gratification.

Time inconsistency occurs because a person's valuation of a consumption bundle changes abruptly when the bundle switches from a future bundle to a present bundle. Specifically, the switch increases utility of the newly present bundle by a factor $(1/\beta)$. In Table 9.2 with $\beta=1/2$, the utility value of the six-apple February bundle doubles from 3 utils from the January vantage point to 6 utils in February. Over the same period, the value of the March bundle doesn't change because it is still in the future. When the February bundle is promoted from future to present status, it loses the downplaying ($\beta < 1$) associated with present bias. This change in status—from future to present—causes inconsistent choices over time.

Time Inconsistency and the Relative Values of Bundles

Present bias causes time inconsistency because the relative values of bundles change over time. Specifically, the relative value of bundles in two successive periods changes when the earlier bundle switches from its status as a future bundle to become the present bundle. Consider the value of the February bundle relative to the value of the March bundle. In January, when both bundles are in the future and downplayed by present bias, the relative value of the February bundle is 3/5:

$$January\ decision: \frac{benefit\ in\ February}{benefit\ in\ March} = \frac{3}{5}$$

When February becomes the present, the February bundle is promoted to present status and loses its β weighting. In contrast, the March bundle is still in the future, so it retains its β weighting. So in February, the relative value of the February bundle doubles to 6/5:

$$February\ decision : \frac{benefit\ in\ February}{benefit\ in\ March} = \frac{6}{5}$$

Because present bias downplays all future events equally (all downplayed by β), the promotion of an event to present status increases its value relative to all future events.

It is worth noting the difference between present bias and conventional discounting. A person with a discount factor δ < 1 has a preference for current consumption over future consumption. For example, if δ = 0.90, one unit of consumption in $t + 1$ is equivalent to 0.90 units of consumption in period t, and this tradeoff occurs for all t and $t + 1$. In other words, the same 90 percent discount factor applies in evaluating periods 0 and 1, or periods 10 and 11, or periods 100 and 101. We can extend the example shown in Table 9.2 to incorporate conventional discounting. Suppose δ = 0.90 and β = 1 (no present bias). In January, when both future bundles are discounted, the relative value of the February bundle is 2/3:

$$January\ decision : \frac{benefit\ in\ February}{benefit\ in\ March} = \frac{0.90 \cdot 6}{0.81 \cdot 10} = \frac{5.40}{8.10} = \frac{2}{3}$$

In February, the February bundle is promoted to present status and loses its δ discounting. In addition, the March bundle is one month closer, so its δ discounting decreases by one period too. As a result, the relative value of the February bundle remains at 2/3:

$$February\ decision : \frac{benefit\ in\ February}{benefit\ in\ March} = \frac{1 \cdot 6}{0.90 \cdot 10} = \frac{6}{9} = \frac{2}{3}$$

Under conventional discounting, the passage of time changes the discounted values of the newly present bundle and all future bundles, so the relative value of a bundle does not change over time. This contrasts with the case of present bias, under which the passage of time eliminates the downplaying of the now-present bundle, which changes the relative value of a bundle over time.

Present Bias and Regret

Another consequence of present bias is regret. For every intertemporal decision, the future eventually becomes the present. When a person looks back on past choices, he or she may regret downplaying future consequences, which are now actual consequences and not subject to present bias. In the example in Table 9.2, the person chooses six apples in February rather than waiting for 10 apples in March. From the February vantage point, the current value of the 10 apples in March is only 5 utils, compared to 6 utils for the February apples. But when March becomes the present, the person might think, "If I had waited, I could have gotten 10 apples instead of six apples. I should have waited."

As we'll see in other intertemporal decisions, regret is a common consequence of present bias. A person subject to present bias often chooses immediate gratification when future gratification would be more gratifying. A person who looks back when the future becomes the present may regret his or her past immediate gratification.

Review the Concepts 9.1

1. Suppose the value of the conventional discount parameter is $\delta = 0.92$ and the value of the present-bias parameter is $\beta = 0.50$. The current value of 100 units of consumption to be received in one year is [___] units. (46, 50, 92, 100)

2. Suppose the value of the conventional discount parameter is $\delta = 0.90$ and the value of the present-bias parameter is $\beta = 1/3$. The current value of 100 units of consumption to be received in two years is [___] units. (27, 30, 50, 81)

3. Present bias causes time inconsistency because plans may change when the [___] becomes the [___]. (past, present; present, future; future, present)

4. The example in Table 9.2 illustrates time inconsistency because a plan developed in [___] to wait until [___] is abandoned in [___]. (January, February, February; January, March, February; February, March, March)

5. Present bias causes time inconsistency because the [___] of bundles in two successive periods changes over time. (numeric value, absolute value, relative value)

6. Use Widget 9.1 (available at www.oup.com/us/osullivanle). As the strength of present bias increases, β [___] and the gap between the two curves [___]. (decreases, narrows; decreases, expands; increases, narrows; decreases, narrows)

7. Use Widget 9.1 (available at www.oup.com/us/osullivanle). As the strength of conventional discounting increases, δ [___] and the curves become [___]. (decreases, flatter; increases, steeper; increases, flatter; decreases, steeper)

9.2 Estimates of Discounting Parameters

Economists use lab experiments and field experiments to estimate the values of the conventional discount factor (δ) and the present-bias parameter (β). Naturally, the values of the two parameters vary from one person to another.

Estimates of Conventional Discounting and Present Bias

There have been dozens of studies that explore the magnitude of conventional discounting and present bias. In the classic study, Richard Thaler asked the question, "What future payment X at time t would make you indifferent between $15 now and X at time t?" For $t = 1$ month, the median response was $X = \$20$, compared to $X = \$50$ for $t = 1$ year and $X = \$100$ for $t = 10$ years. This simple approach provides a useful starting point for estimating the magnitude of conventional discounting and present bias, but the numbers must be interpreted with caution for two reasons.

- *Uncertainty.* Any future payment is uncertain, and a person will naturally assume that the probability of receiving the future payment is less than one. People vary in their assumed probabilities, and people with relatively low assumed probabilities will require relatively large future payments X. In other words, the reported values of X reflect time preferences as well as personal assumptions about probabilities.
- *Diminishing marginal utility of wealth.* Many individuals experience diminishing marginal utility of wealth. A person with rapidly diminishing marginal utility will have a relatively large future payment X. For such a person, additional dollars increase utility by relatively small amounts, so more dollars are required to make the person indifferent about $15 now and X later. In other words, the reported values of X reflect time preferences as well as decreasing sensitivity to gain.

Both factors tend to increase the value of the future payment X, so the responses to the Thaler question are likely to overstate the strength of conventional discounting and present bias.

A number of studies have isolated the effects of present bias from the confounding influences of uncertainty and decreasing sensitivity. Brown, Chua, and Camerer (2009) use lab experiments on thirsty students to estimate the magnitude of present bias with respect to the timing of beverage consumption. Their results suggest a value of the present-bias parameter in the range $\beta = 0.60$ to 0.70. Other studies of present bias cited by Brown, Chua, and Camerer (2009) generate estimates of the present-bias parameter ranging from $\beta = 0.55$ to $\beta = 0.90$. Tanaka, Camerer, and Nguyen (2010) use data from villagers in Vietnam to estimate values of the present-bias parameter. Their results suggest an average value of $\beta = 0.644$.

In a recent study by Augenblick and Rabin (2019), subjects in a lab experiment chose when to complete an unpleasant task—transcribing blurry foreign letters. The authors find strong evidence of present bias, with an estimated value of the present-bias parameter $\beta = 0.83$. The subjects treated all future dates in roughly equal terms, indicating present bias rather than conventional discounting. The results are consistent with the notion that for many decision-makers, time is binary—it is divided into the present and the future, with little or no difference between different future dates.

Economic Experiment: Patience among Mothers and Children

People vary in their degree of patience in waiting for rewards. In the classic experiment to measure a person's patience, the person is asked a series of questions about SS rewards (small and soon) and LL rewards (large and later). For example, we could ask, "Which do you prefer, an SS reward of $100 now, or a LL reward of $101 in one year?" If the answer is the SS reward, we increase the LL value until the person switches to the LL reward. For example, a person could switch at LL = $150. The switching value allows us to compute the person's marginal rate of substitution between a reward now and later, defined as the increase in the future reward required to offset a one-dollar decrease in the current reward:

$$MRS = \frac{LL}{SS}$$

For a person who switches at LL = $150, the marginal rate of substitution (MRS) is 1.50:

$$MRS = \frac{150}{100} = 1.50$$

A large MRS indicates relative impatience, as the person requires a large LL to wait for the reward. In contrast, a small MRS indicates relative patience, as it doesn't take much more money to get the person to wait for the reward.

As we saw in the chapter opener, a recent experiment measured the degree of patience of mothers and their young children (Kosse and Pfeiffer 2013). The researchers ran a SS-LL experiment with monetary rewards for the mothers. On average, the mothers' marginal rate of substitution was MRS = 1.27. On average, a mother was willing to wait one year for a reward that was at least 27 percent larger. The researcher gave each child a choice: either eat the single pack of gummy bears now, or wait until the end of the interview (roughly 50 minutes later) to get two packs of gummy bears. Roughly 22 percent of kids were impatient, and ate the gummy bears immediately, while 78 percent waited for the larger later reward. The researchers found a large positive correlation between the patience of a mother and the patience of her children: patient mothers tend to have patient children. These results provide evidence of the intergenerational transmission of time preferences.

Review the Concepts 9.2

1. An estimate of present bias based on an answer to the future-payment question must be interpreted with caution because of [___]. (diminishing marginal utility, increasing marginal utility, constant marginal utility, uncertainty about a future payment)

2. A plausible range for the value of the present-bias parameter is [___]. (0.10 to 0.40, 0.80 to 1.0, 0.50 to 1.0)

3. An individual in an experiment switches from a $50 small-soon reward (SS) to a large-later reward (LL) when LL = $80. The marginal rate of substitution between a reward now and later is [___]. (0.625, 1, 1.60, 2)

 4. Use Widget 9.2 (available at www.oup.com/us/osullivan1e). You have a contract under which you will receive a payment of $1000 five years from now. Suppose your value for conventional discounting is $\delta = 0.90$. When someone offers to pay you $413 now instead of $1000 five years from now, you realize that you are indifferent between $413 now and $1000 in five years. Your value of the present-bias parameter is $\beta = $ [___]. (0.50, 0.60, 0.70, 0.80)

9.3 Illustrations: Cupcake, Weed, Bucket List

In the next several chapters, we will explore the consequences of present bias in various economic environments. In this introductory chapter, we preview the effects of present bias on three types of decisions.

1. *Food choice.* A hungry person chooses either an apple or a cupcake.
2. *Task completion.* A homeowner decides when to pull a growing weed.
3. *Saving and consumption.* A retiree decides when to spend money to complete items on a bucket list.

Cupcake versus Apple

Consider a hungry consumer who enters a grocery store in search of a snack. Apples are displayed next to a pile of enticing chocolate cupcakes. To simplify matters, suppose the prices of the two goods are equal. The utility from a cupcake is 24 utils, compared to 5 utils from an apple. The consumer has a target body weight, and spends time on a treadmill to avoid gaining weight. Eating an apple doesn't require any treadmill time. In contrast, each cupcake has 600 calories and requires 30 minutes on a treadmill to offset the cupcake calories. Suppose the marginal disutility of treadmill time is 1 util per minute: each minute on the treadmill decreases utility by 1 util.

Consider the choice of a fully rational consumer, defined in this context as a consumer who does not experience present bias. Suppose treadmill time occurs in one week, an interval that is short enough that we can ignore conventional discounting ($\delta = 1$). The payoff from the apple is 5 utils, and the payoff from the cupcake is the consumption benefit (24 utils) minus the disutility of treadmill time (30 utils), or −6 utils:

$$cupcake\ payoff = 24 - 30 = -6\ utils$$

The apple has a higher payoff (5 utils), so a fully rational consumer will choose the apple.

The introduction of present bias decreases the future consequences of current choices. In the apple-cupcake decision, present bias downplays the negative future consequences (treadmill time) and tilts the consumer decision in favor of the cupcake. Suppose the value of the present-bias parameter is $\beta = 1/2$. In this case, present bias downplays the future cost by half, increasing the cupcake payoff to 9 utils:

$$cupcake\ payoff = 24 - \frac{1}{2} \cdot 30 = 9\ utils$$

The cupcake now has a higher payoff (9 utils > 5 utils for the apple), so a consumer subject to present bias chooses the cupcake rather than the apple.

We can quantify the regret for a present-biased consumer who chooses the cupcake instead of the apple. One week after eating the cupcake, the consumer trudges on the treadmill for 30 minutes to burn the cupcake calories. Looking back after the treadmill session, the consumer realizes that the actual payoff from the cupcake is –6 = 4 – 30. The consumer's regret is 11 utils, equal to the difference between the realized utility (–6 with the cupcake) and the forgone apple utility (+5).

As we'll see in later chapters, one response to present bias is to place the benefit and the cost of an economic choice in the same time frame. In our cupcake example, the grocery store could install a treadmill between the apple display and the cupcake display, and require a customer to earn the right to a cupcake by doing treadmill time before getting the cupcake. This approach eliminates the problem of present bias because both benefits and costs are in the present. In our example, a consumer eyeing the treadmill will choose the apple rather than the cupcake. In general, when benefits and costs are experienced during the same time period, present bias does not affect decisions.

Homeowner versus Weed

As a second illustration of the consequences of present bias, consider a homeowner who observes an ugly weed growing rapidly in the back yard. It's January 1, and the homeowner must pull the weed no later than March 1, two months from now. The cost of pulling the weed is the opportunity cost of time spent digging, tugging, and discarding the weed. Suppose the homeowner's opportunity cost is $1 per minute. As shown in Figure 9.1 , the time required to pull the growing weed increases from month to month, from five minutes today ($5 opportunity cost), to eight minutes ($8) in one month, and 14 minutes ($14) in two months. In the absence of present bias, the rational choice is to pull the weed now, incurring a cost of $5 rather than $8 in a month or $14 in two months.

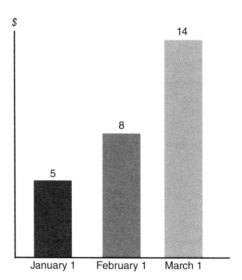

FIGURE 9.1: Rising Cost of Pulling a Weed

A homeowner who experiences strong present bias is likely to delay the weed pull until March. If the value of the present-bias parameter is $\beta= 1/2$, any future cost is downplayed by half. Figure 9.2 shows the cost of the task, as perceived by the homeowner, at the beginning of each month.

- *View on January 1.* The present cost is the true $5 cost of pulling the weed now, but the homeowner downplays the cost of pulling the weed in February to $4 (down from $8). The homeowner decides to delay the weed pull for a month, expecting to incur a cost of $4 in February rather than incurring a cost of $5 in January.
- *View on February 1.* The February cost is now in the present, so the home-owner computes the cost of pulling the weed in the present as $8 (the true cost). Looking ahead one month, the homeowner downplays the March cost to $7 (down from $14). The homeowner decides to delay the weed pull for another month, expecting to incur a cost of $7 on March 1 rather than incurring a cost of $8 on February 1.
- On March 1, the March cost is now in the present, and the homeowner incurs the true cost of $14 to pull the weed.

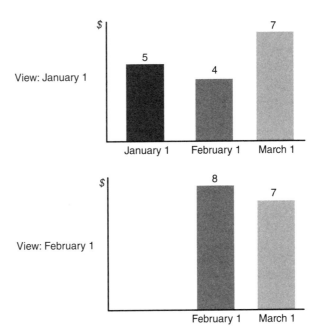

FIGURE 9.2: Present Bias and Procrastination

This example illustrates costly and regrettable procrastination. The cost of the task increases over time, so the fully rational choice is to perform the task now rather than later. Present bias causes the homeowner to delay action, and the cost of completing the task later ($14) exceeds the cost of completing the task now ($5). As the homeowner pulls the weed in March and looks back, he or she will regret delaying the weed pull. We can quantify regret as the $9 difference between the actual $14 cost of pulling the weed in March and the $5 minimum cost. In later chapters, we will take a closer look at procrastination, as well as its inverse, known as preproperation (doing something too soon).

The Bucket List

As a third illustration of present bias, consider a retired person who has a fixed wealth w to spend on travel and various adventure goods. Each item on the bucket list has a price of $1. The retiree has two years to complete the bucket list, so the budget constraint is

$$w = c_1 + c_2$$

where c_1 is consumption this year and c_2 is consumption next year. We assume that $\delta = 1$, meaning that there is no conventional discounting. This assumption does not change the conclusion in a substantive way, but simplifies the calculations and makes the results transparent.

As shown in Figure 9.3, the bucketlister could use the equimarginal principle to allocate the fixed wealth across the two years. To maximize utility, the bucketlister chooses c_1 and c_2 to make the marginal utility of consumption now equal to the marginal utility of consumption later. To simplify matters, we assume that the consumption benefits are symmetric this year and next: there is nothing special about consumption in either year. In Figure 9.3 , the fully rational response is to divide the wealth equally across the two years: In this example, $w = 120$, so the person spends $60 in each time period.

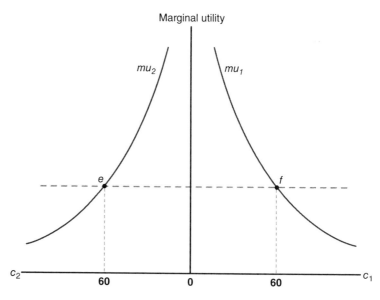

FIGURE 9.3: The Fully Rational Bucketlister

Figure 9.4 shows the implications of present bias represented by $\beta = 1/2$. Present bias decreases the marginal utility of consumption in year 2, shifting the marginal-utility curve downward by half. The equimarginal principle is satisfied at points g and h, with two-thirds of wealth spent in year 1, leaving only one-third for year 2. Present bias tilts preferences in favor of the present, so consumption in year 1 increases at the expense of consumption in year 2.

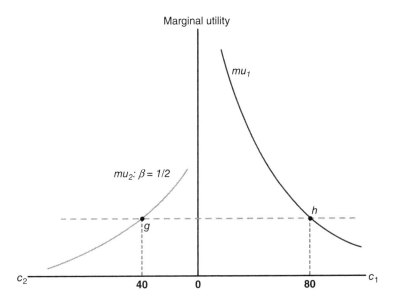

FIGURE 9.4: The Present-Biased Bucketlister

Figure 9.5 shows the bucketlister's regret in the second year, when the future becomes the present. In year 2, present bias is no longer relevant, and the marginal-utility curve for year 2 returns to its position in the absence of present bias (labeled "mu_2: $\beta = 1$"). Regret happens because the experienced marginal utility of consumption in the second year exceeds the experienced marginal utility of consumption in the first year. As shown by point h, the marginal utility of the 80th dollar spent in the first year was 5 utils. As shown by point i, the marginal utility of the 40th dollar spent in the second year is 10 utils. Looking back, the bucketlister realizes that a dollar reallocated from the first year to the second year would generate a net gain of 5 utils.

The lesson from the bucketlister example is that present bias causes regrettable over-spending in the present. In our numerical example with $\beta = 1/2$, the person spends 2/3 of wealth in the first period, and the marginal regret is $mu_2 - mu_1 = 5$ utils. As shown in Math 9.1, these numbers are consistent with a specific utility function that exhibits diminishing marginal utility.

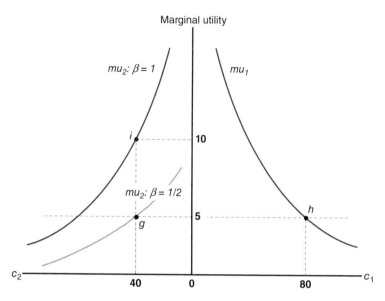

FIGURE 9.5: Bucketlister Regret

Review the Concepts 9.3

1. In the apple-cupcake example, suppose new treadmill technology cuts the time required to off-set the cupcake to 22 minutes. For $\beta = 1/2$, the consumer will choose the [___] and experience regret = [___]. (cupcake, 6 utils; apple, 0 utils; cupcake, 3 utils; cupcake, 11 utils)

2. In the backyard weed example, suppose the cost of pulling the weed doubles in each month, from \$5 in January, to \$10 in February, to \$20 in March. For $\beta = 6/10$, the consumer will pull the weed in [___]. (January, February, March)

3. In the backyard weed example, suppose the cost of pulling the weed doubles in each month, from \$5 in January, to \$10 in February, to \$20 in March. For $\beta = 4/10$, the consumer will pull the weed in [___] and experience regret = \$ [___] (March, 3; January, 0; February, 5; March, 15)

4. In the bucketlister example, suppose present bias becomes weaker, increasing the value of the present-bias parameter to $\beta = 2/3$. A plausible consumption bundle (c_1, c_2) is [___]. ((60, 60), (72, 48), (80, 40), (90, 30))

5. *Comparative statics.* The relationship between β and the bucketlister's consumption in period 2 is [___]. (positive, negative, zero)

Key Terms

conventional discounting
  (exponential), p. 159

present bias, p. 158
time inconsistency, p. 161

Takeaways

1. Suppose $\beta = 0.50$ (present bias) and $\delta = 0.80$ (conventional discounting). The current value of $100 to be received in one year is $40 = 0.50 \cdot 80$. The current value of $100 to be received in two years is $32 = 0.50 \cdot 64$.
2. If a future payment becomes more distant by one time period, the current value under conventional discounting decreases by a factor equal to the discount factor δ.
3. If a future payment becomes more distant by one or more time periods, the current value under present bias does not change.
4. A person subject to present bias shows time inconsistency: at time t, the person makes a plan for the future; at time $t + 1$, the person changes the plan.
5. Present bias causes time inconsistency because the relative values of bundles in two successive periods change when the earlier bundle switches from its status of a future bundle to become the present bundle.
6. Present bias distorts consumer choices in favor of products such as donuts, cigarettes, and other products with relatively high future cost.
7. Present bias can cause regrettable procrastination, as an individual delays completing a task subject to increasing cost.
8. Present bias tilts consumption in favor of consuming now rather than later, leading to later regret.

Discuss the Concepts

1. Conventional Discounting and Present Bias. Bett has two promissory notes: note 1 will be redeemed for $202 in one month; note 2 will be redeemed for $202 in two months. Bett just sold the first note for $150 and sold the second note for $145.

   a. Bett [____] (does, does not) experience present bias.

   b. Bett [____] (does, does not) experience conventional discounting.

2. *Epidemic and MRS.* Suppose the World Health Organization (WHO) announces the emergence of a novel coronavirus in another country. According to epidemiologists, the probability that the virus will cause a pandemic and a one-year shutdown in your area is 0.50. The announcement will [____] (↑, ↓, not change) the large-later payment associated with a small-soon payment of $100. In other words, the announcement will

[___] (↑, ↓, not change) the marginal rate of substitution (MRS) between a reward now and later.

3. *Cupcake and Present Bias.* In the cupcake-apple example, consider Tutherd, a consumer with a value of the present-bias parameter $\beta = 2/3$.

   a. Compared to the example in the text, Tutherd experiences [___] (stronger, weaker) present bias.

   b. Tutherd will choose the [___] (apple, cupcake) because [___].

4. *Comparative Statics: Procrastination.* For the homeowner with the growing weed, suppose $\beta = 0.75$.

   a. On January 1, the homeowner will [___] (pull, not pull) the weed because [___] > [___].

   b. The relationship between β and procrastination is [___]. (positive, negative, zero)

5. *Comparative Statics: Regret.* For the bucketlister, an increase in β [___] (↑, ↓, does not change) the share of wealth spent in period 1 and [___] (↑, ↓, does not change) regret experienced in period 2.

Apply the Concepts

1. *Conventional Discounting versus Present Bias.* A new client for your investment firm announced, "I am indifferent between (i) receiving $40 today and (ii) receiving $100 in five years." Suppose the relatively small current value of $100 in five years is caused by either strong conventional discounting or present bias, but not a combination of the two. In other words, the client has either ($\delta < 1$ and $\beta = 1$) or ($\delta = 1$ and $\beta < 1$).

   a. If $\beta = 1$, $\delta = $ [___]. If $\delta = 1$, $\beta = $ [___]

   b. To determine whether $\delta < 1$ or $\beta < 1$, you can ask the client a single question that has a numerical answer. Your question is [___].

   c. If the answer to your question is $40, the client experiences [___].

2. *Arbitrage and Present Bias.* Use Widget 9.2 (available at www.oup.com/us/osullivan1e). Robin is under contract to receive $600 in 10 years. Robin's values of the discounting parameters are $\delta = 0.90$ and $\beta = 1/2$. Your values are $\delta = 0.90$ and $\beta = 0.80$. Suppose the contract is transferable at zero cost. Design a Pareto improvement under which you and Robin share equally in any gain. The gain per person is $[___].

3. *Banana versus Donut.* A consumer will eat either a banana or a donut. The utility from a banana is 6 utils, and the utility from a donut is 30 utils. Consumption of the donut requires 32 minutes of treadmill time to burn the

extra calories, and the disutility of treadmill time is 1 utils per minute. The consumer will choose the banana if present bias is relatively [___] (weak, strong), with a value of the present-bias parameter β [___] (<, >, =) [___].

4. *Procrastination*. Suppose the cost of performing a task that must be completed no later than $t = 5$ increases exponentially with time: $c(t) = (t+2)^2$, where t is an integer.

   a. A fully rational person will complete the task at $t^* =$ [___] and the cost of completing the task is $[___]. Illustrate.

   b. A person subject to present bias with $\beta = 1/2$ will complete the task at $t^{**} =$ [___]. The person's regret is $[___]. Illustrate.

5. *BucketLister*. Consider a person with two time periods over which to spend wealth $w = \$100$. The utility function is

$$u(c_1, c_2) = a \cdot log[c_1] + b \cdot log[c_2]$$

where log[ ] is the natural logarithm, $a = 300$ and $b = 200$.

   a. For a fully rational person ($\beta = 1$), the solution is $c_1 =$ [___] and $c_2 =$ [___]. Illustrate.

   b. For a person subject to present bias with $\beta = 1/2$, the solution is $c_1 =$ [___] and $c_2 =$ [___]. Illustrate.

   c. In the second period, the person subject to present bias experiences regret, because [___] < [___].

Math Solutions

Math 9.1: Marginal Regret

The utility function is

$$u(c_1, c_2) = a \cdot log[c_1] + b \cdot log[c_2]$$

The expressions for the marginal utility of consumption now and later are

$$mu_1 = \frac{a}{c_1} \qquad mu_2 = \frac{\beta \cdot b}{c_2}$$

Substitute the budget constraint $c_2 = w - c_1$ into the expression for mu_2 and apply the equimarginal rule:

$$\frac{a}{c_1} = \frac{\beta \cdot b}{w - c_1}$$

Solve for the utility-maximizing consumption quantities:

$$c_1^* = \frac{a}{a + \beta \cdot b} \cdot w \qquad\qquad c_2^* = \frac{b \cdot \beta}{a + \beta \cdot b} \cdot w$$

For $a = b = 400$, the consumption bundle for a fully rational person is $(c_1, c_2) = (60, 60)$. For a person subject to present bias with $\beta = 1/2$, the consumption bundle is $(c_1, c_2) = (80, 40)$. To compute marginal regret, substitute consumption quantities of the present-biased person into the expressions for marginal utility, with $\beta = 1$. The regret experienced in period 2 is

$$mu_2 - mu_1 = \frac{400}{40} - \frac{400}{80} = 10 - 5 = 5$$

Time Preferences and Saving

10

Consider the standard warning for state-sponsored lotteries: *"The lottery is a game of chance, and should not be played for investment purposes."* People in the United States spend billions dollars each year on lottery tickets sold by state governments, despite a payback of roughly $0.48 per dollar spent. That translates into a rate of return of −$0.52 per dollar, so a person who regularly plays a lottery is likely to drain a saving account rather than add to it.

Immigrants from Africa and the Caribbean use sou-sous to bring the excitement of lotteries to short-term saving (TheGrio, 2011). A sou-sou collects contributions from its members, and then uses lotteries to award prizes to the members. To illustrate, suppose 20 people form a sou-sou and each person commits to contribute $10 each per month for 20 months. Each month, the winner of a sou-sou lottery gets a $200 prize. Once a person wins a lottery, he or she is no longer eligible to play the monthly lottery. As a result, everyone eventually wins a $200 prize. A sou-sou is an interest-free saving and loan program that promotes saving for two reasons. First, people form sou-sous with family members, friends, and co-workers, so commitments to contribute are likely to be met. Second, people enjoy playing games of chance, and the excitement of winning adds to the benefit of saving.

In the previous chapter we introduced two forms of discounting: conventional discounting and present bias. In this chapter we explore the implications of discounting for a household's decision about how much to consume now and how much to save for later. In the previous chapter, the bucketlister example previews this chapter's discussion of saving. The most obvious application of the now-versus-later decision is saving for retirement, but the framework is applicable to any decision that involves smoothing consumption over time. For example, a household could save for a large purchase such as a car or house, or an adventure seeker could save to finance travel to exotic places.

Learning Objectives: The Explainer

After mastering this chapter, you will be able to explain each of the following statements.

1.   Present bias can increase spending during the working years, and trigger regret during the retirement years.

2.   A saving mandate such as Social Security may fail to increase retirement wealth.

3.   The default option on a retirement plan may be decisive in terms of retirement wealth.

4.   A program known as *Save More Tomorrow* increases saving.

5.   When the future becomes the present, a present-biased and clueless consumer may abandon a consumption plan.

6.   A present-biased and savvy consumer takes costly action to prevent early over-spending.

10.1   Discounting and Intertemporal Choice

We can extend the conventional model of consumer choice to explore the implications of present bias for household saving. Each year, a household decides how much to spend now, and how much to save for future consumption. To focus attention on the role of present bias, we assume that the interest rate on saving is zero, so the only motive for saving is to smooth consumption over two periods. We also assume that the only difference between consumption now (period 1) and later (period 2) is that future consumption is subject to conventional discounting and present bias. This contrasts with consumption choice between different products such as housing and music, when we expect differing preferences for the two goods.

Saving and the Equimarginal Principle

We can use the equimarginal principle to illustrate a household's intertemporal consumption choice. It will be convenient to illustrate the household's intertemporal choice with a specific utility function. The utility function incorporates conventional discounting and present bias:

$$u(c_1, c_2) = \log[c_1] + \delta \cdot \beta \cdot \log[c_2]$$

where log[ ] is the natural logarithm, $\delta < 1$ is the conventional discounting factor, and $\beta < 1$ represents present bias. The household has a fixed wealth w to spend on consumption now (c_1) and later (c_2):

$$w = c_1 + c_2$$

As shown in Math 10.1, the expressions for the marginal utility of consumption now (period 1) and later (period 2) are

$$mu_1 = \frac{1}{c_1} \qquad mu_2 = \frac{\delta \cdot \beta}{c_2}$$

Figure 10.1 illustrates the equimarginal principle for the consumption-saving choice. In the absence of conventional discounting and present bias ($\delta = \beta = 1$), the two marginal-utility curves are symmetric. In this case, consumption now equals consumption later, a case of perfect consumption smoothing. For example, for wealth $w = 120$, the equimarginal principle is satisfied at point i and point j, with $c_1 = c_2 = 60$. The introduction of discounting tilts consumption in favor of period 1. Under conventional discounting measured as $\delta = 2/3$ and present bias measured as $\beta = 1/2$, the marginal-utility curve for consumption later is lower, and the equimarginal principle is satisfied at point b and point a, with $c_1 = 90$ and $c_2 = 30$. The introduction of conventional discounting and present bias increases current consumption at the expense of future consumption.

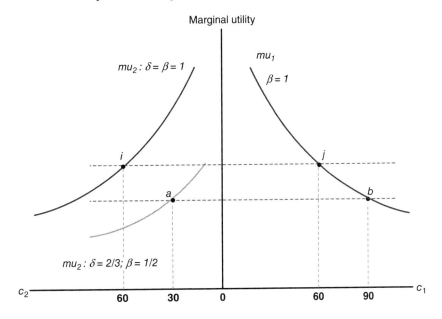

FIGURE 10.1: Equimarginal Principle and Consumption

We can use the equimarginal principle to solve for the utility-maximizing consumption as a function of the parameters. In this case, the two conditions to satisfy the equimarginal principle are (i) the marginal utility of consumption now equals the marginal utility of consumption later, and (ii) total consumption adds up to the fixed wealth: $w = c_1 + c_2$. As shown in Math 10.2, the expressions for the utility-maximizing consumption now and later are

$$c_1^* = \frac{1}{1 + \delta \cdot \beta} \cdot w \qquad c_2^* = \frac{\delta \cdot \beta}{1 + \delta \cdot \beta} \cdot w$$

These expressions are useful because they show consumption now and later as fractions of wealth w. Naturally, the two fractions add to one.

The expressions for consumption now and consumption later show the effects of conventional discounting and present bias on the timing of consumption. In the absence of conventional discounting and present bias, $\delta = \beta = 1$, and the expressions for consumption now and later simplify to

$$c_1^* = c_2^* = \frac{1}{2} \cdot w$$

In this case, the consumer spends half of the wealth in each period. The incorporation of discounting ($\delta < 1$) and present bias ($\beta < 1$) means that more than half of wealth will be consumed now, leaving less than half for later. For example, if $\delta = 2/3$ and $\beta = 1/2$, three-fourths of wealth is spent now, leaving one-fourth for later:

$$c_1^* = \frac{3}{4} \cdot w \qquad c_2^* = \frac{1}{4} \cdot w$$

The magnitude of the tilt toward present consumption is determined by the values of δ and β. As the strength of conventional discounting and present bias increase (as δ decreases or β decreases), c_1 increases at the expense of c_2.

Present Bias and Regret

As we saw in the previous chapter, present bias causes regret. Once the future becomes the present, present bias is no longer relevant. When a household that based its consumption path on $\beta < 1$ looks back, the household will regret its past excessive spending and meager saving. Regret happens when the marginal utility of actual consumption in period 2 exceeds the marginal utility of actual consumption in period 1. As shown in Math 10.3, the ratio of marginal utilities for the actual consumption bundle is determined by the present-bias parameter β:

$$\frac{mu_2}{mu_1} = \frac{1}{\beta}$$

In the absence of present bias, $\beta = 1$ and the marginal utilities are equal, so there is no regret. In contrast, if $\beta < 1$, the marginal utility in period 2 is higher, so there is regret. For example, if $\beta = 1/3$, the marginal utility for consumption in period 2 is three times the marginal utility of consumption in period 1, indicating strong regret.

 We can use Widget 10.1 (available at www.oup.com/us/osullivan1e) to quantify the regret experienced by a person subject to present bias in consumption. Consider a household with $\beta = 6/10$ and no conventional discounting ($\delta = 1$). As shown in Figure 10.2, the utility-maximizing bundle is $c_1 = 75$ and $c_2 = 45$, and the common marginal utility is 4.8 utils. Once the second period arrives and present bias is irrelevant, the actual marginal utility of $c_2 = 45$ is 8 utils:

$$mu_2 = \frac{360}{45} = 8 \text{ utils}$$

Looking back, the household recognizes that the marginal utility of consumption in period 2 (equal to 8 utils) exceeds the marginal utility of consumption in period 1 (equal to 4.8 utils). The ratio of the marginal utilities is

$$\frac{mu_2}{mu_1} = \frac{1}{\beta} = \frac{10}{6} = \frac{8.0}{4.8}$$

If the household could have a redo and reallocate one dollar from period 1 to period 2, utility would increase by 3.2 utils, the difference between the marginal utilities of the two periods.

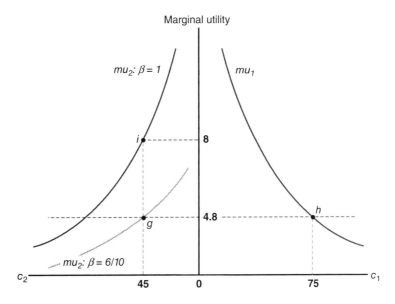

FIGURE 10.2: Present Bias and Regret

Review the Concepts 10.1

1. In a two-period model of consumption, the introduction of conventional discounting and present bias shifts the marginal-utility curve for period [___] [___]. (2, upward; 1, downward; 2, downward; 1, upward)

2. Use the expression for x_2^*. Suppose $\{\delta, \beta, w\} = \{2/3, 3/5, 70\}$. The utility-maximizing consumption in period 2 is $\$[___]$. (10, 20, 35, 50)

3. Use Widget 10.1 (available at www.oup.com/us/osullivan1e). Suppose $\{\delta, \beta\} = \{0.90, 0.62\}$. The utility-maximizing consumption bundle is [___]. ((80, 40), (60, 60), (43, 77), (77,43))

4. Suppose a consumer's present bias is measured by $\beta = 2/3$. For the chosen consumption bundle, the marginal utility in period 2 is [___] times the marginal utility in period 1. (0.67, 1.50, 2, 3)

5. *Comparative statics.* In the two-period consumption model, the relationship between the present-bias parameter β and regret is [___]. (positive, negative, zero)

Saving Mandates and Nudges

In this part of the chapter we take a closer look at a household's consumption-saving choice. We consider the role of public policy in increasing saving.

1. *Mandatory saving.* Social Security taxes in the present and benefits later. An important question is how households respond to mandated increases in saving. Are households passive, or do they take actions that undermine the saving mandate?
2. *Nudge: subtle change in incentives.* The nudge approach exploits the fact that people are inattentive in some circumstances, and suggestible in other circumstances. When people are inattentive or suggestible, subtle changes can increase saving.

Response to Mandate: Active Saver

As we've seen, present bias causes regret when a retired person realizes that his or her meager savings cause a rough transition into retirement years. Suppose the objective of the government is to reduce household regret caused by under-saving during the income-earning years. One option is to use a program like Social Security as a sort of government saving program. A social-security tax reduces current earnings and current consumption; it then repays the contributions in the form of benefits in the retirement years. The program smooths consumption over the citizen's lifetime by decreasing consumption during the working years and increasing consumption during the retirement years.

Consider first a household that will save in the absence of a mandated saving program. Figure 10.3 shows the implications of mandated saving and benefits.

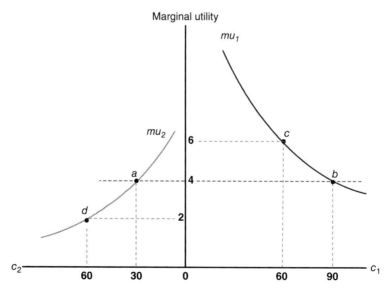

FIGURE 10.3: Mandatory Saving for a Saver Household

In the absence of the tax/benefit system, the household chooses points b and a: the household spends $90 of its $120 wealth and saves $30 for later consumption. Present bias causes a substantial drop in consumption upon retirement—from $90 to $30. Suppose the government imposes a tax of $30 on current consumption and pays the money back in the retirement period. In other words, the tax/payback system smooths consumption, generating $c_1 = c_2 = \$60$. If the household is passive, it will simply accept the smoothed consumption path and reach points c and d.

An attentive household operating in period 1 will notice an opportunity to increase its utility. As shown by point c and point d, the government saving program generates a gap in the marginal utilities of consumption in the two periods. During the first period, the marginal utility of current consumption is 6 utils (point c), compared to a marginal utility of future consumption of 2 utils (point d). A $1 increase in current consumption (and a $1 decrease in future consumption) will generate a net increase in utility of 4 utils. Recall that the household saves $30 of its wealth, so the reallocation could be accomplished by reducing the household's own saving by $1. Applying the same logic, the household will continue to reduce its own saving until it reaches the original utility-maximizing points a and b. In other words, the household's own saving of $30 is replaced by mandated saving of $30: the household changes its behavior to fully offset the effect of Social Security.

Response to Mandate: Non-Saver

Consider next a household that does not save any wealth for future spending. Figure 10.4 shows the consequences of a mandated saving program like Social

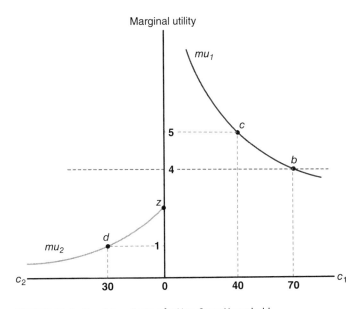

FIGURE 10.4: Mandatory Saving for Non-Saver Household

Security for a non-saver household. In this case, a low-income household spends all its $70 wealth on current consumption, leaving nothing for the future. The marginal utility of the last dollar spent on current consumption (shown by point *b*) exceeds the marginal utility of the first dollar spent on future consumption (shown by point *z*), so all wealth is spent on current consumption. A mandated saving program of $30 moves the household to points *c* and *d*. The new allocation violates the equimarginal rule: the marginal utility of current consumption (shown by point *c*) exceeds the marginal utility of future consumption (point *d*), so the household has an incentive to increase current consumption at the expense of future consumption.

Recall that the household shown in Figure 10.4 does not save any wealth on its own. As a result, it cannot increase current consumption by reducing its saving. An alternative response to the mandated saving under Social Security is to borrow money at the market interest rate and then use Social Security benefits to repay the loan and make interest payments. For each dollar borrowed, c_1 increases by $1 while c_2 decreases by $(1 + r)$, where r is the interest rate for borrowing. For example, if $r = 0.10$, a $1 increase in c_1 decreases c_2 by $1.10. In other words, there is a cost associated with borrowing to weaken the consumption smoothing from Social Security.

Nudges: Defaults, Save More Tomorrow, and Saving Lotteries

In behavioral economics, a nudge is defined as a policy that differs from conventional policies in several respects.

1. A nudge is designed to help people make better decisions for themselves.
2. A nudge does not affect the decisions of fully rational people. For example, a nudge to promote saving does not affect people who are not subject to present bias.
3. A nudge imposes a relatively low cost on everyone.

In the consumption-saving environment, policy-makers have developed two nudges in response to present bias and the resulting low levels of saving.

1. *Default options on employer retirement plans.* Most employers have tax-advantaged retirement plans that generate relatively high rates of return to workers. Under an opt-out policy, each worker is automatically enrolled in the retirement plan, and a worker can take action to drop out of the program. This approach does not harm a worker who would enroll anyway (a worker who does not experience present bias). But for a worker who experiences present bias, the auto-enroll program will increase saving if (i) the worker is inattentive or if (ii) the cost of opting out is sufficiently high.
2. *Commitment to future saving.* Present bias causes problems when the cost of an action is in the present (saving decreases current consumption) but the benefit is in the future (saving increases future consumption). In the decision-making process, the future benefit is downplayed by the present-bias parameter $\beta < 1$, but the current cost is fully in play. Under a

pre-commitment saving program, workers agree that future income will be saved, so the cost of saving (decreased future consumption) will be subject to present bias and downplayed by $\beta < 1$. By placing the cost and benefit of saving in the same time frame (later, not now), the problem of present bias is diminished, so saving increases.

Richard Thaler developed *Save More Tomorrow,* a retirement saving program that reduces the consequences of present bias. A worker agrees today to increase his or her saving rate at a future date, specifically when he or she receives a pay raise. This approach places both the benefit and the cost of saving in the future, so any present bias applies equally to both the benefit and the cost. In one application of the program, the employees of one firm agreed to increase their saving rate by three percentage points when they received their next pay raise. In addition, the workers agree to repeat the boost in saving for up to three additional annual pay raises. Over a four-year period, the average saving rate of participants increased from 3.5 percent of income to 14.6 percent of income.

Another program to promote saving is a prize-linked savings account. Instead of paying interest, a prize-linked saving (PLS) program periodically awards large prizes to savers. The probability that a participant wins a prize is determined by the amount saved in a PLS account: the larger the account balance, the greater the likelihood of winning. PLS programs have been used around the world for roughly 300 years, and they succeed by tapping into people's willingness to pay for a large (potentially life-changing) payoff. For many people, a small chance at a large payoff is more attractive than a small but certain payoff in a conventional saving account.

Recent demonstration projects and experiments have the explored the potential of PLS to boost saving. The *Save to Win* program in Michigan increased saving among participants, more than half of whom had not saved regularly before opening a *Save to Win* account (Kearny et al. 2010). Roughly 6 in 10 participants decreased the money spent on the state lottery. The difference between $20 spent on a state lottery and $20 placed in a *Save to Win* account is that even if a person doesn't win the saving prize, he or she still has $20 in the saving account. In an online experiment, the introduction of a PLS program increased savings by 25 percent (Atalay et al. 2014) The largest increases in savings came from people with zero saving before the introduction of the PLS program. The general conclusion is that saving prizes can boost the savings of low-wealth households.

Review the Concepts 10.2

1. A mandatory saving program such as Social Security may increase consumption during retirement by an amount [____] the mandated amount because participants may [____]. (less than, borrow money; less than, decrease own saving; greater than, increase own saving; greater than, increase own saving)

2. A nudge is defined as a policy that [____]. (allows people to make their own decisions, does not affect the decisions of fully rational people, imposes a relatively low cost, makes decisions for people, imposes a relatively high cost on everyone)

3. The following are examples of nudges for saving: [___]. (commitment to future saving, *Save More Tomorrow*, Social Security, state-sponsored lotteries, opt-out retirement plans)

4. Like other prize-linked savings programs, the *Save to Win* program in Michigan [___]. (increased saving, enrolled people who had not previously saved, diverted money from state-sponsored lotteries)

10.3 Clueless versus Savvy Consumers

So far we have assumed that people who are subject to present bias are not aware of their present bias and its consequences. In other words, people are clueless, so they do not anticipate future regret about their current choices. In behavioral economics, clueless people are sometimes called "naifs." In this part of the chapter, we explore the choices of people who are savvy in the sense that they are self-aware about their present bias. As we'll see, a self-aware person may take actions today to combat present bias and reduce future regret. In behavioral economics, a person who is self aware is sometimes tagged as a "sophisticate."

Three-Period Model of Intertemporal Choice

To explore the strategies of clueless and savvy people, we extend the model of intertemporal choice from two to three periods. As before, each person has a fixed wealth w to allocate to consumption over time. The allocation decisions happen at the beginning of period 1 and the beginning of period 2, and consumption in period 3 is the wealth left over after the first two periods of consumption.

We can use our logarithmic utility function and the equimarginal principle to explore choice in a three-period environment. To simplify matters and focus attention on present bias, we assume (i) there are no interest earnings on saving and (ii) there is no conventional discounting, meaning $\delta = 1$. The utility function is

$$u\left(c_1, c_2, c_3\right) = \theta \cdot \log\left[c_1\right] + \theta \cdot \beta \cdot \log\left[c_2\right] + \theta \cdot \beta \cdot \log\left[c_3\right]$$

where θ is a utility parameter that is common across the three periods and present bias is represented by $\beta < 1$. The budget constraint is

$$w = c_1 + c_2 + c_3$$

Consider the consumer's decision at the beginning of the process (period 1). As shown in Math 10.4, the expressions for marginal utility in the three periods are

$$mu_1 = \frac{\theta}{c_1} \qquad mu_2 = \frac{\theta \cdot \beta}{c_2} \qquad mu_3 = \frac{\theta \cdot \beta}{c_3}$$

In other words, present bias is relevant for periods 2 and 3.

Consider the allocation decision in the absence of present bias. In this case, $\beta = 1$, and the consumer applies the equimarginal principle to choose an allocation that equalize the marginal utility across the three periods:

$$\frac{\theta}{c_1} = \frac{\theta}{c_2} = \frac{\theta}{c_3}$$

In this symmetric case, the consumer maximizes utility by spreading the fixed wealth equally across the three periods:

$$c_1 = c_2 = c_3$$

For example, if wealth is $w = 36$, $c_1 = c_2 = c_3 = 12$.

Consumption Path of the Clueless

Consider the choices of a consumer who experiences present bias but is unaware of the bias. In period 1, the clueless consumer uses the equimarginal principle to make a plan for all three periods. To satisfy the equimarginal rule, $mu_1 = mu_2 = mu_3$:

$$\frac{\theta}{c_1} = \frac{\theta \cdot \beta}{c_2} = \frac{\theta \cdot \beta}{c_3}$$

Present bias applies equally to periods 2 and 3, so $c_2 = c_3$. As shown in Math 10.5, period-one consumption is

$$c_1^* = \frac{1}{1 + 2 \cdot \beta} \cdot w$$

For example, if $\beta = 1/2$, the consumer spends half of wealth in the first period:

$$c_1^* = \frac{1}{1 + 2 \cdot \beta} \cdot w = \frac{w}{2}$$

Under the plan developed in period 1, the other half of wealth is allocated to periods 2 and 3. Therefore, the plan specifies 1/4 of wealth for each of the remaining periods:

$$c_2 = c_3 = \frac{w}{4}$$

Continuing our example with $w = \$36$, consumption in period 1 is $c_1 = 18$, and the planned consumption in periods 2 and 3 is $c_2 = c_3 = 9$.

Figure 10.5 illustrates the plan developed in period 1. Given present bias measured as $\beta = 1/2$, the marginal-utility curves for period 2 and period 3 are lower than the marginal-utility curve of period 1 by half. Applying the equimarginal principle, the marginal utilities are equalized with $c_1 = 18$, $c_2 = 9$, $c_3 = 9$.

Consider the consumer's choice at the start of period 2, after the first period has passed. The clueless consumer makes a plan for spending the leftover wealth in the remaining two periods. The present-bias parameter disappears for the

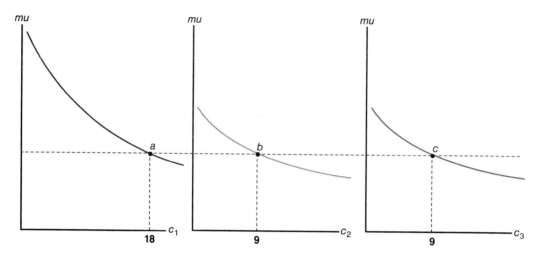

FIGURE 10.5: Consumption Plan Developed before Period One

now-present period 2, and the remaining wealth is allocated to satisfy the equi-marginal principle over the two remaining periods:

$$\frac{\theta}{c_2} = \frac{\theta \cdot \beta}{c_3}$$

This can be rewritten as

$$c_3 = \beta \cdot c_2$$

For example, if $\beta = 1/2$, consumption in period 3 is half the consumption in period 2. In other words, the consumer abandons the original plan under which $c_2 = c_3$. As usual, present bias causes time inconsistency: the plan developed in period 1 is discarded in period 2 because present bias disappears for period 2 but persists for period 3.

Given the wealth left over after period 1, the consumer applies the equi-marginal principle for periods 2 and 3. Math 10.6 derives expressions for the consumption quantities for periods 2 and 3. The consumption in the final period is β times the consumption in period 2, and the leftover money for the last two periods is half of wealth ($w/2$). To summarize, for the clueless consumer with $\beta = 1/2$, consumption decreases each period, from half of wealth, to one-third, to one-sixth:

$$c_1 = \frac{w}{2} \qquad c_2 = \frac{w}{3} \qquad c_3 = \frac{w}{6}$$

In our numerical example with $w = \$36$, the consumption path is (18, 12, 6).

Figure 10.6 illustrates the plan developed in period 2. Given present bias measured as $\beta = 1/2$, the marginal-utility curve for period 3 is lower than the

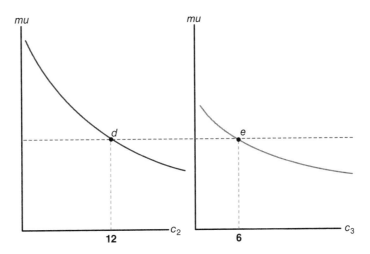

FIGURE 10.6: Consumption Plan Developed before Period Two

marginal-utility curve of period 2 by half. Applying the equimarginal principle, the marginal utilities are equalized with $c_2 = 12$, $c_3 = 6$.

Regret of the Clueless

The clueless consumer adopts a regrettable path of declining consumption. We can quantify the consumer's regret in the final period. Continuing our example with $\beta = 1/2$, suppose the utility parameter is $\theta = 72$. Given the consumption in the third period $c_3 = 6$, the marginal utility of consumption in period 3 is 12 utils:

$$mu_3 = \frac{\theta}{c_3} = \frac{72}{6} = 12 \, \text{utils}$$

Looking back to the second period with consumption $c_2 = 12$, the marginal utility in the second period is only 6 utils:

$$mu_2 = \frac{\theta}{c_2} = \frac{72}{12} = 6 \, \text{utils}$$

Looking back to the first period with consumption $c_1 = 18$, the marginal utility in the first period is only 4 utils:

$$mu_1 = \frac{\theta}{c_1} = \frac{72}{18} = 4 \, \text{utils}$$

The clueless consumer regrets his or her choices because the marginal utility in the last period is twice the marginal utility in the second period, and three times the marginal utility in the first period. A dollar reallocated from period 2 to period 3 would generate twice as much utility (12 utils versus 6 utils). Similarly, a dollar reallocated from period 1 to period 3 would generate three times the utility. The clueless consumer experiences unanticipated regret.

Consumption Path of a Savvy Consumer

Consider next a savvy consumer, defined as a consumer who is aware of his or her present bias. At the start of the three-period time horizon, the savvy consumer develops a consumption plan by applying the equimarginal-principle with $\beta = 1$. In other words, the savvy consumer makes the equimarginal calculations while controlling for present bias. To maximize utility, the marginal utility is equalized across the three periods:

$$\frac{\theta}{c_1} = \frac{\theta}{c_2} = \frac{\theta}{c_3}$$

The result is a consumption plan to spread the fixed wealth evenly over the three periods:

$$c_1 = c_2 = c_3 = \frac{w}{3}$$

For example, if $w = \$36$, the savvy consumer has a consumption plan $c_1 = c_2 = c_3 = 12$. The savvy consumer makes a plan to allocate one-third of wealth to the first period, leaving the other two-thirds for periods 2 and 3.

Will the savvy consumer execute the plan? Being self-aware of present bias does not guarantee self-control. If you are aware of your present bias, that doesn't guarantee that you can overcome it. After the savvy consumer makes the smoothing plan ($c_1 = c_2 = c_3 = w/3$), present bias remains a force. The consumer will be tempted to choose instant gratification over delayed gratification. To execute the smoothing plan, the savvy consumer must take actions in the present to prevent present bias from destroying the plan.

A savvy consumer can take actions that makes some wealth inaccessible until it is needed for the smoothing plan. In the first period, the consumer could allocate one-third of wealth to an asset that cannot be sold until the beginning of period 2, when selling the asset can provide money to finance consumption in the second period. Similarly, one-third of wealth could be locked into an asset to be sold at the start of the third period. In our numerical example, the household could place 12 units of wealth into an asset to be sold at the beginning of period 2, and another 12 units of wealth in an asset to be sold at the beginning of period 3. The purchase and timely sale of the assets allows the consumer to execute the smooth consumption plan. The lock-in of assets is necessary because self-awareness of present bias does not generate self-control.

The purchase and timely sale of assets is an imperfect strategy for combating present bias. Most assets can be sold within a relatively short time, so a consumer may eventually give in to the temptation of instant gratification and sell an asset before the intended sale date. A savvy consumer who anticipates the temptation for instant gratification will purchase assets with relatively high transaction costs, When the transaction cost is high, there is a large penalty from the premature sale of an asset. The penalty from premature sale increases the cost of violating the smooth consumption plan, reducing the temptation to spend now rather than later.

Consider the purchase of a house as a strategy to combat present bias and save for retirement. Although a house can be sold any time, the transaction cost is substantial. In addition to the high cost of executing a large financial transaction, there is a large cost associated with relocating a household and its possessions. In addition, relocation can disrupt a household's social networks, adding to the cost of selling a house. These high transaction costs make a house a good candidate for combating present bias.

Commitment Devices and Saving

A recent study explores the effects of savings programs in the Philippines that allowed savers to commit to specific saving goals (Ashraf, Karlan, and Yin 2006). At the start of the program, each person chose a saving goal, for example, an amount sufficient to replace a leaky roof. Money in the saving account could not be withdrawn until the goal was reached. Each saver had the opportunity to take home a lockbox to encourage daily saving—a sort of piggy bank. The bank kept the keys to the lockboxes, so any money placed in the box was inaccessible until the person brought the lockbox to the bank. The program caused large increases in saving: after a year, the bank-account balance of the average participant was 411 pesos greater than the balance of the average member of a control group, a difference of 82 percent.

Review the Concepts 10.3

1. A person who is not aware of his or her present bias is called [____]. (a naif, thoughtful, savvy, clueless)

2. A person who is aware of his or her present bias is called [____]. (a sophisticate, a clueless dreamer, savvy)

3. In period 1 of our simple three-period consumption model, a clueless consumer who experiences present bias makes a plan under which c_1 [____] c_2 and c_2 [____] c_3. (less than, equal to; greater than, equal to; equal to, greater than; equal to, equal to)

4. In period 2 of our simple three-period consumption model, a clueless consumer who experiences present bias makes a plan under which c_2 [____] c_3 (equal to, less than, greater than)

5. Use Widget 10.1 (available at www.oup.com/us/osullivan1e). Suppose $\beta = 0.60$ and $w = 44$. The chosen consumption path is [____]. ((20, 15, 9), (22, 15, 7), (22, 11, 11), (44/3, 44/3, 44/3))

6. In period 1 of our simple three-period consumption model, a savvy consumer who experiences present bias commits to a plan under which c_1 is [____] c_2 and c_2 is [____] c_3 (greater than, equal to; less than, equal to; equal to, equal to; equal to, greater than)

7. A savvy consumer may purchase a house because [____] decreases the temptation for [____]. (low transaction cost, instant gratification; high transaction cost, delayed gratification; low transaction cost, delayed gratification; high transaction cost, instant gratification)

10.4 | Impulse Control by Pigeons

We've seen that humans combat present bias with various strategies such as asset lock-in. In a classic lab experiment, some pigeons were trained to control their impulses for instant gratification (Ainslie 1974). A small fraction of the pigeons took actions to avoid grabbing an immediate food reward, and these actions allowed them to wait for a later and larger reward.

The birds in the experiment pecked lit keys to get food rewards. The scientist started by training 10 pigeons to peck a red-lit key to get an immediate food reward (one unit of food). The idea is that the birds learned the impulsive behavior: peck a red-lit key to get an immediate reward. The scientists then introduced a larger food reward (three units of food) that could be earned by a bird that did not peck the red-lit key over a time interval of three seconds. In other words, waiting three seconds tripled the food reward. Over the course of the experiment (a total of 20,000 trials) the birds learned about the LL (later larger) reward. Nonetheless, each of the birds chose the SS (smaller sooner) reward at least 95 percent of the time. In other words, none of the birds was able to overcome present bias.

The scientists introduced impulse control in the form of a green-lit key. As shown in Figure 10.7, the experiment starts with a green-lit key (1). If a bird pecks the green key, the red key (2) never appears, meaning that impulse pecking for an immediate reward no longer an option. After a delay of 15 seconds, the bird gets the larger reward. In contrast, if the bird does not peck the green-lit key (1), the red-lit key (2) appears after 7.5 seconds, requiring the bird to either peck (reward = 1 unit) or not peck for three seconds (reward = 3 units).

The introduction of the impulse-control opportunity affected the choice of some pigeons. We can divide the pigeons into two groups.

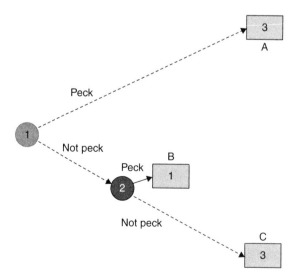

FIGURE 10.7: Pre-Commitment Opportunity for Pigeons

- For most of the pigeons (7 of 10), behavior did not change. They did not peck the green-lit key, and instead waited for the red-lit key, which they pecked for the small reward.
- For 3 of 10 pigeons, behavior changed. These birds acted as if they were savvy about their present bias. They regularly pecked the green-lit key, so they avoided seeing the red-lit key and the uncontrollable impulse to peck at a red-lit key and get an immediate but relatively small reward. As a result, the birds regularly earned the larger reward.

This experiment suggests that with extensive training, some pigeons can learn to control their impulses for instant gratification.

Review the Concepts 10.4

1. In the first stage of the experiment with pigeons, roughly [_____] of the time, pigeons chose the small-soon reward (one unit of food available immediately) rather than the large-later reward (three units of food after waiting three seconds). (20, 50, 60, 95)

2. In the second stage of the experiment with pigeons, 3/10 of the birds acted like they were [____] in the sense that they [____]. (savvy, controlled their impulses; clueless, controlled their impulses; savvy, purchased elaborate bird houses; savvy, invested in GPS devices)

Takeaways

1. In the application of the equimarginal principle to the choice of consumption now (c_1) and later (c_2), the introduction of present bias shifts the marginal-utility curve for c_2 downward, so consumption now increases and consumption later decreases.

2. A policy that mandates a minimum amount of saving (Social Security) is unlikely to affect saving if the initial (pre-mandate) amount saved exceeds the mandated saving amount.

3. A nudge is defined as a policy that (i) allows people to make their own decisions, (ii) does not affect the decisions of fully rational people, and (iii) imposes a relatively low cost.

4. Two nudges have been developed to increase the saving of people subject to present bias: (i) default options in favor of saving and (ii) commitment to future saving.

5. In a three-period model of consumption without conventional discounting, the initial plan of a clueless person is $c_1 > c_2$ and $c_2 = c_3$. On the actual consumption path, $c_2 > c_3$.

6. In a three-period model of consumption without conventional discounting, the initial plan of a savvy consumer is $c_1 = c_2 = c_3$. To execute the plan, a savvy person must purchase assets that cannot be resold until period 2 or period 3.

Discuss the Concepts

1. *Consumption and Regret.* For Wanda, ($\delta = 8/10$, $\beta = 6/10$). For Tula, ($\delta = 1$, $\beta = 1/2$).

   a. [___] consumes a larger fraction of wealth in period 1.

   b. [___] experiences greater regret in period 2.

2. *Mandatory Saving.* Consider an individual with a fixed wealth $w = 120$ to allocate to consumption in two periods. The individual does not experience conventional discounting: $\delta = 1$. The initial saving is $c_2 = 40$. Suppose the government implements a mandatory saving program: a tax of $20 in period 1, and a payment of $20 in period 2. Suppose the individual is attentive and flexible. The program [___] (↑, ↓, does not change) consumption in period 2. During period 2, the individual experiences [___]. (regret, satisfaction with the chosen consumption path)

3. *Consumption Path.* Consider an individual with wealth $w = 60$ to allocate across three periods. The strength of present bias is measured as $\beta = 0.75$, and the individual is clueless about present bias. The consumption path is $c_1 = [\_\_\_]$, $c_2 = [\_\_\_]$, $c_3 = [\_\_\_]$.

4. *WTP for Consumption Contract.* Consider an individual with wealth $w = 60$ to allocate across three periods. The strength of present bias is measured as β. The individual is savvy (self-aware) about his or her present bias, and has an opportunity to sign a binding contract that guarantees $c_1 = c_2 = c_3 = w/3$. The cost of writing and enforcing the contract is T.

   a. To determine the individual's willingness to pay (WTP) for the contract, we need information on [___].

    b. Use Widget 10.1 (available at www.oup.com/us/osullivan1e) to show that the WTP varies with the value of the key parameter.

Apply the Concepts

1. *NGO Spending on Teachers.* You manage an NGO funded by Billinda, whose discounting parameter values are $\delta = 10/11$ and $\beta = 11/20$. The NGO has a fixed sum $w = 63$ to allocate to hiring teachers over two periods: $w = s_1 + s_2$. Billinda's utility function is

$$u(s_1, s_2) = a \cdot \log[s_1] + b \cdot \delta \cdot \beta \cdot \log[s_2]$$

Because of upcoming advances in technology, teachers will be more productive in period 2.

   a. If $a = 20$, a plausible value is $b = [\_\_\_]$. (10, 20, 30)

b. Given the plausible values for a and b, the utility-maximizing values are $s_1 =$ [___] and $s_2 =$ [___]. Illustrate.

c. Suppose Billinda adopts an aggressive meditation program, causing β to increase to $\beta = 11/12$. Given the plausible values for a and b, the utility-maximizing values are $s_1 =$ [___] and $s_2 =$ [___]. Illustrate.

2. *Mandated Saving and MRS.* Consider a household with wealth $w = 60$ and the utility function

$$u\left(c_1, c_2\right) = a \cdot \log\left[c_1\right] + b \cdot \delta \cdot \beta \cdot \log\left[c_2\right]$$

The parameter values are $a = b = 360$, $\delta = 1$, and $\beta = 1/2$. Under a mandated saving program, the government uses a Social Security program to impose a tax of four units of consumption in period 1 and a benefit of three units of consumption in period 2. In other words, the administrative cost of the program is one unit of consumption. Suppose the program decreases c_1 by four units and increases c_2 by 3 units.

a. In the absence of mandated saving, $c_1 =$ [___] and $c_2 =$ [___]. Illustrate.

b. The program [___], (↑, ↓, does not change) lifetime utility from [___] to [___].

3. *Clueless Consumer with $\beta = 2/3$.* Consider the choices of a clueless consumer in a three-period environment. The utility function is

$$u\left(c_1, c_2, c_3\right) = \theta \cdot \log\left[c_1\right] + \theta \cdot \beta \cdot \log\left[c_2\right] + \theta \cdot \beta \cdot \log\left[c_3\right]$$

The parameter values are $\theta = 72$, $\beta = 2/3$, and $w = \$70$.

a. In period 1, the consumption plan for the three periods is $[___], $[___], $[___].

b. In period 2, the consumption plan for the last two periods is $[___], $[___].

4. *Self-Control Potion.* Consider the choices of a consumer in a three-period environment. The utility function is

$$u\left(c_1, c_2, c_3\right) = \theta \cdot \log\left[c_1\right] + \theta \cdot \beta \cdot \log\left[c_2\right] + \theta \cdot \beta \cdot \log\left[c_3\right]$$

The parameter values are $\theta = 72$, $\beta = 1/2$, and $w = \$36$. The consumer has a single dose of a potion that eliminates present bias for a single period.

a. The best time to take the potion is period [___] because [___].

b. The consumer's willingness to pay for the potion is [___] utils.

5. *Save More Tomorrow.* Consider a consumer who is aware of his or her present bias over a three-period lifetime. The utility function is

$$u(c_1, c_2, c_3) = \theta \cdot \log[c_1] + \theta \cdot \beta \cdot \log[c_2] + \theta \cdot \beta \cdot \log[c_3]$$

The parameter values are $\theta = 120$, $\beta = 1/4$, and $w = \$90$. In period 1, the consumer has the opportunity to sign a binding contract that guarantees $c_1 = c_2 = c_3 = w/3$.

   a. In the absence of the contract or other measures to combat present bias, the consumption path is $(c_1, c_2, c_3) = \{\underline{\hspace{1cm}}, \underline{\hspace{1cm}}, \underline{\hspace{1cm}}\}$.

   b. The consumer is willing to pay up to [___] utils for the contract.

6. *Contract for Future Spending.* Consider an individual who does not experience conventional discounting ($\delta = 1$), but experiences present bias, as measured by $\beta = 1/2$.

   a. If wealth increases by \$120 now, the increase in consumption now (period 1) is [___] (>, <, equal to) the increase in consumption later (period 2).

   b. Suppose wealth will increase by \$120 in one year (period 2). Under a contract to be signed today, the increase in consumption in period 2 equals the increase in consumption in period 3. The individual [___] (would, would not) be willing to sign the contract because [___].

7. *Clueless versus Savvy.* Consider an individual with wealth $w = 60$ to allocate across three periods. The strength of present bias is measured as $\beta = 0.75$.

   a. If the individual is clueless about present bias, the consumption path is $c_1 = [\underline{\hspace{0.6cm}}]$, $c_2 = [\underline{\hspace{0.6cm}}]$, $c_3 = [\underline{\hspace{0.6cm}}]$.

   b. Suppose the individual is savvy about his or her present bias, and can sign a contract specifying the consumption path. The consumption path is $c_1 = [\underline{\hspace{0.6cm}}]$, $c_2 = [\underline{\hspace{0.6cm}}]$, $c_3 = [\underline{\hspace{0.6cm}}]$.

8. *Multi-Period Consumption Plan.* Consider a clueless and present-biased consumer with n consumption periods and a symmetric utility function:

$$u(c_1, c_2, \ldots c_n) = \theta \cdot \log[c_1] + \theta \cdot \beta \cdot \log[c_2] + \ldots + \theta \cdot \beta \cdot \log[c_n]$$

Derive an expression for the utility-maximizing consumption in period 1. Use the result from Math 10.6 to check your results: the case $n = 3$ is a special case of the general result.

Math Solutions

Math 10.1: Marginal Utility

The utility function is

$$u(c_1, c_2) = \log[c_1] + \delta \cdot \beta \cdot \log[c_2]$$

Differentiate the utility function with respect to the two choice variables:

$$mu_1 = \frac{1}{c_1} \qquad mu_2 = \frac{\delta \cdot \beta}{c_2}$$

Math 10.2: Utility Maximizing Consumption Now and Later

From Math 10.1, the expressions for marginal utilities are

$$mu_1 = \frac{1}{c_1} \qquad mu_2 = \frac{\delta \cdot \beta}{c_2}$$

Substitute the budget constraint $c_2 = w - c_1$ into the expression for mu_2 and apply the equimarginal rule:

$$\frac{1}{c_1} = \frac{\delta \cdot \beta}{w - c_1}$$

Use algebra to solve for the utility-maximizing c_1:

$$c_1^* = \frac{1}{1 + \delta \cdot \beta} \cdot w$$

Use the budget constraint to solve for the utility-maximizing c_2:

$$c_2^* = \frac{\delta \cdot \beta}{1 + \delta \cdot \beta} \cdot w$$

Math 10.3: Marginal Regret

For actual consumption, present bias is irrelevant ($\beta = 1$), and the marginal utilities are

$$mu_1 = \frac{1}{c_1} \qquad mu_2 = \frac{\delta}{c_2}$$

The ratio of the marginal utilities for actual consumption is

$$\frac{mu_2}{mu_1} = \delta \cdot \frac{c_1}{c_2}$$

Substitute the expressions for the consumption quantities chosen under the influence of present bias ($\beta < 1$):

$$\frac{mu_2}{mu_1} = \delta \cdot \left[\frac{1}{1 + \delta \cdot \beta} \cdot w \right] / \left[\frac{\delta \cdot \beta}{1 + \delta \cdot \beta} \cdot w \right]$$

Cancel the common terms to yield:

$$\frac{mu_2}{mu_1} = \frac{\delta}{\delta \cdot \beta} = \frac{1}{\beta}$$

Math 10.4: Marginal Utilities for Three-Period Model

Apply the rules of differentiating logarithmic functions to the utility function:

$$mu_1 = \frac{\theta}{c_1} \qquad mu_2 = \frac{\theta \cdot \beta}{c_2} \qquad mu_3 = \frac{\theta \cdot \beta}{c_3}$$

Math 10.5: Consumption Now in the Three-Period Model

From the equimarginal rule:

$$\frac{\theta \cdot \beta}{c_2} = \frac{\theta \cdot \beta}{c_3} \Rightarrow c_2 = c_3$$

The budget constraint can be rewritten as

$$c_2 = \frac{w - c_1}{2}$$

Substitute the budget constraint into the expression for the equimarginal rule:

$$\frac{\theta}{c_1} = \frac{2 \cdot \theta \cdot \beta}{w - c_1}$$

Solve for the utility-maximizing consumption in period 1:

$$c_1^* = \frac{1}{1 + 2 \cdot \beta} \cdot w$$

Math 10.6: Utility Maximizing Consumption in Three-Period Model

From the budget constraint, $c_2 = w - c_1 - c_3$. Substitute the expression for c_1 (from Math 10.5) into the budget constraint:

$$c_2 = w - \frac{1}{1 + 2 \cdot \beta} \cdot w - c_3$$

Since $c_3 = \beta \cdot c_2$, the budget constraint in terms of c_3 is

$$c_3 = \beta \cdot \left[w - \frac{1}{1 + 2 \cdot \beta} \cdot w - c_3 \right]$$

Solve for c_3:

$$c_3^* = \frac{2 \cdot \beta^2}{(1+\beta) \cdot (1+2 \cdot \beta)} \cdot w$$

Since $c_3 = \beta \cdot c_2$, we can solve for c_2:

$$c_2^* = \frac{2 \cdot \beta}{(1+\beta) \cdot (1+2 \cdot \beta)} \cdot w$$

11 When to Act

Grabeaux just completed a task in the gig economy and faces a choice: get a $50 check today or get a $55 check in two weeks. If Grabeaux is impatient and chooses the $50 check today, how long will he or she take to cash the check? A recent economic experiment suggests that impatient people procrastinate (Reuben, Sapienza, and Zingales 2015). Three weeks later, Grabeaux thinks, "I could have waited two weeks to receive a bigger check, and then cashed it within a week. In that case, right now I would now have $55 cash in my pocket instead of this wrinkled $50 check." The lesson is that present bias causes both impatience and procrastination.

In this chapter we consider the decision of when to take action—to either incur a cost or collect a benefit. The *when* question is worthy of discussion when (i) the cost to be incurred increases over time or (ii) the benefit to be collected increases over time (O'Donoghue and Rabin 1999). In both cases, present bias distorts the timing of actions and causes later regret. The chapter addresses three key questions.

1. What is the role of present bias in procrastination? Behavioral economists define **procrastination** as waiting to incur a cost when acting early would be better. A procrastinator delays an action, and then later regrets the delay. In the end, the procrastinator thinks, "I should have incurred the cost sooner."

2. What is the role of present bias in preproperation? Behavioral economists define **preproperation** as acting to collect a benefit when waiting would be better. In other words, preproperation is premature action. A preproperator acts too soon, and later regrets the early action. In the end, the preproperator thinks, "I should have waited to collect the benefit."

3. How does an individual's self-awareness about present bias affect procrastination and preproperation? As we'll see, being savvy (self-aware) reduces procrastination, but self awareness can make preproperation worse. In other words, sometimes it is better to be clueless.

To focus attention on present bias, we will assume throughout the chapter that decision-makers are not subject to conventional discounting of future costs and benefits. In other words, the value of the conventional discounting parameter is $\delta = 1$. In the absence of present bias, the current value of a $1 future cost or benefit is $1. This assumption doesn't change the basic logic and conclusions; it makes the results transparent rather than muddied by mixing conventional discounting and present bias.

Learning Objectives: The Explainer

After mastering this chapter, you will be able to explain each of the following statements.

1.   Present bias causes procrastination and later regret.

2.   Self-awareness about present bias tends to decrease procrastination.

3.   Present bias causes preproperation and later regret.

4.   Self-awareness about present bias tends to increase preproperation.

11.1   Procrastination: Waiting Too Long

Consider an individual who must decide when to perform a required task. In Figure 11.1, the cost of performing the task increases over time, from $6, to $10, to $16, and finally to $26. A fully rational individual will compete the task immediately, when the cost of completing the task is lowest. The immediate completion of the task generates a cost of $6, compared to a cost of $26 if the task is completed four months later.

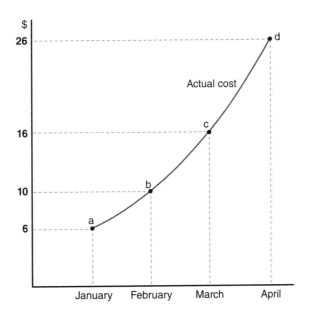

FIGURE 11.1: Increasing Cost of Completing a Task

Present Bias and a Clueless Decision-Maker

Things are not so simple for individuals who are subject to present bias. Consider an individual who is unaware of his or her present bias and unaware of the resulting distortion of decisions. In other words, the individual is clueless about his or her present bias. In behavioral economics, another tag for a **clueless decision-maker** is "naif," indicating that the individual is naive.

Table 11.1 illustrates the decision-making process for an individual with present bias represented by $\beta = 1/2$. The first row of numbers shows the actual costs, as shown in Figure 11.1. The other rows show the perceived costs from different vantage points, when future costs are downplayed by present bias. At the beginning of each month, there is a decision to make: act, or wait to complete the task later. For each month, the decision-maker compares the present cost to the future cost, and delays action if the future cost is lower.

- *January 1: wait and plan to act in February.* The present cost is $6, and present bias downplays all future costs to half their actual values. The downplayed future cost is $5 in February, $8 in March, and $13 in April. The $5 cost in February is less than the $6 present cost, so the individual makes a plan to act in February.
- *February 1: wait and plan to act in March.* Once February is the present, the decision-maker sees the actual $10 cost (up from $5), while all future costs are downplayed by half by present bias. Looking ahead from the February 1 vantage point, the individual makes a plan to act in March, when the downplayed future cost is only $8.
- *March 1: wait and plan to act in April.* Once March is the present, the decision-maker sees the actual $16 cost (up from $8), while the downplayed April cost is only $13. Looking ahead from the March 1 vantage point, the individual makes a plan to act in April.
- *April 1: act.* There is no time left, and the individual completes the task at a present cost of $26.

TABLE 11.1   **Present Bias and Procrastination**

	Cost in $			
	January 1	February 1	March 1	April 1
Actual cost	6	10	16	26
Decision January 1	6	5	8	13
Decision February 1	—	10	8	13
Decision March 1	—	—	16	13
Decision April 1	—	—	—	26

Figure 11.2 illustrates the series of decisions. In addition to the familiar curve showing the time path of the actual cost, the lower curve incorporates

present bias, with $\beta =1/2$. For each future cost, the downplayed (present-biased) cost is half the actual cost. For each vantage point, the dashed arrow shows the present cost and the minimum future cost. For example, in January, the present cost (point a) is higher than the downplayed future cost (point e), so the arrow is negatively sloped. In this example, the arrow is negatively sloped for each decision point (a, b, c), so at the beginning of each month, the individual waits rather than acting. The individual completes the task at the end, when the actual cost is $26.

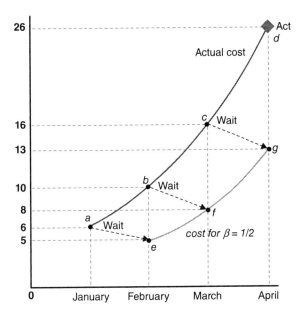

FIGURE 11.2: Rising Cost and Procrastination

As usual, present bias generates two problems for an individual who must decide when to complete a costly task.

- *Time inconsistency.* Although the time path of actual costs does not change, the decision about when to act changes from month to month. The initial plan to act in February is based on the downplaying of February cost. When February arrives, the February cost sheds its future status, and the perceived cost increases. At that point, February seems more costly than March (with its downplayed cost), so the individual abandons the February plan in favor of a March plan. When March arrives, that plan is abandoned in favor of an April plan. A change in the individual's vantage point changes the action plan, resulting in time inconsistency.
- *Regret.* At the end of the process, the individual incurs a cost of $26. The individual regrets not acting at the beginning, when the cost would have been only $6. In other words, present bias causes regrettable procrastination.

Conditions for Procrastination

We can use some simple algebra to identify the conditions that cause procrastination. Consider two successive time periods, 1 (the present) and 2 (the future). An individual will wait if the downplayed future cost is less than the present cost:

$$\beta \cdot c_2 < c_1$$

where c_i is the cost in period i and $\beta < 1$ incorporates present bias. We can rewrite this condition in terms of the growth rate of cost from period 1 to period 2. An individual will wait if

$$\beta \cdot c_1 \cdot (1+g) < c_1$$

where g is the growth rate. For example, if the growth rate is 25 percent per time period, $g = 0.25$. If we divide both sides of the inequality by $c_1 \cdot (1 + g)$, the wait condition simplifies to

$$\beta < \frac{1}{1+g}$$

In other words, an individual will make the misguided choice to wait—procrastinate—when the growth rate is relatively low or if the value of the present-bias parameter is low.

Procrastination is more likely when the growth rate of cost is relatively low. At one extreme, if $g = 0.10$ (a growth rate of 10 percent per time period), the threshold value is $\beta = 10/11$, meaning that any individual with $\beta < 10/11$ procrastinates. A slow growth rate means that it doesn't take much present bias to cause procrastination. In this case, the only non-procrastinators are people with very weak present bias (β between 10/11 and 1). At the other extreme, if $g = 1$ (cost doubles each time period), the threshold value is $\beta = 1/2$, meaning that people with β less than 1/2 procrastinate, but people with higher values of β act immediately rather than waiting. The general lesson is that procrastination is more likely when the cost increases slowly over time.

Review the Concepts 11.1

1. Use the example in Table 11.1. Suppose $\beta = 7/10$. The January decision is to [____] because [____]. (act, 6 < 10; act, 6 < 7; wait, 6 > 5; wait, 6 < 7)

2. The example in Table 11.1 is consistent with a [____] decision-maker because [____]. (clueless, action plans are made and then abandoned; present-biased, future costs are downplayed; savvy, action plans are executed)

3. Present bias is problematic for an individual who must decide when to complete a task subject to rising cost. The problems include [____]. (time inconsistency, regret, delayed action, premature action)

4. A person subject to present bias will procrastinate if present bias is relatively [____] or if the growth rate of cost is relatively [____]. (strong, high; weak, low; strong, low; weak, high)

5. Use Widget 11.1 (available at www.oup.com/us/osullivan1e). Suppose $g = 0.20$. The threshold value for β (the value that separates procrastination from acting immediately) is [____]. (0.50, 0.70, 0.83, 0.90, 1)

6. Use Widget 11.1 (available at www.oup.com/us/osullivan1e). Suppose $\beta = 0.80$. The threshold value for g (the value that separates procrastination from acting immediately) is [____]. (0.20, 0.25, 0.30, 0.40)

11.2   Self-Awareness and Procrastination

Consider next an individual who is aware of his or her present bias and the resulting distortion of the decision of when to act. In other words, the individual is savvy about his or her present bias. In behavioral economics, another tag for a **savvy decision-maker** is "sophisticate." A self-aware individual anticipates the effect of present bias at each stage of the decision-making process. It's important to note that self-awareness does not generate self-control: even a self-aware individual is powerless to overcome present bias in the decision-making moment.

Backward Induction

A self-aware decision-maker uses backward induction to choose when to act. The thought process starts with the final decision-making period and works backward to the present.

- *April 1.* If the individual hasn't acted by April 1, the cost will be $26. From the vantage point of any date before then, the $26 will be downplayed by present bias to $13.
- *March 1.* If the individual hasn't acted by March 1, present bias means that he or she will wait until April because from the March vantage point, the $13 April cost is less than the $16 present cost. A self-aware individual realizes acting on March 1 is not a possibility, because waiting until March means waiting until April. Therefore, the March cost is irrelevant.
- *February 1.* If the individual hasn't acted by February 1, he or she will complete the task then. The self-aware individual recognizes that the March cost is irrelevant. The relevant comparison is the $10 February cost and the $13 April cost (downplayed from $26). The $10 February cost is less than the $13 April cost, so the individual will act in February.
- *January 1.* Acting at the beginning generates a cost of $6. The self-aware individual realizes that delaying to February means acting then, at a cost of $5 (downplayed from $10). The $6 present cost is greater than than the $5 future cost (for February), so the self-aware individual acts will wait, correctly anticipating action in February.

Figure 11.3 illustrates the decision for an individual who is a self-aware about his or her present bias. A self-aware individual realizes that not acting in February ultimately leads to a cost of $26 in April, downplayed to $13 by present bias. The horizontal cost curve that includes point s shows that the downplayed April cost is the cost relevant to the decision on February 1. The individual compares the actual February cost ($10) to the downplayed future cost ($13), and completes the task on February 1. In this example, self-awareness reduces procrastination: the individual completes the task in February rather than waiting until April.

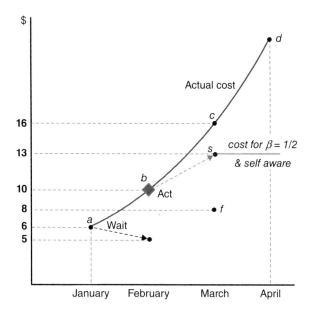

FIGURE 11.3: Self-Awareness Reduces Procrastination

It's important to note that the self-aware individual still experiences present bias. The individual can anticipate present bias but cannot, in the moment a decision is made, do anything about it. So after all that backward induction, the decision on February 1 is still subject to present bias: the individual compares the present cost of $10 in February to $13 for April, not the actual cost equal to $26 in April.

Evidence of Present Bias and Self-Awareness

As noted in an earlier chapter, a recent study by Augenblick and Rabin (2019) estimates the strength of present bias when individuals decide when to complete an unpleasant task—transcribing blurry foreign letters. The authors find strong evidence of present bias, with an estimated value of the present-bias parameter $\beta = 0.83$. On the issue of self-awareness, the authors found little evidence of full self-awareness. But at the individual level, roughly half the participants showed some self-awareness. In summarizing the extent of self-awareness, the authors conclude that participants understood 10–24 percent of their present bias.

Clueless versus Self-Aware: How to Tell the Difference

A recent study provides a clever way to test for self-awareness of present bias (Freeman 2016). At the beginning of each week, a student received a lab assignment that was to be completed in the lab by the end of the week. For some assignments, the lab was open on just two days—Tuesday and Thursday. For other assignments, the lab was open on three days—Tuesday, Wednesday, and Thursday. Consider Kluno, a student who made the following choices.

- *Two lab days.* When the lab was open on just two days (Tuesday and Thursday), Kluno completed the assignment on Tuesday.
- *Three lab days.* When the lab was open on three days (Tuesday, Wednesday, and Thursday), Kluno completed the assignment on Thursday.

In other words, adding the Wednesday option switched Kluno's completion day from Tuesday to Thursday. The question is whether Kluno is clueless or savvy.

Figure 11.4 illustrates Kluno's choice with the two-day and three-day options. The cost of completing the task increases by $6 per day, from $10 on Tuesday, to $16 on Wednesday, to $22 on Thursday. Kluno's present bias is represented by $\beta = 1/2$.

- *Two lab days.* Kluno completes the assignment on Tuesday because Tuesday's $10 is less than Thursday's $11 = $22/2.
- *Three lab days.* On Tuesday, Kluno makes a plan to complete the task on Wednesday because Tuesday's $10 is greater than Wednesday's $8 = $16/2. On Wednesday, Kluno changes the plan, and waits until Thursday because Wednesday's $16 is greater than Thursday's $11 = $22/2.

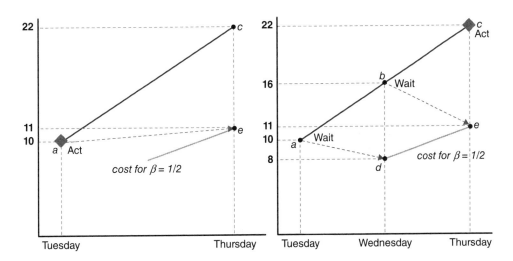

FIGURE 11.4: Test for Clueless versus Savvy

Kluno does not anticipate that he or she will abandon the plan to complete the assignment on Wednesday. Therefore, we conclude that Kluno is clueless—not aware of his or her present bias.

We can contrast Kluno's choice with Saveen, who is self-aware about his or her present bias. Given the option of completing the assignment on Wednesday, Saveen will think ahead to the Wednesday decision. Realizing that present bias experienced on Wednesday will cause a delay until Thursday ($16 > $22/2), Saveen realizes that because of uncontrollable present bias, completing the assignment on Wednesday is logically impossible. Therefore, the Wednesday option is irrelevant and can be ignored. The relevant comparison is Tuesday versus Thursday, and the best choice is Tuesday because $10 < $22/2.

We have a simple test to distinguish between the clueless and the savvy. We can add an intermediate option that is attractive to the clueless (Kluno) but recognized as irrelevant by the savvy (Saveen). The new option causes a clueless individual to (i) make a plan to complete the task at the intermediate date and then (ii) abandon the plan when the intermediate date becomes the present. In contrast, a savvy individual realizes that once the intermediate date becomes the present, the temptation to wait will be irresistible. The savvy individual recognizes that the decision is not between now and a little later (Tuesday versus Wednesday) but actually between now and much later (Tuesday versus Thursday). Tuesday is less costly than Thursday, even after accounting for present bias. In contrast, a clueless individual incorrectly believes that a little later (Wednesday) is a viable option, and acts on this naive belief. Riding a slippery slope, the clueless individual slides through Wednesday and completes the task on Thursday.

Review the Concepts 11.2

1. In Figure 11.3, an individual who is savvy about present bias looks ahead [___] periods to predict how he or she will act. (one, two, three)

2. An individual who is savvy about present bias recognizes that present bias will [___] action at some future dates, so those dates are [___]. (prevent, relevant; prevent, irrelevant; trigger, relevant; trigger, irrelevant)

3. In Figure 11.3, the self-aware individual's regret = [___]. (0, 4, 10, 20)

4. A self-aware individual may procrastinate because self-awareness does not translate into self-[___]. (help, esteem, employment, control)

5. In a study of procrastination on a task of transcribing blurry foreign letters, roughly [___] percent of participants showed some self-awareness of present bias. (1, 10, 50, 90)

6. To test for self-awareness of present bias, we can add an intermediate option that is deceptively attractive to the [___] but irrelevant to the [___]. (clueless, savvy; savvy, clueless)

7. In general, self-awareness of present bias [___] procrastination. (increases, decreases, does not change)

11.3   Preproperation: Acting Too Soon

We turn next to the decision of when to collect a benefit that is increasing over time. As shown in Figure 11.5, the benefit increases each month, starting at $8 and eventually reaching the maximum of $28 in the final month. A fully rational individual will wait until the end of the collection period and collect a $28 benefit on April 1. The benefit of waiting is the $20 gap between the benefit at the end and the benefit at the beginning.

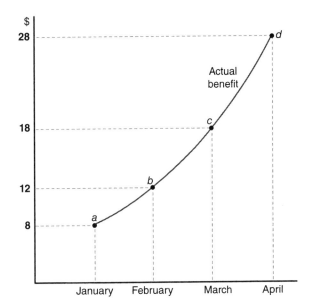

FIGURE 11.5: Increasing Benefit

Present Bias and a Clueless Decision-Maker

Things are not so simple for individuals who are subject to present bias. Consider an individual who is unaware of his or her present bias and the resulting distortion of decision-making. A clueless individual acts under the influence of present bias, and does not anticipate later regret.

Table 11.2 illustrates the decision-making process for an individual with present bias represented by $\beta = 1/2$. The top row of numbers shows the actual benefits, as shown in Figure 11.5. The other rows show benefits after being adjusted for present bias. At the beginning of each time period, the individual looks ahead at the future benefits (downplayed by present bias) and makes a plan to collect the benefit in the period with the highest benefit. At each stage, there is a decision to make: act by collecting the benefit, or wait to collect the benefit later.

- *January 1: wait until April.* The present benefit is $8, compared to a future benefit of $6 in February, $9 in March, and $14 in April. Present bias reduces all future benefit numbers by half, but even after downplaying the benefit in April from $28 to $14, the downplayed benefit exceeds the $8 present benefit. The individual makes a plan to wait until April.

- *February 1: wait until April.* Once February is in the present, the present benefit is $12, while all future benefit numbers are reduced by half by present bias. The downplayed April benefit ($14) still exceeds the $12 present benefit, so the individual stays with the plan to wait until April.
- *March 1: act.* Once March is in the present, the present benefit is $18, while the downplayed April benefit is only $14. The present benefit exceeds the future benefit, so the individual acts and collects an $18 benefit.

TABLE 11.2 **Present Bias and Preproperation**

	Benefit in $			
	January 1	February 1	March 1	April 1
Actual benefit	8	12	18	28
Decision January 1	8	6	9	14
Decision February 1	—	12	9	14
Decision March 1	—	—	18	14
Decision April 1	—	—	—	—

Figure 11.6 illustrates the effects of present bias in collecting a benefit that increases over time. At each stage of the decision-making process, the individual looks ahead to identify the maximum future benefit, which is downplayed because of present bias. When the benefit is increasing over time, the maximum benefit happens in the final period. In Figure 11.6, the maximum benefit is $28 in April, which is downplayed to $14 (point *m*). The maximum downplayed benefit is shown by the horizontal line that includes point *m*.

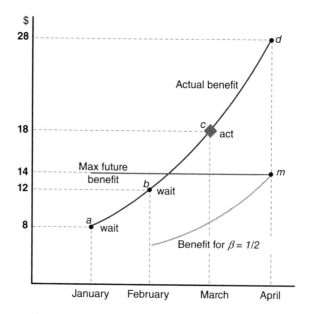

FIGURE 11.6: Rising Benefit and Preproperation

- In the early months, the present benefit ($8 in January and then $12 in February) is less than the downplayed maximum benefit, so the individual waits, anticipating that he or she will collect the benefit in the final period.
- The present benefit increases over time, and the individual will act once it exceeds the downplayed maximum benefit. In Figure 11.6, the individual acts in March because $18 in the present > $14 (the downplayed maximum benefit).

In our example, the individual acts one month early (March instead of April) and collects a benefit of $18 rather than the maximum $28. The term "preproperation" refers to premature action caused by present bias. In our example, the individual preproperates by one month.

As usual, present bias generates two problems for an individual who decides when to collect a benefit that is increasing over time.

- *Time inconsistency.* Although the time path of actual benefits does not change, the decision about when to act changes. The individual first plans to collect the benefit in April. But when March arrives, the individual abandons the plan and collects the benefit in March. Before March 1, the benefits in both March and April were downplayed by present bias. But when March arrives, the March benefit sheds its future status and doubles in perceived value. The increase in value is large enough to cause the individual to collect the benefit rather than waiting.
- *Regret.* At the end of the process, the individual experiences regret equal to the gap between the realized benefit and the maximum benefit. In our example, regret is $10 = $28 – $18.

Conditions for Preproperation

We can use some simple algebra to identify the conditions that lead to preproperation. In the case of increasing benefit, the decision-maker compares the present benefit to the maximum possible future benefit, which is downplayed by present bias. For period i, the individual will make the misguided decision to collect the benefit if the downplayed maximum future benefit is less than the present benefit:

$$\beta \cdot b_{MAX} < b_i$$

where b_i is the benefit in period i and b_{MAX} is the maximum future benefit. We can rewrite this condition in terms of a benefit ratio:

$$\beta < \frac{b_i}{b_{MAX}}$$

In an environment where the benefit grows over time, $b_{MAX} \geq b_i$, so the ratio is less than or equal to one. For example, if the benefit ratio is 9/10 (meaning that b_{MAX} is roughly 11 percent greater than b_i), preproperation happens for the relatively large number of people with $\beta < 9/11$. At the other extreme, if the benefit ratio is 1/3 (meaning that b_{MAX} is three times as large as b_i), preproperation happens only for the relatively small number of people with $\beta < 1/3$. The general lesson is that premature action is more likely when the growth rate of the benefit is relatively low.

We can use the expression for the threshold value of β to predict the choices of an individual facing a given benefit path. For each time period i, compute the ratio (b_i / b_{MAX}) and compare it to the individual's β. If β is less than the benefit ratio, the individual will act prematurely. In contrast, if β exceeds the benefit ratio, the individual will wait for the larger future benefit. In general, an individual will make the fully rational choice to wait if present bias is relatively weak. In the example shown in Figure 11.5, the ratio in March is $18/28 = 0.642$, so an individual with $\beta = 0.75$ will wait for the maximum benefit at the end. For the individual with $\beta = 0.75$, the downplayed future benefit is $21, which exceeds the $18 present benefit in March.

Review the Concepts 11.3

1. Use the example in Table 11.2. Suppose $\beta = 3/4$. The March decision is to [___] because [___]. (act, 18 > 14; wait, 18 < 28; wait, 18 < 21; act, 18 > 17)

2. The example in Table 11.2 is consistent with a [___] decision-maker because [___]. (clueless, action plans are made and then abandoned; present-biased, future benefits are downplayed; savvy, action plans are executed)

3. Present bias is problematic for a person who must decide when to collect a reward that increases over time. The problems include [___] (time inconsistency, regret, premature action, delayed action)

4. A person subject to present bias will preproperate if present bias is relatively [___] or the growth rate of cost is relatively [___]. (strong, high; strong, low; weak, low; weak, high)

5. For a clueless individual, a vision of reaching the final period and the highest benefit is [___]. (realistic, guaranteed, an apparition)

11.4   Self-Awareness and Preproperation

Consider next a savvy individual in an environment of rising benefits. A self-aware individual anticipates the effect of present bias at each stage of the decision-making process. Recall that self-awareness does not translate into self-control: even a self-aware individual is powerless to overcome present bias in the decision-making moment.

Backward Induction

A self-aware decision-maker uses backward induction to decide when to act. The thought process starts with the final decision-making period, and works backward to the present. In Table 11.3, we start at the bottom of the table and work upward.

TABLE 11.3 Preproperation with Self Awareness

	Benefit in $			
	January 1	February 1	March 1	April 1
Actual benefit	8	12	18	28
Decision January 1	8	6	—	—
Decision February 1	—	12	9	—
Decision March 1	—	—	18	14
Decision April 1	—	—	—	28

- *April 1.* If the individual hasn't acted to collect the benefit by April 1, the collected benefit will be $28.
- *March 1.* If the individual hasn't acted by March 1, present bias will cause the individual to collect the $18 benefit in March rather than waiting for the $14 April benefit (downplayed from $28). Because of present bias and unavoidable preproperation, the April benefit is impossible to reach, so a self-aware individual will exclude it from the decision-making process.
- *February 1.* Looking ahead from the February vantage point, the elimination of the April benefit means that the maximum future benefit is the March benefit of $9 (downplayed from $18). If the individual hasn't acted by February 1, present bias will cause the individual to collect the $12 February benefit rather than waiting for the $9 downplayed future benefit in March. Therefore, both the April benefit and the March benefit are excluded from the decision-making process.
- *January 1.* Looking ahead from the January vantage point, the elimination of the March and April benefits means that the maximum future benefit is the February benefit of $6 (downplayed from $12). Acting immediately generates a benefit of $8, so the individual takes action to collect the $8 January benefit rather than waiting for the $6 benefit (downplayed from $12) in February.

Figure 11.7 illustrates the backward induction that leads to immediate action. Looking ahead to the March decision, it seems better to act (benefit = 18) than to wait for April (benefit = 14). Looking ahead to February, it seems better to act (benefit = 12) than to wait for March (benefit = 9). For January, it seems better to act (benefit = 8) than to wait for February (benefit = 6). Therefore, immediate action seems best.

The lesson from Table 11.3 and Figure 11.7 is that self-awareness about present bias can strengthen preproperation. Recall that the clueless individual acted in March and collected a benefit of $18. In other words, the clueless individual preproperates by one month and collects $18. In Table 11.3, the savvy individual acts in January, meaning that he or she preproperates by three months and collects only $8.

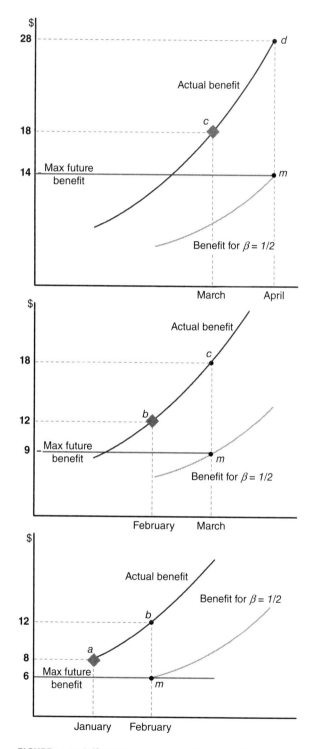

FIGURE 11.7: Self-Awareness Increases Preproperation

Is Being Clueless Better?

Wait a minute! Being clueless is better than being savvy? The problem is that a savvy individual is clever enough to realize that it's impossible to reach the end and get the maximum benefit. In contrast, a clueless individual erroneously believes that reaching the maximum benefit is possible.. A clueless individual waits two months, enticed by the vision of collecting the maximum payment. Although the vision turns out to be an apparition (the clueless individual actually collects the benefit in March, not April), the erroneous belief is useful because it delays the collection of the benefit by two months and increases the benefit from $8 in January to $18 in March. In other words, the benefit of being clueless rather than savvy is $10.

Review the Concepts 11.4

1. In Table 11.3, an individual who is savvy about present bias looks ahead [____] periods to predict how he or she will act. (one, two, three)

2. In Figure 11.7, a savvy individual realizes that collecting the benefit in [____] is a logical impossibility because [____]. (April, 18 > 14; March, 12 > 9; February, 8 > 6)

3. An individual who is savvy about present bias recognizes that present bias will [____] action at some future date, so later dates are irrelevant to the wait/act decision. (prevent, not affect, block, trigger)

4. In Figure 11.7, the self-aware individual's regret = [____]. (4, 10, 20, 22)

5. A self-aware individual may preproperate because self-awareness does translate into self-[____]. (help, control, esteem, employment)

6. Self-awareness of present bias can increases preproperation because a savvy individual is less likely to [____] believe that reaching the maximum reward is [____]. (correctly, impossible; incorrectly, impossible; incorrectly, possible; correctly, possible)

7. In general, self-awareness of present bias [____] preproperation. (increases, decreases, does not affect)

8. For a savvy individual who experiences strong present bias, the thought of reaching the final period and the highest benefit is [____]. (embraced, dismissed, realistic)

Key Terms

clueless decision-maker, p. 202   procrastination, p. 200
preproperation, p. 200   savvy decision-maker, p. 205

Takeaways

1. When the cost of a task is increasing over time, present bias may cause procrastination.

2. Present bias causes (i) time inconsistency and (ii) later regret.

3. An individual subject to present bias will procrastinate if the growth rate of cost is relatively low or if present bias is relatively strong (β is relatively small).

4. Self-awareness of present bias can decrease procrastination because a savvy individual realizes that it will be impossible, in the future, to resist the temptation to delay.

5. When the benefit of an action increases over time, present bias may cause preproperation (premature action).

6. An individual subject to present bias will preproperate if the growth rate of the benefit is relatively low or if present bias is relatively strong (β is relatively small).

7. Self-awareness of present bias can increase preproperation because a savvy individual realizes that it will be impossible to wait long enough to get the maximum benefit.

Discuss the Concepts

1. *Laundry Day Beta.* Lavo has a bag of dirty laundry that must be cleaned today or tomorrow. The laundry facility will be busier tomorrow, so completing the task will require 3 hours, compared to only 1.8 hours today. If Lavo waits until tomorrow, his or her present bias can be measured as $\beta \leq$ [____]. Lavo's regret = [____] hours.

2. *Laundry Day Test.* Lavo has a bag of dirty laundry that must be cleaned today (Monday), Tuesday, or Wednesday. The laundry facility will be busier each day, so completing the task will require 1.8 hours Monday, compared to 3 hours on Tuesday and 5 hours on Wednesday. Lavo's present bias is measured as $\beta = 1/2$.

   a. Lavo will do the laundry on [____] and experience regret = [____] hours.

   b. Suppose the owner of the laundry announces on Sunday that the facility will be open on Monday and Wednesday, but not Tuesday. Lavo will do the laundry on [____] and experience regret = [____] hours.

   c. The answers to (b) indicate that Lavo is [____]. (clueless, savvy).

3. *Clueless Apple Harvester.* A ripening apple gets sweeter each day on the tree, so the utility from consuming it increases from 18 on Monday, to 24 on Tuesday, to 30 on Wednesday. Tutherd's present bias is measured by $\beta = 2/3$.

Tutherd is unaware of his or her present bias. Tutherd will consume the apple on [___] because [___] > [___].

4. *Savvy Apple Harvester.* An ripening apple gets sweeter each day on the tree, so the utility from consuming it increases from 18 on Monday, to 24 on Tuesday, to 30 on Wednesday. Tutherd's present bias is measured by $\beta = 2/3$. Tutherd is aware of his or her present bias. Tutherd will consume the apple on [___] because [___] > [___].

Apply the Concepts

1. *Nudges to Prevent Procrastination.* The cost of completing the task immediately is $10, and the growth rate for the cost is 0.50. Consider a worker with present bias represented by $\beta = 1/2$ who must complete a task on one of the next four days. The firm incurs a $4 cost for each day of delayed action beyond day 1.

   a. Under a delay penalty, the worker pays a penalty d on day 2 if the task is not completed on day 1. In the case of indifference, the worker completes the task immediately. The minimum delay penalty required to nudge the worker to complete the task immediately is $d^* = \$[\_\_\_]$. The gain for the worker is $[___] and the gain for the firm is $[___].

   b. Under an action reward, the worker receives a reward r for completing the task immediately. In the case of indifference, the worker completes the task immediately. The minimum reward required to nudge the worker to complete the task immediately is $r^* = \$[\_\_\_]$. The gain for the worker is $[___] and the gain for the firm is $[___].

2. *Rising Cost: Clueless versus Savvy.* Consider a cost time path $c(t) = 5 + t^2$ for $t = (1, 2, 3, 4, 5)$. The decision-maker is subject to present bias, with $\beta = 1/2$.

   a. A clueless decision-maker (not aware of present bias) will act at $t^* = [\_\_\_]$ and experience regret = $[___]. Illustrate with the relevant numbers.

   b. A clueless decision-maker (not aware of present bias) will make the same choice as a fully rational individual (without present bias) if $\beta \geq [\_\_\_]$. Show your calculations. Illustrate with the relevant numbers.

   c. A savvy decision-maker (aware of present bias) with $\beta = 1/2$ will act at $t^* = [\_\_\_]$. Explain your logic and illustrate with the relevant numbers.

3. *Rising Benefit: Clueless versus Savvy.* Consider a benefit time path $b(t) = t^2$ for $t = (1, 2, 3, 4, 5)$. The decision-maker is subject to present bias.

   a. A clueless decision-maker (not aware of present bias with $\beta = 1/2$) will act at $(t^*) = [\_\_\_]$ and experience regret = $[___]. Illustrate with the relevant numbers.

b. A clueless decision-maker (not aware of present bias) will make the same choice as a fully rational individual (without present bias) if $\beta \geq$ [____]. Show your calculations. Illustrate with the relevant numbers.

c. A savvy decision-maker (self-aware about present bias) with $\beta = 1/2$ will act at $t^* =$ [____] and experience regret = $[____] Explain your logic and illustrate with the relevant numbers.

4. *Pareto Improvement for Preproperation.* Consider a clueless landowner (not aware of his or her present bias with $\beta = 0.40$) who must sell a plot of land now ($t = 1$), or $t = 2$ or $t = 3$. The current ($t = 1$) price of land is $8 and the growth rate is 0.50 per time period. The landowner has a conventional discount factor $\delta = 1$.

   a. The landowner will act at $t^* =$ [____] and collect a benefit of $[____].

   b. Vilfredo is not subject to present bias and has a conventional discount factor $\delta = 1$. Design a Pareto improvement that divides any gain equally between Vilfredo and the landowner. The landowner's payoff changes from $[____] to $[____]. Vilfredo's payoff is $[____].

5. *Yoga for Temporary Cluelessness.* Suppose the time path of the benefit of consuming a product over five days is (55, 57, 72, 90, 120). The value of the present-bias parameter is $\beta = 2/3$.

   a. A clueless individual will collect the benefit at $t^* =$ [____] and experience regret $r^* =$ [____]. Illustrate.

   b. A savvy individual will collect the benefit at $t^{**} =$ [____] and experience regret $r^{**} =$ [____]. Illustrate.

   c. A new yogi has established a daily yoga session that makes a normally savvy individual clueless for the 24 hours following the session. The savvy individual can choose one session over the next five days. The best timing for the yoga session is day [____]. The savvy yoga individual will collect the benefit at $t^{***} =$ [____] and is willing to pay up to $[____] for a yoga session.

Application of Present Bias—Sin Taxes and Fertilizer   **12**

In the 1960s, the liberal activist Zelda Gamson promoted civil rights as a member of the Congress on Racial Equality. As part of her job, she went undercover to expose racial discrimination in housing. For decades, Zelda tried to quit smoking. She engaged in an internal tug-of-war between the part of herself that enjoyed smoking and the other part that knew that smoking was dirty and harmful. After decades of failed attempts to quit smoking, she adopted a new incentive program. She made a solemn pledge that if she ever smoked another cigarette, she would pay a penalty of $5000. As an added incentive, Zelda pledged to send the $5000 to the Ku Klux Klan, an organization she detested. It worked: she never smoked another cigarette.

Source: "Help!" Radiolab, March 9, 2011 (www.radiolab.org)

In this chapter we explore the role of public policy in promoting efficient intertemporal choice. We consider two economic environments where people subject to present bias struggle to make choices that promote with their long-term interests. In the realm of consumer behavior, we explore the effect of present bias in decisions about personally harmful products such as cigarettes and sugar water. In the realm of producer behavior, we explore the effect of present bias on investment in inputs such as fertilizer. In addition, we discuss various actions that can mitigate the ill effects of present bias.

Learning Objectives: The Explainer

After mastering this chapter, you will be able to explain each of the following statements.

1. Present bias tilts consumption in favor of cigarettes and other products that have a relatively high future cost.

2. A savvy consumer of a harmful product can mitigate the effects of present bias by increasing the price of the product.

3. Many smokers and potential smokers support high taxes on cigarettes.

4.   Present bias decreases investment because it decreases the marginal rate of substitution between consumption now and later.

5.   A precisely timed fertilizer subsidy is a nudge aimed at present-biased farmers.

12.1   Personally Harmful Products and Sin Taxes

In this part of the chapter, we explore the role of present bias in the consumption of products that are enticing in the present but personally harmful in the future. For example, cigarettes deliver pleasurable nicotine in the present but cause lung disease in the future. Our model of a personally harmful product is a variation on a model developed by O'Donoghue and Rabin (2003).

A Model of a Personally Harmful Good

Consider a consumer of two products, a personally harmful product (x) and another product (y). The utility function is

$$u(x,y) = a \cdot \log[x] + b \cdot \log[y]$$

where log [ ] is the natural logarithm, x is the quantity of the personally harmful product, and y is the quantity of the other product. We assume that each product has a market price of one. The consumer's budget constraint is

$$w = x + y$$

For each unit of the harmful product consumed today, the consumer incurs a future cost c, so the actual future cost of the harmful product is

$$future\ cost = c \cdot x$$

To simplify matters, we will assume that $a = b = 1$, meaning that the only difference between the two products is that the harmful product has a future cost.

We can use the equimarginal principle to illustrate the consumer's utility-maximizing choice. The decision-making rule is to choose the affordable bundle of the two products that makes the marginal utility per dollar spent on x equal to the marginal utility per dollar spent on y. In casual terms, the consumer chooses a bundle that equates the marginal bang per buck. As shown in Math 12.1, the marginal utilities per dollar for the two products are

$$MU\ per\ dollar\ on\ x = \frac{a}{x \cdot (1+c)} \qquad\qquad MU\ per\ dollar\ on\ y = \frac{b}{y}$$

Each product has a market price of $1, and the harmful product has an additional cost of c per unit. Therefore, for a given quantity, the harmful product has a lower marginal utility per dollar.

Figure 12.1 illustrates the application of the equimarginal principle for a rational consumer. The consumer incorporates the full future cost of a harmful product into its decision. The marginal-utility curve for the harmful product is lower because its future cost is $c > 0$. In this example, the future cost is $c = 3$, and consumer wealth is $w = 60$. The marginal utility per dollar is equalized at points g and h: the consumption of the harmful product is one-fourth the consumption of the regular product.

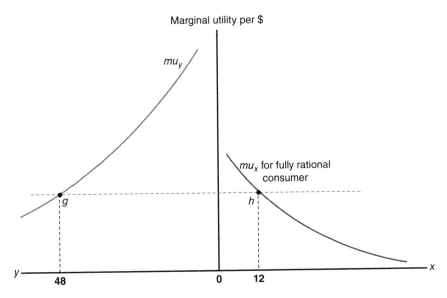

FIGURE 12.1: A Rational Consumer and a Harmful Product

We can derive an expression that shows the consumption of the harmful product relative to the consumption of the other product. As shown in Math 12.2, the utility-maximizing consumption of the harmful product is a fraction of the consumption of the other product:

$$x = y \cdot \frac{1}{1+c}$$

For $c = 0$, the utility-maximizing consumption of the two products are equal: $x = y$. This is sensible because, in the absence of future costs, the two products are equivalent in terms of utility. As the future cost increases (as c increases), the utility-maximizing consumption of the harmful product decreases. For example, if $c = 3$, the consumption of the harmful product is one-fourth the consumption of the regular product.

Present Bias and a Personally Harmful Good

Consider next the effect of present bias on the utility-maximizing consumption bundle. The perceived future cost of the harmful product is determined by the strength of present bias, as measured by $\beta < 1$:

$$perceived\ future\ cost = \beta \cdot c \cdot x$$

For a consumer subject to present bias with $\beta < 1$, the weight on the future cost is relatively low. For example, a person who smokes cigarettes today downplays the future cost associated with emphysema or lung cancer. Similarly, a person who drinks sugary soda today downplays the future costs associated with obesity and related health problems.

Figure 12.2 shows the consequences of present bias on consumer choice. For the harmful product, there are two marginal-utility curves: one for a fully rational consumer ($\beta = 1$), and a second for a consumer with strong present bias ($\beta = 1/3$). Present bias decreases the perceived future cost of the harmful product, so it shifts the marginal-utility curve for the harmful product upward. Applying the equimarginal principle, present bias increases the consumption of the harmful product (from 12 to 20) at the expense of the other product (from 48 to 40). When a consumer underplays the negative future consequences of today's consumption choice, consumption is tilted in favor of the harmful product.

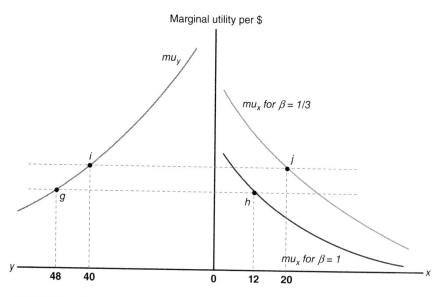

FIGURE 12.2: Present Bias and a Harmful Product

We can use simple algebra to get additional insights into the link between present bias and consumption of the harmful product. As shown in Math 12.3, present bias tilts consumer choice in favor of the harmful product. For $\beta < 1$, the utility-maximizing consumption of the harmful product is a larger fraction of the consumption of the other product:

$$x = y \cdot \frac{1}{1 + \beta \cdot c}$$

As β decreases, the denominator decreases, so the fraction increases.

We can illustrate the tilt in favor of the harmful product with our continuing example. Recall that the future cost per unit of the harmful product is $c = 3$. For a fully rational consumer ($\beta = 1$), the cost of the harmful product is four times the cost of the other product (4 versus 1), and the consumption of the harmful product is one-fourth the consumption of the other product:

$$\beta = 1 \Rightarrow x = \frac{y}{4}$$

In contrast, for a consumer subject to present bias with $\beta = 1/3$, the perceived cost of the harmful product is only twice the cost of the other product (2 versus 1), and the consumption of the harmful product is half the consumption of the other product:

$$\beta = 1/3 \Rightarrow x = \frac{y}{2}$$

In the extreme case with $\beta = 0$, the consumer ignores all the future cost of the harmful product, so the cost of the harmful product equals the cost of the other product (1). As a result, the consumption of the harmful product equals the consumption of the other product:

$$\beta = 0 \Rightarrow x = y$$

Savvy Consumers and Hobbling

Some consumers are self-aware of their present bias and its effects on their consumption of harmful products. A savvy but present-biased consumer can take actions that increase the cost of the product and thus decrease consumption. Some smokers don't keep a stock of cigarettes available for ready use, but instead wait until their desire for a smoke is strong enough to justify a special trip to the store. Another strategy is to purchase a harmful product in small quantities and thus pay a higher unit price. For example, the price per cigarette is higher when purchased by the pack rather than by the carton. As an extreme measure, some consumers purchase individual cigarettes, and thus pay a much higher unit price. These self-imposed hobbling actions increase the cost of consuming a harmful product and at least partly offset present bias.

For some harmful products, self-imposed hobbling is reinforced by public policy. The purchase of cigarettes sometimes requires extra time for a store clerk as they retrieve cigarettes from a special enclosure. Some governments restrict the sale of alcohol to special stores, and others prohibit alcohol sales on certain days of the week. These measures provide special treatment of harmful products, and are designed to increase the cost to a consumer and decrease consumption.

Support for Sin Taxes

Many governments impose relatively high taxes on harmful products such as cigarettes and alcoholic beverages. These taxes receive widespread support, even among potential and actual consumers of the products. A cigarette tax increases the price of cigarettes and decreases the quantity purchased, so smokers benefit from lower future health costs. The health benefits at least partly offset the

smoker's tax liability. For a consumer who quits smoking in response to a cigarette tax, the benefit of lower future health costs comes without any tax liability.
The absence of a tax liability does not mean that the tax is costless to the former
smoker, because he or she experiences a loss of consumer surplus.

How large a tax would be required to fully offset the effects of present bias?
The sum of the perceived future cost ($\beta \cdot c$) and the tax per unit of the product (τ)
must equal the actual future cost of consuming one unit of the product:

$$\beta \cdot c + \tau = c$$

We can solve for the tax rate as a function of the present-bias parameter:

$$\tau* = c \cdot (1 - \beta)$$

In our example, c = $3 and β = 1/3, so a tax of $2 would get the consumer
to choose the fully rational quantity. As shown in Figure 12.3, the tax is zero
in the case of fully rational consumers (β = 1). As present bias gets stronger
(as β decreases) the tax increases, to $1 for β = 2/3 and to $2 for β = 1/3. In the
extreme case of β = 0, a consumer ignores the future cost of the harmful product,
and the sin tax equals the ignored future cost.

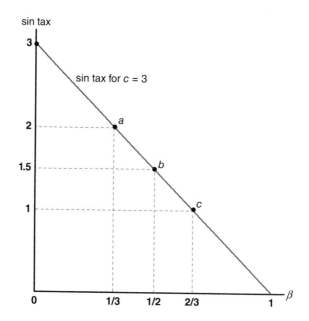

FIGURE 12.3: Present Bias and a Sin Tax

Another advantage of a tax on a harmful product is that it can reduce tax
rates on other products. Suppose the government replaces a tax on a regular product (y) with a tax on cigarettes (x), and total tax revenue does not change. The
revenue-neutral switch to the cigarette tax may improve welfare.

- A sin tax (a tax on a harmful product) can improve efficiency by counteracting the irrational choices caused by present bias.
- A tax on a regular product distorts consumer choice and causes inefficiency, measured as the excess burden of a tax. The elimination of a tax on a regular product eliminates the distortion of consumer choice, and thus improves the efficiency of the economy.

It is possible that a revenue-neutral switch from a tax on a regular product to a tax on a harmful product will improve efficiency. If taxes are required to support public programs, a tax on a harmful product is likely to be more efficient than a tax on other products.

We can relate a sin tax to a tax on pollution. A pollution tax is justified on efficiency grounds because one actor (a polluting firm) ignores the external cost imposed on other actors (air breathers). A pollution tax equal to the marginal external cost of pollution causes the polluter to incorporate the full cost of pollution into the decision-making process. As a result, the volume of pollution decreases and people breathe easier. In the case of a harmful product, there are two actors—a present self and a future self. The present self smokes cigarettes and imposes a cost on the future self. A sin tax will decrease present consumption, and allow the future self to breathe easier. In other words, a sin tax is a sort of intertemporal externality tax.

Review the Concepts 12.1

1. For an initial consumption bundle, the marginal utility for $x = 18$ and the marginal utility for $y = 6$. For each product, the price is 1. This is the utility-maximizing bundle if the additional unit cost of $x = $ [____]. (0, 1, 2, 3).

2. Present bias causes a consumer to [____]. (over-weight future cost, under-weight present benefits, over-weight future cost, under-weight future cost)

3. Present bias [____] the perceived future cost of a harmful product and [____] the consumption of the product. (increases, decreases; decreases, increases; increases, increases; decreases, decreases)

4. Use Figure 12.2. Suppose $c = 3$ and β increases to $\beta = 2/3$. The consumption of x is [____] the consumption of y. (1/3, 1/2, 3/5, 2/3)

5. A consumer who purchases a harmful product in small quantities is revealing self-[____]. (esteem, flattery, awareness, contempt)

6. A smoker is likely to support a cigarette tax if he or she [____]. (is savvy about present bias, experiences relatively strong present bias, is clueless about present bias, experiences relatively weak present bias)

7. A tax on a personally harmful product shifts the [___] cost of consumption to the [___] self. (present, future; future, present; past, future)

 8. Use Widget 12.1 (available at www.oup.com/us/osullivan1e). Suppose $\beta = 0.70$ and you control the price. Your objective is to reach a ratio of x/y roughly equal to the ratio that occurs in the absence of present bias. The appropriate price is roughly [___]. (1.5, 2.0, 2.5, 3, 3.5)

12.2 Present Bias And Fertilizer Investment

Fertilizer is a key input to agriculture, and its use varies significantly around the globe. In recent decades in Asia, the widespread application of fertilizer increased crop yields dramatically. In contrast, many farmers in Africa fail to invest in fertilizer, despite a rate of return greater than 50 percent in some environments. In many African countries, the under-utilization of fertilizer contributes to relatively low agricultural productivity. The traditional response is to subsidize fertilizer for all farmers. As we'll see, behavioral economics suggests a different approach: farmers who are subject to present bias can be nudged into making choices that promote their own long-term interests.

Review of Intertemporal Choice Model

We start our discussion of fertilizer use with a brief review of the conventional model of intertemporal choice, which is typically introduced in a course in intermediate microeconomics. In Figure 12.4, the horizontal axis measures consumption now (c_1) and the vertical axis measures consumption later (c_2).

- *Budget constraint.* The budget line is anchored by the income bundle: consumer income is w_1 in period 1 and w_2 in period 2, generating the endowment point e. The slope of the budget line is the marginal rate of transformation (MRT) between consumption now and later, computed as the increase in future consumption generated by a one-unit decrease in current consumption. When a consumer earns interest income on saving, MRT $= 1 + r$, where r is the interest rate on saving. In this case, when a consumer decreases consumption now by \$1 and places the money in a bank account, the \$1 grows to $(1 + r)$ one period later. In general, MRT measures the market trade-off between consumption now and consumption later. A large MRT indicates a relatively large payoff later from reducing consumption now.
- *Preferences.* An indifference curve shows different bundles of current consumption and future consumption that generate a given utility level. The slope of an indifference curve is the marginal rate of substitution (MRS), defined as the increase in c_2 (consumption later) required to offset, in utility terms, a one-unit decrease in c_1 (consumption now). In other words, the slope shows the consumer's personal trade-off between consumption now and consumption later. A large MRS indicates a relatively high value of consumption now, meaning that a large increase in consumption later is required to offset a one-unit decrease in consumption now.

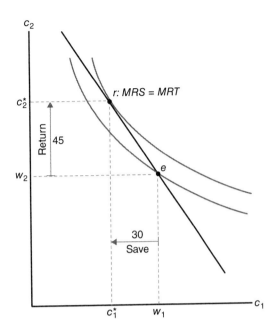

FIGURE 12.4: Intertemporal Consumption Model

A utility-maximizing consumer chooses the feasible consumption bundle that generates the highest utility. The feasible points lie on and below the budget line. In Figure 12.4, utility is maximized at point r, where an indifference curve is tangent to the budget line. The tangency means that the marginal rate of substitution equals the marginal rate of transformation: MRS = MRT. Household saving is shown by the gap between income and consumption in period 1: saving $= w_1 - c_1^*$. In Figure 12.4, household saving is $30. The marginal rate of transformation is MRT $= 1.50$, so a consumer who saves $30 gets $45 in additional consumption later.

Saving is positive because, at the endowment point, the marginal rate of transformation exceeds the household's marginal rate of substitution: MRT > MRS. Starting at point e, MRS $= 1.20$, indicating that the consumer is willing to save $1 if the return is at least $1.20. Because the actual return is MRT $= 1.50$, the first dollar saved returns $0.30 more than the household requires, so saving is sensible. As household saving increases and c_1 decreases, the marginal rate of substitution increases, so the gap between MRT and MRS decreases. At the utility-maximizing point, MRS $= 1.50 =$ MRT. Saving more than $30 is not sensible because beyond point r, MRS > MRT. For the 31st dollar saved, the household requires a return greater than the market provides, so the household stops at point r.

Present Bias and the Fertilizer Investment

We're ready to apply the intertemporal choice model to investment in fertilizer. Figure 12.5 shows a two-period choice model for a farmer who has an opportunity to invest in fertilizer with a rate of return of 50 percent. A farmer who does not use fertilizer produces and consumes w units of food each year, as shown by the endowment point e: $c_1 = c_2 = w$. A second option is to use some of this year's crop to purchase fertilizer to increase next year's crop. To purchase fertilizer, a farmer reduces current consumption by 30 units.

There are trade-offs associated with investment. To determine whether investment is sensible, we compare the marginal rate of transformation to the marginal rate of substitution.

- *MRT = 1.50.* Fertilizer increases next year's output by 45 units, leading to point r. As shown by points e and r, the marginal rate of transformation of current consumption into future consumption is MRT = 1.50 = 45/30. The payback to a 30-unit investment is 45 units.
- *MRS = 1.20.* As shown by point u (on the indifference curve that also includes point e), starting from the endowment point, the farmer's marginal rate of substitution is 1.20 = 36/30. The farmer will be indifferent about a 30-unit investment if the payback is 36 units.

Investment is a rational choice because the farmer's marginal rate of substitution (1.20) is less than the marginal rate of transformation (1.50). The farmer requires a payback of at least 36 units, and the actual payback is 45 units. Investment in fertilizer allows the farmer to reaches point r, which is on a higher indifference curve. As a result, point r generates greater utility for the farmer.

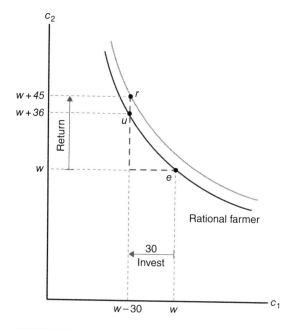

FIGURE 12.5: Rational Farmer Invests in Fertilizer

   We're ready to incorporate present bias into our model of fertilizer investment. As shown in Math 12.4, the marginal rate of substitution equals the ratio of
the marginal utilities of consumption between now and later:

$$MRS = \frac{mu_1}{mu_2}$$

Present bias decreases the marginal utility of consumption later (mu_2) relative
to the marginal utility of consumption now (mu_1), so it increases the marginal
rate of substitution. In other words, a person who downplays the benefit of future
consumption requires a larger increase in future consumption to offset a one-unit
decrease in consumption now.

   Figure 12.6 shows that a farmer subject to strong present bias will not invest
in fertilizer. Present bias increases the marginal rate of substitution, increasing
the slope of the indifference curve. Between point e and point b, the farmer's
marginal rate of substitution is $2.0 = 60/30$. The farmer will be indifferent about
a 30-unit investment if the payback is 60 units. The actual payback is still 45
units, so the present-biased farmer will not invest. In other words, the new MRS
(equal to 2) is greater than the MRT (equal to 1.50), so the farmer will not invest
in fertilizer. The lesson from Figures 12.5 and 12.6 is that present bias increases
the marginal rate of substitution, so it discourages investment in fertilizer.

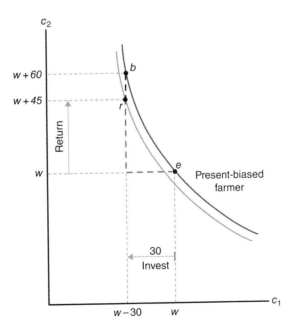

FIGURE 12.6: Present-Biased Farmer Does Not Invest in
Fertilizer

Policy Options: Subsidy versus Nudge

The conventional response to under-investment in fertilizer is a subsidy that reduces the cost of fertilizer to a farmer. In our example, a 50 percent subsidy means that a farmer can get 30 units of fertilizer at a cost of only 15 units of current consumption: the marginal cost of fertilizer decreases. From the farmer's perspective, the marginal rate of transformation increases to MRT = 3 = 45/15. For the present-biased farmer with MRS = 2, the higher MRT means that investment in fertilizer is now attractive. The subsidy makes the MRT greater than the MRS for more farmers, so fertilizer use increases.

The problem with the conventional policy is that not all farmers are present biased. The subsidy decreases the marginal cost of fertilizer for all farmers, including those who are not subject to present bias. The unbiased farmers would purchase fertilizer even without the subsidy, and the subsidy will cause them to buy more fertilizer. This is problematic for two reasons.

- Public funds are transferred to fully rational farmers, requiring either (i) higher taxes on consumer products or income or (ii) cuts in other government programs.
- If fertilizer is normally priced close to its marginal social cost, the subsidy and the resulting lower price will cause inefficiency as rational farmers use more than the efficient quantity of fertilizer.

An alternative policy is a carefully timed nudge. Imagine that at harvest time the government provides a small, short-lived subsidy on fertilizer for next year's crop. Consider a farmer who is savvy and self-aware of his or her present bias in the months between this year's harvest and next year's fertilizing time. The short-lived subsidy provides an opportunity for the farmer to invest in fertilizer at harvest time, precisely when he or she has the most resources available to invest. As reported by Duflo, Kremer, and Robinson (2011), this sort of small and carefully timed subsidy is effective in increasing fertilizer investment by present-biased farmers. In one set of experiments, a program of small, short-lived subsidies increased fertilizer adoption by 14 percent.

Recall that a key feature of a nudge is that it does not distort the behavior of unbiased (rational) decision-makers. A farmer who is not subject to present bias is unlikely to be tempted by the small and short-lived fertilizer subsidy. The rational choice for such a farmer is to invest his or her "fertilizer money" in an interest-bearing account or other productive investment. Such an investment generates income on the fertilizer money between this year's harvest time and next year's fertilizing time. In contrast with a present-biased farmer, the fully rational farmer has the discipline not to raid a bank account between last year's harvest time and next year's fertilizer time.

Review the Concepts 12.2

1. In the conventional model of intertemporal choice, utility is maximized at the (c_1, c_2) bundle where [____]. (the marginal rate of substitution equals the marginal rate of transformation, an indifference curve is tangent to the budget line, $mu_1/mu_2 = MRT$)

2. In the conventional model of intertemporal choice, saving is positive when [____]. ($c_1^* < w_1$, the utility-maximizing point is to the left of the endowment point, $c_1^* > w_1$, the utility-maximizing point is to the right of the endowment point)

3. Present bias [____] the marginal rate of substitution between c_1 and c_2 because present bias [____] the marginal utility of consumption in period 2. (decreases, increases; increases, increases; increases, decreases; decreases, decreases)

4. Present bias decreases the use of fertilizer when it makes the marginal rate of substitution [____] the marginal rate of transformation. (greater than, less than, equal to)

5. A conventional subsidy for fertilizer is problematic because it distorts the choices of [____] farmers. (fully rational, present-biased)

6. An efficient response to under-investment in fertilizer is a [____] subsidy targeted at [____] farmers. (planting-time, present-biased; harvest-time, present-biased; harvest-time, fully rational)

Takeaways

1. In the model of a personally harmful product, present bias increases consumption because the consumer downplays the future cost of the harmful product.

2. In a model of utility maximization with product prices p_1 and p_2, the equimarginal rule is to choose the consumption bundle such that the marginal utility per dollar spent on product 1 (equal to mu_1/p_1) equals the marginal utility per dollar spent on product 2 (equal to mu_2/p_2).

3. A tax on a personally harmful product can improve efficiency by (i) decreasing consumption and (ii) decreasing distortionary taxes on other products.

4. A rational farmer will invest in fertilizer if the marginal rate of transformation (MRT) exceeds the marginal rate of substitution (MRS).

5. Present bias can decrease investment in fertilizer because it increases the marginal rate of substitution between consumption now and later.

6. An alternative to a conventional fertilizer subsidy is a carefully timed subsidy targeted at farmers who experience present bias.

Discuss the Concepts

1. *Harmful Product Numbers.* Consider an economy with two products, a regular product with price $p_y = 1$ and a harmful product with price $p_x = 1$ and future cost $c = 5$. For a fully rational consumer, $x/y = $ [____]. For a present-biased consumer with $\beta = 0.40$, $x/y = $ [____]. Illustrate the case of the present-biased consumer, assuming $y = 30$.

2. *Hobble to Target.* Consider a consumer who experiences strong present bias ($\beta = 1/3$), leading to relatively high consumption of cigarettes. Use a graph like Figure 12.2 to show the effect of purchasing cigarettes one at a time, at a unit price that exceeds the regular unit price (from buying cigarettes by the pack).

3. *Higher Return on Investment.* Using Figure 12.6 as a starting point, suppose the present-biased farmer moves to an area where the return to investment is higher. The farmer will invest if the return/investment ratio is at least [____]. Illustrate.

Apply the Concepts

1. *Present Bias and Hobbling.* Use Widget 12.1 (available at www.oup.com/us/osullivan1e). Consider a harmful product with $p_x = 1$.

    a. The fully rational choice (with $\beta = 1$) is $x^* = $ [____], compared to $x^{**} = $ [____] for a consumer with $\beta = 1/2$.

    b. Suppose the price for an online purchase is $p_x = 1$. Under a hobble strategy, a consumer walks to a store to purchase the product in smaller quantities. Suppose the retail cost per unit of the harmful product is $p_R = 1 + (t/10)$, where t is the number of city blocks traveled for a single unit of the product. To reach a quantity of x^*, the hobble strategy is to choose $t^* = $ [____].

2. *Comparative Statics and the National Detestable Association (NDA).* Consider a person who allocates a fixed budget $w = \$60$ to cigarettes (x_1) and other products (x_2). The marginal utility of cigarettes is $mu_1 = 120/x_1$ and the marginal utility of other products is $mu_2 = 120/x_2$. The prices are $p_1 = p_2 = 1$.

    a. The initial consumption of cigarettes is $x_1^* = $ [____].

    b. Suppose the smoker signs a binding contract under which each cigarette he or she smokes triggers a $2 donation to the NDA. The new cigarette consumption is $x_1^{**} = $ [____].

3. *NGO Fertilizer Program.* Consider a nation where each farmer has the utility function

$$u(c_1, c_2) = \log[c_1] + \delta \cdot \beta \cdot \log[c_2]$$

where $\delta = 10/12$. In the typical village of 60 farmers, the value of β varies from 0.41 to 1.0, with one farmer in each 0.01 interval. In the absence of investment in fertilizer, $c_1 = c_2 = 120$. The marginal rate of transformation for fertilizer is MRT= $\Delta c_2 / \Delta c_1 = 1.60$. Define n as the number of farmers who purchase fertilizer. In your job as an economist for Billinda's NGO, your task is to compute the subsidy required to increase the number of fertilizing farmers.

a. In the absence of a subsidy, n = [____]

b. The subsidy required to double the number of fertilizing farmers is
s = [____].

c. The subsidy required to get all farmers to fertilize is s = [____].

4. *Present Bias and Investment.* Suppose the marginal rate of transformation between c_1 and c_2 is 1.60. For a fully rational farmer, the marginal rate of substitution between consumption now and later is 1.20. For a present-biased farmer, $\beta = 0.50$. Illustrate a case where the fully rational farmer invests, but the present-biased farmer does not. A plausible value for the marginal rate of substitution for the present-biased farmer is MRS = [____].

5. *Fertilizer with Stochastic Present Bias.* Each farmer must decide when to purchase fertilizer for next year's production, either now (this year's harvest time) or later (next year's planting time). The farmer is not subject to conventional discounting, so in the absence of present bias, the marginal rate of substitution between consumption now and later is MRS = 1. The marginal rate of transformation from fertilizer is MRT= $\Delta c_2 / \Delta c_1 = 1.64$. The opportunity cost of purchasing $1 of fertilizer now rather than later is the income forgone in a bank account, $c = 0.25$. Each farmer has a probability p that he or she will experience present bias between now and later, and thus spend any money saved for fertilizer on another product. The utility function is linear, so the marginal utility of consumption is constant.

a. For farmer Haff, $p = 1/2$, so the expected payoff from purchasing $1 of fertilizer now is $[____].

b. For farmer Trey, $p = 3/8$, so the expected payoff from purchasing $1 of fertilizer now is $[____].

c. Describe a "nudge" that (i) gets farmer Trey to voluntarily purchase fertilizer and (ii) is unlikely to distort the behavior of rational farmers.

Math Solutions

Math 12.1: Marginal Utility Per Dollar

Apply the rules for differentiating logarithmic functions to derive expressions for the marginal utility of the two products:

$$\frac{\partial u}{\partial x} = \frac{a}{x}$$

$$\frac{\partial u}{\partial y} = \frac{b}{y}$$

For the harmful product, the unit cost is $p_x + c$. For the other product, the unit cost is p_y. For $p_x = p_y = 1$, the expressions for marginal utility per dollar are

$$MU \ per \ dollar \ on \ x = \frac{a}{x \cdot (1+c)}$$

$$MU \ per \ dollar \ on \ y = \frac{b}{y}$$

Math 12.2: Consumption of a Harmful Product: Fully Rational

From Math 12.1, the marginal utilities per dollar are

$$MU \ per \ dollar \ on \ x = \frac{a}{x \cdot (1+c)}$$

$$MU \ per \ dollar \ on \ y = \frac{b}{y}$$

Apply the equimarginal rule for $a = b$:

$$\frac{1}{x \cdot (1+c)} = \frac{1}{y}$$

Solve for x as a fraction of y:

$$x = y \cdot \frac{1}{1+c}$$

Math 12.3: Consumption of a Harmful Product: Present Bias

Apply the rules for differentiating logarithmic functions to derive expressions for the marginal utility of the two products:

$$\frac{\partial u}{\partial x} = \frac{a}{x}$$

$$\frac{\partial u}{\partial y} = \frac{b}{y}$$

For the harmful product, the unit cost is $p_x + \beta \cdot c$. For the other product, the unit cost is p_y. For $p_x = p_y = 1$, the expressions for marginal utility per dollar are

$$MU \ per \ dollar \ on \ x = \frac{a}{x \cdot (1 + \beta \cdot c)}$$

$$MU \ per \ dollar \ on \ y = \frac{b}{y}$$

Apply the equimarginal rule for $a = b$:

$$\frac{1}{x \cdot (1 + \beta \cdot c)} = \frac{1}{y}$$

Solve for x as a fraction of y:

$$x = y \cdot \frac{1}{1 + \beta \cdot c}$$

Math 12.4: Marginal Rate of Substitution

The total differential of the utility function is

$$du(c_1, c_2) = \frac{\partial u}{\partial c_1} \cdot dc_1 + \frac{\partial u}{\partial c_2} \cdot dc_2$$

where ∂ indicates partial differentiation. Along an indifference curve, utility is constant ($du = 0$), so we can solve for the slope of the indifference curve:

$$\frac{dc_2}{dc_1} = -\frac{\partial u / \partial c_1}{\partial u / \partial c_2}$$

The marginal rate of substitution (the absolute value of the slope of the indifference curve) is the ratio of the marginal utilities:

$$MRS = -\frac{dc_2}{dc_1} = \frac{\partial u / \partial c_1}{\partial u / \partial c_2} = \frac{mu_1}{mu_2}$$

13 Mental Accounting for Consumers

Gasoline is typically sold in three grades that vary in octane level and price—regular, mid-grade, and premium. When gasoline prices decrease, many people switch from regular to premium gasoline. This is puzzling because most modern cars are designed for regular gasoline, and using premium gasoline does not affect performance, fuel efficiency, or engine health (Car Talk 2019). Why do more people waste their money on premium gasoline when the price of gasoline is relatively low?

In this chapter we explore the implications of mental accounting for consumers. As we saw in an earlier chapter, mental accounting is the practice of organizing economic life by setting up separate mental accounts for different aspects of life. Mental shortcuts such as mental accounting allow people to make quick decisions without precise calculations of all the benefits and costs. Some consumers use mental accounting to segregate spending on different classes of products. As we'll see, mental accounting by consumers (i) reduces consumers' flexibility in responding to price changes, (ii) increases the power of coupons, (iii) can make sunk cost relevant, and (iv) helps explain the success of modern ride-hailing services in competition with traditional taxi service.

Learning Objectives: The Explainer

After mastering this chapter, you will be able to explain each of the following statements.

1. Mental accounting causes a consumer to violate the rules for utility maximization.

2. For a product subject to mental accounting, the individual demand curve is negatively sloped.

3. Mental accounting increases the power of coupons to increase consumption.

4. Mental accounting can make sunk cost relevant to decision-making.

5. Mental accounting helps explain the success of modern ride-hailing services (Uber, Lyft) at the expense of traditional taxi service.

6. Mental accounting explains why a decrease in gasoline prices causes many consumers to switch to the premium grade.

13.1 Mental Accounting and Fungibility

Recall from an earlier chapter that mental accounting simplifies the decision-making process by separating economic activities into separate categories or accounts. For example, a person could set up separate mental accounts for regular expenses, annual vacations, and coffee. The fundamental idea of mental accounting is that a person periodically balances each account. For example, a person could place $60 in a coffee account at the beginning of the month, and then buy coffee in the next 30 days to balance the coffee account by the end of the month. Similarly, a person could place $200 each month in a vacation account. At the end of the year, spending $2400 on a vacation would balance the account. In this part of the chapter we explore the implications of mental accounting for (i) consumer budgeting, (ii) incorporating sunk costs into decisions, and (iii) linking the benefits and the costs of a transaction.

Consumer Budgets and Fungibility

Mental accounting decreases a consumer's flexibility in responding to changes in price. Although mental accounts reside in the consumer's head rather than in a bank, the consumer tries to maintain the integrity of the accounting system by not over-spending in any account. For example, if the price of coffee doubles, a consumer with a strict mental account for coffee decreases coffee consumption by half, thus keeping the coffee account in balance. Mental accounting narrows consumer decisions: a mental accountant balances a budget for a specific product rather than balancing the budget for the entire bundle of consumer goods.

Figure 13.1 illustrates the difference between mental accounting and conventional consumer choice. The horizontal axis measures coffee consumption (x_1) and the vertical axis measures the consumption of all other goods (x_2). Consumer income is $w = \$140$. The price of other goods is fixed at $p_2 = 1$, and the price of coffee varies. At the initial coffee price ($2), the consumer maximizes utility at point i, where the marginal rate of substitution equals the price ratio. An increase in the price from $2 to $4 tilts the budget line inward, meaning that the consumer's real income (purchasing power) decreases. Suppose coffee and other goods are normal goods in an economic sense, with positive income elasticities of demand.

1. *Conventional response: Point* j. The increase in price decreases the utility-maximizing quantity of coffee from 30 to 21. The income effect reinforces the substitution effect, decreasing the quantity demanded. The quantity of other goods decreases from 80 to 56, meaning that the consumer shifts spending from other goods to coffee. In this example, total spending on

coffee increases. At point j, the marginal rate of substitution equals the now higher price ratio.

2. *Mental accounting: Point* m. For a mental accountant, total spending on coffee is fixed at $60. The increase in price decreases the quantity of coffee from 30 to 15, a decrease that is just large enough to fully offset the doubling of the price. The fixed spending on coffee means that the quantity of other goods is fixed at 80. The mental accountant confines the response to the higher coffee price to coffee consumption. At point m, the marginal rate of substitution exceeds the now-higher price ratio.

The lesson from Figure 13.1 is that a mental accountant responds in a mechanistic fashion to an increase in price, rather than making choices consistent with conventional utility maximization.

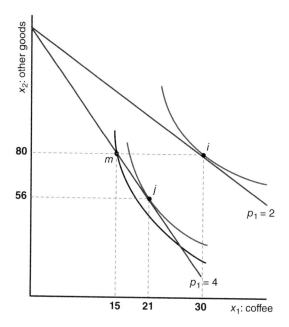

FIGURE 13.1: Mental Accounting versus Conventional Choice

Figure 13.2 shows another plausible response to an increase in the price of coffee. Point h shows the response by a utility-maximizing consumer. The increase in the coffee price causes a relatively large decrease in coffee consumption. In this case, the substitution effect of the price increase is relatively strong, and a utility-maximizing consumer increases the quantity of other goods at the expense of coffee. Spending on coffee decreases, while total spending on other goods increases. In contrast, a mental accountant chooses point m, so the consumption of other goods doesn't change. As before, the mental accountant chooses a bundle at which the marginal rate of substitution is not equal to the price ratio. In this case, the marginal rate of substitution is less than the now higher price ratio.

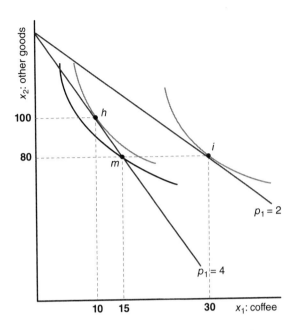

FIGURE 13.2: Mental Accounting versus Conventional Choice: Strong Substitution

Figure 13.3 shows an individual demand curve for a consumer who uses strict mental accounting for coffee consumption. The budget constraint is

$$B = p \cdot q$$

where B is the coffee budget, p is the price of coffee, and q is the quantity of coffee. For a consumer who bases consumption decisions on strict mental accounting, the expression for the demand curve is simple:

$$q = \frac{B}{q}$$

In Figure 13.3, the coffee budget is $B = \$60$. An increase in price from \$2 to \$4 decreases the quantity demanded from 30 to 15.

Mental Accounting and Coupons

Mental accounting also has important implications for consumer responses to coupons. Consider a consumer who regularly spends \$100 in a grocery store. One day the consumer gets a coupon that reduces that day's bill by \$20. How will a utility-maximizing consumer respond to the coupon? Let's assume the consumer's annual income is \$50,000, and the income elasticity of demand for groceries is 1.0.

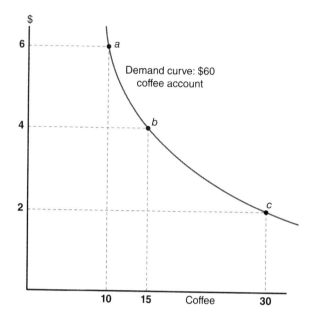

FIGURE 13.3: Mental Accounting and Individual Demand Curve

1. The coupon increases the consumer's real income by 0.04 percent (equal to 20/50,000).
2. Given an income elasticity of 1.0, grocery spending on the coupon day will increase by 0.04 percent—from $100 to $100.04.
3. After using the coupon, the consumer spends only $80.04 of his or her own money, a savings of $19.96.
4. The $19.96 saving is spent on other products over the next year.

In other words, the consumer uses only $0.04 of the coupon on groceries on the coupon day, leaving $19.96 to spend on other products.

Studies of consumer responses to coupons suggest that coupons increase spending on the relevant product by a relatively large amount. Based on a study of online grocery store customers, we would expect a $20 coupon to increase grocery spending on the coupon day by $3.18 (Milkman and Beshears 2009). The relatively large increase in spending is consistent with a mental grocery account that includes deposits from store coupons. For example, a mental accountant could spend an extra $3.18 per week on groceries over roughly 6 weeks to clear a grocery account that is boosted by a $20 coupon.

To further illustrate the response of a mental accountant to coupons, suppose a consumer has planned an all-expense-paid vacation trip with a price tag of $5000. When the consumer goes online to pay for the trip, he or she receives a $1000 coupon to help pay for the trip. Naturally, the money could also be used to purchase extra features such as side trips for skydiving or yoga, special meals, or souvenirs. Suppose the consumer's income over the relevant planing period is

$50,000, and vacation spending is a luxury good, with an income elasticity of demand of 2.0. How will a utility-maximizing consumer respond to the coupon?

1. The coupon increases real income by two percent (equal to 1000/50,000).
2. Given an income elasticity of 1.0, vacation spending will increase by four percent—from $5000 to $5200.
3. After using the coupon, the consumer spends only $4200 of his or her own money, a savings of $800.
4. The $800 saving is spent on other products over the next year.

In other words, the consumer spends one-fifth of the coupon ($200) on the trip, leaving $800 to spend on other goods.

Things are different for a strict mental account with a vacation account. The accountant has already placed $5000 of his or her own money in the vacation account, and then adds the $1000 coupon to the account. To balance the account, spending on the vacation increases to $6000: the accountant adds extra features to spend the full coupon the trip, leaving no surplus money to spend on other goods. For a more casual mental accountant, less than $1000 will be spent on the trip, so some money will be left over to spend on other goods.

Figure 13.4 illustrates the difference between the conventional consumer and a strict mental accountant. The initial utility-maximizing point is *i*, where the marginal rate of substitution equals the price ratio. The consumer has a plan to spend $5000 of the $50,000 income on the trip. The coupon shifts the budget

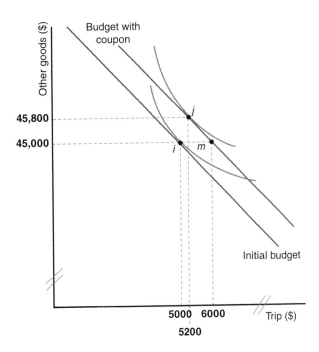

FIGURE 13.4: Mental Accounting and a Coupon

line upward by $1000, and the new utility-maximizing point is j: the utility-maximizing spending increases to $5200. Point m shows the choice of the strict mental accountant: spending on the trip increases from $5000 to $6000. A more casual mental accountant will choose a point between point j and point m.

Review the Concepts 13.1

1. For a conventional (fully rational) consumer, an increase in p_1 may [____] x_2. (↑, ↓, does not change)

2. For a mental-accounting consumer with an account for x_1, an increase in p_1 [____] x_2. (↑, ↓, does not change)

3. For a mental-accounting consumer with an account for x_1, the demand curve for x_1 is [____]. (positively sloped, vertical, horizontal, negatively sloped)

4. For a conventional (fully rational) consumer, a store coupon ($10 off today's purchases) is treated as an increase in [____], and has a relatively [____] effect on today's purchases in the store. (wealth, small; wealth, large; today's budget, large)

5. For a mental-accounting consumer, a store coupon ($10 off today's purchases) has a relatively [____] effect on today's purchases. (tiny, small, large)

13.2 Other Implications of Consumer Mental Accounting

In this part of the chapter we explore several other implications of mental accounting. As we'll see, mental accounting can distort the calculation of benefits and costs, leading to decisions that appear to be irrational.

1. *Sunk cost.* A person who uses mental accounting may incorporate sunk costs (costs incurred in the past) into the decision-making process, thus violating the conventional notion that sunk costs are irrelevant.

2. *Decoupling benefits and costs.* The fundamental rule of benefit–cost analysis is to take an action if the benefit exceeds the cost. Mental accounting can cause a decision-maker to violate this fundamental rule by **decoupling** the benefit and the cost of an action: a person (i) considers the benefit of an action while ignoring the cost, or (ii) considers the cost while ignoring the benefit.

Mental Accounting and Sunk Cost

As we saw in an earlier chapter, sunk cost is defined as a cost incurred in the past. In conventional economic analysis, sunk cost is irrelevant for current decisions.

A decision-maker can't do anything about costs incurred in the past, so a fully rational person ignores sunk costs. In popular language, a rational decision-maker "lets bygones be bygones." But in fact, people regularly incorporate sunk cost in their decision-making.

Richard Thaler (2015) uses a thought experiment to illustrate some subtleties of mental accounting and sunk costs. Suppose you buy a pair of shoes. After a few days of wear, you realize that the shoes are ill-fitting and uncomfortable. It is too late to return the shoes, so the purchase price is a sunk cost. Thaler makes the two conjectures.

1. Although you will wear the shoes, you will eventually discard them. The purchase of the shoes opens a mental account with a negative balance equal to the purchase price. Each time you wear the shoes, the balance in the shoe account becomes a smaller negative number as you incorporate the benefit of wearing the shoes. Eventually, the balance reaches zero, and for a mental accountant, it is time to discard the uncomfortable shoes.
2. The higher the price, the longer you will wear the shoes before discarding them. A higher price for the shoes means that the shoe account starts out with a larger negative balance, so it takes more wearings to accumulate enough benefit to balance the account.

This thought experiment suggests that sunk costs are depreciated over time by actions that offset the sunk cost with benefits.

Decoupling Cost and Benefit: Credit Cards and Ride-Hailing Services

Some forms of mental accounting are highly creative. Under decoupling, a decision-maker separates or "decouples" the cost of an action from the benefit. Consider a consumer in a bookstore who will pay for a book with either cash or a credit card. Paying in cash means that the cost of the book is incurred immediately, meaning that the cost is "coupled" to the benefit of the book. In contrast, paying with a credit card delays the cost of the book for at least a few weeks, so the cost is "decoupled" from the benefit. As we saw earlier in the book, a consumer who experiences present bias downplays a future cost, so paying with a credit card increases the likelihood that the benefit of the book will exceed the perceived cost. As a result, a person paying with a credit card is more likely to purchase the book.

Behavioral economists have explored the brain activity associated with different payment methods. As expected, the parts of the brain responsible for representing the cost of an action are relatively active for cash purchases, and relatively quiet for credit-card purchases. One strategy to combat over-spending with credit cards is to simply remind a consumer that a charge on a credit card must eventually be paid. In one experiment, when consumers paying with credit cards were shown their credit-card statements, the cost-valuation parts of the brain became more active, decreasing the likelihood of purchasing the product. Some organizations have developed mobile apps that remind consumers of their credit-card balances, a practice that reduces present bias by linking the cost and the benefit of a consumer purchase.

As another illustration of decoupling, consider the success of ride-hailing services such as Uber and Lyft and the decline of traditional taxi service. A key feature of the modern services is that credit-card payments are automated—you enter your credit-card information into the system once, before your first ride. Under this prepayment system, the cost of a ride is decoupled from the benefit. In contrast, a traditional taxi requires either a cash payment or an individual credit-card transaction. A second key feature of modern ride-hailing services is that the cost of the ride is determined before you enter the vehicle. In a traditional taxi, the on-board fare meter shows the cost of the ride increasing with distance and time. A taxi rider can see and often hear the fare increasing, so the cost is tightly coupled with the benefit. This is known as the ticking-meter problem. The explicit coupling of cost and benefit in a taxi contrasts sharply with the decoupling in modern services such as Uber and Lyft.

Regular versus Premium Gasoline

As we saw in the chapter opener, a decrease in the price of gasoline causes many people to switch from regular to premium gasoline, despite the fact that most cars are designed for regular gasoline. This puzzling behavior can be explained by mental accounting. Suppose a driver has a mental account for gasoline, with a budget of $90 per month. When gasoline prices are relatively high, the driver spends the entire budget on regular gasoline, buying 15 gallons at $6 per gallon. Suppose the price of regular gasoline decreases from $6 to $4, and the price of premium decreases from $7.50 to $5. In other words, the relative price of premium gasoline remains at 1.25 = 7.50/6.00 = 5.00/4.00.

Consider two responses to lower gasoline prices, a flexible response and the response of a mental accountant with a fixed budget for gasoline.

1. *Flexible consumer.* Increase consumption of regular gasoline from 15 to 20 gallons. Total spending on gasoline decreases from $90 to $80 (equal to $4 . 20). As a result, the consumer has an extra $10 to spend on other products.
2. *Mental accountant with a $90 gasoline account.* Buy 10 gallons of regular gasoline and 10 gallons of premium, and balance the account:

$$\$90 = \$4 \cdot 10 + \$5 \cdot 10$$

In contrast to a mental accountant, a flexible consumer spreads the benefits of lower gasoline prices to other products.

A recent study provides evidence of mental accounting in gasoline consumption (Hastings and Shapiro 2013). Consumers respond to a decrease in gasoline prices by increasing premium consumption by a relatively large amount, so the market share of premium increases. In the opposite direction, an increase in gasoline prices causes a shift away from the premium grade. These results suggests that gasoline consumers use mental accounting in choosing a mix of regular and premium gasoline. When the prices of gasoline changes, much of the action occurs in substitution between regular and premium. This occurs despite the fact that for most cars, there is no performance difference between the regular grade and the more expensive premium grade.

Review the Concepts 13.2

1. A mental accountant walks into a bar, and a friend asks, "Why are you still wearing those uncomfortable shoes?" The accountant responds, "Because they were very [____] when I bought them." (stylish, inexpensive, retro, expensive)

2. Using a credit card is an example of [____] benefits and costs. (coupling, decoupling, cooping, degusting)

3. Ride-hailing services solve the [____]-meter problem by [____] the benefit of a ride and its cost. (ticking, coupling; silent, coupling; ticking, decoupling; hidden, decoupling)

4. For a consumer with a mental account for gasoline, a decrease in gasoline prices triggers a(n) [____] switch [____] gasoline. (inefficient, from regular to premium; efficient, from regular to premium; inefficient, from premium to regular; efficient, from premium to regular)

Key Term

decoupling, p. 242

Takeaways

1. Mental accounting is a system of organizing economic life by setting up mental accounts and periodically balancing the accounts.

2. For a consumer who practices strict mental accounting for product X, an increase in price decreases the quantity of X but does not affect the quantities of other products.

3. For a consumer who practices mental accounting, a coupon is placed in a consumer account, where it triggers a relatively large increase in the consumption of products covered by the account.

4. For a consumer who practices mental accounting, a sunk cost is entered as a negative entry in an account, and the account is balanced when consumption benefit equals the sunk cost.

5. For gasoline consumers who employ mental accounting, changes in gasoline prices may affect the mix of regular and premium gasoline.

Discuss the Concepts

1. *Economic Laws and Rules.* A consumer who bases consumption decisions on mental accounting does not maximize utility in the conventional fashion.

   a. We expect the consumer to [____] (obey, violate) the "law of demand."

   b. We expect the consumer to [____] (satisfy, violate) the utility-maximizing rule MRS $= p_1 / p_2$. Illustrate.

2. *Coupon and Profit.* Consider an online seller with a marginal cost of $0.40 per dollar of products sold. The seller provides a $12 coupon in the check-out process, and each consumer has an opportunity to place more items in his or her shopping bag. In the absence of a coupon, the typical consumer spends $100, while a consumer with a $12 spends $93 and gets $105 worth of products.

   a. On the typical transaction, the coupon [____] (↑, ↓, does not change) the seller's profit by $[____].

   b. The $12 coupon will increase the seller's profit if [____].

3. *Shoe Rebate.* Winceton is a mental accountant who purchased a pair of uncomfortable shoes for $60 and one week later received an unexpected $10 rebate on the shoe purchase. The rebate [____] (↑, ↓, does not change) the number of days Winceton wears the shoes.

4. *Micropayment Browser.* Consider an alternative to modern internet browsers, with all those obnoxious (and often eerily targeted) advertisements. Under a system of micropayments, an individual would pay a small fee for every minute spent browsing in an advertisement-free environment. Suppose the per-minute fee is small enough that the typical user would pay roughly $10 per month. In addition, the total payment over a month would be capped at $20. The prospects for the micropayment browser are [____] (good, bad) because [____].

5. *Concert Prices.* Consider an individual who will purchase an admission ticket to a concert. One option is a $6 seat far from the stage, and a second option is a $24 seat close to the stage. After the individual tentatively decides on the $6 seat, the concert producer announces new prices of $4 (far) and $12 (close).

   a. If the individual switches from a far seat ($4) to a close seat ($12), this is [____] (consistent, inconsistent) with conventional utility maximization because [____].

   b. This scenario is [____] (like, unlike) the gasoline scenario (premium versus regular) because [____].

Apply the Concepts

1. *Mental Accounting and Price Elasticity.* Consider a consumer with mental account for movies, with a fixed budget $b = \$120$. Suppose the price of movies increases from $p_1 = \$8$ to $p_2 = \$12$.

    a. The quantity of movies demanded [___] ($\uparrow$, $\downarrow$, does not change) from $m_1 = [\underline{\quad}]$ to $m_2 = [\underline{\quad}]$.

    b. Illustrate with a conventional consumer-choice model with indifference curves and budget lines.

    c. The price elasticity of demand for movies is [___]. The cross-price elasticity of demand for other goods is [___].

2. *Uncomfortable Shoes.* For Winceton, marginal utility of wealth is constant at 1, and the marginal benefit of wearing a pair shoes is $mu_S = 10 - d$ utils per hour, where d is a measure of discomfort from a bad fit. Winceton's minimum wear time (h^*) for a pair of shoes is the time at which the total benefit equals the total cost. Suppose $d = 2$. An increase in price from $p = \$72$ to $p = \$120$ [___] ($\uparrow$, $\downarrow$, does not change) h* from [___] to [___]. Illustrate.

3. *Will It Float?* Consider a firm that produces one-minute episodes of Will it Float? for a television program. The firm's residual demand curve is $p(q) = a - b \cdot q$ and its cost function is $C(q) = k + c \cdot q$, where q is the number of episodes and s is a sunk cost.

    a. Suppose the firm applies the marginal principle. Derive the expression for the profit-maximizing quantity in terms of the parameters (a, b, c, s). $q^* = [\underline{\quad}]$.

    b. Suppose the firm incorporates sunk cost (s) into its choice of quantity and price. Specifically, the firm chooses the quantity at which marginal revenue equals average cost. Derive the expression for the profit-maximizing quantity in terms of the parameters (a, b, c, s). $q^{**} = [\underline{\quad}]$.

    c. Suppose the values of the parameters are $(a, b, c, s) = (150, 1, 30, 1600)$. Applying the marginal principle, $q^* = [\underline{\quad}]$ and $p^* = [\underline{\quad}]$. For the sunk-cost case, $q^{**} = [\underline{\quad}]$ and $p^{**} = [\underline{\quad}]$.

4. *Mental Accounting for Gasoline.* Consider an individual with a mental account for gasoline, with $b = \$120$. The initial prices are $p_R = \$3$ for regular grade and $p_H = \$5$ for premium (high) grade. For the individual's car, there is no difference between regular and premium gasoline—no difference in engine performance or fuel economy. The individual's initial consumption is $r^* = 40$ and $h^* = 0$. Suppose each price decreases by $1, to $p_R = \$2$ and $p_H = \$4$. Suppose the mental accountant chooses $q_R = q_H$. Design a Pareto improvement that would make both you and the mental accountant better off. To simplify, suppose you share the gain equally

5. *Premium Gasoline Puzzle.* Recall the example of the increase in the quantity of premium gasoline in response to the 2008 decrease in gasoline prices. Consider a household with income $w = \$2000$, $g = 80$ gallons, and $G = 10$ gallons, where g is regular gasoline and G is premium gasoline. Suppose the prices of gasoline decrease from $(p_g, p_G) = (3, 6)$ to $(p_g, p_G) = (2, 4)$. Gasoline is a "normal" good, with a positive income elasticity of demand.

   a. For a consumer choosing the utility-maximizing mix of g and G, substitution effect of the change in gasoline prices [___] (↑, ↓, does not change) g and [___] (↑, ↓, does not change) G.

   b. Suppose the income elasticity of demand for G is 2.0. The predicted change in premium gasoline consumption is $\Delta G = $ [___].

   c. For a gasoline mental accountant, total spending on gasoline is fixed at $\$$[___]. Suppose the accountant responds to the decreases in price by choosing $g = G$. In this case, $g = G = $ [___].

6. *Paying in Advance for a Vacation.* Consumer a consumer with an upcoming nine-day vacation with a total cost of $900. The consumer can either pay a lump sum of $900 or pay $100 each day. The consumer will pay the lump sum if [___]. Illustrate with a utility function.

7. *Paying for Vacations and Appliances.* Many consumers pay in advance for vacations, but pay for home appliances with installment plans that spread the cost of the purchase over several years after the product is delivered. Use the notions of mental accounting to explain these choices.

Loss versus Gain

14

A forester purchased a plot of land for $10 million, a price that equals the value of logs that could be harvested from the land. The value of the land for wilderness services—hiking, gazing, and carbon sequestration—is $12 million. When a wilderness organization offers to buy the land for $12 million, the forester refuses to sell for anything less than $15 million. In other words, the forester declines an offer that would generate a profit of $2 million. How would two prominent thinkers of the nineteenth century react to the forester's seemingly irrational choice?

- Adam Smith, economist and author of *An Inquiry into the Nature and Causes of the Wealth of Nations:* The farmer's refusal to sell is inefficient, and I have a plan that makes everyone better off.

- Charles Darwin, naturalist and author of *On the Origin of Species, by Means of Natural Selection:* The forester is acting just like a capuchin monkey.

This chapter explores a key feature of human psychology—the asymmetry in the influence of loss and gain in decision making. In general, the disutility of loss exceeds the utility of gain: in making decisions, losses loom larger than gains. In more casual terms, the pain of loss exceeds the pleasure of gain. This asymmetry has important implications for decision making. In this chapter, we explore the endowment effect, which tends to increase asking prices for assets and decrease the number of transactions. In later chapters, we explore other behavioral consequences of looming loss.

Learning Objectives: The Explainer

After mastering this chapter, you will be able to explain each of the following statements.

1. In the benefit-cost analysis performed by the brain, the weight of loss exceeds the weight of gain.

2. The greater weight of loss is measured by the parameter $\lambda > 1$.

3.   The endowment effect is explained by the greater weight of loss: λ > 1.

4.   "Thinking like a trader" reduces the weight of loss in financial decisions.

5.   The endowment effect decreases the number of transactions in an economy.

6.   Loss aversion is explained by the greater weight of loss: λ > 1.

14.1   Asymmetric Influences of Loss and Gain

We start our discussion of the asymmetric influences of loss and gain with a brief discussion of studies that explore brain activity. We take a peek inside the brain of an asset owner as he or she thinks about selling an asset. In the benefit-cost analysis performed by the brain, a loss receives a greater weight than a gain.

The Greater Weight of Loss

The **asymmetry between loss and gain** is revealed in studies of brain activity. Neuroscientists have explored what happens in the human brain when an individual contemplates a transaction involving the loss of an asset (Sokol-Hessner, Camerer, and Phelps 2013). Here is a highly simplified version of the brain activity.

1.   The thought of losing the asset causes a spike in the activity of the amygdala, a region of the brain involved in fear and anxiety.
2.   The amygdala activity triggers signals to regions of the brain involved in calculating the benefits and costs of an action such as selling an asset.
3.   The signals from the amygdala increase the weight assigned to loss in the benefit-cost analysis.

The signal-boosting activity of the amygdala increases the perceived cost of losing the asset. There is no analogous booster for the benefit of selling the asset (the value of resources gained from the sale). As a result, the weight assigned to loss exceeds the weight assigned to gain, *ceteris paribus*.

The role of the amygdala in the valuation of loss is illustrated by studies that explore the behavior of individual with disabled amygdalas (De Martino, Camerer, and Adolphs 2010). In one study, subjects made investment choices that generated losses or gains. In making investment choices, the subjects with disabled amygdalas treated losses and gains symmetrically, suggesting that the weight of loss was roughly equal to the weight of gain. In contrast, for subjects with fully functioning amygdalas, the investment choices were consistent with a weight of loss that was roughly 1.76 times the weight of gain.

Measuring the Greater Weight of Loss

Behavioral scientists use the parameter λ to represent the greater weight of loss in the brain's benefit-cost analysis. Under the equal weighting of loss and gain, $\lambda = 1$. As the weight of loss increases in relative terms, λ increases. For example, $\lambda = 2$ indicates that the weight of loss is twice the weight of gain. For $\lambda > 1$, losses loom larger than gains, and the larger the λ, the more ominous the looming loss.

Figure 14.1 illustrates the implications of a greater weight of loss. The horizontal axis measures a change in wealth in monetary terms, and the vertical axis measures utility. In the domain of gain, the slope of the utility curve is one: a one-dollar increase in wealth translates into a utility gain of one util. In the domain of loss, the slope of the curve is $\lambda = 2$: a one-dollar decrease in wealth translates into a utility loss of two utils. Consider a transaction with a $100 loss (point L) and a $120 gain (point G).

- In monetary terms, the transaction is favorable: the benefit ($120) exceeds the cost ($100).
- In utility terms, the transaction is unfavorable: the benefit (120 utils) is less than the cost (200 utils).

Because the loss looms larger than the gain, this transaction won't happen.

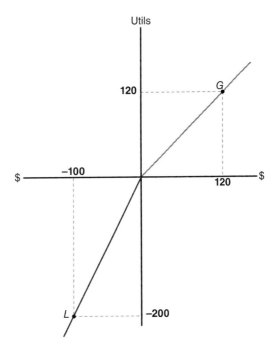

FIGURE 14.1: Loss Aversion

Behavioral scientists use lab experiments and field studies to estimate the value of λ. In a classic study, Tversky and Kahneman (1992) report an estimated value λ = 2.25. Abdellaoui, Bleichrodt, and Paraschiv (2007) summarize the results of studies that generated a range of estimates from 1.79 to 4.80. In a study of 30 individuals, Sokol-Hessner et al. (2009) computed λ values ranging from 0.41 to 3.91, with a mean value of 1.40. These results show that there is substantial variation across individuals in the relative weight of loss.

Reappraisal and the Weight of loss

The greater weight of loss can be self-regulated by process known as "perspective taking" or "reappraisal." In a study by Sokol-Hessner et al. (2009), subjects in the experiment made financial choices that involved possible losses and gains.

1. In the first stage of the experiment, the subjects were encouraged to think about each investment in isolation, much like regular people in everyday investment choices. Their choices revealed an average value of λ = 1.40.
2. In the second stage, the same subjects were instructed to think like professional investors. The instructions included "imagine yourself as a trader" and "treat it as one of many investment decisions, which will sum together to produce a portfolio." Their choices revealed an average value λ = 1.17.

On average, thinking like a trader reduced the relative weight of loss in the decision making process.

The study also measured the subjects' physiological responses to losses and gains. The electrical conductance of skin depends on sweat-gland activity, which in turn depends on emotions such as fear and anxiety. In the normal setting (no self-regulation), the skin-conductance scores for losses exceeded the scores for gains. This indicates that losses generated stronger emotional responses, consistent with boosted fear/anxiety signals from the amygdala. But when subjects engaged in perspective taking by thinking like a trader, the differences between skin-conductivity scores for losses and gains disappeared. This is consistent with the notion that perspective taking can weaken emotional responses to losses.

Review the Concepts 14.1

1. When an individual thinks about selling an asset, the amygdala boosts the brain activity associated with valuing the [___] of the transaction. (benefit, cost, cost and benefit)

2. The relative weight of loss is indicated by the parameter [___] (λ,α,β,δ,ψ).

3. In Figure 14.1, the benefit of the transaction would equal the cost if λ = [___] (1.0, 1.2, 1.5, 2, 5).

4. The relative weight of loss can be reduced by [___]. (reappraisal, perspective taking, acting instinctively, handstands)

14.2 The Endowment Effect

In this part of the chapter we explore the tendency of owners to be possessive. An asset owner may refuse to sell the asset at a price that reflects the asset's economic value. In the chapter opener, the forester's willingness to pay (WTP) for the land was $10 million, equal to the value of harvested logs. As owner of the land, the forester's willingness to accept (WTA) to sell the land is $15 million. This is the **endowment effect**.

> Endowment effect: Willingness to accept > Willingness to pay

In other words, a person demands more to give up an asset (WTA) than he or she would offer to acquire it (WTP).

The endowment effect has been observed in humans, chimpanzees, and capuchin monkeys. Our last common ancestor with capuchin monkeys lived roughly 30 million years ago, meaning that the endowment effect has a long evolutionary history. As we'll see in this part of the chapter, the endowment effect can be explained by looming loss: when a loss receives a greater weight in making decisions ($\lambda > 1$), the willingness to accept for an asset will exceed the willingness to pay (WTA > WTP).

Willingness to Pay versus Willingness to Accept

Consider a potential transaction involving a bicycle. The benefit of possessing a bike is the value of the stream of services generated by the bike. To simplify matters, suppose the value of each bike ride is $2.

- Willingness to pay = $140. If a potential buyer would take 70 bike rides, the benefit of a transaction is $140 = $2 · 70 rides. The potential buyer is willing to pay up to $140 for the bike.
- Willingness to accept = $100. If the current owner of the bike would take only 50 rides, the cost of selling the bike is the $100 value of forgone rides. The current owner is willing to accept any amount greater than $100 for the bike.

If the two people split the difference between WTP and WTA and agree on a price of $120, each is better off by $20. The transaction is a Pareto improvement because each person is better off.

So far in our bicycle example, have considered the benefits and costs of exchange on equal terms. Our simple calculations of WTP and WTA do not account for the greater weight of loss. When the current owner thinks about selling the bike, his or her amygdala fires up, boosting the cost signals to regions of the brain responsible for benefit-cost analysis. If the weight of loss is $\lambda = 2$, the owner's WTA is $200: the owner is willing to sell, but only if the price is twice the amount that he or she was willing to pay for the bike. In this case, the endowment effect generates a willingness to accept that is twice the willingness to pay.

Classic Endowment Experiment

The endowment effect is illustrated with a classic economic experiment involving coffee mugs (Kahneman, Knetsch, and Thaler 1990). A professor gave nice coffee mugs (purchase price $6) to 22 randomly selected students in a class of 44 students. The professor encouraged all the students to inspect the mugs for a few minutes, and then gave them the opportunity to buy and sell mugs. Naturally, students varied in their valuation of the mugs. We expect roughly half of the mug owners to have above-average values, and we'd expect the high-value owners to hang on to their mugs rather than sell them. We expect roughly half the mug owners to have below-average values and we expect these low-value owners to sell their mugs to students with above-average values. On average, we would expect 11 of the 22 mugs to change hands, as half the original owners sell mugs to students with above-average values.

The expectations based on conventional economic analysis were incorrect. On four runs of the experiment, the number of transactions were four, one, two, and two, for an average of 2.25 transactions. In other words, a relatively small number of mugs changed hands. There were few transactions because there was a large gap between mug owners' asking prices (the willingness to accept) and potential buyers' bid prices (willingness to pay). The average willingness to accept was $5.25, compared to an average willingness to pay of $2.25. In other words, the WTA was over twice the WTP. This suggests that mug owners demanded more than twice as much to give up a mug than they would pay to acquire a mug.

Evidence for the Endowment Effect

The endowment effect has been observed in many economic environments for many types of objects. As noted by Dhami (2016), the endowment effect has been documented for college basketball tickets (Carmon and Ariely 2000), gift certificates (Sen and Johnson 1997), and wine (van Dijk and van Knippenberg 1996). Harbaugh, Krause, and Vesterlund (2001) show that school children (ages 5 and 10 years) experience endowment effects, and so do college students. The observed endowment effect was roughly the same for all three age groups. The size of the endowment effect is measured as the ratio of WTA to WTP. Horowitz and McConnell (2002) report that across 45 studies of the endowment effect, the median WTA/WTP ratio is 2.6.

In his survey of behavioral economics, Dhami (2016) summarizes other empirical results concerning the endowment effect.

1. The endowment effect is for objects, not for money. When you take ownership of a $20 bill, your willingness to accept for the bill doesn't change: WTA = WTP = $20. In contrast, taking ownership of a bike is likely to increase your WTA.

2. The endowment effect does not occur for objects that a person expects to hold for a short time. In other words, temporary ownership does not trigger a divergence between WTA and WTP.
3. Trading experience decreases the endowment effect. List (2003) shows that for individuals who trade sport memorabilia (for example, ticket stubs from memorable games), the endowment effect for highly experienced traders (dealers) is weaker than the endowment effect for less experienced traders (non-dealers).

Endowment Effect for Chimpanzees and Capuchin Monkeys

The endowment effect has also been observed in the food choices of chimpanzees. Brosnan et al. (2007) tested the endowment effect by offering chimpanzees two food items—fruit juice and peanut butter. When given a simple choice between the two items, 58 percent of the chimps preferred the juice. But when chimpanzees were endowed with peanut butter and given the opportunity to trade for juice, 79 percent kept the peanut butter.

The endowment effect has also been observed in food-gathering tools. Brosnan et al. (2012) gave chimpanzees two options—a sponge to gather grape juice, and a dipstick to gather maple-flavored oatmeal. When given a simple choice between the two tools, all the chimpanzees preferred the sponge to the dipstick. But when the chimpanzees were endowed with a dipstick and given the opportunity to trade for a sponge, 45 percent kept the dipstick. In contrast, when the chimpanzees were endowed with the sponge, they all kept the sponge rather than trading for the dipstick.

The endowment effect has also been observed in capuchin monkeys (Lakshminaryanan, Chen, and Santos 2008). In stage 1 of the experiment, each monkey received 12 tokens to exchange for fruit discs and cereal chunks. In allocating the tokens between fruit and cereal, the chimps chose roughly equal quantities of the two products (between five and seven tokens spent on each product). In stage 2, the scientists replaced the tokens with actual food: some monkeys received an endowment of 12 fruit discs, and others received an endowment of 12 cereal chunks. The monkeys were then given the opportunity to exchange cereal for fruit, or fruit for cereal. Figure 14.2 shows the results.

1. *Stage 1 (tokens).* Roughly equal division between fruit and cereal.
2. *Fruit endowment.* On average, the monkeys endowed with fruit kept 98 percent of the fruit.
3. *Cereal endowment.* On average, the monkeys endowed with cereal kept 85 percent of the cereal.

On average, only two percent of a fruit endowment was exchanged for cereal. This is consistent with an outcome in which three of four monkeys kept all their endowed fruit, and one in four monkeys traded one unit of fruit for one unit of cereal.

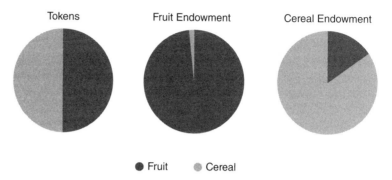

FIGURE 14.2: Endowment Effect for Capuchin Monkeys

The results for chimpanzees and capuchin monkeys suggest that the endowment effect is deeply rooted in our evolutionary history. Our last common ancestor with chimpanzees lived roughly 6 million years ago, and our last common ancestor with capuchin monkeys lived roughly 30 million years ago. The endowment effect presents a puzzle to evolutionary biologists: Why did the endowment effect arise millions of years ago, and why has it persisted for at least 30 million years? Later in the book we explore the role of natural selection in the emergence of the endowment effect.

The Endowment Effect and Exchange

The endowment effect has important implications for asset markets. To illustrate, consider the market for agricultural land. Suppose a farmer earns an annual profit of $200 from a plot of land. If the market interest rate is $r = 0.05$, the farmer's willingness to pay (WTP) for the land is $4000:

$$WTP_1 = \frac{\text{annual rent}}{\text{market interest rate}} = \frac{200}{0.05} = 4000$$

The farmer is willing to pay $4000 in exchange for the rights to earn $200 per year from the land. To buy the land for $4000, the farmer could withdraw $4000 from a bank account that would earn $200 interest per year (0.05 times $4000). The farmer is indifferent at a land price of $4000 because the $200 annual earnings from the land equals the forgone bank earnings.

Suppose for the moment that the farmer does not experience the endowment effect. In this case, the willingness to accept (WTA) to sell the land is $4000: the new owner is willing to sell the land for any price of at least $4000. For example, at a price of $4001, the farmer would earn a profit of $1 on the transaction. A price of $4000 makes the farmer indifferent about selling, so that's the willingness to accept.

Consider the possibility of a market transaction. Suppose a second farmer has an alternative production technology that would generate $300 in annual profit, compared to $200 for the original farmer. The second farmer is willing to pay up to $6000 for the farmland:

$$WTP_2 = \frac{\text{annual rent}}{\text{market interest rate}} = \frac{300}{0.05} = 6000$$

The second farmer is 50 percent more productive and profitable, so the willingness to pay for the farmland is 50 percent higher than the willingness to accept of the first farmer. There is room to negotiate a mutually beneficial exchange: if the two farmers split the difference between the willingness to accept and the willingness to pay and agree on a price of $5000, each farmer will be better off by $1000. The exchange—the change in ownership—is a Pareto improvement because both farmers are better off.

Consider the implications of the endowment effect experienced by the first farmer. The farmer as potential buyer was willing to pay $4000 for the land. But when the farmer takes ownership of the land, the endowment effect comes into play, and the farmer as a potential seller requires more than $4000 to sell the land. To illustrate, suppose the willingness to accept is $8000, or twice the willingness to pay. In this case, the farmer will reject offers of $5000, $6000, $7000, and so on up to $8000. There is no longer room to negotiate a mutually beneficial price, so the farmland remains with the less productive farmer. In general, the endowment effect reduces trade and exchange, reducing the number of transactions in an economy.

Greater Weight of Loss and Loss Aversion

We've seen that the greater weight of loss ($\lambda > 1$) explains the endowment effect. This also explains a phenomenon known as loss aversion. The term "loss aversion" is one of those flexible phrases that can take on different meanings in different contexts. For our discussion, we define **loss aversion** as follows.

> Loss aversion: To avoid a loss equal to x, an individual is willing to forgo a gain equal to $x \cdot \lambda$, where $\lambda > 1$. This is a consequence of the greater weight of loss in the decision-making process: $\lambda > 1$.

If the weight of loss exceeds the weight of gain, an individual needs a larger gain to offset a loss.

If this sounds familiar, it's because the greater weight of loss ($\lambda > 1$) explains both the endowment effect and loss aversion. In each case, a feature of psychology (greater weight of loss) triggers a behavior. For the endowment effect, the willingness to accept exceeds the willingness to pay, meaning that an asset owner demands a premium to give up an asset. For loss aversion, an individual sacrifices a larger gain to avoid a loss.

It is worth noting that the phrase "loss aversion" sometimes refers to greater weight of loss. In other words, "loss aversion" often refers to a feature of psychology ($\lambda > 1$) rather than behavior (To avoid a loss, an individual is willing to forgo a larger gain). When "loss aversion" refers to the feature of psychology ($\lambda > 1$), one implication is that loss aversion causes the endowment effect.

Review the Concepts 14.2

1. The endowment effect is that the willingness to [___] exceeds the willingness to [___]. (pay, accept; accept, pay)

2. A person who experiences the endowment effect demands [___] to give up an object than he or she would offer to acquire it. (more, less, the same amount)

3. In the classic experiment for the endowment effect, the willingness to accept (WTA) was roughly [___] times the willingness to pay (WTP). (1.2, 2, 3, 4, 5)

4. The endowment effect has been observed in [___]. (chimpanzees, capuchin monkeys, three-toed sloths, earthworms)

5. The endowment effect tends to [___] the number of transactions in an economy. (increase, decrease, not change)

Key Terms

asymmetry between loss and gain, p. 250

endowment effect, p. 253

loss aversion, p. 257

Takeaways

1. When an individual considers an action that will generate a loss, activity in the amygdala boosts the brain signals that represent the cost of the action.

2. In the benefit-cost analysis performed by the brain, a loss is assigned a greater weight than a gain: $\lambda > 1$.

3. Reappraisal techniques such as "thinking like a trader" decreases the relative weight of loss.

4. The endowment effect is that the willingness to accept (WTA) exceeds the willingness to pay (WTP): a person demands more to give up an object than he or she would offer to acquire it.

5. The endowment effect has been observed for humans, chimpanzees, and capuchin monkeys.

6. The endowment effect tends to decrease the number of transactions in an economy because the willingness to accept is large relative the willingness to pay.

Discuss the Concepts

1. *Meditation and Efficiency.* Avner owns a plot of land that yields 60 of annual profit. You could deploy superior techniques to generate 150 of annual profit. The market interest rate is 0.10. For Avner, $\lambda = 3$. Vilfredo's Meditation Center offers sessions that decrease the weight of loss from 3 to 2. For the economy, the efficiency gain from enrolling Avner in the meditation program is [___].

2. *Capuchin Feeding.* You are the food manager at a capuchin resort. When given a choice, the monkeys choose roughly equal quantities of fruit and cereal. Today your food supplier made a mistake, delivering 5 boxes of fruit and 1 box of cereal, rather than the usual 3 boxes of each food. Your assistant says, "Uh-oh, we're gonna have some unhappy monkeys today." What's your response?

3. *Car Swap for CO_2 Reduction.* The nation of Ecotopia has developed a pro- gram to swap old high-polluting cars with otherwise identical low-pollution cars. For each car swap, the budgetary cost of the program is $12,000 (for the modern car) plus a negotiated subsidy for the owner of the antiquated car. If the nation swaps 1000 cars, a plausible number for the budgetary cost is [___]. ($12 million, $18 million, $48 million)

Apply the Concepts

1. *Efficient Property Market?* Ona uses old technology on farmland to generate economic profit $\pi_O = \$30$ per year. Newt could apply new technology to the farmland and increase the annual profit to $\pi_N = \$45$. The market interest rate is $r = 0.05$.

   a. In a perfectly rational world, Ona's willingness to accept for the farmland is $WTA_O = \$[\_\_\_]$, compared to Newt's $WTA_N = \$[\_\_\_]$. The social benefit of a transaction is $B = [\_\_\_]$.

   b. Suppose that for Ona, the weight of loss exceeds the weight of gain. A transaction will not occur if $\lambda > [\_\_\_]$.

2. *Think Like a Trader.* Kiren owns an asset that generates an economic profit of $\pi_O = \$100$ per year. Nula could use a patented new technology to generate an annual profit to $\pi_N = \$160$. The market interest rate is $r = 0.05$. For Kiren, the weight of loss is 1.80 times the weight of gain: $\lambda = 1.80$.

   a. A transaction [___] (will, will not) happen because [___] > [___].

   b. After watching a popular movie on financial markets, Kiren starts think- ing like a trader, and λ decreases to $\lambda = 1.30$. A transaction [___] (will, will not) happen because [___] > [___].

3. *Possession is 9/10 of the Law?* Consider an asset (land) that must be divided between two claimants, Abe and Bea Both claimants are grandchildren of the recently deceased title holder, who left no instructions on how to distribute the land. Abe has occupied the land for the last 10 years. For an identical plot of nearby land, the marginal utility of the land is $mu(t_A)=1/t_A$ for Abe and $mu(t_B)=1/t_B$ for Bea. The total acreage is $T = t_A + t_B$, with T=40.

   a. Suppose the weight on loss is three times the weight on gain: $\lambda = 3$. Applying the equimarginal principle, the allocation is t_A = [____] and t_B= [____]. Illustrate.

   b. Suppose a judge enforces the rule that "possession is 9/10 of the law." The allocation is t_A = [____] and t_B = [____]. Illustrate.

   c. If the relative weight of loss is λ, the appropriate legal maxim is "Possession is [____] of the law."

4. *Hatfields versus McCoys.* In 1878, a judge in West Virginia ruled that a pig claimed by both the Hatfields and the McCoys was the property of the Hatfields because the pig was on Hatfield property when the dispute arose. When the disputed pig produces 20 piglets, your job as the clerk is to apply the logic of the relative weight of loss to allocate the piglets to the two families. Deploying an economic experiment to estimate the relative weight of loss, you conclude that $\lambda = 3$ for the Hatfields. The appropriate allocation is [____] piglets for the Hatfields and [____] for the McCoys. Illustrate.

Risk Preferences and Prospect Theory **15**

During a particular type of ear surgery, the main nerves of a patient's tongue are exposed while the patient is awake and alert. In August 1966, two patients (I.J. and S.P.) were good sports, and agreed to participate in experiments during their ear surgeries (Borg et al. 1967; Glimcher 2011). The surgeon poured sugar solutions of varying concentrations onto a patient's tongue, and observed the electrical response (firing rates) of the patient's tongue nerves. As the concentration became stronger, the neuron firing rate increased, but at a decreasing rate. The patients also reported the perceived sweetness of the different concentrations. As the concentration became stronger, the perceived sweetness increased, but at a decreasing rate. In fact, the two relationships between stimulus and response (neural and perception) were similar. In each case, the response was a power function of the stimulus: $f(s) = s^{0.60}$, where s is the sugar concentration, measured in millimolars of sucrose.

This experiment illustrates the notion of *decreasing sensitivity*. As the magnitude of a stimulus increases, the response increases, but at a decreasing rate. For the subjects in the experiment, perceived sweetness increased less rapidly than the actual sugar content. For example, a 10 percent increase in sugar content (a 10 percent increase in sugar per liter) increased the perceived sweetness by roughly six percent. This decreasing sensitivity of perception reflects decreasing sensitivity at the neural level: as the stimulus increased, neuron firing rates increased less rapidly than the actual sugar content.

This is the first of several chapters on prospect theory, a framework for making decisions when there is uncertainty about the benefit or cost of an action. Economists and psychologists developed prospect theory (sometimes known as "cumulative prospect theory") in response to observed human behavior. Prospect theory incorporates several features of human psychology.

1. *Reference point.* Each possible outcome is computed as a gain or a loss relative to a common reference point. The reference point could be the status quo, such as a person's initial wealth.

2. *Decreasing sensitivity to stimulus.* This is illustrated in the chapter opener.

3. *Asymmetry in the influences of loss and gain.* As we saw in the previous chapter, the disutility of loss exceeds the utility of gain. In making decisions that involve loss and gain, there is a greater weight of loss: $\lambda > 1$.

4. *Problems with probabilities.* As we saw in an earlier chapter, human estimation and application of probabilities are often problematic, with several biases coming into play.

This chapter focuses on the first three features, and the next chapter explores the fourth feature.

Learning Objectives: The Explainer

After mastering this chapter, you will be able to explain each of the following statements.

1. Prospect theory incorporates (i) decreasing sensitivity to gain and loss and (ii) a greater weight of loss ($\lambda > 1$).

2. A risk-averse individual will play it safe rather than play a lottery with a monetary value equal to the certain (safe) value.

3. A risk-neutral individual will be indifferent between playing it safe and playing a lottery with a monetary value equal to the certain (safe) value.

4. The strength of risk aversion is determined by (i) decreasing sensitivity to gain and loss and (ii) the relative weight of loss (λ).

5. Experiments show that rats exhibit decreasing sensitivity and a greater weight of loss ($\lambda > 1$).

15.1   Features of Prospect Theory

We will use a simple example of a business start-up to illustrate prospect theory. As explained in a course in microeconomics, we can use a lottery to represent the features of a risky environment. A lottery is a list of n possible outcomes $(x_1, x_2, x_3, \ldots x_n)$ and the associated probabilities $(p_1, p_2, p_3, \ldots p_n)$. We summarize a lottery as

$$L = \{x_1, p_1; x_2, p_2; x_3, p_3; \ldots; x_n, p_n\}$$

To illustrate, suppose you are starting a new firm that could either fail and generate a loss of \$64 or succeed and generate a profit of \$900. If the two outcomes are equally likely, the start-up lottery is

$$L = \{-64, 0.50; 900, 0.50\}$$

In words, the start-up lottery is a 50 percent probability of losing $64 and a 50 percent chance of gaining $900. The conventional approach is to list the outcomes in increasing numerical value, from small to large, with losses listed first. In other words, $x_1 \le x_2 \le x_3 \ldots \le x_n$.

Utility Function for Prospect Theory

Prospect theory uses a specific utility function to translate dollar amounts into utility values. The utility function is a piecewise function of gains ($x > 0$) and losses ($x < 0$):

$$u(x) = x^\mu \text{ for } x \ge 0$$

$$u(x) = -\lambda \cdot (-x)^\mu \text{ for } x < 0$$

There are two parameters in the utility function for prospect theory.

1. *Decreasing sensitivity:* $\mu < 1$. The value of μ determines how rapidly the marginal utility of gain decreases as the magnitude of the gain increases, and how rapidly the marginal disutility of loss decreases as the magnitude of the loss increases. The Greek symbol "mu" (μ) reminds us that the value is related to the marginal utility of gain and the marginal disutility of loss.

   - As the gain increases, utility increases at a decreasing rate, meaning that the marginal utility of gain decreases. Each additional dollar gained adds less to utility than the previous dollar gained.
   - As the loss increases, utility decreases at a decreasing rate, meaning that the marginal disutility of loss decreases. Each additional dollar lost subtracts less from utility than the previous dollar lost.

2. *Greater weight of loss:* $\lambda > 1$. As we saw in an earlier chapter, losses loom larger than gains. The Greek symbol "lambda" (λ) reminds us that the value reflects the greater weight of loss.

Figure 15.1 uses the start-up example to illustrate the prospect utility function. Suppose the parameter values are $\lambda = 2$ and $\mu = 1/2$. Given the equal chances of losing $64 or gaining $900, the utility numbers are

$$u(x) = 900^{1/2} = 30 \text{ utils for gain}$$

$$u(x) = -2 \cdot 64^{1/2} = -16 \text{ utils for loss}$$

As shown by point *b*, for a gain of $x = \$900$, utility = 30 utils. As shown by point *a*, for a loss of $x = -\$64$, utility = −16 utils. In the domain of loss ($x < 0$), the slope of the curve decreases as the loss increases and we move to the left. The curvature reflects the assumption of decreasing marginal disutility of loss. The utility curve is steeper in the domain of loss because $\lambda > 1$, reflecting the greater weight of loss.

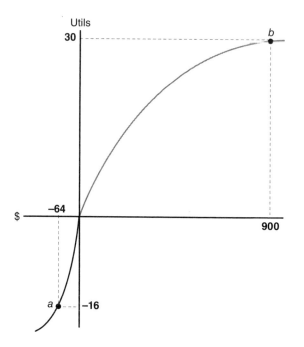

FIGURE 15.1: Utility Function for Prospect Theory

Utility Value and Certainty Equivalent

The next step in applying prospect theory is to compute the full set of measures of a lottery. In this chapter, we assume that utility calculations are based on the actual probabilities of the possible outcomes. The **utility value of a lottery** with two possible outcomes is the weighted sum of the possible outcomes, where the probabilities serve as weights:

$$v(L) = p_1 \cdot u(x_1) + p_2 \cdot u(x_2)$$

Continuing our start-up example (with $\lambda = 2$; $\mu = 0.50$), the utility value of the lottery is 7 utils:

$$v(L) = -\frac{1}{2} \cdot 2 \cdot 64^{1/2} + \frac{1}{2} \cdot 900^{1/2} = -8 + 15 = 7 \, \text{utils}$$

We have computed the value of the lottery in terms of utility, measured in utils. As explained in a course in microeconomics, a more useful measure of a lottery is its certainty equivalent, which measures the value of a lottery in dollars rather than utils. Specifically, the **certainty equivalent of a lottery** is the certain dollar amount that generates the same utility as a lottery. Using $c(L)$ as the symbol for a lottery's certainty equivalent,

$$u(c(L)) = v(L)$$

In words, the utility of the certainty equivalent of a lottery equals the utility value of the lottery.

In our start-up example, the utility function translates dollars into utils by taking the square root of the dollar amount. To translate utils into dollars, we square the util number. In general, if we have an expression for a utility function, we can derive an expression for the certainty equivalent by inverting the utility function. For the square-root utility function,

$$u(x) = x^{1/2} \Rightarrow x = u^2 \text{ or } c(L) = v(L)^2$$

Because the utility value of the start-up lottery is positive, we are operating in the domain of gain. To translate the utility gain in utils into the certainty equivalent in dollars, we use the utility parameter $\mu = 0.50$. The utility value of 7 utils translates into a certainty equivalent of $49:

$$c(L) = v(L)^2 \Rightarrow c(L) = (7)^2 = \$49$$

A certain $49 generates 7 utils, the same as the utility value of the start-up lottery.

$$u(\$49) = 7 \text{ utils}$$

The certainty equivalent of a lottery indicates a person's willingness to pay to play a lottery. For the start-up lottery, a person with a square-root utility function is indifferent between getting $49 for certain and playing the lottery (with equal chances of either losing $64 or gaining $900). The person would be eager to play the lottery if the cost of playing is less than $49, say $36. In this case, the $36 cost of playing is less than the $49 benefit (the certainty equivalent). In contrast, if the cost of playing exceeds $49 (say $64), the person will prefer keeping the $64 rather than playing the lottery. The certainty equivalent makes the person indifferent about playing the lottery, so it is the willingness to pay for the lottery.

Figure 15.2 shows the numbers for the start-up lottery. Point a shows the loss ($x = -\$64$, $u = -16$ utils), and point b shows the gain ($x = \$900$, $u = 30$ utils). The monetary value is $m(L) = \$418$. The utility value is $v(L) = 7$ utils, and the certainty equivalent is $c(L) = \$49$. To summarize, a person with the specified parameter values ($\lambda = 2$ and $\mu = \mu = 0.50$) is willing to pay $49 for the start-up lottery.

The parameter λ plays an important role in determining the certainty equivalent of the start-up lottery. If the weight of loss were to equal the weight of gain ($\lambda = 1$), the utility loss from the $64 loss would be 8 utils rather than 16 utils, and the certainty equivalent of the lottery would be $121. In Figure 15.1, the greater weight of loss is represented by $\lambda = 2$, and the certainty equivalent is only $49. In other words, the greater weight of loss decreases the certainty equivalent of the lottery. The general lesson is that for mixed lotteries (with positive and negative outcomes), potential losses loom large in an individual's willingness to pay to play the lottery.

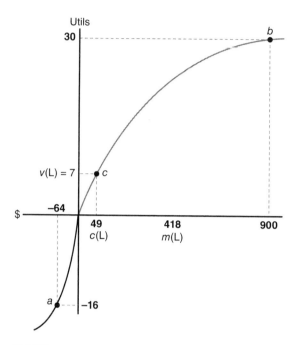

FIGURE 15.2: The Startup Lottery with Prospect Theory

Review the Concepts 15.1

1. The features of prospect theory include [___]. (decreasing sensitivity, greater weight of loss, increasing sensitivity, total wealth, gains and losses)

2. Using Figure 15.2 as a starting point, suppose the gain is $400 (instead of $900) and the loss is $4 (instead of $64). The monetary value of the lottery is $[___] and the utility value of the lottery is [_____] utils. (202, 11; 198, 9; 200, 10; 190, 8)

3. Using Figure 15.2 as a starting point, suppose the gain is $400 (instead of $900) and the loss is $4 (instead of $64). The certainty equivalent of the lottery is $c(L) = $[___]. (64, 81, 121, 100)

4. Use Widget 15.2 (available at www.oup.com/us/osullivan1e). Suppose $\mu = 0.70$ and $\lambda = 1.50$. The certainty equivalent of the lottery is $c(L) = $[___]. (69, 75, 80, 93)

15.2 Risk Aversion and Risk Neutrality

In everyday language, **risk aversion** refers the general inclination of people to avoid taking risks. Using the features of prospect theory, we can define risk aversion precisely. An individual experiences risk aversion if the certainty equivalent of a lottery is less than its monetary value:

$$\text{risk aversion}: c\left(L\right) < m\left(L\right)$$

In contrast, an individual experiences **risk neutrality** if the certainty equivalent equals the monetary value:

$$\text{risk neutrality}: c\left(L\right) = m\left(L\right)$$

In our start-up lottery, the monetary value is $m(L)$ = $418. An individual who is willing to pay $418 to play the lottery ($c(L)$ = $418) is risk neutral, while an individual whose willingness to pay is less than $418 ($c(L)$ < $418) is risk averse.

To get some insights into the difference between risk aversion and risk neutrality, suppose you observe the lottery outcomes for 100 individuals. The lottery has equal chances of loss or gain, so roughly 50 players will be winners and 50 will be losers. The average payoff will be close to the monetary value of the lottery, m(L) = $418. If you are risk-neutral, you will be willing to pay the average payoff ($418) to play the lottery. In contrast, if you are risk-averse, your willingness to pay will be less than the $418 average payoff. A risk-averse individual prefers to "play it safe" rather than taking a risk by playing the lottery.

Risk Aversion and the Risk Premium

The individual whose preferences are illustrated in Figure 15.2 and Figure 15.3 is strongly risk averse. The individual's utility function features decreasing sensitivity to gain and loss: μ = 1/2. The utility function also features a greater weight of loss: λ = 2. The certainty equivalent $c(L)$ = $49 is far less than the monetary value $m(L)$ = $418, so the individual experiences strong risk aversion.

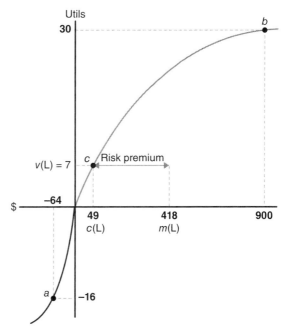

FIGURE 15.3: Risk Aversion and the Risk Premium

We can also compute an individual's risk premium for a particular lottery. The risk premium equals the gap between the **monetary value of a lottery** and its certainty equivalent:

$$\text{risk premium} : r(L) = m(L) - c(L)$$

In Figure 15.3, the individual's risk premium for the start-up lottery is $369:

$$r(L) = \$418 - 49 = \$369$$

The risk premium indicates how much *less than* the monetary value of a lottery an individual is willing to pay to play the lottery. The monetary value equals the average payoff from the lottery: if 100 people played the lottery, the average payoff would be roughly $418. So on average, an individual who pays only $49 to play the lottery will earn a premium of $369 (equal to $418 − $49) as a reward for taking a risk. The $369 difference is the premium required to induce the individual to play the lottery. In general, the stronger an individual's risk aversion, the smaller the certainty equivalent and the larger the risk premium.

Risk Neutrality: Linear Utility and Equal Weight of Loss and Gain

Recall that for a risk-neutral individual, the willingness to pay for a lottery equals its monetary value. Figure 15.4 shows a case of risk neutrality for our start-up lottery. The utility function is linear, indicating constant rather than decreasing sensitivity:

$$u(x) = 10 \cdot x$$

In addition, there is symmetry in the utility effects of loss and gain: $\lambda = 1$, indicating that the weight of loss equals the weight of gain. For this utility function, the utility value of the lottery is 4180 utils:

$$v(L) = \frac{1}{2} \cdot u(-64) + \frac{1}{2} \cdot u(900)$$

$$v(L) = -\frac{1}{2} \cdot 640 + \frac{1}{2} \cdot 9000 = 4180 \, \text{utils}$$

To translate the utility number into the certainty equivalent, we invert the utility function and compute a certainty equivalent of $418:

$$v(L) = 10 \cdot x \Rightarrow c(L) = \frac{1}{10} \cdot v(L)$$

$$c(L) = \frac{1}{10} \cdot 4180 = \$418$$

For this utility function, the certainty equivalent of the lottery equals its monetary value.

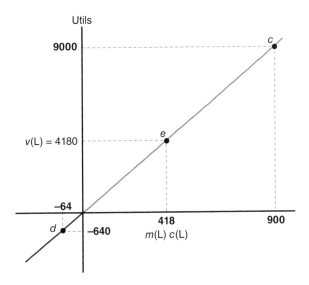

FIGURE 15.4: Risk Neutrality

The lesson from Figure 15.4 is that risk neutrality results from a combination of constant sensitivity to gain and loss and equal weighting of loss and gain. The certainty equivalent equals the monetary value, so the risk premium is zero:

$$risk\ neutrality: c\left(L\right) = m\left(L\right) \Rightarrow r\left(L\right) = 0$$

In the case of constant sensitivity and equal weighting of loss and gain, the risk-neutral individual does not require a premium to play the lottery: the willingness to pay equals the monetary value of the lottery.

Sources of Risk Aversion

So far we have seen two extreme cases of risk aversion. In Figure 15.3, for an individual with the utility parameters $\mu = 1/2$ and $\lambda = 2$, the certainty equivalent is a small fraction of the monetary value of the lottery, indicating strong risk aversion. In Figure 15.4, for an individual with utility parameters $\mu = \lambda = 1$, the certainty equivalent equals the monetary value of the lottery, indicating risk neutrality. These contrasting results indicate that two factors influence the strength of risk aversion: decreasing sensitivity to gain and loss (represented by μ) and the greater weight of loss (represented by λ).

Consider first the influence of the greater weight of loss. As λ increases, the relative weight of loss increases, so the utility loss from the downside of the lottery increases, decreasing the certainty equivalent of the lottery. The risk premium increases, indicating stronger risk aversion. Moving in the opposite direction, as λ decreases, the utility loss from the downside of the lottery decreases, moving the certainty equivalent closer to the monetary value. The decrease in the risk premium indicates weaker risk aversion.

Consider next the influence of decreasing sensitivity. Recall that decreasing sensitivity applies to both the gain and the loss: as the gain increases, utility increases at a decreasing rate; as the loss increases, utility decreases at a decreasing rate. An increase in μ decreases the rate at which utility changes with the dollar gain or loss.

- Gain side. An increase in μ weakens the force of **decreasing sensitivity to gain**, which tends to increase the certainty equivalent of a lottery.
- Loss side. An increase in μ weakens the force of **decreasing sensitivity to loss**, which tends to decrease the certainty equivalent of a lottery.

The net effect of these two forces is logically indeterminate. In general, if the gain is large relative to the loss, an increase in μ increases the certainty equivalent of a lottery, resulting in a smaller risk premium and thus weaker risk aversion.

Review the Concepts 15.2

1. For an individual who experiences risk aversion, [____]. ($m(L) < c(L)$, $c(L) > v(L)$, $c(L) < m(L)$, $v(L) > m(L)$)

2. Using Figure 15.3 as a starting point, suppose the gain is $400 (instead of $900) and the loss is $4 (instead of $64). The risk premium of the lottery is $[____]. (81, 117, 198, 202)

3. For an individual who experiences risk neutrality, [____]. ($c(L) < m(L)$, $c(L) = m(L)$, $c(L) > v(L)$, $v(L) > m(L)$)

4. Using Figure 15.4 as a starting point, suppose the gain is $400 (instead of $900) and the loss is $4 (instead of $64). The certainty equivalent of the lottery is $[____] and the risk premium is [____]. (198, 0; 117, 81; 81, 117; 100, 202)

5. *Comparative statics.* The relationship between λ and risk aversion (as measured by the risk premium) is [____]. (positive, negative, zero)

6. *Comparative statics.* Suppose the gain in a lottery is large relative to the loss. The relationship between μ and risk aversion (as measured by the risk premium) is [____]. (positive, negative, zero)

15.3 The Values of Key Parameters

Prospect theory provides a framework for computing the values of lotteries. As we've seen, the calculations in prospect theory are based on the values of two key parameters: λ for the relative weight of loss, and μ for decreasing sensitivity to gain and loss. In this part of the chapter we discuss the empirical estimates for these parameters and provide a widget (available at www.oup.com/us/osullivan1e) that allows you to compute your own value of μ.

Relative Weight of Loss

Consider the value of λ, the parameter that measures the relative weight of loss. We reported the results of empirical studies of λ in an earlier chapter. In a classic study, Tversky and Kahneman (1992) report an estimated value $\lambda = 2.25$. Abdellaoui, Bleichrodt, and Paraschiv (2007) summarize the results of studies that generated a wide range of estimates for λ, ranging from 1.79 to 4.80. In a study of 30 individuals, Sokol-Hessner et al. (2009) computed λ values ranging from 0.41 to 3.91, with a mean value of 1.40. These results show that there is substantial variation across individuals in the weight of loss relative to the weight of gain.

Decreasing Sensitivity to Gain and Loss

Consider next the value of μ, the parameter that measures the sensitivity to gain and loss. The parameter is often estimated separately for gains and losses. In the classic study of prospect theory, Tversky and Kahneman (1992) report an estimated value $\mu = 0.88$ for both gains and losses. More recently, Abdellaoui, Bleichrodt, and Paraschiv (2007) report an estimated value $\mu = 0.75$ for gains and $\mu = 0.74$ for losses. The estimated values are less than 1.0, indicating decreasing sensitivity gain: the marginal utility of gain decreases as the magnitude of the gain increases. The estimated values of μ for gains and losses are close, indicating rough symmetry in decreasing sensitivity.

Behavioral economists use lab experiments to estimate the values of μ for gains. Here is the prompt from a person running an experiment to estimate μ for gains.

> I'll flip a coin. If it's heads, I'll give you $100. If it's tails, I'll give you nothing. Or, we can forget about flipping the coin, and I'll give you $20 for certain. It's your choice—a coin flip with equal chances of $100 or nothing, or $20 for sure.

What's your response? If you choose the coin flip instead of the certain $20, how about a certain $21? If that doesn't work, how about a certain $22? If that doesn't work, how about a certain $23? If the proposed certain amount continues to increase, eventually you will switch from the coin flip to the certain amount. Your switch number is your certainty equivalent for the coin-flip lottery.

We can use some simple algebra to derive a formula to convert an observed certainty equivalent into the implied value of the utility parameter μ. Consider first a gain lottery, with x > 0. As shown in Math 15.1, the value of μ that is consistent with a person's certainty equivalent is

$$\mu = \frac{\log[p]}{\log[c] - \log[x]}$$

where log [ ] is the natural logarithm, p is the probability of the gain x, and c is the person's certainty equivalent.

We can use the equation for μ for any specified lottery and any person's certainty equivalent. For example, suppose $(x, p, c) = (100, 0.50, 25)$: for a 50–50 chance of winning \$100, a person is willing to pay \$25. Substituting the values into the formula for μ,

$$\mu = \frac{\log[0.50]}{\log[25] - \log[100]} = 0.50$$

In this case, we have the familiar square-root utility function $u(x) = x^{1/2}$. A person with a larger certainty equivalent has a larger value of μ. For example, for a person whose certainty equivalent is $c(\text{L}) = \$40$, the implied parameter value is $\mu = 0.756$. For a person whose certainty equivalent equals the \$50 monetary value, $\mu = 1$, indicating constant sensitivity rather than decreasing sensitivity to gain. To compute your personal μ, use the coin-flip prompt to compute your certainty equivalent, and substitute your certainty equivalent into the equation for μ.

Behavioral economists also use lab experiments to estimate the values of μ for a loss lottery, with $x < 0$. To illustrate, imagine that you owe \$100 in taxes, and the tax collector makes you an offer:

> I'll flip a coin. If it's heads, you pay \$100. If it's tails, you pay nothing, and your tax liability disappears. Or, we can forget about flipping the coin, and you pay \$50 for certain. It's your choice—a coin flip with equal chances of paying \$100 or nothing, or pay \$50 for sure.

If you choose the coin flip instead of the certain \$50, how about a certain \$49? If that doesn't get you to choose the certain outcome, how about a certain \$48? If that doesn't work, how about a certain \$47? For what certain amount will you be indifferent between the coin flip and the certain amount? The indifferent amount is your certainty equivalent of the loss lottery.

The equation used to compute μ from a gain lottery also applies to a loss lottery. For a loss lottery, $x < 0$ and $c < 0$, so we must mind the minus signs.

$$\mu = \frac{\log[p]}{\log[-c] - \log[-x]}$$

For example, suppose $(x, p, c) = (-100, 0.50, -25)$: to avoid a 50–50 chance of losing \$100, a person is willing to sacrifice \$25. Plugging the values into the expression for μ,

$$\mu = \frac{\log[0.50]}{\log[25] - \log[100]} = 0.50$$

In this case, we have the familiar square-root utility function in the domain of loss: $u(x) = -(-x^{1/2})$. A person with a smaller certainty equivalent (a larger negative number) has a larger value of μ. For example, for a certainty equivalent of $-\$40$, $\mu = 0.756$. For a person whose certainty equivalent equals the $-\$50$ monetary value, $\mu = 1$, indicating constant rather than decreasing sensitivity to loss. To compute your μ, use the coin-flip prompt from the tax collector to compute your certainty equivalent, and substitute your certainty equivalent into the equation for μ.

Measuring Sensitivity to Stimulus

As we saw in the chapter opener, psychologists measure the relationship between stimulus and response, focusing on perceptions. For example, as the actual sugar content of a solution increases, the perceived sweetness increases, but at a decreasing rate. To measure the relationship between stimulus and perceptions, psychologists use the bisection method. To start the experiment, the scientist exposes the subject to a low stimulus (low sugar concentration) and a high stimulus (high concentration). Then the scientist asks the subject to choose a stimulus that is halfway between the low stimulus and the high stimulus (an intermediate sugar concentration). The typical subject chooses an intermediate stimulus that is closer to the low stimulus than to the high stimulus, indicating decreasing sensitivity to the stimulus.

Figure 15.5 illustrates the bisection method for the sweetness experiment. The horizontal axis measures the actual sugar concentration. The vertical axis measures the subject's responses to the varying concentration in terms of perception (perceived sweetness). Point L shows the subject's perceived sweetness for

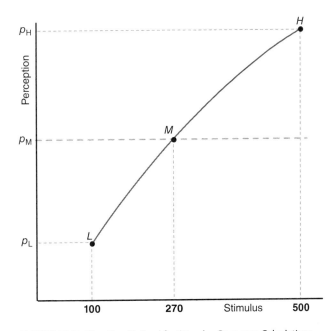

FIGURE 15.5: Bisection Method for Stimulus-Response Calculations

the low concentration (p_L for a concentration of 100 mM), and point H shows the subject's perceived sweetness for the high concentration (p_H for a concentration of 500 mM). After tasting the low concentration and the high concentration, the subject chooses a sugar concentration that he or she perceives to be halfway between the low concentration and the high concentration. In graphical terms, the subject picks a point on the thick dashed line, which lies half way between p_L (perceived sweetness of the low concentration) and p_H (perceived sweetness of the high concentration).

We can use the subject's choice of the intermediate concentration to determine whether he or she experiences decreasing sensitivity to sugar concentrations. For the typical subject, the intermediate concentration is roughly 270 mM (point *M*). To close half the gap between the perceived low sweetness and the perceived high sweetness, a relatively small increase over the low concentration will suffice. The subject perceives a concentration of 270 mM to be halfway between a concentration of 100 mM and a concentration of 500 mM. Starting from the low concentration, the subject is relatively sensitive to the sugar content, so it takes a relatively small increase in the concentration to close half the perception gap. In contrast, a person with constant sensitivity would choose an intermediate concentration of 300 mM.

The bisection method has been used to measure the sensitivity to all sorts of stimuli. The relationship between stimulus and response is summarized in a power function.

$$perceived\ stimulus = \left(actual\ stimulus\right)^r$$

A value $r < 1$ indicates decreasing sensitivity. As noted in the chapter opener, the power function for sweetness is

$$perceived\ sweetness = \left(sugar\ concentration\right)^{0.60}$$

Stevens (1961) estimated stimulus–response relationships for warmth, cold, lifted weights, pressure, vibration, and white noise. Stevens concluded that the responses to these stimuli were subject to decreasing sensitivity. For example, the power function for warmth is

$$perceived\ warmth\ of\ a\ large\ patch\ of\ skin = \left(skin\ temperature\right)^{0.70}$$

Economic Experiment: Risk Preferences and Cognitive Ability

A recent economic experiment explores the relationship between risk preferences and cognitive ability (Dohmen et al. 2010). Participants made choices between (i) a certain payment of *X* euros and (ii) a lottery with a 50 percent chance of a payment of 300 euros. Starting from *X* = 40 euros, most participants chose the lottery over the certain payment of 40 euros. As the certain payment increased, some participants switched from the lottery to the certain payment. A person who quickly switched from the lottery to the certain payment revealed his or her reluctance to take risks. For example, a person who switched at 60 euros prefers 60 euros for certain to a 50 percent chance of 300 euros. A person who didn't switch until the certain payment reached 140 euros revealed a greater willingness to take risks.

The purpose of the experiment was to determine the relationship between cognitive ability and risk preferences. Cognitive ability was measured by scores on a widely used intelligence test. On average, the switching point for the participants was 100 euros. For people with below-average cognitive ability, the switching point was lower, indicating a greater reluctance to take risk. For people with above-average cognitive ability, the switching point was higher, indicating a greater willingness to take risk.

Review the Concepts 15.3

1. Studies of the greater weight of loss ($\lambda > 1$).suggest that there is [___] variability in λ across individuals. (little, a modest amount, substantial)

2. Consider a gain lottery with a 50 percent chance of winning $60. Rudy's certainty equivalent is $15, and Newt's certainty equivalent is $30. Plausible values for the utility parameter μ are [___] for Rudy and [___] for Newt. (1, 0.50; 0.50, 1; 0.80, 0.20)

3. Consider a gain lottery with a 50 percent chance of winning $60. Mid's certainty equivalent is $24. A plausible value for the utility parameter μ is [___]. (0.25, 0.50, 0.75, 1)

4. Consider a loss lottery with a 50 percent chance of losing $40. Rudy's certainty equivalent is –$10, and Newt's certainty equivalent is –$20. Plausible values for the utility parameter μ are [___] for Rudy and [___] for Newt. (1, 0.50; 0.50, 1; 0.80, 0.20)

5. Use Widget 15.3 (available at www.oup.com/us/osullivan1e). Suppose an individual is willing to pay $40 for a 50 percent chance of a $100 gain. The implied value of the utility parameter is $\mu = $ [___]. (0.24, 0.50, 0.76, 1)

6. Consider an experiment that used the bisection method to test for decreasing sensitivity. The low stimulus is 10 and the high stimulus is 40. We conclude that a subject has decreasing sensitivity if he or she chooses an intermediate stimulus [___]. (less than 25, greater than 25, equal to 25)

15.4 Risk Preferences for Rats

So far we have explored risk preferences of humans. An important question is whether other members of the animal kingdom share the key features of prospect theory—reference dependence, decreasing sensitivity to gain and loss, and greater weight of loss. In this part of the chapter, we explore the risk preferences of rats.

A recent study suggests that the decisions made by rats in an uncertain environment are consistent with the key features of prospect theory (Constantinople,

Piet, and Brody 2018). Thirsty lab rats chose between certain and uncertain water rewards, with flashing lights conveying the probabilities of the uncertain rewards and auditory clicks conveying the volumes of water for both certain and uncertain rewards. After extensive training for the visual and auditory cues, the authors ran hundreds of trials on 48 rats.

The general conclusion is that prospect theory applies to rats. For the rats as a whole, there are several conclusions.

- *Reference dependence.* Rats who regularly experienced relatively large rewards treated relatively small rewards as losses rather than gains. For a rat who becomes acclimated to large rewards, gaining just a little is treated as a loss.
- *Decreasing sensitivity.* The rats experienced decreasing sensitivity to gain and loss. The median estimate is $\mu = 0.54$, which is roughly consistent with a square-root utility function.
- *Greater weight of loss.* The median estimate is $\lambda = 1.66$, meaning that the disutility of loss was roughly 1.66 times the utility of gain.

Figure 15.6 shows the estimated value function for the rats. The value function exhibits decreasing sensitivity to gain and loss (as reflected in the curvature of the utility curve) and greater weight of loss (a steeper curve in the domain of loss).

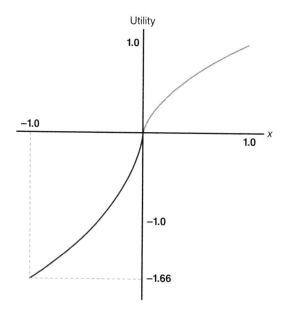

FIGURE 15.6: Value Function for Rats

The study also tracked the choices of individual rats, and revealed substantial variation in risk preferences across rats.

- *Sensitivity to gain and loss.* Although as a whole the rats experienced decreasing sensitivity, a relatively small number of rats experienced increasing sensitivity, with value of μ greater than one.
- *Relative weight of loss.* As a whole the rats experienced greater weight of loss ($\lambda > 1$). But for 44 percent of the rats, $\lambda < 1$, indicating that the disutility of loss was less than the utility of gain.

The study also showed that for rats, history matters. For an individual rat, a recent history of rewards affected the shape of the utility curve. After a rat was lucky enough to receive a reward, the curvature of the utility function decreased (the utility curve became closer to linear), indicating less rapidly decreasing sensitivity to gain and loss. Overall, the lab experiment suggests that risk preferences are not stable traits, but instead reflect a rat's reward experience.

Review the Concepts 15.4

1. A recent study of decision-making by rats in uncertain environments reveals [____]. (greater weight of loss, increasing sensitivity, decreasing sensitivity, loss neutrality)

2. Use Figure 15.6. The utility curve is steeper in the domain of loss, indicating [____]. (greater weight of gain, decreasing sensitivity, increasing sensitivity, greater weight of loss)

3. Use Figure 15.6. The utility curve in the domain of gain has a decreasing slope, indicating [____]. (constant sensitivity, decreasing sensitivity, lower weight of gain, increasing sensitivity)

Key Terms

certainty equivalent of a lottery, p. 264
decreasing sensitivity to gain, p. 270
decreasing sensitivity to loss, p. 270
monetary value of a lottery, p. 268
risk aversion, p. 266
risk neutrality, p. 267
utility value of a lottery, p. 264

Takeaways

1. Prospect theory incorporates decreasing sensitivity to gain: the marginal utility of a gain decreases as the magnitude of the gain increases.

2. Prospect theory incorporates decreasing sensitivity to loss: the marginal disutility of a loss decreases as the magnitude of the loss increases.

3. Prospect theory incorporates greater weight of loss ($\lambda > 1$): the disutility of loss exceeds the utility of gain.

4. An individual is risk averse if the certainty equivalent of a lottery is less than its monetary value, and is risk neutral if the certainty equivalent of a lottery equals its monetary value.

5. The the strength of risk aversion is determined by decreasing sensitivity (μ) and the relative weight of loss (λ).

6. The bisection method measures the relationship between stimulus and response, providing evidence of decreasing sensitivity to stimuli such as sweetness, warmth, cold, and pressure.

7. Experiments show that rats exhibit reference dependence, decreasing sensitivity, and greater weight of loss.

Discuss the Concepts

1. *Comparative Statics.* Suppose the start-up lottery is for your new food cart in a city. Starting from the lottery shown in Figure 15.2, consider the effects of following changes.

   a. A potential competitor relocates a nearby food cart, increasing your probability of success to 0.75. The certainty equivalent [____] ($\uparrow$, $\downarrow$, does not change) to $[____].

   b. A new housing development in the neighborhood increases the number of potential customers, increasing the gain to $1156. The certainty equivalent [____] ($\uparrow$, $\downarrow$, does not change) to $[____].

   c. The long-term lease for the food-cart pad doubles in length, increasing the loss to $100. The certainty equivalent [____] ($\uparrow$, $\downarrow$, does not change) to $[____].

2. *Highest Bidder.* Imagine that you are selling a stake in your start-up company to the highest bidder. The associated lottery is the start-up lottery in Figure 15.1. Rootone has a square-root utility function and loss neutrality, with $\lambda = 1$. Linthree has a linear utility function $u(x) = 10 \cdot x$ and greater weight of loss, with $\lambda = 3$.

a. Rootone's bid is [____]. Illustrate.

b. Linthrees bid is [____]. Illustrate.

3. *Neighborly Certainty Equivalent.* Use Widget 15.3 (available at www.oup. com/us/osullivan1e) to compute the value of your utility parameter μ for gain. Suppose you are offered a lottery with a 25 percent chance of a \$144 gain. Your willingness to pay is $c(L) = $ [____]. Use the results from three neighbors to plot four points on a curve showing the relationship between μ (on the horizontal axis) and the certainty equivalent (on the vertical axis).

4. *Rat Certainty Equivalent.* Consider the results of the experiments with thirsty lab rats.

a. The typical rat would be indifferent between a lottery with equal chances of gaining 36 ounces or losing 4 ounces and a certain [____] ounces.

b. Suppose, as an approximation, we assume $\mu = 0.50$ and $\lambda = 2$. The resulting certainty equivalent would be [____] (>, <, =) to the value computed in (a) because [____].

Apply the Concepts

1. *Your Certainty Equivalent and the Start-Up Lottery.* Determine your values for the relevant parameters of prospect theory. Your value for $\mu = $ [____] and your value for $\lambda = $ [____]. Based on these values, your certainty equivalent for the start-up lottery is $c(L) = $ [____]. Your willingness to pay (certainty equivalent) is [____] (>, <, =) to the text example $c(L) = \$49$ because [____].

2. *Euro Lottery and the Start-Up Lottery.* Consider the experimental results for the euro lottery L{0,0.50, 300, 0.50}. Recall that the average switching price was 100 euros.

a. The average switching price is consistent with a value of $\mu = $ [____].

b. Suppose $\lambda = 2$. For the average participant in the euro lottery, the certainty equivalent of the start-up lottery = \$ [____].

c. The average participant in the euro lottery is willing to pay [____] (more, less) than the person in the text example because [____].

3. *Linear Utility and the Start-Up Lottery.* Consider an individual with linear utility function $u(x) = 2 \cdot x$ and $\lambda = 3$. The utility value of the start-up lottery (in the text) is $v(L) = $ [____]. The certainty equivalent is $c(L) = $ [____] and the risk premium is $r(L) = $ [____]. The individual experiences risk [____].

4. *Loss Neutrality and and the Start-Up Lottery.* Consider an individual with the square-root utility function and $\lambda = 1$. The utility value of the start-up

lottery (in the text) is $v(L) = $ [___]. The certainty equivalent is $c(L) = $ [___] and the risk premium is $r(L) = $ [___]. The individual experiences risk [___].

5. *Willingness to Pay for a Gain Lottery.* Consider a lottery in which there is a 40 percent chance of gaining $100. The utility function is $u(x) = x^{1/2}$, where x is the money gained.

   a. The monetary value of the lottery is $m(L) = \$$ [___].

   b. The certainty equivalent of the lottery is $c(L) = \$$ [___].

   c. The willingness to pay is less than the monetary value because [___].

6. *Aging, Weight of Loss, and Certainty Equivalent.* Use Widget 15.4 (available at www.oup.com/us/osullivan1e). Consider the lottery L = {−100, 0.80; 2000, 0.20}. For Ochocho at age 30, the parameter values are $\{\mu, \lambda\} = \{0.88, 1.30\}$.

   a. The monetary value of the lottery is $m(L) = \$$ [___]. The utility value of the lottery is $v(L) = $ [___] utils. The willingness to pay for the lottery is $c(L) = \$$ [___].

   b. Illustrate with a graph that shows the numbers from (a) as well as (i) the utility of the gain and (ii) the utility of the loss.

   c. Suppose that as Ochocho ages, the value of λ increases by 0.01 per year. At age 60, Ochocho's willingness to pay for the lottery is $c(L) = \$$ [___].

7. *Billinda's Meditation Program.* For Billinda the philanthropist, utility is determined by the number of malaria cases in Tanzania, with $\mu = 1/2$. A proposed project has equal chances of (i) decreasing the number of malaria cases by 900 (a gain) and (ii) increasing the number of malaria cases by 36 (a loss).

   a. Suppose Billinda experiences greater weight of loss, with $\lambda = 2.50$. The willingness to pay for the project is $\$$ [___].

   b. Suppose Billinda enrolls in an aggressive meditation program. If the meditation program eliminates the greater weight of loss, the willingness to pay changes to $\$$ [___].

8. *How Many Shares?* Use Widget 15.4 (available at www.oup.com/us/osullivan1e). In your job as an investment advisor, your clients have a common relative weight of loss, with $\lambda = 1.5$. Your clients vary in the curvature of their utility functions, with μ varying uniformly between 0.71 and 0.90, with one client in each 0.01 interval (a total of 20 clients) You have the opportunity to sell each client one unit of stock, described by the lottery L = {−100, 0.80; 2000, 0.20}. The purchase price of the stock is $126.

   a. Ochocho, a client with $\mu = 0.88$, is willing to pay $\$$ [___] for the stock lottery. Illustrate with a graph that shows all the relevant values.

   b. The stock will be relatively attractive to a client with a relatively [___] (large, small) values of μ. You will sell [___] units to your clients.

Math Solution

Math 15.1

The certainty equivalent of a lottery with probability p of winning a prize x is

$$c = \left(p \cdot x^{\mu} \right)^{1/\mu} \Rightarrow c = p^{1/\mu} \cdot x$$

Raise each side to the power μ to get

$$c^{\mu} = p \cdot x^{\mu}$$

Take the natural logarithm of each side:

$$\mu \cdot \log[c] = \log[p] + \mu \cdot \log[x]$$

Solve for μ:

$$\mu = \frac{\log[p]}{\log[c] - \log[x]}$$

16 Problems with Probability

Imagine a conversation between a medical doctor and parent about vaccinating a child. Reliable data from a website shows that 1 in 14,000 children who receive the vaccine will experience seizures. Both the parent and the doctor are familiar with the data. The doctor also has many years of experience in vaccinating children, and does not recall any seizures among vaccinated children. Would you expect the parent and the doctor to agree on the advisability of vaccination? As we'll see in this chapter, it is likely that the parent will over-weight the probability of a seizure, while the doctor may under-weight the probability. The key difference is that the parent learns the probability by description (the reliable web data), while the doctor incorporates his or her experience with child vaccinations (Hertwig et al. 2004; Glimcher, 2011).

This chapter presents the fourth feature of prospect theory: **probability weighting**. In computing the certainty equivalent of a lottery, the sensible approach is to use the actual known probabilities of various outcomes. But instead, many people use decision weights that are not equal to the probabilities. As we saw in an earlier chapter, humans are not skillful in (i) estimating the probabilities of alternative outcomes and (ii) applying probabilities in decision-making. In general, prospect theory is based on the observation that people systematically over-weight rare (low probability) outcomes and under-weight common (high probability) outcomes. As we'll see, this observation is consistent with learning probabilities by description.

Learning Objectives: The Explainer

After mastering this chapter, you will be able to explain each of the following statements.

1. In prospect theory, a decision-maker over-weights rare (low-probability) outcomes and under-weights common (high-probability) outcomes.

2. Depending on how an individual learns probabilities, rare events may be over-weighted or under-weighted.

3. The numbers-game puzzle can be solved by (i) over-weighting of rare events and (ii) weak decreasing sensitivity to gain.

4. The longshot puzzle can be solved by (i) over-weighting of rare events and (ii) weak decreasing sensitivity to gain.

16.1 Probability in Prospect Theory

Behavioral economists have documented many puzzles in the way humans estimate probabilities and apply probabilities to decision-making. Prospect theory incorporates this puzzling human behavior into the calculations of the utility value and certainty equivalent of a lottery. In the previous chapter, we computed the utility value of a lottery as

$$v(\text{L}) = p_1 \cdot u(x_1) + p_2 \cdot u(x_2) + p_3 \cdot u(x_3) + \ldots + p_n \cdot u(x_n)$$

where p_i is the probability of outcome i and the utility function $u(x_i)$ translates a monetary value x_i into a utility value (in utils). In prospect theory, the utility value is computed as

$$v(\text{L}) = w_1 \cdot u(x_1) + w_2 \cdot u(x_2) + w_3 \cdot u(x_3) + \ldots + w_n \cdot u(x_n)$$

where w_i is the decision weight associated with outcome i. It is tempting to assume that $w_i = p_i$, that is, the decision weight of an outcome equals its probability. Prospect theory is based on the observation that individuals systematically over-weight rare (low-probability) outcomes and under-weight common (high-probability) outcomes. In other words, for low-probability outcomes, $w_i > p_i$, while for high-probability outcomes, $w_i < p_i$.

Prelec Probability Weighting

The Prelec function shows the relationship between probabilities p_i and decision weights w_i in prospect theory. A simple version of the Prelec function is

$$w(p) = E^{-(-\log[p])^\phi}$$

where E is the base of the natural logarithm (approximately 2.718) and log[ ] is the natural logarithm. The parameter ϕ determines the nonlinearity of the weighting function. For $\phi = 1$, the weights equal the actual probabilities: $w_i = p_i$. In contrast, for $\phi < 1$:

- low-probability outcomes are over-weighted: $w_i > p_i$ for low p_i
- high-probability outcomes are under-weighted: $w_i < p_i$ for high p_i

In a widely cited study of probability weighting, Wu and Gonzalez (1996) estimate a value of $\phi = 0.74$.

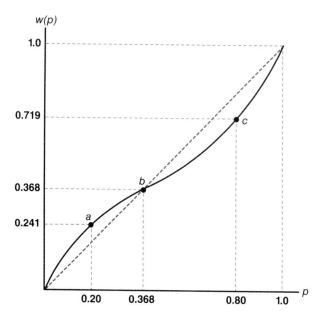

FIGURE 16.1: Probability Weighting

Figure 16.1 shows a Prelec weighting function with $\phi = 0.75$. The horizontal axis shows the probability p and the vertical axis shows the decision weight $w(p)$. The weighting curve is the solid curve that has the shape of an inverted S. The dashed diagonal shows the undistorted weights: $w_i = p_i$. For relatively low probabilities, the decision weight exceeds the probability. For example, point a shows that for a probability $p = 0.20$, the weight is $w(p)=0.241$. For relatively high probabilities, the decision weight is less than the probability. For example, point c shows that for a probability $p = 0.80$, the weight is $w(p)=0.719$. For some intermediate probability, the decision weight equals the probability. In Figure 16.1, the weight equals the probability for $p = 0.368$. For this class of Prelec weighting functions, the crossing point is $1/E$.

Psychological Foundations

Tversky and Kahneman (1992) explore the psychological foundations for the shape of the Prelec probability weighting function. Suppose that for relatively low probabilities, the reference point for a decision-maker is a probability of zero (impossible). A person thinking about a relatively low probability compares the probability of 0.00 (impossible) to the probability of 0.01 (possible but highly unlikely). The shift from "impossible" to "possible" makes the step from 0.00 to 0.01 appear to be relatively large. The next step, from 0.01 to 0.02 appears to be smaller because the shift is from "possible but highly unlikely" to "possible and a bit more likely than highly unlikely." This is an example of decreasing sensitivity to change: the decision-maker is more sensitive to a change from 0.00 to 0.01 than to a change from 0.01 to 0.02. The Prelec curve is concave for low probabilities, indicating decreasing sensitivity to increases in the probability.

In Figure 16.1, the logic of decreasing sensitivity applies to probabilities from 0.00 to 0.368. As the probability increases, the decision weight increases, indicating that a decision-maker incorporates the higher probability into the decision weight. But as the distance from "impossible" increases, decreasing sensitivity means that the effect of each 0.01 increment in probability decreases. For example, for a probability $p = 0.10$, the distance from the "impossible" reference point is twice the distance for a probability of $p = 0.05$, but decision weight is less than twice as large. Stated another way, the increase in probability from 0.00 to 0.05 is more significant to the decision-maker than the increase in probability from 0.05 to 0.10.

Gonzales and Wu (1999) use surveys to get insights into the phenomenon of decreasing sensitivity to changes for low probabilities. Imagine that you are participating in two lotteries. Lotto5 offers a 5 percent chance of winning $250. Lotto30 offers a 30 percent chance of winning $250. Which of the following changes is more significant?

- You can improve your chance of winning Lotto5 from 5 percent to 10 percent.
- You can improve your chance of winning Lotto30 from 30 percent to 35 percent.

In a survey of undergraduates, 75 percent viewed the first option (increase from 5 percent to 10 percent) as a more significant change. The sensitivity to a given increase in probability (an increase of 0.05) decreases as the starting probability increases: an increase from 0.05 to 0.10 is more powerful than an increase from 0.30 to 0.35.

Consider the shape of the curve for high probabilities. Suppose that for relatively high probabilities, the reference point for a decision-maker is a probability of 1.00 (certainty). A person thinking about a relatively high probability compares the probability of 1.00 (certain) to the probability of 0.99 (uncertain but highly likely). The shift from "certainty" to "uncertain" makes the step from 1.00 to 0.99 appear to be relatively large. The next step, from 0.99 to 0.98 appears to be smaller because the shift is from "uncertain but highly likely" to "uncertain but slightly less likely." This is an example of decreasing sensitivity to change: the decision-maker is more sensitive to a change from 1.00 to 0.99 than to a change from 0.99 to 0.98. As shown in Figure 16.1, as we move away from the certainty outcome ($p = 1.00$), the Prelec curve becomes progressively flatter, indicating decreasing sensitivity to movement away from the certainty outcome.

A Closer Look at Rare Events

A recent study of the insurance market explores the over-weighting of rare events (Barseghyan et al. 2013). The study focuses on events that trigger insurance claims, such as automobile accidents and residential damage from storms. The study explores the over-weighting by insurance consumers for events with probabilities that range from zero to 0.16. As shown in Figure 16.2, insurance buyers over-weight rare events, and the largest over-weighting occurs for the rarest (lowest-probability) events. For example, the decision weight is 0.08 for a probability of 0.02, compared to a decision weight of 0.11 for a probability 0.05 and a decision weight of 0.18 for a probability 0.16.

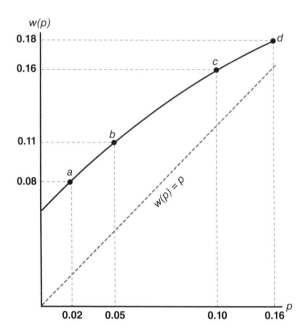

FIGURE 16.2: Probability Weighting for Insurance Claims

Figures 16.1 and 16.2 show different patterns of probability weighting for rare events. In Figure 16.1, the Prelec weighting curve is steeper than the dashed line (showing $w(p) = p$) up to and beyond a probability of 0.16. In Figure 16.2, the weighting curve is flatter than the dashed line. For probabilities close to zero, the Prelec curve shows weights close to zero, while the curve in Figure 16.2 shows decision weights close to 0.06. The nature and magnitude of probability weighting is a topic of ongoing work by behavioral economists. Many questions remain unanswered, and behavioral economists are developing models to measure probability weighting and understand its origin.

Review the Concepts 16.1

1. In prospect theory, the utility value of a lottery is computed with [____]. (a utility function, outcome values, outcome probabilities, decision weights)

2. Prospect theory is based on the assumption that an individual [____] rare events and [____] common events. (under-weights, over-weights; over-weights, under-weights; over-weights, properly weights, under-weights, properly weights)

3. The mis-weighting of rare events can be explained by [____] sensitivity to changes. (increasing, decreasing, constant)

4. In an experiment on changing the probability of winning a lottery, well over half the subjects said that an increase from 5 percent to 10 percent was [____] significant when compared to an increase from 30 percent to 35 percent. (more, less, equally)

5. Use Widget 16.1 (available at www.oup.com/us/osullivan1e). Suppose the value of the Prelec parameter is $\phi = 0.75$. For an outcome with a probability $p = 0.01$, the decision weight is roughly [___] times the probability. (1, 2, 4, 6, 10)

6. A study of insurance claims provides evidence that insurance buyers [___] rare events, and the greatest mis-weighting occurs for the [___] probability events. (over-weight, highest; over-weight, middle; over-weight, lowest; under-weight, lowest)

16.2   Learning by Description versus Learning by Experience

Consider the distinction between learning probabilities by description and learning through experience. In most of the lab experiments used to determine the curvature of the Prelec probability-weighting curve, subjects learn the probabilities by description. The scientist describes the features of lotteries, including the probabilities of possible outcomes, and then observes the choices of the subject. For example, consider a pair of lotteries.

$$L_G = \{0, 0.90; 32, 0.10\}$$

$$L_C = \{3, 1\}$$

The scientist's descriptions are simple: lottery G provides a 10 percent chance of a $32 payoff, and lottery C is a certain payoff of $3. Based on these descriptions, a subject can choose between the lotteries. By varying the described probability and the payouts, a scientist can determine the curvature of the subject's Prelec curve.

An alternative approach is to allow subjects to learn the probabilities through experience. Instead of giving a subject a list of probabilities that describe the lotteries, the scientist sets up a learning environment. In the learning phase, a subject repeatedly presses two buttons on a computer, one for lottery G and a second for lottery C. For each press of the C button, the computer screen shows "$3." Repeated presses of the C button during the learning phase will make it clear that pressing button C in the choice phase will generate a certain reward of $3. For the G button, one of every ten presses signals a $32 gain, while nine of ten presses signals the zero outcome. Repeated presses of the G button will show the one-in-ten chance of getting $32. In the learning phase, subjects can press the buttons as many times as they like before moving on to make an actual choice.

Hertwig et al. (2004) ran a series of experiments, with six decisions involving lotteries that varied in probabilities and payoffs. Each subject was randomly assigned to one of two groups: descriptive learning or experiential learning. For the decision about lottery G versus lottery C, the two methods of learning generate different patterns of decision weighting.

1. *Descriptive learners.* Roughly 48 percent of descriptive learners chose lottery G. In other words, roughly half the subjects chose a gamble with a monetary value of $3.20 rather than choosing a certain $3.00.
2. *Experiential learning.* Only 20 percent of experiential learners chose G. In other words, 80 percent of the subjects chose a certain $3.00 rather than a gamble with a monetary value of $3.20.

One interpretation of these results is that learning by experience rather than by description generates lower decision weights for rare events. An experiential learner who places a lower weight on the rare event of winning $32 is more likely to choose the certain payment.

Based on this experiment and five other experiments, the authors conclude that descriptive learning and experiential learning generate different patterns of decision weighting.

> In the case of decisions from description, people make choices as if they over-weight the probability of rare events, as described by prospect theory. We found that in the case of decisions from experience, in contrast, people make choices as if they under-weight the probability of rare events. (Hertwig et al. 2004, 534)

Studies of animal behavior confirm that experiential learning generates similar bias in other animals. Animal experiments rely on experiential learning rather than descriptive learning because we haven't yet figured out how to describe lotteries to monkeys, mice, and insects. A study of foraging bumblebees (Real, 1991) suggests that bumblebees under-weight rare events (probability = 0.20) and over-weight common events (probability = 0.80). In other words, humans and bumblebees who learn probabilities from experience exhibit the same bias in incorporating probabilities into decisions.

Glimcher (2011) discusses the neuroscience of experiential learning of probabilities. Animals use the frequencies of past events to guide their actions. For example, suppose a particular action by a lab animal triggers a reward once every 20 trials. If the animal had permanent memories, the animal would base any future actions on an assumed reward probability of 0.05. But memories are not permanent, and of course a forgotten event does not play a role in estimating probabilities. Glimcher notes that for the typical lab animal, a memory lasts roughly ten trials. For example, a reward on trial 3 will be almost completely forgotten by trial 13. As a result, a lab animal in a 1-in-20 reward system will have no memory of past rewards on roughly half the trials. So we can expect the animal to systematically under-weight the reward in the decision-making process, and act as if the reward probability is less than the actual 0.05.

> That means that if a large reward occurs with low probability, under typical conditions it will have only a brief influence on average estimates of value. Under such conditions, low-probability events will thus be underrepresented and high-probability events overrepresented in the long-term average estimate of value that drives behavior. (Glimcher 2011, 386)

Naturally, humans are different from lab animals, but we do share the feature of impermanent memories. When we learn probabilities from experience, we can expect a similar under-weighting of low-probability events.

Recall the chapter opener about the conversation about vaccinating a child. The parent learns the probability of seizures by description, from a reliable source of information. Based on the study by Hertwig et al. (2004) and a follow-up study by Barron and Ursino (2013), we would expect the parent to over-weight the rare event. Therefore, we expect parents to be less inclined to vaccinate the child. In contrast, a doctor who draws on experience to infer the likelihood of the rare event may under-weight the rare event. In general, when an individual (human, bumblebee, or lab animal) learns a probability by experience, rare events are likely to be under-represented in the decision-making process.

Review the Concepts 16.2

1. Individuals who learn about lotteries from description typically [____] rare events. (over-weight, under-weight, properly weight)

2. Individuals who learn about lotteries from experience typically [____] rare events. (over-weight, under-weight, properly weight)

3. When a medical doctor and a parent disagree about the wisdom of a vaccinating a child, the disagreement could be because the parent learns probabilities by [____] while a doctor also learns from [____]. (description, experience; experience, description)

16.3   Solving Puzzles with Probability Weighting

In this part of the chapter we use the notion of probability weighting to solve two puzzles from the gambling world. The **numbers-game puzzle** is that people play games of chance with a monetary payback that is less than the cost of playing. The **longshot puzzle** is that racetrack bettors are biased in favor of horses with relatively low probabilities of winning.

The Numbers-Game Puzzle

In a traditional neighborhood numbers game, a player specifies a bet (say $20) and chooses a three-digit number from 000 to 999. The winning number for a day is the last three digits of the total amount bet that day at the local race-track. The payout is 600:1, meaning that a $20 bet on the winning number pays $12,000. The numbers game (sometimes called the numbers racket) was popular in many neighborhoods, and accepted bets as low as one cent. In New York and other cities, the illegal game was managed by organized crime, and employed people as runners, lookouts, accountants, and bankers (*New York Times* 1964). The state of Massachusetts developed its own numbers game to compete with illegal neighborhood games. To entice people to switch to the lawful game, the state increased the payout to roughly 700:1, meaning that a $20 bet on the winning number paid $14,000.

A few quick calculations suggest that both versions of the numbers game are losing propositions. The probability of choosing the winning three-digit number is 1/1000. For a $20 bet, the monetary value of the illegal version is $12 (equal to $12,000/1000) and the monetary value of the legal version is a bit higher at $14 (equal to $14,000/1000). So why pay $20 for an expected monetary payback of only $12 or $14? As noted in the standard warning for state-sponsored gambling, "the numbers game is a game of chance, and should not be played for investment purposes." But why play at all, given that you expect, on average, to lose $6 for each $20 bet?

Solving the Numbers-Game Puzzle

Consider a person who plays a neighborhood numbers game with a bet of $20. A bettor has one chance in 1000 to be the winner, so the numbers-game lottery for a $20 bet is

$$L = \{0, 0.999; 12,000, 0.001\}$$

The monetary value is less than the $20 cost of playing:

$$m(L) = 0.001 \cdot 12,000 = 12$$

For the utility value of the lottery, let's start with the linear utility function $u(x) = x$. Using the objective probabilities as decision weights, the utility value and certainty equivalent of the lottery are

$$v(L) = 0.001 \cdot 12,000 = 12 \, \text{utils} \qquad c(L) = v(L) = \$12$$

Recall that the certainty equivalent is the willingness to pay to play a lottery. In this case, the $12 willingness to pay is less than the $20 bet, so it's puzzling that people play the numbers game.

We can solve the numbers-game puzzle with probability weighting. Suppose the decision weight assigned to the numbers lottery is $w(0.001) = 0.005$, or five times the actual probability. This over-weighting of the rare event of winning increases the utility value and the certainty equivalent of the numbers-game lottery:

$$v(L) = 0.005 \cdot 12,000 = 60 \, \text{utils} \qquad c(L) = v(L) = \$60$$

The over-weighting of the rare event of winning increases the willingness to pay for the lottery to $60. For a person who over-weights the winning outcome by a factor of five, placing a $20 bet is no longer a puzzle.

What about bettors who experience decreasing sensitivity to gain? The numbers game is a gain lottery, and people experience decreasing marginal utility of gain. For $\mu = 0.83$, the utility function is

$$u(x) = x^{0.83}$$

In Figure 16.3, point i shows the winning outcome: a $12,000 gain translates into a utility gain of 2431 utils (roughly). As shown by point j, with a decision weight $w = 0.005$, the utility value is 12.15 utils:

$$v(L) = 0.005 \cdot u(12,000) = 0.005 \cdot 2431 = 12.15 \, \text{utils}$$

As shown by point k, the certainty equivalent is (roughly) $20.27:

$$c(L) = v(L)^{1/0.83} = 12.15^{1/0.83} = \$20.27$$

The certainty equivalent (the willingness to pay to play the lottery) just barely exceeds the $20 bet, so we've solved the numbers-game puzzle for a person with $\mu \geq 0.83$ and a decision weight that is five times the actual probability of 0.001.

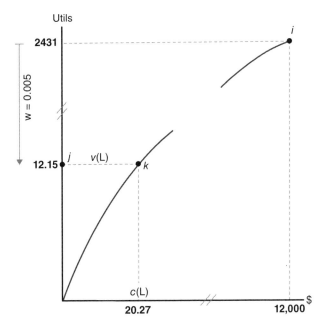

FIGURE 16.3: Solving the Numbers-Game Puzzle

Our calculations show two characteristics of people who play the numbers game. First, a player may over-weight the low probability of winning. Second, a player may experience constant sensitivity to gain (linear utility) or moderately decreasing sensitivity to gain. In our example with a decision weight $w = 0.005$, playing the numbers game will appear to be wise if μ is at least 0.83. For a person with stronger decreasing sensitivity to gain (a smaller value of μ), playing the numbers game will appear to be wise only if the decision weight is greater than 0.005. In general, we can solve the numbers-game puzzle for people with (i) relatively large over-weighting of the rare event of winning and (ii) relatively weak decreasing sensitivity to gain.

The Longshot Puzzle

Racetrack bettors place a relatively large number of bets on longshots—defined as horses with low probabilities of winning. A recent study of betting on British horse races computes the payoffs from betting on horses with different probabilities of winning (Jullien and Salanie 2000). In Figure 16.4, the horizontal axis shows the probability that a horse wins a race, and the vertical axis shows the expected payback from a $1 bet. For all probabilities shown, the payback is less than $1, so bettors lose money on average. The payback is the lowest for the lowest probability: the expected payback for a probability of 0.05 is $0.50, meaning that the average bettor loses $0.50 on a $1 bet on a longshot. For a horse with a probability of 0.10, the payback is $0.75, so the average bettor loses only $0.25 per $1 bet. The payback is higher for a horse with a probability 0.20, (payback = $0.90), so the average bettor loses only $0.10 per $1 bet.

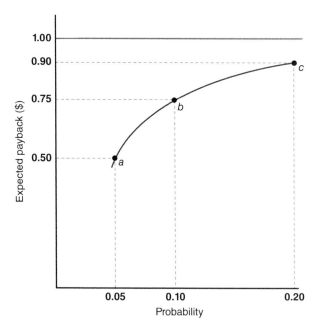

FIGURE 16.4: Racetrack Paybacks

Why would people bet on a longshot with a 1-in-20 chance of winning? Suppose that when a longshot wins, a person who bet $30 on the longshot gets $300. The longshot lottery is

$$L = \{0, 0.95; 300, 0.05\}$$

The monetary value is $15, or only half the cost of playing:

$$m(L) = 0.05 \cdot 300 = \$15$$

Consider a bettor with the linear utility function $u(x) = x$. Suppose we use the objective probabilities as decision weights. In this case, the utility value and certainty equivalent of the lottery are

$$v(L) = 0.05 \cdot 300 = 15 \, \text{utils} \qquad c(L) = v(L) = \$15$$

The certainty equivalent (the willingness to pay to play) is less than the $30 bet, so placing a bet is irrational.

The longshot puzzle can be solved by incorporating probability weighting. As shown in Figure 16.2, a probability of 0.05 generates a decision weight 0.11. As shown by the Prelec calculator, a probability of 0.05 and a parameter value $\phi = 0.74$ generates a decision weight 0.105, rounded to 0.11. Suppose the racetrack bettor uses a decision weight of 0.11 for the probability 0.05. In this case, the utility value and certainty equivalent are

$$v(L) = 0.11 \cdot 300 = 33 \, \text{utils} \qquad c(L) = v(L) = \$33$$

In other words, probability weighting makes the certainty equivalent greater than the $30 bet, so it appears to be a wise bet.

What about bettors who experience decreasing sensitivity to gain? A bet on a horse race is a gain lottery, and people experience decreasing marginal utility of gains. Suppose the bettor experiences mildly decreasing sensitivity to gain, and the value of the utility parameter is $\mu = 0.96$. The utility function is

$$u(x) = x^{0.96}$$

In Figure 16.5, point i shows the winning outcome: a gain of $300 is 239 utils (roughly). A shown by point j, with a decision weight $w = 0.11$, the utility value is 26.27 utils:

$$v(L) = 0.11 \cdot u(300) = 0.11 \cdot 239 = 26.27 \, \text{utils}$$

We invert the utility function to compute the certainty equivalent of the lottery. As shown by point k, the certainty equivalent is (roughly) $30.10:

$$c(L) = v(L)^{1/0.96} = 26.27^{1/0.96} = \$30.10$$

The certainty equivalent (the willingness to pay to play the lottery) exceeds the $30 bet, so we've solved the longshot puzzle. For a person with $\mu = 0.96$ and a decision weight of 0.11 (compared to a probability of 0.05), the longshot looks like a wise bet, but just barely.

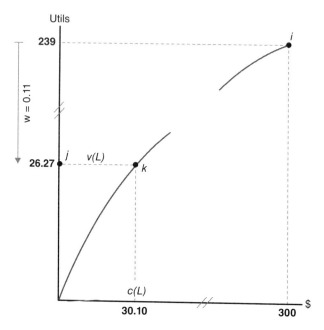

FIGURE 16.5: Solving the Longshot Puzzle

Our calculations show that longshot bettors share two characteristics with people who play neighborhood numbers games. First, a longshot bettor may over-weight the low probability that the longshot will win. Second, a longshot bettor may experience constant sensitivity to gain (linear utility) or mildly decreasing sensitivity to gain. Under the assumption that a probability of 0.05 is over-weighted to 0.11, the longshot will appear to be a wise bet if μ is at least 0.96. For a person with stronger decreasing sensitivity to gain (a smaller value of μ), the longshot bet will appear to be wise only if the decision weight is greater than 0.11. In general, we can solve the longshot puzzle for people with (i) relatively large over-weighting of the rare event of a longshot win and (ii) relatively weak decreasing sensitivity to gain.

Review the Concepts 16.3

1. In a traditional neighborhood numbers game, the monetary value of a $10 bet is $[___]. (3, 5, 6, 10, 12)

2. Suppose the decision weight in a three-digit numbers game is five times the actual probability, and the payoff is 600:1. In the case of linear utility $u(x) = x$, the certainty equivalent of a $10 bet is $[___]. (10, 15, 30, 60)

3. We can solve the numbers-game puzzle for individuals with relatively [___] over-weighting of rare outcomes and relatively [___] decreasing sensitivity to gain. (weak, strong; strong, strong; strong, weak; weak, weak)

4. Consider a $10 bet on longshot horse with a probability of winning 0.05 and a payout $140. The monetary value of the bet is $[___]. (5, 7, 10, 14)

5. Consider a $10 bet on longshot horse with a probability of winning 0.05 and a payout $140. Suppose the decision weight is twice the actual probability. In the case of linear utility $u(x) = x$, the certainty equivalent of the bet is $[___]. (7, 10, 14, 96)

6. We can solve the longshot puzzle for individuals with relatively [___] over-weighting of rare outcomes and relatively [___] decreasing sensitivity to gain. (weak, strong; strong, weak; strong, strong; weak, weak)

Key Terms

longshot puzzle, p. 289   numbers-game puzzle, p. 289   probability weighting, p. 282

Takeaways

1. In a world of uncertain benefits and costs, humans have trouble in (i) estimating probabilities and (ii) applying known probabilities to decision-making.

2. In prospect theory, a decision-maker over-weights rare (low-probability) outcomes and under-weights common (high-probability) outcomes.

3. An individual who learns probabilities by description is likely to over-weight rare events.

4. An individual who learns probabilities by experience, is likely to under-weight rare events.

5. The numbers-game puzzle is that people play a lottery with a monetary value that is less than the price of playing.

6. The numbers-game puzzle can be solved by (i) strong over-weighting of rare events and (ii) relatively weak decreasing sensitivity to gain.

7. The longshot puzzle is that racetrack bettors are biased in favor of horses with relatively low probabilities of success.

8. The longshot puzzle can be solved by (i) strong over-weighting of rare events and (ii) relatively weak decreasing sensitivity to gain.

Discuss the Concepts

1. *Probability Weighting and WTP.* Consider a legal game that offers of 0.01 probability of winning $300. Newt is risk-neutral, with utility function $u(x) = x$. Newt uses Prelec probability weighting, with $\phi = 0.72$. Suppose Newt actually pays 4/5 of his willingness to pay, and plays the game 1000 times. His total spending is $[___]. A plausible value for his total winnings is $[___]. (1000, 3000, 5000, 6000)

2. *Experiential Probability.* Consider a legal game that offers a 0.01 probability of winning $300. All players are risk-neutral, with utility function $u(x) = x$. The players learn about the chance of winning in repeated practice rounds, each with a 1 in 100 chance of indicating a "win." On average, the most plausible value for a player's willingness to pay is $c(L) = [___]. (0, greater than zero but less than $3, greater than $3)

3. *Racetrack Player versus Venture Capitalist.* You have an investment opportunity with a 1/50 chance of a gain of $100,000. You have received two bids, $1900 and $3000. One bid comes from a racetrack player who regularly bets on longshots. A second bid comes from a successful venture capitalist who makes hundreds of investments each year. Match the bids with the potential investors.

Apply the Concepts

1. *Numbers Game and the Gambler's Paradox.* You run a daily 0–99 numbers game (choose a number from 0 through 99) with probability of winning of 1/100, and a payout ratio 75:1. Each possible bettor has a linear utility function in the domain of gain. Each bettor places a $20 bet. People vary in their decision weights for the numbers lottery. Over the range 0.014 to 0.024, there are 30 people in each 0.001 interval. An indifferent person does not play the game.

   a. The number of bettors per day is $b^* = [___]$.

   b. Your daily expected profit is $[___].

   c. Suppose the possible bettors experience the gambler's paradox (also known as the erroneous law of small numbers). In a particular week, there were no winners for the first five days of the week. Your expected profit on day six will be relatively [___] (high, low) because [___]. Illustrate with an numerical example.

2. *Shut Down the Numbers Racket?* Consider a three-digit numbers game with a 600:1 payout. The typical operator collects $1000 per day in bets, pays out $600, and earns a profit of $400. The typical operator could instead earn

$100 for certain on a lawful job. As the new economist for the city, your task is to determine the monetary penalty f for running a numbers game. Your objective is to compute the penalty that is just large enough to convert the typical numbers operator into a lawful worker. Suppose a caught operator forfeits the day's profit: the operator has already paid $600 to the winners, and the authorities confiscate the $400 profit for the day. The probability of catching an operator on any given day is 0.10. Assume that the operator (i) has a square-root utility function, (ii) uses decision weights equal to the probabilities, and (iii) experiences symmetry in the utility effects of loss and gain ($\lambda = 1$).

a. The operator's daily lottery is L = [___].

b. The threshold penalty is $f^* = $ [___].

3. *Longshot and Decision Weights.* Consider a horse-race lottery for a longshot, a horse with a relatively low probability of winning: L ={0, 0.99; 100, 0.01} . The price of joining the lottery (buying a betting slip on the longshot) is $4. For three bettors, compute the decision weight such that the certainty equivalent of the lottery equals its price.

a. Lynn has a linear utility function, with μ =1. The threshold decision weight is $w_1 = $ [___].

b. Root has a square-root utility function, with $\mu = 1/2$. The threshold decision weight is $w_2 = $ [___].

c. Septocho has a nonlinear utility function, with μ =7/8. The threshold decision weight is $w_3 =$[___].

4. *Racetrack Profit.* A racetrack has a race between a longshot (win probability = 1/10) and a favorite (win probability = 5/6). Bettors have a common utility function, with $\mu = 1$. The decision weights are 0.25 for the longshot and 0.75 for the favorite.

a. Suppose the prize per dollar bet equals the monetary value of the lottery: $g_L = $ $10 for the longshot and $g_F = $ $1.20 for the favorite. The willingness to pay for a longshot lottery (a $1 bet on a longshot) is $c_L = $ [___]. The willingness to pay for a favorite lottery (a $1 bet on a favorite) is $c_F = $ [___].

b. Suppose the racetrack chooses prizes to make bettors indifferent. The prize for the longshot lottery is $g_L = $ [___] and the prize for the favorite lottery is $g_F = $ [___].

c. Suppose there are 100 bets of $1 each on longshots. The racetrack profit on longshots = [___].

d. Suppose there are 100 bets of $1 each on favorites. The racetrack profit on favorites = [___].

17 Prospect Theory and Asset Markets

Consider two individual buyers in the housing market. Winnie lives in a city where housing prices have increased over the last 10 years, while Lois lives in a city where housing prices have decreased. Each buyer will negotiate directly with a seller to agree on a price. What question should Winnie definitely ask the seller? What question should Lois definitely *not* ask the seller? Hint: It's the same question.

This chapter uses prospect theory to gain insights into the markets for assets such as stocks, bonds, land, and houses. We start by reviewing the notions of risk aversion and risk neutrality, and introducing the notion of **risk seeking**. Then we use the features of prospect theory to solve two puzzles about asset markets.

1. *Disposition puzzle.* In an asset market with a recent history of increasing prices, a seller's asking price is relatively low, and assets sell quickly. In an asset market with a recent history of decreasing prices, a seller's asking price is relatively high, and assets sell slowly.

2. *Equity premium puzzle.* The average return to stocks is roughly six times the average return to bonds. Why don't investors shift money from bonds to more lucrative stocks?

Learning Objectives: The Explainer

After mastering this chapter, you will be able to explain each of the following statements.

1. House buyers prefer markets where (i) prices have recently increased and (ii) sellers base their asking prices on hindsight.

2. For a real-estate agent, an unfavorable market is one where (i) prices have recently decreased and (ii) sellers base their asking prices on hindsight.

3. In a housing market with perfectly rational sellers, past housing prices are irrelevant.

4. The equity premium puzzle can be explained by loss aversion.

Decreasing Sensitivity and Attitudes toward Risk

We start this chapter with a closer look at the notion of **decreasing sensitivity** to gain and loss, a key feature of prospect theory. As we saw in an earlier chapter, decreasing sensitivity to gain causes risk aversion. We extend our discussion of decreasing sensitivity to show that decreasing sensitivity to loss causes risk seeking. This discussion sets the stage to solve the disposition puzzle.

Decreasing Sensitivity to Gain and Risk Aversion

Consider a landowner in a market where land prices are expected to either increase or not change. For example, suppose the current price is $100, and the probability that the price will increase to $164 is 0.50. The landowner faces a gain lottery because the price may increase by $64, but it won't decrease. The gain lottery is summarized as

$$L_G = \{0, 0.50; 64, 0.50\}$$

The monetary value of the lottery is $32:

$$m(L_G) = \frac{1}{2} \cdot 0 + \frac{1}{2} \cdot 64 = \$32$$

Given the 50 percent chance of a $64 increase in price, the expected monetary gain is $32.

The next step is to compute the utility value and certainty equivalent of the gain lottery. To simplify the calculations, we use the square-root utility function, which incorporates decreasing sensitivity to gain:

$$u(x) = x^{1/2}$$

As shown in Figure 17.1, the possible gain is $64 and the possible utility gain is 8 utils (point g), so the utility value of the gain lottery is 4 utils:

$$v(L_G) = \frac{1}{2} \cdot 0 + \frac{1}{2} \cdot 64^{1/2} = \frac{1}{2} \cdot 8 = 4 \text{ utils}$$

As we saw in an earlier chapter, we use the certainty equivalent of a lottery to translate utility into dollars. As shown by the pivot point h, the certainty equivalent is $16:

$$c(L_G) = 4^2 = \$16$$

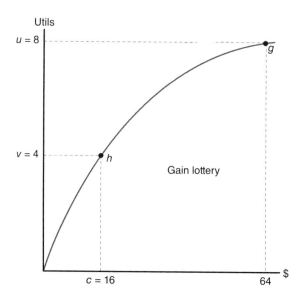

FIGURE 17.1: Certainty Equivalent for the Gain Lottery

Recall that the certainty equivalent of a lottery is the willingness to pay to play the lottery. The $16 certainty equivalent indicates that the landowner willing to pay $16 to play the lottery. Playing the lottery means the landowner does not sell the land today, but instead hangs on to the land to get either $100 or $164 later. The alternative to playing the lottery is to play it safe and sell today. A landowner's reservation price is the lowest possible price at which he or she will sell today. The reservation price equals the current price plus the certainty equivalent of the lottery, equal to $116 in the gain lottery:

$$\hat{p}_G = current\ price + certainty\ equivalent = \$100 + \$16 = \$116$$

The reservation price makes the landowner indifferent between selling today (a gain of $16 over the current market price) and playing the lottery (a certainty equivalent of $16). If someone offers a price of at least $116, the landowner will play it safe and sell today. Otherwise, the landowner will take a risk, playing the lottery to get equal chances of either $100 or $164.

Recall that a decision-maker is risk averse if the certainty equivalent of a lottery is less than the monetary value of the lottery.

$$risk\ aversion: c(L) < m(L)$$

In our gain lottery, the certainty equivalent is $16, compared to a monetary value of $32. The landowner is willing to pay only $16 to play a lottery with an expected monetary payoff of $32. This indicates a general aversion to taking risks.

Decreasing Sensitivity to Loss and Risk Seeking

Consider next a landowner in a land market where prices are expected to either not change or decrease. For example, suppose the current price is $164, and there is a

50 percent chance that the price will decrease to $100. The landowner faces a loss lottery because the price may decrease, but it won't increase. The loss lottery is

$$L_L = \left[-64, 0.50; 0, 0.50\right]$$

The monetary value of the loss lottery is –$32:

$$m(L_L) = -\frac{1}{2} \cdot 64 + \frac{1}{2} \cdot 0 = -\$32$$

Given the 50 percent chance of a $64 decrease in price, the expected monetary loss is $32.

The next step is to compute the utility value and certainty equivalent of the loss lottery. The utility function incorporates decreasing sensitivity to loss:

$$u(x) = -\left(-x^{1/2}\right)$$

In Figure 17.2, the possible utility change is -8 utils (point i), so the utility value of the loss lottery is –4 utils:

$$v(L_L) = -\frac{1}{2} \cdot 64^{1/2} = -\frac{1}{2} \cdot 8 = -4 \, \text{utils}$$

The certainty equivalent of the loss lottery is –$16 (shown by the pivot point j).

$$c(L_L) = -\left(4^2\right) = -\$16$$

Recall that the certainty equivalent of a lottery is the willingness to pay to play the lottery. A negative certainty equivalent indicates that an individual is willing

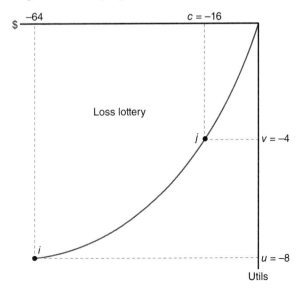

FIGURE 17.2: Certainty Equivalent for the Loss Lottery

to pay to *avoid* playing the lottery. To avoid playing the loss lottery, a landowner sells the land today. The question is, "How much is the landowner willing to lose (relative to the current price) in selling the land today?" The answer is $16, the willingness to pay to *avoid* playing the loss lottery. The reservation price is

$$\hat{p}_L = current\ price + certainty\ equivalent = \$164 - \$16 = \$148$$

If someone offers the landowner a price of at least $148, the landowner will play it safe and sell today. Otherwise, landowner will take a risk, playing the lottery with equal chances of either $100 or $164.

It will be useful to introduce the notion of risk seeking. A decision-maker is risk seeking if the certainty equivalent of a lottery is greater than the monetary value.

$$Risk\ seeking: c(L) > m(L)$$

In a market with decreasing prices, the landowner's certainty equivalent is –$16 and the monetary value is –$32, meaning that the landowner is risk seeking. The landowner is willing to pay only $16 to avoid playing a lottery that, on average, generates a monetary loss of $32. In other words, to get the landowner to play it safe by selling today, the offered price must be at least $148. The relatively high reservation price is an indication of risk seeking: for all offered prices up to $148, the landowner will take the risk.

Constant Sensitivity and Risk Neutrality

As an alternative to decreasing sensitivity to gain and loss, consider the implications of constant sensitivity. We can represent constant sensitivity to gain and loss with a linear utility function. Suppose the utility function for both gains and losses is

$$u(x) = \frac{x}{8}$$

For this utility function, the change in utility per dollar gained or lost is constant at 1/8.

Consider the gain lottery in an environment of constant sensitivity to gain. Recall that the gain lottery is a gain of $64 with probability 0.50. The upper part of Figure 17.3 shows the linear utility curve for the gain lottery. As before, the monetary value of the gain lottery is $32.

$$m(L_G) = \frac{1}{2} \cdot 0 + \frac{1}{2} \cdot 64 = \$32$$

The utility value of the gain lottery is 4 utils:

$$v(L_G) = \frac{1}{2} \cdot 0 + \frac{1}{2} \cdot \frac{64}{8} = \frac{1}{2} \cdot 8 = 4\ utils$$

The certainty equivalent of the gain lottery (shown by the pivot point h) is $32:

$$c\left(L_G\right) = 4 \cdot 8 = \$32$$

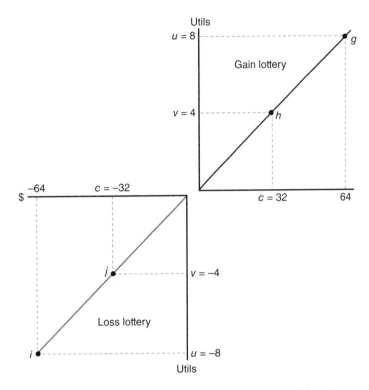

FIGURE 17.3: Certainty Equivalent with Constant Sensitivity to Gain and Loss

Consider the loss lottery in an environment of constant sensitivity to loss. Recall that the loss lottery is a loss of $64 with probability 0.50. The lower part of Figure 17.3 shows the utility curve for the loss lottery. As before, the monetary value of the loss lottery is –$32.

$$m\left(L_G\right) = -\frac{1}{2} \cdot 64 + \frac{1}{2} \cdot 0 = -\$32$$

The utility value of the loss lottery is –4 utils:

$$v\left(L_G\right) = -\frac{1}{2} \cdot \frac{64}{8} + \frac{1}{2} \cdot 0 = -\frac{1}{2} \cdot 8 = -4 \, \text{utils}$$

The certainty equivalent of the loss lottery (shown by the pivot point j) is –$32:

$$c\left(L_G\right) = -4 \cdot 8 = -\$32$$

As we saw in an earlier chapter, a decision-maker is risk neutral if the certainty equivalent of a lottery equals the monetary value of the lottery.

$$risk\ neutrality: c(L) = m(L)$$

In the case of constant sensitivity, the certainty equivalent of the gain lottery equals the $32 monetary value. The landowner is willing to pay $32 to play a gain lottery with an expected monetary payoff of $32, indicating a general neutrality to taking risk. Similarly, the certainty equivalent of the loss lottery equals the −$32 monetary value. The landowner is willing to pay $32 to avoid playing a lottery with an expected monetary payoff of −$32.

In the case of constant sensitivity to gain and loss, the reservation price for the gain lottery equals the reservation price for the loss lottery. For the gain lottery, a reference price of $100 generates a reservation price of $132:

$$\hat{p}_G = \$100 + certainty\ equivalent = \$100 + \$32 = \$132$$

For the loss lottery, a reference price of $164 generates a reservation price of $132:

$$\hat{p}_L = \$164 + certainty\ equivalent = \$164 - \$32 = \$132$$

In the case of constant sensitivity to gain and loss, the two price paths generate the same reservation price.

Review the Concepts 17.1

1. For land with a current price of $60, the future price will be either $60 or $96, and each future price is equally likely. The utility function is $u(x) = x^{1/2}$. The monetary value of the gain lottery is $m(L) = \$[\_\_]$, and the certainty equivalent of the gain lottery is $c(L) = \$[\_\_]$. (15, 10; 18, 18; 18, 9)

2. An individual who experiences decreasing sensitivity to gain and faces a gain lottery is risk-[__] because the certainty equivalent of a lottery is [__] its monetary value. (seeking, less than; averse, greater than; seeking, greater than; averse, less than)

3. For land with a current price of $60, the future price will be either $24 or $60, and each future price is equally likely. The utility function is $u(x) = x^{1/2}$. The monetary value of the loss lottery is $m(L) = \$[\_\_]$ and the certainty equivalent of the loss lottery is $c(L) = \$[\_\_]$. (−15, −10; −18, −9; −18, −18)

4. An individual who experiences decreasing sensitivity to loss and faces a loss lottery is risk-[__] because the certainty equivalent of a lottery is [__] its monetary value. (seeking, greater than; averse, less than; averse, greater than; seeking, less than)

5. For land with a current price of $60, the future price will be either $60 or $96, and each future price is equally likely. The utility function is $u(x) = x/6$. The monetary value of the gain lottery is $m(L) = \$[\underline{\quad}]$, and the certainty equivalent of the gain lottery is $c(L) = \$[\underline{\quad}]$. (18, 9; 18, 18; 15, 15)

6. An individual who experiences constant sensitivity to gain and loss is risk-[___] because the certainty equivalent of a lottery is [___] its monetary value. (neutral, less than; averse, less than; neutral, equal to; seeking, less than)

17.2 The Disposition Puzzle

In conventional economic analysis, past events are irrelevant to current choices. For example, if you paid $164 for an asset last year, this "sunk cost" is irrelevant in your decision about whether to sell the asset today. In the language of economics, sunk costs are irrelevant. In regular language, it is sensible to "let bygones be bygones." This is consistent with fully rational behavior: we can't change past events, so it is sensible to ignore sunk costs and other bygones. Although "let bygones be bygones" is sound advice from parents and "sunk costs are irrelevant" is sound advice from economics professors, many individuals don't think that way. Instead, many people systematically incorporate sunk costs and other bygones into their decision-making, so they allow past events to influence current choices.

In this part of the chapter we explore the origins of the **disposition puzzle** and its solution. There are two parts to the disposition puzzle.

- In an asset market with a recent history of increasing prices, a seller's asking price is relatively low, and assets sell quickly.
- In an asset market with a recent history of decreasing prices, a seller's asking price is relatively high, and assets sell slowly.

As we'll see, one factor in the disposition puzzle is hindsight on the part of asset sellers. A seller who deploys hindsight uses the past purchase price of an asset as the reference price, and calculates possible gains and losses relative to the purchase price. In other words, the seller ignores the advice to "let bygones be bygones" and instead incorporates sunk cost into the calculations of the asking price. In a world of decreasing sensitivity to gain and loss, hindsight causes the disposition puzzle.

To illustrate the disposition puzzle, we will use a hypothetical housing market in two environments. In one case, the price of housing has a recent history of increasing. In the second case, the price of housing has a recent history of decreasing. Our numerical example uses the same numbers as deployed in the gain and loss lotteries for the land market.

Reservation Price in a Winner Market

When house sellers use hindsight in their calculations, the recent history of housing prices matters. Figure 17.4 shows price paths in a housing market where prices recently increased. Each homeowner purchased a house at a price p_0 = $100 in the recent past, and the current price is p_1 = $164. In this market, a homeowner who uses hindsight to focus on the past purchase price feels like a winner in the housing market: the homeowner paid $100, and the price recently increased to $164. For convenience, let's call this a winner market. Looking to the future, the price in the next period (p_2) will be either $100 or $164, and each future price is equally likely.

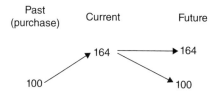

Past (purchase)	Current	Future
	164	164
100		100

FIGURE 17.4: Time Path of House Prices in a Winner Market

The homeowner in a winner market faces a lottery with equal chances of a future price of either $100 or $164. For a homeowner who uses hindsight to choose the reference price, the lottery is a gain lottery. There are equal chances of either gaining $64 (the $164 future price is $64 greater than the $100 purchase price) or no change (the $100 future price equals the purchase price). As we saw earlier in the land-market example, the certainty equivalent of the gain lottery is $16. The owner's reservation price equals the reference price (the past purchase price) plus the certainty equivalent, or $116:

$$\hat{p}_{win} = past\ purchase\ price + certainty\ equivalent = \$100 + \$16 = \$116$$

The reservation price is a homeowner's asking price to sell the house. If someone offers a price greater than or equal to the $116 reservation price, the homeowner will play it safe and sell today. Otherwise, the homeowner will take a risk by playing a lottery with equal chances of either $100 or $164.

Reservation Price in a Loser Market

Things are different in a market with a recent history of decreasing prices. Figure 17.5 shows price paths in a housing market where the current price is less than the past purchase price. Each homeowner purchased a house at a price p_0 = $164 in the recent past, and the current price is p_1 = $100. In this market, a homeowner who uses the past purchase price as a reference price feels like a loser in the housing market: the homeowner paid $164 for a house, and the current price is only

$100. For convenience, let's call this a loser market. Looking to the future, the future price p_2 will be either $100 or $164, and each future price is equally likely.

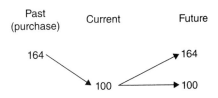

FIGURE 17.5: Time Path of House Prices in a Loser Market

The homeowner in the loser market faces a lottery with equal chances of a future price of either $100 or $164. A homeowner who uses the past purchase price as the reference price faces a loss lottery. There are equal chances of either losing $64 (a $100 future price is $64 less than the purchase price) or no change (a $164 future price equals the purchase price). As we saw earlier in the land-market example, the certainty equivalent of the loss lottery is –$16. The owner's reservation price equals the reference price (the past purchase price) plus the certainty equivalent, or $148:

$$\hat{p}_{\text{lose}} = past\ purchase\ price + certainty\ equivalent = \$164 - \$16 = \$148$$

The reservation price is a homeowner's asking price to sell the house. If someone offers a price greater than or equal to the $148 reservation price, the homeowner will play it safe and sell today. Otherwise, the homeowner will take a risk by playing a lottery with equal chances of either $100 or $164.

Reservation Prices and Time on the Market

We've seen that in two markets with identical prospects for future prices, homeowners have different reservation prices. Although in each market, the future price will be either $100 or $164, the reservation prices are different.

- *Winner market.* The reference price is the $100 past purchase price, and the reservation price is $116. The risk-averse homeowner is inclined to accept a certain gain rather than taking a risk. To persuade a homeowner in a winner market to play it safe by selling today, a relatively low price ($116) will suffice.
- *Loser market.* The reference price is the $164 past purchase price, and the reservation price is $148. The risk-seeking homeowner is inclined to take a risk rather than accepting a certain gain. To persuade a homeowner in a loser market to play it safe by selling today, a relatively high price ($148) is required.

Consider the implications of the two reservation prices on the marketing time for houses in the two markets. Suppose homeowners in each market offer houses for sale, and their asking prices equal their reservation prices. In the winner market, the asking price will be $116, compared to $148 in the loser market. Naturally, a low-price house in the winner market will sell quickly, while a high-price house in the loser market will take a long time to sell.

We have a solution to the disposition puzzle. In a market with a recent history of increasing prices, the reservation price will be relatively low, and the asset will sell quickly. In a market with a recent history of decreasing prices, the reservation price will be relatively high, and the asset will take a long time to sell. This solution to the disposition puzzle deploys two features of prospect theory.

- *Gains and losses are defined relative to a reference point.* The past purchase prices differ, so the reference prices differ too. A homeowner who feels like a winner (current price > purchase price) has a lower reservation price and sells sooner. A homeowner who feels like a loser (current price < purchase price) has a higher reservation price and takes longer to sell the house.
- *Decreasing sensitivity to gain and loss.* Decreasing sensitivity to gain means that a homeowner who feels like a winner is risk averse, and accepts a relatively low price to avoid risk. Decreasing sensitivity to loss means that a homeowner who feels like a loser is risk seeking, and requires a relatively high price to play it safe.

Evidence for the Disposition Puzzle

A study of the Boston housing market provides evidence for the disposition effect in the market for condominiums (Genesove and Mayer 2001). The study compares prices and market times in loser markets (recent history of decreasing prices) to prices and market times in winner markets (recent history of increasing prices).

- *Higher asking prices.* The authors computed the gaps between asking prices and equilibrium prices. In loser markets, the average gap between the asking price and the equilibrium price was roughly 35 percent, compared to a gap of only 12 percent in winner markets.
- *More time on the market.* The authors computed the percent of houses that sold within 180 days of being listed. In loser markets, fewer than 30 percent of houses sold within 180 days, compared to over 60 percent in winner markets.

Review the Concepts 17.2

1. The disposition puzzle is that a seller's asking price is relatively low in a market with recently [____] prices, and relatively high in a market with recently [____] prices. (decreasing, increasing; increasing, stable; stable, decreasing; increasing, decreasing)

2. One part of the disposition puzzle is that in a market with recently decreasing prices, an asset spends a relatively [___] time on the market. (short, long)

3. A seller's reservation equals a reference price plus [___]. (certainty equivalent of gain or loss lottery, a target gain)

4. For a fully rational seller, the reference price is [___] (the past purchase price, the average of the purchase price and the current price, the current market price)

5. For a seller who deploys hindsight, the reference price is [___]. (the past purchase price, the current market price, the average of the purchase price and the current price)

6. For a house with a current price of $96, the past purchase price is $60. The future price will be either $60 or $96, and each future price is equally likely. The utility function is $u(x) = x^{1/2}$. For an asset owner who uses hindsight about housing prices, the reference price is $[___] and the reservation price is $[___]. (96, 87; 60, 69; 78, 78)

7. For a house with a current price of $60, the past purchase price is $96. The future price will be either $60 or $96, and each future price is equally likely. The utility function is $u(x) = x^{1/2}$. For an asset owner who uses hindsight about housing prices, the reference price is $[___] and the reservation price is $[___]. (60, 69; 78, 78; 96, 87)

<h2>17.3　Disposition Puzzle Disappears?</h2>

We've seen that the disposition puzzle can be solved with two features of prospect theory. First, decision-makers evaluate lotteries in terms of gains and losses defined by reference prices. When homeowners use the past purchase price as a reference price, their incorporation of sunk cost changes their computed reservation prices. Second, there is decreasing sensitivity to gains and losses, resulting in choices guided by risk aversion and risk seeking. In this part of the chapter, we see what happens when (i) homeowners base their choices on current prices rather than the past purchase prices, and (ii) the sensitivity to gain and loss is constant.

Let Bygones Be Bygones

What would happen if a homeowner changed his or her reference price from the past purchase price to the current price? Perhaps a homeowner takes an economics course and learns that sunk costs are irrelevant. In other words, the homeowner decides to let bygones be bygones, and uses the current price as the reference price in the calculation of the reservation price.

Consider first a homeowner in a city with a recent history of increasing prices. The adoption of the bygones approach means that the reference price is now $164 rather than $100. The homeowner switches to a loss lottery (the price will either stay at $164 or decrease to $100) and and the reservation price is $148. In other words, when the homeowner switches his or her reference price to the current price, the reservation price increases from $116 to $148. As a participant in a loss lottery, the household is now in the realm of risk seeking, leading to a higher reservation price.

Recall that in a city with a recent history of increasing prices (winner market), the disposition effect is that prices are relatively low, and houses sell quickly. The adoption of the bygones approach increases the reservation price, so houses take a longer time to sell. When sellers base their decisions on the current market price rather than the past purchase price, the disposition effect in a winner market disappears.

The same logic applies, in reverse, to a homeowner in a city with a recent history of decreasing prices. The adoption of the bygones approach means that the reference price is now $100 rather than $164. As a result, the homeowner switches to a gain lottery (the price will either stay at $100 or increase to $164), and the reservation price decreases from $148 to $116. As a participant in a gain lottery, the household is now in the realm of risk aversion, leading to a lower reservation price.

Recall that in a city with a recent history of decreasing prices (loser market), the disposition effect is that prices are relatively high, and houses sell slowly. The adoption of the bygones approach decreases the reservation price, so houses take a shorter time to sell. When sellers base their decisions on the current market price rather than the past purchase price, the disposition effect in a loser market disappears.

Recall the chapter opener on home buyers in different cities. Winnie is buying a house in a city with a recent history of increasing prices. To get the low price ($116) Winnie must find a seller who acts like a winner and uses the past purchase price ($100) as the reference price. To encourage a seller to act like a risk-averse winner with a low reservation price, Winnie can ask, "So, how much did you pay for this house 10 years ago?"

Things are different for Lois, who is buying a house in a city with a recent history of decreasing prices. To get the low price ($116) Lois must find a seller who uses the current price ($100) as the reference price. To avoid triggering thoughts of the past purchase price ($164), Lois must avoid Winnie's question about the past. For Lois, the best strategy is to focus the seller's attention on the present.

Constant Sensitivity to Gain and Loss

Consider next the role of decreasing sensitivity in the disposition puzzle. To show the role of decreasing sensitivity, we can switch to the case of constant sensitivity to gain and loss. As shown in Figure 17.3, when the sensitivity to gain and loss is constant, the certainty equivalent of a gain lottery equals the monetary value, and the same is true for a loss lottery. As a result, the reservation price in a winner market equals the reservation price in a loser market. It doesn't matter whether a homeowner uses $100 or $164 as the reference price. In each case, the reservation price is $132, equal to the average of the two prices. When the reservation prices are equal, there is no disposition puzzle.

Review the Concepts 17.3

1. For house with a current price of $96, the past purchase price is $60, the future price will be either $60 or $96, and each future price is equally likely. The utility function is $u(x) = x^{1/2}$. For an asset owner who is perfectly rational, the reference price is $[___] and the reservation price is $[___]. (60, 69; 78, 78; 96, 87)

2. For house with a current price of $60, the past purchase price is $96, the future price will be either $60 or $96, and each future price is equally likely. The utility function is $u(x) = x^{1/2}$. For an asset owner who is perfectly rational, the reference price is $[___] and the reservation price is $[___]. (96, 87; 60, 69; 78, 78)

3. Suppose you are a house buyer in a market where prices recently increased. If given a choice between a perfectly rational seller and a seller who operates with hindsight, you will get a lower price if you choose the [___]. (perfectly rational seller, hindsight seller)

4. Suppose you are a house buyer in a market where prices recently decreased. If given a choice between a perfectly rational seller and a seller who operates with hindsight, you will get a lower price if you choose the [___]. (perfectly rational seller, hindsight seller)

5. The future price of a house will be either $60 or $96, and each future price is equally likely. The utility function is linear: $u(x) = x$. For an asset owner whose reference price is $60, the reservation price is $[___]. For an asset owner whose reference price is $96, the reservation price is $[___]. (69, 87; 87, 69; 78, 78)

17.4 The Equity Premium Puzzle

The **equity premium puzzle** is that the rate of return on stocks (equities) exceeds the rate of returns on bonds by a large margin. Based on decades of data, the annual real rate of return on stocks is roughly six percent, compared to one percent on bonds. These are equilibrium rates of return, meaning that investors are indifferent between the two financial instruments, despite the fact that the return on stocks is six times higher. This is a puzzle because we would expect profit-seeking investors to shift funds out of bonds into more lucrative stocks.

A higher return to stocks is not surprising. The variability of stock prices exceeds the variability of bond prices, meaning that an investment in stocks carries more risk than an investment in bonds. A greater risk translates into a larger risk premium and a higher rate of return, so we expect a higher rate of return on stocks. Nonetheless, the 6:1 return ratio is much larger than we can explain with conventional notions of risk aversion.

Greater Weight of Loss and Loss Aversion

As we saw in an earlier chapter, a key feature of human psychology is that losses loom larger than gains. In other words, the disutility of loss exceeds the utility of gain. This feature is incorporated into prospect theory with the parameter $\lambda > 1$, the relative weight of loss. Recall the definition for loss aversion:

> Loss aversion: To avoid a loss equal to x, an individual is willing to forgo a gain equal to $x \cdot \lambda$, where $\lambda > 1$. This is a consequence of the greater weight of loss in the decision-making process: $\lambda > 1$.

As we'll see in this part of the chapter, we can use loss aversion to solve the equity premium puzzle. To focus on the influence of loss aversion, we will assume that investors have linear utility functions. In other words, investors experience constant sensitivity to gain and loss. The utility function is

$$u(x) = x \quad for\ x \geq 0$$

$$u(x) = -\lambda \cdot (-x) \quad for\ x < 0$$

Loss Aversion Solves the Equity Premium Puzzle

Table 17.1 provides a simple example of a bond and a stock. Suppose each asset has a purchase price of $100, and for each asset, a loss just as likely as a gain. In other words, the probability of each outcome is 0.50. For the bond, the possible loss is $3 and the possible gain is $6. In other words, the bond price could decrease to $97 or increase to $106. For the stock, the possible loss is $18 and the possible gain is $36 (a price of $82 or $136). The lotteries are

$$L_{BOND} = \left\{-3, \frac{1}{2}; 6, 1/2\right\} \qquad L_{STOCK} = \left\{-18, 1/2; 36, 1/2\right\}$$

As shown in the fourth column of the table, the expected monetary value of the bond lottery is $1.50, compared to $9.00 for the stock. Given the $100 purchase price, the rate of return for the bond is 1.50 percent, compared to 9 percent for the stock. In other words, the rate of return on the stock is six times the rate of return on the bond.

The sixth column of Table 17.1 computes the utility values of the two assets for $\lambda = 2$. In the utility calculations, a loss gets twice as much weight as a gain. For each asset, the monetary loss is half the monetary gain, so the utility value is zero. The common utility value means that investors will be indifferent between the two assets, despite the much higher monetary rate of return on stocks. In other words, a much higher rate of return is sustainable: investors do not have an incentive to shift from bonds (rate of return = 1.5 percent) to stocks (rate of return = 9%).

TABLE 17.1 **Equity Premium Puzzle Solved**

Asset	Loss	Gain	Monetary value	Rate of return	Utility value: $\lambda = 2$
Bond	3	6	$1.50 = -(1/2) \cdot 3 + (1/2) \cdot 6$	1.50%	$0 = -2 \cdot (1/2) \cdot 3 + (1/2) \cdot 6$
Stock	18	36	$9 = -(1/2) \cdot 18 + (1/2) \cdot 36$	9%	$0 = -2 \cdot (1/2) \cdot 18 + (1/2) \cdot 36$

Figure 17.6 illustrates the equity premium puzzle and its solution. The bond is represented by point *B* (a monetary gain of $6 translates into a utility gain of 6 utils) and point *b* (a monetary loss of $3 translates into a utility loss of 6 utils). With equal chances of a gain or a loss, the utility value of the bond is zero. The stock is represented by point *S* (a monetary gain of $36 translates into a utility gain of 36 utils) and point *s* (a monetary loss of $18 translates into a utility loss of 36 utils). With equal chances of a gain or a loss, the utility value of the stock is zero. The two financial instruments have the same utility value of zero, despite the higher monetary rate of return for the stock (9% = 9/100 versus 1.5% = 1.50/100).

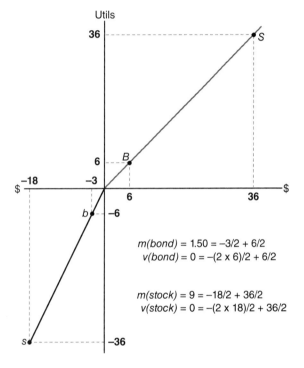

$m(bond) = 1.50 = -3/2 + 6/2$
$v(bond) = 0 = -(2 \times 6)/2 + 6/2$

$m(stock) = 9 = -18/2 + 36/2$
$v(stock) = 0 = -(2 \times 18)/2 + 36/2$

FIGURE 17.6: Equity-Premium Puzzle Solved with Loss Aversion

It's important to note that we have solved the equity premium puzzle with loss aversion caused by a greater weight of loss. We have assumed constant marginal utility of gains and constant marginal disutility of loss, so the utility function is linear. Therefore, decreasing sensitivity in the domains of gain and loss do not enter the calculations. A more comprehensive look at the equity premium puzzle would include loss aversion (greater weight of loss) as well as decreasing sensitivity with respect to gain and loss. The introduction of decreasing sensitivity ($\mu < 1$) has two implications.

1. We can solve the equity premium puzzle with a lower weight of loss ($1 < \lambda < 2$).
2. Decreasing sensitivity alone cannot solve the equity premium puzzle: if $\lambda = 1$, the puzzle persists.

For the adventuresome student, the exercises at the end of the chapter provide opportunities to demonstrate these implications.

Professional Traders: Too Much Information?

A recent study explores the role of information updates on the behavior of professional financial traders (Larson, List, and Metcalfe 2016). Hundreds of professional traders signed up for a beta test of a trading platform for a mutual fund that tracked the relative value of the US dollar. The researchers separated traders into two groups.

1. *Frequent updates.* For traders in the frequent group, prices and portfolio values were updated every second.
2. *Infrequent updates.* For traders in the infrequent group, prices and portfolio values were updated every four hours.

Both groups had perfect flexibility in trading: each trader could buy and sell assets at any time. In other words, the only difference between the two groups was the frequency of information updates.

The study shows that the frequency of information updates has a large effect on trading behavior and profit. Traders who received frequent updates invested 27 percent of their portfolio in high-risk assets, compared to 33 percent for traders who received infrequent updates. In other words, frequent updating decreases investment in high-risk assets. The difference in high-risk investing generated a large difference in the profits from trading: the average profit of traders with infrequent updates was 53 percent higher than the average profit of traders with frequent updates. The lesson is that sometimes it's better to have less information.

Review the Concepts 17.4

1. The equity premium puzzle is that the return to stocks is roughly [___] times the return on bonds, a difference that is too [___] to be explained by conventional notions of risk aversion. (3, large; 2, small; 10, large; 6, large)

2. Use Figure 17.6. Suppose the possible gain from the stock is $24 and the possible gain from the bond is $4. For each asset, the possible loss is half the possible gain. The monetary value of the bond is m(bond) = [___]. The monetary value of the stock is m(stock) = [___]. (2, 12; 1, 6; 4, 24)

3. Use Figure 17.6. Suppose the possible gain from the stock is $24 and the possible gain from the bond is $4. For each asset, the possible loss is half the possible gain. The utility value of the bond is v(bond) = [___]. The utility value of the stock is v(stock) = [___]. (1, 6; 2, 12; 0, 0)

4. The equity premium puzzle is solved by [___]. (loss aversion, greater weight of gain, risk aversion, clown aversion, greater weight of loss)

5. The equity premium puzzle can be solved by showing that a stock lottery with six times the [___] value of a bond lottery can have the same [___] value. (monetary, utility; utility, monetary)

6. A study showed that more frequent updates on investment portfolios [___] investment in high-risk assets and [___] average profit. (increased, increased; decreased, decreased; decreased, increased; increased, decreased)

Key Terms

decreasing sensitivity, p. 299
disposition puzzle, p. 305
equity premium puzzle, p. 311
risk seeking, p. 298

Takeaways

1. *Disposition puzzle.* In an asset market with a recent history of increasing prices, the seller's asking price is relatively low, and assets sell quickly.

2. *Disposition puzzle.* In an asset market with a recent history of decreasing prices, the seller's asking price is relatively high, and assets sell slowly.

3. The disposition puzzle is solved by (i) hindsight by sellers and (ii) decreasing sensitivity to gain and loss.

4. The disposition puzzle disappears when sellers use the current market price as the reference price.

5. The disposition puzzle disappears when we replace decreasing sensitivity (to gain and loss) with constant sensitivity.

6. The equity premium puzzle is that the average return of stocks is roughly six times the average return on bonds.

7. The equity premium puzzle is solved by the greater weight of loss and the resulting loss aversion.

8. A study of trading behavior suggests that frequent updating on asset prices decreases investment in high-risk assets.

Discuss the Concepts

1. *Hindsight or Bygones.* Last year you purchased a bicycle for $164, and the current market price for similar bicycles is $100. The future price will be either $100 or $164, and each price is equally likely. You have the familiar

square-root utility function. Your reservation price for the bicycle is [___].
Illustrate.

2. *Sales Commission.* You are a real-estate broker for sellers, and you are paid a commission equal to three percent of the selling price of each property sold. Your new client purchased his or her house at a price less than the current market price. You can anticipate receiving a relatively [___] (small, medium, large) commission in a relatively [___] (short, medium, long) time.

3. *Reappraisal and Bonds versus Stocks.* Recall the discussion of reappraisal and perspective-taking in an earlier chapter. Using Table 17.1 as a starting point, suppose a reappraisal program decreases λ to 3/2.

   a. Add a column to the table: utility value: $\lambda = 3/2$

   b. The decrease in the relative weight of loss triggers a shift in investment from [___] to [___].

Apply the Concepts

1. *Condo Sale.* Five years ago, Shorty and Tatt purchased identical units in a condominium complex, and each paid $136. Shorty has a short memory and has forgotten the purchase price. Tatt cannot forget the price, a result of a forearm tattoo, "Never Forget: Condo purchase price = $136." Today an identical unit sold for $100. Looking ahead, there is a 50 percent chance of a market price of $100 and a 50 percent chance of a market price of $136. Shorty and Tatt have the familiar square-root utility function for gain and loss. Suppose both owners offer their units for sale.

   a. Tatt's reservation price is $[___] and Shorty's reservation price is $[___].

   b. Tatt has a [_____] (higher, lower) reservation price because he or she has a [___] attitude.

   c. Suppose the number of days a house is on the market is five times the gap between the reservation price and the fully rational reservation price. Tatt's house will be on the market for $d^* = $ [___] days.

2. *Sell Now or Later?* Consider a homeowner who purchased a house for $600. The current market price is $456. The future price could be $600 or $200, and each possible future price is equally likely. The homeowner's utility function is the familiar square-root utility function.

   a. If the homeowner is fully rational, the reference price is $[___] and the reservation price is [___]. The rational choice is to [___] (sell now, sell later) because [___] > [___]. Show your calculations. Illustrate.

   b. If the homeowner uses the purchase price as the reference price, the reservation price is [___]. The rational choice is to [___] (sell now, sell later) because [___] > [___]. Show your calculations. Illustrate.

3. *Winner Asset Numbers.* You will buy a house in a city where the price of housing has increased over the last decade from $100 to $244. Looking forward, there are equal chances of a future price of either $100 or $244. Bygones uses the current price as the reference price, while Hindsight uses the past purchase price as the reference price. The utility function is the familiar square-root utility function. Bygone's reservation price is $[___] and Hindsight's reservation price is $[___]. Illustrate.

4. *Memory Boost?* Suppose you have the power to influence the strength of homeowner memories in your city. To promote the rapid sale of properties that come on the market, you should

   a. increase the strength of memories when [___]

   b. decrease the strength of memories when [___]

5. *Aging, Loss Aversion, and Stocks versus Bonds.* You provide financial advice. Lin Ere, a client with a utility function that is linear in gain and loss. At age 30, Lin's λ =1.30, and the value increases with age: for each year, λ increases by 0.01.

$$\lambda = 1 + \frac{y}{100}$$

   where y is Lin's age in years.

   a. Consider a bond lottery L_B = {–5, 0.50; 10, 0.50}. Draw a curve showing the certainty equivalent of the bond lottery as a function of Lin's age, with two values computed, for age = 30 and age = 90.

   b. Consider a stock lottery L_S = {–20, 0.50; 36, 0.50}. Draw a curve showing the certainty equivalent of the stock lottery as a function of Lin's age, with two values computed, for age = 30 and age = 90.

   c. The threshold age (at which you advise Lin to switch from one financial instrument to the other) is age = [___].

6. *Billinda's Meditation.* Your task is to allocate $30 donated by the philanthropist Billinda to scientific projects that vary in potential payoffs, but have the same probability of success p = 1/2. For project A, the potential loss $20 and the potential gain is $70. For project B, the potential loss is $10 million, and the potential gain is $50. Billinda's utility function is $u(x) = x$.

   a. The monetary value of project A is m_A = $[___], compared to m_B = $[___] for project B.

   b. Suppose Billinda experiences loss aversion, with λ = 3. The utility-maximizing choice is project [___] because [_____]. Illustrate with a graph like Figure 17.6, and include the relevant numbers.

c. Suppose that in an attempt to reduce the weight of loss, Billinda enrolls in an aggressive meditation program. Billinda will be indifferent between the two projects if $\lambda = $ [____].

7. *Decreasing Sensitivity and the Equity Premium Puzzle.* Consider a bond with a purchase price of $200 that has equal changes of a loss of $4 or a gain of $16. Consider a stock with a purchase price of $200 that has equal chances of a loss of $25 and a gain of $100.

a. The monetary value of the bond lottery is $m(L_B) = $ [____]. The monetary value of the stock lottery is $m(L_S) = $ [____].

b. Suppose investors have linear utility functions: $u(x) = x$. The utility value of the bond lottery equals the utility value of the stock lottery if the value of the loss-aversion parameter is $\lambda = $ [____].

c. Suppose $\lambda = 1$ and $u(x) = x^{1/2}$ for loss and gain. The utility value of the stock lottery is [_____] utils, compared to [____] utils for the bond lottery.

d. Suppose $\lambda = 1$ and $u(x) = x^{1/20}$ for loss and gain. The utility value of the stock lottery is [_____] utils, compared to [____] utils for the bond lottery.

Prospect Theory and Insurance

18

Imagine that as you and your fellow students enter the classroom, a behavioral economist gives each student $10, and says that he or she will flip an unbiased coin to determine whether everyone gets to keep the money. If the coin shows "heads," everyone keeps the money; if the coin shows "tails," everyone returns the money. The economist also offers coin-flip insurance. At a price of X, you can purchase an insurance policy that guarantees that you'll keep your $10 regardless of the outcome of the coin flip. What is your X? In other words, how much would you be willing to pay for the insurance? Write down your willingness to pay in a secure location, and later in the chapter you can get insights into your risk preferences in the domain of loss.

This chapter explores some implications of prospect theory for insurance markets. The motivation for buying insurance is to reduce the losses from unfavorable outcomes such as floods, fire, and theft. As a result, the calculation of the benefits and costs of insurance occur in the domain of loss. Recall that a key feature of prospect theory is decreasing sensitivity to loss. In the first part of the chapter we explore the implications of decreasing sensitivity for the decision to purchase insurance. The second part of the chapter explores the implications of probability weighting, the tendency of people to over-weight rare outcomes and under-weight common outcomes.

Learning Objectives: The Explainer

After mastering this chapter, you will be able to explain each of the following statements.

1. For a homeowner who experiences decreasing sensitivity to loss, the willingness to pay for hazard insurance is less than an insurance company's break-even price.

2. The over-weighting of rare events increases the willingness to pay for insurance.

3. Many homeowners who are required to purchase insurance purchase high-coverage (small-deductible) plans despite their higher prices.

4. A relatively small insurance deductible will be sensible for a homeowner who (i) over-weights rare events and (ii) experiences relatively weak decreasing sensitivity to loss.

18.1 Decreasing Sensitivity and the Willingness to Pay for Insurance

Consider a person who faces a loss lottery. The person owns a $100 bike that has a positive probability of being stolen. The reference point for the bike owner is the status quo—the bike has not been stolen. The unfavorable outcome of the loss lottery is the $100 loss if the bike is stolen. A bike owner can avoid the loss by purchasing bike-theft insurance. If the bike is stolen, the insurance company pays $100 to replace the bike. In this part of the chapter we explore the rationale for purchasing insurance against a loss such as bike theft. As we'll see, for a person who experiences decreasing sensitivity to loss, insurance looks like a losing proposition.

Decreasing Marginal Disutility of Loss

Consider a person who experiences decreasing marginal disutility of loss. The loss of the first dollar is more painful than the loss of the second dollar, which is more painful than the loss of the third dollar, and so on. Figure 18.1 shows a utility curve in the domain of losses, with utility (in utils) as a function of a monetary loss x (in dollars). As the magnitude of the loss increases (as we move to the

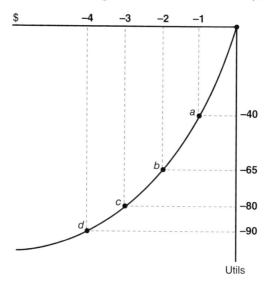

FIGURE 18.1: Decreasing Marginal Disutility of Loss

left along the horizontal axis) the slope of the utility curve decreases, indicating decreasing marginal disutility of loss. The marginal disutility of the first dollar lost is 40 utils (point *a*), compared to 25 utils for the second dollar lost (65 − 40), then 15 utils for the third dollar lost (80 − 65), and so on.

To illustrate the implications of decreasing marginal disutility, suppose there is a one-fifth chance that a $100 bike will be stolen. The bike-theft lottery is

$$L = \{-100,\ 0.20;\ 0,\ 0.80\}$$

The monetary value of the lottery is −$20 = −100 · 0.20. Suppose the utility function in the domain of loss is the familiar square-root utility function.

$$u(x) = -\left(-x^{1/2}\right)$$

For a $100 bike, the utility loss from theft is

$$u(x) = -\left(100^{1/2}\right) = -10\,\text{utils}$$

The utility value of the lottery is

$$v(L) = -10 \cdot \frac{1}{5} + 0 \cdot \frac{4}{5} = -2\,\text{utils}$$

Figure 18.2 shows the features of the bike-theft lottery. Point *a* shows the theft outcome in dollar terms (−$100), and point *b* shows the theft outcome in utility terms (−10 utils). The utility value of the lottery is −2 utils (on the vertical axis), computed as one-fifth the utility loss from bike theft (−10 utils). The monetary value of the lottery is shown by the dashed line at −$20.

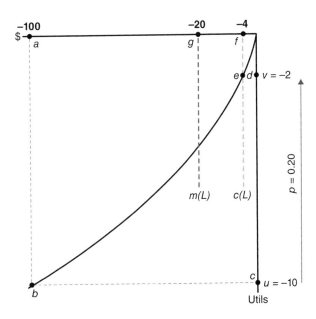

FIGURE 18.2: Measures of Bike-Theft Lottery

Certainty Equivalent and Willingness to Pay for Insurance

For a loss lottery, the certainty equivalent is the certain monetary loss that generates the same utility loss as the lottery. To translate the utility of a lottery into its certainty equivalent, we invert the utility function. The certainty equivalent of the theft lottery is –$4:

$$c(L) = -v(L)^2 \Rightarrow c(L) = -(2)^2 = -\$4$$

In other words, a certain loss of $4 is just as painful as playing a lottery with a one-fifth chance of losing $100. In Figure 18.2, the certainty equivalent is shown by point f: a 2-util loss from the lottery translates into a certain monetary loss of $4. The certainty equivalent of a loss lottery is the willingness to pay to avoid playing the lottery. In the bike-theft lottery, the owner would be willing to pay up to $4 to avoid facing a one-fifth chance of losing the $100 bike.

Figure 18.2 shows the counter-clockwise path of calculations from the $100 loss to the $4 certainty equivalent. We start on the horizontal ($) axis at point a and then move counter-clockwise, taking several steps to return to the horizontal axis. To compute the utility value of the $100 loss, we go to point b and then to point c. To compute the utility value of the lottery, we go to point d. To compute the $4 certainty equivalent, we go to point e and then to point f. To summarize, the path is

$$a \rightarrow b \rightarrow c \rightarrow d \rightarrow e \rightarrow f$$

Willingness to Pay for Insurance versus Break-Even Price

Consider the perspective of a firm that provides bike-theft insurance. Suppose we ignore any management cost of providing insurance, and assume that the insurance policy covers the full loss. The break-even (zero-profit) price for an insurance firm is the price just high enough to cover the insurance firm's cost of replacing stolen bikes. The break-even price is simply the negative of the monetary value of a loss lottery:

$$break\text{-}even\ price = -m(L)$$

In our bike-theft example, the break-even price is $20:

$$break\text{-}even\ price = -m(L) = 100 \cdot 1/5 = \$20$$

To illustrate, an insurance firm that sells five insurance policies will get $100 in revenue from its customers. On average, the insurance company will reimburse one in five customers for a bike theft, so the cost of serving five customers is $100. The break-even price is sometimes known as the "fair" price of insurance.

For a bike owner who experiences decreasing marginal disutility of loss, it is irrational to purchase insurance at the break-even price. In our example, the bike owner's willingness to pay is only $4, which falls short of the $20 break-even price for insurance. In Figure 18.2, the willingness to pay is shown by point f, and the break-even price is shown by point *g*. The rational choice for the bike owner is to play the bike-theft lottery rather than buying insurance.

A person who experiences decreasing sensitivity to loss (decreasing marginal disutility of loss) is a risk seeker rather than a risk avoider. Our bike owner can either pay $20 for insurance, or face a one-in-five chance of losing $100. Naturally, the pain of losing $100 is greater than the pain of losing $20, but the $20 loss is certain, while the chance of the $100 loss is only one in five. For a bike owner who experiences decreasing marginal disutility, a $100 loss is less than five times more painful than a $20 loss. Therefore, it is sensible to take the one-in-five risk of losing $100 rather than bearing the certain pain of paying $20 for insurance.

Economic Experiment: Willingness to Pay for Insurance

The chapter opener uses a classroom experiment to illustrates the willingness to pay for insurance. Friedl, Lima de Miranda, and Schmidt (2014) ran the experiment with a group of 149 students. Each student received an initial endowment of 10 euros, and everyone either kept or lost the endowment, depending on the outcome of a single coin toss. Each student chose a willingness to pay for insurance. The range of WTP was 4.00 euros to 6.25 euros, and the average WTP was 4.14 euros. The distribution of the willingness to pay was as follows.

- WTP < 5 euros: 44 percent
- WTP = 5 euros: 41 percent
- WTP > 5 euros: 15 percent

These results are consistent with variation across students in the curvature of the utility function in the domain of loss. The monetary value of the coin-flip lottery is –5 euros, a result of a 50 percent chance of losing 10 euros. In other words, the break-even price for insurance is 5 euros. For the 44 percent of students who were not willing to pay the break-even price, a plausible explanation is decreasing sensitivity to loss (decreasing marginal disutility of loss). For the 41 percent of students who were willing to pay the break-even price, a plausible explanation is constant sensitivity to loss (constant marginal disutility of loss). For the remaining 15 percent who were willing to pay more than the break-even price, a possible explanation is increasing sensitivity to loss (increasing marginal disutility of loss).

Review the Concepts 18.1

1. Using Figure 18.2 as a starting point, suppose the value of the bike is $225. The certainty equivalent of the bike-theft lottery is *c*(L) = $[___]. (–45, –15, –9, –3)

2. Using Figure 18.2 as a starting point, suppose the value of the bike is $225. The break-even price for bike-theft insurance is $[___]. (9, 15, 45, 112.50)

3. An asset owner who experiences decreasing sensitivity to loss is risk-[___] and the willingness to pay for insurance is [___] the break-even price of insurance. (seeking, greater than; seeking, less than; averse, less than; neutral, equal to)

4. Use Widget 18.1 (available at www.oup.com/us/osullivan1e). Suppose the probability of loss is 0.30 and $\mu = 0.75$. The gap between the willingness to pay for insurance and the break-even price = $[___]. (30, 35, 40, 45)

5. Use Widget 18.1 (available at www.oup.com/us/osullivan1e). Suppose the probability of loss is 0.20. As μ increases, the gap between the willingness to pay for insurance and the break-even price [___], and disappears for $\mu = $ [___]. (does not change, 0.50; increases, 1; decreases, 0.75; decreases, 1)

Probability Weighting and Insurance Puzzles

In this part of the chapter we extend our discussion of insurance markets to incorporate the fifth feature of prospect theory—probability weighting. We've seen that for an individual who experiences decreasing sensitivity to loss, the willingness to pay for insurance is less than the break-even price. And yet many people voluntarily purchase insurance against all sorts of losses. This part of the chapter shows that probability weighting can offset the effects of decreasing sensitivity, causing property owners to purchase insurance against loss.

Decreasing Sensitivity and Probability Weighting

As we saw in an earlier chapter, many decision-makers over-weight rare (low-probability) events. In the market for property insurance, homeowners over-weight events such as floods, windstorms, and other foul weather. To illustrate the implications for insurance decisions, consider the owner of a house with a value of $100,000. Suppose that each year there is a 1-in-20 chance that a flood will destroy the house. The flood lottery is

$$L = \{-100,000, 0.05; 0, 0.95\}$$

The monetary value of the lottery is –$5000:

$$m(L) - \$5000 = -\$100,000 \cdot 0.05$$

Therefore, the break-even price for insurance is $5000. The question is whether a homeowner will purchase flood insurance for $5000 to avoid a 1/20 chance of losing $100,000.

Figure 18.3 illustrates the calculation of the willingness to pay for flood insurance. We assume that the homeowner experiences decreasing sensitivity to loss, with a value for the utility parameter $\mu = 0.77$. The calculations follow the usual counter-clockwise path, starting with the $100,000 loss at point a and ending at the –$2043 certainty equivalent at point f.

$$u(x) = -100,000^{0.77} = -7079 \text{ utils}$$

$$v(L) = -7079 \cdot 0.05 = -354 \text{ utils}$$

$$c(L) = -(354)^{1/0.77} = -\$2043$$

For this homeowner with strong decreasing sensitivity, the $2043 willingness to pay for insurance is less than the $5000 break-even price. In this case, the homeowner plays the flood lottery rather than buying insurance to cover flood losses.

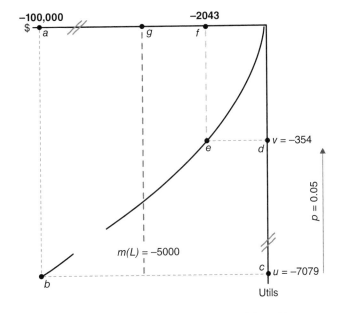

FIGURE 18.3: Willingness to Pay Less Than the Break-Even Price

Consider the implications of over-weighting rare events like a flood. Over-weighting makes the unfavorable event look worse, so it increases the willingness to pay for flood insurance. Suppose the homeowner uses a decision weight of 0.10, or twice the actual probability. This over-weighting makes the certainty equivalent of the flood lottery a larger negative number. In this case, the certainty equivalent of the flood lottery changes to –$5027.

$$v(L) = -7079 \cdot 0.10 = -708 \text{ utils}$$

$$c(L) = -(708)^{1/0.77} = -\$5027$$

The willingness to pay for insurance ($5027) now exceeds the $5000 break-even price by a small margin, so the homeowner will purchase insurance to avoid playing the flood lottery.

Figure 18.4 illustrates the calculations for the case of probability weighting. As usual, the path is counter-clockwise, starting with the $100,000 loss at point a and ending at the –$5027 certainty equivalent at point F. Comparing Figure 18.4 to 18.3, the counter-clockwise paths diverge after point c. The over-weighting of the flood means that the next step after point c is point D (for $w = 0.10$) rather than point d (for $p = 0.05$). The lower utility value of the lottery (a larger negative number) translates into a certainty equivalent of –$5027 (path from D to E to F) compared to –$2043 in the absence of probability weighting.

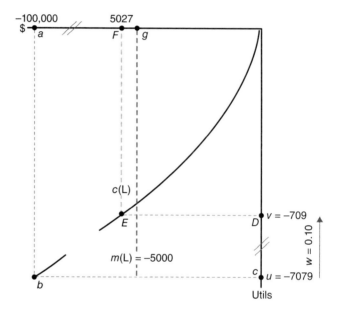

FIGURE 18.4: Willingness to Pay Exceeds the Break-Even Price

Conflicting Forces: Decreasing Sensitivity and Probability Weighting

The lesson from Figures 18.3 and 18.4 is that a homeowner experiences conflicting forces in deciding whether to purchase hazard insurance.

- *Decreasing sensitivity.* Decreasing sensitivity to loss decreases the willingness to pay for insurance: the stronger the decreasing sensitivity, the lower the willingness to pay.
- *Probability weighting.* The over-weighting of a rare event increases the willingness to pay for insurance.

The homeowner is engaged in a tug-of-war between decreasing sensitivity and probability weighting. A homeowner will purchase insurance if the over-weighting of the rare event is stronger than decreasing sensitivity.

Figure 18.5 illustrates the trade-offs between decreasing sensitivity and probability weighting. The figure is for a loss lottery with an actual probability

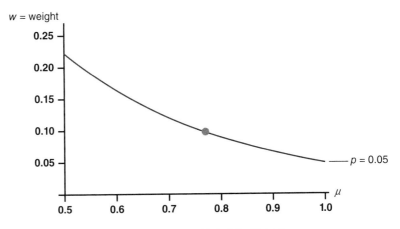

FIGURE 18.5: Decreasing Sensitivity versus Probability Weighting

of loss $p = 0.05$. The horizontal axis shows the value of the utility parameter μ over the range $\mu = 1/2$ (for a square-root utility function) to $\mu = 1$ (for a linear utility function). The vertical axis measures the decision weight w. The curve shows the weight required to make the willingness to pay for insurance equal to the break-even price. At the lower end of the curve, $\mu = 1$ (constant sensitivity), and the threshold weight equals the actual probability $p = 0.05$. As μ decreases, we move upward along the curve: as μ decreases and the strength of decreasing sensitivity increases, the threshold weight increases. In other words, the stronger the decreasing sensitivity to loss, the larger the over-weighting required to get a homeowner to purchase insurance. The point on the curve shows the combination ($\mu = 0.77$, $w = 0.10$). Figure 18.4 shows that for this combination, the willingness to pay for insurance is close to the break-even price.

We can use some simple algebra to represent the conflicting forces in a decision about whether to purchase insurance. As shown in Math 18.1, the decision weight that makes the willingness to pay for insurance equal to the break-even price is determined by the actual probability of loss p and the utility parameter μ:

$$\hat{w} = p^{\mu}$$

To compute the threshold decision weight $\hat{w}$, we raise the probability of loss to a power equal to μ. For linear utility ($\mu = 1$), the threshold decision weight equals the probability. As the strength of decreasing sensitivity increases and μ decreases, the decision weight for a given loss probability increases. To illustrate, suppose the probability of loss is $p = 0.09$.

- *Constant sensitivity.* For $\mu = 1$, the threshold decision weight is $\hat{w} = p = 0.09$.
- *Strong decreasing sensitivity.* For $\mu = 1/2$, the threshold decision weight is $\hat{w} = 0.30$, or roughly 3.33 times the loss probability.
- *Middling decreasing sensitivity.* For $\mu = 3/4$, the threshold decision weight is $\hat{w} = 0.122$, or roughly 1.35 times the loss probability.

An increase in μ increases the willingness to pay for insurance as the decreasing sensitivity to loss weakens. An increase in the decision weight increases the willingness to pay for insurance because homeowner acts as if the flood or other natural disaster is more likely.

The Hazard-Insurance Puzzle

The **hazard-insurance puzzle** is that homeowners systematically under-insure against losses from floods, earthquakes, tornadoes, hurricanes, and other natural disasters. When hazard insurance is subsidized by the government, a homeowner pays less than the break-even price, but many homeowners fail to purchase hazard insurance at the subsidized price. As we've seen, a homeowner considering insurance is engaged in a tug-of-war between decreasing sensitivity (which decreases the willingness to pay) and probability weighting (which increases the willingness to pay). We expect that people who don't buy subsidized hazard insurance experience relatively strong decreasing sensitivity to loss and relatively weak probability weighting.

The Insurance-Deductible Puzzle

Another puzzle in the insurance market is that many homeowners choose relatively expensive policies with relatively high levels of coverage (Sydnor 2010. Under a conventional mortgage contract, the bank requires the borrower to purchase homeowner insurance to cover property damage from natural events such as earthquakes, hurricanes, and floods. The **insurance-deductible puzzle** is that when a bank requires a homeowner to buy insurance, the typical homeowner doesn't choose a low-price policy with relatively low coverage, but instead chooses a high-price policy with a high level of coverage.

Consider a homeowner who is required by a bank to purchase hazard insurance with a maximum deductible of $1600. The $1600 deductible means that the homeowner is responsible for the first $1600 of an insurance claim. For example, if a windstorm causes $3000 in damage, the homeowner bears $1600 of the repair cost, leaving $1400 to be paid by the insurance company. For a homeowner who will not voluntarily purchase insurance, it might seem sensible to choose the insurance policy with the minimum coverage ($1600 deductible) and the lowest possible price. But in fact, many homeowners purchase policies with smaller deductibles and thus higher prices: a policy with a smaller deductible is more costly to the insurance company, so the homeowner pays a higher price. The insurance-deductible puzzle is that many homeowners choose low-deductible policies despite their higher prices.

To illustrate the inclination of homeowners to choose high-price policies with low deductibles, we consider an extreme case. For a homeowner with an insurance policy with a $1600 deductible, the windstorm lottery is

$$L = \{-1600, 0.05; 0, 0.95\}$$

Imagine that a homeowner with a $1600 deductible purchases a supplementary insurance policy that pays the full $1600 deductible in the event of property damage. The supplementary insurance policy eliminates the homeowner's responsibility to pay for any property damage. The break-even price for $1600 worth of supplementary insurance is the negative of the monetary value of the lottery:

$$break\text{-}even\ price = -m(L) = 0.05 \cdot 1600 = \$80$$

An insurance company that charges a price of $80 for $1600 coverage will break even. For the insurance company as a whole, the $80 payments from customers will cover the payouts to the five percent of customers who file insurance claims, each with a $1600 payout from the insurance company.

Figure 18.6 shows the calculations of the willingness to pay for supplementary insurance for a homeowner who experiences decreasing sensitivity and probability weighting. The value of the utility parameter is $\mu=0.77$ and the decision weight is 0.10, or twice the actual probability. As usual, the counter-clockwise path is

$$a \rightarrow b \rightarrow c \rightarrow D \rightarrow E \rightarrow F$$

The $80.43 willingness to pay exceeds (just barely) the $80 break-even price. In this case, the tug-of-war between decreasing sensitivity and probability weighting is won by probability weighting, so the homeowner will purchase supplementary insurance to avoid playing the windstorm lottery. The utility value and certainty equivalent are computed as

$$v(L) = 0.10 \cdot u(-1600) = -\cdot 0.10 \cdot 293 = -29.3\,utils$$

$$c(L) = -(29.3)^{1/0.77} = -\$80.43$$

Figure 18.6 shows how probability weighting increases the willingness to pay for insurance. The first three points in the counter-clockwise path (points a, b, and c) are unaffected by probability weighting. The difference in the computation paths starts after point c. In the absence of probability weighting, the additional steps are points d, e, and f. Under a decision weight of 0.10, the homeowner acts as if the flood is twice as likely. The utility value is shown by point D ($w = 0.10$) rather than by point d ($p = 0.05$). As a result, the certainty-equivalent point is point F rather than point f, meaning that the willingness to pay for insurance greater than the $80 break-even price.

In the example illustrated in Figure 18.6, the willingness to pay for insurance is just barely greater than the break-even price. In other words, probability weighting is just strong enough to offset the force of decreasing sensitivity. This is consistent with the expression for the threshold decision weight. Recall that to make the willingness to pay for insurance equal to the break-even price, $\hat{w} = p^{\mu}$. For a homeowner with $\mu = 0.77$ and an actual probability of loss $p = 0.05$, the threshold decision weight is 0.0996:

$$\hat{w} = 0.05^{0.77} = 0.0996$$

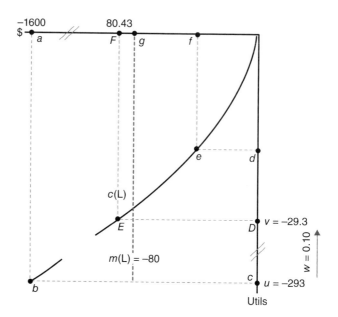

FIGURE 18.6: Willingness to Pay Exceeds the Break-Even Price

In Figure 18.6, a decision weight of $w = 0.10$ is just a bit above the threshold, so the willingness to pay exceeds the break-even price by a small margin. The willingness to pay would be less than the break-even price if (i) probability weighting were a bit weaker (say a decision weight of 0.09 instead of 0.10) or (ii) decreasing sensitivity were a bit stronger (say $\mu = 0.75$ instead of 0.77). The lesson is that a low deductible will be relatively attractive to homeowners with (i) relatively weak decreasing sensitivity and (ii) relatively strong probability weighting.

Review the Concepts 18.2

1. For a homeowner, decreasing sensitivity to loss tends to [___] the willingness to pay for hazard insurance, and over-weighting rare events tends to [___] the willingness to pay. (increase, decrease; not affect, increase; decrease, increase; increase, not affect)

 2. Use Widget 18.2 (available at www.oup.com/us/osullivan1e). Suppose $\mu = 0.75$, indicating middling decreasing sensitivity to loss. The homeowner will voluntarily purchase hazard insurance if the decision weight is at least [___] times the actual probability of loss. (1.5, 2, 3.2, 4)

3. Homeowners who don't buy subsidized hazard insurance experience [___] decreasing sensitivity to loss and [___] probability weighting. (strong, weak; weak, strong)

4. The insurance-deductible puzzle is that when a bank requires a homeowner to buy insurance, the typical homeowner chooses an [___] policy with a [___] level of coverage. (inexpensive, low; expensive, high)

5. In Figure 18.6, the utility value of the lottery with the actual probability is shown by point [___], while the utility value of the lottery with the decision weight is shown by point [___]. (*D, d; c, D; D, E; d, D*)

6. In Figure 18.6, the effect of probability weighting is shown by the switch (or switches) from [___]. (point *f* to point *F*, point *d* to point *D*)

7. A low insurance deductible will be relatively attractive to homeowners with (i) relatively [___] decreasing sensitivity and (ii) relatively [___] probability weighting. (strong, weak; weak, strong; strong, strong)

Key Terms

hazard-insurance puzzle, p. 328   insurance-deductible puzzle, p. 328

Takeaways

1. For a homeowner who uses actual probabilities to compute the values of lotteries, decreasing sensitivity to loss means that the willingness to pay for insurance is less than the break-even price.

2. There are conflicting forces in the willingness to pay for insurance: decreasing sensitivity to loss decreases the willingness to pay, while probability weighting increases the willingness to pay.

3. The hazard-insurance puzzle is that many homeowners under-insure against rare losses from natural hazards such as floods, earthquakes, and tornadoes.

4. The hazard-insurance puzzle is solved by (i) relatively strong decreasing sensitivity to loss and (ii) relatively weak over-weighting of rare events.

5. The insurance-deductible puzzle is that many homeowners who are required to purchase hazard insurance purchase high-price policies with high levels of coverage (small deductibles).

6. A relatively small insurance deductible will be sensible for a homeowner with (i) relatively strong over-weighting of rare events and (ii) relatively weak decreasing sensitivity to loss.

Discuss the Concepts

1. *Insurance Subsidy.* The probability that Ocho's $400 bike will be stolen is 0.20. Ocho experiences decreasing sensitivity with $\mu = 0.80$ and bases insurance decisions on the actual probabilities of loss. To get Ocho to purchase theft insurance at the break-even price, he or she will require a subsidy of $[____]. Illustrate.

2. *Threshold Decision Weight.* The probability of a natural disaster that will destroy Ocho's $250,000 house is 0.01. Ocho experiences decreasing sensitivity with $\mu = 0.80$. Ocho will be indifferent about hazard insurance if the decision weight is $w = [\_\_\_]$. Use Widget 18.2 (available at www.oup.com/us/osullivan1e) to verify your number.

3. *Supplementary Insurance.* Consider the supplementary insurance example with a lottery L = {–1600, 0.05; 0, 0.95}. Ocho experiences decreasing sensitivity with $\mu = 0.80$.

   a. Ocho will.be indifferent about supplementary insurance if the decision weight is $w = [\_\_\_]$.

   b. This weight is [____] (>, <, =) the weight for text example because [____].

Apply the Concepts

1. When you purchase a new phone for $225, you have an opportunity to purchase insurance that replaces the phone at zero cost when it is lost or stolen. Over the next year, the probability of loss or theft is 0.20. The break-even price for insurance is $[____]. Suppose you experience decreasing sensitivity to loss and base your insurance decisions on the actual probabilities of loss. You [____] (will, will not) purchase insurance at the break-even price. Illustrate with numbers.

2. *Personal WTP for Insurance.* Use Widget 18.1 (available at www.oup.com/us/osullivan1e). Suppose the probability that your $400 bike is stolen is 0.20. Use your personal value of μ to compute your willingness to pay for bike-theft insurance. You are willing to pay roughly [____] percent of the break-even price.

3. *Skydiving Insurance as a Public Good?* Your life-insurance office is close to the landing zone for skydivers, where the probability of death from a skydive is 0.25. The death of a diver would generate a wealth loss of $80 for the diver's domestic partner. The death of the diver would also generate losses from lost companionship, for the partner and the diver's cousins. A $64 parade in honor of the deceased diver would offset the loss in companionship for each person who watches the parade, including the partner and the cousins. The utility function in the domain of loss is $u = -(-x^{1/2})$, with $x < 0$.

a. The break-even price for a full payout of the partner's loss ($144) is $[____].

b. It is [____] (rational, irrational) for the partner to buy life insurance at the break-even price because [____]. Illustrate.

c. Each cousin is willing to pay $[____] for an insurance policy with a payout of $144, which includes $64 for a parade. The skydiver will be insured if he or she has at least [____] cousins.

4. *Hazard Insurance Subsidies.* Your task is to compute the cost of subsidies for flood insurance in an area where the annual probability of losing a $200,000 house to a flood is 0.01. Homeowners vary in their values of μ, with a uniform distribution of 40 homeowners between $1 = 0.61$ and $\mu = 1.0$. Your objective is to get eight homeowners to purchase insurance. The budgetary cost of the subsidy program is $[____] $= 8 \times$ $[____].

5. *Insurance for Insurance Deductible.* Consider a homeowner with an insurance policy with a $1600 deductible and a probability of a claim of 0.10. Your task is to compute the homeowner's willingness to pay for an insurance policy that pays the $1600 deductible in the event of a claim.

a. The break-even price of insurance is $p_0 = $[____].

b. Consider a homeowner with decreasing sensitivity to loss ($\mu = 0.50$) and decision weights equal to probabilities. The willingness to pay for deductible insurance is WTP* = $[____].

c. Consider a homeowner with decreasing sensitivity to loss ($\mu = 0.50$) and a decision weight of 0.20 (twice the probability). The willingness to pay for deductible insurance is WTP** = $[____].

Math Solution

Math 18.1

Consider a loss lottery L = {x, p; 0, 1–p}, where $x < 0$. The monetary value is

$$m(L) = -p \cdot x$$

With decision weight w, the utility value is

$$u(L) = -w \cdot (-x)^{\mu}$$

The certainty equivalent is

$$c(L) = \left[u(L) \right]^{1/\mu} = -w^{1/\mu} \cdot x$$

The certainty equivalent equals the monetary value if

$$p \cdot x = w^{1/\mu} \cdot x$$

Divide each side by x to get

$$p = w^{1/\mu}$$

Solve for the decision weight that makes the certainty equivalent to the monetary value:

$$\hat{w} = p^{\mu}$$

Reference Points and Goals

19

In the game of golf, the winner is the player who takes the fewest strokes to complete a course of 18 holes. There is an official "par" for each hole, defined as the number of strokes that a highly skilled player should take to complete the hole. The par for a particular hole is determined by the length of the hole (from the tee to the pin) and the presence of obstacles such as water, sand, and trees. The typical championship golf course has a mix of par-3, par-4, and par-5 holes.

A recent study explores the effects of changing par numbers on the performance of professional golfers (Elmore and Urbaczewski 2019). Suppose course officials decrease the par number on a particular hole from 5 to 4. For a professional golfer who played the hole at the original par 5, would you expect the change in the par number to increase, decrease, or not change the player's score—the number of strokes to complete the hole?

A key feature of prospect theory is that decision-makers use reference points to calculate the benefits and costs of alternative actions. Setting a goal for a particular activity establishes a reference point. For example, a bike messenger in a hilly city could set a goal of working five grueling hours on a particular day. The goal of five hours is a reference point for the messenger. If the messenger falls short of the goal, there is a psychological cost—a loss. As we'll see, the introduction of goals makes marginal analysis more complex and interesting.

Learning Objectives: The Explainer

After mastering this chapter, you will be able to explain each of the following statements.

1. For an individual with a goal, the marginal-benefit curve for an activity may be positively sloped.

2. Once an individual reaches a goal, he or she is likely to be unresponsive to small changes in marginal benefit or marginal cost.

3. For a taxi driver, a daily income goal is likely to be inferior to a weekly income goal.

4. As part of a strategy to break a bad habit, an individual could get information about how to donate money to the NDA (the National Detestable Association).

19.1 Goals and the Marginal Principle

We will explain the implications of setting a goal with an example from a labor market. Suppose you work as a bicycle messenger in a hilly city and have flexible hours—you choose how many hours to work on a particular day. How would a daily goal for hours of work affect your utility-maximizing hours?

Figure 19.1 shows the conventional approach to choosing the utility-maximizing number of hours. The negatively sloped curve shows the conventional marginal-benefit curve for earning income as a messenger. Income buys material goods (food, housing, books, entertainment), and the material marginal-benefit curve is negatively sloped, reflecting diminishing marginal utility in the consumption of material goods. The positively sloped curve shows the marginal cost of work, which is positively sloped under the assumption that each additional hour of work is more costly than the previous hour. Rising marginal cost could reflect the cumulative effects of physical effort or boredom. The material marginal benefit equals the marginal cost at point a, so the utility-maximizing number of hours is h^*.

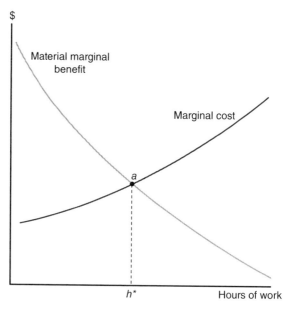

FIGURE 19.1: The Marginal Principle

Goal-Related Marginal Benefit

To explore the implications of a goal, suppose you set a goal of $H = 5$ hours of work on a particular day. If you fall short of the goal, you experience a loss of R. For example, if $R = \$32$, falling short of the goal is equivalent to losing $32. The goal adds another benefit to working. The goal-related benefit of working one additional hour is that you give yourself a chance of reaching your goal. If instead you quit for the day, the probability of reaching the goal is zero, and you will experience a $32 loss from falling short.

To incorporate a goal into marginal analysis, we compute the goal-related marginal benefit of working an additional hour. The benefit of working another hour is that it increases the likelihood that you will reach a goal and thus avoid the cost of falling short. In fact, working an additional hour increases the probability of reaching the goal from zero (if you stop) to a positive number (if you keep working).

The goal-related marginal benefit depends on the probability of reaching the goal and the benefit of reaching the goal. Suppose that once you work an additional hour, the probability of eventually reaching the goal is $p(h)$. The benefit of reaching the goal is R, equal to the avoided cost of falling short. The goal-related marginal benefit is

$$mb_G(h) = p(h) \cdot R$$

Suppose you have worked one hour, and must decide whether to work the second hour, which would leave three additional hours to reach your goal. Suppose the probability that you will take the final three steps to your goal (working hours three, four, and five) is one-eighth. Reaching the goal avoids a loss of $32, so the goal-related marginal benefit of working the second hour is $4:

$$mb_G(2) = \frac{1}{8} \cdot 32 = \$4$$

Working the second hour gives you a one-eighth chance of avoiding a $32 loss, so the goal-related marginal benefit is $4.

How does the probability of reaching the goal change as the number of hours worked increases and the goal gets closer? One possibility is that as you get closer to the goal, the probability of reaching the goal increases. In other words, the fewer the additional steps required to reach the goal, the greater the likelihood of eventually reaching the goal. In our discussion we assume that the closer the goal, the greater the probability of reaching it.

Figure 19.2 shows a positively sloped goal-related marginal benefit curve for a goal $H = 5$ and $R = \$32$. As the goal gets closer and the probability of reaching to goal increases, the marginal benefit increases, from $4 for the second hour, to $8 for the third hour, $16 for the fourth hour, and $32 for the fifth hour. Working the fifth hour (as opposed to stopping at four hours) increases your probability of reaching the goal from zero to one, so the benefit is the $32 loss avoided. Once the goal is reached, the goal-related marginal benefit drops to zero, as shown by the horizontal line on the horizontal axis beyond five hours. Math 19.1 shows the mathematics behind the rising probability of reaching the goal.

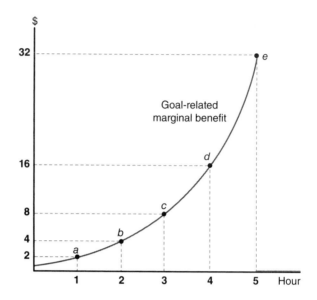

FIGURE 19.2: Goal-Related Marginal Benefit

Full Marginal Benefit and Choice

Figure 19.3 illustrates the marginal-benefit curves for a bike messenger. The negatively sloped curve that includes point *m* shows the conventional material marginal benefit from earning income. The lower curve shows the marginal

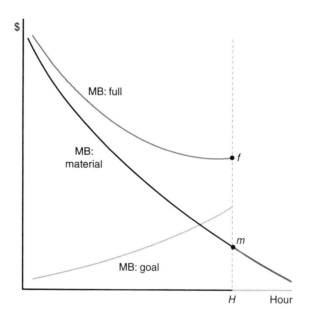

FIGURE 19.3: The Full Marginal Benefit of an Activity

benefit associated with getting closer to the goal. The upper curve shows the full marginal benefit, the sum of the material and goal-related marginal benefits. The gap between the upper curve (full marginal benefit) and the curve showing the material marginal benefit equals the goal-related marginal benefit. For h beyond the goal H, the goal-related marginal benefit is zero, so the full marginal benefit equals the material marginal benefit.

Figure 19.4 shows the implications of goal orientation for decision-making. The conventional marginal-benefit curve shows the material marginal benefit of work, and the marginal principle is satisfied at point *a*, with h^* hours. The full marginal-benefit curve lies everywhere above the marginal-cost curve. For each hour up to the goal, the marginal benefit exceeds the marginal cost, so the rational choice is to reach the goal of $H = 5$ hours. Once the goal is achieved, the goal-related benefit disappears, and the benefit from working comes exclusively from material benefits. Beyond the goal $H = 5$, the material marginal benefit is less than the marginal cost (point *m* is below point *c*), so the rational choice is to stop at the goal.

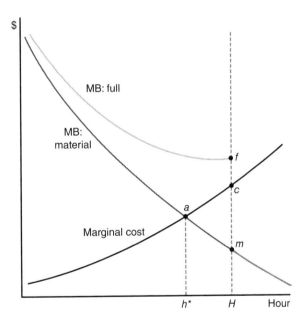

FIGURE 19.4: Work Hours and the Marginal Principle

The introduction of goal orientation makes marginal analysis more complex and interesting. We can highlight four implications of goal orientation.

1. *No intersection.* Because the marginal-benefit curve is not continuous, it is possible—as in Figure 19.4—that a marginal-benefit curve will not intersect the marginal-cost curve. When the full marginal-benefit curve is above the marginal-cost curve for all quantities up to and including the goal, the rational choice is the goal quantity.

2. *Increased quantity.* When a worker reaches the conventional quantity $h*$ (where the material marginal benefit equals the marginal cost), the goal-related marginal benefit may cause the worker to go beyond $h*$ to reach the goal and avoid the loss associated by falling short of the goal.

3. *Unresponsive to changes in marginal cost.* For a person who has reached a goal, there may be a large gap between the full marginal benefit and the marginal cost. As a result, a modest shift in the marginal-cost curve is unlikely to change the rational choice: the decision-maker is likely to continue to reach the goal and stop there. To get the decision-maker to either exceed or fall short of the goal, a relatively large change in the marginal cost is required.

4. *Unresponsive to changes in material marginal benefit.* For a person who has reached a goal, there may be a large gap between the full marginal benefit and the marginal cost. As a result, a modest shift in the material marginal-benefit curve is unlikely to change the rational choice: the decision-maker is likely to continue to reach the goal and stop there. To get the decision-maker to either exceed or fall short of the goal, a relatively large change in the material marginal benefit is required.

Goals on the Golf Course

In the chapter opener, the question is whether a change in the par number for a golf hole will change a player's score on the hole. At first glance, it is sensible to think that the score won't change. After all, the golfer's objective is to minimize the number of strokes on each hole, and a change in a par number on a particular hole should not affect the player's strategy. But in fact, the change in the par number decreased the average score by roughly 0.11 strokes (Elmore and Urbaczewski 2019).

As we saw in an earlier chapter, a key feature of human psychology is that losses loom larger than gains. In other words, the disutility of loss exceeds the utility of gain. This feature is incorporated into prospect theory with the parameter $\lambda > 1$, the relative weight for loss. Recall the definition for loss aversion:

> Loss aversion: To avoid a loss equal to x, an individual is willing to forgo a gain equal to $x \cdot \lambda$, where $\lambda > 1$. This is a consequence of the greater weight for loss in the decision-making process: $\lambda > 1$.

On the golf course, the observed decrease in the average score illustrates the power of goals to motivate behavior. The par number establishes a goal for the golfer. Falling short of the goal generates a loss, and for a golfer who experiences loss aversion, the loss is relatively large. When the par number decreases from five to four, taking a fifth stroke means falling short of the goal and incurring a relatively large loss. The greater the strength of loss aversion (the larger the value of λ), the greater a golfer's incentive to avoid taking the fifth stroke. Golfers respond by finishing the hole with fewer strokes.

Another study of golfing explores the performance of golfers on two types of putts (short-distance strokes to finish the hole): par putts and birdie putts (Pope and Schweitzer 2011).

- A successful par putt allows the golfer to reach par. An unsuccessful par putt means that the golfer will exceed par and suffer a relatively painful loss from falling short.
- A successful birdie putt means the golfer scores one stroke better than par.

The authors examined 2.5 million putts by professional golfers. Holding the degree of difficulty constant, golfers have greater success on par putts than on birdie putts. This suggests that golfers experience loss aversion, and boost their efforts and skill to avoid missing a par putt and falling short of the par goal. If the typical top-20 player duplicated his or her par-putt accuracy on birdie putts, the player's tournament score would increase by roughly one stroke in a 72-hole tournament, increasing his or her annual earnings by roughly $640,000.

Review the Concepts 19.1

1. Your reward from reaching the top of a 10-floor building is $50. The probability of reaching the top is $f/10$, where f is the floor you've reached. The marginal benefit for floor 1 is $[___] and the marginal benefit for floor 8 is $[___]. (45, 10; 5, 5; 5, 40; 10, 10)

2. If the probability of reaching a goal increases as the goal gets closer, the goal-related marginal benefit [___]. (increases, decreases, does not change)

3. The introduction of a goal for some activity [___] the marginal benefit and [___] the utility-maximizing level of the activity. (decreases, decreases; increases, increases; increases, decreases; decreases, increases)

4. An individual who achieves a goal is likely to be [___] to a small change in marginal cost because at the goal, marginal benefit is [___] marginal cost. (unresponsive, equal to; responsive, equal to; unresponsive, less than; unresponsive, greater than)

5. An individual who achieves a goal is likely to be [___] to a small increase in material marginal benefit because beyond the goal, marginal cost is [___] material marginal marginal benefit. (unresponsive, equal to; responsive, equal to; unresponsive, less than; unresponsive, greater than)

6. Professional golfers have greater success on [___] putts, providing evidence for the power of [___]. (par, goals; birdie, exceeding expectations; long, positive thinking)

19.2 Applications: Rainy-Day Taxis and Abstinence

The framework of goal-oriented decision-making can be applied to all sorts of economic choices. In this part of the chapter, we apply the framework to address two questions.

1. Why is it so difficult to get a taxi ride on a rainy day?
2. How does a personal abstinence goal affect the prospects for success?

Rainy-Day Taxis

We can use the notion of goal orientation to solve the puzzle of why it is so difficult to find a taxi on a rainy day (Camerer et al. 1997). On a day with foul weather, the demand for taxi service is relatively high as some travelers switch from walking or biking to riding taxis. As a result, taxi drivers have less idle time between rides, so the hourly payoff from driving a taxi (the taxi wage) is relatively high. The puzzle is that when foul weather increases the taxi wage, the number of taxis on the streets actually decreases. In other words, taxi drivers respond to an increase in the wage by working fewer hours.

Figure 19.5 illustrates the decision-making process for a taxi driver, with and without a daily income goal. The material marginal benefit incorporates the consumption benefits of goods purchased with an additional hour of earnings. The positively sloped marginal-cost curve intersects the material marginal-benefit curve at point a, so in the absence of a goal, the rational choice is four hours of driving.

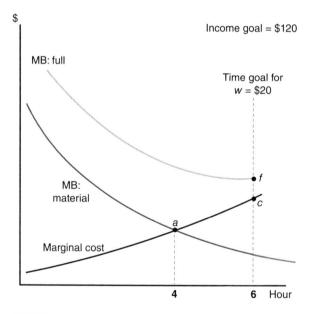

FIGURE 19.5: Income Target for Taxi Drivers

An income goal may change the driver's choice. Suppose the driver sets an income goal of $120 for the day. For an hourly wage of $20, the $120 income goal translates into a time goal of six hours. For a driver subject to loss aversion from a greater weight for loss, falling short of the goal will be particularly costly. The goal-related marginal benefit equals the benefit of moving one step closer to the goal and thus avoiding the loss from falling short of the goal. The full marginal benefit is the sum of the material marginal benefit and the goal-related marginal benefit. As shown by points f and c, the full marginal benefit exceeds the marginal cost for up to six hours, so the taxi driver meets the $120 income goal by working six hours.

Consider the effects of foul weather. An increase in the wage (a result of less idle time between rides) means that it takes fewer hours to reach an income goal. For example, if the wage increases to $24, the $120 income goal translates into a time goal of five hours. As shown in Figure 19.6, the increase in the wage has several effects on the marginal benefit of taxi drive time.

1. The vertical goal line shifts to the left, from six hours to five hours.
2. The material marginal-benefit curve shifts upward, a result of the increase in the wage.
3. The goal-related marginal-benefit curve shifts upward because there are fewer steps (fewer hourly decisions) to reach the goal.
4. The full marginal-benefit curve shifts upward.

A taxi driver reaches the income goal by working fewer hours—five hours instead of six. On a rainy day, taxi drivers reach their income goals earlier in the day, so the number of taxis on the streets decreases.

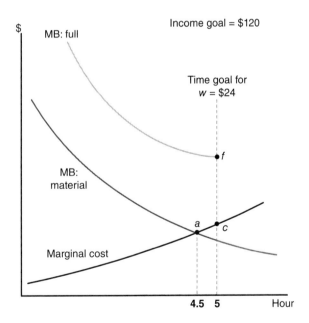

FIGURE 19.6: Rain Decreases Taxi Hours

Inefficiency and a Pareto Improvement

For some taxi drivers, the daily income goal is inefficient. The problem is not with the adoption of a goal; the problem is that the goal is narrow. A driver with a daily goal misses an opportunity to fully exploit high wages on rainy days. Table 19.1 provides a simple example, with a regular (sunny day) wage = $20 and a rainy-day wage = $40. Over the three-day period, there is one rainy day and two sunny days.

- *Daily goal.* The driver works three hours on the rainy day and six hours on each sunny day, for a total of 15 hours. The total income is $360 = 3 \cdot 120$.
- *Three-day goal = $360.* The driver works six hours on the high-wage rainy day, and only three hours on each sunny day, for a total of 12 hours. The total income is $360 = 240 + 2 \cdot 60$.

This example identifies a Pareto improvement: A driver who switches from a daily income goal to a three-day goal is better off because he or she can earn the same income with fewer work hours.

Abstinence

We can use the framework of goal orientation to gain insights into efforts to break bad habits such as physical inactivity or excessive consumption. Consider Bev, who wants to break her habit of spending $6 each day on an unhealthy beverage. Bev sets an abstinence goal of going 10 consecutive days without the beverage. If she falls short of her abstinence goal by drinking even one unit of the beverage in the next 10 days, she will donate money to the NDA (National Detestable Association). For example, if Bev is an environmentalist, her donation could go to an organization that promotes burning coal. Bev's commitment to donate money to an organization she detests generates a relatively large loss from falling short of her abstinence goal.

Consider first the benefit side of Bev's abstinence campaign. The material marginal benefit of a day of abstinence is the $6 worth of other goods she can consume instead. The goal-related benefit is that if Bev abstains on a particular day, she gives herself a chance of reaching her goal. If she instead takes a drink, the probability of reaching the goal is zero, so she contributes money to the NDA. The goal-related marginal benefit of abstinence equals the loss from falling short of the goal (R) times the probability of reaching the goal.

$$mb_G(d) = R \cdot p(d)$$

TABLE 19.1 **Daily Goal versus 3-Day Goal**

	Daily Goal		3-Day Goal	
	Hours	Income	Hours	Income
Rain Day: wage = 40	3	120	6	240
Sun Day 1: wage = 20	6	120	3	60
Sun Day 2: wage = 20	6	120	3	60
Total	15	360	12	360

where d is the number of days of abstinence so far. For example, suppose that if Bev abstains on day 6, the probability she will reach the 10-day goal is one-third. If the loss is $R = \$30$, the goal-related marginal benefit for day 6 is

$$\$10 = \$30 \cdot (1/3)$$

Figure 19.7 shows the three marginal-benefit curves for the abstinence program. The material marginal-benefit curve is horizontal at the $6 savings per day. The goal-related marginal-benefit curve is positively sloped: as Bev gets closer to the goal (as *the number of days of abstinence* increases), the probability of reaching the goal increases, so the goal-related marginal benefit increases. The full marginal benefit of abstinence is the sum of the material and goal-related marginal benefits. The full marginal-benefit curve is positively sloped, reflecting the constant material marginal benefit and the rising goal-related marginal benefit. Once the goal is reached at D days, the goal-related marginal benefit is zero, so the full marginal benefit equals the material marginal benefit.

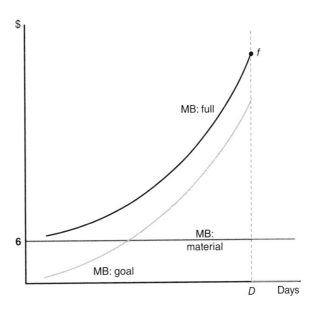

FIGURE 19.7: The Full Marginal Benefit of Abstinence

We can apply the marginal principle to Bev's abstinence campaign. In Figure 19.8, the marginal-cost curve is positively sloped, reflecting the notion that abstinence becomes progressively more difficult and costly. The abstinence goal is decisive in the sense that it increases Bev's days of abstinence.

1. *No goal.* In the absence of a goal, Bev bases her decision on the material marginal benefit of $6 per day. She will abstain for only d^* days, when the material marginal benefit equals the marginal cost.

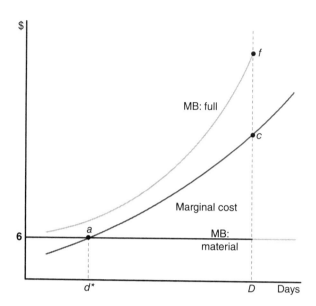

FIGURE 19.8: Reaching the Abstinence Goal

2. *Goal.* Starting from $d*$ days, the full marginal benefit exceeds the marginal cost, so an additional day of abstinence is rational.

In this case, Bev reaches her goal because the full marginal-benefit curve is above the marginal-cost curve for all days up to the abstinence goal D. Bev reaches her goal and thus avoids the loss associated with falling short of the goal—donating money to the NDA.

Review the Concepts 19.2

1. A taxi driver with a daily income goal drives [____] hours on a rainy day because the hourly payoff is [____]. (fewer, low; fewer, high; more, high)

2. As a taxi driver with a daily income goal gets closer to reaching the goal, the goal-related marginal benefit is likely to [____]. (increase, decrease, not change)

3. A taxi driver is unlikely to exceed an income goal because once the goal is reached, the marginal benefit of taxi time [____]. (is constant, increases, decreases abruptly)

4. A switch from a daily income goal to a multi-day income goal can [____] total work hours because it allows a taxi driver to exploit [____] wages on rainy days. (increase, high; decrease, low; decrease, high)

 5. Use Widget 19.1 (available at www.oup.com/us/osullivan1e). On a day with two units of rain, the taxi time is roughly [____], compared to [____] on a dry day. (4.77, 3.75; 5.71, 8; 6.17, 8)

6. An individual with an abstinence goal is unlikely to exceed the goal because once the goal is reached, the marginal benefit of abstinence [___]. (decreases abruptly, is constant, increases)

7. If Bev switches the recipient of any donation from NDA to NAA (National Admirable Association), the switch shifts her marginal-benefit curve [___] and [___] her likelihood of reaching the goal. (upward, increases; downward, increases; upward, decreases; downward, decreases)

Takeaways

1. A goal-related marginal-benefit curve is likely to be positively sloped because the closer the goal, the higher the probability of reaching it.

2. For an individual who achieves a goal, the full marginal benefit is likely to exceed the marginal cost.

3. An individual who achieves a goal is likely to be unresponsive to small changes in marginal cost and marginal benefit.

4. The rainy-day taxi puzzle is that when wages are relatively high, the quantity of taxi services supplied is relatively low.

5. The solution to the rainy-day taxi puzzle is that a driver who sets a daily income goal will work fewer hours when the wage is high.

6. A switch from a daily income goal to a multi-day goal is likely to be a Pareto improvement because it allows a worker to exploit high wages.

7. If the material marginal benefit of abstinence is constant, the full marginal-benefit curve is likely to be positively sloped.

8. An individual will achieve an abstinence goal if the full marginal-benefit curve is above the marginal cost from zero to the goal.

Discuss the Concepts

1. *Increasing Marginal Benefit.* Gull has a goal of mastering a new skill (second language, musical instrument, labor technique). There are five steps in the process, and the reward from completing all five steps is $R = 96$. At each step, Gull assumes that the probability of completing each additional step is $\theta = 1/2$. For example, when Gull decides whether to take step 2, he or she assumes that (i) the probability of taking step 3 is 1/2, (ii) the probability of taking step 4 is 1/2, and so on up to the last step. Draw the marginal-benefit curve for steps 1 through 5.

2. *Skill Goal.* Gull has a goal of mastering a new skill (second language, musical instrument, labor technique). There are five steps in the process, and the reward from completing all six steps is $R = 80$. At each step, Gull assumes that the probability of completing each additional step is $\theta = 1/2$. Each step is more costly than the previous step: $mc = s^2$, where s is the step number. Draw the marginal-benefit curve and the marginal-cost curve. Gull [___] (will, will not) reach the goal because [___].

3. *A More Efficient Goal?* Consider a taxi driver with a daily income target $y = 120$. Half the work days are rainy, with $w_H = 30$, and half the work days are sunny, with $w_L = 20$. Describe an alternative work strategy that satisfies the income target over several days and makes the driver better off.

4. *Abstinence Overreach.* Suppose Bev's objective is to abstain from a drinking habit for five days. The material marginal benefit is $2, and the marginal cost is $mc(d) = d^2$. At each step, Bev assumes that the probability of completing each additional step is $\theta = 1/2$. The reward from completing the abstinence goal is $96.

   a. Bev [___] (will, will not) achieve her goal because [___]. Illustrate.

   b. Suppose Bev increases her abstinence target by two days, from five days to seven days. For day 3, the marginal benefit of abstinence is $mb(3) = $ [___]

   c. Bev [___] (will, will not) achieve her goal because [___]. Illustrate.

Apply the Concepts

1. *Increase Work Time.* A firm's objective is to get the typical employee to work nine hours per day. The wage is fixed at $w = $144. The material benefit of work time is $b_m = w \cdot \log[h]$ and the marginal cost of work time is $mc(h) = 4 \cdot h$, where $\log[\ ]$ is the natural logarithm and h is daily work hours. Define h^* as the number of work hours at which the material marginal benefit equals the marginal cost. The firm will choose a reward (R) for a worker who reaches $H = 9$. Assume that for each hour beyond h^*, the probability that a goal-oriented worker will work one more hour (take one more step toward the goal) is $\theta = 1/2$.

   a. The material marginal benefit equals the marginal cost at $h^* = $ [___] hours. Illustrate.

   b. Suppose $R = $40. The worker [___] (will, will not) work at least one hour beyond h^* because [___]. Illustrate.

   c. Suppose $R = $40. The worker [___] (will, will not) reach the goal because [___] and [___]. Illustrate.

 2. *Rainfall for Equal Hours.* Use Widget 19.1 (available at www.oup.com/us/osullivan1e). Under what circumstances will regular drivers (without a daily earnings goal) work the same number of hours as goal-oriented drivers? The rainfall is [___] inches and the wage is $[___].

3. *Ten Days Beerless.* Brewster has a daily $20 beer habit, but every year sets a goal of not drinking beer for 10 days in a row. If he falls short of the abstinence goal, he donates R to an organization he detests. The material marginal benefit of abstinence is $20, and the marginal cost of abstinence is mc $= 4 \cdot a$, where a is the number of days without beer. Define a^* as the days of abstinence at which the material marginal benefit equals the marginal cost. Starting from a^*, the probability of taking the next step (another day of abstinence during the 10-day period) is constant at $\theta = 1/2$.

   a. The material marginal benefit equals the marginal cost $a^* =$ [____]. Illustrate.

   b. Brewster will go at least one day beyond a^* if $R^* \geq$ $[____]. Illustrate.

   c. Given the reward computed in (b), he [____] (will, will not) meet the goal because [____], [____], [____], [____].

4. *Wipeout.* Consider a contestant on the television program *Wipeout.* The contestant must complete six stages of the game to win a prize R. At each stage, there are random acts of unkindness (balls thrown, logs swung, trap doors sprung) such that the probability of making it to the next stage is $\theta = 1/2$. The contestant's marginal cost is mc$(s) = s^2$, where s is the stage number. The minimum prize such that a contestant achieves the goal of $S = 6$ is $R^* =$ [____]. Illustrate.

5. *Swag for a Radio Pledge Drive.* Consider a public radio station with a membership fee $c =$ $68 and a goal of $M = 20$ new members. The probability of success is $p(m, M) = 0.50 + 0.02 \cdot m$, where m is the number of new members. The personal reward from participating in a successful pledge drive is $R =$ $100.

   a. In the absence of swag, the marginal benefit of joining equals the marginal cost at $m^* =$ [____], and the number of new members is $m^{**} =$ [____]. Illustrate.

   b. The station will use swag to ensure a successful pledge drive. The minimum swag value per new member is $[____]. The minimum total cost of swag cost is $[____]. Illustrate.

Math Solution

Math 19.1: Probability of Reaching the Goal

The goal-related marginal benefit is

$$mb_G(h) = p(h) \cdot R$$

Define θ as the probability of taking one more step, assumed to be the same for each step. For example, if $\theta = 1/2$, the probability of taking the second step once you've taken the first is 0.50. Similarly, the probability of taking the third step once you've taken the second is 0.50. After working h hours, there are $(H - h)$ additional steps required to reach the goal H. The probability of reaching the goal after working h hours is

$$p(h) = \theta^{H-h}$$

For $H = 5$, the probability increases as h increases:

$$p(1) = (1/2)^{5-1} = 1/16 \qquad\qquad p(2) = (1/2)^{5-2} = 1/8$$

$$p(3) = (1/2)^{5-3} = 1/4 \qquad\qquad p(5) = (1/2)^{5-5} = 1$$

For a fixed value of R, the goal-related marginal benefit increases as the goal gets closer. For $R = \$32$, mb_G increases from \$2, to \$4, to \$8, to \$16, to \$32.

Natural Selection and Co-Evolution of Genes and Culture

20

Consider the curious mating behavior of the redback spider, a relative of the black-widow spider (Futuyma 2013). As part of the mating process, a male redback spider does a headstand on the female's belly, and then somersaults into her mouth and is consumed. This behavior is certainly inconsistent with the utility-maximizing behavior we study in economics. And the somersaulting appears to violate the notion of survival of the fittest. As we'll see in this chapter, the persistence of somersaults among male redback spiders illustrates the difference between a conventional model of utility maximization and a model of behavior grounded in evolutionary biology.

This is the first of several chapters on the roles of natural selection and culture in shaping human behavior. In a species experiencing **natural selection**, one genetic type has a relatively high reproduction rate, so its share of the population increases over time. To illustrate, suppose that in an environment with poisonous snakes, there are two types of chimpanzees. Type K has keen vision and readily detects a nearby snake, while type R has regular vision. A chimp with keen vision is more likely to avoid snakebites and more likely to survive to adulthood and produce many offspring. Some of the children will inherit the chimp's keen vision, so they will produce a relatively large number of grandchildren. Over time, the greater reproductive success of type-K chimps increases its share of the population. In casual terms, nature selects for keen vision because the trait increases reproductive success, also known as "**reproductive fitness**" or simply **fitness**.

The genetic makeup of modern humans (*Homo sapiens*) reflects the legacy of millions of years of natural selection. The first members of the *Homo* genus emerged roughly 2.4 million years ago (Henrich 2016), and the genetic makeup of modern humans reflects natural selection over the long hunter-gatherer era from the early days of the *Homo* genus until the development of agriculture roughly 12,000 years ago. Although natural selection has continued in the last 12,000 years, the time since the development of agriculture is only 0.50 percent of our evolutionary history as a member of the *Homo* genus. In later chapters, we will use models of the hunter-gatherer environment to explore possible links between the genetic makeup of our hunter-gatherer ancestors and modern behavior. The behavioral topics include cooperation, time preferences, loss aversion, risk aversion, and the endowment effect.

This chapter explains some key concepts from environmental biology. We explain how genetic mutations fuel natural selection and the evolution of a species. Our discussion highlights the difference between utility maximization in economics and reproductive fitness in biology. As we'll see, genes are not destiny because environmental conditions affect how genes work. As a result, genes are responsible for context-dependent tendencies, potentials, and vulnerabilities. Moreover, human behavior results from an enormously complex interplay of instinctive urges and thoughtful deliberation, with cultural practices and social norms sometimes playing an important role.

This chapter also discusses the interdependence of genes and culture. Starting in the hunter-gatherer era, human evolution has included the co-evolution of genes and culture. Changes in genetic material and cultural practices are complementary: they build on each other to promote reproductive fitness. For example, genetic changes in the human digestive system promoted the cultural practice of milking cows and camels. In our discussion of human evolution, the co-evolution of genes and culture is a recurring theme.

Learning Objectives: The Explainer

After mastering this chapter, you will be able to explain each of the following statements.

1. **Genetic mutations cause natural selection, which causes biological evolution.**

2. **The geometric mean provides a useful measure of reproductive fitness.**

3. **For reproductive fitness, steady (a constant reproduction rate) is superior to varying (a variable reproduction rate).**

4. **An individual's genetic makeup is one of many factors in determining behavior.**

5. **Genes and culture have co-evolved in an interdependent fashion.**

20.1 Background Concepts from Evolutionary Biology

Evolutionary biology is the study of how organisms change over time. Before we start our discussion of the connection between natural selection and human behavior, it will be useful to provide a brief overview of some key concepts and terms in evolutionary biology. After a formal discussion of the key scientific terms, we present a simple analogy that illustrates the concepts.

DNA, Genetic Mutations, and Natural Selection

DNA is a molecule that carries instructions on how to build and maintain the cells of an organism. A **gene** is a distinct portion of an organism's DNA. Some genes provide instructions for cells, in effect telling cells what to do. For example, we have a gene for eye color, and there are several variants (known as **alleles**) for the eye-color gene: blue, brown, green, and so on. When the eye-color gene has the green variant, the gene provides instructions on how to make green eyes. Regulator genes react to the environment, and produce proteins labeled "transcription factors" that turn other genes on or off. So to get green eyes, the eye-color gene must be set to "green" and must be turned on by a regulator gene.

The **genome** of an organism is its complete set of genetic material—all the genes and other material that constitute the organism's DNA sequences. At the individual level, a human's genome is a set of instructions on how to use the available resources to build and operate a human body. As shown by the Human Genome Project, each human has roughly 20,500 genes. The genomes of any two humans differ by less than one percent, and the small differences are responsible for differences in physical features (height, eye color), susceptibility to disease, and other traits. It is important to note that most traits are polygenic, meaning that each trait is determined by many genes. For example, a study of human height showed that a person's height is determined by variants in hundreds of genes (Sapolsky 2018). If you think you are too short or too tall, you can't blame a single gene.

A genetic mutation is a random change in DNA. Genes are transmitted by heredity from one generation to the next, but in the process, mistakes (replication errors) happen. A genetic mutation results in a new genetic type—a new bundle of genes and variants. Mutations happen in both types of genes— regulator genes and other genes. On average, a newborn human has roughly 70 new mutations (Keightley 2012). Roughly two percent of the new mutations are harmful, while roughly 0.02 percent are are potentially advantageous. Futuyma (2013) estimates that in a population of one million humans, roughly 20,000 potentially useful mutations will arise in each generation.

Genetic mutations provide the raw material for natural selection, defined as differences in reproduction rates (Futuyma 2013). In casual terms, natural selection means that one genetic type of a species reproduces at a greater rate than a second genetic type. When a genetic mutation is favorable in a particular environment, natural selection causes the mutation to propagate in the population. For example, if a genetic mutation generates keen vision for a single chimp in a snaky environment, the chimp with keen vision will live longer and produce more offspring than other chimps. The keen-vision mutation will be passed on to numerous children, who will in turn have relatively long lives and produce a relatively large number of offspring. The numerous children will pass on the mutation to numerous grandchildren. Over time, the share of the chimp population with the keen-vision mutation will increase.

What about harmful mutations? Although harmful mutations are more numerous than favorable mutations, natural selection causes harmful mutations to disappear from a population. An organism with a harmful mutation will produce a relatively small number of offspring, and the offspring who inherit the harmful gene will in turn produce a relatively small number of offspring. Over time, the share of the population with the harmful mutation will decrease.

Natural selection sets the stage for evolution, defined in terms of the population shares of different genetic types (Futuyma 2013). A favorable genetic mutation can cause natural selection in favor of a particular genome (a higher reproduction rate), which causes evolution—an increase in the population share of the genome. It's important to note that genetic mutations are random. As a result, natural selection and evolution are not the results of any design process, but instead reflect the cumulative effects of favorable random replication errors. A popular quip among evolutionary biologists is

> Evolution is a tinkerer, not an inventor.

A relatively large share of genetic tinkering happens in mutations of regulator genes, the genes that turn other genes on or off.

Illustration: A Fire-Building Manual

To illustrate the notion of a genome as a set of inherited instructions to accomplish tasks, consider the task of building a fire without modern conveniences such as a match or a lighter. A fire-building manual is a list of instructions, and the simplest manual has just three steps: (i) rub two dry sticks together until you see smoke; (ii) place dry moss close to the smoke until the moss starts to smoke; (iii) blow the smoke until a flame appears. Like a genome, the fire-building manual tells an organism how to accomplish a task.

Suppose a fire-building manual washes up on the beach of an isolated island whose inhabitants don't know how to build a fire. A single human who uses the fire manual will have a survival advantage over other humans because fire provides warmth and cooking capability. As a result, the person with the fire manual is likely to have more offspring. Suppose the parent copies the fire manual and gives a copy to each child. The copied fire manual gives each child a survival advantage, generating a relatively large number of grandchildren. Each child copies the copy of the fire manual and gives each grandchild a copy, so the fitness-enhancing manual is passed on to the next generation. Over time, the fire-capable humans will increase the share of the population with fire skills codified in copied and recopied fire manuals.

Suppose that the transmission of the fire manual from one generation to the next is subject to random mistakes. The replication errors include spelling errors and word substitutions. Consider three types of replication errors.

1. *Harmless errors may persist.* If a parent spells the word "see" as "seee," the error will not prevent the child from building fires and getting the fitness advantage of the manual. We expect this error to be copied and recopied because it is harmless. In the human genome, harmless genetic mutations can persist without consequences.

2. *Harmful errors disappear.* Suppose a parent makes a random mistake by using the word "suck" instead of "blow." If a child following the erroneous instructions ("suck the smoke") dies from smoke inhalation, that child will not produce any offspring. In this case, there are no children to inherit the

defective manual, so the harmful error disappears from the fire manual. For the human genome, a random mutation that disrupts the operation of the human body will be short lived because individuals whose genomes encode harmful instructions will have relatively few offspring.

3. *Beneficial errors propagate.* Suppose a parent makes an error by using the word "rocks" instead of "sticks." Imagine that the child who uses the erroneous instructions ("rub two rocks") has a ready supply of quartz and other rocks that generate a spark when rubbed together. Less time and effort is required to start a fire with rocks and sparks, so a person using rocks will have an fitness advantage over people using sticks. The rock person will produce more offspring, each of whom gets a manual from the parent that codifies the rock method rather than the stick method. The rock method generates a higher reproduction rate, so the rocker share of the population will increase. The beneficial error is codified in the fire manual because, over time, rocks replace sticks in the fire manual. For the human genome, a random mutation that improves reproductive fitness will propagate as individuals whose genomes encode the beneficial instructions produce a relatively large number of offspring.

The fire-manual analogy illustrates the role of genetic changes and natural selection in human evolution. Although harmful mutations are more numerous than beneficial mutations, natural selection tends to eliminate harmful mutations and promote beneficial mutations. Over millions of years, random genetic mutations provide plenty of new raw material for natural selection and evolution.

Review the Concepts 20.1

1. Favorable genetic mutations tend to [___], while unfavorable genetic mutations tend to [___]. (propagate, disappear; disappear, propagate)

2. Evolution is a [___], not a [___]. (designer, tinkerer; tinkerer, designer; scripted process, random process)

3. Natural selection is defined in terms of [___], while evolution is defined in terms of [___]. (population shares, reproduction rates; survival rates, life spans; reproduction rates, population shares)

20.2 A Closer Look at Fitness and Evolution

It will be useful to define and illustrate the notion of reproductive fitness, or fitness for short. The formal definition is the success of an entity in reproducing: the average contribution of a genome to the next generation or succeeding generations. To illustrate, consider the fitness of type-K chimpanzees. Suppose the original chimp with a genome that encodes keen vision (sometimes called the founder) has two children, and passes on the keen-vision genome to each child. Suppose each child has two children, each of whom inherits the genome. After two generations, the population of type-K chimpanzee is four, the number of grandchildren of the original type-K chimpanzee (the founder). After three generations, the population is eight, as each of the four grandchildren has two offspring, generating eight great-grandchildren of the founder.

Figure 20.1 illustrates population over three generations. The population at generation t equals the number of individuals with the genome. We start with a single individual (the founder) at $t = 0$, and each individual produces s offspring and then dies. The circles represent the time path of population for our chimpanzee example, with $r = 2$ offspring per parent. In each period, the population doubles, from one in period 0, to two in period 1, to four in period 2, and eight in period 3. The single individual from $t = 0$ has two children, four grandchildren, and eight great-grandchildren. The diamonds shown the time path for $r = 3$: the population increases by a factor of three in each period, from 1 to 3 to 9 to 27. In the language of mathematics, the population numbers are subject to geometric progression.

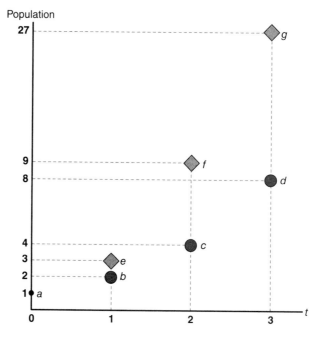

FIGURE 20.1: Population over Three Generations

Fitness, Natural Selection, and Evolution

We can use the example in Figure 20.1 to illustrate the connections between natural selection and evolution. Suppose we start with one chimpanzee of each type: one chimp of type K, and one chimp with regular vision (type R). Suppose the reproduction rate for type-K chimps is $r_K = 3$, compared to $r_R = 2$ for chimps with regular vision (type R).

1. *Natural selection.* We have natural selection because the two genomes have different reproduction rates: $r_K > r_R$.
2. *Evolution.* We have **biological evolution** because the population shares of the two genomes change over time. Specifically, the higher reproduction rate of genome K means that its population share increases from one generation to the next.

In Figure 20.2, the population share of type-K chimps increases, from 50 percent at $t = 0$ (equal to 1/2), to 60 percent at $t = 1$ (equal to 3/5), to roughly 69 percent at $t = 2$ (equal to 9/13), to roughly 77 percent at $t = 3$ (equal to 27/35).

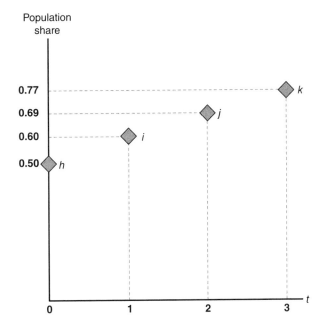

FIGURE 20.2: Natural Selection and Evolution

Fitness Contests and Geometric Mean Fitness

In this part of the chapter, we introduce **geometric mean fitness**, a metric for reproductive fitness developed by evolutionary biologists (Dempster [1955]; Lewontin and Cohen. 1969; Gillespie [1977]; Frank and Slatkin [1990]; Cohen 1993; Yoshimura and Jansen [1996]). This metric allows the direct comparison of the relative fitness of two genomes, allowing us to predict the outcome of a fitness contest between two competing genomes. The genome with the greater geometric mean fitness wins the fitness contest, so its share of the population increases over time.

As we've seen, the reproduction process is a geometric series that is described by its reproduction rates (offspring per parent). For a genome with a constant reproduction rate of two, the geometric series is (1, 2, 4, 8, ...), while for a genome with a constant reproduction rate of three, the geometric series is (1, 3, 9, 27 ...). Define r_t as the reproduction rate in period t. For a genome that starts with a single unit (one individual) in period 0, the geometric mean fitness of the genome is

$$g\left(r_1, r_2, r_3, \ldots, r_T\right) = \left(r_1 \cdot r_2 \cdot r_3 \ldots r_T\right)^{1/T}$$

To compute the geometric mean fitness, we multiply all the r_t values, and raise the product to the power $1/T$. To illustrate, suppose the series of reproduction rates for a genome is (1, 2, 3, 4). The geometric mean fitness of the genome is

$$g(1, 2, 3, 4) = (1 \cdot 2 \cdot 3 \cdot 4)^{1/4} = 24^{1/4} = 2.21336$$

The geometric mean fitness is the constant reproduction rate required to generate the same final population as a series with varying reproduction rates. In this case, the series with varying rates generates a population of $24 = 1 \cdot 2 \cdot 3 \cdot 4$, while a series with a constant rate of 2.21336 generates a population of $24 = 2.21336^4$. Math 20.1 provides definitions of the **geometric mean** and the arithmetic mean.

Geometric mean fitness provides a useful metric for reproductive fitness. Consider genome C, with a constant reproduction rate of three offspring per parent. For $r_1 = r_2 = 3$, the geometric mean is 3:

$$g(3, 3) = (3 \cdot 3)^{1/2} = 3^{1/2} = 3$$

Naturally, the geometric mean equals the constant reproduction rate. Consider genome V, with varying reproduction rates: $r_1 = 2$ and $r_2 = 4$. In other words, the initial parent has two offspring, and each child has four offspring, so there are eight grandchildren. The geometric mean fitness is 2.83:

$$g(2, 4) = (2 \cdot 4)^{1/2} = 2.83$$

The lower geometric mean for genome V is consistent with its smaller final population: the final population of genome C is $9 = 3 \cdot 3$, compared to $8 = 2 \cdot 4$ for genome V. Genome C has a larger geometric mean fitness, so it will win a fitness contest against genome V.

It is worth highlighting the difference between the geometric mean and the more common arithmetic mean, also known as the simple average. For genome C, the arithmetic mean is 3:

$$A(3, 3) = \frac{1}{2} \cdot (3 + 3) = 3$$

For genome V with $(r_1, r_2) = (2, 4)$, the arithmetic mean is 3:

$$A(2, 4) = \frac{1}{2} \cdot (2 + 4) = 3$$

The two genomes have the same arithmetic mean (3) but different geometric means (3.00 versus 2.83). Although the two genomes have the same average growth rate (arithmetic mean = 3), the genome with the constant reproduction rate has greater fitness (geometric mean fitness = 3, compared to 2.83).

Wait a minute! The two genomes have the same average reproduction rate, but genome C has greater reproductive fitness? In Figure 20.3, the population path for genome C $(r_1 = r_2 = 3)$ is point a to point b (three children in period 1) to point c (nine grandchildren in period 2). For genome V $(r_1 = 2; r_2 = 4)$, the population path is point a to point d (two children in period 1) to point e (eight grandchildren in period 2). Although the two genomes have the same average reproduction rate of three offspring per parent, population is greater with a constant reproduction rate: $9 > 8$. This is consistent with a larger geometric mean fitness for genome C: $3 > 2.83$. Note that we get the same result if the sequence of reproduction rates for genome V are reversed. If $r_1 = 4$ and $r_2 = 2$, there will be four children and nine grandchildren.

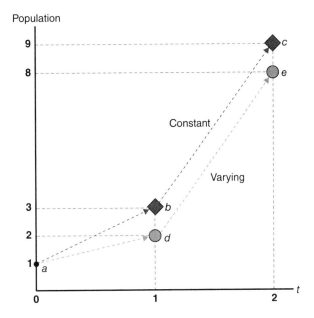

FIGURE 20.3: Constant versus Varying Reproduction

This result is a fundamental consequence of the geometric progression at the heart of reproduction (Dempster [1955]; Gillespie [1977]; Frank and Slatkin [1990]).

> A constant reproduction rate generates greater fitness than a variable reproduction rate with the same arithmetic mean.

As we'll see in later chapters, this result has important consequences for several features of human behavior. In particular, the result provides insights into the role of evolution in the emergence of time preferences, loss aversion, and risk aversion.

Economics versus Biology: Spider Somersaults

Our discussion of evolutionary biology highlights a key difference between economics and biology. In conventional economic analysis, we usually assume that a person's objective is to maximize his or her utility, which is determined by material consumption. In casual terms, the objective is to use material goods to maximize personal happiness. In biology, natural selection means that an organism acts as if its objective is to maximize its contribution to the gene pool by maximizing the number of descendants, including children, grandchildren, great-grandchildren, and so on. Nature selects for traits that promote reproductive fitness, meaning that surviving genomes have the highest reproduction rates. In casual terms, the biological imperative is to maximize the number of offspring. This is captured in an evo-bio quip from Richard Dawkins:

> The chicken is only an egg's way for making more eggs.

The curious mating behavior of the redback spider illustrates the difference between conventional utility maximization and reproductive fitness in biology. After mating, the male somersaults into the female's mouth to be eaten. This behavior decreases the male spider's material consumption to zero, but increases the fraction of the female's eggs that are fertilized by the suicidal male. In other words, the payoff from spider suicide is more offspring. Nature selects for male somersaulting because the trait increases reproductive fitness. A somersaulting male passes on the genome encoded for somersaulting to his numerous male descendants, who in turn somersault and produce numerous offspring with the somersaulting genome.

The redback spider raises interesting questions about human behavior. Suppose we observe human behavior that is obviously inconsistent with the objective of maximizing lifetime material well-being. For example, suppose a prime-age male uses all his retirement money and a huge bank loan to buy a flashy sports car that increases his attractiveness to females. Suppose the result is more offspring now and a miserable retirement later. The question is whether the seemingly irrational behavior reflects a biological imperative to increase the person's contribution to the gene pool. Is a flashy sportscar like a redback somersault?

Review the Concepts 20.2

1. Figure 20.1 illustrates [___] and Figure 20.2 illustrates [___]. (evolution, natural selection; natural selection, evolution).

2. The series of reproduction rates for a genome is (2, 3). The geometric mean is [___] and the arithmetic mean is [___]. (2.50, 2.50; 2, 3; 2.449, 2.50; 5, 5)

3. A [___] reproduction rate generates greater fitness than a [___] reproduction rate with the same arithmetic mean. (constant, variable; variable, constant)

4. Genome C has a constant series of reproduction rates: (2, 2, 2, 2). Genome V has a variable series: (1, 3, 1, 3). The number of great-grandchildren for a founder of genome C is [___], compared to [___] great-grandchildren for genome V. (8, 9; 9, 16; 16, 9; 16, 16)

20.3 Genes, Environment, Norms, Culture, and Cognition

It's important to note that a individual's genetic makeup influences but does not determine behavior. In this part of the chapter, we briefly discuss some subtleties in the influence of genes on decision-making. We also explore the role of thoughtful deliberation in the decision-making process.

Genes and the Environment

Consider first the role of environmental conditions on behavior. As explained by Sapolsky (2018), there are all sorts of interactions between genes and their environments.

> It is not meaningful to ask what a gene does, just what it does in a particular environment.

The classic example is the so-called "warrior gene," a variant on a particular gene (MAO-A) that is positively correlated with violent behavior ... sometimes. Adults with the gene variant who also experienced severe childhood abuse are more violent than the average person. But people with the "warrior" gene who did not experience childhood trauma are roughly average in terms of violent behavior. The environment matters because childhood trauma triggers stress-related chemicals that cause regulator genes to activate the MAO-A variant, resulting in above-average violent behavior.

An individual's genetic makeup is a key factor in behavior, but other factors are important. Sapolsky (2018) makes several observations about the influence of genes on behavior.

1. All behavioral traits are influenced to some extent by genes.
2. Individual differences in behavior are influenced to some extent by genes.

3. Genes are responsible for context-dependent tendencies, potentials, and vulnerabilities.

In other words, a person's genetic makeup can tilt preferences and behavior in one direction, but other factors come into play in the complex tug-of-war that determines behavior.

Genes and Culture

As explained by Henrich (2016), the human genome has shaped human culture, and human culture has shaped the human genome. In other words, the modern human genome is a product of the co-evolution of genes and culture. To illustrate, consider the cultural phenomenon of domesticating mammals such as cows and goats for their milk (Henrich 2016). Before the domestication of milkable mammals roughly 12,000 years ago, the only source of lactose sugars for humans was maternal milk. The human genome deployed regulator genes to encode a shut-off of lactose processing at roughly five years of age, the age at which most youngsters have finished nursing. The shut-off was sensible because it preserved valuable resources for other uses: why support a system for processing something that is not consumed after age five?

The domestication of milkable mammals changed the human genome. Milk from cows, goats, horses, and camels provided an additional source of lactose. In order to tap the new source, the human genome had to undergo changes that allowed people beyond the age of five to process lactose. A genetic mutation of a regulator gene responsible for the traditional lactose shut-off accomplished the task: the mutation disrupted the shut-off process, allowing a person with the mutation to process lactose into late childhood and adulthood (lactase persistence). Individuals whose genomes encoded lactase persistence tapped a new source of nutrition—milk from cows and other mammals—and their superior nutrition translated into more offspring. Some of the numerous offspring inherited the favorable genetic feature and passed it on to some of their numerous offspring. The higher reproduction rates of genomes that encoded lactase persistence caused the trait to propagate in populations that domesticated milkable mammals.

The emergence of lactase persistence illustrates the interdependence of genes and culture. One interesting feature of lactase persistence is that it emerged independently in several areas, and each instance was triggered by a different genetic mutation (Henrich 2016). The trait emerged first in Africa, then later in Europe, then still later in the Arabian Peninsula. Naturally, the timing of emergence matched the timing of domestication of milkable mammals. The last of the domesticated mammals was the camel in the Arabian Peninsula. Roughly one-third of the world's population has genomes encoded for lactase persistence, meaning that over a period that is relatively short in evolutionary terms (12,000 years), a cultural practice caused substantial changes in the human genome.

Evolutionary biologists have identified a large number of genes that have been affected by culture. In other words, lactase persistence is one of many examples of the co-evolution of genes and culture. In summarizing the lessons from evolutionary biology, Gintis (2011) notes that "Gene-culture coevolution is responsible for human other-regarding preferences, a taste for fairness, the capacity to empathize, and the salience of morality and character virtues."

Genes and Social Norms

As discussed earlier in the book, social norms sometimes play an important role the decision-making process. In the words of Adam Smith (1759):

> The all-wise Author of Nature has … taught man to respect the sentiments
> and judgements of his brethren … Our continued observations upon the
> conduct of others insensibly (unconsciously) lead us to form to ourselves
> certain general rules concerning what is fit and proper either to be done or
> to be avoided.

As explained by Henrich (2016), humans instinctively internalize social norms, a result of natural selection that favored genomes that helped individuals navigate complex social environments where "some of the most frequent and dangerous pitfalls involved violating social norms."

Scientists have identified some genetic features that influence social interactions (Way and Lieberman 2010). One gene involved in the brain's serotonin system encodes responses to stressful life events such as divorce, the death of a loved one, and hurricanes. A variant of the gene is associated with a greater risk of depression in response to stressful life events, but only if the person does not have strong social support. For example, for a person with the variant who experiences a hurricane and weak social support, the risk of depression is over four times greater than the risk for a person without the variant. But the depression risk is not significantly different when the person with the variant has strong social support. People with the variant are also more sensitive to positive life events that are social in nature. To summarize, the gene variant means that social interaction inhibits the ill effects of stressful events and promotes the enjoyment of positive events. This promotes social engagement, which of course requires a person to observe the social norms of a group.

Scientists have also identified genes in the brain's opioid system that encode social sensitivity (Way and Lieberman 2010). One gene encodes a person's sensitivity to exclusion from social interactions. A variant of the genes is associated with increased sensitivity to social exclusion. Scientists observed brain activity when a subject was excluded from a virtual ball-tossing game (Cyberball) with two supposed others. The exclusion caused a spike of neural activity in parts of the brain responsible for physical pain. The authors summarize the implications: "This greater sensitivity to cues of rejection and greater concern over the consequences of rejection could lead to the subjugation of self-interest for the interest of the in-group" (Way and Lieberman 2010, 206) In other words, the heightened sensitivity to social exclusion increases the incentive to observe social norms in order to avoid the pain of exclusion.

Instinctive Urges versus Thoughtful Deliberation

As discussed in earlier chapters, human behavior results from an enormously complex interplay of instinctive urges and thoughtful deliberation. In Chapter 2, we considered the apple-or-cupcake decision. The instinctive urge to grab the enticing cupcake is a result of natural selection over millions of years when food resources were scarce. Thoughtful deliberation enters the decision-making process if a person stops to think about the future health consequences of a cupcake, including diabetes and heart disease. In some cases, thoughtful deliberation wins the battle against instinctive urges, and the person steps away from the cupcake. When the instinctive urge wins the battle, the person chooses instant gratification, and perhaps regrets the choice later.

We can sometimes see the results of thoughtful deliberation in actions that are designed to avoid temptation. We saw some of these avoidance strategies in earlier chapters. Some people go out of their way to avoid walking by cupcake displays, donut shops, and other sources of enticing but harmful products. Some smokers try to control their habit by purchasing one cigarette at a time, a practice that increases the price of the harmful good and decreases the quantity consumed. Some people lock their wealth in houses and other assets that are costly to sell, making it easier to overcome the urge to impulsively spend money now rather than saving for retirement.

Review the Concepts 20.3

1. *True or false.* Genes determine behavior. [___] (true, false)

2. *True or false.* All behavioral traits are influenced to some extent by genes. [___] (true, false)

3. *True or false.* Individual differences in behavior are affected by genes. [___] (true, false)

4. Genes are responsible for context-dependent [___]. (tendencies, potentials, vulnerabilities)

5. The co-evolution of genes and culture is illustrated by the domestication of [___]. (cows, horses, goats, camels)

6. *True or false.* Richard Dawkins said, "The egg is only a chicken's way for making more chickens." [___] (true, false)

7. Gene-culture evolution is responsible for [___]. (a taste for fairness, the capacity to empathize, the salience of morality)

8. *True or false.* Humans instinctively internalize social norms. [___] (true, false)

9. Scientists have identified genes that promote [___]. (social interaction, sensitivity to exclusion)

Key Terms

allele, p. 353
biological evolution,
   p. 357
DNA, p. 353

gene, p. 353
genome, p. 353
geometric mean, p. 358
geometric mean fitness, p. 357

natural selection, p. 351
reproductive fitness (or fitness),
   p. 351

Takeaways

1. Genetic mutations provide the raw material for natural selection, defined as differences in reproduction rates of different genetic types.

2. Natural selection causes biological evolution, defined as changes over time in the population shares of different genetic types.

3. Nature selects for traits that promote reproductive fitness, meaning that surviving genomes are the ones with the highest reproduction rates: the chicken is an egg's way of making more eggs.

4. Evolution reflects the cumulative effects of favorable random replication errors: evolution is a tinkerer, not an inventor.

5. A person's genetic makeup influences but does not determine behavior.

6. Genes and culture are interdependent: the human genome has shaped human culture, and human culture has shaped the human genome.

7. Humans instinctively internalize social norms, which play an important role in some decisions.

8. Human decisions result from an enormously complex interplay of instinctive urges and thoughtful deliberation.

Discuss the Concepts

1. *Constant versus Varying Reproduction.* Genome C has a constant reproduction rate $r = 4$.

   a. Starting with a founder at $t = 0$, the population path of the genome is [___], [___], [___], [___]. Illustrate.

   b. Genome V has a varying reproduction rate, alternating between $r = 3$ and $r = 5$. Genome [___] will win the fitness contest between C and V because [___].

2. *Fitness Equivalence.* Genome S has a constant reproduction rate $r = 6$. Genome E has a varying reproduction rate, alternating between $r_L = 4$ and r_H. Consider a three-period model, with $t = (0, 1, 2)$ and a founder at $t = 0$.

   a. For fitness equivalence, $r_H = $ [___]. Illustrate.

   b. The arithmetic mean for genome E = [___], which is (>, <, =) the arithmetic mean for S.

   c. The geometric mean for genome E = [___], which is [___] (>, <, =) the geometric mean for S.

Apply the Concepts

1. *Natural Selection and Evolution.* Consider an environment with two genomes, one with a relatively low reproduction rate ($r_L = 2$) and a second with a relatively high reproduction rate ($r_H = 4$).

   a. Draw a graph like Figure 20.1 to show the population paths of the two genomes. Start with a founder at $t = 0$ and draw the paths up to $t = 3$.

   b. Draw a graph like Figure 20.2 to show the population share of the genome with the high reproduction rate.

   c. There is natural selection because [___]. There is evolution because [___].

2. *Geometric versus Arithmetic Mean.* Consider an environment with two genomes, one with a constant reproduction rate ($r_1 = r_2 = 4$) and a second with a varying reproduction rate ($r_1 = 2, r_2 = 6$).

   a. Draw a graph like Figure 20.3 to show the population paths of the two genomes. Start with a founder at $t = 0$ and draw the paths up to $t = 2$.

   b. For the genome with the constant reproduction rate, the arithmetic mean growth rate is [___] and the geometric mean growth rate is [___].

   c. For the genome with the varying reproduction rate, the arithmetic mean growth rate is [___] and the geometric mean growth rate is [___].

Math Solution

Math 20.1: Geometric Mean versus Arithmetic Mean

Both the geometric mean and the arithmetic mean indicate the central tendency of a set of numbers. The geometric mean is the *n*th root of the product of *n* numbers. For a set of numbers $(x_1, x_2, x_3, \ldots x_n)$, the geometric mean is

$$g(x_1, x_2, x_3, \ldots x_n) = [x_1 \cdot x_2 \cdot x_3 \ldots x_n]^{1/n}$$

The arithmetic mean is the sum of a set of n numbers divided by the count of numbers in the set. For a set of numbers $(x_1, x_2, x_3, \ldots x_n)$, the arithmetic mean is

$$a(x_1, x_2, x_3, \ldots x_n) = [x_1 + x_2 + x_3 \ldots + x_n] \cdot \frac{1}{n}$$

Cooperation

21

Our last common ancestor with chimpanzees lived roughly six million years ago. Somewhere along the evolutionary path between then and now, genetic mutations caused humans and other members of the *Homo* family to develop prominent sclera, also known as "the whites of our eyes." As we'll see, the whites of our eyes help explain why humans are highly collaborative and cooperative. In contrast, chimpanzees and other primates don't have prominent sclera, so they lack a key tool for communication and cooperation.

This chapter explores the role of natural selection and culture in the emergence of cooperation and collaboration as human traits. As we look back millions of years in the evolutionary history that shaped humans, we see that natural selection favored genomes that promoted cooperation as a behavioral trait. Human cooperation has been boosted by the co-evolution of genes and culture, as well as cultural learning. Cooperation helps explain why humans dominate the world, while our closest evolutionary relative—the chimpanzee—plays a relatively small role in world affairs. Humans have other-regarding preferences that often trigger cooperation. In contrast, chimps are largely self-regarding creatures that compete in situations where humans cooperate.

As noted earlier in this book--and emphasized by many wise authors--an individual's genetic makeup is one of many factors that influence behavior. Among the other factors are cultural practices, social norms, and personal experience. In addition, the influence of genes is mediated by the environment: move a genome to a different environment, and behavior may change. As we discuss natural selection and its implications for genomes, remember that although genes influence behavior, other forces of varying power are also in play.

Learning Objectives: The Explainer

After mastering this chapter, you will be able to explain each of the following statements.

1. Compared to chimpanzees, young humans are more inclined to share the rewards from collaboration, and more likely to punish non-cooperative behavior.

2. Under the assumption of diminishing marginal fitness, the sharing of harvests smooths consumption and increases reproductive fitness.

3. Genetic changes facilitated cooperation among humans, promoting the co-evolution of genes and culture.

4. Cultural learning from faithful imitation promotes cooperation.

21.1 Humans versus Chimpanzees

The evolutionary paths of humans and chimpanzees diverged roughly six million years ago. The divergent evolutionary paths generated differences in physiology and behavior. In this part of the chapter, we explore some key behavioral differences between young humans and chimpanzees. We contrast the frequently cooperative nature of young humans with the largely competitive nature of chimpanzees.

Cooperation: Skills and Motivation

As explained by Tomasello (2019), a key difference between humans and chimpanzees is that humans regularly cooperate and collaborate in the pursuit of a shared goal, but chimps do not.

* *Skills for cooperation and collaboration.* Young humans have the skills to engage their caregivers and other infants. For example, one-year-olds (i) follow the gaze of an adult to share a visual experience, (ii) laugh to share happy thoughts, and (iii) point to an object with an index finger to share interest or provide useful information. In contrast, chimps don't follow gazes, don't laugh unless tickled, and don't point to objects to share interest or provide information.
* *Motivation for cooperation and collaboration.* Young humans actively seek cooperative tasks such as back-and-forth ball rolling and other cooperative fun. When given a choice between working for a reward individually or in a group, young humans regularly choose the team approach. In contrast, chimpanzees prefer to work and play alone. It is possible to get chimps to join a team, but only if the team approach generates a larger per-capita reward.

A simple experiment demonstrates the difference between humans and chimps in terms of cooperation (Behne et al. 2012). A one-year-old faces three overturned buckets with a treat (gummy bears) under one bucket. When an adult points to the bucket that hides the treat, the kid flips the bucket and retrieves the treat. The infant has the social skills required to interpret the adult's action. When roles are reversed (the kid knows where the treat is, but the adult does not), a kid will eagerly point out the bountiful bucket to an adult. In other words, the cooperation skills of a young human go both ways.

The bucket experiment has a very different outcome with young chimps (Tomasello 2006). When a human adult points to the bucket covering a treat (a grape), the chimp does not react. This tells us that the chimp is clueless about the helpful gesture. But when the adult lunges toward the bucket that hides the treat, the chimp reacts instantly, and lunges too. The chimp behavior is consistent with competitive rather than cooperative instincts: the chimp views the human as a competitor for food, and a human lunge triggers a chimp lunge to get to the treat first. This competitive orientation is consistent with self-regarding preferences.

Sharing

Another difference between humans and chimpanzees is that young humans share the fruits of cooperative endeavors, but chimps do not. This difference is illustrated by the rope-pulling experiment we discussed in Chapter 2 (Hamann et al. 2011).

- If two three-year-old humans pull the two ends of a rope simultaneously, the cooperative effort delivers a total of four toys (marbles) to the kids.
- If only one kid pulls the rope, the rope runs through the mechanism without delivering any treats.

Kids quickly figure out how to cooperate to get the treats. When by chance one kid gets more marbles than the other, the lucky kid typically transfers marbles to the other kid to equalize the payoffs. For example, a kid who gets three marbles typically gives one marble to the other kid. When the lucky kid is greedy (tries to keep three marbles), the unlucky kid typically protests the unequal allocation, and the greedy kid typically relents and equalizes the reward.

Recall that the key to sharing is collaboration. As shown in Figure 21.1, when youngsters collaborate to get the reward, equal sharing happens in 75 percent of trials. In contrast, when the youngsters work in parallel to get rewards, equal sharing happens in only 25 percent of trials. The authors note, "Taken together,

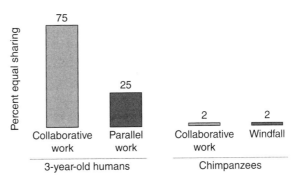

FIGURE 21.1: Equal Sharing for Young Humans and Chimpanzees

these studies show that collaborative work encourages equal sharing in children much more than does working in parallel or acquiring resources in a windfall" (Hamann et al. 2011, 328).

What about chimpanzees? To implement the rope-pulling experiment for chimpanzees, experimenters replace marbles with food, and the chimps quickly figure out how to cooperate to get the food. But in contrast with young humans, chimps don't share food to equalize the payoffs. As shown in Figure 21.1, a lucky chimp equalized the reward in only two percent of trials. If a dominant chimp gets most of the grapes, it typically keeps them. If a lower-ranking chimp gets most of the grapes, there is a chance that a dominant chimp will take the grapes. The lack of sharing means that cooperation among chimps is not sustainable: a chimp who doesn't get any grapes quickly loses interest in the task and walks away, so neither chimp gets any more grapes.

The rope-pulling experiment suggests that sharing the fruits of a cooperative activity is instinctive in humans but not in chimpanzees. Although young humans have limited opportunities to learn social norms by observing and learning from adults, equal sharing is standard behavior. When the standard is violated, most shortchanged infants protest, and most greedy infants relent and divide the reward equally. Experiments in a wide variety of cultural environments generate the same results, suggesting that the equal sharing of a reward generated by cooperation is a human universal, at least for three-year-olds (Tomasello 2019). Later in life, older children absorb social norms that vary from one culture to another, and differences in sharing behavior emerge.

As another illustration of the difference between humans and chimps in sharing, consider the allocation of a harvest from hunting and gathering (Tomasello 2019, Boehm 2012, Blurton Jones 1991). Human hunter-gatherers hunted in groups and shared the harvest in roughly equal terms: each hunter received roughly the same quantity. Chimpanzees hunt and gather in groups, but do not share the harvest equally. Instead, the harvest is allocated by (i) first touch (the first chimp to touch the harvested edible gets the largest share) and (ii) dominance (the dominant chimp gets to feed first). For example, when a group of foraging chimps finds a bountiful fruit tree, the chimps clamber up the tree to establish individual harvest territories, and the first climbers get the most bountiful territories. When dominant chimps enter the scene, they displace some lower-ranked chimps. For meat harvests, a chimpanzee that claims the harvest under the first-touch rule sometimes shares the meat with a few allies. This sharing is strategic, as it helps to balance power against other hungry chimps.

Bearing a Cost to Enforce Norms

Another key feature of young humans is a willingness to bear a cost to punish norm violators. As we saw in the puppet experiment in an earlier chapter, youngsters are willing to enforce social norms. As we saw in an earlier chapter, we can use the ultimatum game to explore how people respond to an unequal distribution of resources. Recall that in an ultimatum game, two players decide how to divide a fixed endowment. One person (the proposer) proposes how to divide the endowment, and if the second person (the responder) rejects the proposal, each person gets nothing.

As we saw in an earlier chapter, adult responders reject relatively low offers, even though rejection means getting nothing. For example, suppose the endowment is $100. The typical responder would reject an offer of $20 because the proposer's greed (taking $80 of $100) violates the responder's standard of fairness. In other words, the responder is willing to sacrifice $20 to avoid a transaction that violates his or her sense of fairness.

Figure 21.2 shows the results of ultimatum experiments with chimpanzees and humans (Falk, Fehr, and Fischbacher 2003; Jensen, Call, and Tomasello 2007). For the chimpanzees, a proposer divides 10 raisins between proposer and responder. How do chimpanzees respond to a proposal of eight for the proposer and only two for the responder? In this case, responding chimps rejected only two percent of the unequal offers. In an equivalent experiment for humans, the proposer divides $10 between proposer and responder. How do humans respond to a proposal of $8 for the proposer and only $2 for the responder? In this case, human responders rejected 45 percent of the unequal offers. Experiments with five-year-old humans show that like adults, youngsters reject unequal offers (Wittig, Jensen, and Tomasello 2013). This suggests that humans, young and old, have other-regarding preferences that incorporate a sense of fairness, and are willing to sacrifice material benefits to block allocations that violate a social norm of sharing.

We can summarize our discussion of the differences between chimpanzees and young humans with several observations about cooperation in young humans.

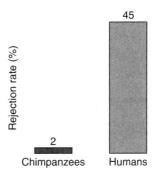

FIGURE 21.2: Responder Rejection Rates in the Ultimatum Game

1. Cooperation is possible. Youngsters have the skills required to (i) signal their intentions to adults and (ii) interpret the signals of adults.
2. Cooperation is rewarding. Youngsters are motivated to engage adults and other youngsters.
3. Cooperation is sustainable. Youngsters share the gains from cooperation, so each individual has an incentive to continue the cooperative activity.

4. Non-cooperative behavior triggers punishment. Youngsters are willing to sacrifice material gains to punish individuals who violate the social norm of sharing.

Review the Concepts 21.1

1. Your objective is to use the minimum effort to get a subject to retrieve a treat under a bucket. For a young human subject, you [_____] the bucket. For a chimpanzee subject, you [____] the bucket. (lunge toward, point at; tap dance on, do a handstand on; point at, lunge toward)

2. [____] share the rewards of collaboration, but [____] do not. (young humans, chimpanzees; chimpanzees, young humans)

3. *True or false.* As shown by the ultimatum game, chimpanzees are willing to incur a cost to punish norm violators. [____] (true, false)

21.2 Consumption and Production Benefits of Cooperation

We've seen that human behavior includes two features that promote cooperation. First, humans instinctively share the rewards from collaboration. Second, humans are willing to bear a cost to punish individuals who violate a social norm of sharing. As we saw in an earlier chapter, the second feature inhibits or eliminates free riding on public goods. In other words, human behavior features **strong reciprocity** in an environment of collaboration.

In this part of the chapter, we explore the benefits of cooperation in a hunter-gatherer environment. There are two key benefits.

1. *Consumption smoothing.* If the harvest of an individual hunter-gatherer is large but infrequent, group sharing smooths consumption over time, increasing reproductive fitness.
2. *Increased productivity.* If there are economies of scale in hunting and gathering, forming a production team increases average productivity, increasing nutritional and reproductive fitness.

These two advantages explain how natural selection can favor genomes that promote cooperation as a behavioral trait.

In a natural-selection model, we translate nutrition into reproductive fitness. Consider a bundle of nutrients consumed at a particular time. The function $g(x)$ translates nutrients in a bundle of size x into reproductive fitness, with diminishing returns to nutrition. Figure 21.3 shows the reproductive fitness per bundle as a function of the size of the bundle. For example, reproductive fitness could be measured as the number of children or grandchildren. As x increases, fitness increases at a decreasing rate.

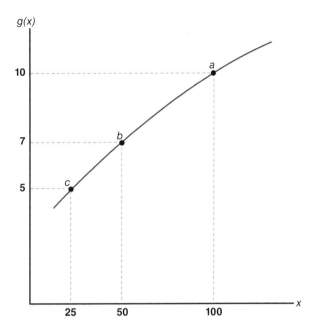

FIGURE 21.3: Benefits of Consumption Smoothing

As a starting point, consider a hunter-gatherer environment where genomes promote self-regarding preferences. Each hunter-gatherer instinctively consumes everything he or she harvests—there is no sharing beyond the narrowly defined kin group of mate and offspring. We can describe such a person as having the KiY (keep it for yourself) genome. Suppose each individual gets a large harvest once every month—a hunter captures an antelope, a scavenger finds a carcass, or a gatherer finds a large cache of wild tubers. As shown by point a in Figure 21.3, the monthly harvest is $x = 100$, and the individual's reproductive fitness is

$$fitness(solo) = 1 \cdot g(100) = 10$$

Benefits from Consumption Smoothing

Consider the effects of a set of random genetic mutations that produce a genome that promotes cooperation. Suppose two people in the tribe carry a gene variant (an allele) that triggers paying it forward. A person with the PIF (pay it forward) genome gives half of a harvest to a hungry person—someone who has not recently harvested food. Suppose Ona and Tula have the PIF genome. At the beginning of each month, Ona harvests 100 units of food and gives 50 units to Tula. Two weeks later, Tula reciprocates by giving half of a harvest to Ona. The sharing arrangement means that each person gets two 50-unit bundles of food rather than a single 100-unit bundle.

Figure 21.3 shows the reproductive benefits of sharing harvests. As shown by point *b*, the reproductive fitness per bundle is $g(50) = 7$. Each individual gets two bundles per month, so food sharing generates fitness per individual equal to 14:

$$fitness\left(member, group\ of\ 2\right) = 2 \cdot g\left(50\right) = 2 \cdot 7 = 14$$

Under the assumption of diminishing marginal fitness, a pair of 50-unit bundles (one every two weeks) provides better reproductive fitness than a single monthly bundle of 100 units. Therefore, the reproductive fitness of an individual with PIF genome will exceed the reproductive fitness of an individual with the KiY genome.

The greater reproductive fitness of individuals with the PIF genome will cause the advantageous genetic mutation to propagate in the population. An individual with the PIF genome will will produce more offspring. Some of the numerous children will inherit the PIF genome and the resulting fitness advantage, and will produce a relatively large number of offspring, some of whom will inherit the PIF genome. Numerous children will produce numerous grandchildren, and the share of the population with the PIF genome will increase. In contrast, the genome that promotes self-regarding preferences will decline in importance and may disappear.

As the PIF genome spreads, it may generate larger cooperative groups. For example, suppose four people form a PIF sharing group. Over the course of a month, each person (i) harvests 100 units and shares 75 units with others, and (ii) gets three transfers of 25 units from other members of the group. As shown by point *c* in Figure 21.3: each smaller bundle generates $g(25) = 5$ units of reproductive fitness, and four smaller bundles generate total reproductive fitness per individual of 20:

$$fitness\ (member,\ group\ of\ 4) = 4 \cdot g(25) = 4 \cdot 5 = 20$$

In other words, each member of a four-person sharing team has twice the reproductive fitness of a solo hunter. The greater reproductive fitness means that the PIF genome will propagate in the population.

Benefits from Economies of Scale

So far our discussion of cooperation has focused on the benefits from consumption smoothing. Cooperation may also increase productivity. To illustrate, suppose a solo hunter chases an antelope for several hours before harvesting the bundle of nutrients. In contrast, a team of four hunters can surround the antelope and converge to harvest the nutrients in one-sixth the time. In a given time period, the four-hunter team harvests six times as much as a solo hunter. This is an example of economies of scale: a four-fold increase in inputs causes a six-fold increase in output. Similarly, a group of four gatherers could be more systematic than a solo gatherer in searching for tubers. If the switch to group gathering more than quadruples the harvest, economies of scale in gathering increase productivity. Economies of scale increase the benefit of cooperation, increasing the reproductive fitness of the PIF genome.

Review the Concepts 21.2

1. In a hunter-gatherer environment, cooperation promotes [____]. (consumption smoothing, increased productivity)

2. Use Figure 21.3 as a starting point. If $g(25) = 6$, food sharing by a team of four hunters generates fitness = [____] each. (10, 12, 20, 24)

3. Economies of scale happen when a [____] increase in all inputs causes a [____] increase in the quantity produced. (proportionate, proportionate; proportionate, greater than proportionate; greater than proportionate, proportionate)

Co-Evolution of Genes and Culture

We've seen that humans are inclined to cooperate and collaborate, and that this behavior is beneficial in terms of reproduction. In this part of the chapter, we provide a brief sketch of the evolutionary history of humans and our *Homo* ancestors over hunter-gatherer era that started roughly 2.4 million years ago. The key question is, "Why did humans and our evolutionary ancestors evolve for cooperation and collaboration?" The emergence of cooperation in humans and our evolutionary ancestors resulted from the co-evolution of genes and culture across thousands of generations (Bowles and Gintis 2011; Henrich 2016; Tomasello 2019). In other words, cooperation resulted from many genetic mutations that provided fitness advantages in specific cultural environments. The cultural environments evolved over time along with genetic material, so cooperation resulted from the co-evolution of genes and culture.

The relevant evolutionary history starts roughly 1.8 million years ago with climate change. The genus *Homo* emerged roughly 2.4 million years ago as a byproduct of roughly 20 million years of natural selection and evolution of the great apes. One of the early members of the *Homo* family was *Homo erectus,* which emerged roughly 1.8 million years ago. Shortly after the emergence of *Homo erectus*, changes in the earth's climate increased competition for food resources, with terrestrial monkeys such as baboons encroaching on *Homo erectus* territories (Tomasello 2019). The increased competition set the stage for natural selection to generate creatures whose genomes promoted behavior that increased reproduction rates in the more competitive environment. In casual terms, the time was right to try something different—it was time for some evolutionary tinkering.

Genes and Culture

Genetic mutations that promoted cooperation increased reproductive fitness. To illustrate, consider the sclera, the opaque portion of the eye (Tomasello et al. 2007). The human sclera is prominent because it is white, and is large relative to the human iris. The human sclera is often tagged as "the whites of the eyes." In contrast, for the roughly 200 other primate species, the sclera is not easy to see because it is dark in color, and small relative to the iris. The prominent human sclera promotes cooperation: the whites of our eyes make it easier to see where people are looking, making it easier to communicate and cooperate. In contrast, chimp sclera are small and dark, so chimps are ill-equipped to communicate and cooperate by following the gazes of fellow chimps. Somewhere along the six-million-year evolutionary path from our last common ancestor with chimpanzees to modern humans, genetic mutations generated prominent sclera, and natural selection favored genomes that generated this tool of cooperative behavior.

Naturally, the prominent sclera is one of many genetic changes that promote cooperation and collaboration in humans. Cooperation requires a person to (i) send signals of his or her intentions to other people and (ii) interpret signals from others. The signaling and interpretation of intentions requires a sophisticated brain. Genetic mutations over millions of years increased the processing power and bandwidth of the *Homo* brain, making cooperation and collaboration possible. For example, the brain of a modern human is roughly three times the size of the brain of a chimpanzee.

Many changes in the human genome occurred simultaneously with changes in culture. Consider two cases of co-evolution of genes and culture.

1. *Spears and shoulders.* The cultural practice of group hunting with spears was accompanied by anatomical changes in the shoulders that increased throwing power and accuracy. Individuals whose genomes generated the best hunting shoulders produced more offspring, and passed on the superior shoulder-building genes to the next generation,
2. *Fire and stomachs.* The cultural practice of cooking by fire was accompanied by a reallocation of body-building resources from stomachs and intestines to brains. Cooking moved a large part of nutrient processing outside the body, allowing bigger brains and greater reproductive success.

Natural selection favored genomes that promoted cooperation, so cooperative genomes propagated in *Homo* populations (West-Eberhard 1979). Individuals who lacked either the relevant cognitive ability or a sharing attitude were excluded from food-gathering teams, so they didn't survive to pass their genes to the next generation. In a curious twist on evolutionary biology, competition with baboons triggered cooperation among members of the *Homo* family.

Cultural Learning

Consider next the role of cultural learning. As we saw in an early chapter, faithful imitation facilitates cultural learning across generations. Although it may be impossible for a single individual to figure out how to transform a rock into a spear point, the cumulative innovation over many generations provided the necessary technology to perform the task. The first innovation may have been to toss a nearby rock against a rock face and look for suitable shards. Later innovations included several refinements (Henrich 2016):

- Search for suitable rocks (such as flint and obsidian)
- Develop hard hammers for coarse shaping and soft hammers for precise shaping
- Use antlers for precise pressure flaking

We can illustrate the role of cultural learning with a simple thought experiment. Suppose you have a genome that promotes cooperation. Imagine that a time-travel machine transports you to a hunter-gatherer environment roughly 1.8 million years ago, when competition from baboons is causing *Homo erectus* to pursue new food opportunities. Herds of antelope are positioned to be tapped by cooperative hunters. Unfortunately, you have arrived at a time before the development of the culture and technology of group hunting. It's up to you to promote cooperative hunting. What's your plan?

You have a number of learning tasks to complete before you can be an effective cooperative hunter. Here are some of your required tasks.

1. Fabricate a spear from a tree branch and a rock
2. Practice your spear-throwing technique to achieve the speed and accuracy required to take down a fleeing antelope
3. Fabricate a water container to sustain you and your partner on the five-hour pursuit of an antelope that you will separate from the herd (persistence hunting)
4. Fabricate a set of saws and knives to transform a captured antelope into edible food
5. Start a fire to cook the meat

For the typical modern human, this list of required tasks is daunting. Even over a lifetime, it may be impossible for an individual to develop all the tools, techniques, and skills required to harvest and process an antelope for consumption. How do you transform a tree branch into an aerodynamic spear? How do you make a rock into a spear point? How do you train yourself to throw a spear effectively? How do you make a water container to quench your thirst on a long hunt? How do you make saws and knives from rocks and bones? How do you start a fire? The simple lesson is that in the absence of knowledge and skills embodied in a culture of collective hunting, the prospects for group hunting are dim.

What if you could reset the time-travel clock for roughly 400,000 years ago? This is about the time that *Homo heidelbergensis* emerged as perhaps the first member of the *Homo* family to engage in cooperative food gathering. By that time, hunter-gatherer cultures had developed most of the tools for group hunting and food processing, so you could use tools developed over many generations of hunters. In addition, you could observe successful hunters and learn hunting techniques that had been passed from one generation to the next for thousands of years.

Summary: Co-Evolution of Genes and Culture

The emergence of cooperation as a trait of humans and other members of the *Homo* family resulted from the co-evolution of genes and culture. Cultural learning allowed the accumulation of knowledge across generations. Over thousands of generations, there were fitness contests between competing sets of genomes and cultural practices. The winners of the fitness contests were the genomes and cultural practices that were most successful in terms of reproductive fitness.

Review the Concepts 21.3

1. In contrast with other primate species, humans have [____]. (relatively large brains, a keener sense of smell, prominent sclera, sharper teeth)

2. The relatively high level of cooperation among humans is caused in part by our [____]. (relatively small digestive systems, relatively large brains, superior physical strength, skills in probability, prominent sclera)

3. Match a cultural practice with the related genetic change: fire (F), group hunting (GH), lactase persistence (LP), milkable mammals (MM), powerful shoulders (PS), small stomachs (SS). [____] (F and SS, GH and PS, MM and LP; F and LP, GH and PS, MM and PS; F and SS, GH and LP, MM and PS)

4. The tools of group hunting were developed across thousands of generations by [____] that facilitated [____]. (mechanical engineers, learning in schools; faithful imitation, cultural learning)

Key Term

strong reciprocity, p. 372

Takeaways

1. The key difference between humans and chimpanzees is that humans regularly cooperate and collaborate.

2. The overturned-bucket experiment shows that young humans have a cooperative orientation, while chimpanzees have a competitive orientation.

3. The rope-pulling experiment suggests that the equal sharing of the rewards from collaboration is instinctive in young humans.

4. The ultimatum game shows that young humans are willing to incur a cost to punish norm violators, but chimpanzees are not.

5. In a hunter-gatherer environment, cooperation by sharing harvests increases fitness because of the benefits of consumption smoothing and economies of scale.

6. The emergence of cooperation in humans and their evolutionary ancestors resulted from the co-evolution of genes and culture across thousands of generations.

7. Faithful imitation promotes cultural learning across generations.

Discuss the Concepts

1. *Consumption Smoothing.* Consider a hunter-gatherer environment where the fitness function is $g(x) = x^{1/2}$ where x is the nutritional content of a bundle of food. A solo hunter harvests $x = 225$, and hunting is subject to constant returns to scale. The fitness of a solo hunter is [____]. The fitness of a member of a hunter group with nine members is [____]. Illustrate.

2. *Shoulder Selection.* Genome W has a constant reproduction rate $r_w = 2$. Genome S has better shoulders for throwing spears, and has a constant reproduction rate $r_s = 3$. At $t = 0$, the population of genome W is $n_w = 5$, and the population of genome S is $n_s = 1$. The population of genome S will exceed the population of genome W at t = [____]. Illustrate.

Apply the Concepts

1. *Consumption Smoothing and Economies of Scale.* Consider a tribe of hunter-gatherers with fitness per bundle $g(x) = x^{1/2}$ where x is the size of the bundle. For a solo hunter, the monthly harvest is $x = 144$.

   a. Consider the case of constant returns to scale in production. For a four-hunter group that shares harvests, the fitness per hunter is [____] compared to [____] for a solo hunter. Illustrate.

   b. Suppose that because of economies of scale, the harvest per hunter for a four-hunter team is $x_4 = 196$. The fitness per hunter in a four-hunter group is [____] compared to [____] for a solo hunter. Illustrate.

2. *Fitness-Maximizing Hunting Team.* Consider a hunter-gatherer economy with scale economies. The fitness function for each member of a hunting team is

$$f(q, n) = n \cdot \left(\frac{n^{\sigma} \cdot x}{n} \right)^{\mu}$$

   where x is the harvest of a solo hunter and n is the number of people on the hunting team. Suppose $x = 100$, $\mu = 1/2$, and $\sigma = 1/4$.

   a. The expression for the marginal benefit of a hunter for the team is. mb(n) = [_____]. Illustrate.

   b. Suppose the marginal cost of an additional member of a hunting team is two. The fitness-maximizing number of hunters on a team is $n^* = $ [____]. Illustrate.

22 Loss Aversion and Time Preferences

You and a friend just received the results of your DNA tests. Most of your ancestors come from a region of the world where long ago the return on investment in food production (hunting, gathering, cultivation) was relatively low. In contrast, most of your friend's ancestors come from a region where the return on investment in food production was relatively high. How would you expect these differences in ancestry to affect (i) the likelihood of smoking cigarettes and (ii) saving for retirement and other long-term plans? Who is more likely to smoke, and who is likely to save more?

This chapter explores the possible roles of natural selection and culture in two types of human behavior discussed earlier in the book.

- *Loss aversion.* As we saw in earlier chapters, the disutility of loss exceeds the disutility of gain. This causes loss aversion: to avoid a loss of x, an individual is willing to forgo a gain of $x + \Delta$.

- *Short-term orientation.* As we saw in earlier chapters, there is substantial variation across individuals in time preferences. For an individual with a **short-term orientation (STO)**, the time path of consumption is tilted in favor of the present. In contrast, an individual with a **long-term orientation (LTO)** is more inclined to sacrifice current consumption to increase future consumption.

As a starting point for our discussion of the link between natural selection modern behavior, recall a key result from our earlier discussion of natural selection.

> A constant reproduction rate generates greater fitness than a variable reproduction rate with the same arithmetic mean.

As we'll see, this simple observation provides insights into loss aversion and a short-term orientation.

As noted earlier in this book—and emphasized by many wise authors—an individual's genetic makeup is one of many factors that influence behavior. Among the other factors are cultural practices, social norms, and personal experience. In addition, the influence of genes is mediated by the environment: move a genome to a different environment, and behavior may change. As we discuss natural selection and its implications for genomes, remember that although genes influence behavior, other forces of varying power are also in play.

Learning Objectives: The Explainer

After mastering this chapter, you will be able to explain each of the following statements.

1.   In an environment where the gain of a fluctuating system equals the loss, natural selection favors genomes that encode loss aversion.

2.   In an environment where the gain of a fluctuating system exceeds the loss by a large margin, natural selection favors genomes that encode loss neutrality or weak loss aversion.

3.   In an environment with a relatively low return on investment, natural selection favors genomes that encode a short-term orientation.

4.   In an environment with a relatively high return on investment, natural selection favors genomes that encode a long-term orientation.

5.   There is evidence that the agricultural productivity experienced by your distant ancestors influence your time preferences and behaviors such as saving and smoking.

22.1   Natural Selection and Loss Aversion

In this part of the chapter, we explore the role of natural selection in loss aversion. Recall that loss aversion is caused by a feature of psychology: the disutility of loss exceeds the utility of gain. In other words, losses loom larger than gains. As explained in an earlier chapter, loss aversion is a possible explanation of the endowment effect, which has been observed in humans, chimpanzees, and capuchin monkeys. Our last common ancestor with capuchin monkeys lived roughly 30 million years ago, so it is possible that loss aversion in primates goes back at least 30 million years, long before the emergence of the first members of the *Homo* genus roughly 2.4 million years ago.

In this chapter, our discussion of loss aversion occurs in a world of certainty. As usual, we use the parameter $\lambda > 1$ to measures the strength of loss aversion. The value is greater than one to represent the greater weight of loss. As we've seen in earlier chapters, there is substantial variation in the strength of loss aversion across individuals.

Steady versus Fluctuating Reproduction

Consider an environment with two systems for generating nutrition. One system provides a steady number of calories; a second system provides the same average number of calories, but the number fluctuates from one period to the next.

1. *Fluctuating nutrition.* Some nutritional resources are sensitive to weather and climate, so the number of calories is likely to fluctuate from one period to the next.
2. *Steady nutrition.* Some nutritional resources are less susceptible to variations in weather and climate, so the number of calories doesn't change from one period to the next.

In our simple model, the link between nutrition and reproductive fitness is straightforward. A steady flow of calories generates a constant reproduction rate of $r = 3$ offspring per parent. In contrast, a fluctuating flow of calories generates a fluctuating reproduction rate, either a low rate (r_L) or a high rate (r_H). This is obviously an abstraction from reality, and in a more realistic model, the connection between nutrition and reproduction would be more complex.

Our example of the steady and fluctuating nutrition systems provides a useful framework for a discussion of loss aversion. Suppose the steady system is a reference point for a decision-maker. An individual who switches from the steady system to the fluctuating system experiences a loss and a gain.

- *Loss*: $L = r - r_L$. This is the difference between the steady reproduction rate and the low rate under the fluctuating system.
- *Gain*: $G = r_H - r$. This is the difference between the high rate under the fluctuating system and the steady reproduction rate.

Gain Equals the Loss

Consider first an environment where the gain equals the loss. Suppose the low reproduction rate is $r_L = 2$ and the high reproduction rate is $r_H = 4$. The gain $(G = 4 - 3)$ equals the loss $(L = 3 - 2)$.

In Figure 22.1, the population path of the steady system is $a \rightarrow b$ (three children in period 1) and then $b \rightarrow c$ (nine grandchildren in period 2). For the fluctuating system, the path is $a \rightarrow d \rightarrow e$. There are two children in period one and eight grandchildren in period two. Recall that the geometric mean of reproduction rates is a measure of reproductive fitness. The geometric mean of the fluctuating system is 2.83:

$$g(2, 4) = (2 \cdot 4)^{1/2} = 2.83$$

Naturally, the geometric mean of the steady system equals the constant rate of three offspring per parent:

$$g(3,3) = (3 \cdot 3)^{1/2} = 9^{1/2} = 3$$

The lower geometric mean for the fluctuating system is consistent with its smaller final population: 8 (shown by point *e*) < 9 (shown by point *c*).

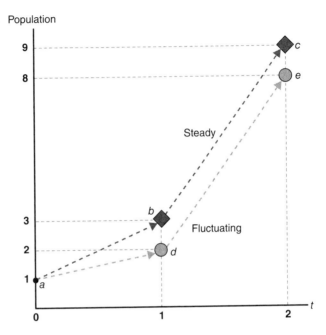

FIGURE 22.1: Population Paths with Common Arithmetic Mean

We turn next to the implications of the two systems for natural selection. Suppose there are two genomes in the population.

1. Genome S encodes strong loss aversion, with $\lambda = 3$. The disutility of loss is three times the utility of gain. When the gain of the fluctuating system equals the loss, an individual with strong loss aversion will choose the steady system. It is possible to get these individuals to choose the fluctuating system, but the gain must be at least three times the loss.

2. Genome N encodes loss neutrality, with $\lambda = 1$. The disutility of loss equals the utility of gain. When the gain of the fluctuating system equals the loss, the individual will be indifferent between the two systems.

Natural selection favors the genome that causes individuals to instinctively choose the system with greater reproductive fitness. In our example, the steady system has greater geometric fitness (3 > 2.83). Individuals with genome S instinctively choose the steady system, so they experience relatively high fitness—a relatively large number of grandchildren. In contrast, individuals with genome N are indifferent between the two systems, and half of them will choose the inferior fluctuating system. This means that on average, the reproductive fitness of individuals acting on genome N will be lower. As a result, genome S will propagate in the population, while genome N will disappear.

Figure 22.2 summarizes the results of the case with a common arithmetic mean. Each rectangle indicates the population of a genome. The upper panel shows the initial equal distribution of the population across the two genomes. The lower panel shows the effects of natural selection: the population of a genome S (strongly loss averse) grows at the expense of genome N (loss neutral).

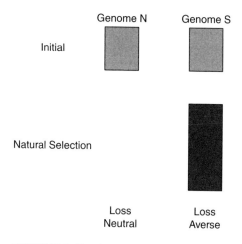

FIGURE 22.2: Population Shares with Common Arithmetic Mean

Why does the loss-neutral genome disappear from the population? It's not a result of inferior intelligence, because individuals in our simple model act on instincts, not cognition. In this specific environment—with the loss equal to the gain—the fluctuating approach generates fewer grandchildren. So a genome that causes individuals to instinctively choose the inferior fluctuating system will lose the fitness contest to a genome that causes individuals to instinctively choose the superior steady system. In this specific environment, the loss-averse genome wins the fitness contest because it steers its individuals away from the inferior fluctuating system.

Gain Exceeds the Loss

Consider next an environment where the gain exceeds the loss by a large margin. Suppose the high reproduction rate is $r_H = 5$, while the low reproduction rate remains at $r_L = 2$. In Figure 22.3, the path for the fluctuating system is $a \to d$ (two children in period 1) and then $d \to e$ (ten grandchildren in period 2). Combining a low reproduction rate $r_L = 2$ and a high rate $r_H = 5$, the gain/loss ratio is

$$\frac{gain}{loss} = \frac{r_H - r}{r - r_L} = \frac{5 - 3}{3 - 2} = 2$$

where $r = 3$ is the steady reproduction rate. The geometric mean of the fluctuating system is 3.16:

$$g(2, 5) = [2 \cdot 5]^{1/2} = 3.16$$

Compared to the steady system, the fluctuating system has a greater geometric mean (3.16 > 3). The higher geometric mean for the fluctuating system is consistent with its larger final population: 10 (shown by point e) > 9 (shown by point c).

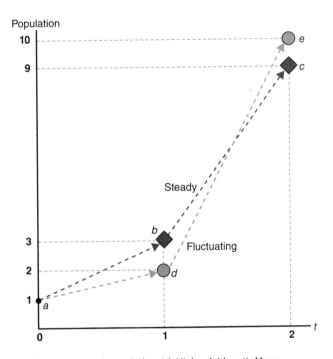

FIGURE 22.3: Population Paths with Higher Arithmetic Mean

In an environment where the gain is twice the loss, the loss-neutral genome will survive, while the genome that encodes strong loss aversion will disappear.

1. *Loss neutrality* (genome N, with $\lambda = 1$). Individuals whose genomes encode loss neutrality instinctively choose the superior fluctuating system because the gain/loss ratio is greater than one. Their choice of the superior system confers a fitness advantage, so the loss-neutral genome propagates in the population.
2. *Strong loss aversion* (genome S, with $\lambda = 3$). Individuals whose genomes encode strong loss aversion instinctively choose the inferior steady system. For individuals with $\lambda = 3$, the disutility of loss is three times the utility of gain, and the fluctuating system offers a gain that is only twice as large.

Their choice of the inferior steady system confers a fitness disadvantage, so the genome disappears.

Figure 22.4 summarizes the results of the case of a relatively large gain. Each rectangle indicates the population of a genome. The upper panel shows the initial equal distribution of the population across the two genomes. The lower panel shows the effects of natural selection: the population of a genome N (loss neutral) grows at the expense of genome S (loss averse).

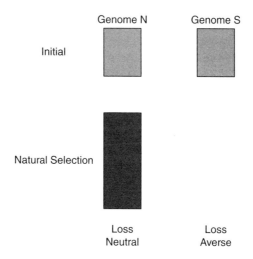

FIGURE 22.4: Population Shares with Higher Arithmetic Mean

Fitness Equivalence

We turn next to the issue of fitness equivalence. Given values for the steady reproduction rate (r) and a low reproduction rate for the fluctuating system (r_L), we can compute the high reproduction rate for the fluctuating system (r_H) that equalizes the reproductive fitness of the two systems. As shown in Math 22.1, for fitness equivalence,

$$r_H = \frac{r^2}{r_L}$$

For example, for $r = 3$ and $r_L = 2$, the fitness-equivalent high reproduction rate is 4.50:

$$r_H = \frac{9}{2} = 4.50$$

The fitness equivalence is confirmed by the geometric mean:

$$g(2, 4.50) = (2 \cdot 4.50)^{1/2} = 3$$

In Figure 22.5, the low reproduction rate is 2 and the high reproduction rate is 4.50. The fluctuating system generates nine grandchildren, the same as the steady system.

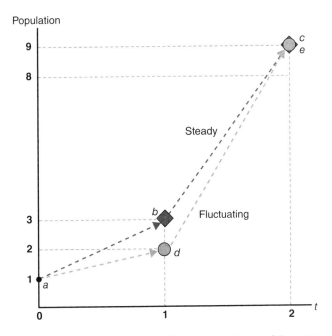

FIGURE 22.5: Fitness of the Steady System Equals Fitness of Fluctuating

We can also compute the fitness-equivalent gain/loss ratio. For $r_H = 4.50$, the gain/loss ratio is 1.50:

$$\frac{gain}{loss} = \frac{r_H - r}{r - r_L} = \frac{4.50 - 3}{3 - 2} = 1.50$$

This is the threshold gain/loss ratio: for any ratio less than 1.50, the steady system is superior; for any ratio greater than 1.50, the fluctuating system is superior.

We can extend our model to incorporate a continuum of gain/loss ratios. Suppose the continuum runs from 1 to 2.10. Consider the implications of a gain/loss ratio = 1.20. This is less than the fitness-equivalent gain/loss ratio (1.50), so the steady system has greater reproductive fitness.

- *Winners: genomes of individuals who choose the steady system.* The winners include genomes that encode loss aversion strong enough to steer individuals away from fluctuating system with a gain/loss ratio of 1.20. In terms of the loss-aversion parameter, $\lambda \geq 1.20$.
- *Losers: genomes of individuals who choose the inferior fluctuating system.* The losers include genomes that encode loss neutrality ($\lambda = 1$) and

genomes that encode loss aversion weak enough that it can be overcome by a gain/loss ratio of 1.20. Individuals who are weakly loss averse can be enticed into choosing the inferior fluctuating system. In terms of the loss-aversion parameter, $\lambda \leq 1.20$.

This case is shown in Figure 22.6. The column on the left above the gain/loss ratio = 1.20 shows the winning genomes in dark gray ($\lambda \geq 1.20$) and the losing genomes in light gray ($\lambda \leq 1.20$).

Consider next the implications of a gain/loss ratio = 1.80. This is greater than the fitness-equivalent gain/loss ratio (1.50), so the fluctuating system has greater reproductive fitness.

- *Winners: genomes of individuals who choose the fluctuating system.* The winners include genomes that encode loss neutrality and genomes that encode loss aversion weak enough to be overcome by a gain/loss ratio of 1.80. In terms of the loss-aversion parameter, the winners have $\lambda \leq 1.80$.
- *Losers: genomes of individuals who choose the steady system.* The losers include genomes that encode strong loss aversion–strong enough that it cannot be overcome by a gain/loss ratio of 1.80. The strongly loss averse choose the inferior steady system despite the large gain/loss ratio. In terms of the loss-aversion parameter, the losers have $\lambda \geq 1.80$. For example, for a genome that generates $\lambda = 3$, a gain/loss ratio of 1.80 will not be large enough to offset a disutility of loss that is is three times the utility of gain.

This case is shown in Figure 22.6. The column on the right above the gain/loss ratio = 1.80 shows the winner genomes in dark gray ($\lambda \leq 1.80$) and the loser genomes in light gray ($\lambda \geq 1.80$).

Environmental Conditions and Genetic Mixes

We've seen that environmental conditions affect natural selection and the genetic mix of a population. In environments where the gain/loss ratio of the fluctuating system is relatively low, the steady system generates greater reproductive fitness, and natural selection favors genomes that encode loss aversion. In contrast, in environments where the gain-loss ratio is relatively high, natural selection *disfavors* genomes that encode strong loss aversion because they steer individuals away from the *superior* fluctuating system. In environments with a relatively high gain-loss ratio, natural selection favors genomes that encode loss neutrality and mild loss aversion.

What are the implications for modern genomes and behavior? Modern human genomes have been shaped by natural selection over thousands of years. As we saw in an earlier chapter, there is substantial variation in the strength of loss aversion across modern humans. It is possible that the varying environments that shaped the genomes of our ancestors have contributed to variation in the strength of loss aversion in modern humans. Recall that genes influence but do not determine behavior: an individual's genetic makeup is one of many factors in the decision-making process.

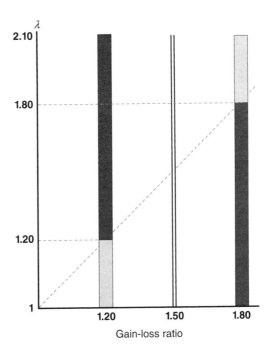

FIGURE 22.6: Winner and Loser Genomes

Review the Concepts 22.1

1. When two nutrition systems—steady and fluctuating—generate the same average reproduction rate, reproductive fitness is greater under the [____] system, as shown by a larger [____] mean. (fluctuating, geometric; steady, arithmetic; steady, geometric; fluctuating, arithmetic)

2. For the threshold gain/loss ratio of a fluctuating system, the two systems have the same [____]. (number of grandchildren, arithmetic mean, number of children, geometric mean)

3. When the gain/loss ratio of a fluctuating system is less than the fitness-equivalent ratio, a [____] genome survives and a [____] genome disappears. (loss-averse, loss-neutral; loss-neutral, loss-averse)

4. When the gain/loss ratio of a fluctuating system is greater than the fitness-equivalent ratio, a [____] genome survives and a [____] genome disappears. (strongly loss-averse, loss-neutral; loss-neutral, strongly loss-averse)

5. A loss-neutral individual makes a fitness-reducing choice when the gain/loss ratio is [____]. (less than the fitness-equivalent ratio, greater than the fitness-equivalent ratio, less than 1, equal to 1)

6. A strongly loss-averse individual makes fitness-reducing choices when the gain/loss ratio is [____]. (a bit greater than the fitness-equivalent ratio, a bit less than the fitness-equivalent rate, 1, much greater than the fitness-equivalent ratio)

7. Use Widget 22.1 (available at www.oup.com/us/osullivan1e). Suppose $r = 5$ for the steady system, so for the fluctuating system, $r_L = 4$. The threshold value for r_H is roughly [____], and the threshold gain/loss ratio is roughly [____]. (7.00, 2.00; 6.50, 1.50; 6.00, 1.00; 6.25, 1.25)

22.2   Natural Selection, Culture, and Time Preferences

In earlier chapters we explored the notion of time preference, the trade-off between consumption now and consumption later. In general, people are willing to sacrifice some consumption now in exchange for greater consumption later. We measure this subjective trade-off with the marginal rate of substitution (MRS) between consumption now and consumption later.

- *Short-term orientation.* An individual with a relatively large MRS places a relatively high value on current consumption, and thus requires a relatively large reward (an increase in future consumption) to invest (a decrease in current consumption). In other words, a large MRS indicates a short-term orientation.
- *Long-term orientation.* An individual with a relatively small MRS places a relatively low value on current consumption, and thus requires a relatively small reward to invest. In other words, a small MRS indicates a long-term orientation.

In this part of the chapter, we explore the role of natural selection and cultural practices in the emergence of time preference as a behavioral trait.

Trade-Offs from Investment

In a discussion of natural selection, a long-term perspective—more than one generation—is required. To keep things simple, we will look forward two generations. Consider a pre-industrial economy where individuals have the opportunity to invest resources in the production of food. An individual sacrifices now and collects the rewards of the investment later. In our multi-generation model, an individual sacrifices offspring now to provide resources to support more offspring in the next generation.

As shown in Figure 22.7, we can modify our example of the steady and fluctuating systems to accommodate investment. Suppose that in the absence of investment, the time path of population is shown by the steady system. The reproduction rate is constant at $r = 3$: the quantity produced is consumed by the current generation, and producers do not invest any resources for future generations. The population path is shown by points a, b, and c.

We can use the fluctuating system to represent the population path under an investment program. Suppose the founder (the original person alive at $t = 0$) allocates resources (time and material) to develop an irrigation system. The cost of

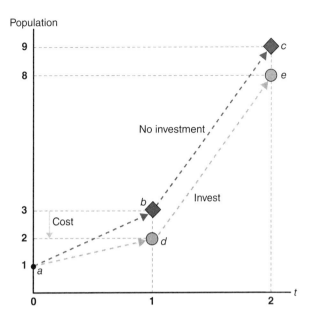

FIGURE 22.7: Fitness and Investment: Low Productivity

the investment is a smaller harvest over the founder's lifetime: time spent on the irrigation system comes at the expense of hunting, gathering, and cultivating. The decrease in the current harvest means the founder can support fewer children. The payoff from the investment comes later, in the form of bigger harvests for the next generation (the founder's children). The increase in the future harvest means that each of the founder's children can support more grandchildren.

Low Investment Productivity

As a starting point, suppose there is a one-for-one trade-off in terms of reproduction rates. A founder who allocates time to an irrigation system can support only two offspring, so $r_1 = 2$. In the next generation, greater productivity allows each parent to support four children, so $r_2 = 4$. As shown in Figure 22.7, the population path is point a to d to e, generating 8 grandchildren. Compared to the non-investment scenario, the investment scenario has the same arithmetic mean (A(3, 3) = A(2 ,4)) and a lower geometric mean:

$$g(3,3) = (3 \cdot 3)^{1/2} = 9^{1/2} = 3$$

$$g(2,4) = (2 \cdot 4)^{1/2} = 8^{1/2} = 2.83$$

The lower geometric mean indicates lower reproductive fitness for the investment program. In Figure 22.7, the investment program generates 8 grandchildren, compared to 9 without investment.

Consider the implications for natural selection. Suppose there are two genomes, one that encodes a short-term orientation, and a second that encodes a long-term orientation.

- *Short-term orientation.* Individuals do not invest.
- *Long-term orientation.* Individuals instinctively invest.

In the case of relatively low investment productivity (one-for-one trade-off), investment decreases reproductive fitness. Individuals with the STO genome don't invest and have more grandchildren, and their greater fitness (3 > 2.83) will cause the STO genome to propagate in the population at the expense of the LTO genome. The lesson is that in an environment with a relatively low return on investment, the genome that encodes a short-term orientation will propagate in the population.

High Investment Productivity

Figure 22.8 shows what happens in an environment where the productivity of investment is higher. Suppose the irrigation project increases the future reproduction rate to $r_2 = 5$, while the cost of investment continues to be a one-unit decrease in the number of children for the founder, from $r = 3$ to $r_L = 2$. In the high-productivity environment, the investment program generates 10 grandchildren,

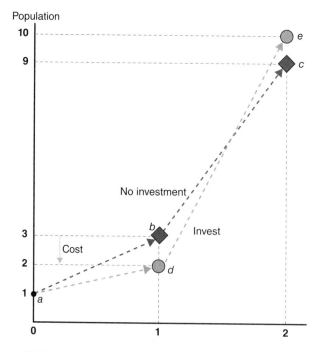

FIGURE 22.8: Fitness and Investment: High Productivity

compared to 9 without investment. Combining a low reproduction rate $r_1 = 2$ and a high rate $r_2 = 5$, the arithmetic mean of the investment program is 3.50:

$$A(2, 5) = 3.50$$

The geometric mean of the investment program is 3.16:

$$g(2, 5) = [2 \cdot 5]^{1/2} = 3.16$$

Compared to the no-investment system, the investment program has a greater arithmetic mean (3.50 > 3) and a greater geometric mean (3.16 > 3).

Consider the implications of high investment productivity for natural selection. As before, we have two genomes, STO and LTO.

1. *STO.* Individuals with a genome that encodes a short-term orientation will not invest. The fitness level is 3 = g(3, 3), with 9 grandchildren.
2. *LTO.* Individuals with a genome that encodes a long-term orientation will instinctively invest. The fitness level is 3.16 = g(2, 5), with 10 grandchildren.

The greater fitness of genome LTO means that the genome will propagate in the population, and the STO genome will disappear. The lesson is that in an environment with a relatively high return on investment, the genome that encodes a long-term orientation will propagate in the population.

The key lesson is that time preferences can be shaped by natural selection. In an environment with a relatively low return on investment, genomes with a short-term orientation win the fitness contest: when the payoff to investment is low, non-investors survive. In contrast, in an environment with a relatively high return to investment, genomes with a long-term orientation win the fitness contest: when the payoff to investment is high, investors survive. There is more investment in a high-productivity environment because natural selection generates a population that is dominated by individuals with a long-term orientation.

We can relate our discussion of natural selection and investment to conventional economic analysis of investment. In a conventional model, individuals use cognition (full benefit-cost analysis) to make rational choices. A high return to investment triggers more investment because utility-maximizing individuals invest more. In our model of natural selection and instinctive behavior, a high return to investment triggers more investment because the survivors have a long-term orientation.

Lessons from Historical Data

Galor and Ozak (2016) explore the link between ancestral productivity and modern time preferences. The authors show that modern humans whose ancestors experienced relatively high agricultural productivity during the pre-industrial period are more likely to have a long-term orientation. The link between high ancestral productivity and present-day long-term orientation reflects both natural selection and culture.

> The theory highlights the effect of crop yield on the gradual propagation of traits for higher long-term orientation due to the forces of natural selection and cultural evolution. (p. 3087)

Given the short time span of their data, the authors emphasize the role of cultural evolution.

> While 350–500 years (i.e., 18–25 generations) … is perhaps a short (but not implausible) period for genetic changes in the composition of traits, it is a sufficient time period for cultural evolution of traits, reflecting the process of learning to delay gratification as well as the vertical and horizontal transmission of long- term orientation (p. 3088).

As we saw earlier in this book, human evolution includes the co-evolution of genes and culture. Recall our discussion of the co-evolution of human shoulder muscles for throwing spears and the cultural practice of group hunting. The two forces are complementary. A group of chimpanzees that adopted group-hunting techniques to hunt a mastodon would fail because chimpanzee shoulders are not capable of throwing spears. A single human with spear-throwing muscles would fail in a mastodon hunt because success requires cooperation with other humans. The results of Galor and Ozak are consistent with the co-evolution, over thousands of years preceding the pre-industrial period covered by their data, of (i) genes that promote a long-term orientation and (ii) complementary cultural practices. The authors suggest that over the last 18-25 generations, cultural practices have (i) continued to evolve, and (ii) supported the transmission of a long-term orientation from one generation to the next

The authors use data on saving behavior and smoking to show the link between ancestral agricultural productivity and present-day time orientation. The evidence for the inheritance of a long-term orientation is that modern humans whose ancestors lived in high-productivity environments have relatively high saving rates and relatively low cigarette consumption. In contrast, short-term orientation is more prevalent in modern humans whose ancestors lived in low-productivity environments. The short-term orientation is reflected in relatively low saving rates and relatively high cigarette consumption. In other words, if your distant ancestors experienced a relatively high return to agricultural investment, you are more likely to save more and smoke less, ceteris paribus.

How does a short-term orientation play out in the modern world? Things have changed since the pre-industrial period, when a short-term orientation promoted fitness in low-return environments. The cost of a short-term orientation has changed for several reasons.

1. *Retirement saving.* Most people live longer than they work, and a short-term orientation can lead to meager retirement saving and a rough transition from working to retirement.
2. *Food supply.* Food is inexpensive and readily available, and a short-term orientation can lead to excessive consumption and later health problems.

3. *Harmful goods.* Cigarettes and other drug-delivery systems are inexpensive and readily available, and a short-term orientation can lead to the consumption of addictive goods and later health problems.

We can relate the notion of short-term orientation to our discussion of present bias in earlier chapters. Individuals who experience present bias places a relatively small weight on future consequences, and may make decisions that they may regret. The Galor-Ozak results suggest that regrettable choices may be in part a legacy of natural selection and cultural evolution. But it's important to note that a person's genetic makeup influences rather than determines behavior. As we've seen in earlier chapters, an individual who experiences present bias can use thoughtful deliberation to develop strategies to avoid regrettable choices.

Review the Concepts 22.2

1. A relatively large marginal rate of substitution (MRS) between consumption now and later results in [____]. (short-term orientation, long-term orientation, neutral time orientation)

2. In a model of natural selection, the investment question is "Will investment increase [____]?" (the number of children, material benefits next year, the number of grandchildren)

3. In the low-productivity environment shown in Figure 22.7, investment [____] the number of grandchildren because the [____] mean of [____] is greater. (decreases, arithmetic, investment; increases, geometric, investment; decreases, geometric, non-investment; decreases, geometric, non-investment)

4. In an environment of relatively low investment productivity, a genome that encodes [____] will win a fitness contest. (short-term orientation, long-term orientation, neutral time orientation)

5. In the high-productivity environment shown in Figure 22.8, investment [____] the number of grandchildren because the [____] mean of [____] is greater. (increases, arithmetic, investment; decreases, geometric, non-investment; increases, geometric, investment; increases, geometric, non-investment)

6. In an environment of relatively high investment productivity, a genome that encodes [____] will win a fitness contest. (short-term orientation, long-term orientation, neutral time orientation)

7. The Galor-Ozak results suggest that modern humans whose ancestors lived in high-productivity environments have relatively [____] saving rates and relatively [____] cigarette consumption. (low, high; average, average; high, average; average, high; high, low)

8. The Galor-Ozak results suggest that if your distant ancestors experienced a relatively low return on investment, you are likely to save [____] the average person, and smoke [____] the average person, ceteris paribus. (more than, less than; less than, more than; about the same as, about the same as; less than, about the same as)

9. *True or false.* Modern present bias may be in part be a legacy of natural selection over thousands of years. [____] (true, false)

10. *True or false.* An individual who experiences present bias as an instinctive urge can develop strategies to avoid regrettable choices. [____] (true, false)

Key Terms

long-term orientation (LTO),
  p. 380

short-term orientation (STO),
  p. 380

Takeaways

1. When the arithmetic mean reproduction rate of a fluctuating system equals the constant reproduction rate of a steady system, natural selection favors genomes that encode loss aversion.

2. For fitness equivalence, the geometric mean fitness of the fluctuating system equals the geometric mean fitness of the steady system.

3. When the gain/loss ratio of a fluctuating system is relatively small, natural selection favors genomes that encode strong loss aversion, while genomes that encode loss neutrality disappear.

4. When the gain/loss ratio of a fluctuating system is relatively large, natural selection favors genomes that encode loss neutrality, while genomes that encode strong loss aversion disappear.

5. A large marginal rate of substitution (MRS) between consumption now and later causes a short-term orientation, while a small MRS causes a long-term orientation.

6. In an environment where the return on investment is relatively low, natural selection favors a short-term orientation.

7. In an environment where the return on investment is relatively high, natural selection favors a long-term orientation.

8. There is evidence that differences in time preferences among modern humans reflect in part differences in productivity experienced by their ancestors.

9. The Galor-Ozak results suggest that for modern humans whose ancestors lived in high-productivity environments, saving rates are relatively high, and cigarette consumption is relatively low.

Discuss the Concepts

1. *Threshold Gain/Loss.* Consider an environment where a steady nutrition system generates a constant reproduction rate $r = 10$. The fluctuating system generates $r_L = 8$ and r_H with equal frequency.

   a. The threshold high reproduction rate is $r_H = $ [____] and the threshold gain/loss ratio is [____].

b. Suppose $r_H = 13$. A genome that encodes strong loss aversion with $\lambda = 2$ will [___] (survive, disappear). A genome that encodes weak loss aversion with $\lambda = 1.10$ will [___] (survive, disappear).

2. *Which Genome Disappears?* Use Widget 22.1 (available at www.oup.com/us/osullivan1e). Consider an environment where a steady nutrition system generates a constant reproduction rate $r = 8$. The fluctuating system generates $r_L = 5$ and r_H with equal frequency.

    a. The threshold high reproduction rate is $r_H = $ [___] and the threshold gain/loss ratio is [___].

    b. Suppose $r_H = 12$. A genome that encodes middling loss aversion with $\lambda = 1.50$ will [___] (survive, disappear).

3. *STO versus LTO.* Consider an environment where in the absence of investment, the reproduction rate is constant at $r = 4$. Investment in period one decreases the reproduction rate in period 1 to $r_1 = 2$ and increases the reproduction rate in period 2 to r_2. A geneome that encodes short-term orientation will disappear if $r_2 > $ [___].

Apply the Concepts

1. *Steady versus Fluctuating.* Suppose a steady nutrition system generates a constant reproduction rate of five. For a fluctuating system, $(r_L, r_H) = (3, 9)$.

    a. Starting with a founder at $t = 0$, illustrate the population paths for $t = (0, 1, 2)$. The fitness of the steady system is [___] and the fitness of the fluctuating system is [___].

    b. The gain/loss ratio = [___].

    c. The geometric mean fitness is [___] for the steady system and [___] for the fluctuating system.

    d. Natural selection favors with genomes that encode [___]. (choose one or more: loss neutrality, weak loss aversion, strong loss aversion)

2. *Natural Selection for Loss Neutrality.* Suppose a steady nutrition system generates a constant reproduction rate of $r = 5$. For a fluctuating system, $r_L = 3$ and r_H is unknown. Define G as the reproduction gain/loss ratio:

$$G = \frac{r_H - r}{r - r_L}$$

The population is initially divided equally between (i) individuals whose genomes encode loss aversion and the choice of a steady nutrition system, and (ii) individuals whose genomes encode loss neutrality and the choice of any fluctuating system with $G \geq 1$. Consider the eventual mix of genomes in the environment.

a. Use a graph to show the relationship between G (on the horizontal axis) and the share of the population with the loss neutral genome (s_{LN}) on the vertical axis).

b. For $G = 1$, $s_{LN} = $ [____]. For $G = 2$, $s_{LN} = $ [____].

c. The threshold value of G (separating dominance by loss aversion and domi-nance by loss neutrality) is [____].

3. *Return on Investment.* Consider an environment where, in the absence of investment, the reproduction rate is constant at $r = 6$. Investment in period 1 decreases the reproduction rate in period 1 to $r_1 = 4$ and increases the repro-duction rate in period 2 to $r_2 = 10$.

a. Starting with a founder at $t = 0$, illustrate the population paths for $t = (0, 1, 2)$. The fitness of the no-investment program is [____] and the fitness under the investment program is [____].

b. The geometric mean fitness is [____] for the no-investment program and [____] for the investment program.

c. Natural selection favors genomes that encode [____] (short-term orientation, long-term orientation).

4. *Natural Selection for LTO.* Consider an environment where, in the absence of investment, the reproduction rate is constant at $r = 6$. Investment in period 1 decreases the reproduction rate in period 1 to $r_1 = 4$ and increases the repro-duction rate in period 2 to r_2. Define R as the reproduction payback ratio:

$$R = \frac{r_2 - r}{r - r_1}$$

The population is initially divided equally between individuals whose genomes encode never invest (STO) and individuals whose genomes encode always invest (LTO). Consider the eventual mix of genomes in the environment.

a. Use a graph to show the relationship between R (on the horizontal axis) and the share of the population with the LTO genome (s_L) on the vertical axis.

b. For $R = 1$, $s_L = $ [____]. For $R = 2$, $s_L = $ [____].

c. The threshold value of R (separating dominance by STO and dominance by LTO) is [____].

Math Solution

Math 22.1: Fitness Equivalence

The geometric mean fitness of the fluctuating system (with F for fluctuating) is

$$g_F\left(r_L,r_H\right)=\left(r_L\cdot r_H\right)^{1/2}$$

where r_L is the reproduction rate for the loss and r_H is the reproduction rate for the gain. Naturally, the geometric mean fitness of the steady system (with S for steady) equals r, the steady reproduction rate:

$$g_S\left(r,r\right)=\left(r\cdot r\right)^{1/2}=r$$

The values of the fitness index are equal if

$$r=\left(r_L\cdot r_H\right)^{1/2}$$

Solve for r_H in terms of r and r_L:

$$r_H=\frac{r^2}{r_L}$$

In the text example, $r=3$ and $r_L=2$. The fitness-equivalent value of the high reproduction rate is 4.50:

$$r_H=\frac{9}{2}=4.50$$

23 Natural Selection and Risk Preferences

A female white cabbage butterfly must decide where to lay its eggs (Yoshimura and Jansen 1996). One option is a cabbage field, where a bountiful supply of nutrients means that 100 eggs will mature into butterflies, but only if the farmer avoids spraying pesticide. There is a 10 percent chance of a pesticide spritz that will kill all the larva, so the expected value of the farm location is 90 offspring: $90 = 0.90 \cdot 100$. A second option is a wild location, where harsh conditions mean that only 50 eggs will mature into butterflies. The wild option has a certain outcome of 50 offspring.

Which option will produce the greatest reproductive fitness? The farm option is enticing because it has a larger expected value of offspring: $90 > 50$. A risk-neutral female butterfly would choose the risky farm option because putting all the eggs in one basket (the cabbage field) maximizes the expected value of offspring. But real butterflies are risk averse, so they place some eggs in the wild environment. The survival rate in the wild is lower, but there is no risk from a pesticide spritz. This suggests that the butterfly genome encodes risk aversion: a butterfly instinctively lays eggs in an environment that is less productive $(50 < 90)$.

This chapter uses simple models of natural selection to explore the connection between investment environments and risk preferences. We address two questions.

1. What sort of environments generate genomes that encode strong risk aversion? Recall that a strongly risk-averse individual requires a large premium to take a risk. For example, a strongly risk-averse individual may be willing to pay only half the expected monetary value of a risky startup enterprise.

2. What sort of environments generate weak risk aversion and risk neutrality? Recall that a weakly-neutral individual requires only a small premium to take a risk. For example, a weakly risk-averse individual may be willing to pay 90 percent of the expected monetary value of a risky startup enterprise.

The answers to these questions provide insights into modern risk preferences.

As noted earlier in this book—and emphasized by many wise authors—an individual's genetic makeup is one of many factors that influence behavior. Among the other factors are cultural practices, social norms, and personal experience. In addition, the influence of genes is mediated by the environment: move a genome to a different environment, and behavior may change. As we discuss natural selection and its implications for genomes, remember that although genes influence behavior, other forces of varying power are also in play.

Learning Objectives: The Explainer

After mastering this chapter, you will be able to explain each of the following statements.

1. In an environment where the reward from risk taking is relatively small, natural selection favors genomes that encode risk aversion.

2. In an environment where the reward from risk taking is relatively large, natural selection favors genomes that encode risk neutrality and mild risk aversion.

3. In an environment where playing it safe causes a zero reproduction rate, natural selection favors genomes that encode risk seeking.

4. The dark-eyed junco has flexible risk preferences, and switches between risk aversion and risk seeking as environmental conditions change.

23.1   Small Reward and Risk Aversion

Consider a hunter-gatherer environment where there is uncertainty with respect to nutrition and the number of offspring. As usual, we use lotteries to represent uncertainty. The lottery could be a hunting expedition with two possible outcomes.

1. *High outcome: hunting success.* A successful hunt generates enough additional nutrition that the hunter can support three offspring. The reproduction rate is $r_H = 3$.
2. *Low outcome: hunting failure.* A failed hunt depletes the hunter's nutritional resources, so the hunter can support only one offspring. The reproduction rate is $r_L = 1$.

To simplify the calculations, we assume that the two outcomes are equally likely: the probability of each outcome is 1/2.

The alternative to playing the lottery is to play it safe and choose a certain outcome. Suppose that under the certain outcome, a hunter has sufficient resources to support two offspring. The certain reproduction rate is r = 2. For example, an individual could play it safe by tapping reliable sources of nutrition. In our hunter-gatherer environment, an individual could gather tubers, hunt small animals, and be certain to get enough resources to support two offspring.

Geometric Mean Fitness

A key issue concerns the measurement of reproductive fitness in an uncertain environment. The consensus among biologists is that the appropriate metric is geometric mean fitness: " … [natural] selection in settings with intergenerational variance in the number of offspring dictates the maximization of the geometric mean" (Kolodny and Stern 2017, 4). As noted by Saether and Engen (2015, 275), in a natural-selection contest, "… the type with the largest value of the long-run growth rate … always will be the winner, such that evolution maximizes the geometric mean fitness." Yoshimura et al. (2009) explore the mathematics of natural selection and fitness in an environment of uncertainty.

Consider an uncertain world with two possible outcomes, r_L and r_H. If the probability of r_L (low outcome) is p and the probability of r_H (high outcome) is $(1 - p)$, the geometric mean fitness is

$$G(r_L, r_H) = r_L^p \cdot r_H^{1-p}$$

If the two outcomes are equally likely ($p = 1/2$), the geometric mean fitness is

$$G(r_L, r_H) = r_L^{1/2} \cdot r_H^{1/2}$$

A hunter-gatherer can take a risk by playing the offspring lottery. There are two outcomes in the lottery, with $r_L = 1$ and $r_H = 3$. We assume that each outcome is equally likely, so the lottery is

$$lottery = \left[1, \frac{1}{2}; 3, \frac{1}{2}\right]$$

The expected value of the lottery (the analog of the arithmetic mean) is 2:

$$expected\ value(1,3) = \frac{1}{2} \cdot 1 + \frac{1}{2} \cdot 3 = 2$$

The geometric mean fitness of the lottery is 1.73:

$$G(1,3) = 1^{1/2} \cdot 3^{1/2} = 1.73$$

Which is better from a reproduction standpoint, playing the lottery or playing it safe? Playing it safe generates a certain reproduction rate $r = 2$, so naturally, the geometric mean fitness of the safe strategy is 2:

$$G(2) = 2$$

The safe strategy has a greater fitness (2 > 1.73), so in terms of reproductive fitness, playing it safe is better than playing the lottery.

Wait a minute! The fitness of the safe strategy exceeds the fitness of the risky strategy? For both strategies, the average number of offspring per parent is two: the safe strategy has $r = 2$, while the risky strategy has equal chances of either 1 or 3. The surprise is that the safe strategy has greater fitness, despite the common expected reproduction rate (arithmetic mean) of 2. This result will not be a surprise to evolutionary biologists, who recognize that variance in reproduction rates decreases fitness (Dempster 1955; Frank and Slatkin 1990).

> A constant reproduction rate generates greater fitness than a variable reproduction rate with the same arithmetic mean.

In our model, the two strategies have the same expected reproduction rate of 2 offspring per parent, but the safe strategy (constant reproduction rate) has a larger geometric mean, indicating greater reproductive fitness than the risky strategy (variable reproduction rate).

Natural Selection and Risk Aversion

As a starting point for a discussion of natural selection, consider a simple case of three genomes. Two genomes encode risk aversion, one with weak risk aversion and a second with strong risk aversion. For both risk-averse genomes, if the expected value of the lottery equals the certain value, an individual plays it safe by choosing the certain outcome. A third genome encodes risk neutrality: if the expected value of the lottery equals the certain value, an individual is indifferent between playing it safe and taking a risk.

As usual, natural selection favors the genome with the greater reproductive fitness. In our example, the safe strategy has greater fitness: 2 > 1.73. The individuals with the risk-averse genomes instinctively choose the safe strategy, and thus have greater fitness. In contrast, individuals with the risk-neutral genome are indifferent between the two strategies, so we expect half of them to choose the inferior risky strategy. The misguided choices of risk-neutral individuals generate lower reproductive fitness, so the genome that encodes risk neutrality will disappear. In Figure 23.1, the genome that encodes risk neutrality disappears (light gray), while genomes that encode risk aversion survive (dark gray).

Why does the risk-neutral genome eventually disappear from the population? It's not a result of inferior intelligence, because individuals are acting on instincts, not cognition. Risk-averse individuals don't win the natural-selection contest because they are smarter, but because their genomes encode instinctive behavior that is appropriate for a specific environment. In this case, the expected value of the lottery equals the certain outcome, so the safe strategy generates greater fitness. The instinct to play it safe is a winning strategy in this specific environment.

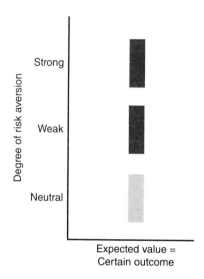

FIGURE 23.1: Surviving and Disappearing Genomes: Small Reward

Review the Concepts 23.1

1. An individual whose genome encodes risk aversion [____] (plays it safe, plays a lottery, is indifferent between playing it safe and playing a lottery).

2. An individual whose genome encodes risk neutrality [____] (plays it safe, plays a lottery, is indifferent between playing it safe and playing a lottery).

3. Suppose the expected value of a risky strategy equals the certain reproduction rate. Reproductive fitness is greater under the [____] strategy, as shown by its [____] geometric mean fitness. (risky, greater; safe, greater; safe, lower; risky, lower)

4. Suppose the expected value of a risky strategy equals the certain reproduction rate. Individuals whose genomes encode [____] instinctively choose the safe strategy, and individuals whose genomes encode [____] are instinctively indifferent between the two strategies. (risk aversion, risk neutrality; risk neutrality, risk aversion)

5. Suppose the expected value of a risky strategy equals the certain reproduction rate. A genome that encodes [____] wins the fitness contest, and a genome that encodes [____] disappears. (risk neutrality, risk aversion; risk aversion, risk neutrality)

23.2 | Large Reward and Risk Neutrality

We turn next to an environment with a larger reward from successful hunting. Suppose the hunting target shifts from small deer to large deer. The large-reward lottery has a larger upside potential because a successful hunt generates a larger bundle of nutrients, allowing the hunter to support more offspring

Greater Fitness for Risk Takers

A switch to the large-reward environment changes the hunting lottery and the reproductive fitness of the risky strategy. If the high outcome is $r_H = 5$ offspring, the lottery is

$$lottery = \left\{1, \frac{1}{2}; 5, \frac{1}{2}\right\}$$

Given the low outcome $r_L = 1$ and the high outcome $r_H = 5$, the expected value of the lottery is three offspring:

$$expected\ value(1,5) = \frac{1}{2}\cdot 1 + \frac{1}{2}\cdot 5 = 3$$

As in the earlier case, the alternative to the offspring lottery is a certain outcome under which an individual has sufficient resources to support two offspring. In this large-reward environment, the expected value of the risky strategy exceeds the certain outcome: 3 > 2.

In the large-reward environment, the fitness of the risky strategy exceeds the fitness of the safe strategy. The fitness of the risky strategy is 2.24:

$$G(1,5) = 1^{1/2}\cdot 5^{1/2} = 2.24$$

The fitness of the safe strategy is still G(2,2) = 2, so the risky strategy generates greater reproductive fitness. The large payoff from taking risks means that risk takers produce more offspring than individuals who instinctively choose the safe strategy.

Natural Selection Favors Risk Taking

Consider the implications of the large-reward environment for the risk-neutral genome. An individual with a risk-neutral genome will take a risk if the expected value of the risky strategy is at least as large as the certain outcome. In the large-deer environment, the expected value of the lottery exceeds the certain value (3 > 2), so a risk-neutral individual will take the risk. In the large-deer environment, the reproductive fitness of the risky strategy exceeds the fitness of the safe strategy (3.24 > 2). So in taking a risk, the risk-neutral individual has a fitness advantage rather than a disadvantage. The genome that encodes risk-neutrality will survive in the high-reward environment.

What are the prospects for risk-averse genomes in the large-reward environment? We can refine our notion of risk aversion by giving our hunter-gatherers a bit of cognition in decisions about taking risks. Suppose the typical hunter-gatherer cannot compute geometric means, but has an intuitive sense of expected value. Although a risk-averse individual is generally inclined to play it safe, he or she will take a risk if the reward is large enough to overcome his or her general aversion to taking chances. Recall that there are two risk-averse genomes, one that encodes weak risk aversion and a second that encodes strong risk aversion.

Suppose that an individual will take a risk if the gap between the expected value of the risky strategy and the certain outcome is sufficiently large. In our example, the gap is 50 percent of the certain value:

$$gap = \frac{expected\ value - certain}{certain} = \frac{3-2}{2} = 0.50$$

For an individual with weak risk aversion, it doesn't take much of a gap between the expected value of the lottery and the certain outcome to trigger risk taking. Suppose that an individual with weak risk aversion will take a risk if the gap is at least 20 percent. For the hunting lottery with the large reward (large deer), the gap is 50 percent. Therefore, a weakly risk-averse individual will take the risk. Because the large-deer lottery generates greater reproductive fitness than the certain outcome (3.24 > 2), genomes that encode weak risk aversion will survive in the high-reward environment.

What about an individual whose genome encodes strong risk aversion? The individual won't take a risk unless the expected value of the risky strategy exceeds the certain outcome by a large margin. Suppose that an individual with strong risk aversion requires a gap of at least 60 percent to take a risk. This minimum gap exceeds the 50 percent gap, so an individual with strong risk aversion will not take the risk, but instead will play it safe by choosing the certain outcome. Because the safe strategy generates lower fitness than the risky strategy (2 < 3.24), genomes that encode strong risk aversion will disappear.

Figure 23.2 shows the surviving and disappearing genomes for the large-reward environment. In an environment where the expected value of the lottery is 50 percent greater than the certain outcome, a genome that encodes risk neutrality survives (dark gray), along with a genome that encodes weak risk aversion. In contrast, a genome that encodes strong risk aversion disappears (light gray).

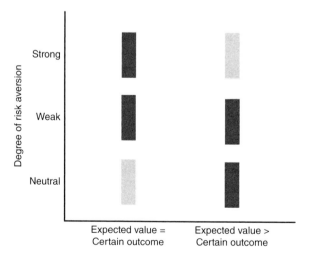

FIGURE 23.2: Fitness in Different Environments: Small versus Large Reward

We've seen that in a large-reward environment, natural selection favors genomes that cause individuals to take risks rather than playing it safe. Genomes that encode risk neutrality and weak risk aversion survive, but genomes that encode strong risk aversion disappear. Genomes that encode strong risk aversion disappear because strongly risk-averse individuals do not take risks even when the payoff from risk taking is relatively high. In a large-reward environment, the winners in the fitness contest are genomes that encode risk taking.

Fitness Equivalence

Figure 23.3 shows an iso-fitness curve for the fitness level generated by the safe strategy. The curve shows the different combinations (r_L, r_H) that generate a fitness level $G = 2$ for the risky strategy. Point a shows the safe strategy, with $r = 2$. Point b shows the small-reward (small-deer) outcome, with a fitness level $G(1, 3) = 1.73$. The fitness is less than the fitness from the safe strategy, so the point lies below the iso-fitness curve. Point c shows the large-reward (large-deer) outcome, with a fitness level $G(1, 5) = 2.24$. The fitness is greater than the fitness from the safe strategy, so the point lies above the iso-fitness curve. Point d shows that in an environment with $(r_L, r_H) = (1, 4)$, the risky strategy generates the same fitness as the safe strategy: $G(1, 4) = 2$.

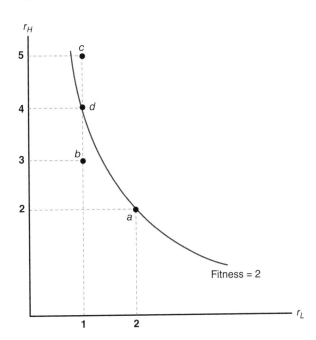

FIGURE 23.3: Fitness Equivalence and the Iso-Fitness Curve

We can use some simple calculations to verify the fitness equivalence of points a and d. The fitness level of $(r_L, r_H) = (1, 4)$ is 2:

$$G(1, 4) = 1^{1/2} \cdot 4^{1/2} = 2$$

The expected value of the lottery is 2.50:

$$A(1, 4) = \frac{1}{2} \cdot 1 + \frac{1}{2} \cdot 4 = 2.50$$

For fitness equivalence, the expected value of the risky strategy exceeds the certain outcome ($r = 2$). For risk taking to achieve the same reproductive fitness as the certain outcome, the expected reward of the risky strategy (the expected value) must exceed the certain reward of the safe strategy.

The iso-fitness curve in Figure 23.3 is negatively sloped and convex. Math 23.1 shows how to compute the fitness-equivalent pairs (r_L, r_H) for a given certain outcome r. As r_L increases, the value of r_H required to maintain a fixed fitness level decreases at a decreasing rate. In addition, an increase in the fitness of the safe strategy shifts the curve upward: to support a greater fitness level, larger values of r_L and r_H are required.

Risk Aversion in Bonobos, Shrews, and Other Creatures

The last common ancestor of humans and bonobos lived roughly 6 million years ago. In a recent experiment (Heilbronner et al. 2008), bonobos were given a choice between a certain reward of four grapes or a lottery with equal chances of either one or seven grapes. In this case, the expected value of the lottery equals the certain reward. The bonobos could play it safe or take a risk by playing the lottery. The bonobos chose the certain reward on roughly 72 percent of the trials, revealing risk aversion. Other studies have shown risk aversion in wasps, bumblebees, blue jays, rats, shrews, and rhesus monkeys (Kacelnik and Bateson 1996).

Review the Concepts 23.2

1. In an environment with a relatively large reward for risk taking, the risky strategy will have [___] reproductive fitness, as indicated by a larger [___] mean fitness. (greater, arithmetic; lesser, geometric; greater, geometric; lesser, arithmetic)

2. In an environment with a relatively large reward for risk taking, individuals whose genomes encode risk neutrality and weak risk aversion choose the [___] strategy, which has [___] fitness. (risky, greater; risky, lower; safe, greater; safe, lower)

3. In an environment with a relatively large reward for risk taking, individuals whose genomes encode strong risk aversion instinctively choose the [___] strategy, which has [___] fitness. (risky, greater; safe, lower; risky, lower; safe, greater)

4. In an environment with a relatively large reward for risk taking, genomes that encode [___] propagate in the population, and a genome that encodes [___] disappears. (risk neutrality and

weak risk aversion, strong risk aversion; strong risk aversion, risk neutrality and weak risk aversion)

5. A risky strategy is fitness-equivalent to a safe strategy if [___] of the risky strategy equals the reproduction rate of the safe strategy. (expected value, arithmetic mean, geometric mean fitness)

23.3   Subsistence and Risk Seeking

So far we have used a simple example of an offspring lottery with positive reproduction rates. What happens when the environment is so unfavorable that "playing it safe" leads to reproductive doom? In an environment where the nutrition provided by the certain outcome is below the minimum level required to reproduce, natural selection may favor genomes that encode risk seeking rather than risk aversion.

Subsistence and Risk Preferences

Figure 23.4 shows the relationship between nutrition and reproductive fitness for a bird. The horizontal axis measures nutrition as the number of seeds consumed, and the vertical axis measures reproductive fitness. For example, fitness could be measured as the number of descendants after several generations.

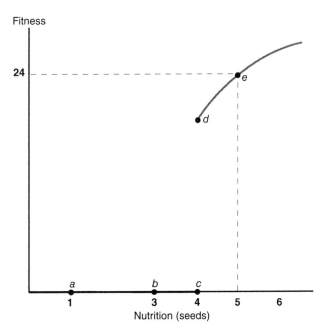

FIGURE 23.4: Subsistence and Risk Seeking

The subsistence level is four seeds, meaning that an individual that gets fewer than four seeds does not produce any offspring. For nutrition levels up to the subsistence quantity, the fitness curve is horizontal at zero (from the origin to point *c*). Beyond the subsistence level, reproductive fitness is positive, and increases with the number of seeds at a decreasing rate: an increase in nutrition increases the number of descendants.

Consider a bird that has two options. One option is to get three seeds for certain: the bird could fly to a tree that has three seeds available for consumption. As shown by point *b* in Figure 23.4, this nutrition level is below the subsistence level, so the bird's reproductive fitness is zero. A second option is to play a lottery with equal chances of either one seed or five seeds. The lottery is

$$L = \left\{ 1, \frac{1}{2}; 5, \frac{1}{2} \right\}$$

For example, a bird could fly to a tree that has either one or five seeds available for consumption.

In Figure 23.4, the high outcome is shown by point *e* (fitness > 0), and the low outcome is shown by point *a*. In contrast with the certain strategy, the risky strategy provides a positive probability of producing offspring. In terms of nutrition, the expected value of the lottery is 3 seeds:

$$expected\ value(1,5) = \frac{1}{2} \cdot 1 + \frac{1}{2} \cdot 5 = 3$$

We can contrast the reproductive prospects of risk-seeking and risk-averse genomes. In our example, the expected value of the lottery (3 seeds) equals the certain harvest.

- Risk seeking genome. Recall that a risk-seeking individual prefers playing a lottery to receiving a certain payment equal to the expected value of the lottery. A genome that encodes risk seeking will cause a bird to choose the lottery, the strategy that generates a positive probability of producing offspring.
- Risk averse genome. Recall that a risk-averse individual prefers a certain payment to playing a lottery with an expected value equal to the certain payment. A genome that encodes risk aversion will cause a bird to choose the certain harvest, the strategy that generates a zero probability of producing offspring.

The general lesson is that in an environment with highly unfavorable conditions, a genome that encodes risk seeking may propagate in the population.

The Flexible Risk Preferences of Juncos

The dark-eyed junco is a bird species that is common across much of temperate North America. A study of the bird's risk preferences illustrates how environmental conditions affect the bird's risk-taking behavior (Caraco 1981).

When conditions are highly unfavorable and nutrients are scarce, the birds exhibit risk seeking. But when nutrients are plentiful, the birds exhibit risk aversion, and play it safe rather than taking risks.

To test the risk behavior of juncos in an unfavorable environment, the biologists fed the birds at a rate below the subsistence level. The idea was to get the birds to believe that they were on the path to starvation. Then the biologists gave the birds a choice between a certain outcome (three seeds) and a risky strategy (equal chances of one or five seeds). In this case of being primed for a starvation environment, the birds chose the risky strategy in 19 of 21 trials. In other words, most juncos threatened with starvation take risks rather than choosing certain rewards. In a grim nutritional environment, a genome that encodes risk seeking has a fitness advantage because risk taking provides a positive probability of producing offspring.

Biologists also explored junco risk preferences in a bountiful environment. In this case, they fed the birds at a rate exceeding the subsistence level. The ideas was to get the birds to believe that they were on a sustainable path, with no concerns about survival. Then the biologists gave the birds the same choice between a certain outcome (three seeds) and a risky strategy (equal chances of one or five seeds). In this case of being primed for a bountiful environment, the birds choose the certain reward in 26 of 34 trials, revealing risk aversion. The birds chose the risky strategy in only two trials, and were indifferent in the remaining trials. Like many other creatures, most juncos play it safe when survival is not an issue.

These experiments suggest that the junco genome encodes flexible risk preferences. Juncos are risk-averse in favorable conditions, but risk seeking in unfavorable conditions. This sort of flexible behavior has been observed in other species, including bumblebees, sparrows, and common shrews (Kacelnik and Bateson 1996).

Review the Concepts 23.3

1. An individual whose genome encodes risk seeking [___]. (plays it safe, plays a lottery, is indifferent between playing it safe and playing a lottery)

2. Consider an unfavorable nutritional environment where the certain outcome generates a zero reproduction rate. Natural selection favors risk [___]. (seeking, neutrality, aversion)

3. The dark-eyed junco has flexible risk preferences: the birds display [___] in a favorable nutrition environment and [___] in an unfavorable nutrition environment. (risk seeking, risk aversion; risk neutrality, risk aversion; risk aversion, risk seeking; risk aversion, risk neutrality)

Takeaways

1. A risk-averse individual plays it safe (chooses the certain outcome) rather than playing a lottery with an expected value equal to the certain outcome.

2. In an uncertain environment, geometric mean fitness is a suitable metric for reproductive fitness.

3. If the expected reproduction rate of a risky strategy equals the certain rate, a genome that encodes risk aversion propagates in the population, while a genome that encodes risk neutrality disappears.

4. A genome wins a fitness contest because individuals with the genome instinctively choose the strategy with greater reproductive fitness in a specific environment.

5. In an environment with a relatively large reward for risk taking, the expected reproduction rate of the risky strategy exceeds the certain rate.

6. In an environment with a relatively large reward for risk taking, genomes that encode risk neutrality and weak risk aversion propagate in the population, while a genome that encodes strong risk aversion disappears.

7. In an unfavorable nutritional environment where the certain outcome generates a reproduction rate of zero, natural selection favors risk seeking.

Discuss the Concepts

1. *Certain versus Risky Strategy.* Consider an environment where a certain nutrition strategy generates a reproduction rate $r = 6$. The risky strategy generates $r_L = 4$ and $r_H = 8$ with equal probability.

   a. A genome encoded for [___] (risk neutrality, risk aversion) will win a fitness contest because [___].

   b. The two strategies would be equivalent in terms of reproductive fitness if $r_L = 4$ and $r_H = $ [___].

2. *Risky versus Certain Strategy.* Consider an environment where a certain nutrition strategy generates a constant reproduction rate $r = 6$. The risky strategy generates $r_L = 4$ and $r_H = 10$ with equal probability. A genome encoded for [___] (risk neutrality, risk aversion) will win a fitness contest because [___].

Apply the Concepts

1. *Numbers for Chapter Opener.* Consider the chapter opener. Consult Math 23.1 for the general expression for geometric mean fitness. Recall that the probability of the low outcome is 1/10 and the probability of the high outcome is 9/10. The fitness of the certain outcome (50 eggs on a wild site) is $G(50) = 50$.

   a. Suppose a butterfly lays all 100 eggs on the farm, so $(r_L, r_H) = (0, 100)$. The fitness of the risky strategy is $G(0, 100) = $ [___]. The [___] (farm, wild) strategy is superior in terms of fitness.

b. Suppose a butterfly chooses a mixed strategy, with 80 eggs on the farm and 10 surviving eggs (out of 20 laid) on the wild site. In other words, $(r_L, r_H) =$ (10, 80). The fitness of this mixed strategy is $G(10, 80) = $ [___]. The [___] (farm, wild, mixed) strategy is superior in terms of fitness.

2. *More Favorable Lottery.* Consider an offspring lottery with equal chances of either one or six offspring per parent. As in the text, the certain outcome is $r = 2$. Initially, there are three genomes that encode risk behavior: risk neutrality (RN), weak risk aversion (WRA), and strong risk aversion (SRA). For WRA, taking a risk is instinctive if the expected value of the lottery is at least 10 percent greater than the certain outcome. For SRA, taking a risk is instinctive if the expected value of the lottery is at least twice the certain outcome.

   a. The fitness of the lottery is $G(1,6) = $ [___], compared to $G(2) = $ [___] for the certain outcome.

   b. Genome RN [___] (will, will not) survive because [___].

   c. Genome WRA [___] (will, will not) survive because [___].

   d. Genome SRA [___] (will, will not) survive because [___].

3. *Lottery 3–7.* Consider an offspring lottery with equal chances of either three or seven offspring per parent. The certain outcome is $r = 5$.

   a. The fitness of the certain outcome is $G(5) = $ [___], compared to $G(3, 7) = $ [___] for the lottery.

   b. Suppose the value of r_L is fixed at $r_L = 3$. For fitness equivalence, the value of r_H must be at least [___].

   c. Draw the iso-fitness curve and identify two points on the curve.

4. *Lottery 3–7 with Higher Probability of Success.* Consider an offspring lottery with a 20 percent chance of three offspring per parent and an 80 percent chance of seven offspring per parent. The certain outcome is $r = 6.2$.

   a. The fitness of the lottery is $G(3, 7) = $ [___], compared to $G(6.2) = $ [___] for the certain outcome.

   b. Suppose the value of r_L is fixed at $r_L = 3$. For fitness equivalence, the value of r_H must be at least [___].

5. *Genome Survival.* Consider an offspring lottery with a 20 percent chance of three offspring per parent and an 80 percent chance of 10 offspring per parent. The certain outcome is $r = 6.2$. An individual with weak risk aversion will take a risk if the expected value of the risky strategy is at least 20 percent higher than the certain outcome. An individual with strong risk aversion will take a risk if the expected value of the risky strategy is at least 40 percent greater than the certain outcome.

   a. The fitness of the lottery is $G(3, 10) = $ [___] compared to $G(6.2) = $ [___] for the certain outcome.

   b. A genome that encodes risk neutrality [___] (will, will not) survive because [___].

   c. A genome that encodes weak risk aversion [___] (will, will not) survive because [___]

   d. A genome that encodes strong risk aversion [___] (will, will not) survive because [___].

Math Solution

Math 23.1:   Fitness Equivalence

The geometric mean fitness of a risky strategy with equal chances of r_L and r_H is

$$G(r_L, r_H) = r_L^{1/2} \cdot r_H^{1/2}$$

where r_L is the reproduction rate for the low outcome and r_H is the reproduction rate for the high outcome. The fitness of the certain outcome with reproduction rate r is

$$G(r) = r$$

The fitness of the risky strategy will equal the fitness of a safe strategy if

$$r = r_L^{1/2} \cdot r_H^{1/2}$$

To derive an expression for the iso-fitness curve, solve for r_H in terms of r and r_L:

$$r_H = \frac{r^2}{r_L}$$

The iso-fitness curve is negatively sloped and convex: as r_L increases, the value of r_H required to maintain a fixed fitness level decreases at a decreasing rate. In addition, an increase in certain reproduction rate (and certain fitness) r shifts the curve upward. In our example with $r = 2$, the equation for the iso-fitness curve is

$$r_H = \frac{4}{r_L}$$

Bargaining and the Endowment Effect 24

> Nobody ever saw a dog make a fair and deliberate exchange of one bone for another with another dog. … But man has almost constant occasion for the help of his brethren, and it is in vain for him to expect it from their benevolence only. He will be more likely to prevail if he can interest their self-love in his favour, and show them that it is for their own advantage to do for him what he requires of them.
>
> —Adam Smith, *An Inquiry into the Nature and Causes of the Wealth of Nations*

This chapter explores a possible connection between the endowment effect and bargaining in a hunter-gatherer exchange economy. The key issue is whether the endowment effect generates fitness benefits for humans in a hunter-gatherer exchange economy. If so, it is possible that modern humans who experience the endowment effect are acting on instincts that were encoded in the genomes of their hunter-gatherer ancestors.

> endowment effect: willingness to accept (WTA) > willingness to pay (WTP)

In other words, a person demands more to give up an asset (WTA) than he or she would offer to acquire it (WTP).

Learning Objectives: The Explainer

After mastering this chapter, you will be able to explain each of the following statements.

1. In a hunter-gatherer exchange economy, exchange allows balanced consumption and increases the reproductive fitness of hunters and gatherers.

2. The endowment effect increases an individual's bargaining power, increasing his or her equilibrium fitness at the expense of others.

3. The fitness advantage of a genome that encodes the endowment effect will cause the genome to propagate in a population.

4. For an economy as a whole, the endowment effect causes imbalanced consumption and lower reproductive fitness.

A Hunter-Gatherer Exchange Economy

In this part of the chapter we introduce a simple model of a hunter-gatherer exchange economy. The model incorporates key features of the environment during the millions of years over which natural selection shaped the human genome. The model comes from Huck, Kirchsteiger, and Oechssler (2005). We use the model to explore the connection between natural selection and the endowment effect.

Hunter-Gatherer Fitness

Consider a hunter-gatherer economy with two types of people: hunters (H) and gatherers (G). For example, a hunter could catch fish (x for xobos), while a gatherer could collect tubers (y for yams). At the end of each day, a hunter and a gatherer have an opportunity to exchange products. Suppose each hunter harvests one kilo of fish, and each gatherer harvests one kilo of tubers. The common fitness function shows how bundles of fish and tubers translate into nutrition and thus reproductive fitness:

$$f(x,y) = x^{1/2} + y^{1/2}$$

For example, if there is no exchange, each person will keep the harvested fish or tubers. In this case, each person has a fitness of one:

$$f_H = x^{1/2} = 1^{1/2} = 1 \qquad f_G = y^{1/2} = 1^{1/2} = 1$$

In contrast, if the two people divide the harvests equally (1/2 kilo of each product for each person), each person's fitness is roughly 1.41:

$$f_H = x^{1/2} + y^{1/2} = 0.50^{1/2} + 0.50^{1/2} = 1.41$$

$$f_G = x^{1/2} + y^{1/2} = 0.50^{1/2} + 0.50^{1/2} = 1.41$$

In other words, a balanced diet is superior to an exclusive diet. As a result, the two people have an incentive to exchange fish and tubers. The superiority of a balanced diet results from the fitness function, which exhibits diminishing marginal fitness for each product.

Edgeworth Box and Gains from Exchange

Figure 24.1 uses an Edgeworth box to illustrate the hunter-gatherer economy. The width of the box is 1 kilogram of fish, and the height is 1 kilogram of tubers.

- *Hunter orientation point: southwest corner.* A move to the right increases the hunter's fish consumption, and a move upward increases the hunter's tuber consumption.
- *Gatherer orientation point: northeast corner.* A move to the left increases fish consumption, and a move downward increases tuber consumption.

Point *e* shows the endowment point, with all the fish (1 kilo) harvested by the hunter and all the tubers (1 kilo) harvested by the gatherer. Point *i* shows the allocation with equal division of the two products: each person gets 0.50 kilo of fish and 0.50 kilo of tubers. Point *j* shows an allocation under which the hunter gets more than half of both goods: the hunter gets 0.80 kilo of fish and 0.60 kilo of tubers, while the gatherer gets only 0.20 kilo of fish and only 0.40 kilo of tubers.

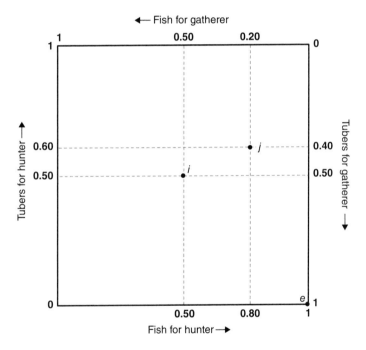

FIGURE 24.1: Edgeworth Box for an Exchange Economy

In a system of voluntary exchange, people will trade away from the endowment point if exchange increases the fitness of each person. Figure 24.2 shows the indifference curves and at-least-as-good sets for the endowment point.

- *Hunter.* The black indifference curve shows the bundles of fish and tubers that generate the same fitness as the endowment point *e*. For any allocation to the northeast of the indifference curve, the hunter's fitness is higher. For example, the fitness level at the endowment point is 1 util, compared to roughly 1.41 at point *i*. Utility is even higher for the hunter at point *j* because the hunter gets more fish and more tubers.

- *Gatherer.* The light-gray indifference curve shows the bundles of fish and tubers that generate the same fitness level as the endowment point *e*. For any allocation to the southwest of the indifference curve, the gatherer's fitness is higher. For example, the fitness level at the endowment point is 1 util, compared to roughly 1.41 at point *i*. At point *j*, the gatherer's fitness is greater than 1.0 because point *j* is to the southwest of the endowment indifference curve. But the gatherer's fitness at point *j* is lower than fitness at point *i* because at point *j*, the gatherer gets less of both goods.

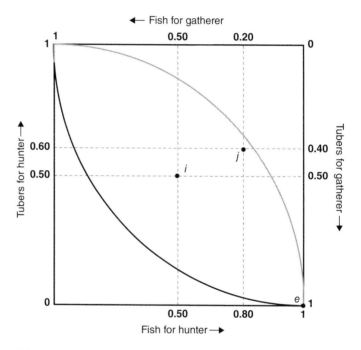

FIGURE 24.2: Endowment, Indifference Curves, and At-Least-as-Good Sets

Bargaining and Equilibrium

When the two people meet for the exchange of fish and tubers, they will bargain over how to divide the two products. In Figure 24.3, the equilibrium is at the center of the Edgeworth box at point *i*. The black curve shows the hunter's indifference curve for the endowment fitness level. The light-gray curve shows the gatherer's indifference curve for the endowment fitness level. The equilibrium exchange rate is 1 kilo of tubers per kilo of fish. Each person exchanges half of his or her endowment for an equal quantity of the other good, so each person gets half of each product. In other words, we get a symmetric equilibrium, with the same outcome for each person. Each person reaches the maximum nutritional fitness $f_H = f_G = 1.41$, an improvement over the fitness level of 1.0 in the absence of exchange.

What is the intuition for the symmetric Nash equilibrium? The solution to the bargaining process is at the center of the area between the two endowment indifference curves, meaning that the two people share equally in the gain from

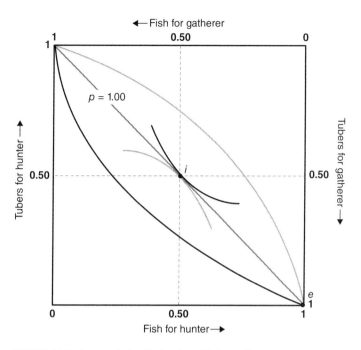

FIGURE 24.3: Symmetric Equilibrium in an Exchange Economy

exchange. This is sensible because the two people have the same fitness function, which is symmetric with respect to the two products. In a hunter-gatherer economy, we would expect the people involved in exchange to have similar genomes, so the assumption of a common fitness function is reasonable. We also assume that the two people are equally skilled in bargaining.

For the equilibrium allocation shown in Figure 24.3, each person maximizes fitness, subject to a budget constraint. The budget line starts at the endowment point (e), and its slope is the exchange rate, the rate at which the two people exchange tubers for fish. In Figure 24.3, the slope of the budget line is one, indicating a one-for-one exchange of tubers for fish. In other words, the price of one kilo of fish is one kilo of tubers. As explained in a course in intermediate microeconomics, a utility-maximizing consumer chooses the product bundle at which the marginal rate of substitution (MRS) between two products equals the price ratio. At the equilibrium point i, the hunter's MRS (the slope of the indifference curve) equals the price ratio (the slope of the budget line). Similarly, the gatherer's MRS equals the price ratio. Each person equates his or her MRS to the common price ratio, so each person maximizes fitness.

In a formal analysis of the hunter-gatherer model, we could use the **Nash bargaining solution**, a concept from cooperative game theory. Math 24.1 summarizes the Nash solution concept for a simple exchange economy. A formal analysis of our simple hunter-gatherer model, with symmetric preferences and endowments, generates a symmetric Nash equilibrium. In the Nash equilibrium, the exchange rate is one, and the two products are divided equally between the two people. As a result, there is a common fitness level $f_H = f_G = 1.41$.

Review the Concepts 24.1

1. In the model of the exchange economy, a balanced diet is [___] to an exclusive diet because the utility function features [___] marginal fitness for each product. (superior, constant; inferior, increasing; superior, diminishing; equivalent, constant)

2. In the Edgeworth box, the area between the endowment-point indifference curves shows the allocations that [___]. (increase the fitness of the hunter and decrease the fitness of the gatherer, increase the fitness of the hunter and the gatherer, decrease the fitness of the hunter and the gatherer)

3. Under a system of voluntary exchange, the hunter and the gatherer will trade to a point in the Edgeworth box where [___]. (the hunter MRS equals the gatherer MRS, the hunter MRS equals the exchange rate, the indifference curves are tangent)

24.2   Natural Selection: Bargaining Outcomes

We can use the model of the hunter-gatherer economy to explore the role of natural selection in the emergence of the endowment effect. The analytic framework comes from Huck, Kirchsteiger, and Oechssler (2005). At first glance, it may appear that a person with a genome that encodes the endowment effect has a fitness disadvantage. As we saw in an earlier chapter, the endowment effect reduces the number of transactions: a person who experiences the endowment effect has fewer opportunities for mutually beneficial exchange. That sounds like a fitness disadvantage, and we know that natural selection eliminates harmful features of a genome. This raise an important question.

Why has the endowment effect persisted, despite its harmful effects?

Endowment Effect and Nash Equilibrium

As a starting point, suppose a hunter-gatherer economy has reached the symmetric Nash equilibrium for several consecutive time periods. Suppose that a hunter then experiences a genetic mutation that causes the hunter to become oddly possessive of harvested fish. The hunter's utility is the sum of fitness and the endowment effect:

$$u_H(x, y) = x_H^{1/2} + y_H^{1/2} + e_H \cdot x_H$$

where x_H is the hunter's quantity of fish and the endowment effect is represented by $e_H > 0$. For each kilo of the fish held by the hunter after exchange, there is a utility boost of $e_H > 0$. For example, if $e_H = 1/5$, the utility boost from keeping the daily harvest is $1/5 \times 1$ kilo of fish, or 1/5 util. In the other direction, for each unit of fish sacrificed in exchange for tubers, the hunter experiences a utility loss equal to e_H. The hunter has a new trade-off: the exchange of fish for tubers may increase fitness by providing a more balanced diet, but also causes a utility loss because of the endowment effect.

Figure 24.4 uses an Edgeworth box to illustrate the endowment effect with $e_H = 1/2$. The endowment effect increases the hunter's value of fish, so it increases the hunter's marginal rate of substitution of fish for tubers. Starting from the endowment point, the hunter sacrifices fish to get tubers, and the endowment effect means the hunter requires more tubers to give up each fish. The hunter's endowment indifference curve pivots upward, indicating an increase in the marginal rate of substitution.

Consider the implications for the equilibrium in the hunter-gatherer economy. Suppose that the Nash solution is at the center of the area between the indifference curve of the hunter and the indifference curve of the gatherer. In other words, the two people share equally the gain from exchange. In Figure 24.4, point k shows the center of the area between the indifference curves.

- *Hunter.* The hunter gets 71 percent of the fish and 42 percent of the tubers.
- *Gatherer.* The gatherer gets 29 percent of the fish and 58 percent of the tubers.

The exchange rate (price) is 1.44 kilos of tubers per kilo of fish: the hunter exchanges 0.29 kilo of fish to get 0.42 kilo of tubers. At the equilibrium, the indifference curves are tangent, and the marginal rate of substitution for each person equals the equilibrium price of 1.44.

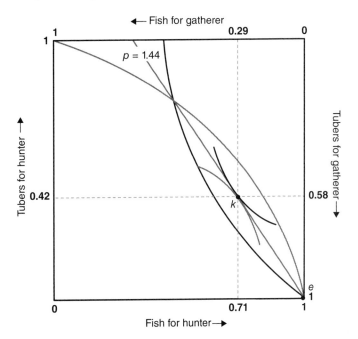

FIGURE 24.4: Nash Solution with Hunter Endowment Effect

The endowment effect increases the fitness of the hunter at the expense of the gatherer. The fitness levels are computed as

$$f_H = x_H^{1/2} + y_H^{1/2} = 0.71^{1/2} + 0.42^{1/2} = 1.49$$

$$f_G = x_G^{1/2} + y_G^{1/2} = 0.29^{1/2} + 0.58^{1/2} = 1.30$$

The endowment effect provides a fitness advantage to the hunter because the hunter's higher marginal rate of substitution distorts the bargaining process in the hunter's favor. The equilibrium price of fish increases, so the hunter gets more tubers per fish. Intuitively, the oddball hunter really likes his fish and drives a harder bargain in sacrificing fish to get tubers. The result is a higher price for fish and a better bargaining outcome for the hunter.

Consider the implications of the endowment effect for natural selection. In our simple two-person example, the oddball hunter acts instinctively in the bargaining process, and achieves a higher level of nutritional fitness. The superior nutrition translates into greater reproductive fitness: the hunter will produce a relatively large number of offspring. Some of the offspring will inherit the genome that encodes the endowment effect, and they will pass on the genome to the next generation. Naturally, we expect some of the offspring to be hunters and others to be gatherers, so over time the endowment effect will spread to both occupations. At the same time, people with a genome that does not encode the endowment effect will fare badly in exchange, so they have inferior nutrition and thus lower reproductive fitness. Over time, the share of the population with the endowment-effect genome will increase.

Disagreement Value and the Nash Bargaining Solution

We can use the concept of the **Nash disagreement value** to provide additional insights into the fitness advantage of the endowment effect. The disagreement value is defined as the utility level achieved by a person if the two people fail to reach a bargaining agreement. In casual terms, the disagreement value is the utility generated by the fall-back position. When bargaining fails, each person keeps his or her endowment—one kilo of fish for the hunter and one kilo of tubers for the gatherer. If the hunter experiences an endowment effect, the disagreement values in our example are

$$u_H \left(disagree \right) = x^{1/2} + e_H = 1^{1/2} + e_H = 1 + e_H$$

$$u_G \left(disagree \right) = y^{1/2} = 1^{1/2} = 1$$

The hunter's disagreement value is boosted by the endowment effect $(e_H > 0)$. For example, if $e_H = 1/5$, the hunter's disagreement value is 1.20, compared to 1.00 for the gatherer. As a result, the hunter has less to lose if bargaining breaks down. The hunter can use the superior fallback position to negotiate a

more favorable exchange, with a higher price for fish. A higher fish price means more food for the hunter, and thus a higher fitness level. Math 24.2 shows how to incorporate the endowment effect into the Nash bargaining solution.

The Endowment Effect and Group Fitness

We've seen that an endowment effect for an individual generates a fitness advantage that propagates in the population. Suppose that eventually, everyone in the economy experiences an endowment effect of the same strength. In this case, the bargaining power of a gatherer will equal the bargaining power of a hunter, and the Nash disagreement values will be equal as well. The result is a symmetric equilibrium that differs from the symmetric equilibrium that occurs in an economy without an endowment effect. The endowment effect tilts consumption bundles in favor of the product harvested by an individual: hunters consume more fish, and gatherers consume more yams. In other words, the endowment effect generates imbalanced consumption for both hunters and gatherers.

Recall that with the symmetric fitness function, fitness is maximized with a balanced consumption, with equal quantities of the two products. Because the endowment effect eventually generates imbalanced consumption for everyone in the hunter-gatherer economy, it decreases the common fitness level. Figure 24.5 shows an example from Widget 24.1 (available at www.oup.com/us/osullivan1e). The endowment effect is represented by $e_H = e_G = 0.50$. For the typical hunter, the consumption of fish is over three times the consumption of tubers (0.78 versus 0.22). The typical gatherer has the same imbalance in favor of tubers. The common utility is 1.352, compared to 1.41 in the absence of the endowment effect. The lesson is that although the endowment effect increases the fitness of an individual, it decreases the common fitness of the population.

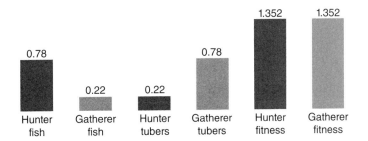

FIGURE 24.5: The Endowment Effect Decreases Common Fitness

Egalitarian Economy and the Endowment Effect

Our discussion suggests that bargaining in a hunter-gatherer economy contributes to the propagation of a genome that encodes the endowment effect. An interesting question is whether a society that does not use bargaining to allocate resources will experience the endowment effect. A recent paper by Apicella et al. (2014) addresses this question with a study of the Hazda people, an isolated hunter-gatherer group in Tanzania. The group is fully egalitarian, with equal sharing of food and thus no bargaining. The authors show that the group does not experience the endowment effect. This result is consistent with the theory of Huck, Kirchsteiger, and Oechssler (2005) that the endowment effect can be explained by bargaining in a hunter-gatherer economy.

Review the Concepts 24.2

1. An endowment effect experienced by the hunter [___] the hunter's MRS of fish for tubers, causing the endowment indifference curve to pivot [___]. (increases, downward; decreases, upward; decreases, downward; increases, upward)

2. An endowment effect experienced by the hunter [___] the equilibrium exchange rate (tubers per fish) and tilts consumption and fitness in favor of the [___]. (decreases, gatherer; increases, hunter; increases, gatherer; decreases, hunter)

3. An endowment effect that originates as a single genetic mutation is likely to [___]. (disappear, have no effect, propagate).

4. An endowment effect experienced by the hunter [___] the hunter's disagreement value. (increases, decreases, does not affect)

5. An increase in the hunter's disagreement value [___] the hunter's bargaining power and and tilts equilibrium consumption and fitness in favor of the [___]. (increases, gatherer; decreases, hunter; increases, hunter; decreases, gatherer)

6. Suppose everyone in an exchange economy experiences an equally strong endowment effect. Consumption is [___]. Compared to an economy without an endowment effect, the equilibrium fitness is [___]. (imbalanced, higher; imbalanced, lower; balanced, lower; balanced, higher)

7. Use Widget 24.1 (available at www.oup.com/us/osullivan1e). Suppose the hunter's endowment effect is represented by $e_H = 0.40$. The hunter gets [___] percent of the fish and [___] percent of the tubers. The hunter's utility is higher by roughly [___]. (68, 44, 0.17; 60, 40, 0.10)

Key Terms

Nash bargaining solution, p. 419   Nash disagreement value, p. 422

Takeaways

1. The endowment effect is that the willingness to accept exceeds the willingness to pay: a person demands more to give up an object than he or she would offer to acquire it.

2. The endowment effect increases the marginal rate of substitution between the possessed good and other goods, improving the bargaining position of the person with the endowment effect.

3. In a hunter-gatherer environment, a genome encoded for the endowment effect has a bargaining advantage that increases reproductive fitness.

4. If a genome that encodes the endowment effect propagates, the equilibrium is characterized by imbalanced consumption and lower economy-wide reproductive fitness.

Discuss the Concepts

1. *Unbalanced Consumption.* Consider a hunter-gatherer exchange economy with one unit of x and one unit of y. The common fitness function is $f(x,y) = x^{1/2} + y^{1/2}$. Suppose the allocation is (3/4, 1/4) for the hunter and gatherer and (1/4, 3/4) for the gatherer.

   a. The allocation is Pareto [____].

   b. Design a Pareto improvement.

2. *Weak Endowment Effect.* Use Widget 24.1 (available at www.oup.com/us/osullivan1e). Suppose the hunter experiences an endowment effect, with $e_H = 0.20$. The equilibrium allocation is [____] for the hunter and [____] for the gatherer. The hunter's fitness is [____], compared to [____] for the gatherer.

3. *Endowment Effect versus Self-Sufficiency.* Consider two independent hunter-gatherer economies. In economy S (for specialized), each individual specializes in one product (either $x = 1$ or $y = 1$) and engages in exchange, given a common endowment effect $e_H = e_G = 0.50$. In economy D (for diversified), each individual is self-sufficient, with $x_D = y_D$. In economy D, there is no exchange, so there is no endowment effect.

   a. Define total productivity in economy D as $q = x_D + y_D$. We expect q to be [____] ($< 1, > 1, = 1$) because [____].

   b. Reproductive fitness will be greater in economy D if [____]. Provide a numerical example.

Apply the Concepts

1. *Exchange Rate and Fitness.* Consider a two-person exchange economy with the common fitness function $f(x,y) = x^{1/2} + y^{1/2}$. The hunter harvests one kilogram of fish and the gatherer harvests one kilogram of tubers. Suppose the hunter experiences an endowment effect, and the outcome of the Nash bargaining is an exchange rate of 1.5 grams of tubers per gram of fish. Suppose the hunter exchanges one-quarter kilo of fish for tubers. The fitness of the hunter is $f(x_H, y_H) =$ [_____]. The fitness of the gatherer is $f(x_G, y_G) =$ [_____].

2. *Nash Bargaining Solution.* Consider the Nash bargaining function $N(x, y)$ in Math 24.2. Suppose the value of the endowment-effect parameter for the hunter is $e_H = 1/5$. For the gatherer, $e_G = 0$. Solve for the Nash equilibrium, either using conventional optimization techniques or Widget 24.1 (available at www.oup.com/us/osullivan1e).

   a. The consumption bundles are $(x_H, y_H) =$ [_____] and $(x_G, y_G) =$ [_____].

   b. The fitness values are $f_H =$ [_____] and $f_G =$ [_____].

   c. The exchange rate is [_____] grams of tubers per gram of fish.

3. *Land Bridge and Natural Selection.* Tribe E occupies an isolated island, and the tribe's genome encodes the endowment effect, with $e_H = e_G = 0.50$. Tribe F occupies a nearby isolated island, and the tribe's genome does not encode the endowment effect: $e_H = e_G = 0$. The two tribes are equal in population. The two island are separated by a channel that hosts creatures whose genome encodes an aquatic lifestyle and fire-breathing extermination of humans. Suppose change in climatic conditions decreases sea levels, generating a land bridge that connects the islands: two isolated islands become a single island. Suppose the tribes do not interbreed, so each genome remains distinct.

   a. Predict the implications of the land bridge for the genetic composition of the new island. Over time, what happens to the population shares of the two genomes?

   b. Illustrate your answer with a simple numerical example with the common fitness function $f(x, y) = x^{1/2} + y^{1/2}$.

4. Specialized versus Diversified. Consider two independent hunter-gatherer economies. In economy S (for specialized), each individual specializes in one product (either $x = 1$ or $y = 1$) and engages in exchange, given a common endowment effect $e_H = e_G = 0.50$. In economy D (for diversified), each individual is self-sufficient, with $x_D = y_D = 0.40$. In economy D, there is no exchange, so there is no endowment effect.

   a. In economy D, $x_D + y_D < 1$. This is evidence of the productivity benefit of [_____].

   b. Reproductive fitness is greater under [_____] (S, D): [_____] > [_____].

c. The two systems are equivalent in terms of reproductive fitness for $x_D = y_D$ = [____].

5. *Endowment Effect, Fitness, and Transactions.* Consider a genetic mutation that encodes a common endowment effect in a particular genome.

   a. The mutation [____] (increases, decreases, does not change) the fitness of the genome.

   b. Relate your answer to our earlier discussion of the implications of the endowment effect on the the number of transactions in an economy.

Math Solutions

Math 24.1: Nash Equilibrium with Common Utility Function

Consider an exchange economy with two goods (x, y) and endowments $(1, 0)$ for A and $(0, 1)$ for B. In other words, A starts with all the x and B starts with all the y. The utility functions are $u_A(x, y)$ and $u_B(x, y)$. For each person, the gain from exchange is the utility generated by the bundle generated by exchange minus the utility from the endowment:

$$v_A(x,y) = u_A(x,y) - u_A(1,0) \qquad v_B(x,y) = u_B(x,y) - u_B(0,1)$$

The Nash bargaining solution is the allocation that maximizes the product of the gain functions:

$$N(x,y) = v_A(x,y) \cdot v_B(x,y)$$

In the case of a common utility function, the Nash bargaining solution is an equal division of the two goods: each person gets $x = y = 1/2$.

Math 24.2: Nash Bargaining Equilibrium

The hunter's gain function incorporates nutritional fitness, the endowment effect, and the disagreement value:

$$v_H(x,y) = x_H^{1/2} + y_H^{1/2} + e_H \cdot x_H - (1 + e_H)$$

The gatherer does not experience an endowment effect, so the gain function is

$$v_G(x, y) = x_G^{1/2} + y_G^{1/2} - 1$$

The Nash function is the product of the two gain functions:

$$N(x,y) = v_H(x,y) \cdot v_G(x,y)$$

Use the resource constraints to simplify to two equilibrium variables (x_H and y_H). In an economy with one unit of each good,

$$x_G = 1 - x_H \qquad y_G = 1 - y_H$$

The Nash function is

$$N(x,y) = \left(x_H^{1/2} + y_H^{1/2} + e_H \cdot x_H - (1 + e_H) \right) \cdot \left((1 - x_H)^{1/2} + (1 - y_H)^{1/2} - 1 \right)$$

We can use conventional optimization methods to solve for the values of x_H and y_H that maximize the value of the Nash function, given a value for the endowment-effect parameter e_H.

GLOSSARY

advantaged inequity Inequity resulting from greater wealth: Bett experiences advantaged inequity relative to Alf if Bett's wealth exceeds Alf's wealth. Measured by parameter γ.

allele A gene variant, such as green for the eye-color gene.

anchoring effect A person's valuation of an object is positively correlated with recently generated—and perhaps irrelevant—numbers.

asymmetry between loss and gain In decision making, the weight for loss exceeds the weight for gain. The relative weight for loss is $\lambda > 1$.

availability heuristic Strong memories are more readily recalled and have a relatively large effect on the estimated probability of an event.

biological evolution A change over time in the population shares of different genetic types.

certainty equivalent of a lottery The certain value that generates utility equal to the utility value of a lottery.

choice variable A variable whose value is chosen by a decision-maker.

clueless decision-maker An individual who is not aware of his or her present bias. Sometimes labeled "naif."

cognitive bias A systematic pattern of faulty thinking that tilts a person's decision-making in a predictable direction.

comparative statics Shows the effect of a change in the value of a parameter on the value of a choice variable or an equilibrium variable.

conditional cooperation An individual links his or her contribution to a public good to the contribution of others.

confirmation bias A person is selective in acquiring information, focusing on information that confirms prior beliefs.

conventional discounting (exponential) The current value of \$1 to be received one period later is $\delta < 1$. The current value of \$1 to be received t periods later is δ^t.

cultural learning The transmission of knowledge from one generation to the next.

decoupling A decision-maker separates the cost of an action from its benefit.

decoy effect The presence of an object B- that is clearly inferior to object B increases the likelihood that a person will prefer B to an otherwise equivalent object A.

decreasing sensitivity As the magnitude of a change increases, a person experiences a progressively smaller marginal effect.

decreasing sensitivity to gain As the magnitude of a gain increases, the marginal utility per dollar gained decreases. Measured by the parameter $\mu < 1$.

decreasing sensitivity to loss As the magnitude of a loss increases, the marginal disutility per dollar lost decreases. Measured by the parameter $\mu < 1$.

default effect People often passively accept the default option rather than carefully evaluating the merits of alternative options.

dictator game A person decides how much of a gain to share with another person.

disdvantaged inequity Inequity resulting from lesser wealth: Bett experiences disadvantaged inequity relative to Alf if Bett's wealth is less than Alf's wealth. Measured by parameter ε.

disposition puzzle In an asset market with a recent history of increasing prices, a seller's asking price is relatively low, and assets sell quickly. In an asset market with a recent history of decreasing prices, a seller's asking price is relatively high, and assets sell slowly.

DNA A molecule that carries instructions on how to build and maintain the cells of an organism.

endowment effect The willingness to accept exceeds the willingness to pay: a person demands more to give up an object than he or she would offer to acquire it.

equal-sharing price The price that divides the gain from exchange equally between consumer and producer.

equilibrium variable The value is determined within the market or other economic environment.

equimarginal principle To allocate a fixed amount of a resource to competing uses, choose the feasible bundle (adding-up constraint) that equates the marginal benefit across the competing uses (**equimarginal rule**).

equimarginal rule The marginal benefit of a resource in one use equals the marginal benefit in the other use.

equity-premium puzzle The rate of return on stocks (equities) exceeds the rate of return on bonds by a large margin.

exponential discounting The current value of $1 to be received one period later is $\delta < 1$. The current value of $1 to be received t periods later is δ^t.

faithful imitation Imitating a trusted authority in executing all the steps in a production process without questioning the relevance of individual steps.

fitness The success of an entity in reproducing: the average contribution of a genome to the next generation or succeeding generations.

free rider A person who gets a benefit from a good but does not pay for it.

gambler's fallacy The erroneous belief that the probability of a random event is determined by the past frequency of the event.

gene A distinct portion of an organism's DNA.

genome An organism's complete set of genetic material—all the genes and alleles that constitute the organism's DNA sequences.

geometric mean $g(x_L, x_2, x_3, \dots x_n) = (x_L \cdot x_2 \cdot x_3 \cdot \dots \cdot x_n)^{1/n}$

geometric mean fitness $g(r_1, r_2, r_3, \dots r_T) = (r_1 \cdot r_2 \cdot r_3 \cdot \dots \cdot r_T)^{1/T}$ where r_t is a reproduction rate.

hazard-insurance puzzle Many homeowners underinsure against rare losses from natural hazards such as floods, earthquakes, and tornadoes.

insurance-deductible puzzle Many homeowners who are required to purchase hazard insurance purchase policies with relatively high levels of coverage (low deductibles).

long-term orientation (LTO) A relatively low value on current consumption and thus a small marginal rate of substitution (MRS).

longshot puzzle Racetrack bettors are biased in favor of horses with low probabilities of winning.

loss aversion To avoid a loss equal to x, an individual is willing to forgo a gain equal to $x \cdot \lambda$, where $\lambda > 1$. This is a consequence of the greater weight for loss in decision making: $\lambda > 1$.

marginal benefit The additional benefit from a one-unit increase in the activity.

marginal cost The additional cost from a one-unit increase in the activity.

marginal principle Choose the level of an activity where the marginal benefit equals the marginal cost.

matching pennies A game in which the matcher wins if both players make the same choice (H-H or T-T) and the mismatcher wins if they make different choices (H-T or T-H).

mental accounting A system of organizing economic life under which resources such as income, wealth, and time are segregated into separate accounts.

monetary value of a lottery The weighted sum of the monetary values of different outcomes of a lottery. The weights are the probabilities of the outcomes.

Nash bargaining solution The allocation that maximizes the product of the gain functions of the bargainers.

Nash disagreement value The utility level achieved by a person when two parties fail to reach a bargaining agreement.

Nash equilibrium An allocation such that there is no incentive for unilateral deviation.

natural selection The differential reproduction of classes of entities that differ in one or more characteristics.

numbers-game puzzle People play the numbers game despite a negative monetary value for the lottery.

opportunity cost (*economic cost*) The value of a resource in its next-best use.

other-regarding preferences An individual considers the consequences of his or her decisions on other individuals.

over-imitation The imitation of irrelevant steps in a production process.

overconfidence effect A person over-estimates his or her productivity in a task or in cognitive processing.

parameter (choice environment) A variable whose value is beyond the control of the decision-maker.

parameter (equilibrium environment) A variable whose value is determined outside the market under consideration.

Pareto efficiency A situation in which there are no Pareto improvements.

Pareto efficient allocation An allocation for which there are no Pareto improvements.

Pareto improvement A reallocation that makes at least one person better off without making anyone worse off.

Pareto inefficient allocation An allocation for which there is a Pareto improvement.

pay it forward (PIF) Each consumer voluntarily pays for another consumer.

pay what you want (PWW) Each consumer chooses a price to pay for a product, sometimes constrained by a minimum price.

preproperation Acting to collect a benefit when waiting would be better.

present bias The current value of $1 to be received any time in the future is $\beta < 1$.

probability weighting The decision weight for an outcome differs from the actual probability. In prospect theory, people over-weight rare (low-probability) outcomes and under-weight common (high-probability) outcomes.

procrastination Waiting to incur a cost when acting early would be better.

public good A good that is (i) nonrival (one person's benefit does not reduce another person's benefit) and (ii) nonexcludable (impractical to exclude people who don't pay).

reproductive fitness The success of an entity in reproducing: the average contribution of a genome to the next generation or succeeding generations.

risk aversion The certainty equivalent of a lottery is less than the monetary value of the lottery.

risk neutrality The certainty equivalent of a lottery equals the monetary value of the lottery.

risk seeking The certainty equivalent of a lottery exceeds the monetary value of the lottery.

savvy decision-maker An individual who is aware of his or her present bias. Sometimes labeled "sophisticate."

self-regarding preferences An individual ignores the consequences of his or her decisions on other individuals.

short-term orientation (STO) A relatively high value on current consumption and thus a large marginal rate of substitution (MRS).

social capital The features of social organization that improve cooperation and promote efficiency.

social norm A context-specific rule for the behavior of members of a social group.

strong reciprocity A tendency to voluntarily cooperate and to punish individuals who do not cooperate.

third-party punishment An individual with no direct stake in an interaction between individual 1 and individual 2 incurs a cost to punish a norm violator.

time inconsistency A plan for future consumption is discarded rather than executed.

trust game An investor transfers resources to a producer, who increases the value of the resources and transfers a share of the new value to the investor.

ultimatum game A proposer proposes how much of a gain to share with a responder. If the responder rejects the proposal, each person gets nothing.

utility value of a lottery The weighted sum of the utility values from different outcomes of a lottery. The weights are normally the probabilities of the outcomes. In prospect theory, the weights are related to, but not necessarily equal to, the probabilities of the outcomes.

REFERENCES

Abdellaoui, M., H. Bleichrodt, and C. Paraschiv. 2007. Loss aversion under prospect theory: A parameter-free measurement. *Management Science* 57 (5): 1659–87.

Adams, P. A., and Adams, J. K. 1960. Confidence in the recognition and reproduction of words difficult to spell. *The American Journal of Psychology* 73 (4): 544–52.

Ainslie, G. W. 1974. Impulse control in pigeons. *Journal of the Experimental Analysis of Behavior* 21 (3): 485–89.

Akerlof, George A., and Rachel E. Kranton. 2000. Economics and identity. *Quarterly Journal of Economics* 115 (3): 715–53.

Akerlof, George A., and Rachel E. Kranton. 2005. Identity and the economics of organizations. *Journal of Economic Perspectives* 19 (1): 9–32.

Akerlof, George A., and Rachel E. Kranton. 2008. Identity, supervision, and work groups. *American Economic Review: Papers and Proceedings* 98 (2): 212–17.

Andreoni, James, and B. Douglas Bernheim. 2009. Social image and the 50–50 norm: A theoretical and experimental analysis of audence effects. *Econometrica* 77 (3): 1607–36.

Apicella, Coren, Eduardo Azevedo, Nicholas Christakis, and James Fowler. 2014. Evolutionary origins of the endowment effect: Evidence from hunter-gatherers. *American Economic Review* 104:1793–805.

Ashraf, Nava, Dean Karlan, and Wesley Yin. 2006. Tying Odysseus to the mast: Evidence from a commitment savings product in the Philippines. *Quarterly Journal of Economics* 121:635–72.

Asturias, Jose. 2006. Why do individuals contribute to public radio? Scholarly Commons, University of Pennsylvania.

Atalay, Kadir, Fayzan Bakhtiar, Stephen Cheung, and Robert Slonim. 2014. Savings and prize-linked savings accounts. *Journal of Economic Behavior & Organization* 107:86–106.

Augenblick, Ned, and Matthew Rabin. (2019). An experiment on time preference and misprediction in unpleasant tasks. *Review of Economic Studies* 86:941–75.

Barron, G., and G. Ursino. 2013. Underweighting rare events in experience-based decisions: Beyond sample error. *Journal of Economic Psychology* 39:278–86.

Barseghyan, Levon, Francesca Molinari, Ted O'Donoghue, and Joshua C. Teitelbaum. 2013. The nature of risk references: Evidence from insurance choices. *American Economic Review* 103:2499–529.

Behne, T., U. Liszkowski, M. Carpenter, and M. Tomasello. 2012. Twelve-month-olds' comprehension and production of pointing. *British Journal of Development Psychology* 30:359–75.

Bellemare, Charles, and Shearer, Bruce. 2009. Gift giving and worker productivity: Evidence from a firm-level experiment. *Games and Economic Behavior* 67:233–44.

Belot, Michele, Vincent P. Crawford, and Cecilia Heyes. 2013. Players of matching pennies automatically imitate opponents' gestures against strong incentives. *PNAS* 110:2763–68.

Berg, Joyce, John Dickhaut, and Kevin McCabe. 1995. Trust, reciprocity, and social history. *Games and Economic Behavior* 10:122–42.

Blurton Jones, N. G. 1991. Tolerated theft: Suggestions about the ecology and evolution of sharing, hoarding, and scrounging, Chapter 7 in *Primate Politics*, edited by G. Schubert and R. D. Masters. Carbondale: Southern Illinois University Press.

Boehm, Christopher. 2012. *Moral Origins: The Evolution of Virtue, Altruism, and Shame.* New York: Basic Books.

Borg, G., H. Daimant, L. Strom, and Y. Zotterman. 1967. The relation between neural and perceptual intensity: A comparative study on the neural and psycholphysical response to taste stimuli. *Journal of Physiology* 192 (13): 13–20.

Bowles, S., and H. Gintis. 2011. *A Cooperative Species: Human Reciprocity and Evolution.* Princeton University Press.

Boyd, Robert, Samuel Bowles, and Herbert Gintis. 2010. Coordinated punishment of defectors sustains cooperation and can proliferate when rare. *Science* 328:617–20.

Brosnan, S. F., O. D. Jones, M. Gardner, S. P. Lambeth, and S. J. Schapiro. 2012. Evolution and the expression of biases: Situational value changes the endowment effect in chimpanzees. *Evolution and Human Behavior* 33 (4): 378–86.

Brosnan, S. F., O. D. Jones, M. C. Mareno, A. S. Richardson, S. P. Lambeth, and S. J. Schapiro. 2007. Endowment effect in chimpanzees. *Current Biology* 17:1–4.

Brown, Alexander L., Eric Zhikang Chua, and Colin F. Camerer. 2009. Learning and visceral temptation in dynamic saving experiments. *Quarterly Journal of Economics* 124 (1): 197–231.

Camerer, Colin, Linda Babcock, George Loewenstein, and Richard Thaler. 1997. Labor supply of New York City cabdrivers: One day at a time. *Quarterly Journal of Economics* 112: 407–41.

Car Talk. 2019. Premium vs. regular. https://www.cartalk.com/content/premium-vs-regular-1.

Caraco, Thomas. 1981. Energy budgets, risk, and foraging preferences in dark-eyed juncos (junco hymalis). *Behavioral Ecology and Sociobiology* 8:213–17.

Carmon, Z, and Ariely, D. 2000. Focusing on the foregone: How value can appear so different to buyers and sellers. *Journal of Consumer Research* 27 (3): 360–70.

Charness, Gary, Ninghau Du, and Chun-Lei Yang. 2011. Trust and trustworthiness reputations in an investment game. *Games and Economic Behavior* 72:361–75.

Chen, Daniel L., Tobias J. Moskowitz, and Kelly Shue. 2016. Decision making under the gambler's fallacy: Evidence from asylum judges, loan officers, and baseball umpires. *Quarterly Journal of Economics* 131:1181–242.

Cohen, D. 1993. Fitness in random environments, in *Adapation in Stochastic Environments*, edited by J. Yoshimura and C. W. Clark. New York: Springer-Verlag.

Conlisk, John. 2011. Professor Zak's empirical studies on trust and oxytocin. *Journal of Economic Behavior and Organization* 78:160–6.

Connolly, Terry, Jochen Reb, and Edgar E. Kausel. 2013. Regret salience and accountability in the decoy effect. *Judgment and Decision Making* 8:136–49.

Constantinople, Christine M., Alex T. Piet, and Carlos D. Brody. 2018. An analysis of decision under risk in rats. bioRxiv. https://doi.org/10.1101/446575.

Cook, Richard, Geoffrey Bird, Gabriele Lunser, Steffen Huck, and Cecilia Heyes. 2012. Automatic imitation in a strategic context: Players of rock-paper-scissors imitate opponents' gestures. *Proceedings of the Royal Society B* 279:780–6.

Dean, L.G., R.L Kendal, S.J. Schapiro, B. Thierry, K.N. Laland. 2012. Identification of the social and cognitive processes underlying human cumulative culture. *Science* 335: 1114-1118.

De Martino, B., C. F. Camerer, and R. Adolphs. 2010. Amygdala damage eliminates monetary loss aversion. *Proceedings of the National Academy of Sciences USA* 107 (8): 3788–92.

Dempster, E. R. 1955. Maintenance of genetic heterogeneity. *Cold Spring Harbor Symposium Quantitative Biology* 20:25–32.

Dhami, Sanjit. 2016. *The Foundations of Behavioral Economic Analysis.* Oxford University Press.

Dohmen, Thomas, Armin Falk, David Huffman, and Uwe Sunde. 2010. Are risk aversion and impatience related to cognitive ability? *American Economic Review* 100:1238–60.

Duflo, Esther, Michael Kremer, and Jonathan Robinson. 2011. Nudging farmers to use fertilizer: Evidence from Kenya. *American Economic Review* 101:2350–90.

Elmore, Ryan, and Andrew Urbaczewski. 2019. Loss aversion in professional golf. https://ssrn.com/abstract=3311649 or http://dx.doi.org/10.2139/ssrn.3311649.

Engel, Christoph. 2011. Dictator games: A meta study. *Experimental Economics* 14:583–610.

Ensminger, Jean, and Joseph Henrich. 2014. *Experimenting with Social Norms*. New York: Russell Sage Foundation.

Falk, Armin, Ernst Fehr, and Urs Fischbacher. 2003. On the nature of fair behavior. *Economic Inquiry* 41: 20–26.

Fehr, Ernst, and Klaus Schmidt. 1999. A theory of fairness, competition, and cooperation. *Quarterly Journal of Economics* 114:817–68.

Fehr, Ernst, and Klaus Schmidt. 2004. A theory of fairness, competition, and cooperation, in *Advances in Behavioral Economics*, edited by Colin Camerer, George Loewenstein, and Matthew Rabin, Chapter 9. Princeton University Press.

Fehr, Ernst, and Klaus Schmidt. 1999. A theory of fairness, competition, and cooperation. *Quarterly Journal of Economics* 114:817–68.

Fehr, Ernst, and Simon Gachter. 2000. Cooperation and punishment in public goods experiments. *American Economic Review* 90:980–94.

Fischbacher, U., C. M. Fong, and E. Fehr. 2009. Fairness, errors, and the power of competition. *Journal of Economic Behavior and Organization* 72:527–45.

Frank, Steven A., and Montgomery Slatkin. 1990. Evolution in a variable environment. *The American Naturalist* 136 (2): 244–60.

Freeman, David. 2016. Revealing naivete and sophistication from procrastination and preproperation. Simon Fraser Department of Economics Working Paper 16–11.

Friedl, Andreas, Katharina Lima de Miranda, and Ulrich Schmidt. 2014. Insurance demand and social comparison: An experimental analysis. *Journal of Risk and Uncertainty* 48: 97–109.

Futuyma, Douglas. 2013. *Evolution*. 3rd ed. Sinauer Associates: Sunderland, MA: Sinauer Associates.

Galor, Oded, and Omer Ozak. 2016. The agricultural origins of time preferences. *American Economic Review* 106:3064–106.

Genesove, David, and Christopher Mayer. 2001. Loss aversion and seller behavior: Evidence from the housing market. *Quarterly Journal of Economics* 116:1233–60.

Gillespie, John H. 1977. Natural selection for variances in offspring numbers: A new evolutionary principle. *The American Naturalist* 111:1010–14.

Gintis, H. 2011. Gene-culture coevolution and the nature of human sociality. *Philosophical Transactions of the Royal Society* 366:878–88.

Glimcher, Paul W. 2011. *Foundations of Neuroeconomic Analysis*. Oxford University Press.

Gneezy U., and J. List. 2006. Putting behavioral economics to work: Testing for gift exchange in labor markets using field experiments. *Econometrica* 74:1365–84.

Gneezy, Uri. 2002. Does high wage lead to high profits? An experimental study of reciprocity using real effort. University of Chicago Working Paper.

Gonzales, Richard, and George Wu. 1999. On the shape of the probability weighting function. *Cognitive Psychology* 38:129–66.

Gouldner, Alvin W. 1960. The norm of reciprocity: A preliminary statement. *American Sociological Review* 25:161–78.

Greenberg, Spencer, and Seth Stephens-Davidowitz. You are not as good as kissing as you think. But you are better at dancing. *New York Times*, April 6, 2019, page SR2.

Hamann, K., F. Warneken, J. R. Greenberg, and M. Tomasello. 2011. Collaboration encourages equal sharing in children but not in chimpanzees. *Nature* 476 (7360): 328–31.

Harbaugh, William T., Kate Krause, and Lise Vesterlund. 2001. Are adults better behaved than children? Age, experience, and the endowment effect. *Economic Letters* 70:175–81.

Hastings, Justine S., and Jesse M. Shapiro. 2013. Fungibility and consumer choice: Evidence from commodity price shocks. *Quarterly Journal of Economics* 128:1149–98.

Haun, D. B, Y. Rekers, and M. Tomasello. 2014. Children conform to the behavior of peers; Great apes stick with what they know. *Psychological Science* 25:2160–67.

Heilbronner, Sarah R., Alexandra G. Rosati, Jeffrey R. Stevens, Brian Hare, and Marc D. Hauser. 2008. A fruit in the hand or two in the bush? Divergent risk preferences in chimpanzees and bonobos. *Biology Letters* 4:246–49.

Henrich, Joseph. 2016. *The Secret of Our Success: How Culture Is Driving Human Evolution, Domesticating our Species, and Making Us Smarter.* Princeton University Press.

Henrich, Joseph. 2020. *The Weirdest People in the World.* New York: Farrar, Straus, and Giroux.

Henrich, Joseph, Jean Ensminger, Abigail Barr, and Richard McEalreath. 2014. Major empirical results: Markets, religion, community size, and the evolution of fairness and punishment. In *Experimenting with Social Norms*, edited by Jean Ensminger and Joseph Henrich, Chapter 4. New York: Russell Sage Foundation.

Hertwig, R., G. Barron, E. U. Weber, and I. Erev. 2004. Decisions from experience and the effect of rare events in risky choice. *American Psychological Society* 18:534–39.

Horner, Victoria, and Andrew Whiten. 2005. Causal knowledge and imitation/emulation switching in chimpanzees (Pan troglodytes) and children (Homo sapiens). *Animal Cognition* 8:164–81.

Horowitz, J. K., and K. E. McConnell. 2002. A review of WTA/WTP studies. *Journal of Environmental Economics and Management* 44 (3): 426–47.

Huck, Steffen, George Kirchsteiger, and Jorg Oechssler. 2005. Learning to like what you have—Explaining the endowment effect. *The Economic Journal* 115:680–702.

Jensen, K., J. Call, and M. Tomasello. 2007. Chimpanzees are rational maximizers in an ultimatum game. *Science* 318: 107–109.

Johnson, N. D., and A. A. Mislin. 2011. Trust games: A meta-analysis. *Journal of Economic Psychology* 32:865–89.

Jordan, Jillian, Katherine McAuliffe, and David Rand. 2016. The effects of endowment size and strategy method on third party punishment. *Experimental Economics* 19:741–63.

Jullien, Bruno, and Bernard Salanie. 2000. Estimating preferences under risk: The case of racetrack betting. *Journal of Political Economy* 108:503–30.

Jung, Minah H., Leif D. Nelson, Ayelet Gneezy, and Uri Gneezy. 2014. Paying more when paying for others. *Journal of Personality and Social Psychology* 107:414–31.

Kacelnik, Alex, and Melissa Bateson. 1996. Risky theories—The effects of variance on foraging decisions. *American Zoology* 36:402–34.

Kahneman, D., J. L. Knetsch, and R. H. Thaler. 1990. Experimental tests of the endowment effect and the Coase theorem. *Journal of Political Economy* 98 (6): 1325–48.

Kahneman, Daniel. 2011. *Thinking Fast and Slow.* New York: Farrar, Straus, and Girox.

Kahneman, Daniel, and Amos Tversky. 1979. Prospect theory: An analysis of decision under risk. *Econometrica* 47:263–91.

Kearny, Melissa Schettini, Peter Tufano, Jonathan Guryan, and Erik Hurst. 2010. Making savers winners: An overview of prize-linked savings products. National Bureau of Economic Research Working Paper 16433.

Keightley Peter. 2012. Rates and fitness consequences of new mutations in humans. *Genetics* 190:295–304.

Kimbrough, Erik O., and Alexander Vostroknutov. 2016. Norms make preferences social. *Journal of the European Economic Association* 14:608–38.

Kolodny, O., and Stern, C. (2017). Evolution of risk preference is determined by reproduction dynamics, life history, and population size. *Science Reports* 7 (9364); 1–13.

Kosse, Fabian, and Friedhelm Pfeiffer. 2013. Quasi-hyperbolic time preferences and their intergenerational transmission. *Applied Economic Letters* 20:983–86.

Kube, Sebastian, Michel Andre Marechal, and Clemens Puppe. 2006. Putting reciprocity to work: Positive versus negative responses in the field. Economics Department, University of St. Gallen.

Kube, Sebastian, Michel Andre Marechal, and Clemens Puppe. 2013. Do wage cuts damage work morale? Evidence from a natural field experiment. *Journal of the European Economic Association* 11:853–70.

Laibson, David. 1998. Life-cycle consumption and hyperbolic discount functions. *European Economic Review* 42:861–71.

Lakshminaryanan, V, M. Keith Chen, and Laurie R. Santos. 2008. Endowment effect in capuchin monkeys. *Philosophical Transactions of the Royal Society* 363: 3837–3884.

Larson, Francis, John A. List, and Robert D. Metcalfe. 2016. Can myopic loss aversion explain the equity premium puzzle? Evidence from a natural field experiment with professional traders. NBER Working Paper 22605.

Latty, Tanya, and Madeliene Beekman. 2011. Irrational decision-making in an ameoboid organism: Transitivity and context-dependent preferences. *Proceedings of the Royal Society B* 278:307–12.

Levati, M. Viittoria. 2006. Explaining private provision of public goods by conditional cooperation: An indirect evolutionary approach. *Metroeconomica* 57:68–92.

Lewis, Michael. 2015. *The Undoing Project*. New York: W.W. Norton & Company.

Lewontin, R. C., and D. Cohen. 1969. On population growth in a randomly varying environment. *Proceedings of the National Academy of Sciences: Zoology* 62:1056–60.

List, John. 2003. Does market experience eliminate market anomalies? Quarterly Journal of Economics. 118: 47–71.

Lyons, Derek, Andrew Young, and Frank Keil. 2007. The hidden cost of overimitation. *PNAS* 104 (50): 19751–56.

Mackie, Gerry, and John LeJeune. 2009. Social dynamics of abandonment of harmful practices: A new look at the theory. UNICEF Innocenti Working Paper.

Malmendier, Ulrike, and Klaus M. Schmidt. 2017. You owe me. *American Economic Review* 107:493–526.

Mauss, Marcel. 1924. *The Gift: The Form and Reason for Exchange in Archaic Societies.* London: Routledge & Kegan Paul. Translated by W. D. Halls. (London: Routledge, 1990).

McGuigan, Nichola, Jenny Makinson, and Andrew Whiten. 2011. From over-imitation to super-copying: Adults imitate causally irrelevant aspects of tool use with higher fidelity than young children. *British Journal of Psychology* 102:1–18.

Milkman, Katherine L., and John Beshears. 2009. Mental accounting and small windfalls: Evidence from an online grocer. *Journal of Economic Behavior and Organization* 71:384–94.

Nave, Gideon, Colin Camerer, and Michael McCollough. 2015. Does oxytocin increase trust in humans? A critical review of research. *Perspectives on Psychological Science* 10 (6): 772–89.

New York Times. 1964. Dimes make millions for numbers racket; 600–1 payoff lures 500,000 a Day to Make Bets Here. *New York Times*, June 26, 1964, p. 1.

O'Donoghue, Ted, and Matthew Rabin. 1999. Doing it now or later. *American Economic Review* 89:3–24.

O'Donoghue, Ted, and Matthew Rabin. 2003. Studying optimal paternalism, illustrated by a model of sin taxes. *American Economic Review* 93:186–91.

Oosterbeek, Hessel, Randolph Sloof, and Gijs van de Kuilen. 2004. Cultural differences in ultimatum game experiments: Evidence from a meta-analysis. *Experimental Economics* 7:171–88.

Phelps, E., and R. A. Pollak. 1968. On second-best national savings and game-equilibrium growth. *Review of Economic Studies* 35:185–99.

Pope, Devin G., and Maurice E. Schweitzer. 2011. Is Tiger Woods loss averse? Persistent bias in the face of experience, competition, and high stakes. *American Economic Review* 101:129–57.

Rabin, Matthew, and Dimitri Vayanos. 2010. The gambler's and hot-hand fallacies: Theory and application. *Review of Economic Studies* 77:730–88.

Rand, D. G., J. D. Greene, and M. A. Mowak. 2012. Spontaneous giving and calculated greed. *Nature* 489:427–30.

Real, Leslie A. 1991. Animal choice behavior and the evolution of cognitive architecture. *Science* 253:980–7.

Reuben, Ernesto, Paola Sapienza, and Luigi Zingales. 2015. Procrastination and impatience. *Journal of Behavioral and Experimental Economics* 58:63–76.

Robbins, Erin, and Philippe Rochat. 2011. Emerging signs of strong reciprocity in human ontogeny. *Frontiers in Developmental Psychology* 353:1–14.

Rustagi, Devesh, Stefanie Engel, and Michael Kosfeld. 2010. Conditional cooperation and costly monitoring explain success in forest commons management. *Science* 330:961–64.

Saether, Bernt-Erik, and Steinar Engen. 2015. The concept of fitness in fluctuating environments. *Trends in Ecology and Evolution* 30: 273–81.

Salali, Gul Deniz, Myriam Juda, and Joseph Henrich. 2015. Transmission and development of costly punishment in children. *Evolution and Human Behavior* 36:86–94.

Sapolsky, Robert M. (2018). *Behave: The Biology of Humans at Our Best and Worst*. Penguin.

Sen, S., and E. J. Johnson. 1997. Mere-possession effects without possession in consumer choice. *Journal of Consumer Research* 24 (1): 105–17.

Shafir, Sharoni, Tom A. Waite, and Brian H. Smith. 2002. Context-dependent violations of rational choice in honeybees (Apis mellifera) and gray jays (Perisoreus canadensis). *Behavioral Ecology and Sociobiology* 51:180–87.

Smith, Adam (1759, 1976). *The Theory of Moral Sentiments*. edited by D. D. Raphael and A. L. Macfie. Glosgow Edition of the Works and Correspondence of Adam Smith. Oxford University Press.

Smith, Adam (Glasgow Edition, 1982). *The Theory of Moral Sentiments*. Indianapolis: Liberty Fund.

Sokol-Hessner, P., C. F. Camerer, and , E. A. Phelps. 2013. Emotion regulation reduces loss aversion and decreases amygdala responses to losses. *Scan* 8:341–50.

Sokol-Hessner, P., M. Hsu, N. G. Curley, M. R. Delgado, C. F. Camerer, and E. A. Phelps. 2009. Thinking like a trader selectively reduces individuals' loss aversion. *Proceedings of the National Academy of Sciences USA*. 106 (13): 5035–40.

Stevens, S. S., 1961. To honor Fechner and repeal his law. *Science* 133:80–86.

Suetens, Sigrid, Claus B. Galbo-Jørgensen, and Jean-Robert Tyran. 2016. Predicting lotto numbers: A natural experiment on the gambler's fallacy and the hot-hand fallacy. *Journal of the European Economic Association* 14 (3): 584–607.

Svenson, Ola. 1981. Are we all less risky and more skillful than our fellow drivers? *Acta Psychologica* 47:143–48.

Sydnor, Justin. 2010. (Over)insuring modest risks. *American Economic Journal: Applied Economics* 2:177–99.

Tanaka, Tomomi, Colin F. Camerer, and Quang Nguyen. 2010. Risk and time preferences: Linking experimental and household survey data from Vietnam. *American Economic Review* 100:557–71.

Thaler, Richard. 1999. Mental accounting matters. *Journal of Behavioral Decision Making* 12:183–206.

Thaler, Richard. 2015. *Misbehaving: The Making of Behavioral Economics*. New York: W.W. Norton.

Thaler, Richard, and Cass Sunstein. 2009. *Nudge: Improving Decisions about Health, Welfare and Happiness*. Penguin Books.

TheGrio. 2011. "Sou-sou": Black immigrants bring saving club stateside. https://thegrio.com/2011/05/20/sou-sou-black-immigrants-bring-savings-club-stateside/.

Tomasello, M. 2006. Why don't apes point? in *Roots of Human Sociality: Culture, Cognition, and Interaction*, edited by N. J. Enfield and S. C. Levinson, pp. 506–30. Oxford: Berg.

Tomasello, M. 2019. *Becoming Human: A Theory of Ontogeny*. Cambridge, MA: Harvard University Press, Belknap Press.

Tomasello, M., B. Hare, H. Lehmann, and J. Call. 2007. Reliance on head versus eyes in the gaze following of great apes and human infants: the cooperative eye hypothesis. *Journal of Human Evolution* 52:314–20.

Tversky, Amos, and Daniel Kahneman. 1992. Advances in prospect theory: Cumulative representation of uncertainty. *Journal of Risk and Uncertainty* 5:297–323.

Tversky, Amos, and Daniel Kahneman. 1971. Belief in the law of small numbers. *Psychological Bulletin* 76 (2): 105–10.

Tversky, Amos, and Daniel Kahneman. 1974. Judgment under uncertainty: Heuristics and biases. *Science* 185 (4157): 1124–31.

Tversky, Amos, and Daniel Kahneman. 1992. Advances in prospect theory: Cumulative representation of uncertainty. *Journal of Risk and Uncertainty* 54: 297–323.

van Dijk, E., and van Knippenberg, D. 1996. Buying and selling exchange goods: Loss aversion and the endowment effect. *Journal of Economic Psychology* 17 (4): 517–24.

Warneken, F., K. Lohse, A.P. Melis, and M. Tomasello. 2011. Young children share the spoils after collaboration. *Psychological Science* 22 (2): 267–73.

Way, Baldwin M., and Matthew D. Lieberman. 2010. Is there a genetic contribution to cultural differences? Collectivism, individualism and genetic markers of social sensitivity. *Social Cognitive and Affective Neuroscience* 5:203–11.

West-Eberhard, M. J. 1979. Sexual selection, social competititon, and evolution. *Proceedings of the American Philosophical Society* 51 (4): 222–34.

Wiessner, Polly. 2002. Hunting, healing, and hxaro exchange. A long-term perspective on !Kung (Ju/'hoansi) large-game hunting. *Evolution and Human Behavior* 23:407–36.

Wittig, R. M., K. Jensen, and M. Tomasello. 2013. Five-year-olds understand fair as equal in a mini-ultimatum game. *Journal of Experimental Child Psychology* 116 (2): 324–37.

Wu, G., and R. Gonzalez. 1996. Curvature of the probability weighting function. *Management Science* 42 (12): 1676–90.

Yoshimura, Jin, Yumi Tanaka, Tatsuya Togashi, Shigehide Iwata, and Kei-ichi Tainaka. 2009. Mathematical equivalence of geometric mean fitness with probabilistic optimization under environmental uncertainty. *Ecological Modelling* 220:2611–17.

Yoshimura, Jin, and Vincent A.A. Jansen. 1996. Evolution and population dynamics in stochastic environments. *Resource Population Ecology* 38:165–82.

INDEX

Note: Tables are indicated by a *t,*
    Figures are indicated by a *f.*

abstinence goals, 342–44, 342*t,*
    343*f,* 344*f*
action timing. *See* timing of action
active saver households, 182–83,
    182*f*
advantaged inequity, 44, 68
alleles, 351
Amazon Mechanical Turk
    (MTurk), 53
amygdala, 250
ancestral productivity, modern time
    preferences and, 391–93
anchoring effect, 40
Andreoni-Bernheim theory, of
    50-50 norm, 22
apple or cupcake conflict, 34–35
arithmetic mean, 356–57, 364
asset lock-in, saving and, 190–91
asset markets
    disposition puzzle and, 296, 297,
      303–8
    endowment effect and, 256–57
    equity premium puzzle and, 296,
      309–12
    prospect theory for, 296
asymmetry between loss and gain,
    250–52, 262, 263
availability heuristic, 41–42

backward induction
    preproperation and, 212–13, 213*t,*
      214*f*
    procrastination and, 205–6, 206*f*
bargaining
    endowment effect and, 413, 422
    equilibrium and, 416–17, 417*f*
    Nash bargaining solution, 417,
      420–21, 425–26
    natural selection and, 418–22
behavior
    dictator game and variation in
      sharing, 50–52, 51*f*
    environment and, 365

genes and, 359–60, 365
    pro-social, 2, 44, 68, 94
behavioral economics. *See also spe-*
    cific topics
    concept of, 1–2
    economics compared to, 16–17
    workhorse model of, 2
beneficial errors, in fire-building
    manual analogy, 353
benefit–cost analysis, 16–17
benefits and costs, decoupling,
    242–44
bias. *See* cognitive biases; present
    bias
bike theft lottery, 319–21, 320*f*
biological decision-making, decoy
    effect and, 30
biological evolution, 355
biology, economics compared to,
    358
bisection method, for stimulus-
    response calculations, 273–74,
    274*f*
bonobos, risk aversion in, 406
brain activity, loss and, 250
break-even price, willingness to pay
    for insurance versus, 320–23,
    323*f,* 324*f*
bucketlist decisions, present bias
    and, 170–71, 170*f,* 171*f,* 172*f*
budgets, fungibility and, 237–39
butterflies, risk aversion in, 398
bygones, sunk costs as, 303, 307–8

capuchin monkeys, endowment
    effect in, 253, 255–56, 256*f*
cash payments, decoupling costs
    and benefits of, 243–44
certainty equivalent of a lottery,
    264–66, 266*f,* 297–302, 298*f,*
    299*f,* 301*f,* 319, 320*f*
chimpanzees
    collaboration in humans com-
      pared to, 365
    cooperation in humans compared
      to, 365–66

endowment effect in, 255–56
    as hunter-gatherers, 368
    natural selection and, 349
    norm-violation costs in humans
      compared to, 368–70, 369*f*
    over-imitation by humans com-
      pared to, 148–49, 149*f*
    reproductive fitness of, 353–54,
      354*f*
    sclera in humans compared to,
      365, 373–74
    sharing in humans compared to,
      367–68, 367*f*
    social learning in humans com-
      pared to, 153–54
    in ultimatum game compared to
      humans, 369, 369*f*
choice environment (parameter), 10
choice variable, 10
clueless decision-makers (naifs)
    benefits of savvy decision-makers
      compared to, 215
    consumption path of, 187–89,
      188*f,* 189*f*
    preproperation and, 209–11
    present bias and, 202–3,
      209–11
    present bias of savvy decision-
      makers compared to, 207–8,
      207*f*
    procrastination and, 202–3
    regret of, 189
    three-period model of intertempo-
      ral choice for, 186–87
coffee mugs experiment, endow-
    ment effect and, 254
cognitive ability, risk preferences
    and, 274–75
cognitive biases
    anchoring effect and, 40
    confirmation bias and, 40–41
    decoy effect and, 28–30, 29*f*
    definition of, 28
    overconfidence effect and, 41
    present bias and, 2, 30–31
    probability and, 32–33

collaboration. *See also* cooperation
  in humans compared to chimpan-
    zees, 365
  motivation for, 366
  sharing and, 20–21, 21*f*
  skills for, 366
  strong reciprocity in environment
    of, 370
  workplace reciprocity and, 113
commitment devices, saving and,
  191
common fitness, endowment effect
  and, 421, 421*f*
comparative statics, 8, 10–11
compartmentalization, 26
conditional cooperation, 94, 99,
  106–7
confirmation bias, 40–41
conformity
  imitation and, 147–50, 148*f*, 149*f*
  matching pennies game and,
    149–50
  social norms and, 22
Congress on Racial Equality, 219
constant sensitivity
  to gain and loss, in disposition
    puzzle, 308
  risk neutrality and, 300–302, 301*f*
consumer budgets, fungibility and,
  237–39, 238*f*, 239*f*
consumer choice, conventional,
  mental accounting compared to,
  237–39, 238*f*, 239*f*
consumer mental accounting. *See*
  mental accounting
consumption smoothing, 370–72,
  371*f*
conventional consumer choice,
  mental accounting compared to,
  237–39, 238*f*, 239*f*
conventional discounting
  estimates of, 164–65
  present bias and, 158–60, 159*t*,
    163
  time inconsistency and, 163
cooperation. *See also* collaboration
  co-evolution of genes and culture
    and, 373–76
  consumption smoothing benefits
    with, 370–72, 371*f*
  cultural learning and, 374–75
  economies of scale benefits with,
    370, 372
  in humans compared to chimpan-
    zees, 365–66

motivation for, 366
natural selection and, 365
sharing and, 367–68, 367*f*
skills for, 366
costs and benefits, decoupling,
  242–44
coupons, mental accounting and,
  239–42, 240*f*, 241*f*
credit card payments, decoupling
  costs and benefits of, 243–44
crosswalk experiment
  rule-following and, 19–20, 19*f*
  ultimatum game and, 60
cultural evolution, 35
cultural learning
  cooperation and, 374–75
  faithful imitation and, 151–54
  imitation and, 146
  punishment and, 23–24
culture, 3
  ancestral productivity, modern
    time preferences and, 391–93
  genes and, 350, 360–61, 373–76
  time preferences, natural selection
    and, 388–93
cupcake versus apple decision,
  present bias and, 167–68

Darwin, Charles, 249
Dawkins, Richard, 358
decision justification, decoy effect
  and, 29
decoupling costs and benefits, mental accounting and, 242–44
decoy effect, 28–30, 29*f*
decreasing contributions, path of,
  104–5, 105*f*
decreasing marginal disutility of
  loss, 318–19, 318*f*
decreasing sensitivity
  to gain and loss, 271–73
  to gain and loss, in disposition
    puzzle, 306
  to gain and risk aversion, 297–98,
    298*f*
  hazard-insurance puzzle and, 326
  insurance-deductible puzzle and,
    326–28, 328*f*
  to loss and risk seeking, 298–300,
    299*f*
  probability weighting and, 283
  probability weighting versus, for
    insurance, 324–26, 325*f*
  in prospect theory, 261, 263
  risk aversion and, 270

willingness to pay for insurance
  and, 318–21
default options, 27
  on employer retirement plans, 184
deliberation, thoughtful, 34–35, 362
depression, 361
descriptive learning, experiential
  learning compared to, 285–87
dictator game
  history of, 49
  market engagement and, 61–62, 62*f*
  participant variation and, 51–52
  sharing behavior variation in,
    50–52, 51*f*
  structure and results of, 49–50,
    50*f*
  third-party punishment in, 53–54,
    53*f*
  trust game compared to, 73
  ultimatum game compared to, 60
  utility maximization and, 50–51,
    51*f*, 67
diminishing marginal utility of
  wealth, 165
disadvantaged inequity, 44, 68–70
disagreement value, Nash, 420–21
discounting. *See also* conventional
  discounting; present bias
  exponential, 159
  intertemporal choices and, 178–81
disposition puzzle, 296, 297
  constant sensitivity to gain and
    loss in, 308
  decreasing sensitivity to gain and
    loss in, 306
  evidence for, 306
  gains and losses relative to refer-
    ence points in, 306
  parts of, 303
  reservation price and time on
    market in, 305–6
  reservation price in loser market
    in, 304–5, 305*f*
  reservation price in winner mar-
    ket in, 304, 304*f*
  sunk costs as bygones in, 307–8
DNA, 351
domestication of milkable mammals, 360–61
doubling apples, present bias and,
  160–61

economic cost, opportunity cost
  and, 4
economics, traditional

behavioral economics compared
to, 16–17
biology compared to, 358
economies of scale, cooperation
and benefits of, 370, 372
Edgeworth box, for hunter-gatherer
exchange economy, 414–16,
415f, 416f
efficiency
Pareto, 8, 11–12
in trust game, 83
efficient allocation, Pareto, 11
efficient contributions, 99–103,
101f, 102f, 110–11
effort
norm sensitivity and, 119–21, 120f
utility maximization of, 116–18,
117f, 118f
wage increases for increased,
112–13, 123–24, 124f
egalitarian economy, endowment
effect and, 422
emotional memories, 42
employer retirement plans, default
options on, 184
endowment effect
bargaining and, 413, 422
in capuchin monkeys, 253,
255–56, 256f
in chimpanzees, 255–56
classic experiment of, 254
common fitness and, 421, 421f
concept of, 253
egalitarian economy and, 422
evidence of, 254–55
exchange and, 256–57, 413
hunter-gatherer exchange economy and, 414–17, 415f, 416f, 417f
loss aversion and, 257
Nash disagreement value and,
420–21
Nash equilibrium and, 418–20,
419f
persistence of, 418
WTP versus WTA in, 253
enforcement, of social norms,
22–24. See also norm-violation
costs; punishment
environment
behavior and, 365
gain equals loss, 380–82, 381f,
382f
gain exceeds loss, 382–84, 383f,
384f
genes and, 359–60, 378–79

loss aversion and conditions of,
387
risk preferences and, 398–99
strong reciprocity in collaboration, 370
environmental biology, 350
equal contributions, 99, 103–4, 111
equal-sharing norm (50-50 norm)
Andreoni-Bernheim theory of, 22
marginal cost of violating, 66–67
equal-sharing price, 132–36
equilibrium
bargaining and, 416–17, 417f
comparative statics and, 8, 10–11
investor's norm sensitivity in trust
game and, 82–83, 82f, 83f
Nash, 8–10, 9f, 25, 96–97, 418–20,
419f
responder, in ultimatum game,
56–58, 56f, 67
variable, 10–11
equilibrium environment (parameter), 10
equimarginal principle
applications of, 7–8
definition of, 6
illustration of, 6–7, 7f
personally harmful products and,
220–21, 221f
saving and, 178–80, 179f
equimarginal rule, 6, 7
equity premium puzzle, 296
concept of, 309
greater weight of loss and,
309–10
loss aversion and, 309–12, 310t,
311f
professional traders, information
updates and, 312
Ethiopia, 94
evolution, 3, 35. See also natural
selection
biological, 355
cultural learning, cooperation
and, 374–75
of genes and culture, 373–76
genetic mutations and natural
selection in, 352, 365
of humans, 349–50
reproductive fitness, natural selection and, 354–55, 355f
evolutionary biology
concepts of, 350–52
definition of, 350
illustration of, 352–53

exchange, endowment effect and,
256–57, 413
exchange economy, of hunter-
gatherers, 414–17, 415f, 416f,
417f
experiential learning, descriptive
learning compared to, 285–87
exploitation, voluntary contributions and, 98–99
exponential discounting, 159. See
also conventional discounting
eye-color genes, 351

faithful imitation, 146
cultural learning and, 151–54
definition of, 151
manioc production processes and,
151–53
social learning and, 152–54
Fehr-Schmidt inequity cost, 44,
68–70, 69f
fertilizer investment
intertemporal consumption model
and, 226–27, 227f
nudges for, 230
present bias and, 227–29, 228f,
229f
subsidies for, 226, 230
trade-offs associated with, 228
50-50 norm. See equal-sharing norm
fire-building manual analogy,
352–53
fitness. See reproductive fitness
fitness contests, 355–58, 357f
fitness equivalence, 412
loss aversion and, 384–87, 385f,
386f
risk preferences and, 405–6, 405f
fluctuating reproduction, steady
reproduction versus, 380–85
food supply, time preferences and,
392
free-rider problem
economic experiments with,
96–99, 97f
exploitation and, 98–99
Nash equilibrium and, 96–97
public broadcasting pledge drives
and, 139–41, 140f, 141f
punishment for, 106–7
self-regarding preferences and, 95
unbridled self-love and, 106
frequent information updates, professional traders and, 312
frequent rule followers, 20

full trust game, 85–86, 85*f*
fungibility
  consumer budgets and, 237–39,
    238*f*, 239*f*
  mental accounting and, 237–42
future gratification, immedi-
    ate gratification compared to,
    163–64
future savings, commitment to,
    184–85

gain
  asymmetry between loss and,
    250–52, 262, 263
  constant sensitivity to, in disposi-
    tion puzzle, 308
  decreasing sensitivity to, 271–73
  decreasing sensitivity to, in dispo-
    sition puzzle, 306
  decreasing sensitivity to risk aver-
    sion and, 297–98, 298*f*
  reference points for, in disposition
    puzzle, 306
  risk neutrality, equal loss and,
    269, 269*f*
gain equals loss environment,
    380–82, 381*f*, 382*f*
gain exceeds loss environment,
    382–84, 383*f*, 384*f*
gambler's fallacy, 32–33, 33*f*
gambling puzzles
  longshot puzzle, 287, 290–92,
    290*f*, 292*f*
  numbers-game puzzle, 287–90,
    288*f*
Gamson, Zelda, 219
gasoline prices, mental accounting
    and, 244–45
genes
  behavior and, 359–60, 365
  culture and, 350, 360–61, 373–76
  definition of, 351
  environment and, 359–60,
    378–79
  eye-color, 351
  loss aversion and mixes of, 387
  natural selection and, 350
  regulator, 351
  social norms and, 361
genetic mutations, 351–52, 365,
    373–74
genetics, 35
genomes
  definition of, 351
  fitness contests of, 355–58, 357*f*

geometric mean, 356, 364
geometric mean fitness, 355–58,
    357*f*, 400–401
gift exchange, workplace reciproc-
    ity and, 113, 126–27, 127*f*
goals
  for abstinence, 342–44, 342*t*,
    343*f*, 344*f*
  benefits of, 337–38, 337*f*
  on golf course, 338–39
  loss aversion and, 338
  marginal benefit related to,
    335–37, 336*f*, 342–43, 343*f*
  marginal cost and, 337–38, 337*f*,
    343–44, 344*f*
  marginal principle and, 334–39,
    334*f*
  motivation and, 338
  probability of reaching, 347–48
  rainy-day taxis and, 339–42, 340*f*,
    341*f*
  reference points and, 333
Golden Rule, 44
golf course, goals on, 338–39
group norms, identity, self-image
    and, 115–16

harmful errors, in fire-building
    manual analogy, 352–53
harmful mutations, 351
harmful products. *See* personally
    harmful products
harmful social norms, 25
harmless errors, in fire-building
    manual analogy, 352
hazard-insurance puzzle, 326
Hazda people, 422
height, human, 351
heuristics (mental shortcuts)
  availability, 41–42
  uses of, 2–3, 26–27
hobbling, self-imposed, 223
homeowner versus weed decision,
    present bias and, 168–70, 168*f*,
    169*f*
Homo genus, 349–50, 365, 373
Human Genome Project, 351
humans
  collaboration in chimpanzees
    compared to, 365
  cooperation in chimpanzees com-
    pared to, 365–66
  height of, 351
  as hunter-gatherers, 368
  natural selection and, 349–50

norm-violation costs in chimpan-
    zees compared to, 368–70, 369*f*
  over-imitation by, 147–48, 148*f*
  over-imitation by chimpanzees
    compared to, 148–49, 149*f*
  sclera in chimpanzees compared
    to, 365, 373–74
  sharing in chimpanzees compared
    to, 367–68, 367*f*
  social learning in chimpanzees
    compared to, 153–54
  strong reciprocity in collaboration
    environment of, 370
  in ultimatum game compared to
    chimpanzees, 369, 369*f*
hunter-gatherers
  consumption smoothing benefits
    in cooperation of, 370–72, 371*f*
  economies of scale benefits in
    cooperation of, 370, 372
  exchange economy of, 414–17,
    415*f*, 416*f*, 417*f*
  humans and chimpanzees as, 368
  large reward and risk neutrality
    in, 402–6, 404*f*, 405*f*
  small reward and risk aversion in,
    399–401, 402*f*

identity
  group norms, self-image and,
    115–16
  of insiders compared to outsiders,
    119, 119*f*
  management, 113, 121
imitation
  conformity and, 147–50, 148*f*,
    149*f*
  cultural learning and, 146
  faithful, 146, 151–54
  over-imitation, 146–49, 148*f*, 149*f*
immediate gratification, future
    gratification compared to,
    163–64
impartial spectators, Smith on, 18,
    84
imperfect information in work-
    place, 114–15
impermanent memories, 287
improvements, Pareto, 11–12,
    114–15, 341–42
increased productivity, 370, 372
individual utility maximization. *See*
    utility maximization
inefficient allocation, Pareto, 11
inequity aversion, 44

inequity cost, Fehr-Schmidt, 44, 68–70, 69*f*
information updates, professional financial traders and, 312
infrequent information updates, professional traders and, 312
An Inquiry into the Nature and Causes of the Wealth of Nations (Smith), 413
insider identity, outsider identity compared to, 119, 119*f*
instant gratification, present bias and, 31
instinctive urges, 34–35
  thoughtful deliberation compared to, 362
insurance, 317
  break-even price versus willingness to pay for, 320–23, 323*f*, 324*f*
  certainty equivalent and willingness to pay for, 319, 320*f*
  decreasing sensitivity and willingness to pay for, 318–21
  decreasing sensitivity versus probability weighting for, 324–26, 325*f*
  experiment for willingness to pay for, 321
  hazard-insurance puzzle and, 326
  insurance-deductible puzzle and, 326–28, 328*f*
  probability weighting and, 322–28
insurance-deductible puzzle, 326–28, 328*f*
intertemporal choices, 2. *See also* present bias
  consumption model of, 226–27, 227*f*
  definition of, 157
  discounting and, 178–81
  public policy and, 219
  three-period model of, 186–87, 198–99
  types of, 157–58
investor's decision, in trust game, 79–80, 80*f*
investor's sharing norm, in trust game, 81–84, 82*f*, 83*f*

Ju/'hoansi, hunting practices of, 35
juncos, risk preferences of, 408–9

Kimbrough-Vostroknutov utility function, 55

labor-management practices. *See also* workplace
  of identity management, 113
  of wage increases for increased effort, 112–13
lactase persistence, 360–61
large reward, risk neutrality and, 402–6, 404*f*, 405*f*
law of large numbers, 32
law of small numbers, 32–33
learned norms, 24
learning, by description and experience, 285–87
linear utility, risk neutrality and, 268–69, 269*f*
longshot puzzle, 287, 290–92, 290*f*, 292*f*
long-term orientation (LTO), 378, 388, 390–92
loser market, reservation price in, disposition puzzle and, 304–5, 305*f*
loss
  amygdala activity and, 250
  asymmetry between gain and, 250–52, 262, 263
  constant sensitivity to, in disposition puzzle, 308
  decreasing marginal disutility of, 318–19, 318*f*
  decreasing sensitivity to, 271–73
  decreasing sensitivity to, in disposition puzzle, 306
  decreasing sensitivity to risk seeking and, 298–300, 299*f*
  endowment effect and, 253–57
  greater weight of, 250, 257
  measuring weight of, 251–52, 251*f*
  power of, 2–3
  prospect theory and relative weight of, 271
  reappraisal weight of and, 252
  reference points for, in disposition puzzle, 306
  risk neutrality, equal gain and, 269, 269*f*
loss aversion
  causes of, 378, 379
  endowment effect and, 257
  equity premium puzzle and, 309–12, 310*t*, 311*f*
  environmental conditions and, 387
  fitness equivalence and, 384–87, 385*f*, 386*f*

in gain equals loss environment, 380–82, 381*f*, 382*f*
in gain exceeds loss environment, 382–84, 383*f*, 384*f*
genetic mixes and, 387
goals and, 338
natural selection and, 379–87
reproductive fitness and, 380–85
lottery
  certainty equivalent of, 264–66, 266*f*, 297–302, 298*f*, 299*f*, 301*f*, 319, 320*f*
  monetary value of, 268
  utility value of, 264–66, 266*f*
LTO (long-term orientation), 378, 388, 390–92
Lyft, 244

Makinson, Janet, 148
mandatory saving, 182–84, 182*f*, 183*f*
manioc production processes, faithful imitation and, 151–53
MAO-A variant, 359
marginal benefit
  goal-related, 335–37, 336*f*, 342–43, 343*f*
  in microeconomics, 4, 5, 5*f*
  of norm-sensitive producer in trust game, 92–93
  in utility maximization with social norms, 47–48, 48*f*
marginal cost
  of equal-sharing norm violation, 66–67
  goals and, 337–38, 337*f*, 343–44, 344*f*
  in microeconomics, 4, 5, 5*f*
  of norm-sensitive producer in trust game, 92–93
  in utility maximization with social norms, 47–48, 48*f*
marginal principle
  goals and, 334–39, 334*f*
  in microeconomics, 4–6, 5*f*
marginal rate of substitution (MRS), 38–39, 166, 226–30, 235, 388
marginal rate of transformation (MRT), 226–30
marginal reasoning, 4–8
marginal regret, 175–76, 197–98
market engagement, social norms and, 61–62, 62*f*, 63*f*
matching pennies game, 146
  conformity and, 149–50

material benefits
  efficient contributions and, 101–2,
    101*f*
  equal contributions and, 103
  norm-violation cost trade-off
    with, 46–47, 47*f*
  in trust game, 77, 81–82
  in ultimatum game, 55–57, 55*f*,
    56*f*
  voluntary prices and, 134–35,
    134*f*
McGuigan, Nicola, 148
memories
  emotional, 42
  impermanent, 287
  permanent, 286
  recent, 41
mental accounting, 2–3
  benefits of, 236
  concept of, 26–27, 237
  conventional consumer choice
    compared to, 237–39, 238*f*,
    239*f*
  coupons and, 239–42, 240*f*,
    241*f*
  decoupling costs and benefits and,
    242–44
  fungibility and, 237–42
  gasoline prices and, 244–45
  sunk cost and, 242–43
  uses of, 236
mental shortcuts (heuristics)
  availability, 41–42
  uses of, 2–3, 26–27
meta-analysis, of ultimatum game,
  59
microeconomics
  efficiency in, 8, 11–12
  equilibrium in, 8–11, 25
  equimarginal principle in, 6–8, 7*f*
  key concepts in, 1
  marginal principle in, 4–6, 5*f*
  opportunity cost in, 4
milkable mammals, domestication
  of, 360–61
minimum prices, 132
monetary value of a lottery, 268
motivation
  for cooperation and collaboration,
    366
  goals and, 338
MRS (marginal rate of substitution),
  38–39, 166, 226–30, 235, 388
MRT (marginal rate of transformation), 226–30

MTurk (Amazon Mechanical Turk),
  53
mutations, genetic, 351–52, 365,
  373–74

naifs. *See* clueless decision-makers
Nash bargaining solution, 417,
  420–21, 425–26
Nash disagreement value, 420–21
Nash equilibrium
  common utility function and, 425
  endowment effect and, 418–20, 419*f*
  free-rider problem and, 96–97
  harmful social norms and, 25
  in microeconomics, 8–10, 9*f*
natural selection, 3, 35
  ancestral productivity, modern
    time preferences and, 391–93
  bargaining and, 418–22
  chimpanzees and, 349
  cooperation and, 365
  fitness equivalence and, 384–87,
    385*f*, 386*f*
  in gain equals loss environment,
    380–82, 381*f*, 382*f*
  in gain exceeds loss environment,
    382–84, 383*f*, 384*f*
  genes and, 350
  genetic mutations and, 351–52, 365
  high investment productivity and,
    390–91, 390*f*
  humans and, 349–50
  hunter-gatherer exchange econ-
    omy and, 414–17, 415*f*, 416*f*, 417*f*
  loss aversion and, 379–87
  low investment productivity and,
    389–90, 389*f*
  reproductive fitness and, 349,
    354–55, 355*f*
  risk aversion and, 401, 402*f*,
    403–5, 404*f*
  risk neutrality and, 403–5, 404*f*
  time preferences, culture and,
    388–93
  trade-offs from investment and,
    388–89, 389*f*
non-saver households, 183–84, 183*f*
norm psychology, 24–25
norm sensitivity
  efficient contributions and, 102–3,
    102*f*
  effort and, 119–21, 120*f*
  equal contributions and, 103
  of insiders compared to outsiders,
    119, 119*f*

of investor, in trust game, 82–83,
  82*f*, 83*f*
of producer, in trust game, 79, 79*f*,
  92–93
of proposer, in ultimatum game,
  58
of responder, in ultimatum game,
  55–56, 55*f*
voluntary prices and, 135, 135*f*
norm-violation costs
  conditional cooperation and, 107
  efficient contributions and, 101–2,
    101*f*
  equal contributions and, 103
  in humans compared to chimpan-
    zees, 368–70, 369*f*
  of insiders compared to outsiders,
    119, 119*f*
  material benefit trade-off with,
    46–47, 47*f*
  public broadcasting pledge drives
    and, 140, 140*f*
  punishment and, 22–24, 52–58
  Smith on, 106
  in trust game, 77, 81–82
  in ultimatum game, 55–57, 55*f*,
    56*f*
  voluntary prices and, 134–35,
    134*f*
nudges
  for fertilizer investment, 230
  saving and, 182, 184–85
numbers-game puzzle, 287–90,
  288*f*

On the Origin of Species (Darwin),
  249
opportunity cost, 4
original trust game, 86–87, 87*f*
other-regarding preferences, 17, 20
outsider identity, insider identity
  compared to, 119, 119*f*
overconfidence effect, 41
over-imitation, 146
  by chimpanzees compared to
    humans, 148–49, 149*f*
  by humans, 147–48, 148*f*
oxytocin, trust game and, 88

parameter (choice environment), 10
parameter (equilibrium environ-
  ment), 10
Pareto, Vilfredo, 11
Pareto efficiency, 8, 11–12
Pareto efficient allocation, 11

Pareto improvements
  determining, 11–12
  perfect information in workplace and, 114–15
  rainy-day taxis, goals and, 341–42
  social norms and, 115
Pareto inefficient allocation, 11
path of decreasing contributions, 104–5, 105*f*
patience of mothers and children experiment, 165–66
pay it forward (PIF), 131, 137, 137*f*
payoffs to members, public broadcasting pledge drives and, 138–39, 139*f*
pay what you want (PWW), 131–37, 137*f*
perfect information in workplace, 114–15
permanent memories, 286
personally harmful products
  consumption of, 234–35
  equimarginal principle and, 220–21, 221*f*
  model of, 220–21
  present bias and, 221–23, 222*f*, 234–35
  savvy decision-makers and, 223
  self-imposed hobbling and, 223
  sin taxes for, 223–25
  time preferences and, 393
perspective taking, 252
PIF (pay it forward), 131, 137, 137*f*
pigeons, impulse control and, 192–93, 192*f*
pledge drives. *See* public broadcasting pledge drives
PLS (prize-linked saving), 185
pollution taxes, sin taxes compared to, 225
pre-commitment by pigeons, present bias and, 192–93, 192*f*
Prelec probability weighting, 281–82, 282*f*
premium versus regular gasoline, 244–45
preproperation
  backward induction and, 212–13, 213*t*, 214*f*
  clueless decision-makers and, 209–11
  conditions for, 211–12
  definition of, 200
  increasing benefit of, 209, 209*f*, 210*f*

premature timing of action and, 200, 209–15
present bias and, 209–11, 210*f*, 210*t*
regret and, 211
savvy decision-makers, self-awareness and, 212–15, 213*t*, 214*f*
time inconsistency and, 211
present bias, 2
  asset lock-in and, 190–91
  bucket list decisions and, 170–71, 170*f*, 171*f*, 172*f*
  clueless decision-makers and, 186–89, 187*f*, 188*f*, 202–3, 209–11
  of clueless decision-makers compared to savvy decision-makers, 207–8, 207*f*
  concept of, 30–31
  conventional discounting and, 158–60, 159*t*, 163
  cupcake versus apple decision and, 167–68
  definition of, 158
  diminishing marginal utility of wealth and, 165
  doubling apples and, 160–61
  estimates of, 164–65
  fertilizer investment and, 227–29, 228*f*, 229*f*
  homeowner versus weed decision and, 168–70, 168*f*, 169*f*
  instant gratification and, 31
  patience of mothers and children experiment and, 165–66
  personally harmful products and, 221–23, 222*f*, 234–35
  preproperation and, 209–11, 210*f*, 210*t*
  procrastination and, 31, 169–70, 169*f*, 202–3, 202*t*, 203*f*
  regret and, 163–64, 171, 172*f*, 180–81, 181*f*, 203, 211
  savvy decision-makers and, 186–87, 190–91, 206
  sin taxes and, 224, 224*f*
  time inconsistency and, 161–63, 162*t*, 203, 211
  uncertainty and, 165
prices. *See* voluntary prices
prize-linked saving (PLS), 185
probability
  cognitive biases and, 32–33

gambler's fallacy and, 32–33, 33*f*
  problems with, 262
  of rare events, 32
  of reaching goals, 347–48
probability weighting
  decreasing sensitivity and, 283
  decreasing sensitivity versus, for insurance, 324–26, 325*f*
  of descriptive learning versus experiential learning, 285–87
  hazard-insurance puzzle and, 326
  insurance and, 322–28
  insurance-deductible puzzle and, 326–28, 328*f*
  for longshot puzzle, 287, 290–92, 290*f*, 292*f*
  for numbers-game puzzle, 287–90, 288*f*
  Prelec, 281–82, 282*f*
  problems with, 280
  psychological foundations of, 282–83
  of rare events, 283–84, 284*f*
procrastination
  backward induction and, 205–6, 206*f*
  clueless decision-makers and, 202–3
  conditions for, 204
  definition of, 200
  present bias and, 31, 169–70, 169*f*, 202–3, 202*t*, 203*f*
  regret and, 157, 203
  rising cost of, 201, 201*f*, 203, 203*f*
  savvy decision-makers, self-awareness and, 205–8
  time inconsistency and, 203
  timing of action delayed by, 200–208
producer's sharing norm, in trust game, 76–80, 78*f*, 79*f*
product choice, 157
productivity, increased, 370, 372
professional traders, information updates and, 312
profit, wages and, 124
pro-social behavior, 2
  social norms and, 44, 68
  voluntary contributions and, 94
prospect theory, 3
  for asset markets, 296
  asymmetry between loss and gain in, 262, 263

prospect theory (*continued*)
  bisection method measuring sensitivity to stimulus in, 273–74, 274f
  decreasing sensitivity in, 261, 263
  decreasing sensitivity to gain and loss in, 271–73
  disposition puzzle and, 296, 297, 303–8
  equity premium puzzle and, 296, 309–12
  features of, 262–66
  insurance and, 317–28
  probability weighting in, 280–93
  reference points in, 261, 333
  relative weight of loss in, 271
  risk aversion in, 266–70, 267f
  risk neutrality in, 267–69, 269f
  risk preferences and cognitive ability in, 274–75
  risk preferences for rats and, 275–77, 276f
  startup lottery with, 264–66, 266f
  utility function for, 263, 264f
  values of key parameters in, 270–75
psychology, probability weighting foundations in, 282–83
public broadcasting pledge drives
  choosing length of, 141–42, 142f
  free-rider problem and, 139–41, 140f, 141f
  norm-violation costs and, 140, 140f
  payoffs to members and, 138–39, 139f
public goods
  conditional cooperation and, 94, 99, 106–7
  definition of, 94
  efficient contributions to, 99–103, 101f, 102f, 110–11
  equal contributions to, 99, 103–4, 111
  free-rider problem and, 96–99, 97f
  free-rider punishment and, 106–7
  non-excludable feature of, 95
  non-rival feature of, 94
  path of decreasing contributions to, 104–5, 105f
  social norms and, 99–105
  voluntary contributions supporting, 95
public policy
  for fertilizer investment, subsidies versus nudge, 230

intertemporal choices and, 219
pollution taxes and, 225
saving and, 182
sin taxes and, 223–25, 224f
punishment
  conditional cooperation and, 107
  cultural learning and, 23–24
  for free-rider problem, 106–7
  norm-violation costs and, 22–24, 52–58
  for social norm violators, 22–24
  third-party, 53–54, 53f, 62
PWW (pay what you want), 131–37, 137f

quasi-hyperbolic discount function, 158–60

racetrack bettors, longshot puzzle and, 287, 290–92, 290f, 292f
Radiolab, 219
rainy-day taxis, goals and, 339–42, 340f, 341f
rare events
  probability of, 32
  probability weighting of, 283–84, 284f
rats, risk preferences for, 275–77, 276f
reappraisal, weight of loss and, 252
recent memories, 41
reciprocity
  strong, 370
  workplace, 113–15, 125–27, 127f
redback spider somersaults, 358
reference points
  gains and losses relative to, in disposition puzzle, 306
  goals and, 333
  in prospect theory, 261, 333
regret
  of clueless decision-makers, 189
  marginal, 175–76, 197–98
  preproperation and, 211
  present bias and, 163–64, 171, 172f, 180–81, 181f, 203, 211
  procrastination and, 157, 203
  saving and, 158, 180–81, 181f
regular versus premium gasoline, 244–45
regulator genes, 351
reproductive fitness (fitness). *See also* fitness equivalence
  of chimpanzees, 353–54, 354f

definition of, 353
endowment effect and common, 421, 421f
geometric mean, 355–58, 357f
high investment productivity and, 390–91, 390f
hunter-gatherer exchange economy and, 414–17
loss aversion and, 380–85
low investment productivity and, 389–90, 389f
natural selection and, 349, 354–55, 355f
risk preferences and, 403
utility maximization compared to, 358
reservation price, in disposition puzzle
  in loser market, 304–5, 305f
  time on market and, 305–6
  in winner market, 304, 304f
retirement savings, time preferences and, 177, 392
return fractions, in trust game, 79
revenue neutral switch, with sin taxes, 224–25
ride-hailing services, decoupling costs and benefits of, 244
risk aversion
  in bonobos, 406
  in butterflies, 398
  decreasing sensitivity to, 297–98, 298f
  decreasing sensitivity to gain and, 270
  definition of, 266
  natural selection and, 401, 402f, 403–5, 404f
  risk premium and, 267–68, 267f
  small reward and, 399–401, 402f
  sources of, 269–70
risk neutrality
  constant sensitivity and, 300–302, 301f
  definition of, 267
  equal gain and loss in, 269, 269f
  large reward and, 402–6, 404f, 405f
  linear utility and, 268–69, 269f
  natural selection and, 403–5, 404f
risk preferences, 3
  cognitive ability and, 274–75
  environment and, 398–99
  fitness equivalence and, 405–6, 405f
  of juncos, 408–9

for rats, 275–77, 276f
reproductive fitness and, 403
subsistence and, 407–8, 407f
risk premium, 267–68, 267f
risk seeking, 296
concept of, 300
decreasing sensitivity to loss and, 298–300, 299f
subsistence and, 407–9, 407f
rope-pulling experiment, 20–21, 21f, 62, 367–68
rule breakers, 20
rule-following, crosswalk experiment and, 19–20, 19f

Save More Tomorrow program, 185
Save to Win program, 185
saving
asset lock-in and, 190–91
commitment devices and, 191
equimarginal principle and, 178–80, 179f
future, commitment to, 184–85
mandatory, 182–84, 182f, 183f
nudges and, 182, 184–85
prize-linked, 185
public policy and, 182
regret and, 158, 180–81, 181f
time preferences and retirement, 177, 392
savvy decision-makers (sophisticates)
backward induction and, 205–6, 206f, 212–13, 213t, 214f
benefits of clueless decision-makers compared to, 215
consumption path of, 190–91
definition of, 190
personally harmful products and, 223
preproperation and, 212–15, 213t, 214f
present bias and, 206
present bias of clueless decision-makers compared to, 207–8, 207f
procrastination and, 205–8
three-period model of intertemporal choice for, 186–87
sclera, in chimpanzees and humans, 365, 373–74
self-awareness, 200. See also savvy decision-makers
backward induction and, 205–6, 206f, 212–13, 213t, 214f
preproperation and, 212–15, 213t, 214f

present bias and, 206
present bias of cluelessness compared to, 207–8, 207f
procrastination and, 205–8
self-domestication, 24–25
self-image, identity, group norms and, 115–16
self-imposed hobbling, 223
selfish motives, 16–17, 44
self-love, unbridled, 106
self-regarding preferences, 16, 87
free-rider problem and, 95
PWW and, 132
sensitivity. See also decreasing sensitivity; norm sensitivity
constant, risk neutrality and, 300–302, 301f
constant, to gain and loss, in disposition puzzle, 308
to stimulus, bisection method measuring, 273–74, 274f
serotonin, 361
sharing
collaboration and, 20–21, 21f
dictator game and, 50–52, 51f
equal-sharing norm and, 22, 66–67
in humans compared to chimpanzees, 367–68, 367f
trust game and investor's norm of, 81–84, 82f, 83f
trust game and producer's norm of, 76–80, 78f, 79f
trust game in absence of, 75
wages and, 122–23, 123f
short-term orientation (STO), 378, 388, 390–93
sin taxes
for personally harmful products, 223–25
pollution taxes compared to, 225
present bias and, 224, 224f
revenue neutral switch with, 224–25
support for, 223–24
small reward, risk aversion and, 399–401, 402f
Smith, Adam
on endowment effect and exchange, 413
on impartial spectators, 18, 84
on norm-violation costs, 106
on social norms, 18, 22, 45, 48, 52, 361
smoking cessation, 219

social capital
definition of, 83
social norms and, 115
trust as component of, 72
trust game and, 83–84, 87–88
trust system for, 88
workplace reciprocity and, 114–15
social exclusion, 361
social learning, faithful imitation and, 152–54
social norms. See also norm-violation costs; sharing
conformity and, 22
crosswalk experiment and, 19–20, 19f, 60
definition of, 18
dictator game and, 49–54, 50f, 51f, 53f
efficient contributions and, 99–103, 101f, 102f
enforcement of, 22–24
equal contributions and, 99, 103–4
equal-sharing (50–50), 22, 66–67
genes and, 361
gift exchange and, 113, 126–27, 127f
harmful, 25
identity, self-image and group, 115–16
internalization of, 361
market engagement and, 61–62, 62f, 63f
material benefit, norm-violation cost trade-offs with, 46–47, 47f
Pareto improvements and, 115
path of decreasing contributions and, 104–5, 105f
pro-social behavior and, 44, 68
self-domestication and, 24–25
Smith on, 18, 22, 45, 48, 52, 361
social capital and, 115
social preferences and, 17–25
trust game and investor's sharing, 81–84, 82f, 83f
trust game and producer's sharing, 76–80, 78f, 79f
trust game in absence of sharing, 75
utility maximization with, 45–49, 48f
voluntary contributions to public goods and, 99–105
in workplace, 112–13

social preferences, 2
  other-regarding preferences and, 17, 20
  social norms and, 17–25
Social Security, 182–84
sophisticates. *See* savvy decision-makers
spending wealth, 158
startup lottery, with prospect theory, 264–66, 266*f*
steady reproduction, fluctuating reproduction versus, 380–85
stimulus, bisection method measuring sensitivity to, 273–74, 274*f*
STO (short-term orientation), 378, 388, 390–93
strict rule followers, 20
strong reciprocity, 370
subsidies, for fertilizer investment, 226, 230
subsistence, risk seeking and, 407–9, 407*f*
sunk costs
  as bygones, 303, 307–8
  mental accounting and, 242–43

Tanzania, 422
taxes
  pollution, 225
  sin, 223–25, 224*f*
taxis
  decoupling costs and benefits of ride-hailing services and, 244
  goals of rainy-day, 339–42, 340*f*, 341*f*
Thaler, Richard, 30–31, 160, 164, 185, 243
The Theory of Moral Sentiments (Smith), 18
third-party punishment, 53–54, 53*f*, 62
thoughtful deliberation
  for apple or cupcake conflict, 34–35
  instinctive urges compared to, 362
three-period model of intertemporal choice, 186–87, 198–99
time inconsistency
  conventional discounting and, 163
  present bias and, 161–63, 162*t*, 203, 211
  procrastination and, 203
time on market, reservation price and, in disposition puzzle, 305–6

time preferences, 2
  ancestral productivity and modern, 391–93
  food supply and, 392
  high investment productivity and, 390–91, 390*f*
  low investment productivity and, 389–90, 389*f*
  LTO, 378, 388, 390–92
  MRS and, 388
  natural selection, culture and, 388–93
  personally harmful products and, 393
  retirement savings and, 177, 392
  STO, 378, 388, 390–93
  trade-offs from investment and, 388–89, 389*f*
timing of action. *See also* preproperation; procrastination
  preproperation and premature, 200, 209–15
  procrastination delaying, 200–208
transaction cost, trust reducing, 72
transcription factors, 351
trust
  oxytocin and, 88
  as social capital component, 72
  transaction cost reduced with, 72
  trustworthiness compared to, 73–74
trust game
  in absence of sharing, 75
  in consumer world, 87
  dictator game compared to, 73
  efficiency in, 83
  experiments and implications of, 84–88
  full, 85–86, 85*f*
  investor's decision in, 79–80, 80*f*
  investor's sharing norm in, 81–84, 82*f*, 83*f*
  norm sensitive investor in, 82–83, 82*f*, 83*f*
  norm sensitive producer in, 79, 79*f*, 92–93
  original, 86–87, 87*f*
  oxytocin and, 88
  producer's sharing norm in, 76–80, 78*f*, 79*f*
  return fractions in, 79
  social capital and, 83–84, 87–88
  structure of, 74–75, 75*f*
  trust compared to trustworthiness in, 73–74

ultimatum game compared to, 73
  utility maximization in, of investor, 81–82
  utility maximization in, of producer, 76–79, 78*f*, 92
  at work, 87–88
trust system, for social capital, 88
trustworthiness
  factors of, 86
  trust compared to, 73–74

Uber, 244
ultimatum game
  crosswalk experiment and, 60
  dictator game compared to, 60
  equilibrium responder in, 56–58, 56*f*, 67
  humans compared to chimpanzees in, 369, 369*f*
  market engagement and, 62, 63*f*
  meta-analysis of, 59
  norm-sensitive proposer in, 58
  norm-sensitive responder in, 55–56, 55*f*
  results from, 59–60
  structure of, 54, 54*f*
  trust game compared to, 73
  utility maximization in, 56–57, 56*f*
unbridled self-love, 106
uncertainty, present bias and, 165
utility function
  Nash equilibrium and common, 425
  for prospect theory, 263, 264*f*
utility maximization, 2
  coupons, mental accounting and, 239–42, 240*f*, 241*f*
  dictator game and, 50–51, 51*f*, 67
  efficient contributions and, 100–103, 101*f*, 102*f*, 110–11
  equal contributions and, 103, 111
  reproductive fitness compared to, 358
  with social norms, 45–49, 48*f*
  three-period model of intertemporal choice and, 198–99
  in trust game, of investor, 81–82
  in trust game, of producer, 76–79, 78*f*, 92
  in ultimatum game, 56–57, 56*f*
  voluntary prices and, 133–36, 134*f*, 145
  wages and, 124, 124*f*

workplace effort and, 116–18, 117*f*, 118*f*
utility value of a lottery, 264–66, 266*f*

violence, "warrior gene" and, 359
voluntary contributions
    efficient, 99–103, 101*f*, 102*f*, 110–11
    equal, 99, 103–4, 111
    exploitation concerns with, 98–99
    free-rider problem and, 96–99, 97*f*
    free-rider punishment and, 106–7
    path of decreasing, 104–5, 105*f*
    pro-social behavior and, 94
    public goods supported by, 95
    social norms and, 99–105
voluntary prices
    equal-sharing price and, 132–36
    minimum prices and, 132
    norm sensitivity and, 135, 135*f*
    norm-violation costs and, 134–35, 134*f*
    PIF, 131, 137, 137*f*

public broadcasting pledge drives and, 138–42
PWW, 131–37, 134*f*, 135*f*, 137*f*
self-regarding preferences and, 132
utility maximization and, 133–36, 134*f*, 145

wages
    increased effort for higher, 112–13, 123–24, 124*f*
    as motivational tool, 122
    profit and, 124
    rainy-day taxis, goals and, 340–41, 340*f*, 341*f*
    sharing and, 122–23, 123*f*
    utility maximization and, 124, 124*f*
"warrior gene," 359
when to act. *See* timing of action
Whiten, Andrew, 148
willingness to accept (WTA), 253–57. *See also* endowment effect

willingness to pay (WTP). *See also* endowment effect
    endowment effect and, 253–57
    for insurance, 318–21, 318*f*, 320*f*
winner market, reservation price in, disposition puzzle and, 304, 304*f*
workplace
    effort in, 112–13, 116–21, 117*f*, 118*f*, 120*f*, 123–24, 124*f*
    gift exchange in, 113, 126–27, 127*f*
    identity in, 113, 115–16, 119, 119*f*, 121
    perfect or imperfect information in, 114–15
    profit and, 124, 124*f*
    reciprocity, 113–15, 125–27, 127*f*
    social norms in, 112–13
    trust game in, 87–88
    wages in, 112–13, 122–24, 123*f*, 124*f*
WTA (willingness to accept), 253–57. *See also* endowment effect
WTP. *See* endowment effect; willingness to pay